The
Anarchists

The
Anarchists

Edited by
Irving Louis Horowitz
With a new introduction by the editor

AldineTransaction
A Division of Transaction Publishers
New Brunswick (U.S.A.) and London (U.K.)

Library of Congress Catalog Number: 200504982
ISBN: 0-202-30768-9
Printed in the United States of America

Library of Congress Cataloging-in-Publication Data

The anarchists / Irving Loius [i. e. Louis] Horowitz, editor ; with a new introd. by the editor.
    p. cm.
   Includes bibliographical references and index.
   ISBN 0-202-30768-9 (alk. paper)
   1. Anarchists. 2. Dissenters. I. Horowitz, Irving Louis.

HX826.A55   2005
335'.8'0922—dc22   2005040982

To the memory of a great libertarian
G.D.H. Cole, who pointed out the basic truth:
"The Anarchists . . . were anarchists because
they did not believe in an
anarchical world."

contents

Reconsidering The Anarchists: 2005 Introduction to the Transaction Edition

The dedicated researcher will find more than one hundred thousand entries and just about one thousand definitions for the term "anarchists" in the search engines available in electronic format. At first blush, this in itself would serve to disqualify the republication of an older 1964 anthology on *The Anarchists*. But on deeper probing, the overlapping of such definitions does little to change matters in the course of time. One can take as an operational definition the idea put forth by many of these websites that anarchism is simply the doctrine of a free society—where no force is necessary to establish or uphold freedom and liberty. Therefore, I should like to dedicate these new introductory pages to explain what has or rather has not happened in the past forty years to make this effort timely, rather than obsolete.

One critical element that makes the reproduction of such a volume more than anachronistic is that although the word anarchism ends, like so many other grandiose terms, with an "ism" – the usual ploy for ideological labels –it serves to highlight a set of powerfully held beliefs about human beings and social systems. Anarchism is less an ideology than a sentiment. It is indeed an ideal type – a statement of a system rarely to be found in a universe of nation-states or even non-governmental agencies. Unless one prefers as a definition of anarchy its presumed equivalencies for sheer chaos, it is more customarily a statement of a system in which laws are few, rules of conduct expressed by individuals rather than imposed by collectivities, and a society guided by ethical conduct rather than power concentration.

This is perhaps best expressed by the need of almost all commentators to constantly think of anarchism in hyphenated terms or in regional geographic terms. As a result we find clusters of people in select nations identified with Christianity, community, gender, religion – in short the full gamut of ascribed features of a human being that actually do exist. So at least one conception of anarchism is as a moral extension of being born into or acquiring a particular religion, nation, sex, race, and seeking to make a common ground with those who hold fast to the ethical tenets of political minimalism. This makes for a reasonable starting point. But such a definition also defines a variety of movements – from humanism to libertarianism – that also laid claim to a moral high ground for internalized personal behavior.

This volume is somewhat unique in that it owes its origins less to an interest in anarchism as such, so much as to a rounding out of a trilogy of works on revolutionary doctrines concocted by the late C. Wright Mills toward the close of his life. Initially, it was conceived as a trilogy with basic texts on Marxists, Trotskyites, and anarchists. The first volume, on *The Marxists,* Mills lived to complete, and curiously advance copies of the anthology shipped in March 1962, sadly the very month and week that he passed away at the age of forty-four-plus years.

The second volume, on the Trotskyites, Mills had barely sketched out in the rough. It fell to the late Isaac Deutscher, properly enough, to actually bring the volume to completion. As the outstanding biographer of Leon Trotsky, Deutscher was closer to the Trotskyites than Mills, who while earlier in his life had some modest flirtations with Trotsky, especially with Fourth International circles in the New York City area, clearly lost interest in the didacticism and dogmatism of the Trotskyites as a group. While retaining some association with Dwight Macdonald, who also drifted away from Fourth International standards of conduct, both he and Mills retained a life-long sense of opposition to Stalinist Russia and to Stalinism as such. This animus for the Stalinists, and preference for Marxists who retained a lively pragmatic sense of the West, were evident in *The Marxists*, nonetheless, such a vision had little impact on Deutscher's fine volume. One suspects that it would nonetheless have retained Mills's general approbation – given his high respect for Deutscher personally, and for the combination of revolutionary fervor and intellectual skills Trotsky himself exhibited, which Mills certainly tried to simulate with respect to his writings on Cuba between 1959-1961.

The third and final volume, *The Anarchists*, was not even worked up as an outline by Mills. Its need came from his strong belief in the Franco-Italian mode of sociology, especially the study of mass movements, irrational leaders and interest driven organizational dynamics. Figures like Georges Sorel, Roberto Michels, and Gaetano Mosca, among others attracted Mills. His studies of actual anarchist movements had not yet begun. Having myself completed *Radicalism and the Revolt Against Reason: The Political Sociology of Georges Sorel* in 1961, Richard Huett, the lovely man who ran Dell-Delta at the time, suggested that I take on editing the third and final volume, and complete the task of the trilogy. I did so with pleasure. It was a final statement of support for Wright, fulfilling at least in part his intellectual legacy, and allowing for an appreciation of what his thinking meant in my own development.

While Wright Mills was too much of a curmudgeon to have a tight "circle," his umbilical cord did have some carry. In relation to the trilogy of *The Marxists, The Trotsky Reader,* and *The Anarchists* this became apparent after his demise. Wright met Isaac Deutscher in England, when he was visiting professor at Sussex and living in London. They got on well, differing cultural styles notwithstanding. In turn, I met Deutscher during my own tour of duty as visiting lecturer at the London School in 1961. We met several times at his London flat, in the company of Isaac's wife. On one such occasion Ralph Miliband, who was another good friend to Mills in those final years, joined us. We were all readers and reviewers of the various drafts of *The Marxists*.

From the posthumous correspondence, it is evident that the close textual analysis that I performed was somewhat different than the wide-ranging commentary by Deutscher. Mills, in turn, was very kind in citing my contribution and also in referring the readers to *Radicalism and the Revolt Against Reason* that had appeared early in 1961, when *The Marxists* was under preparation. I do not know for certain, but suspect that Mills discussed handling the trilogy in the event of his inability to complete the project with Dick Huett – we were able to honor the contracts signed for each of the volumes, and complete the task. That said, I have no idea what Wright would have thought about how I handled the topic of anarchism, the choice of contributors, or the views I expressed. But of course in retrospect, I would like to think he would give his overall approval, amidst shouts of particular dismay.

Preparing this volume was also a learning process unto itself: Anarchism was both more amorphous but with a much richer tradition in literary, cultural, and economic formations than Trotskyism, or arguably, even Marxism itself. And immersing myself in its literature was a yearlong task. The end results are what are herein presented. Because of the commercial publication of the work, the need to emphasize literary and cultural pieces was a foremost consideration. Happily, the quality of writing was up to and often beyond the ideology of anarchism as such. Doing this work also dovetailed with a rising interest in the State, that is, in Behemoth as the epitome of state power, state terror, and indeed state benevolence. To study the history and current status of the anarchists permitted me to enlarge my scope beyond conflict theory to conflict practice. Hence doing this volume, far from being diversionary, was central to my evolution as a political sociologist.

It would be a mistake to think that the subject of this trilogy was simply an intellectual brainstorm of editors and publishers. The Spanish Civil War served not only as a preliminary battleground between the political forces of fascism and democracy, but as a testing ground for those global elements that came together to resist the Franco regime between 1936-1939. The so-called Left was united in its opposition to the overthrow of the Spanish Republic by the forces of tradition and dictatorship, but in little else. Within the foreign brigades in particular that gathered in Spain, the forces of Marxism (or at least its Third International gathered under the Stalinist umbrella), those of Trotskyism (or at least its Fourth International gathered under the far more nominal and looser leadership of Leon Trotsky in exile), and those of anarchism (often more indigenous to Spanish soil, but also drawn from largely European sources whose linkages to varieties of communist rule were weak, if at all extant), the three radical factions that gathered under the Spanish Republican cause prepared to do battle with each other as well as against the Falangist enemy. It was this historical and empirical back-

ground that formed the deep-seated source of anarchism as a
political movement no less than as a psychological state of
mind.

It is intriguing to note that Yasir Arafat, like Enrico
Malatesta one hundred years earlier, was identified as an anarchist in a variety of press reports. Despite the obvious difference between an individual who is leader of a national
and ethnic movement and one who was an outsider to actual
political power, it raises the specter of the individual disrupting social systems if not historical processes as such. For
whatever the event: the capacity of the person to assassinate,
terrorize, and eliminate leaders, and when required, followers, does link a good deal of anarchist history. The relation of
the anarchist "deed" with the Moslem "martyr" is arguably
as much a difference of labels as it is of actual performance.
As societies become increasingly complex, political leadership is central to the conduct of public affairs and policy. In
short, vulnerabilities increase, and anarchical responses, activities lacking state authorization entirely or possessing only
tacit support also show a corresponding increase.

In consequence of these political developments, the
anarch is yoked with its opposite, the *behemoth* more powerfully than ever. As state power increases, its essential reliance on weapons and officers of law and order, become as
important as any imagined democratic consensus. Conflict
theory is the umbilical chord of revolutionary doctrines, of
theories which presume that change is a function of the action of the few and the proud and the brave, rather than those
masses who go about their business quietly, vote for candidates, and accept outcomes based on premises of majority
rules and arguably, minority rights. Indeed, the moral claim
of many human rights non-governmental organizations is
the need for action when sovereign states fail to act – as in
cases of clear evidence of genocide. In this sense, anarchist
theory – whatever its variations – and these are discussed in
detail in *The Anarchists* – may have individualistic premises
of action, but often end up in collectivist forms of system
maintenance when the legal machinery fails its citizens. Utopian communities that start with premises of minimalist rule
or top down instruction frequently end up with dissension,
conflict, leadership struggles, and animosities that cannot be

resolved within communitarian frameworks. Since anarchism lacks a theory of democratic consensus – the very theory it defines as its enemy, or in its more benign form, as its nemesis – places its advocates outside the mainstream of the polity.

There are serious consequences of this lack of legitimacy. They foster uncertainty with those who profess anarchism: the felt need for solidarity leads to a strongly hyphenated approach. The unity of anarchist groups often reside less in a commitment to bottom-up decision making without instruction, inhibition, or coercion, and more on common background variables, such as religion, culture, ethnicity, or movement inspired beliefs in environmental protection or animal rescue. What such hyphenated categories result in are smaller circles of converts rather than large-scale outreach. Even when the anarchists were involved in trade union activities, such as the International Workers of the World in the early decades of the twentieth century, the actual location of influence was restricted to small pockets in select geographical terrains or pockets of association. This is not a critique of anarchism in action as such, but it serves to remind us that it is an "ism" that has more in common with an American tradition of voluntary associations than broad-based notions of economic and political organization.

In order to compensate for this obvious shortcoming in its doctrinal commitments, anarchism often represents itself as a hyphenated doctrine: anarcho-syndicalism, communist anarchism, individualist anarchism, religious anarchism, and communitarian anarchism. And while these sort of ad hoc approaches make anarchism as such a more palatable option to behemoth, it has failed to attract any but small numbers of individuals to palliatives. Trade unionists, itinerant peasants, religious communes, all display the red flag of anarchy, but they simply come upon the hard truth that they survive and expand in a world of economic organization and political administration that such small clusters do not have the capacity to destroy, and indeed, do not possess the ability to survive independent of such formal systems. Even non-governmental organizations exhibit patterns of behavior that simulate government organization rather than mechanisms for the destruction of state power.

By the same token, social-psychological characteristics of anarchism tend to attract young people who are alienated from mainstream activities or occupations. And this connection of the young with anarchism dates back to the European tradition as well; what might be called its moral characteristics. To start with, it takes courage, fortitude, energy – all of the verities associated with young people—to engage in acts that are dangerous and risky – ranging from bank hold-ups to attempted assassinations. But it also feeds the ambitions within anarchism of individualism in actions and collectivism in organization. Anarchism brings back into the political process words like heroism and risk – terms of endearment to the young and the striving. The slogan of the post-1960s generation – that history is bunk – is imitative of the old Henry Ford belief that technology can overcome all deterministic and inherited beliefs. This polarity itself pits the person against the machine. Still, if it seems that the stratification factors of anarchists are closely aligned with those of terrorists, one can only respond that a necessary condition is not sufficient for the commission of deeds viewed by high society or the state as lawful in character.

In present-day, twenty-first-century terms, the anarchists are at one end of the needle on human rights, whereas the statists are at the other end, advocates of human obligations. In classical philosophical terms, the anarchists can find solace and comfort in Nietzsche, whereas the behemoths find support in Hegel. Anarchism does not pass away because these deep valuation themes of personal freedom, choice, and instinct are rooted in psychological needs that exist in all human beings; whatever the strength of the Leviathan. At the same time, the value requirements of public law, necessity, and obedience to higher callings are also part of the human make-up. That for the most part, human beings operate within such extremes, and in search of some sort of balance that permits life to go on in a predictable and secure fashion – but not to the degree that personal elements are entirely expunged. The importance of examining the anarchist tradition is thus not simply an idle academic exercise, but a way for us all to test the limits of tolerations and the potential for change that fails to solicit full-fledged public sponsorship.

The key element then in the continuing vibrancy of anarchism goes to the heart of the public choice versus public
policy advocates. If the historical destiny of advanced economies, and such a movement from capitalism to socialism is
irrevocable, why should any person become involved in social action? Indeed what becomes of any notion of heroism
much less freedom as such? With its attendant risks and li-
abilities – in aiding and abetting the negation of what deter-
minists and historicists deemed to be inevitable – anarchism
provides a frame of reference that individuals of all persua-
sions and beliefs must ultimately wrestle with, if they are to
aim for a public role in social consensus.

The anarchist responses have been many, varied, and tor-
tured: it is essential to "speed up" the historical processes
described as inevitable, personal participation is part of such
a notion of the inevitable, the individual is a moral actor and
hence derives therapeutic advantages in revolutionary participation, and finally, the utilitarian notion that where any
individual stands in the historical drama unfolding depends
upon activity or passivity. But all such tormented scholastic
explanations fall apart once it became apparent that there are
transitions of society from secularism to clericalism (as in
Iran in 1979) and from communism to capitalism (as in the
bulk of Eastern Europe in 1989-91). Not only were such reverse transitions feasible, they happened with starling cultural suddenness: Iranian women, long the bellwether of
gender equity in the Middle East, were readily converted to
the shawl (*chador*) and a retreat from the working process in
short order. And at the same time, Kuwaitis who swore allegiance and waved flags on behalf of a dictator in Iraq were
quickly converted to the principles and premises of American democracy once the alien armies were driven away. Voting procedures, competing political parties, and
constitutional norms were more difficult to implement, but
at least became the rhetoric of the streets.

In effect, history was preempted by policy, that is to say
the notion of inevitabilities in the social process gave way to
changes made by, and with the full responsibilities, of the
people involved. Without "laws" of historical materialism to
fall back on, dictators and their would-be successors were
unable to punish people for their ideology, for the idea of

holding views contrary to the infallibilities and inevitabilities being paraded forth for the citizen as whole. In such a
context, the individual as anarchist could reclaim the stage
of making the very history deemed central to the revolutionary process.

This was clearly a key part of the thought of many classical nineteenth-century anarchists like Georges Sorel. But they
were nearly uniformly the idea of a free society—where no
force is necessary to establish or uphold freedom and liberty.
They were laboring under the belief that socialism indeed
was the next stage in human evolution. It was an agenda
built upon the abolition of the state, of capitalism, of exploitation, and of evolution as such if need be. Hence, these
classical figures were unable to draw the proper conclusions
from their own theorizing, that is, from the idea that regimes
– whatever their character – were a function of manifest psychological desires, rather than a consequence of hidden historical forces operating behind the backs of men.

Ultimately, the psychological need for a measure of choice
in decision making is the key to the irritating anarchist survival – such that it is – in the ideological arena and the
private realm. It demonstrates, if more evidence is needed,
that extreme determinisms were inconsequential to real social change, and that decisions made by individual, families,
clans, were crucial in larger decisions about where and how
to live. Such a lesson is not easy to acquire, especially amongst
those for whom the dogma of certainty remains particularly
high. So even as Marxism and Trotskyism in theory, and
socialism and communism in system, come upon very hard
times, the anarchist tradition manages to remain an intriguing, albeit imperfect, way of thought – if not necessarily a
viable way of life.

But if the thirst for personal liberty maintains anarchism
on the fringes of political discourse, it is the equally compelling demand for social order that prevents it from being put
into practice. For it is not the *commission* of acts of cruelty,
mayhem, and where deemed necessary, murder, that is at the
heart of the anarchist project, but the *justification* of such
actions in the name of an abstract higher morality. We are
asked to believe, once more, that worthy goals can be reached
through the performance of ignoble and even brutal instru-

ments. This break in the means-ends continuum makes skeptics of the very people who presumably will be beneficiaries of the anarchist credo. The search for a more perfect union is reason enough why anarchism continues to serve as a ghost in the social machinery. However, the quotidian need for a predictable and civil social reality compels such anarchical tendencies to remain for the most part a harmless, curious ghost in an old closet rather than one more thorn in the flesh of human existence.

Irving Louis Horowitz
November 12, 2004

Note to the reader: A small number of books appeared after publication of *The Anarchists* that, in my opinion, merit the attention of those wishing to pursue the issues raised further. I was especially impressed by the following titles:

Paul Avrich, *Anarchist Portraits* (Princeton, NJ: Princeton University Press, 1988), 308 pp.

Daniel Guerin, *No Gods/No Masters* (Oakland, CA: AK Press, 1997), 294 pp.

Corinne Jacker, *The Black Flag of Anarchy: Antistatism in the United States* (New York: Charles Scribners' Sons, 1968), 211 pp.

John L. Stanley, *The Sociology of Virtue: The Political and Social Theories of Georges Sorel* (Berkeley and Los Angeles: University of California Press, 1981). 387 pp.

Laurence R. Veysey, *The Communal Experience: Anarchist and Mystical Communities in Twentieth Century America* (Chicago: University of Chicago Press, 1978), 512 pp.

Acknowledgments

Let me first record the fact that I shall speak in these pages not as an anarchist, but as a social scientist in search of what the late Robert E. Park used to refer to as the "big news." This entails a constant search for valuable contributions and insights, whatever their sources, that can serve to enlarge the scope and content of the scientific study of society. The anarchist tradition is a particularly fruitful, and frightfully neglected, source in the common human effort to overcome manipulation with the only genuinely effective instrument we have—clarification.

My sympathies for the anarchists shall not be disguised. But neither shall I neglect to make clear the reasons for the virtual disappearance of anarchism as an "organized" social movement, a disappearance due not simply to a contradiction in terms, but more impressively, as a contradiction in the social processes as such. The collapse of anarchism as a social movement does not signify its annihilation as an intellectual force. Ideas are not so readily subject to obsolescence as institutions. This prime lesson, taught by the anarchists themselves, should caution us against a ready dismissal of anarchism as a pragmatic failure. The anarchist does not live in terms of criteria of success and neither should his views be judged in such terms. We inhabit a world of dismal success and heroic failure. That the anarchist posture fits into the latter category is not necessarily a charge against him. This sort of orientation may not qualify me as a bona fide anarchist, but it is my belief that at least it does not disqualify me from writing on and introducing the reader to the wealth of anarchist literature.

The original idea for this volume is, I unashamedly confess, not mine. As long ago as 1950, C. Wright Mills was interested in preparing a reader on "Anarchists, Criminals, and Deviants." This was never done. Unquestionably, Mills had second thoughts on the subject. In the passage of time between 1950 and 1960, Mills added a unique international dimension to his sociological orientation. So that by 1961 his vision of anarchism was more in keeping with the political sources of this doctrine and less tied to a sociological formalism that considered anarchism to be an expression of "deviant behavior." Mills came to consider anarchism as one of the three major "pivots" of Marxism, the other two being social democracy and bolshevism. He intended to produce a radical "trilogy": The Marxists, The Trotskyists, and The Anarchists. His untimely death in March, 1962, cut short any possibility of his completing this enterprise. And as a matter of fact, while he was already focusing attention on Trotsky and his followers, he left not even a scrap of paper on the anarchists.

I mention this not only to pay an intellectual debt of honor to Wright Mills, but also to take full responsibility for the execution and excerpts of *The Anarchists*. The views expressed in my introductory study, with whatever shortcomings they contain, are mine alone. Indeed, my own view is that anarchism, far from being a "pivot" of Marxism as Mills believed, is an effort to fashion a radical alternative to the Marxist tradition in its orthodox forms. And I think that the historical careers of the anarchists, as well as their theoretical moorings, give substance to this statement. If anything, nineteenth- and twentieth-century forms of anarchism are a self-conscious "minority" report on the progress of man in contrast to the "majority" report filed by the Marxists.

If the reader keeps in mind the fact that *The Anarchists*, when initially delivered to the publishers, was much longer, then this same reader will hopefully not be too severe with me for "obvious omissions. I have tried to compensate for these gaps and defects by providing a *Postscript* of the questions most often asked of anarchists, the kinds of answers they in turn most frequently provide, and finally, my own beliefs on these matters of controversy and conjecture.

—IRVING LOUIS HOROWITZ
Washington University
St. Louis, Missouri

part one

the theory

Introduction

1. Natural Man and Political Man

From its historical beginnings a linguistic ambiguity resides in what the term "anarchism" signifies. The ambiguity is not exclusively a failing of language. It is a consequence of the claims and counterclaims, currents and crosscurrents that necessarily plague a social movement dedicated to "propaganda of the deed" and "scientific liberation from political myth" simultaneously. The anarchists are theorists and terrorists, moralists and deviants, and above all, political and antipolitical.

If we examine the matter from a purely definitional viewpoint, we find the concept of anarchy raising up two contrasting visions. On one hand, it describes a negative condition, that which is unruly or disorganized, that which is not controlled or controllable. Sociologists might say that a condition of anarchy prevails when any event is unstructured or lacking in norms, such as spontaneous crowd behavior. These negative connotations of anarchism have penetrated the scientific literature no less than the popular literature. Nonetheless, there is also a popular positive notion of anarchy as conscious rebellion. What is entailed is a view of anarchy as "un-rule" because formal rule systems are unnecessary and superfluous in the governing of normal men. The phenomenon of altruism, or self-sacrifice of personal ambitions, indicates that spontaneous behavior is not synonymous with irrational behavior. We are thus confronted with a negative concept of anarchy as a condition of unruliness in contrast to a positive view of anarchy as the superfluity of rules.

Anarchist negation is embodied by an event, or an agency of events, such as the group, which rejects external pressures in the form of adjustment to a context of prevailing norms or superimposed rules. Conversely, positive anarchism,

anarchy as affirmation, means the "internalization" of rules
to such a high degree as to do away with the need for external constraint altogether. This ambiguity in anarchism has
as its theoretical underpinning an idealization of natural
man in contrast and in opposition to civilized man.

One of the confusions, at least, is not so much the work of
anarchism as of the commentators on anarchism who consider it to be exclusively a historical movement or a political
organism. Some historians see the demise of anarchism in
1914, or with the absorption of anarchist ideals by social reformers and the awakening of "social conscience" in the middle classes.[1] Others consider anarchist ideas to have been absorbed by mass union and political movements.[2] And still
others place the final death agony of anarchism in 1939, with
the collapse of the Spanish Republic.[3] What seems to bind
the historical school is a consensus that, however fuzzy the
beginnings of anarchism might have been, there is no question about its definite terminal point. The plain truth is that
as a historical force, anarchism never had much of a reality.
When Bakunin spoke of three thousand anarchists in Lyons,
he considered this an extraordinary achievement. And even
in Republican Spain, the anarchist "organization," *Federación Anarquista Ibérica,* could claim only a fractional (and
factional) membership.

What characteristically distinguishes anarchism from
other radical movements is precisely the low premium placed
on immediate political success, and the high premium placed
on the fashioning of a "new man" in the womb of the old society. The great Italian anarchist, Errico Malatesta, who
bridges 19th- and 20th-century European thought as few of
his peers did, put the matter directly:

> Our belief is that the only way of emancipation and of
> progress is that all shall have the liberty and the means of
> advocating and putting into practice their ideas—that is
> to say, anarchy. Thus, the more advanced minorities will

[1] Barbara W. Tuchman, "The Anarchists," *The Atlantic.* Vol. 211, No. 5
(May, 1963), pp. 91–110.
[2] G. D. H. Cole, *Socialist Thought: Marxism and Anarchism, 1850–1890.*
London: Macmillan & Co. Ltd., 1954, pp. 315–60.
[3] George Woodcock, *Anarchism: A History of Libertarian Ideas and Movements.* Cleveland and New York: The World Publishing Co., 1962, esp.
pp. 393–8.

persuade and draw after them the more backward by the force of reason and example.[4]

The classical anarchists, Bakunin, Malatesta, Sorel, Kropotkin, have a shared consensus in anarchism as a "way of life" rather than as a "view of the future." What is offered is a belief in "natural man" as more fundamental and historically prior to "political man."

Civilization is viewed as a series of impediments and obstructions preventing the natural man from realizing himself. This represents an inversion of Hobbes' doctrine of the "war of every man against every man." In Hobbes, the Leviathan exists for the exclusive purpose of curbing "the solitary, poor, nasty, brutish, and short" character of natural man. From the anarchist standpoint, Rousseau's doctrine of the natural goodness of man is only a partial solution to the problems presented in Hobbes' view of human nature. For whether man is "good" or "brutish" is less important to the anarchist than what men do to preserve their inner core. Rousseau shares with the power theorists the idea that self-preservation requires men to contract out their private rights. The Rousseau paradox is that to gain survival entails a loss of humanity. Rights are swallowed up by obligations. The State absorbs Civil society. Natural man is outflanked and outmaneuvered by society.

The anarchist rebuttal to this line of reasoning is that to make a contract, which is an involuntary act to begin with, is really to compromise the natural man. If man is really good, then the purpose of life, in contrast to the purpose of politics, ought to be the restoration of the natural condition of human *relations* at whatever level of human *development* thus far achieved. This is not exclusively a matter of internalizing felt needs, but no less, a form of shedding that which is superfluous and unnecessary. Intrinsic to anarchism is an asceticism and an ascetic mood. One finds the anarchist as a historical figure to be a person very close to "natural" values and "fundamental" living conditions. Their attitudes toward matters of food, shelter, sexuality, and the generalized expression of human needs in the social economy are simply that all needs can be satisfied once the "natural laws of so-

[4] Errico Malatesta, in *Le Réveil* (1906), as quoted in G. D. H. Cole, *op. cit.*, pp. 356–7.

ciety" shed the impediments of civilization. This sublime
faith in the natural in contrast to the social accounts to a
considerable degree for the central peculiarity of anarchism
—the absence of a well worked-out commitment to economic
development.

Precisely because economics in its advanced form must
necessarily cope with problems of affluence, consumer and
producer demands, distribution of goods, allocation of natural resources, etc., the anarchist tends to consider economic
prognostication as catering to both the impossible (because
prediction is unfeasible for future social systems) and the unnecessary (since any "rational" economy would center on
"production for use"). Even in its specifically economic
form, such as in the work of Pierre Joseph Proudhon, anarchism makes little attempt to chart the contours of a rational
economy. Proudhon's critique of property relations is everything Marx said it was: abstract, grandiose in statement, and
rhetorical in content. Piecework is described as the "deprivation of the soul," machinery becomes the "protest against
homicidal labor," and economic history as such becomes a
"sequence of ideas."[5] Even those later figures, like Bakunin
and Kropotkin, who accepted the main contours of socialist
economics, did so more as an instrument by which the restoration of the feudal workshop could be achieved rather than
as a guide to the study of economic realities.

There is a perennial tension between the naturalistic character of anarchism and its emergent participation in socialist
currents. On frankly moral grounds the anarchists opposed
the stratification of men into classes. Social classes violate
the natural equality of men in their psychological-biological
characteristics. Anarchism tends to distinguish wage laborers
from factory owners in terms of the moral properties of
work rather than the alienative features of class relations. A
strong pietistic religious element is present: work is good,
idleness is evil; the poor are noble while the rich are sinful.
Men are naturally equal, while they are socially stratified.
Real and legitimate differences are obscured by social position and by family property. Anarchist man sees differences

[5] Pierre Joseph Proudhon, *What is Property: An Inquiry into the Principles of Right and of Government.* New York: Humboldt Publishing Co., 1891;
and *Système des contradictions économiques ou philosophie de la misère.*
Paris: Guillaumin, 1846. In contrast, see the critique by Karl Marx, *The
Poverty of Philosophy* (1847). New York: International Publishers, 1935.

in terms of the quality of mind of each person, the degree of self-realization and self-fulfillment, and the extent of socialization. Capitalist man is the accommodating man: solicitous when profits are at stake, brutal when workers are at stake, cruel when the social system is at stake.

The anarchist image of life is in terms of a moral drama, a drama in which individuals are pitted against social systems. It is little wonder, then, that the anarchist has an apocalyptic attitude toward social classes. Abolish class relations, and the natural man will come to fructification. This attitude toward classes is comparable to the approach that nudists take to clothing. Eliminate clothing, and all people will immediately perceive the absurdity of clothing, as well as its harmful psychological by-products, such as repression and guilt. So, too, runs the anarchist argument. Abolish social classes, and the absurdity of class distinctions will immediately become manifest. The absurd by-products of the class system—oppression of the poor by the rich, impoverishment of the many on behalf of the few, etc.—will give way to the new dawning. Just how this process will install an economy of abundance and distributive justice becomes a matter for future generations to discuss. Just as it would be metaphysics to discuss the problems that would occur in a world of naked people, so too, the anarchist holds the socialists to be metaphysicians for attempting to anticipate the problems as well as the contours of a society without exploitation and an economy without classes.

This tension between "naturalism" and "socialism" is also present in the anarchist stance toward politics. The whole world of politics is itself an embodiment of authority, of arbitrary power. At some level the definition of politics is necessarily linked to the exercise or restraint of power. The whole concept of politics has as its perfect social expression superordination and subordination, just as in the previous illustration the whole notion of economics has as its basis, mastery and slavery. Once again then, the reason the anarchists take an antipolitical position, not simply against certain forms of politics, but against the content of politics as such, is that the notion of superordination and subordination, resting as it does on a social concept to justify power, is a superfluity, a civilized manner for expressing the social fact of inequality. The point of view of most anarchists is that the doctrine of

self-interest arises only at that point when the interests of society are schismatic or bifurcated. When it is seen or felt
that the self is something other than the society, only at that
point does hedonism become a force.

The political doctrines of anarchism are totalistic. They are
anti-egoistic, because egoism is an expression of civilization.
It is antifatalist, because fatalism violates individual liberty.
The propensity of natural man is voluntary association based
on the practice of mutual aid. The concept of mutual aid,
while sharing many properties of altruism, differs from the
latter since altruism implies conscious surrender of self in an
egotistical milieu. Mutual aid is socially systematized. There
is no longer any psychology of egotism in anarchist society,
and therefore altruism cannot have a psychological base.
One wouldn't perform an altruistic act. One performs social
acts at all levels—whether in defense of self or on behalf of
other persons. Psychology as a division among men will be
broken down in the anarchist world. There will then be a
possibility of a truly human association that at the same time
overcomes the distinction between the public and the private.

This utilitarian "mutual aid" aspect of anarchism is dominant and fully expressed from Godwin to Tolstoy. It was particularly suitable as the ultimate expression of the plight of
the modern peasantry. Collectivist anarchism departs from
this social stress to the idea of the individual's war against the
state as a form of self-preservation. The ever-enlarged scope
of bureaucratic domination has led anarchism to emphasize
the need to survive under the pressures and censures of
society.

What characterizes contemporary anarchism, as contrasted with earlier forms, is the highly personal nature of
the revolt against authority. There might very well be a sense
in which the anarchism of intellectuals is a very special vari-
ant of anarchism. It possesses three distinguishing qualities:
1) emphasis on individual responses, on the "politics of
truth"; 2) rejection of professionalism and departmental
academicism; and 3) belief in the sanctity of the "private
life." In the intellectual's powerful sense of the distinction
between public and private, which D. H. Lawrence in particular has pointed out, and the image of the fighting private
intellectual there is perhaps an anomic kind of anarchism, if
one may speak of *anomie* in this connection.

In its classical model, the notion of the fighting romantic against the world is antithetical to anarchism as a theory, but quite in keeping with the "deviant" psychological characteristics of the anarchists as people. The anarchist as a person tends to be highly deviant, closely allied to the criminal sectors in European society, and to the *lumpenproletariat* in the United States, the tramps, hoboes, and rummies. While the anarchist does not define himself as a criminal (criminality is seen as a form of lower-class egotism—excusable rather than practicable) he does not consider the criminal, as does the bourgeois, to be "an enemy of society." Indeed, they have close dealings since anarchists have at times hired out as professional criminals to commit assassinations and bank robberies in Italy and Spain. But the anarchist who steals does not do so for his own self-interest. He carefully allocates funds making very sure that nothing is used for creature comforts. He will kill, but he is very careful not to harm anyone who is innocent from the viewpoint of the class struggle. He will cajole, but not for the purpose of keeping the reigns of power. The goal, however ill-defined, is all-important. And the means used in its attainment (the overthrow of the state and of the class system) are moral in virtue of these aims. Therefore, the means used are conditioned only by the question of efficiency of realizing the ends. No ethic is attached to them. Clearly, the anarchist is not a pragmatist. He does not accept the idea that there is a means-ends continuum. The purposes of violence determine its good or its evil character—and not the fact of violence as such. This dichotomization gives to the anarchist the appearance of criminality, while distinguishing his essence. It also provides for a life-style that is often awkward and difficult to manage —since he must work with egotists while maintaining his altruism; and cooperate with derelicts while urging a "new man" theory of social change; and he must oppose totalitarianism in theory while maintaining authoritarian personality traits in his personal habits and behavior.

The fundamental development of anarchism as a social agency for change and as an intellectual mood reached full expression in the nineteenth century. It is not inconsequential to take note of the philosophical climate and technological level surrounding this development. The philosophical point of view underlying classical anarchism is not so much Hegel's dialectics as it was Kant's ethics. The only true morality that the anarchist would recognize is one in which there would no longer be a distinction between what is done for one's self and what is done for others.

A derivative of this is the antitechnological claims of anarchism. These turn out to be fundamentally petty bourgeois or peasant. The notion of community was very strong in utopian varieties of community life. Small-scale farming and small-scale industry, where there was indeed intimacy and rapport between the people at work, where work itself was an organizing principle and a viable one, were a vital principle of life writ large. This combination of the technology of the small factory and the small farm, combined as it was with this highly rationalistic Kantian image of what a moral man defines the communal obligation to be, reveals the anarchist as antitechnological in his stance just as previously he is described as antipolitical and anti-economic. He is total in his commitment to a social ethic in which the personality is part and parcel of that social view. And the alienation of men from the sources of their labor, and from the machine directly, violates this social ethic. The fact that anarchism in its most distilled form is the idea of the brotherhood of man and the *naturalness* of this equality, any separatist movement, such as nationalism or racialism, that has imaginary pressures from the exploiting strata of every state has to be sharply opposed. The main evil of nationalism is not solely that it breeds wars, but that it does so because nationalism is *unnatural*. Civilization sets up arbitrary differentiations so that national distinctions intensify and exaggerate factors making for conflict: patriotic gore, class animus, racial purity. They are unreal and susceptible to dissolution and alteration. Their only reality derives from the power relations that are caused by class domination and legal rationalization.

The philosophic stance of anarchism is juxtaposed against the power relations of society. Anarchism is a commitment to the idea of nature, to the belief that nature is an "essence," while society is an "accident." It stands in contrast to the idea of existence because the concept of existence, as it has unfolded in both Marxist and Existentialist thought, involves problems of revolution, of change in terms of other men, in terms of a fundamental theory of the redistribution of power, in terms of the redistribution of wealth rather than the notion of wealth as such. So that the difference between socialism and anarchism is primarily a difference between those who would abolish the forms of social relations as they now exist, and those who would abolish the content of all hitherto existing class society. The socialist has ultimate visions of future society through the redistribution of power, property, etc. The anarchist sees any such compromise as stillborn and doomed to perpetuate in new form the same divisions that have riven society historically. For the anarchist, the root of the problem is society; for the socialist, the root of the problem is class. This helps explain, in addition to the fierce personality clashes, the bitterness between socialists and anarchists. Their philosophical and ideological premises differ despite the superficial acceptance by both of a communal economy. It is shallow to say that the difference between anarchists and socialists is tactical, i.e., that socialists would postpone the abolition of the state while the anarchists want to abolish the state now. What underlies this tactical difference are contrasting theories of human nature.

Anarchists regard socialists as corrupted by the political structure since they accept the premises of the bourgeois state: order, constitutional limits, parliamentary procedure, etc., in order to wrest power. By failing to destroy power, they are corrupted by it and perpetuate the state they are pledged to overthrow. The anarchist assumption is that to better civilization is a subtle form of corruption, of self-delusion. What is required is abolition, not improvement. Not even the word "revolution" really encompasses the anarchist ideal. Revolution is the idea of the radical change in the forms of life. The anarchist notion of abolition is more profoundly radical in its implications because of the distinctions between contamination through the acceptance of the forms of civilization and regeneration through the breaking of such civilized forms. The socialist changes society, leaving inherited civilization intact. He reforms its worst abuses. His arguments are for a higher development of civilization. The anarchist rejects the inherently constricting and corrupting nature of civilization and demands total reconstruction of the human condition. It means to annihilate sociological, economic, and political features of human life that we have come to consider fixed. The practical socialist claims no more than the right to humanize and equalize the power structure. The impractical anarchist claims to do no less than liquidate State power as such.

2. The Anarchist Ambiguity

We inherit many stereotyped notions about political movements. Perhaps one of the most common is that of the bearded, bomb-throwing, and blasphemous anarchist. And though the more priggish devotees of anarchism would wish to deny that any truth inheres in the stereotype, even historical truth, it must be admitted frankly that, like most stereotypes, this one has much to recommend itself. From the *Narodniki* in Czarist Russia, to the anarchist mine workers of Catalonia and Asturias in Spain, to the "wobblies" of the IWW in the western part of the United States, anarchist social movements have been violent in practice if not always in "theory." To be sure, anarchism traditionally counterposes the "force" of the Nation-State against the principled "violence" of the great unwashed.[1] But the brute fact remains that a cornerstone of anarchism has been its militant and spontaneous activism.[2]

On the other side, the anarchist literature (and we must face the fact at the outset that anarchism is in this day and age more of a literature than a movement) frequently operates out of a sweeping stereotype of its own: a view of the social system as inhabited by alienated proletarians, anomic professionals, and anxiety-ridden policy makers. This, too, is a stereotype with considerable punch behind it. Indeed, the two-pronged anarchist attack—upon a bourgeois society become insipid and infirm with age, and upon a socialist State become more corrupt and bureaucratized than even the most ossified form of capitalism—is not restricted to anarchists

---

[1] Georges Sorel, *Reflections on Violence.* Glencoe (Ill.): The Free Press, 1950, pp. 247–48; and also his *Matériaux d'une theorie du prolétariat* (3rd edition). Paris: Marcel Riviere, 1929, p. 67.

[2] Even so humane an anarchist as Emma Goldman wrote: "Does not the end justify the means? What if a few should have to perish? The many could be made free and could live in beauty and comfort." See her autobiography, *Living My Life.* New York: Alfred A. Knopf, 1931, p. 88.

by any means. A spate of literature, from analytic to poetic, bristles with the same charges. The social sciences have taken over the anarchist claims against bureaucracy with its trenchant critique of the dysfunctional nature of the organizational life.[3]

We are not done with a settlement of what anarchism stands for by a simple cataloguing of social systems it opposes. For on such matters anarchism stands close to the entire frontal assault made on capitalism—from nostalgic conservatism to utopian socialism. The classic definition of anarchism is that as an ideology and as a philosophy it stands for the immediate liquidation of all State authority. But the close observer will immediately perceive that this is a negative recommendation rather than a positive option. It is a central purpose of this work to elicit, through both text and commentary, the chief principles and aims of anarchism. For it is upon these positive recommendations that anarchism as a body of social theory either stands or falls.

The American now lives in what sociologists have termed the "overdeveloped society." Social scientists have sternly warned us that the bureaucratic machinery that makes this overdeveloped society tick is fast approaching a condition of diminishing returns. The organizational complex has substituted a chain of command for individual initiative, automatic salary escalations for promotions based on personal merit, problems of communication for differences of class, and an overall bureaucratic pathos in place of treating issues as they arise in each instance. The psychiatrists have put us on notice that this bureaucratic machinery has taken a huge toll in disrupting normal human impulses and relations. The economists have been no less clear in pointing out that the costs of supporting this Leviathan are paid for by keeping the largest portion of humanity in a socially underdeveloped condition.

In the face of this matrix of public issues and private agonies, the dominant human response to this giganticism has been a retreat to the private world of friends and family, where the home becomes not so much the castle as the fortress against any further penetration by the monster State.

[3] For recent examples, see Robert Presthus, *The Organizational Society.* New York: Alfred A. Knopf, 1962, pp. 287–323; and William H. Whyte, Jr., *The Organization Man.* New York: Simon and Schuster, 1956, esp. pp. 155–85.

But at the same time this dichotomization of life rests on the total separation of public policy and personal ethics, on an acceptance of the permanent existence of the manipulative State and the manipulated Man. Recent studies of the American electorate indicate how complete is this passive acceptance of the situation. Political parties are described in terms of the "same difference," while outrages to public sensibilities are met with a definite solution: "Go fight City Hall." In this situation, the good American becomes the clever American: the man who can "stay out of trouble," the man who can "work the system" rather than one who fights the system. Admittedly, this is painting with a broad brush. Nonetheless, it is hard to escape the realities of the overdeveloped society, if only because there is no clear alternative and life must continue.

Given such a set of public factors—of the complex organizational apparatus, of the deterioration in citizen participation through voluntary association—it scarcely requires any feats of mind to show that modern industrial life is incompatible with the anarchist demand for the liquidation of State authority. Anarchism can be no more than a posture. It cannot be a viable political position. This is said at the outset so that the reader concerned exclusively with problems of political decision-making can return the book and demand a refund. Indeed, if such a simple refund can be made without the wild snarls of credit memoranda!

One can afford to be forthright about discouraging the exclusively political-minded because this audience is miniscule to begin with. It is precisely this fact—the ineluctable separation of the American overdeveloped society from the underdeveloped science of politics—that still makes anarchism an interesting, if ambiguous, point of view. For the bulk of our public have little beyond postures by which to live in any event. And it helps to explore a literature that unpretentiously declares itself nothing but a posture, an attitude of mind and a style of life. Indeed, anarchism has become, in this generation, an effort to stay the hand of the "iron law of bureaucracy," an attempt to fashion a personal code of ethics that consciously refuses either to abide by the rules or to work such rules to personal "businesslike" advantage.

In terms of the social forces utilizing the anarchist credo and posture a remarkable transvaluation of values has occurred. In the eighteenth century, the chief advocates of anarchism were recruited from the European peasantry, with its plethora of utopian communities, religious societies, and aristocratic idealists, all poised against the onslaught and inevitable victory of the industrial capitalist system and its political affiliate, the Leviathan. In the nineteenth century, anarchist doctrine found a new home among the working classes of industrial Europe. In the specialized trades, in the trade unions, and in working-class voluntary social associations, anarchist principles took on new vigor. But once again the wave of organization swept "spontaneous" working-class anarchism into the dustbin of history. The complete victory of trade unionism and social democracy in Western Europe, and of bureaucratic State socialism in Eastern Europe, further separated anarchist doctrine from proletarian practice.

Nonetheless, anarchism has proven to be a stubborn if self-conscious minority posture. Modern life has created its own standards of success and failure. And there are enough "failures" to fill any ten mass movements, much less the anarchist posture. The rebirth of anarchism in the twentieth century has been due to a general disaffiliation of "intellectuals" and "professionals" from the general celebration of the affluent society. This portion of society, while enlarged as a consequence of the growing need for expertise and exact knowledge, has also been the most defeated victim of overdevelopment. The man of knowledge has been "on tap" but rarely "on top." Knowledge has been effectively separated from power, just as clarification has been isolated from manipulation.[4]

In consequence of this very bifurcation, modern society has created the first collectivity of natural anarchists, people who are resistant to absorption within the Establishment and whose antipolitical rejection of affiliation is part of the self-definition of an intellectual. The bases of intellectual activity require spontaneity in a world of precision and order, individuality in a universe of collective responses, risk-taking in an organizational arrangement geared to "line" and "staff." Because of this polarization of social life, anarchism has remained a factor in modern societies. The intellectual is antipolitical by social training and personal habit. The anarchist

[4] *Cf.* C. Wright Mills, *Power, Politics and People,* edited by Irving L. Horowitz. New York: Oxford University Press, 1963, pp. 599–613.

is antipolitical by intellectual conviction. The wedding of these two elements defines the scope of present-day anarchism.

The great anarchist Peter Kropotkin anticipated this fusion of intellect and anarchy when he outlined the basis of scientific activity:

> There is one point on which Anarchism is absolutely right. It is in considering the study of social institutions as a chapter of natural science; when it parts forever with metaphysics; and when it takes for its method of reasoning the method that has served to build up all modern science and natural philosophy. If this method be followed, errors into which Anarchists may have fallen will be easily recognized. But to verify our conclusions is only possible by the scientific inductive-deductive method, on which every science is built, and by means of which every scientific conception of the universe has been developed.[5]

Whatever its defects, anarchism has attempted to adhere to the canons of scientific method. And whether by conscious decision or by indirection, intellectual activity has become increasingly anarchist in posture. Thus, however "ambiguous" the anarchist legacy may be, it remains a useful one and a needed one.

3. A Typology of Anarchist Strategies and Beliefs

However contemptuous contemporary anarchists may be concerning the ordinary standards of political success and failure, within its own frame of reference, anarchism reduplicates this general concern for political realities no less than political truths. This is expressed with admirable clarity by Kropotkin in his work on the French Revolution. He points out that anarchism is not only a series of brilliant ideas, but an historical entity as well:

[5] Peter Kropotkin, *Modern Science and Anarchism*. London: Freedom Press, 1912, pp. 92–3.

All through the Great Revolution the communist idea
kept coming to the front. . . . Fourierism descends in a
direct line from L'Ange on one side and from Chalier on
the other. Babeuf is the direct descendant of ideas which
stirred the masses to enthusiasm in 1793; he, Buonarotti,
and Sylvain Maréchal have only systematized them a little
or even merely put them into literary form. But the secret
societies organized by Babeuf and Buonarotti were the
origin of the *communistes matérialistes* societies which
Blanqui and Barbès conspired under the *bourgeois* monarchy of Louis-Philippe. Later on in 1866, the International Workingmen's Association appeared in the direct
line of descent from these societies. . . . There is therefore a direct filiation from the *Enragés* of 1793 and the
Babeuf conspiracy of 1795 to the International Workingmen's Association of 1866–1878.[1]

In examining the basic forms of anarchism we do not
mean to imply the existence of eight distinct doctrines. What
is at stake is not so much alternative models of the good society as distinctive strategies for getting there. Therefore
the differences in forms of anarchism involve details of priority rather than programmatic rhetoric. Should the first
step include or exclude violence? Should the State be liquidated as a consequence of workers' organization from below,
or must the first stage in organizing a system of mutual aid
be in terms of first liquidating the State? Should anarchism
strive for victory through numbers or through conspiratorial
techniques? It might appear strange that an *ism* that has generally never been in a position to muster any significant political support should be so preoccupied with principles and
programs. Yet, historically, it is a characteristic feature of
minority movements, unburdened as they are with problems
of the exercise of political power, to be schismatic and factional in relation to their principles and precepts. The struggle for purity is as essential to political messianism as the sacrifice of principles is characteristic of actual rule.

Furthermore, it is evident that while anarchism has undergone integral transformations in terms of changing demands
placed upon it by the inner dialogue, the converse is no less

[1] Peter Kropotkin, *The Great French Revolution: 1789–1793*. London: William Heinemann, Ltd., 1909, pp. 579–80.

the case: anarchism is subject to changes in terms of differing historical circumstances. The Godwinists' concern for
universal justice was a direct outgrowth of the English bourgeois Revolution with its exceptional concern for the juridical forms of change. The Bakuninists' sanction of organizational terror was likewise framed in the spirit of Russian
Narodniki, who saw no other possible means of toppling the
autocracy. The impulse behind the doctrines of violence pro-
pounded by Malatesta and Sorel was clearly a disillusionment
with organizations as such, with their "oligarchical" tendencies that Robert Michels so brilliantly summed up in *Political
Parties.* Present pacifist varieties of anarchism likewise reveal a response to the concentration of armed power in the
hands of the emissaries of government, and hence a need to
fashion tactics that can circumvent this monumental fact
without destroying anarchists as such. The "rage to live" that
is witnessed in the writings of literary anarchists is just as
true to the canon of rebellion to State tyranny as earlier
forms; however it sees individual acts of terror as hopelessly
meaningless in an age that takes systematic extermination of
populations for granted.

Thus it is that the types of anarchism that have evolved
represent a double response: to the internal tensions and
strains of doctrine, and no less to the changing social circumstances in which anarchism found itself at given historical
periods. What is revealed in the varieties of anarchism are
different seats of social and class support, contrasting attitudes towards the utility of political combat, different psychological and philosophical supports, and contrasting organizational methods. This may not produce theoretical
coherence or, for that matter, success in the public arena,
but it does prevent the kind of doctrinal stultification and
stagnation that has overcome a good many *isms* that at one
time or another could claim a far larger number of adherents.
And this very fact must appear as a central feature of the
anarchist tradition.

UTILITARIAN ANARCHISM: The first conscious form of anarchism represented a compound of nostalgia and utopianism
—a natural enough consequence of a doctrine developed by
an enlightened sector of the aristocracy and later employed
by the *sansculottes.* Utilitarian anarchy ever remained an

expression by the declassé wealthy on behalf of the under-privileged of society. The poor had not yet learned to speak for themselves, so an element of surprise is ever present in the writings of Helvetius, Diderot, and Godwin, that there should be an ever widening distinction between rich and poor, between social gain and social responsibility. The utilitarian anarchism even of a Saint-Simon was not so much a form of rational consciousness as it was a form of embarrassment in search of guilt alleviation. The solution was to be reason—the manufacture of reasonable creatures from below, and the appeal to rational authorities from above. Self and society, private and public, ruler and ruled were all to be united under the banner of reason, in the path of which stood the accursed State.

As befitted men of sensibility and good sense, not the direct action of masses, but the edict of rational rulers was to be the central agency for eliminating, first the iniquities of the State, and later the State itself. The equation was relatively simple: education plus legislation equals the good society. The present tendency is to offer a perfunctory dismissal of these earliest expressions of anarchist sentiment; and clearly modern experience offers sound reasons for this. Nonetheless, it should be recalled that utilitarian anarchism did a great deal to shape the modern vision of human nature as plastic and progressive. It understood, indeed, that men can be rendered happier by a more reasonable social order and that they would be more orderly rather than less so, given a more equitable distribution of power and wealth.

Still, this eighteenth-century form of anarchism suffered from the deformations and exaggerations of the aristocratic sector that gave it original shape and that remained present even when it was taken over by the conspiratorial elements within utilitarian anarchism. So volitional a creature was man, according to this view, that historical forces simply dissolved. Just as the slate could be wiped clean, so too was society to be cleansed of its repressive mechanisms. Cultural antecedents, malignant classes, vested interests, competition for power, each and all were to be eliminated in the wave of reasonableness, that was to overtake rational and responsible men. From Helvetius to Godwin, the assumption was clearly that knowledge and truth could overcome ignorance and interests. What Kingsley Martin wrote of the utilitarians in

general has a particular relevance in understanding the apocalyptic antihistorical basis of the early anarchists. "They never
dreamed that if men were offered the truth they would not
leap for it, that if they were told ugly facts they would prefer
pleasant lies, that if reasonable ideals were offered them they
would continue to act as their fathers had done; they did not
see that the follies of the past were not only imposed but
ingrained, that men carried their history not only on their
backs but in their heads."[2] It might be added that when the
recognition of these historical truths became manifest, the
aristocracy that fashioned the early versions of anti-State
chose to sacrifice its revolutionary awareness and to preserve
its inherited privileges. The decline of utilitarian anarchism
was a consequence of a double force: the rise of the consciousness of poverty by the propertyless; and the growth of
compromise rather than criticism as the path chosen by the
dwindling aristocracy to maintain its privileged place in the
empire of Capital.

PEASANT ANARCHISM. The other major current in early anarchism had as its basis the gigantic European peasantry,
which, despite the process of industrialization, remained the
largest single class in Western society down through the nineteenth century. Indeed, the process of industrialization led to
a celebration of the verities and the virtues of the land. From
Thomas Münzer to Charles Fourier there was a pervasive and
widespread sentiment that capitalism meant the growth of
external authority and not the age of progress the bourgeois
spokesmen were so fond of heralding. Unlike the utilitarian
anarchists, the peasant anarchists put little faith in reform
from above. Instead, they urged a withdrawal from the State
as such and the setting up of informal communities based on
principles of mutual assistance and social service.

The anarchist communities represented an effort to escape
the profanation of all values under capitalism, and to avoid
the liberalist solutions put forth by capitalist apologists. The
industrial process and the wealth it produced, far from being
a liberating agent, was for the peasant anarchists the ultimate
form of human degradation.

In describing the individual and organization in utopian

[2] Kingsley Martin, *French Liberal Thought in the Eighteenth Century*,
London: Ernest Benn, Ltd., 1929, p. 191.

ideology, J. L. Talmon shows just what the peasant spirit held to be most sinful in the capitalist spirit. In it one can see the moral bases of later socialisms:

> The capitalist system, which claims to be wholly purposeful, encourages wasteful parasitism, and is in turn to a large extent fed on it. There are the throngs of innumerable middlemen, agents, lawyers, useless clerks, who eat at the expense of others, without producing anything useful. Their whole raison d'etre is to incite their begetters and bread givers to greater and more refined acts of rapacity and fraud, and to stultify the victims thereof. The State machinery, gendarmes and army, tax collectors and magistrates, customs officers and civil servants, allegedly existing to "protect" society from commercial piracy and abuse, are in fact the accomplices and instruments of the fraudulent conspiracy.[3]

In such a situation, any appeal to the reasonableness of the holders of power and wealth must appear absurd. The peasant anarchists had little regard for the philosophers and their liberal sophistication. They tended to emphasize the curative power of work, especially of productive cultural work.

But in this emphasis on peasant verities they came upon the inherited concerns of the Church and its interests in preserving and salvaging the souls of the poor. Thus, peasant anarchism was compelled to pay special attention not only to the bourgeois liberal enemy, but also to the religious and conservative "enemy." In Fourier, it took the form of a critique of ascetic and repressive morality. Such an outlook only perverted the truly human gains of mutual aid in the communities of land by making man into "a creature of insatiable cupidity." The goodly peasant must therefore avoid not only the lures of the City of Man, but also the perversions of the City of God—or rather the construction of Providential Will given by corrupt, property-holding clerical forces.

The high regard in which later anarchist spokesmen, such as Proudhon and Bakunin, held the peasantry, marks one of the great watersheds between anarchism and bolshevism. For

---

[3] Jacob L. Talmon, *Political Messianism: The Romantic Phase.* London: Secker and Warburg, 1960, pp. 127–36.

what is involved is nothing short of the difference between a theory of peasant revolution and a theory of proletarian revolution. The polemics of Lenin against Sismondi, and of Stalin against the Russian *Narodniki,* can only be appreciated in a context in which the peasantry remained the largest portion of backward Imperial Russia, a portion that not a few socialists felt was being dangerously downgraded in the formation of a revolutionary movement.

The peasant anarchist vision of the European peasant as an independent, hard-working, creative, and potentially radical creature, contrasted most sharply with the official socialist vision of this same creature as a "troglodyte," a self-seeking petty-bourgeois, whose vision of the world was restricted to the sight of his fields. Leaving aside the special features of the Western European peasantry (which tended to confirm the Marxist image rather than that held by Bakunin), it remains a fact that most present-day revolutions in the Third World[4] have a very definite peasant character. The theory of proletarian revolution has had to be bent to a considerable extent to take account of this mass peasant force—that far from being a selfish and willing pawn of industrial capitalism, it has proven to be far more revolutionary than the Marxian tradition has ever officially acknowledged. Nevertheless, it must be acknowledged that the anarchist view of the Western European peasant was far more rosy than the facts warrant. And even though anarchism may not have worshiped at the shrine of petty-bourgeois life as such, through the medium of a "bourgeoisified" peasantry, it certainly did respond to petty-bourgeois values—individualism, enterprise, dissociation, and antipolitics. The failure of the peasantry of Europe to respond to anarchist impulses was, after all, the definitive answer to those who saw the solution in a withdrawal from rather than combat with, the State.

ANARCHO-SYNDICALISM. If the anarchism of aristocratic utilitarians was often aggressive and intellectualist about the less vital questions of the day—such as vegetarianism, free love, and a universal language—and the anarchism of the peasants moved in a narrow and parochial circle entailing negative attitudes toward the processes of industrialization and urbani-

---

[4] The newly emerging States of Asia and Africa and the rapidly developing States of Latin America.

zation, the anarchism practiced and preached by radical trade unionism proved of a sounder variety. It was first and foremost based on the realities of nineteenth-century European life; and it drew its support from the struggles between classes that was at the center of the historic drama. As one writer put it: "Anarcho-syndicalism is *par excellence* the fighting doctrine of the organized working class, in which the spirit of enterprise and initiative, physical courage and the taste for responsibility have always been highly esteemed." [5]

The marriage of unionism and anarchism in Europe was a natural consequence of the fear and hostility the more articulate factory workers felt concerning the "Bourgeois State." The organizational apparatus of skilled workers in particular often developed in conscious opposition to the State. The *Bourses du Travail* in France became a "State within a State," as did the Swiss watchmaking guilds. The expansion of union activities of working-class life contributed to a mass political awakening by virtue of its very emancipation from politics as such. Fernand Pelloutier in particular gave theoretical substance to anarcho-syndicalism by connecting the economic struggle of classes with the direct political struggle to emancipate mankind from the State. The new men of labor were to assume all positive State functions, from the protection of proletarian rights to education in the possible forms of mutual cooperation. Anarchy was to be made over into a social force first and an ideological force second. The proletariat was to replace the peasant and the ideologue alike as the central element in the struggle against the bourgeois state. [6]

The growth of anarcho-syndicalism was greatly assisted by a new turn toward the problems of tactics in social revolution —something notable for its absence in older anarchist postures. The fusion of socialism and unionism was seen as functionally complete in the general strike. This was not viewed either as a strike for summer wages, or as a widespread attempt to garner political concessions from the State. While the possibilities of immediate gains were not denied, the essence of the general strike was to evoke the deepest class allegiances and obligations of the workers. As economic strife between classes would become more intense, the meaning of

[5] Leo Moulin, *Socialism of the West*. Translated by Alfred Heron. London: Victor Gollancz, Ltd., 1948, p. 137.

[6] Cf. Fernand Pelloutier, *Histoire des Bourses du Travail*, Paris, 1902, esp. pp. 70–71, 184–9.

the general strike would become manifest. The anarcho-syndicalist strike would entail direct worker participation in a broad social and economic upheaval. It would become an instrument for compelling the State to abandon its place on the historical stage to the direct association of the wage-earning class. For the most part, revolutionary unionism, such as that practiced by the International Workers of the World in the United States and the General Confederation of Labor in France, did not view the general strike as a replacement of the traditional economic strike. Rather, it was to supercede all pragmatic "short-run inspired" strikes. Keynoting this approach was an intense disdain and a flat rejection of anything that the government or opposing politicians were willing to concede the workers. The general strike was antipolitical, conceived of as part of the permanent social revolution.[7]

The new wave of optimism that gripped anarchist circles in the late nineteenth century soon gave out. The workers cared less for political strikes than for economic strikes; less about the general strike and more about the wages of sin and the hours of leisure. The State proved quite as adept at absorbing proletarian interests as it earlier did bourgeois interests. The State as a mediative power obviated and blunted the sharp edge of anarchist criticism of the State as oppressor. The immense growth of an impersonal bureaucracy, the extension of the administrative aspects of State authority to cover worker interests, cut deeply into anarchist pretensions at forging a spontaneous mass movement of insurgency.

It was not simply the continued vigor of the State that caused anarcho-syndicalism to be short-lived. Nor, for that matter, can the dismal failure of this form of proletarian anarchism be attributed to the moral corruption of the working class as such. The deeper answers are to be found in the faulty formulations of the anarcho-syndicalists themselves. Their problems ran along three pivotal paths: 1) They tended to approach socialism as a reality around the corner, rather than a long-range process of social reorganization. Beyond the general strike no precepts or principles were enunciated. 2) Anarcho-syndicalism abandoned the tasks of organization —preferring ready-made agencies of working-class life that

[7] Irving L. Horowitz, *Radicalism and the Revolt Against Reason.* London: Routledge and Kegan Paul, Ltd., 1961, esp. pp. 23–38.

were essentially unprepared (and unwilling) to engage in direct revolutionary action. Revolutions are not spontaneous events; they are made by men. And men in their turn either lead them to the promised land or turn them away from the implications of large-scale revolution. 3) Finally, anarcho-syndicalism failed to offer sound sociological or psychological reasons for getting men to act. It failed to distinguish between the ends of action and the stimuli to action. The simple announcement that a world without a State will be the outcome of a general strike neither proves that this will indeed be the result nor is it likely to stimulate men to maintain and sustain a political act beyond the initial failures.

Anarcho-syndicalism, which was itself a response to the disillusionment of appeals to monarchical rulers, and with parliamentary socialists, created its own forms of disillusionment as the workers increasingly turned toward the State as a mediative force in their conflict with the bourgeoisie. Anarcho-syndicalism sought to engage in mass politics while at the same time it wanted to escape the evils of political contamination. The paradox proved too great for the doctrine to resolve; and it was increasingly compelled to flee from the State, rather than defeat the State in a general contest of class wills.

With the collapse of anarcho-syndicalism, anarchism as a class ideology increasingly gave way to anarchism as personal-moral redemption. Anarchism became a form of conduct rather than an instrument of class politics.

COLLECTIVIST ANARCHISM. Anarchism had within itself one remaining burst of *political* energy, that with which the names of Bakunin, Kropotkin, and the First International are connected. It is to be distinguished from communist anarchism as preached by Malatesta. What it really hinges very much upon is "freeing" anarchism from a class base and placing it upon a mass base. The rhetoric of class is retained, but it is clear from the contents of the Bakuninist message that the concept of proletarian is more a matter of self-definition than of economic position in the factory system. In collectivist anarchism, the words "proletariat," "peasantry," "rabble," "people," and even *"lumpenproletariat"* are interchangeable. The battle line was drawn between the people and the State. Nationalism replaced the bourgeoisie as the

great *bête noire* of the century. What was begun by the
French Revolution of 1789 was to be completed by modern
revolutions, such as the Paris Commune—the destruction of
the Nation-State. Collectivist anarchism took firm hold of the
humanist aspect of socialism—and accused the class theorists
of violating the double purpose of socialism: the "smashing"
of State power and the creation of voluntary associations
along internationalist lines.

The position of Bakunin is particularly emphatic in summing up collectivist anarchist sentiments. The central elements are that the poor already carry the germs of true collective life and that the social revolution is prefigured by the
life-style of the very poor. The passage is worth quoting in
full, since the differences between Bakunin and Marx were
stated with full clarity.

> By the *flower of the proletariat,* I mean above all, that
> great mass, those millions of non-civilized, disinherited,
> wretched and illiterates whom Messrs. Engels and Marx
> mean to subject to the paternal regime of *a very strong gov-
> ernment,* to employ an expression used by Engels in a letter
> to our friend Cafiero. Without doubt, this will be for their
> own salvation, as of course all governments, as is well-
> known, have been established solely in the interests of the
> masses themselves. By the flower of the proletariat I mean
> precisely that eternal "meat" for governments, that great
> *rabble of the people* ordinarily designated by Messrs. Marx
> and Engels by the phrase at once picturesque and contemp-
> tuous of *"lumpenproletariat,"* the "riff-raff," that rabble
> which, being very nearly unpolluted by all bourgeois civili-
> zation carries in its heart, in its aspirations, in all the neces-
> sities and the miseries of its collectivist position, all the
> germs of the Socialism of the future, and which alone is
> powerful enough today to inaugurate the Social Revolution
> and bring it to triumph.[8]

At the core of collectivist anarchism lies the consideration
that the State claims as its victim society as a whole, the exploited mass as a whole, and not just any particular class. To
be sure, under certain conditions the factory workers may

[8] Michael Bakunin, *Marxism, Freedom and the State.* Translated and
edited by K. J. Kenafick. London: Freedom Press, 1950, p. 48.

receive the harshest treatment, but it is no less the case that historic conditions exist in which the factory worker may suffer far less as a result of the manipulative capacity of the State than other social factors. Therefore, the task of socialism is a collective one, since communism is a collective need. The purpose of the State is to break up the solidarity of all the oppressed—from the *lumpenproletariat* to the peasantry —and hence the role of the anarchists is essentially to prevent this catastrophic process from gaining success. It can do this best by exposing the hoax of patriotism, the chauvinism inherent in the system of nations, the duplicity involved in doling out favors to one exploited group over another.

Collectivist anarchism is thus seen as a continuation of the human as against the inhuman, a break with class theory and class solutions. The State principle is particularistic—favoring one group over another, exploiting the many on behalf of the few. The anarchist principle is its dialectical opposite. It is universalistic—favoring society as against the State, the great mass as against the very few. Collectivist anarchism is basically a midpoint between the class consciousness of the early pioneers and the humanistic consciousness of the present century. In Bakunin, one sees the constant swing of a pendulum: an attempt to retain the theory of the struggle of classes, but no less an attempt to broaden it so as to be universal in its inclusiveness. Here one also finds the effort to develop a broad-based politics, but no less an appeal to individual integrity and initiative as against politics in its profane practice.

The moralization of politics takes place through the general application of the principle of freedom (people) as the chief force opposed to the principle of authority (the State). Unfortunately for collectivist anarchism, the appeal to everyman had even less success than the appeal to class-man. Its very universalism and moralism deprived it of any fighting core, of any "advanced sector." A wish-fulfillment element was clearly present: collectivism was viewed not so much as a future condition of man as a present status assigned to the masses by the State. The powerless, designated as noble, good, true, and healthy, really had no need of further organization on such a theory. In their very wretchedness they were internally purified. Those furthest "outside of civilization," those most deviant with respect to conventional norms of behavior,

were good. In such a situation, the need for specific measures
became unnecessary. The dissolution of Bakuninist organization in Spain and Italy was perhaps brought about as much
by the celebration of the poor as by the damnation of the rich.
In short, it lacked a theory of alienation, and hence the need
for practical steps to overcome this condition.

It remains important to note the insight of collectivist
anarchism concerning the character of State power. If it was
indeed a moralistic, and even petty-bourgeois outcry against
State authority, the fact was that political solutions did not
resolve the paradox of authority by simply transferring coercive power from one class to another. The People's State or
the Proletarian Dictatorship did not exactly mark a vast improvement over the Aristocratic State or the Bourgeois State,
in terms of the reduction of public intervention over private
lives. On this point Bakunin scored heavily. The widening of
the State apparatus, whether through evolution or revolution,
to include the proletariat and the displacement of one class
by another class does indeed have significance of a libertarian
character.

The French Revolution may have been "aborted" by the
bourgeoisie. But it is hard to doubt that significant changes
took place to better man's lot. Universal enfranchisement, a
system of juridical checks on power, vast improvements in
the services rendered by the State to its Citizenry, may not
constitute the perfect resolution of human ailments, but it
did constitute real improvement. In this sense, collectivist
anarchism missed the point of social revolution—which is
that revolution is an adventure into new possibilities, and not
an ultimate resolution. It continues historic processes, but
does not resolve them in a final messianic burst of popular
virtue. In opposing the "cult of the State" with the "cult of
freedom," collectivist anarchism sharpened the differences
between Behemoth and Anarch—but it contributed little to
maximize the area of human options and social reorganization.

CONSPIRATORIAL ANARCHISM. The general failure of anarchism to make an impression upon the population as a whole,
and the corresponding growth in the centralization and
bureaucratization of the Nation-State, placed anarchism in a
crisis condition. By the close of the nineteenth century, cer-

tain clear patterns had emerged: 1) Class *membership* no
longer corresponded to class *interests*—the factory workers
were not so much concerned with the acquisition of political
power as they were with gaining a "fair share" of economic
wealth. 2) Industrial technology undermined and outflanked
anarchism by transferring the seat of power from the small
artisan workshop to the big impersonal factory. What was
increasingly required was counterorganization and not withdrawal from political society. Under such conditions as these,
the anarchism of involvement received a new emphasis.

Conspiratorial anarchism acts on the premise that the
State exists by force, by the actual or legal terrorization of the
masses. The State is able to do this with small numbers since
it has the force of arms behind it. Conspiratorial anarchism
thus sought to emulate and simulate the techniques of the
ruling class. The force of the State would be met with the
violence of the Anarch. The conspirators hoped to "speed
up" the collapse of State power by a process of systematic
assassination of the rulers and stimulating widespread insurrection. The last part of the century saw the techniques of
violence raised to a principle throughout Europe and
America.

The United States has the distinction of having the most
violent and turbulent labor history in the Western world and,
at the same time, one of the least theory-involved publics.[9] In
this situation, the United States offered fertile soil for conspiratorial anarchism. The arrival in the United States of
Johann Most provided just the sort of theoretical support
necessary to inflame working-class violence. Most's booklet
of 1885 has as its instructive and definitive title: *Science of
Revolutionary Warfare—A Manual of Instruction in the Use
and Preparation of Nitroglycerine, Dynamite, Gun-Cotton,
Fulminating Mercury, Bombs, Fuses, Poisons, Etc. Etc.* One
can only wonder what the *etceteras* refer to. Johann Most was
clearly infatuated with the direct response of force to the
bourgeoisie. Listen to the following eulogy offered by Most:

> In giving dynamite to the downtrodden millions of the
> globe science has done its best work. The dear stuff can be
> carried in the pocket without danger, while it is a formid-

---

[9] Richard Hofstadter, *Anti-Intellectualism in American Life.* New York:
Alfred A. Knopf, 1963.

able weapon against any force of militia, police, or detectives that may want to stifle the cry for justice that goes
forth from the plundered slaves. It is something not very
ornamental, but exceedingly useful. It can be used against
persons and things. It is better to use it against the former
than against bricks and masonry. It is a genuine boon for
the disinherited, while it brings terror and fear to the rob-
bers. A pound of this good stuff beats a bushel of ballots
all hollow—and don't you forget it. Our lawmakers might
as well try to sit down on the crater of a volcano or on the
point of a bayonet as to endeavor to stop the manufacture
and use of dynamite. It takes more than justice and right
than is contained in laws to quiet the spirit of unrest.[10]

But the use of violence to counter the force of the State,
wherever it occurred—in the Haymarket affair, in Coxey's
Army, the American Federation of Labor Dynamiters, Cen-
tralia Steel unionization, by the Wobblies of the West—all
came to a frustrating and dismal end. The organizational
power of the State could not be overwhelmed by the disorganized power of direct action. In America as in Europe, the
conspiratorial anarchists were hunted as criminals and punished with a vengeance reserved for murderers and kidnap-
pers. The State unleashed a steady stream of counter violence
that finally dissipated anarchist strength (and not incidentally, a good deal of socialist power). The State, in the form
of the legislative groupings, for its part began to respond to
industrial violence by increasing the pressure on all sides for
nonviolent methods of resolution. Laws protecting the rights
of workingmen considerably mitigated the class war of the
previous period. In addition, new forces of unification arose.
Nationalism, engendered by the First World War, superceded
labor strife. Class unity was restored. The Union was saved.

A serious drawback to conspiratorial anarchism lies in the
difficulty of establishing the difference between ordinary
crime and a principal case of regicide. The bomb outrage of
Emile Henry in 1894 was condemned by fellow conspirators
as the act of an ordinary bandit. Confusion was always occasioned by a division of opinion on this or that assassination.
The assassination of Princess Elizabeth was condemned by

[10] Johann Most, as cited in Louis Adamic, *Dynamite: The Story of Class
Violence in America*. New York: The Viking Press, 1934, p. 47.

some as foolish and by others as necessary. Similarly, the assassination of President McKinley had the same effect in the United States. Violence simply has no definition of limits. As Masaryk reminds us: "We must not forget that anarchism is a menace to the very anarchists themselves, that Kropotkin and Reclus were [themselves] threatened with death by anarchists." The line between egoistic criminality and altruistic assassination was crossed so often that this type of conspiratorial approach degenerated into sheer chaos. "The Metaphysics of anarchism becomes indeterminist; miracle plays its ancient role in the anarchist chaos; anarchist philosophers become poets; anarchist politicians develop into utopians." [11]

One might readily consider conspiratorial anarchism a short-lived failure. And measured in terms of the achievements it registered, this is so. The conspirators, however, raised to a new level of consciousness the plight of the lower depths of society. It produced extensive protective labor legislation. It implanted the juridical problem of the special quality of politically inspired coercion in contrast to the egoistic terror of the professional criminal. Above all, it accelerated a consideration of social and economic legislation relating to women, children, minority and immigrant groups. If this took place in an atmosphere of hostility to anarchism, it must also be said that anarchism for its part made a more radical political posture feasible throughout Europe and America.

But for the anarchists themselves, conspiratorial techniques created yet an additional schismatic and factional element. The needs of the twentieth century moved revolutionaries into a more concerted effort to connect strategies to general ideologies. This in turn led to an extended period of working-class political organization that had little to do with the anarchists. Drawn from declassé elements in society, from students, intellectuals, semiprofessionals, and artisans, conspiratorial anarchists never had the kind of connection to proletarian life that could produce any kind of direct impact that might allow for a socialist renaissance. Violence gave way to organization. In the United States, Eugene Victor Debs' socialism took a commanding post. In France, Jean Jaurés became the acknowledged leader of proletarian

---

[11] Thomas Garrigue Masaryk, *The Spirit of Russia: Studies in History, Literature and Philosophy*. New York: The Macmillan Co., 1955 (second edition), Vol. II, pp. 393–9.

action (over and above the animosities of his anarchist critics). In Russia, the *Narodniki* gave way to the Marxism of Plekhanov, Martov, and Lenin—to organizational socialism. What further insured the abandonment of conspiratorial anarchism is that the organizational socialists absorbed, rather than cancelled, nonparliamentary methods. The tactic of illegality, while rarely resorted to in European socialism, was never abandoned as a possible ploy. The rhetoric, if not the content, of violence was thus made part of the general program of contemporary socialism—of Marxism.

COMMUNIST ANARCHISM. The cross-fertilization of radical ideas produced a form of anarchism that was at once a theoretical response to the extreme anti-intellectualism of the conspiratorial factions, and no less a practical response to the extreme intellectualism of the First International. The leading exponent of communist anarchism is unquestionably Errico Malatesta. Malatesta attempted to apply the principles of direct action early in his career. In a movement characteristic of Francisco Juliao's Peasant Leagues in Brazil, he headed a small group of armed men in 1874 that had the explicit purpose of liberating the peasantry of Southern Italy from the domination of State and Church. He encouraged the peasantry to seize the land and set up workers' collectives. This experiment in political independence through direct action was a constant theme in Malatesta's life. The fact that the insurrectionary movement was suppressed and overwhelmed each time it was attempted did not discourage Malatesta, or, for that matter, lead him to revise his positive estimate of the possibilities of revolution.

The main point in the principles of communist anarchism is that violence should be intrinsic and organic to the goals sought. First, if force was to be used it should not be a hit-and-run affair, but a concerted effort by the entire social class or sector of that class that had achieved revolutionary consciousness. Second, Malatesta sought to eschew the heavy premium on parliamentarism that was ever characteristic of the First International. Third, there was a rejection of the anti-Marxism of Bakunin and Kropotkin. While no criticisms were made directly, a large gulf existed between the collectivism of Bakunin and the communism of Malatesta. The fact is that Bakunin hardly could be said to have escaped the

leadership cult that gripped most anarchist factions in the
First International. Malatesta and his allies Sergei Stepniak
and Carlo Cafiero saw themselves as activists first, and as
leaders last. It was to be an activism conditioned by scientific
socialism, by the laws of historical evolution, and by the
exacting labors necessary to forge a revolutionary apparatus
—in short by Marxism rather than Bakuninism.

Communist anarchism was not opposed to violence on
principle, but it was opposed to a form of violence that was
not at the same time educative and instrumental in gaining
lasting advantages for the oppressed. "Certainly, in the present state of mankind, oppressed by misery, stupefied by
superstition and sunk in degradation, the human lot depends
upon a relatively small number of individuals. Of course, not
all men will be able to rise in a moment to the height of
perceiving their duty, or even the enjoyment of so regulating
their own action that others will also derive the greatest
possible benefit from it. But because the thoughtful and guiding forces at work in society are few, that is no reason for
paralyzing them still more, and for the subjection of many
individuals to the direction of a few." [12] If Bakunin sought to
be the Marx of anarchism, so in like manner Malatesta can
be considered the Saint-Simon of anarchism. The focus of
communist anarchism was on organizing the mass of exploited for a general assault on the capitalist-feudal bastions.
And to do this, "armchair" techniques were no better than
"violent" techniques. Both had to be subsumed in a sociological appreciation of the general struggle between classes.

Communist anarchism comes close to urging some form of
political organization if anarchism is not to be dissolved by
parliamentary maneuvers. When Malatesta asks rhetorically
how to solve the problem of self-government and self-
regulation, he inquires bitingly: "To elect a government of
geniuses by the votes of a mass of fools?" While this is a
sword intended to cut through the arguments of parliamentary socialists, it also reflects his belief in political action,
which is at the same time organized action.

The main energies theoretically of communist anarchism
is in proving that human nature is plastic enough for self-
regulation without the need of State authority. As such, he

[12] Errico Malatesta, *Anarchy* (1907). London: Freedom Press, 1949 (eighth
edition), p. 38.

anticipated Lenin's distinction between techniques of command and techniques of administration. Unlike many of his fellow anarchists, Malatesta distinguished between legitimate authority and illicit power. And as such, communist anarchism gave special priorities to separating those who have a "functional" role in society and those who have an "exploitive" role.

> A governor is a privileged person, because he has the right to command others, and to avail himself of the force of others to fulfill his own ideas and desires. An administrator or technical director is a worker like others, in a society where all have equal opportunities of development, and all can be at the same time intellectual and manual workers; when there are no other differences between men than those derived from diversity of talents, and all work and all social functions give an equal right to the enjoyment of social advantages. The functions of government are, in short, not to be confounded with administrative functions, as they are essentially different. That they are today so often confused is entirely on account of the existence of economic and political privilege.[18]

Communist anarchism distinguishes itself from collectivist anarchism by urging the abolition of government by the proletarians in the name of all mankind. Malatesta felt that "it would be better to use the expression 'abolition of the State' as little as possible," since the State is only the federal expression of governmental rule. And what anarchism ought to strive for is the elimination of external coercion at any level—local, regional, or national—and hence, for the elimination of government of men and its displacement by the regulation of things. The arguments adduced against those who maintain that men are selfish by nature, that regulation inadvertently spills over into rule, and that the State may be manipulated to workers' demands, are treated in the customary anarchist way. Psychological plasticity, social altruism, and self-consciousness are all bastions against the corruption of anarchy.

There is an interesting anticipation of Durkheim's ideas on the *Division of Labor* in Malatesta's work. Anarchism is to be

[18] Errico Malatesta, *op. cit.*, p. 30.

guaranteed in the first place by each person's performing a useful function; in the second place, by elimination of all distinctions between town and country; and in the third place, by what Durkheim called the "collective conscience," that form of social solidarity guaranteed by a consensus of interests and sentiments. Underlying communist anarchism is the same sort of philosophical telos operative in mercantile capitalism. Since each man knows that his own interests are directly plugged into social interests, he will himself assure accord with the principle of the greatest happiness for the greatest numbers. But it is precisely the factual dubiousness of utilitarianism that casts a long shadow over anarchism on the "left" no less than mercantilism on the "right." It was difficult enough to cast a net and catch *one good man,* as the Encyclopedists sought to do. But for a net to be large enough to catch *all good men* was more than doctrine could support. The equation of all society with the common search for happiness leaves out of the reckoning the alternative definitions of happiness that men harbor. As a result, the theoretical collapse of communist anarchism was inevitable. What held it in its course for any length of time proved to be the saintly charismatic qualities of its leaders; the rational behavior of its followers had little importance. The irony of communist anarchism is that in practice it rested so heavily for its support on the strength of its leaders, and so little on the revolutionary mass of the poor. The advantages of Leninism, of communism without anarchism, is that it made no such felicitous assumptions about the goodness of men, the spontaneity of social revolution, or the capacity of a quick conversion from one social system to another without strife. That such advantages dissolved with the emergence of Stalinist absolutism may show just why Malatesta mistrusted any form of State communism. But in the course of events, this has to be reckoned a small comfort to one who made such great sacrifices for his convictions.

INDIVIDUALIST ANARCHISM. At the same time that European anarchism was undergoing a steady ramification, with an emphasis on mass strikes, general revolutionary violence, and developing some of the organizational features of political life, there arose a highly personalistic anarchism in America. Inspired more by Max Stirner than by Bakunin, Kropotkin, or the "Latin" wing of anarchism, this variety of anarchism is distinguished by viewing the "ego" or the "person" as the repository of all that is human and self-determining, and the State as the repository of all that is inhuman and oppressive. While it shares with utilitarian anarchism a reliance on utilitarian philosophy, the extremely personalistic turn it gave to utility theory marked it decisively apart from this early form, as utilitarianism in general is marked by two distinct stages: the French "sociological" variety and the English "psychological" variety. And like the English school of utilitarianism, the point of crossover between individualist anarchism and extreme conservatism was not always easy to define. Indeed, if Stirner provided individualist anarchism with its original rationale, it was the conservative critique of the State made by Jeremy Bentham and later Herbert Spencer that provided this strain of anarchism with its sense of righteousness.

Individualist anarchism shared a vocabulary of sentiments and a theory of natural law with the classical conservatives. A cataloguing of what this form of anarchism involved is not unlike a reckoning of the features one encounters in reading Lord Acton, Alexis de Toqueville, or Brooks Adams. Rather than recount the separate achievements of the leading figures of individualist anarchism, let us see what such disparate figures as Max Stirner and his American exponents, Josiah Warren, Lysander Spooner, and Benjamin R. Tucker, have in common.[14]

1) The individualist anarchists believed that a collective society in any form was impossible without leading to an authoritarian system. They thus adhered to the concept of private property or individual proprietorship, insofar as this embraced no more than the total product of individual labor.

2) The purpose of society is to preserve the sovereignty of every individual without exception. Thus, all human associations based on limiting sovereignty, particularly the State, must be curbed and eventually eliminated.

3) The principle of mutualism was to be arrived at on a voluntary basis and in this way: through a withdrawal from

[14] For a most useful compendium, see James J. Martin, *Men Against the State*. DeKalb, (Ill.): The Adrian Allen Associates, 1953; also see Eunice Minette Schuster, *Native American Anarchism: A Study of Left-Wing American Individualism*, Northampton (Mass.): Smith College Studies in History, 1932.

all agencies and institutions of an involuntary kind, undermine all juridical and legislative authority.

4) The principle of individuality requires the absolute equality of the sexes, the absolute equality of the races, and the absolute equality of labor for its success. Thus, anarchism must seek the extinction of interest, rent, dividends, profits, except as represented by work done.

5) The system of democracy, of majority decision, is held null and void. Any impingement upon the natural rights of the person is unjust and a symbol of majority tyranny. No rightful authority can be external to individual consent, and all such authority legitimizes civil disobedience, resistance, and even destruction.

6) Any definition of liberty begins and concludes with the liberty of the weaker party in a nation. Since the majority always appropriates the right to legislate and enforce legislation, the true and basic test of liberty is always the right to disobey and violate such legislation.

In many ways individualist anarchism found its natural home in the frontier spirit of America. It was the perfect embodiment of "worldly asceticism" and represented a secularization of the Protestant ethos and the capitalist spirit of thrift and trust. In Europe, the anarchists found themselves involved increasingly in socialist politics and adopting a class position. It was the socialists, especially the Marxists, who attempted to purge the anarchists from the radical ranks. In America, the situation was reversed. The anarchist found himself increasingly espousing petty-bourgeois causes, the rights of individual proprietorship. As such, the anarchists became the first consistent critics of socialism in America.

William Bradford Greene expressed the antisocialist bias most directly. "In socialism, there is but one master, which is the State; but the State is not a living person, capable of suffering and happiness. Socialism benefits none but the demagogues, and is emphatically, the organization of universal misery. Socialism gives us but one class, a class of slaves." [15] This passage might as easily have been written by William Lecky. And indeed, the *History of European Morals* contains not a few phrases of such an order. Benjamin Tucker, perhaps the best known and certainly the most

[15] William Bradford Greene, *Equality,* West Brookfield (Mass.), 1849, pp. 70–1.

prolific of individualist anarchists, said of Marx at the time
of his death that he was the most "bitter of all enemies of
anarchism." And in turn Tucker pledged anything that
would combat Marxism, which "represented the principle
of authority which we live to combat." [16] Nor were the differences between individualist anarchism and all forms of
collectivism matters of principle alone. The tactic of violence
—propaganda by the deed—was vehemently opposed by
men like Tucker. Speaking of the violent wing of American
anarchism, of Spies, Parsons, Fischer, and Berkman, he
wrote that "if the revolution comes by violence, and in
advance of light, the old struggle will have to be begun
anew." [17]

Individualist anarchism sought to preserve the principle
of rights over law, and hence supported, at least passively, the
anarchists indicted by the law courts for their acts of violence.
But it also sought to make anarchism a respectable doctrine.
And so it opposed the principles of violence and the acts
defined as criminal that the European wave of collectivist and
conspiratorial anarchists brought with them to the new
world. Anarchism thus carried within itself a microscopic
reflection of the general struggle going on throughout the
nineteenth century in America between nativism and foreign-
ism. Tucker went to rather desperate lengths to show anarchism in the most respectable light. He presented an analysis of
the subscription list of his publication *Liberty,* according to
occupational and professional ranking (perhaps the first
such example of mass-communications research done in the
United States!) to show that anarchists are not criminal either
in fact or in theory.

The anarchism of Tucker, Spooner, and Josiah Warren
disintegrated for many reasons. Among the most immediate
was the loss of nativism as a progressive value. Increasingly,
it became subject to chauvinistic and conservative leanings;
and correspondingly, it came to fear and loathe the introduction of unionism and political organization of the for-
eign-born as the direct consequence of mass democracy. Individualist anarchism thus joined intellectual bonds with
know-nothingism—with that variety of anti-intellectualism

[16] Benjamin R. Tucker, *Liberty,* II (April 14, 1883). Cited in James J.
Martin, *op. cit.,* p. 219.
[17] Benjamin R. Tucker, *Liberty,* VIII (July 30, 1892). Cited in James J.
Martin, *op. cit.,* p. 255.

which soon lost the need for intellectualist postures as such. Second, the very individualism of the American nativist anarchists made the establishment of "a central clearing house" out of the question. Pockets of anarchism soon became transformed into small literary clubs. The championing of private enterprise as the bulwark of State monopoly, made by near anarchists like Karl Heinzen, rendered anarchism useless for the advancement of working-class interests; and superfluous, even absurd, as a rationalization of the ideology of laisser-faire capitalism.[18]

If individualist anarchism made sense in 1870, with the rise of political-boss rule, the collapse of reconstruction, the centralization of authority through the liquidation of local self-government, it lost all meaning in an era of uncontrolled big business. In the early 1930s, with the country in a catharsis over the depression and with mass unemployment on an unparalleled scale, the last voice of individual anarchism that of Charles Erskine Scott Wood, was being raised in an outcry: "too much government." This at a point where even corporate barons were ready to support federal legislation for the amelioration of the crisis in the American economy. The conclusion of Wood's work makes plain the pathetic outcome of individualist anarchism:

> We are interfered with and accustomed to control and dictation from the cradle to the grave in thought, speech and act, in work and play, in morals and manners, in habits and costumes. If in anything we seem free, it is only because our despot is indifferent and has not yet chosen to dictate. Always there was that much freedom to the most servile peoples. The soul of freedom, the understanding of what is the true sphere of government, the aroused defiance against all tyranny, the resentful, angry resistance of free men to every invasion of their god-given rights, is dead. . . . We do not fight that others may have freedom in the opinions we hate. We reverence the policeman's club because it is "law"—when in fact it is generally only the policeman's will, conscious of the brutal power of the State back of him; and every instinct should teach us that

[18] See Carl Wittke, *Against the Current: The Life of Karl Heinzen.* Chicago: The University of Chicago Press, 1945, pp. 247–9; also Eunice M. Schuster, *op. cit.*, pp. 124–5.

most law is oligarchic despotism, and no law is entitled to blind obedience.[19]

But pathetic or not, this kind of minority report cuts two ways. If it resists the encroachments of government in such matters of welfare as social security legislation and federal health insurance, it no less stands as a constant reminder that the State has no right to tyrannize minority opinion under any conditions—since, in fact, the State has no "rights" per se that are not surrendered by or expropriated from individuals. Libertarianism and conservatism are the paradoxical consequences of individulist anarchism: Roger Baldwin and Barry Goldwater are both products of its ideology to one degree or another. And if no doctrine could possibly survive such dichotomous results, it remains true that individualist anarchism put the case against Behemoth most starkly. The aberration and absurdity it yielded is hence nothing but the logical outcome of the arguments it put forth.

PACIFIST ANARCHISM. While most anarchists did not avail themselves of terrorist tactics, few spokesmen of classical anarchism cared to deny its efficiency. But with the historical collapse of anarchism and its complete separation from political involvement, it became possible for their remaining number to return to a more pristine, if pietistic, view; all the more so since the absence of any fruitful intercourse with the socialists limited the range of their dialogue and still further the range of their influence. Those among the anarchists whose position rested on persuasion attempted to create models of community action to prove that the "vision" is attainable. Indeed, in the work of Gandhi, the idea of pacifism as the essential way to a truthful life is casually related to the view that a truthful life must itself exclude proprietary and monetary claims of any type.

The view of the State found in anarchist pacifism corresponds to that of most traditional varieties of anarchism. In Gandhi's view, the State has three functions in the exploitative process: first, it serves as a mechanism for the distribution of goods and services; second, as a mechanism for the resolution of conflict among its members; and third, as an

[19] C. E. S. Wood, *Too Much Government.* New York: The Vanguard Press, 1931, p. 266.

instrument for safeguarding the "national interest" in a world of competitive and conflicting petty interests. But it was also his view that these functions which the State performs are corrupted by the very nature of the State as sovereign. Nation-States rest on coercion, not reason or humanity. Constantly even the positive ambitions of the State are being thwarted by the means it must employ, by force and violence. The problems of a society are no different than the problems of the individuals a society contains. Since the very nature of State authority is the enrichment of private wealth and not the public good, the only legitimate task of the State is its self-liquidation. In place of State power there is to be a "world federation established by agreement." [20]

A similar viewpoint emerged in the work of Tolstoy. Tolstoy was confronted by a "holy Russia" in which the collective conscience of the wealthy classes was reserved for Sunday sermons; while during the rest of the week they were concocting ways to exploit further the nominally emancipated peasantry. But in the bosom of this growing Leviathan, a popular anarchistic ethos emerges. For Tolstoy, it takes the form of pure Christianity, a religion that substitutes for the irrational and the violent "a new comprehension of life" in which no person will "employ violence against anyone, and under no consideration." But anarchist pacifism is aware that this new comprehension of life is none too readily appreciated by State power, by those benefiting from coercion. This is the basis of political terror.

> The governments and the ruling classes do not now lean on the right, not even on the semblance of justice, but on an artificial organization, which with the aid of the perfections of science, encloses all men in the circle of violence, from which there is no possibility of tearing themselves away. [21]

This circle of violence is made possible by the use of several means. The first is the massive intimidation of the people by falsely representing the State as inalienable and so "inflicting the severest penalties for any attempt at changing

[20] *Cf. The Wit and Wisdom of Gandhi.* Edited by Homer A. Jack. Boston: Beacon Press, 1951, pp. 120–1.
[21] Leo Tolstoy, *The Kingdom of God Is Within You.* New York: Thomas Y. Crowell, 1905, p. 199.

it." Second is the bribery by the State of civil bureaucracy and military officialdom. These bribes are ultimately paid for in the heavy taxation of the populace. Third is the hypnotic effect of the State—its concerted effort to distort and deprive common men of cultural and scientific knowledge. The circle of violence is completed by the brutalization of a certain segment of the people into unthinking beasts, willing to do the bidding of any master. Given these new idols of the cave, any attempt to change social systems through violence ends in the abyss of a blood bath. The world of the State is one in which virtue is made synonymous with force and irrationality.[22]

For both Tolstoy and Gandhi, the history of class society bears witness to the fact that violence has never established its opposite, a consensual society. It only intensifies and institutionalizes the uses of violence. The impasse of violence can only be broken in the triumph of conscience, in the release of the natural propensities of people to cooperate with one another and to love each other. The anarchist element emerges in pacifism as a direct confrontation of man and the State. Obedience to a government is considered a negation of religious principles. As Tolstoy put it: "A man who unconditionally promises in advance to submit to laws which are made and will be made by men, by this very promise renounces Christianity." [23] The individualism inherent in the pacifist reply to violence becomes a pronounced renunciation of the social contract and of State authority as such. In this way, anarchism and pacifism were wedded in history and in theory.

At the basis of anarchist pacifism is the idea that as long as sovereign Nation-States exist, the possibility of resolving the dilemma of egoism and altruism, force and harmony, war and peace, remains nil. The very existence of separate States implies the use of force to resolve every major issue. Just as individuals must strive to go beyond the passions of the ego, Tolstoy and Gandhi implore men, as political beings, to move beyond the confines of the State and its by-products—force and aggression. Universal Man can be fulfilled only in Universal Society.

[22] *Cf.* Irving L. Horowitz, "Tolstoy and Gandhi: The Pacifist Dream," *The Idea of War and Peace in Contemporary Philosophy*. New York: Paine-Whitman, 1957, pp. 89–106.
[23] *Cf.* Leo Tolstoy, in "Gandhi-Tolstoy Correspondence," *Iscus* (India), Vol. II, No. 1 (1955), p. 13–14.

The difficulty with pacific anarchism is that it can no more escape the commitments to a specific milieu in which the State exists than can other forms of the doctrine. Whatever its subjective intentions, it is clear that pacific anarchism is a politically involved position. Historically, it was the basic instrument for achieving national liberation in India. But in that very act, emerged the Indian *State*. Pacifism, while a call to nonviolent action, was no less an instrument of large-scale social conflict. And to insure the success of the revolutionary movement meant the consecration and sanctioning of the coercive State after the revolution. The use of armies, policemen, and "agents of the State" had to be given a large priority. Hence, pacifism in the state of political victory involved itself in the betrayal of its anarchist premises.

The problem of anarchist pacifism is not simply that the anarchist aspect tended to be submerged in the hue and cry of nationalistic passions, but no less in its assumptions about the *fixed* goodness of man. The pacifist techniques, elevated as they were to innate principles of human nature, came into the conflict with the fact that pacifism is a *learned* technique. It no more demonstrates the superiority of pacifism's gaining its victory than conspiratorial anarchism demonstrated the superiority of violence. The argument from human nature always comes upon the possibility of being contravened by the facts of human behavior. Thus it is that the anarchist position as a "pure" doctrine gave way to a series of tactical preferences—violence, pacifism, conspiracy, collectivism, communism, etc.—that only further emphasized the contradictions between anarchy as a way of life and as a goal of men. The very victories of pacifist techniques only further exposed the anarchist dilemmas. It is perhaps in the nature of anarchism that it can never have any real "victory" without sacrificing its principles. By the same token, it can never suffer any ultimate defeats either.

4. The Revolutionary Deed and the Redemptive Spirit

If, as Santayana says, anarchy is a momentary sporadic enjoyment of change underlying a paradise of order, it is equally true that for the anarchist the Leviathan is but a celebration of order underlying a world of change. Basic to anarchism is a general theory of action. And the test of significant action is the rejuvenation of personal existence. Significant change occurs only through the direct confrontation of class actors. The dialogue is determined by social interests, the stage setting provided by the State, and the resolution guaranteed by the absurdities of the present.

The necessity for participation, for direct action, is a *modus operandi* of anarchism. Action may not guarantee the successful conclusion of a conflict, and long-range prediction is out of the question for most anarchists; what is guaranteed is personal redemption. Social equilibrium tends to be viewed with a certain suspicion and alarm not because of political factors so much as personal factors. Equilibrium resolves itself in terms of rationalized authority. The "rules" of a society tend to become deified into the "rights" of society. The very perpetuation of formalistic rules thus comes to depend upon the willingness of men to become alienated with respect to work processes and anomic with respect to social interaction. The anarchist demand for action is at its source an insistence on the psychological values of spontaneity. The revolutionary deed is useful *in its nature,* over and above political success or failure, precisely because action with a moral purpose is redemptive.

What should not be confused are the terms "action" and "conflict." The existence of conflict is a consequence of incompatibilities of class and power. The existence of action is a volitional response to conflict. As such, humanized man, active man, dedicates himself to the removal of sources of conflict. What underlies the anarchist faith is indeed a restoration of order. It is a holistic view in which the desirability of voluntary association provides the ground of social action. The host of anarchist "little societies"—from agricultural associations in Catalonia to proletarian *Bourses* in France— was an attempt to put into practice the idea of moral redemption through the release of natural impulses. The socialization process is held essential to personal liberty. The concept of personal redemption through a counterprocess of withdrawal is alien to the anarchist tradition.

The belief that the closer one is to natural behavior, the more proximate man is to the good society, is a common theme of nineteenth-century romanticism. The anarchists, along with the utopians, simply sought to put this strain of romanticism to the test. The secretary of The Social Freedom Community of Chesterfield, Virginia, filed the following report in 1874:

> We hold to the unity of interests, and political, religious, and social freedom; and believe that every individual should have absolute control of herself or himself, and that, so long as they respect the same freedom in others, no one has the right to infringe on that individuality. We have no constitution or by-laws; ignore the idea of man's total depravity; and believe that all who are actuated by a love of truth and a desire to progress (and we will knowingly accept no others), can be better governed by love and moral suasion than by any arbitrary laws. Our government consists in free criticism. We have a unitary home.[1]

Nor should it be thought that such principles can have no application to industrial society. The argument from the inherent egoism of human nature is clearly the weakest link in the critique of anarchism. The Council of Aragon was an illustration in pre-Franco Spain of anarchist organization along "natural" lines.

> Libertarian principles were attempted in the field of money and wages. Wages were paid by a system of coupons exchangeable for goods in the cooperatives. Wages were based on the family unit: a single producer was paid the equivalent of 25 pesetas; a married couple with only one working, 35 pesetas, and four pesetas weekly additional for each child. This system had a serious weakness, particularly while the rest of Spain operated on a system of great disparity in wages between manual and professional workers, since that prompted trained technicians to migrate from Aragon. For the time being, however, ideological conviction, inspiring the many technicians and professionals in the libertarian organizations, more than made up for this weakness.[2]

It is undoubtedly the case that such social and economic

---

[1] Charles Nordhoff, *The Communistic Societies of the United States* (1875). New York: Hillary House Publishers, 1960, p. 357.

[2] Felix Morrow, *Revolution and Counter-Revolution in Spain.* New York: Pioneer Publishers, 1938, pp. 142–3.

equalization runs *counter to the* general tendency toward
differential reward for differential work. But it must likewise
be noted that it is precisely this general tendency toward
status factors (urban rather than rural, engineer rather than
technician, etc.) that anarchism sought to challenge.

The idea of a natural man continues to inform the heirs of
anarchism. There is a considerable body of European social
scientists, especially the Franco-Italian group gathered about
the Center of the Sociology of Cooperation, who have made
the concept of voluntary association a cornerstone of its researches. The problems of getting people to make sound use
of their time, the task of overcoming the anomic characteristic of industrial society, the forms of stimulating the spontaneous action of small groups in a world of bureaucratic
manipulation, planning to overcome the gaps between peasant and city dwellers—all of these, while now stripped of
apocalyptic trappings and ideological baggage, remain central tasks of social theory and social practice alike.[3]

Most anarchists would question the possibility of successfully reconciling the impulse to voluntary association with a
society increasingly determined by impersonal mechanisms
of persuasion and coercion. The continuing preeminence of
associations guaranteed by coercive measures—by either the
force of arms or the symbolic power of law and contract—
only intensifies the alienation of industrial man from his
natural inclinations. Supporting this anarchist line of reasoning is the steady decline of the influence and nuclear membership in voluntary associations. The town council has
given way to the urban planner; the political party has given
way to the policy maker; and the voluntary association as
such has given way to centralized bureaucracy. Impersonal-
ism and professionalism, essential features of a developed industrial society, have perhaps done more to deprive anarchism of any contemporary vigor than all of the repressive
measures of all of the modern garrison States.

In this situation the anarchist appeal might appear helpless
were it not for a singular fact of our times: the very weight
of modern industrial organization reveals a series of dysfunctional elements. Work becomes routinized. Bureaucracy

---

[3] *Cf.* Albert Meister, "Community Development and Community Centers," *International Review of Community Development,* No. 1 (1958), pp.
123–6.

tends to dull initiative. Automation intensifies the difference between effort expended and results achieved. And leisure tends to be anomic, tending toward excitation without meaning, to a breakdown in long-range goals as such.

The large problem that comes into focus at the sociological end of the spectrum is therefore the possibilities of rejuvenation. What is the effective scope of change? Is change possible at the purely individual level? Can a voluntary basis of agreement be reached at the national or international level? Traditionally, anarchism has been a failure, in part because it was never able to see the practice of men as extending beyond face-to-face relations. Organizationally, it never got beyond immediate primary group associations. And when it did foster and formulate an organizational network, it then became subject to the structural features of a social system that it ostensibly set about to overturn. When anarchism became large-scale, as it did in Italy in the nineteenth century and in Spain during the twentieth century, it employed the techniques of mass persuasion, which made it subject to Michels' "iron law of oligarchy."

Part of the dilemma is built into the anarchist ethos of voluntarism. The scope of rejuvenation is always highly restrictive and restricted. It was restricted to that level of primary associations which would allow for the interplay of forces without the creation of a bureaucracy or a rationalized hierarchy. On the other hand, it was also restrictive in the sense that whatever its aims of becoming a national movement managed to gain in terms of support, it laid itself open to the charges of exercising the known pressures of the existing social order for its own ends. Interestingly enough, a movement of such vast scope and anarchist potential as Gandhism, in a period when it became a consolidated political force, when it had the responsibility of running the society, at that point the ideal of a "cottage society" gave way to the clamor of industrial society, and pacifism itself gave way to a new form of benevolent Statism. The whole purpose of anarchistic pacifism became subverted in the practical everyday needs of manning borders, training an army, developing a bureaucratic force, becoming a world power. Anarchism seems to have intrinsic to itself a contradiction between a sociological view of personal redemption and a belief in the ultimate subversion of individuality by a society.

The anarchist concept of internationalism was never made clear. Rather it developed the notion of the breakup of nationalisms. The shape of international order or the idea of international cooperation is held to be a consequence of the absence of competition between dictatorial involuntary associations. In contradistinction to bourgeois notions of internationalism, such as protective associations on a multinational level (e.g., the European economic community) or the Marxist socialist view of national self-determination of proletarian states, the anarchists juxtapose the idea of internationalism as a necessary consequence of voluntary life. The liquidation of involuntary activity means the liquidation of nationalism and the maturation of the true community of man. But you do not have an anarchist scheme as in most varieties of universalism or federalism. Such instruments of peace as a world court are themselves held to be agencies of supercoercion. And supercoercion is not a realized internationalism because competition between nations would remain. Class exploitation is a form of superordination—but not the exclusive form. The anarchist idea of revolution has two phases: the first phase is the abolition of social classes and the second is the rising force of voluntary association between men, bringing about a rejuvenation. The anarchists were among the first to be critical of industrialism in its capitalist forms. They were the first to explore the weaknesses in bolshevik revolution. There is a *theoretical* soundness to most anarchist criticism of existing social orders. If one reads Berkman or Goldman on the repressive character of bolshevism, one cannot help but admire their predictive acumen. On the other hand, one is always left a bit discontented by the type of criticism that can never be wrong because it is always dealing in the realm of what *ought* to be. Anarchism is an argument of perfection against an imperfect world. It scoffs at attempts to make an imperfect world a little less so. Its very totality gives it a rightness in the abstract. But this totality deprives it of concreteness. Anarchists are right in their critique of existing social orders. But the issues are not quite joined. How do you get from an oppressive social system to one a little less so?

The victories of industrialism and urbanism led to considerable changes in anarchist doctrine. The Proudhonian critique of property had an appeal to propertyless peasants, whereas the later Kropotkin emphasis on an anarchism of social need both universalized it and served to reorient it toward proletarian aims. Withdrawal from harsh bourgeois realities into Stirner's *Gemeinschaft* paradise of total egoism —the community of fate which sustained the early anarchist belief in the natural goodness of man—gave way to increased involvement in *Gesellschaft* imperfections, to the society of interests based on mistrust of this natural goodness, to a contractual relationship. And it must be said that the only time anarchism became a "world historic force" coincided precisely with this new emphasis on class exploitation and class redemption.[4] But this historic period proved as ineffectual in general as the wranglings of Bakunin in the International. The anarchist doctrine of *smashing* State power never admitted of a strategy and theory for the *maintenance* of power. The purpose of involvement was continually beclouded by a strong moralizing belief in the dangers of contamination that stem from such involvement.

Liberation in the anarchist lexicon always retained a negative quality. It remained liberation *from* rather than liberation *through*. Tolstoy wanted to be liberated from all national governments. Sorel wanted to be liberated from all political parties. Stirner wanted to be liberated from all social requirements. In this way, anarchism insured its marginality, which was not unlike the marginality of coffeehouse European intellectuals. Both preferred the underground to the firing line of politics. Redemption was to be personal. Like the intellectuals, immortality was insured by moral rightness rather than by political victory.

The ideology of negation is not an adequate tool for class rebellion. It is a fact of the age that no class, *qua* class, can exist without the action generated by ideological thinking. For that reason, intellectuals as a class can never be galvanized into a form of independent activity. On the other hand, it is the only class that can survive strictly on the unmasking tradition—on the tradition of uncovering the weaknesses in political myth and social ideology as such. Given the anarch-

---

[4] That anarchism reaches its maximum practicality in relation to a concept of class rather than personal exploitation is made clear by comparing such different forms of anarchism as those preached in China and Latin America. See and compare, Robert A. Scalapino and George T. Yu, *The Chinese Anarchist Movement.* Berkeley Institute of International Studies, 1961; and S. F. Simon, "Anarchism and Anarcho-Syndicalism in South America," *Hispanic American Historical Review,* Vol. XXVI (Feb., 1946), pp. 38–59.

ist propensity to this kind of exposé, an "alliance" of anarchism and intellectualism might have been expected to materialize.

What prevented an association of intellectuals and anarchists is therefore a complex question. Two processes in particular seem to attract attention. In the first place, the historic tendencies of intellectuals were to cancel themselves in the direction of academicism and professionalism. That is, the intellectuals were the historic forerunners of the present-day teachers, welfare workers, researchers, etc. And while a tension remains between the intellectual and the academic, the process of cross-fertilization between them served to enhance the status of both. And more, it tended to make the intellectual increasingly cautious and responsible in the types of criticism he offered. His view of life became separated from his work performance, with the latter increasingly defining his "role-set." The slogan of the modern intellectual became the separation of fact and value. More and more, the search for facts gave the intellectual the kind of special information and special consciousness that made professionalism possible. And from professionalism to respectability is a short hop indeed—especially since the striving for professionalism is itself partially motivated by precisely the impulse to respectability—to a high status ranking.

The second master trend that prevented too close an 'association with anarchism is the historic apathy, indeed antipathy, for deeds, and certainly for the "propaganda of the deed." Anarchist and socialist shibboleths about the unity of theory and practice remain largely mythical. The intellectual sees political action as corrupting thought. Indeed, the whole of the sociology of knowledge from Dilthey to Mannheim can be seen against a background that believed that action is the fundamental basis for the "distortion of truth." Intellectualism developed its own ideology—the guardianship of the truth over and against political ideologies. The anarchist celebration of social myths, political slogans, and propaganda of destruction were viewed as techniques for manipulating the rebellion of the oppressed. Anarchist martyrdom always seemed to carry with it infliction of suffering upon others—particularly men of learning. As such, the anarchist was viewed as a slave of his own activism—violence always threatened to spill over into regicide, and self-sacrifice into the sacrifice of others. Anarchism was viewed as a labyrinth of tactics and terror which it was the job of intellectuals to transcend if not actually to eliminate. Thus, the process of redemption for intellectuals came to be defined as the politics of exposure rather than liberation from politics as such.

On the other side, the anarchists were undergoing certain sociological processes that similarly moved them away from any informal concordat with intellectuals. We have already spoken of the marginality and negative definitions of freedom that anarchists are bound by. These definitions, when translated into action, made the anarchists arch "normbreakers." They became the foes of organized society and the friends of social deviance. As such, they were hardly distinguishable from criminals. Certain "non-utilitarian" theories of crime—crime committed not to secure the direct objects of theft and vandalism but as a reaction against bourgeois society—share with anarchism a principled attitude toward crime. Even if we accept Emile Durkheim's brilliant commentaries on the necessity of crime for social change, and the definition by a given society of what a crime is, it is clear that anarchists can hardly accept the indecisiveness of intellectuals—of a portion of society that remains relatively low on any risk-taking scale. Anarchists thus rationalized the gap between themselves and intellectuals by indicating that the indecisive nature of intellectual behavior stemmed from their hazy interests as a social subclass. Therefore, even their sanctimonious doctrine of separating facts from values was held to be a reflection of weakness rather than of principle.

This directly feeds the plaint of anarchists that intellectuals are betrayed by their own quest for knowledge. When Dostoyevsky noted that the "direct, legitimate fruit of consciousness is inertia, that is, conscious sitting with-the-hands-folded," he gave expression to this antagonism of the anarchist for men who could never be direct. The consequence of reflection is ultimately self-reflection—and this soon leads to an academic narcissism. The whole force of anarchist "anti-intellectualism" is not so much a critique of ideas as it is a condemnation of the "man of ideas." The "deed" was after all what stimulated new ideas, and so the deed was held paramount.

There was a peculiar, if rather esoteric, dialogue that went on between the intellectuals and anarchists of the *fin de siècle*. For in this dialogue was forged the sophisticated anarchism that made distinctions between myth making and truth gathering, between the credo of revolution and the results of revolution, and between mechanisms of persuasion and instruments of discovery. And in this dialogue the anarchist, by a peculiar dialectic of history, gave rise to its own form of superintellectualism. For in the hands of Michels, Sorel, Griffueles, and Lagardelle, Merlino, and Labriola, the Franco-Italian school of anarchism gave rise, out of its very search for a rational revolution that could engage irrational man, to a new form of sociological intellectualism —i.e., to the Franco-Italian school of social and political science—sometimes referred to as the "neo-Machiavellian tradition."

This cross-fertilization of anarchy and intellect attests to how close, in point of origin and inspiration (if not in point of conviction) anarchism and social science once were. I might here venture bold and suggest that the history of nineteenth-century social science has as one of its master threads its critical dialogue with anarchism. The "golden mean" of Spencerian sociology, the "social solidarity" of Durkheim, the "iron law of oligarchy" of Michels, these and many more can have little meaning until an accounting of the specter of anarchism—at least as the most extreme consequence of socialism—is fully made. The "redemptive spirit" of anarchism was absorbed in intellectually inspired reform. The "revolutionary specter" was absorbed in the general sweep of modern liberalism—in trade unionism, parliamentary democracy, and rapid mobility through the open social system. Between them, less than little was left for the anarchist to do battle against. Withdrawal once again became the leitmotif of anarchism.

While the social sources of intellectualism are profoundly anti-moralistic in contrast to anarchism, they turn a full circle, moving in opposite directions, and meet. The "meeting place" is their shared critical view of the present, a common need to see the present as *a moment in* history rather than as *the moment of* history, and a common need to make the better serve as the critic of the good.

IRVING LOUIS HOROWITZ

section one

Anarchism as a Critique of Society

Denis Diderot   The Fall of Natural Man[1]

Denis Diderot (1713–1784)   Diderot was born in Langres, France, the son of a cutler. After his education by the Jesuits he came to Paris to continue his education for a life in the Church. There his interests turned away from religion and toward law. When he would not continue his studies in this field, it is believed that his father refused to support him. He turned to free-lance writing, journalism, and translation. In 1743 he was wed to a highly conventional girl. This marriage proved to be unhappy to the bohemian and brilliant Diderot, who was further frustrated by the need to support his family with badly paid translating work. One of his chief claims to fame was the planning and editing of the great French Encyclopedia. This latter enterprise owes much of its success to the zealous efforts of Diderot on its behalf. He became part of the ranks of the philosophers and devoted his entire life to the exposition and dissemination of liberal ideas. He was a materialist philosopher and a leading spokesman for the French Revolution. He vehemently rejected authority and tradition as obstacles to free inquiry. First a deist and then an athiest, he was convinced that religous intolerance was the great enemy of mankind. In opposition to most of his fellow philosophers, he rejected enlightened despotism. He advocated a parliamentary monarchism in which

[1] From "Supplement au Voyage de Bougainville," by Denis Diderot. Translated from French by Jonathan Kemp, in *Diderot: Interpreter of Nature*. New York: International Publishers Co., Inc., Copyright © 1963. London: Lawrence & Wishart, 1943. By permission of the publishers.

representation would be elected by propertied classes. He advocated a national education system in which tuition, food, and books would be provided as well as subsidies to the families of impoverished students. *Philosophic Thoughts* appeared in 1746. It was condemned and burnt. He wrote *Promenade for a Skeptic* in 1747, which was denounced to the police. He suffered repression and even a brief imprisonment for his radical views. Among his chief works are, *Thoughts on the Explanation of Nature, Rameau's Nephew, Conversation between D'Alembert and Diderot, Elements of Physiology.*

He was the father of a large family. At the arrival of the Europeans, he looked disdainfully at them, showing neither astonishment, fear nor curiosity. They accosted him. He turned his back on them, and withdrew into his hut. His silence and his anxiety revealed his thoughts only too well: he lamented within himself for the great days of his country, now eclipsed. At the departure of Bougainville, when the inhabitants ran in a crowd to the shore, clinging to his garments, embracing his companions and weeping, the old man came forward with a stern air and said:

"Weep, poor folk of Tahiti, weep! Would that this were the arrival and not the departure of these ambitious and wicked men. One day you will know them better. One day they will return, in one hand the piece of wood you now see attached to the belt of this one, and the other grasping the blade you now see hanging from the belt of another. And with these they will enslave you, murder you or subject you to their extravagances and vices. One day you will serve under them, as corrupted, as vile, as loathsome as themselves.

"But I console myself; I am reaching the end of my journey; I shall not live to see the calamity I foretell. Oh people of Tahiti! Oh my friends! You have a means to escape this tragic future; but I would rather die than counsel it. Let them go their ways, let them live."

Then, addressing himself to Bougainville, he continued:

"And you, chief of these brigands who obey you, quickly take your vessel from our shores. We are innocent, we are happy; and you can only spoil our happiness. We follow the pure instincts of nature; and you have tried to wipe its impress from our souls. Here everything belongs to everybody. You have preached to us I know not what distinctions

between "mine" and "thine." Our daughters and our wives
are common to us all. You have shared this privilege with us;
and you have lighted passions in them before unknown. They
have become maddened in your arms; you have become
ferocious in theirs. They have begun to hate each other; you
have slain each other for them, and they have returned to us
stained with your blood.

"We are a free people; and now you have planted in our
country the title deeds of our future slavery. You are neither
god nor demon; who are you, then, to make slaves? Orou!
You understand the language of these men, tell us all, as you
have told me, what they have written on this sheet of metal:
'This country is ours.' This country yours? And why? Because
you have walked thereon? If a Tahitian landed one day on
your shores, and scratched on one of your rocks or on the
bark of your trees: 'This country belongs to the people of
Tahiti'—what would you think?

"You are the strongest! And what of that? When someone
took one of the contemptible trifles with which your vessel
is filled, you cried out and you were revenged. Yet at the
same time in the depths of your heart you plotted the theft
of a whole country! You are not a slave; you would suffer
death rather than be one; yet you want to enslave us. Do you
think the Tahitian does not know how to defend his liberty
and to die? The Tahitian you want to seize like a wild animal
is your brother. You are both children of nature; what right
have you over him that he has not over you? When you came,
did we rush upon you, did we pillage your ship? Did we
seize you and expose you to the arrows of our enemies? Did
we yoke you with the animals for toil in our fields? No. We
respected our own likeness in you. Leave us to our ways;
they are wiser and more honest than yours. We do not want
to barter what you call our ignorance for your useless civilization. Everything that is necessary and good for us we
possess. Do we deserve contempt, because we have not
known how to develop superfluous wants? When we hunger,
we have enough to eat; when we are cold we have wherewith
to clothe us. You have been in our huts; what is lacking there,
in your opinion? You may pursue as far as you like what
you call the comforts of life; but allow sensible people to
stop, when they would only have obtained imaginary good
from the continuation of their painful efforts. If you per-

suade us to exceed the narrow limits of our wants, when shall
we ever finish toiling? When shall we enjoy ourselves? We
have reduced the sum of our annual and daily labors to the
least possible, because nothing seems to us preferable to
repose. Go to your own country to agitate and torment yourself as much as you like; leave us in peace. Do not worry us
with your artificial needs nor with your imaginary virtues.
Look on these men; see how upright, healthy, and robust
they are. Look on these women; see how upright, healthy,
fresh, and beautiful they are. Take this bow; it is my own.
Call one, two, three, or four of your friends to help you and
try to bend it. I can bend it myself, alone. I till the soil. I
climb mountains. I pierce the forest. I can run a league on
the plains in less than an hour. Your young companions
would be hard put to follow me, yet I am more than ninety
years old.

"Woe unto this island! Woe to these people of Tahiti and
to all who will come after them, woe from the day you first
visited us! We should know only one disease; that to which
all men, animals, and plants are subject—old age; but you
have brought us another; you have infected our blood.

"It will perhaps be necessary to exterminate our daughters,
wives, children, with our own hands; all those who have
approached your women; those who have approached your
men.

"Our fields shall be soaked with the foul blood which has
passed from your veins into ours; or else our children, condemned to nourish and perpetuate the evil which you have
given to the fathers and mothers, will transmit it for ever
to their descendants. Villains! You will be the guilty ones;
guilty either of the ravages of disease that will follow the
fatal embraces of your people, or of the murders which we
shall commit to stop the spread of the poison.

"You speak of crimes! Do you know any more enormous
than your own? What is your punishment for him who kills
his neighbor?—death by the sword; what is your punishment
for the coward who poisons?—death by fire. Compare your
crime to his; tell us then, poisoner of whole peoples, what
should be the torment you deserve? But a short while ago,
the young Tahitian girl yielded herself to the transports and
embraces of the Tahitian youth; waited impatiently until her
mother, authorized by her having reached the age of mar-

riage, should remove her veil and make naked her breast.
She was proud to excite the desire and to attract the amorous
glances of unknown men, of relatives, of her brother. Without dread and without shame, in our presence, in the midst
of a circle of innocent Tahitians, to the sound of flutes, between the dances, she accepted the caresses of the one to
whom her young heart and the secret voice of her senses
urged her. The idea of crime and the peril of disease came
with you. Our enjoyments, once so sweet, are now accompanied by remorse and terror. That man in black who stands
near you listening to me, has spoken to our lads. I do not
know what he has said to our girls. But our lads are hesitant;
our girls blush. Plunge if you will into the dark depths of
the forest with the perverse companion of your pleasure;
but let the good and simple Tahitians reproduce themselves
without shame, under the open sky, in the full light of day.
What finer and more noble feeling could you put in place of
that with which we have inspired them, and which animates
them now? They think that the moment to enrich the nation
and the family with a new citizen is come, and they glory in
it. They eat to live and to grow; they grow in order to multi-
ply and they find in it nothing vicious nor shameful.

"Listen to the continuation of your crimes. You had
hardly come among our people than they became thieves.
You had scarcely landed on our soil, than it reeked with
blood. That Tahitian who ran to meet you, to receive you
crying 'Taio! friend, friend,' you slew. And why did you slay
him?—because he had been taken by the glitter of your
little serpents' eggs. He gave you of his fruits; he offered you
his wife and daughter, he ceded you his hut; yet you killed
him for a handful of beads which he had taken without
having asked. And the people? At the noise of your mur-
derous shot, terror seized them, and they fled to the mountains. But be assured that they would not have waited long
to descend again. Then you would all have perished, but for
me. Ah! why did I pacify them, why did I hold them back,
why do I still restrain them, even now? I do not know; for
you deserve no pity; for you have a ferocious soul which will
never feel it. You have wandered, you and yours, everywhere
in our island. You have been respected; you have enjoyed
all things; you have found neither barrier nor refusal in your
ways; you have been invited within, you have sat, and all the

abundance of our country has been spread before you. When you desired young girls, only excepting those who had not yet the privilege of unveiling their faces and breasts, their mothers have presented to you all the others, quite naked. You have possessed the tender victim of the duties of hospitality; flowers and leaves were heaped up for you and her; musicians sounded their instruments; nothing has spoiled the sweetness, nor hindered the freedom of your caresses nor of hers. They have sung the anthem exhorting you to be a man, and our child to be a woman, yielding and voluptuous. They danced around your couch. And it was when you came from the arms of this woman, after experiencing on her breast the sweetest of all intoxications, that you slew her brother, friend, or father.

"You have done still worse. Look over there, see that enclosure bristling with weapons. These arms which have menaced only your enemies are now turned against our own children. See these unhappy companions of our pleasures. See their sadness, the grief of their fathers and the despair of their mothers. They are those condemned to die, either by our hands or by the diseases you have given them.

"Away now, unless your cruel eyes revel in the spectacle of death. Go now, go; and may the guilty seas which spared you on your voyage hither, absolve themselves and avenge us, by engulfing you before you return.

"And you, oh people of Tahiti! Go into your huts, go, all of you; and let these strangers as they leave hear only the roar of the tide and see only the foam of its fury whitening a deserted shore."

He had scarcely finished before the crowd of people had disappeared. A vast silence reigned over the whole island, and only the keen whistling of the wind and the dull sound of the breakers along the shore could be heard. One might have said that the air and the sea, conscious of the voice of the aged man, were moved to obey him.

Errico Malatesta **Anarchism and Government**[1]

Errico Malatesta (1853–1932)   Malatesta gave some sixty years to

[1] From *Anarchy,* by Errico Malatesta. London: Freedom Press, 1907.

the anarchist movements of Europe. As a medical student at
the University of Naples he embraced Republicanism and shortly
thereafter became a socialist and member of the First International. It was in this association that he befriended and came
under the influence of Bakunin. He pressed constantly for the
principles of direct action, land seizure, and the general strike.
He organized a number of insurrections and workers' revolts. He
delivered anti-State speeches at many anarchist gatherings at an
international level. He thus laid down important features of
communist anarchism and anarchist tactics that had a great impact on the movement. Malatesta was a wealthy man who put
his entire fortune at the disposal of the cause. He won the militant support of broad sections of his countrymen whose demonstrations and strikes on his behalf saved him from death and
imprisonment a number of times. In Argentine exile and again
in the United States he published radical newspapers. He took
part in the Xeres insurrection in Spain, in the General Strike
of 1895 in Belgium, spent years of exile and imprisonment in
England, France, and Switzerland. It was in 1907 that he
attended the anarchist congress at Amsterdam and made speeches
on anarchist organization that were to shape the anarchist
movement. Kropotkin left us a picture of his life in exile:
"Without even so much as a room that he could call his own,
he would sell sherbet in the streets of London to get his living,
and in the evening write brilliant articles for the Italian papers.
Imprisoned in France, released, expelled, recondemned in Italy,
confined to an island, escaped, and again in Italy in disguise;
always in the hottest of the struggle. . . ."
  Through the systematic destruction of its finest radical leader-
ship, Italy moved on to the eventual victory of fascism.
Malatesta remained in Italy, under house arrest, until he died.
The authorities ordered his body thrown into a common grave.
His best known political statement in English is his pamphlet
Anarchy.

                              Anarchy is a word that comes
from the Greek, and signifies, strictly speaking, "without
government": the state of a people without any constituted
authority.
  Before such an organization had begun to be considered
possible and desirable by a whole class of thinkers, so as to
be taken as the aim of a movement (which has now become
one of the most important factors in modern social warfare),
the word "anarchy" was used universally in the sense of dis-

order and confusion, and it is still adopted in that sense by the ignorant and by adversaries interested in distorting the truth.

We shall not enter into philological discussions, for the question is not philological but historical. The common interpretation of the word does not misconceive its true etymological signification, but is derived from it, owing to the prejudice that government must be a necessity of the organization of social life, and that consequently a society without government must be given up to disorder, and oscillate between the unbridled dominion of some and the blind vengeance of others.

The existence of this prejudice and its influence on the meaning that the public has given to the word is easily explained.

Man, like all living beings, adapts himself to the conditions in which he lives, and transmits by inheritance his acquired habits. Thus, being born and having lived in bondage, being the descendant of a long line of slaves, man, when he began to think, believed that slavery was an essential condition of life, and liberty seemed to him impossible. In like manner, the workman, forced for centuries to depend upon the good-will of his employer for work, that is, for bread, and accustomed to see his own life at the disposal of those who possess the land and capital, has ended in believing that it is his master who gives him food, and asks ingenuously how it would be possible to live, if there were no master over him?

In the same way, a man whose limbs had been bound from birth, but who had nevertheless found out how to hobble about, might attribute to the very bands that bound him his ability to move, while, on the contrary, they would diminish and paralyze the muscular energy of his limbs.

If then we add to the natural effect of habit the education given him by his master, the parson, the teacher, etc., who are all interested in teaching that the employer and the government are necessary, if we add the judge and the policeman to force those who think differently—and might try to propagate their opinions—to keep silence, we shall understand how the prejudice as to the utility and necessity of masters and governments has become established. Suppose a doctor brought forward a complete theory, with a thousand ably invented illustrations, to persuade the man with bound limbs that, if his limbs were freed, he could not walk, or even live. The man would defend his bands furiously and consider anyone his enemy who tried to tear them off.

Thus, if it is believed that government is necessary and that without government there must be disorder and confusion, it is natural and logical to suppose that anarchy, which signifies absence of government, must also mean absence of order.

Nor is this fact without parallel in the history of words. In those epochs and countries where people have considered government by one man (monarchy) necessary, the word "republic" (that is, the government of many) has been used precisely like "anarchy," to imply disorder and confusion. Traces of this meaning of the word are still to be found in the popular languages of almost all countries.

When this opinion is changed, and the public are convinced that government is not necessary, but extremely harmful, the word "anarchy," precisely because it signifies "without government," will become equal to saying "natural order, harmony of the needs and interests of all, complete liberty with complete solidarity."

Therefore, those are wrong who say that anarchists have chosen their name badly, because it is erroneously understood by the masses and leads to a false interpretation. The error does not come from the word, but from the thing. The difficulty which anarchists meet in spreading their views does not depend upon the name they have given themselves, but upon the fact that their conceptions strike at all the inveterate prejudices which people have about the function of government, or "the state," as it is called.

Before proceeding further, it will be well to explain this last word (the "State") which, in our opinion, is the real cause of much misunderstanding.

Anarchists generally make use of the word "State" to mean all that collection of institutions, political, legislative, judicial, military, financial, etc., by means of which the management of their own affairs, the guidance of their personal conduct, and the care of ensuring their own safety are taken from the people and confided to certain individuals, and these, whether by usurpation or delegation, are invested with the right to make laws over and for all, and to constrain the public to respect them, making use of the collective force of the community to this end.

In this case the word "State" means "government," or, if you like, it is the abstract expression of which government is the personification. Then such expressions as "Abolition of the State," or "Society without the State," agree perfectly with the conception which anarchists wish to express of the destruction of every political institution based on authority, and of the constitution of a free and equal society, based upon harmony of interests, and the voluntary contribution of all to the satisfaction of social needs.

However, the word "State" has many other meanings, and among these some that lend themselves to misconstruction, particularly when used among men whose sad social position has not afforded them leisure to become accustomed to the subtle distinctions of scientific language, or, still worse, when adopted treacherously by adversaries, who are interested in confounding the sense, or do not wish to comprehend it. Thus the word "State" is often used to indicate any given society, or collection of human beings, united on a given territory and constituting what is called a "social unit," independently of the way in which the members of the said body are grouped, or of the relations existing between them. "State" is used also simply as a synonym for "society." Owing to these meanings of the word, our adversaries believe, or rather profess to believe, that anarchists wish to abolish every social relation and all collective work, and to reduce man to a condition of isolation, that is, to a state worse than savagery.

By "State" again is meant only the supreme administration of a country, the central power, as distinct from provincial or communal power, and therefore others think that anarchists wish merely for a territorial decentralization, leaving the principle of government intact, and thus confounding anarchy with cantonal or communal government.

Finally, "State" signifies "condition, mode of living, the order of social life," etc., and therefore we say, for example, that it is necessary to change the economic state of the working classes, or that the anarchical State is the only State founded on the principles of solidarity, and other similar phrases. So that if we say also in another sense that we wish

to abolish the State, we may at once appear absurd or
contradictory.

For these reasons, we believe that it would be better to use
the expression "abolition of the State" as little as possible,
and to substitute for it another, clearer and more concrete—
"abolition of government."

The latter will be the expression used in the course of this
essay.

We have said that anarchy is society without government.
But is the suppression of government possible, desirable, or
wise? Let us see.

What is the government? There is a disease of the human
mind, called the metaphysical tendency, that causes man,
after he has by a logical process abstracted the quality from
an object, to be subject to a kind of hallucination that makes
him take the abstraction for the real thing. This metaphysical
tendency, in spite of the blows of positive science, has still
strong root in the minds of the majority of our contemporary
fellowmen. It has such influence that many consider government an actual entity, with certain given attributes of reason,
justice, equity, independent of the people who compose the
government.

For those who think in this way, government, or the State,
is the abstract social power, and it represents, always in the
abstract, the general interest. It is the expression of the rights
of all and is considered as limited by the rights of each. This
way of understanding government is supported by those
interested, to whom it is an urgent necessity that the principle
of authority should be maintained and should always survive
the faults and errors of the persons who exercise power.

For us, the government is the aggregate of the governors,
and the governors—kings, presidents, ministers, members of
parliament, and what not—are those who have the power to
make laws regulating the relations between men, and to force
obedience to these laws. They are those who decide upon and
claim the taxes, enforce military service, judge and punish
transgressors of the laws. They subject men to regulations,
and supervise and sanction private contracts. They monopo-
lize certain branches of production and public services, or, if
they wish, all production and public service. They promote
or hinder the exchange of goods. They make war or peace
with the governments of other countries. They concede or

withhold free trade and many things else. In short, the governors are those who have the power, in a greater or lesser degree, to make use of the collective force of society, that is, of the physical, intellectual, and economic force of all, to oblige each to their (the governors') wish. And this power constitutes, in our opinion, the very principle of government and authority.

But what reason is there for the existence of government?

Why abdicate one's own liberty, one's own initiative in favor of other individuals? Why give them the power to be the masters, with or against the wish of each, to dispose of the forces of all in their own way? Are the governors such exceptionally gifted men as to enable them, with some show of reason, to represent the masses and act in the interests of all men better than all men would be able to act for themselves? Are they so infallible and incorruptible that one can confide to them, with any semblance of prudence, the fate of each and all, trusting to their knowledge and goodness?

And even if there existed men of infinite goodness and knowledge, even if we assume what has never happened in history and what we believe could never happen, namely, that the government might devolve upon the ablest and best, would the possession of government power add anything to their beneficent influence? Would it not rather paralyze or destroy it? For those who govern find it necessary to occupy themselves with things which they do not understand, and, above all, to waste the greater part of their energy in keeping themselves in power, striving to satisfy their friends, holding the discontented in check, and mastering the rebellious.

Again, be the governors good or bad, wise or ignorant, how do they gain power? Do they impose themselves by right of war, conquest, or revolution? If so, what guarantees have the public that their rules have the general good at heart? In this case it is simply a question of usurpation, and if the subjects are discontented, nothing is left to them but to throw off the yoke by an appeal to arms. Are the governors chosen from a certain class or party? Then inevitably the ideas and interests of that class or party will triumph, and the wishes and interests of the others will be sacrificed. Are they elected by universal suffrage? Now numbers are the sole criterion, and numbers are clearly no proof of reason, justice, or capacity. Under universal suffrage the elected are those who know best how to take in the masses. The minority, which may happen to be the half minus one, is sacrificed. Moreover, experience has shown it is impossible to hit upon an electoral system that really ensures election by the actual majority.

Many and various are the theories by which men have sought to justify the existence of government. All, however, are founded, confessedly or not, on the assumption that the individuals of a society have contrary interests, and that an external superior power is necessary to oblige some to respect the interests of others, by prescribing and imposing a rule of conduct, according to which the interests at strife may be harmonized as much as possible, and according to which each may obtain the maximum of satisfaction with the minimum of sacrifice. If, say the theorists of the authoritarian school, the interests, tendencies, and desires of an individual are in opposition to those of another individual, or perhaps all society, who will have the right and the power to oblige the one to respect the interests of the other or others? Who will be able to prevent the individual citizen from offending the general will? The liberty of each, they say, has for its limit the liberty of others: but who will establish those limits, and who will cause them to be respected? The natural antagonism of interests and passions creates the necessity for government, and justifies authority. Authority intervenes as moderator of the social strife and defines the limits of the rights and duties of each.

This is the theory; but to be sound the theory should be based upon an explanation of facts. We know well how in social economy theories are too often invented to justify facts, that is, to defend privilege and cause it to be accepted tranquilly by those who are its victims. Let us here look at the facts themselves.

In all the course of history, as in the present epoch, government is either brutal, violent, arbitrary domination of the few over the many, or it is an instrument devised to secure domination and privilege to those who, by force, or cunning, or inheritance, have taken to themselves all the means of life, and first and foremost the soil, whereby they hold the people in servitude, making them work for their advantage.

Governments oppress mankind in two ways, either directly, by brute force, that is physical violence, or indirectly, by depriving them of the means of subsistence and thus reducing them to helplessness. Political power originated in the first method; economic privilege arose from the second. Governments can also oppress man by acting on his emotional nature, and in this way constitute religious authority. There is no reason for the propagation of religious superstitions but that they defend and consolidate political and economic privileges.

In primitive society, when the world was not so densely populated as now and social relations were less complicated, if any circumstance prevented the formation of habits and customs of solidarity, or destroyed those which already existed and established the domination of man over man, the two powers, political and economic, were united in the same hands—often in those of a single individual. Those who by force had conquered and impoverished the others, constrained them to become their servants and to perform all things for them according to their caprice. The victors were at once proprietors, legislators, kings, judges, and executioners.

But with the increase of population, with the growth of needs, with the complication of social relationships, the prolonged continuance of such despotism became impossible. For their own security the rulers, often much against their will, were obliged to depend upon a privileged class, that is, a certain number of cointerested individuals, and were also obliged to let each of these individuals provide for his own sustenance. Nevertheless they reserved to themselves the supreme or ultimate control. In other words, the rulers reserved to themselves the right to exploit all at their own convenience, and so to satisfy their kingly vanity. Thus private wealth was developed under the shadow of the ruling power, for its protection and—often unconsciously—as its accomplice. The class of proprietors arose, and, concentrating little by little into their own hands all the means of production, the very fountains of life—agriculture, industry, and exchange—ended by becoming a power in themselves. This power, by the superiority of its means of action and the great mass of interests it embraces, always ends by subjugating more or less openly the political power, that is, the government, which it makes its policeman.

This phenomenon has been repeated often in history. Every time that, by military enterprise, physical brute force has taken the upper hand in society, the conquerors have shown the tendency to concentrate government and property in their own hands. In every case, however, because the government cannot attend to the production of wealth and overlook and direct everything, it finds it necessary to conciliate a powerful class, and private property is again established. With it comes the division of the two sorts of power, that of the persons who control the collective force of society, and that of the proprietors, upon whom these governors become essentially dependent, because the proprietors command the sources of the said collective force.

Never has this state of affairs been so accentuated as in modern times. The development of production, the immense extension of commerce, the extensive power that money has acquired, and all the economic results flowing from the discovery of America, the invention of machinery, etc., have secured such supremacy to the capitalist class that it is no longer content to trust to the support of the government and has come to wish that the government shall emanate from itself; a government composed of members from its own class, continually under its control and specially organized to defend it against the possible revenge of the disinherited. Hence the origin of the modern parliamentary system.

Today the government is composed of proprietors, or people of their class so entirely under their influence that the richest do not find it necessary to take an active part themselves. Rothschild, for instance, does not need to be either M.P. or minister, it is enough for him to keep M.P.'s and ministers dependent upon him.

In many countries, the proletariat participates nominally in the election of the government. This is a concession which the *bourgeois* (i.e., proprietory) class have made, either to avail themselves of popular support in the strife against royal or aristocratic power, or to divert the attention of the people from their own emancipation by giving them an apparent share in political power. However, whether the bourgeoisie foresaw it or not, when first they conceded to the people the right to vote, the fact is that the right has proved in reality a mockery, serving only to consolidate the power of the bourgeoisie, while giving to the most energetic only of the proletariat the illusory hope of arriving at power.

So also with universal suffrage—we might say, especially

with universal suffrage—the government has remained the servant and police of the bourgeois class. How could it be otherwise? If the government should reach the point of becoming hostile, if the hope of democracy should ever be more than a delusion deceiving the people, the proprietory class, menaced in its interests would at once rebel and would use all the force and influence that come from the possession of wealth, to reduce the government to the simple function of acting as policeman.

In all times and in all places, whatever may be the name that the government takes, whatever has been its origin, or its organization, its essential function is always that of oppressing and exploiting the masses, and of defending the oppressors and exploiters. Its principal characteristic and indispensable instruments are the policeman and the tax collector, the soldier and the prison. And to these are necessarily added the time-serving priest or teacher, as the case may be, supported and protected by the government, to render the spirit of the people servile and make them docile under the yoke.

Certainly, in addition to this primary business, to this essential department of governmental action other departments have been added in the course of time. We even admit that never, or hardly ever, has a government been able to exist in a country that was at all civilized without adding to its oppressing and exploiting functions others useful and indispensable to social life. But this fact makes it nonetheless true that government is in its nature a means of exploitation, and that its origin and position doom it to be the defense of a dominant class, thus confirming and increasing the evils of domination.

The government assumes the business of protecting, more or less vigilantly, the life of citizens against direct and brutal attacks; acknowledges and legalizes a certain number of rights and primitive usages and customs, without which it is impossible to live in society. It organizes and directs certain public services, such as the post, preservation and construction of roads, care of the public health, benevolent institutions, workhouses, etc., and poses as the protector and benefactor of the poor and weak. But to prove our point it is sufficient to notice how and why it fulfills these functions. The fact is that everything the government undertakes is always inspired with the spirit of domination and intended to defend, enlarge, and perpetuate the privileges of property and of those classes of which government is the representative and defender.

A government cannot rule for any length of time without hiding its true nature behind the pretence of general utility. It cannot respect the lives of the privileged without assuming the air of wishing to respect the lives of all. It cannot cause the privileges of some to be tolerated without appearing as the custodian of the rights of everybody. "The law" (and, of course, those who have made the law, i.e., the government) "has utilized," says Kropotkin, "the social sentiments of man, working into them those precepts of morality, which man has accepted, together with arrangements useful to the minority —the exploiters—and opposed to the interests of those who might have rebelled, had it not been for this show of a moral ground."

A government cannot wish the destruction of the community, for then it and the dominant class could not claim their wealth from exploitation; nor could the government leave the community to manage its own affairs, for then the people would soon discover that it (the government) was necessary for no other end than to defend the proprietory class who impoverish them, and would hasten to rid themselves of both government and proprietory class.

Today, in the face of the persistent and menacing demands of the proletariat, governments show a tendency to interfere in the relations between employers and work people. Thus they try to arrest the labor movement and to impede with delusive reforms the attempts of the poor to take to themselves what is due to them, namely, an equal share of the good things of life that others enjoy.

We must also remember that on one hand the bourgoisie, that is, the proprietory class, make war among themselves and destroy one another continually, and that, on the other hand, the government, although composed of the bourgeoisie and, acting as their servant and protector, is still, like every servant or protector, continually striving to emancipate itself and to domineer over its charge. Thus, this seesaw game, this swaying between conceding and withdrawing, this seeking allies among the people and against the classes, and among the classes against the masses, forms the science of the governors and blinds the ingenuous and phlegmatic, who are always expecting that salvation is coming to them from on high.

With all this, the government does not change its nature. If it acts as regulator or guarantor of the rights and duties of each, it perverts the sentiment of justice. It justifies wrong and punishes every act that offends or menaces the privileges of the governors and proprietors. It declares just and *legal* the most atrocious exploitation of the miserable, which means a slow and continuous material and moral murder, perpetrated by those who have on those who have not. Again, if it administers public services, it always considers the interests of the governors and proprietors, not occupying itself with the interests of the working masses, except insofar as is necessary to make the masses willing to endure their share of taxation. If it instructs, it fetters and curtails the truth, and tends to prepare the minds and hearts of the young to become either implacable tyrants or docile slaves, according to the class to which they belong. In the hands of the government everything becomes a means of exploitation, everything serves as a police measure, useful to hold the people in check. And it must be thus. If the life of mankind consists in strife between man and man, naturally there must be conquerors and conquered, and the government, which is the means of securing to the victors the results of their victory and perpetuating those results, will certainly never fall to those who have lost, whether the battle be on the grounds of physical or intellectual strength, or in the field of economics. And those who have fought to secure to themselves better conditions than others can have, to win privilege and add dominion to power, and have attained the victory, will certainly not use it to defend the rights of the vanquished, and to place limits to their own power and to that of their friends and partisans.

The government—or the State, if you will—as judge, moderator of social strife, impartial administrator of the public interests, is a lie, an illusion, a Utopia, never realized and never realizable. If, in fact, the interests of men must always be contrary to one another, if, indeed, the strife between mankind had made laws necessary to human society, and the liberty of the individual must be limited by the liberty of other individuals, then each one would always seek to make his interests triumph over those of others. Each would strive to enlarge his own liberty at the cost of the liberty of others, and there would be government. Not simply because it was more or less useful to the totality of the members of society to have a government, but because the conquerors would wish to secure to themselves the fruits of victory. They would wish effectually to subject the vanquished and relieve themselves of the trouble of being always on the defensive, and they would appoint men, specially adapted to the business, to act as police. Were this indeed actually the case, then humanity would be destined to perish amid periodical contests between the tyranny of the dominators and the rebellion of the conquered.

But fortunately the future of humanity is a happier one, because the law that governs it is milder.

Thus, in the contest of centuries between liberty and authority, or, in other words, between social equality and social castes, the question at issue has not really been the relations between society and the individual, or the increase of individual independence at the cost of social control, or vice versa. Rather it has had to do with preventing any one individual from oppressing the others; with giving to everyone the same rights and the same means of action. It has had to do with substituting the initiative of all, which must naturally result in the advantage of all, for the initiative of the few, which necessarily results in the suppression of all the others. It is always, in short, the question of putting an end to the domination and exploitation of man by man in such a way that all are interested in the common welfare, and that the individual force of each, instead of oppressing, combating, or suppressing others, will find the possibility of complete development, and everyone will seek to associate with others for the greater advantage of all.

From what we have said, it follows that the existence of a government, even upon the hypothesis that the ideal government of authoritarian socialists were possible, far from producing an increase of productive force, would immensely diminish it, because the government would restrict initiative to the few. It would give these few the right to do all things, without being able, of course, to endow them with the knowledge or understanding of all things.

In fact, if you divest legislation and all the operations of government of what is intended to protect the privileged, and what represents the wishes of the privileged classes alone, nothing remains but the aggregate of individual governors. "The State," says Sismondi, "is always a conservative power which authorizes, regulates, and organizes the conquests of progress (and history testifies that it applies them to the profit of its own and the other privileged classes) but never does it inaugurate them. New ideas always originate from beneath, are conceived in the foundations of society, and then, when divulged, they become opinion and grow. But they must always meet on their path, and combat the constituted powers of tradition, custom, privilege and error."

In order to understand how society could exist without a government, it is sufficient to turn our attention for a short space to what actually goes on in our present society. We shall see that in reality the most important social functions are fulfilled even nowadays outside the intervention of government. Also that government only interferes to exploit the masses, or defend the privileged, or, lastly, to sanction, most unnecessarily, all that has been done without its aid, often in spite of and in opposition to it. Men work, exchange, study, travel, follow as they choose the current rules of morality or hygiene; they profit by the progress of science and art, have numberless mutual interests without ever feeling the need of any one to direct them how to conduct themselves in regard to these matters. On the contrary, it is just those things in which there is no governmental interference that prosper best and give rise to the least contention, being unconsciously adapted to the wish of all in the way found most useful and agreeable.

Nor is government more necessary for large undertakings, or for those public services which require the constant co-operation of many people of different conditions and countries. Thousands of these undertakings are even now the work of voluntarily formed associations. And these are, by the acknowledgement of everyone, the undertakings that succeed the best. We do not refer to the associations of capitalists, organized by means of exploitation, although even they show capabilities and powers of free association, which may extend until it embraces all the peoples of all lands and includes the widest and most varying interests. We speak rather of those associations inspired by the love of humanity, or by the passion for knowledge, or even simply by the desire for amusement and love of applause, as these represent better such groupings as will exist in a society where, private property and internal strife between men being abolished, each will find his interests compatible with the interests of everyone else and his greatest satisfaction in doing good and pleasing others. Scientific societies and congresses, international lifeboat and Red Cross associations, laborers' unions, peace societies, volunteers who hasten to the rescue at times of great public calamity, are all examples, among thousands, of that power of the spirit of association which always shows itself when a need arises or an enthusiasm takes hold, and the means do not fail. That voluntary associations do not cover the world and do not embrace every branch of material and moral activity is the fault of the obstacles placed in their way by governments, of the antagonisms created by the possession of private property, and of the impotence and degradation to which the monopolizing of wealth on the part of the few reduces the majority of mankind.

The government takes charge, for instance, of the postal and telegraph services. But in what way does it really assist them? When the people are in such a condition as to be able to enjoy and feel the need of such services they will think about organizing them, and the man with the necessary technical knowledge will not require a certificate from a government to enable him to set to work. The more general and urgent the need, the more volunteers will offer to satisfy it. Would the people have the ability necessary to provide and distribute provisions? Never fear, they will not die of hunger waiting for a government to pass laws on the subject. Wherever a government exists, it must wait until the people have first organized everything, and then come with its laws to sanction and exploit what has already been done. It is evident that private interest is the great motive for all activity. That being so, when the interest of every one becomes the interest of each (and it necessarily will become so as soon as private property is abolished), then all will be active. If they work now in the interest of the few, so much more and so much better will they work to satisfy the interests of all. It is hard to understand how anyone can believe that public services indispensable to social life can be better secured by order of a government than through the workers themselves who by their own choice òr by agreement with others carry them out under the immediate control of all those interested.

Certainly in every collective undertaking on a large scale there is need for division of labor, for technical direction, administration, etc. But the authoritarians are merely playing with words, when they deduce a reason for the existence of government, from the very real necessity for organization of labor. The government, we must repeat, is the aggregate of the individuals who have received or have taken the right or the means to make laws, and force the people to obey them. The administrators, engineers, etc., on the other hand, are men who receive or assume the charge of doing a certain work. Government signifies delegation of power, that is, abdication of the initiative and sovereignty of everyone into the hands of the few. Administration signifies delegation of work, that is, the free exchange of services founded on free agreement.

Pierre Joseph Proudhon **Property and Revolution**[1]

Pierre Joseph Proudhon (1809–1865) Proudhon was one of the few great revolutionary leaders of genuinely plebeian origin, his father having been a barrel-maker. Scholarship aid enabled him to pursue his studies. In 1840, in Paris, his pamphlet *What Is Property?* was published and created a sensation with the thesis that property is theft and an impossibility. His further publications gave him a wide reputation as a radical. Involved with radical politics and in his contact with the Marxists, he soon rejected their doctrine, seeking rather a middle way between socialist theories and classical economics. He supported a notion of free credit and equitable exchange. In 1848 he attempted to found a people's bank. His activities led to his imprisonment. His *De la justice dans la révolution et dans l'église,* an attack on Church and State, led to his flight to Brussels. On his return to Paris he continued his writings, despite ill health, till the end of his life. He wrote his *De la capacité politique des classes ouvrières,* which was published a few months after his death. This work had an influence upon the

[1] From *What Is Property: An Inquiry into the Principle of Right and of Government,* by Pierre Joseph Proudhon. Translated from the French by Benjamin R. Tucker. New York: The Humboldt Publishing Company, 1890.

French workers in the International. They defended his solutions, which aimed at free credit and equality of exchange without a dictatorship of the proletariat. Marx first admired this enemy of property, then attacked him, thereby undermining his prestige and virtually eclipsing him until the syndicalist Fernand Pelloutier revived interest in his theories by falling back on his work. Proudhon published many works in jurisprudence, political economy, on the State and property. Among them are: *System of Economic Contradictions or the Philosophy of Poverty, Confessions of a Revolutionary, The Principle of Federation and the Need to Rebuild the Revolutionary Party.*

    If I were asked to answer the following question: "What is slavery?" and I should answer in one word, "It is murder," my meaning would be understood at once. No extended argument would be required to show that the power to take from a man his thought, his will, his personality, is a power of life and death; and that to enslave him is to kill him. Why, then, to this other question: "What is property?" may I not likewise answer, "It is robbery," without the certainty of being misunderstood, the second proposition being no other than a transformation of the first?

I undertake to discuss the vital principle of our government and our institutions, property: I am in my right. I may be mistaken in the conclusion that shall result from my investigations: I am in my right. I think best to place the last thought of my book first: still I am in my right.

Such an author teaches that property is a civil right, born of occupation and sanctioned by law; another maintains that it is a natural right, originating in labor—and both of these doctrines, totally opposed as they may seem, are encouraged and applauded. I contend that neither labor, nor occupation, nor law, can create property; that it is an effect without a cause: am I censurable?

But murmurs arise! *Property is robbery!* This is the war cry of '93! That is the signal of revolutions!

Reader, calm yourself. I am no agent of discord, no firebrand of sedition. I anticipate history by a few days. I disclose a truth whose development we may try in vain to arrest. I write the preamble of our future constitution. This proposition which seems to you blasphemous—property is robbery—would, if our prejudices allowed us to consider it, be recognized as the lightening rod to shield us from the coming thunderbolt; but too many interests stand in the way!—Alas! Philosophy will not change the course of events. Destiny will fulfill itself regardless of prophecy. Besides, must not justice be done and our education be finished?

Property is robbery!—What a revolution in human ideas! "Proprietor" and "robber" have been at all times expressions as contradictory as the beings whom they designate are hostile; all languages have perpetuated this opposition. On what authority, then, do you venture to attack universal consent and give the lie to the human race? Who are you, that you should question the judgment of the nations and the ages?

Of what consequence to you, reader, is my obscure individuality? I live, like you, in a century in which reason submits only to fact and to evidence. My name like yours is TRUTH-SEEKER. My mission is written in these words of the law: "Speak without hatred and without fear; tell that which thou knowest!" The work of our race is to build the temple of science, and this science includes Man and Nature. Now truth reveals itself to all. Today to Newton and Pascal, tomorrow to the herdsman in the valley and the journeyman in the shop. Each one contributes his stone to the edifice, and, his task accomplished, disappears. Eternity precedes us. Eternity follows us. Between two infinites, of what account is one poor mortal that the century should inquire about him?

Disregard then, reader, my title and my character, and attend only to my arguments. It is in accordance with universal consent that I undertake to correct universal error. From the *opinion* of the human race I appeal to its *faith*. Have the courage to follow me and, if your will is untrammelled, if your conscience is free, if your mind can unite two propositions and deduce a third therefrom, my ideas will inevitably become yours. In the beginning by giving you my last word, it was my purpose to warn you, not to defy you; for I am certain that, if you read me, you will be compelled to assent. The things of which I am to speak are so simple and clear that you will be astonished at not having perceived them before, and you will say: "I have neglected to think." Others offer you the spectacle of genius wresting Nature's secrets from her and unfolding before you her sublime messages. You will find here only a series of experiments upon "justice" and "right," a sort of verification of the weights and measures of your conscience. The operations shall be conducted under your very eyes and you shall weigh the result.

Nevertheless, I build no system. I ask an end to privilege, the abolition of slavery, equality of rights, and the reign of law. Justice, nothing else; that is the alpha and omega of my argument. To others I leave the business of governing the world.

One day I asked myself: Why is there so much sorrow and misery in society? Must man always be wretched? And not satisfied with the explanations given by the reformers—these attributing the general distress to governmental cowardice and incapacity, those to conspirators and *émeutes,* still others to ignorance and general corruption—and weary of the interminable quarrels of the tribune and the press, I sought to fathom the matter myself. I have consulted the masters of science. I have read a hundred volumes of philosophy, law, political economy, and history. Would to God that I had lived in a century in which so much reading had been useless! I have made every effort to obtain exact information, comparing doctrines, replying to objections, continually constructing equations and reductions from arguments, and weighing thousands of syllogisms in the scales of the most rigorous logic. In this laborious work, I have collected many interesting facts, which I shall share with my friends and the public as soon as I have leisure. But I must say that I recognized at once that we had never understood the meaning of these words, so common and yet so sacred: "justice," "equity," "liberty"; that concerning each of these principles our ideas have been utterly obscure. And in fact, that this ignorance was the sole cause, both of the poverty that devours us and of all the calamities that have ever afflicted the human race.

My mind was frightened by this strange result. I doubted my reason. What! said I, that which eye has not seen, nor ear heard, nor insight penetrated, you have discovered! Wretch, mistake not the visions of your diseased brain for the truths of science! Do you not know (great philosophers have said so) that in points of practical morality universal error is a contradiction?

I resolved then to test my arguments, and in entering upon this new labor I sought an answer to the following questions:

Is it possible that humanity can have so long and so universally been mistaken in the application of moral principles?
How and why could it be mistaken? How can its error, being
universal, be capable of correction?

These questions, on the solution of which depended the
certainty of my conclusions, offered no lengthy resistance to
analysis. It will be seen, in Chapter V of this work, that in
morals, as in all other branches of knowledge, the gravest
errors are the dogmas of science; that even in works of
justice, to be mistaken is a privilege that ennobles man; and
that whatever philosophical merit may attach to me is infinitely small. To name a thing is easy. The difficulty is to
discern it before its appearance. In giving expression to the
last stage of an idea, an idea that permeates all minds, that
tomorrow will be proclaimed by another if I fail to announce
it today, I can claim no merit save that of priority of utter-
ance. Do we eulogize the man who first perceives the dawn?

Yes, all men believe and repeat that equality of conditions
is identical with equality of rights; that "property" and
"robbery" are synonymous terms; that every social advantage accorded, or rather usurped, in the name of superior
talent or service is iniquity and extortion. All men in their
hearts, I say, bear witness to these truths. They need only
to be made to understand it.

Before entering directly upon the question before me, I
must say a word of the road that I shall traverse. When
Pascal approached a geometrical problem, he invented a
method of solution. To solve a problem in philosophy a
method is equally necessary. Well, by how much do the
problems of which philosophy treats surpass in the gravity
of their results those discussed by geometry! How much
more imperatively, then, do they demand for their solution
a profound and rigorous analysis!

It is a fact placed ever beyond doubt, say the modern
psychologists, that every perception received by the mind
is determined by certain general laws that govern the mind;
is molded so to speak, in certain types preexisting in our
understanding, and which constitutes its original condition.
Hence, say they, if the mind has no innate *ideas*, it has at
least innate *forms*. Thus, for example, every phenomenon is
of necessity conceived by us as happening in *time* and *space*.
That compels us to infer a cause of its occurrence. Every-

thing that exists implies the ideas of "substance," "mode," "relation," "number," etc. In a word, we form no idea that is not related to some one of the general principles of reason, independent of which nothing exists.

These axioms of the understanding, add the psychologists, these fundamental types, by which all our judgments and ideas are inevitably shaped, and which our sensations serve only to illuminate, are known in the schools as "categories." Their primordial existence in the mind is today demonstrated. They need only to be systematized and catalogued. Aristotle recognized ten. Kant increased the number to fifteen. Mr. Cousin has reduced it to three, to two, to one, and the indisputable glory of this professor will be due to the fact that, if he has not discovered the true theory of categories, he has, at least, seen more clearly than anyone else the vast importance of this question—the greatest and perhaps the only one with which metaphysics has to deal.

I confess that I disbelieve in the innateness not only of *ideas,* but also of *forms* or *laws* of our understanding. And I hold the metaphysics of Reid and Kant to be still further removed from the truth than that of Aristotle. However, as I do not wish to enter here into a discussion of the mind, a task that would demand much labor and be of no interest to the public, I shall admit the hypothesis that our most general and most necessary ideas—such as "time," "space," "substance," and "cause"—exist originally in the mind, or at least are derived immediately from its constitution.

But it is a psychological fact nonetheless true, and one to which the philosophers have paid too little attention, that habit, like a second nature, has the power of fixing in the mind new categorical forms derived from the appearances that impress us, and by them usually stripped of objective reality, but whose influence over our judgments is no less predetermining than that of the original categories. Hence we reason by the *eternal* and *absolute* laws of our mind, and at the same time by the secondary rules, ordinarily faulty, that are suggested to us by imperfect observation. This is the most fecund source of false prejudices, and the permanent and often invincible cause of a multitude of errors. The bias resulting from these prejudices is so strong that often, even when we are fighting against a principle that our mind thinks false, that is repugnant to our reason, and of which our conscience disapproves, we defend it without knowing it, we reason in accordance with it, and we obey it while attacking it. Enclosed within a circle, our mind revolves about itself, until a new observation, creating within us new ideas, brings to view an external principle that delivers us from the phantom by which our imagination is possessed.

Thus, we know today that, by the laws of a universal magnetism whose cause is still unknown, two bodies (no obstacle intervening) tend to unite by an accelerated impelling force that we call "gravitation." It is gravitation that causes unsupported bodies to fall to the ground, that gives them weight, and that fastens us to the earth on which we live. Ignorance of this cause was the sole obstacle that prevented the ancients from believing in the antipodes. "Can you not see," said St. Augustine after Lactantius, "that, if there were men under our feet, their heads would point downward, and that they would fall into the sky?" The bishop of Hippo, who thought the earth flat because it appeared so to the eye, supposed in consequence that, if we should connect by straight lines the zenith with the nadir in different places, these lines would be parallel with each other; and in the direction of these lines he traced every movement from above to below. Thence he naturally concluded that the stars were rolling torches set in the vault of the sky, that, if left to themselves, they would fall to the earth in a shower of fire; that the earth was one vast plain, forming the lower portion of the world, etc. If he had been asked by what the world itself was sustained, he would have answered that he did not know, but that to God nothing is impossible. Such were the ideas of St. Augustine in regard to space and movement, ideas fixed within him by a prejudice derived from an appearance, and which had become with him a general and categorical rule of judgment. Of the reason that bodies fall his mind knew nothing. He could only say that a body falls because it falls.

With us the idea of a fall is more complex. To the general ideas of space and movement that it implies, we add that of attraction or direction towards a center, which gives us the higher idea of cause. But if physics has fully corrected our judgment in this respect, we still make use of the prejudice of St. Augustine. And when we say that a thing has *fallen,* we do not mean simply and in general that there has been an effect of gravitation, but specially and in particular that it is towards the earth, and *from above to below,* that this movement has taken place. Our mind is enlightened in vain. The imagination prevails and our language remains forever incorrigible. To "descend from heaven" is as incorrect an expression as to "mount to heaven." And yet this expression will live as long as men use language.

All these phrases—"from above to below"; "to descend from heaven"; "to fall from the clouds," etc.—are henceforth harmless, because we know how to rectify them in practice. But let us deign to consider for a moment how much they have retarded the progress of science. If, indeed, it be a matter of little importance to statistics, mechanics, hydrodynamics, and ballistics that the true cause of the fall of bodies should be known and that our ideas of general movements in space should be exact, it is quite otherwise when we undertake to explain the system of the universe, the cause of tides, the shape of the earth and its position in the heavens. To understand these things we must leave the circle of appearances. In all ages there have been ingenious mechanicians, excellent architects, skillful artillerymen. Any error, into which it was possible for them to fall in regard to the rotundity of the earth and gravitation, in no wise retarded the development of their art. The solidity of their buildings and accuracy of their aim was not affected by it. But sooner or later they were forced to grapple with phenomena, which the supposed parallelism of all perpendiculars erected from the earth's surface rendered inexplicable. Then also commenced a struggle between the prejudices that for centuries had sufficed in daily practice, and the unprecedented opinions that the testimony of the eyes seemed to contradict.

Thus, on the one hand, the falsest judgments, whether based on isolated facts or only on appearances, always embrace some truths whose sphere, whether large or small, affords room for a certain number of inferences, beyond which we fall into absurdity. The ideas of St. Augustine, for example, contained the following truths: that bodies fall towards the earth, that they fall in a straight line, that either the sun or the earth moves, that either the sky or the earth turns, etc. These general facts always have been true. Our science has added nothing to them. But, on the other hand, its being necessary to account for everything, we are obliged to seek for principles more and more comprehensive. That is why we have had to abandon successively, first the opinion that the world was flat, then the theory that regards it as the stationary center of the universe, etc.

If we pass now from physical nature to the moral world, we still find ourselves subject to the same deceptions of appearance, to the same influences of spontaneity and habit. But the distinguishing feature of this second division of our knowledge is, on the one hand, the good or the evil that we derive from our opinions; and, on the other, the obstinacy with which we defend the prejudice that is tormenting and killing us.

Whatever theory we embrace in regard to the shape of the earth and the cause of its weight, the physics of the globe does not suffer. And, as for us, our social economy can derive therefrom neither profit nor damage. But it is in us and through us that the laws of our moral nature work. Now these laws cannot be executed without our deliberate aid and, consequently, unless we know them. If, then, our science of moral laws is false, it is evident that, while desiring our own good, we are accomplishing our own evil. If it is only incomplete, it may suffice for a time for our social progress, but in the long run it will lead us into a wrong road and will finally precipitate us into an abyss of calamities.

Then it is that we need to exercise our highest judgments. And, be it said to our glory, they are never found wanting. But then also commences a furious struggle between old prejudices and new ideas. Days of conflagration and anguish! We are told of the time when, with the same beliefs, with the same institutions, all the world seemed happy. Why complain of these beliefs? Why banish these institutions? We are slow to admit that that happy age served the precise purpose of developing the principle of evil that lay dormant in society. We accuse men and gods, the powers of earth and the forces of Nature. Instead of seeking the cause of the evil in his mind and heart, man blames his masters, his rivals, his neighbors, and himself. Nations arm themselves and slay and exterminate each other until equilibrium is restored by the vast depopulation, and peace again rises from the ashes of the combatants. So loath is humanity to touch the customs of its ancestors and to change the laws framed by the founders of communities and confirmed by the faithful observance of the ages.

Nihil motum ex antiquo probabile est: Distrust all innovations, wrote Titus Livius. Undoubtedly it would be better were man not compelled to change, but what! Because he is born ignorant, because he exists only on condition of gradual self-instruction, must he abjure the light, abdicate his reason, and abandon himself to fortune? Perfect health is better than convalescence. Should the sick man, therefore, refuse to be cured? "Reform, reform!" cried, ages since, John the Baptist and Jesus Christ. "Reform, reform!" cried our father fifty years ago. And for a long time to come we shall shout, "Reform, reform!"

Seeing the misery of my age, I said to myself: Among the principles that support society, there is one that it does not understand, that its ignorance has vitiated and that causes all the evil that exists. This principle is the most ancient of all. For it is a principle of revolutions to tear down the most modern principles and to respect those of long standing. Now the evil by which we suffer is anterior to all revolutions. This principle, impaired by our ignorance, is honored and cherished. For if it were not cherished, it would harm nobody. It would be without influence.

But this principle, right in its purpose, but misunderstood: this principle, as old as humanity, what is it? Can it be religion?

All men believe in God; this dogma belongs at once to their conscience and their mind. To humanity God is a fact as primitive, an idea as inevitable, a principle as necessary as are the categorical ideas of cause, substance, time, and space to our understanding. God is proven to us by the conscience prior to any inference of the mind; just as the sun is proven to us by the testimony of the senses prior to all the arguments of physics. We discover phenomena and laws by observation and experience. Only this deeper sense reveals to us existence. Humanity believes that God is; but in believing in God, what does it believe? In a word what is God?

The nature of this notion of Divinity—this primitive, universal notion, born in the race—the human mind has not yet fathomed. At each step that we take in our investigation of Nature and of causes, the idea of God is extended and

exalted. The further science advances, the more God seems
to grow and broaden. Anthropomorphism and idolatry constituted of necessity the faith of the mind in its youth, the
theology of infancy and poesy. A harmless error, if they had
not endeavored to make it a rule of conduct, and if they had
been wise enough to respect the liberty of thought. But having made God in his own image, man wished to appropriate
Him still further. Not satisfied with disfiguring the Almighty,
he treated Him as his patrimony, his goods, his possessions.
God, pictured in monstrous forms, became throughout the
world the property of man and of the State. Such was the origin of the corruption of morals by religion and the source of
pious feuds and holy wars. Thank heaven, we have learned to
allow everyone his own beliefs. We seek for moral laws outside the pale of religion. Instead of legislating as to the nature
and attributes of God, the dogmas of theology, and the destiny of our souls, we wisely wait for science to tell us what to
reject and what to accept. God, soul, religion—eternal
objects of our unwearied thought and our most fatal aberrations, terrible problems whose solution, forever attempted,
forever remains unaccomplished—concerning all these questions we may still be mistaken, but at least our error is harmless. With liberty in religion, and the separation of the
spiritual from the temporal power, the influence of religious
ideas upon the progress of society is purely negative; no
law, no political or civil institution being founded on religion.
Neglect of duties imposed by religion may increase the
general corruption, but it is not the primary cause. It is
only an auxiliary or result. It is universally admitted, and
especially in the matter that now engages our attention, that
the cause of the inequality of conditions among men—of
pauperism, of universal misery, and of governmental em-
barrassments—can no longer be traced to religion. We must
go further back and dig still deeper.

But what is there in man older and deeper than the
religious sentiment? There is man himself; that is, volition
and conscience, free will and law, eternally antagonistic.
Man is at war with himself. Why?

"Man," say the theologians, "transgressed in the beginning;
our race is guilty of an ancient offense. For this transgression
humanity has fallen. Error and ignorance have become its
sustenance. Read history. You will find universal proof of

this necessity for evil in the permanent misery of nations. Man suffers and always will suffer. His disease is hereditary and constitutional. Use palliatives, employ emolients. There is no remedy."

Nor is this argument peculiar to the theologians. We find it expressed in equivalent language in the philosophical writings of the materialists, believers in infinite perfectibility. Destutt de Tracy teaches formally that poverty, crime, and war are the inevitable conditions of our social state; necessary evils, against which it would be folly to revolt. So, call it "necessity of evil" or "original depravity," it is at bottom the same philosophy.

"The first man transgressed." If the votaries of the Bible interpreted it faithfully, they would say: "man originally transgressed," that is, made a mistake. For "to transgress," "to fail," "to make a mistake" all mean the same thing.

"The consequences of Adam's transgression are inherited by the race; the first is ignorance." Truly, the race, like the individual, is born ignorant. But, in regard to a multitude of questions, even in the moral and political spheres, this ignorance of the race has been dispelled. Who says that it will not depart altogether? Mankind makes continual progress toward truth, and light ever triumphs over darkness. Our disease is not then absolutely incurable. And the theory of the theologians is worse than inadequate. It is ridiculous since it is reducible to this tautology: "Man errs because he errs." While the true statement is this: "Man errs because he learns." Now, if man arrives at a knowledge of all that he needs to know, it is reasonable to believe that, ceasing to err, he will cease to suffer.

But if we question the doctors as to this law, said to be engraved upon the heart of man, we shall immediately see that they dispute about a matter of which they know nothing; that, concerning the most important questions, there are almost as many opinions as authors; that we find no two agreeing as to the best form of government, the principle of authority, and the nature of right; that all sail haphazard upon a shoreless and bottomless sea, abandoned to the guidance of their private opinions, which they modestly take to be right reason. And, in view of this medley of contradictory opinions, we say: "The object of our investigations is the law, the determination of the social principle. Now the politicians, that is, the social scientists, do not understand each other. Then the error lies in themselves, and as every error has a reality for its object, we must look in their books to find the truth that they have unconsciously deposited there."

Now, of what do the lawyers and the publicists treat? Of "justice," "equity," "liberty," "natural law," "civil laws," etc. But what is justice? What is its principle, its character, its formula? To this question our doctors evidently have no reply. For otherwise their science, starting with a principle clear and well-defined, would quit the region of probabilities, and all disputes would end.

What is justice? The theologians answer: "All justice comes from God." That is true. But we know no more than before.

The philosophers ought to be better informed. They have argued so much about justice and injustice! Unhappily, an examination proves that their knowledge amounts to nothing, and that with them—as with the savages whose every prayer to the sun is simply "O! O!"—it is a cry of admiration, love, and enthusiasm. But who does not know that the sun attaches little meaning to the interjection "O!" That is exactly our position toward the philosophers in regard to justice. Justice, they say, is a "daughter of Heaven"; "a light that illumines every man who comes into the world"; "the most beautiful prerogative of our nature"; "that which distinguishes us from the beasts, and likens us to God"—and a thousand other similar things. What, I ask, does this pious litany amount to? To the prayer of the savages: "O!"

All the most reasonable teachings of human wisdom concerning justice are summed up in that famous adage: "Do unto others that which you would that others should do unto you; do not unto others that which you would not that others should do unto you." But this rule of moral practice is unscientific. What have I a right to wish that others should do or not do to me? It is of no use to tell me that my duty is equal to my right, unless I am told at the same time what my right is. Let us try to arrive at something more precise and positive.

Justice is the central star that governs societies, the pole around which the political world revolves, the principle and regulator of all transactions. Nothing takes place between men save in the name of *right*, nothing without the invocation of justice. Justice is not the work of the law. On the contrary, the law is only a declaration and application of *justice* in all circumstances where men are liable to come in contact. If, then, the idea that we form of justice and right were ill-defined, if it were imperfect or even false, it is clear that all our legislative applications would be wrong, our institutions vicious, our politics erroneous. Consequently there would be disorder and social chaos.

This hypothesis of the perversion of justice in our minds and, as a necessary result, in our acts, becomes a demonstrated fact when it is shown that the opinions of men have not borne a constant relation to the notion of justice and its applications; that at different periods they have undergone modifications. In a word, that there has been progress in ideas. Now, that is what history proves by the most overwhelming testimony.

Eighteen hundred years ago, the world, under the rule of the Caesars, exhausted itself in slavery, superstition, and voluptuousness. The people—intoxicated and, as it were, stupefied by their long-continued orgies—had lost the very notion of right and duty. War and dissipation by turns swept them away. Usury and the labor of machines (that is, of slaves), by depriving them of the means of subsistence, hindered them from continuing the species. Barbarism sprang up again, in a hideous form, from this mass of corruption, and spread like a devouring leprosy over the depopulated provinces. The wise foresaw the downfall of the empire, but could devise no remedy. What could they think indeed? To save this old society it would have been necessary to change the objects of public esteem and veneration, and to abolish the rights affirmed by a justice purely secular. They said: "Rome has conquered through her politics and her gods. Any change in theology and public opinion would be folly and sacrilege. Rome, merciful toward conquered nations, though binding them in chains, spared their lives. Slaves are the most fertile source of her wealth. Freedom of the nations would be the negation of her rights and the ruin of her finances. Rome, in fact, enveloped in the pleasures and gorged with the spoils of the universe, is kept alive by victory and government. Her luxuries and her pleasures are the price of her conquests. She can neither abdicate nor dispossess herself." Thus Rome had the facts and the law on her side. Her pretensions were justified by universal custom and the law of nations. Her institutions were based upon idolatry in religion, slavery in the State, and epicurism in private life. To touch those was to shake society to its foundations, and, to use our modern expression, to open the abyss of revolutions. So the idea occurred to no one; and yet humanity was dying in blood and luxury.

All at once a man appeared, calling himself "The Word of God." It is not known to this day who he was, whence he came, nor what suggested to him his ideas. He went about proclaiming everywhere that the end of the existing society was at hand, that the world was about to experience a new birth; that the priests are vipers, the lawyers ignoramuses, and the philosophers hypocrites and liars; that master and slave were equals, that usury and everything akin to it was robbery, that proprietors and idlers would one day burn, while the poor and pure in heart would find a haven of peace.

This man—"The Word of God"—was denounced and arrested as a public enemy by the priests and the lawyers, who well understood how to induce the people to demand his death. But this judicial murder, though it put the finishing stroke to their crimes, did not destroy the doctrinal seeds that "The Word of God" had sown. After his death, his original disciples traveled about in all directions, preaching what they called the "good news," creating in their turn millions of missionaries. And, when their task seemed to be accomplished, dying by the sword of Roman justice. This persistent agitation, the war of the executioners and martyrs, lasted nearly three centuries, ending in the conversion of the world. Idolatry was destroyed, slavery abolished, dissolution made room for a more austere morality, and the contempt for wealth was sometimes pushed almost to privation. Society was saved by the negation of its own principles, by a revolution in its religion, and by violation of its most sacred rights. In this revolution, the idea of justice spread to an extent that had not before been dreamed of, never to return to its original limits. Heretofore justice had existed only for the masters. It then commenced to exist for the slaves.

Nevertheless, the new religion at that time had borne by no means all its fruits. There was a perceptible improvement of the public morals, and a partial release from oppression.

But, other than that, the *seeds sown by the Son of Man*, having fallen into idolatrous hearts, had produced nothing save innumerable discords and a quasi-poetical mythology. Instead of developing into their practical consequences the principles of morality and government taught by "The Word of God," his followers busied themselves in speculations as to his birth, his origin, his person, and his actions. They discussed his parables, and from the conflict of the most extravagant opinions upon unanswerable questions and texts that no one understood, was born "theology"—which may be defined as the "science of the infinitely absurd.

The truth of Christianity did not survive the age of the apostles. The Gospel, commented upon and symbolized by the Greeks and Latins, loaded with pagan fables, became literally a mass of contradictions. And to this day the reign of the "infallible Church" has been a long era of darkness. It is said that the gates of hell will not always prevail, that "The Word of God" will return, and that one day men will know truth and justice. But that will be the death of Greek and Roman Catholicism, just as in the light of science disappeared the caprices of opinion.

The monsters that the successors of the apostles were bent on destroying, frightened for a moment, reappeared gradually, thanks to the crazy fanaticism, and sometimes the deliberate connivance, of priests and theologians. The history of the enfranchisement of the French communes offers constantly the spectacle of the ideas of justice and liberty spreading among the people, in spite of the combined efforts of kings, nobles, and clergy. In the year 1789 of the Christian era, the French nation, divided by caste, poor and oppressed, struggled in the triple net of royal absolutism, the tyranny of nobles and parliaments, and priestly intolerance. There was the right of the king and the right of the priest, the right of the patrician and the right of the plebeian; there were the privileges of birth, province, communes, corporations, and trades. And, at the bottom of all, violence, immorality, and misery. For some time they talked of reformation. Those who apparently desired it most favoring it only for their own profit, and the people were to be the gainers, expecting little and saying nothing. For a long time these poor people, either from distrust, incredulity, or despair, hesitated to ask for their

rights. It is said that the habit of serving had taken the
courage away from those old communes, which in the
Middle Ages were so bold.

Finally a book appeared, summing up the whole matter
in these two propositions: "What is the third estate?—Nothing. What ought it to be?—Everything." Someone added by
way of comment: "What is the king?—The servant of the
people."

This was a sudden revelation. The veil was torn aside, a
thick bandage fell from all eyes. The people commenced to
reason thus:

If the king is our servant, he ought to report to us.

If he ought to report to us, he is subject to control.

If he can be controlled, he is responsible.

If he is responsible, he is punishable.

If he is punishable, he ought to be punished according to
his merits.

If he can be punished according to his merits, he can be
punished with death.

Five years after the publication of the brochure of Sieyès,
the third estate was everything. The king, the nobility, the
clergy, were no more. In 1793, the nation, without stopping
at the constitutional fiction of the inviolability of the sovereign, conducted Louis XVI to the scaffold. In 1830, it accompanied Charles X to Cherbourg. In each case, it may have
erred, in fact, in its judgment of the offense. But, in right, the
logic that led to its action was irreproachable. The people,
in punishing their sovereign, did precisely that which the
government of July was so severely censured for failing to
do when it refused to execute Louis Bonaparte after the affair of Strassburg. They struck the true culprit. It was an
application of the common law, a solemn decree of justice
enforcing the penal laws.

The spirit that gave rise to the movement of '89 was a spirit
of negation; that, of itself, proves that the order of things
that was substituted for the old system was not methodical or
well considered; that, born of anger and hatred, it could not
have the effect of a science based on observation and study;
that its foundations, in a word, were not derived from a profound knowledge of the laws of Nature and society. Thus the
people found that the republic, among the so-called new
institutions, was acting on the very principles that they had

intended to destroy. We congratulate ourselves, with inconsiderate enthusiasm, on the glorious French Revolution, the regeneration of 1789, the great changes that have been effected, and the revision of institutions: a delusion, a delusion!

When our ideas on any subject, material, intellectual, or social, undergo a thorough change in consequence of new observations, I call that movement of the mind "revolution." If the ideas are simply extended or modified, there is only "progress." Thus the system of Ptolemy was a step in astronomical progress, that of Copernicus was a revolution. So, in 1789, there was struggle and progress; revolution there was none. An examination of the reforms that were attempted proves this.

The nation, so long a victim of monarchical selfishness, thought to deliver itself forever by declaring that it alone was sovereign. But what was monarchy? The sovereignty of one man. What is democracy? The sovereignty of the nation, or, rather, of the national majority. But it is, in both cases, the sovereignty of man instead of the sovereignty of the law, the sovereignty of the will instead of the sovereignty of reason; in one word, the passions instead of justice. Undoubtedly, when a nation passes from the monarchical to the democratic state, there is progress, because in multiplying the sovereigns we increase the opportunities of reason to substitute itself for the will. But in reality there is no revolution in the government, since the principle remains the same. Now we have the proof today that, with the most perfect democracy, we cannot be free.

Nor is that all. The nation-king cannot exercise its sovereignty itself. It is obliged to delegate it to agents. This is constantly reiterated by those who seek to win its favor. Be these agents five, ten, one hundred, or a thousand, of what consequence is the number and what matters the name? It is always the government of man, the rule of will and caprice. I ask what this pretended revolution has revolutionized?

We know, too, how this sovereignty was exercised; first by the Convention, then by the Directory, afterwards confiscated by the Consul. As for the Emperor, the strong man so much adored and mourned by the nation, he never wanted to be dependent on it. But, as if intending to set its sovereignty at defiance, he dared to demand its suffrage: that is, its abdication, the abdication of this inalienable sovereignty, and he obtained it.

But what is sovereignty? It is, they say, the "power to make laws." Another absurdity, a relic of despotism. The nation had long seen kings issuing their commands in this form: "for such is our pleasure." It wished to taste in its turn the pleasure of making laws. For fifty years it has brought them forth by myriads; always, be it understood, through the agency of representatives. The play is far from ended.

The definition of sovereignty was derived from the definition of the law. The law, they said, is "the expression of the will of the sovereign": then, under a monarchy, the law is the expression of the will of the king. In a republic, the law is the expression of the will of the people. Aside from the difference in the number of wills, the two systems are exactly identical. Both share the same error, namely, that the law is the expression of a will. It ought to be the expression of a fact. Moreover, they followed good leaders. They took the citizen of Geneva for their prophet, and the *contrat social* for their Koran.

Bias and prejudice are apparent in all the phrases of the new legislators. The nation had suffered from a multitude of exclusions and privileges. Its representatives issued the following declaration: "All men are equal by nature and before the law"; an ambiguous and redundant declaration. "Men are equal by nature": Does that mean that they are equal in size, beauty, talents, and virtue? No; they meant, then, political and civil equality. Then it would have been sufficient to have said: "All men are equal before the law."

But what is equality before the law? Neither the constitution of 1790, nor that of '93, nor the granted charter, nor the accepted charter, have defined it accurately. All imply an inequality in fortune and station incompatible with even a shadow of equality in rights. In this respect it may be said that all our constitutions have been faithful expressions of the popular will. I am going to prove it.

Formerly the people were excluded from civil and military offices. It was considered a wonder when the following high-sounding article was inserted in the Declaration of Rights: "All citizens are equally eligible to office; free nations know no qualifications in their choice of officers save virtues and talents."

They certainly ought to have admired so beautiful an idea.
They admired a piece of nonsense. Why, the sovereign people, legislators, and reformers see in public offices, to speak
plainly, only opportunities for pecuniary advancement. And,
because it regards them as a source of profit, it decrees the
eligibility of citizens. For of what use would this precaution
be, if there were nothing to gain by it? No one would think
of ordaining that none but astronomers and geographers
should be pilots, nor of prohibiting stutterers from acting at
the theater and the opera. The nation was still aping the kings.
Like them it wished to award the lucrative positions to its
friends and flatterers. Unfortunately, and this last feature
completes the resemblance, the nation did not control the
list of livings. That was in the hands of its agents and representatives. They, on the other hand, took care not to thwart
the will of their gracious sovereign.

This edifying article of the Declaration of Rights, retained
in the charters of 1814 and 1830, implies several kinds of
civil inequality; that is, of inequality before the law: inequality of station, since the public functions are sought only for
the consideration and emoluments that they bring; inequality
of wealth, since, if it had been desired to equalize fortunes,
public service would have been regarded as a duty, not as a
reward; inequality of privilege, the law not stating what it
means by "talents" and "virtues." Under the empire, virtue
and talent consisted simply in military bravery and devotion
to the emperor. That was shown when Napoleon created his
nobility and attempted to connect it with the ancients. Today, the man who pays taxes to the amount of two hundred
francs is virtuous. The talented man is the honest pickpocket.
Such truths as these are accounted trivial.

The people finally legalized property. God forgive them,
for they know not what they did! For fifty years they have
suffered for their miserable folly. But how came the people,
whose voice, they tell us, is the voice of God and whose conscience is infallible—how came the people to err? How happens it that, when seeking liberty and equality, they fell back
into privilege and slavery? Always through copying the ancient regime.

Formerly, the nobility and the clergy contributed towards
the expenses of the State only by voluntary aid and gratuitous gift. Their property could not be seized even for debt—

while the plebeian, overwhelmed by taxes and statute labor, was continually tormented, now by the king's tax gatherers, now by those of the nobles and clergy. He whose possessions were subject to *mortmain* could neither bequeath nor inherit property. He was treated like the animals, whose services and offspring belong to their master by right of accession. The people wanted the conditions of *ownership* to be alike for all. They thought that everyone should *enjoy and freely dispose of his possessions, his income, and the fruit of his labor and industry.* The people did not invent property. But as they had not the same privileges in regard to it that the nobles and clergy possessed, they decreed that the right should be exercised by all under the same conditions. The more obnoxious forms of property—statute labor, mortmain, *maîtrise,* and exclusion from public office—have disappeared. The conditions of its enjoyment have been modified. The principle still remains the same. There has been progress in the regulation of the right. There has been no revolution.

These, then, are the three fundamental principles of modern society, established one after another by the movements of 1789 and 1830: 1) *Sovereignty of the human will;* in short, *despotism.* 2) *Inequality of wealth and rank.* 3) *Property*—above JUSTICE, always invoked as the guardian angel of sovereigns, nobles, and proprietors; JUSTICE, the general, primitive, categorical law of all society.

William Godwin

The Rights of Man and the Principles of Society [1]

William Godwin (1756–1836) William Godwin was a political philosopher who, while in the ministry for which he was trained, had cast off his Toryism and Calvinism and achieved a place of first importance as the interpreter to England of the French Encyclopedists. His ideal society is intensely equalitarian and a complete anarchy, although he tolerated the idea of a loosely knit democratic transition that would witness the withering of the State. Strongly antiviolence and completely

[1] From *An Enquiry Concerning Political Justice and Its Influence on General Virtue and Happiness,* by William Godwin. London: 1793.

rationalistic he carried his doctrine to the point of total alteration in human relations. Ignoring economics and starting from
a highly individualistic psychology, he argued for education and
social conditioning as the chief factors in character formation.
His chief work, *Enquiry Concerning Political Justice,* develops
the thought of the prerevolutionary school, is strongly influenced by Helvetius, and is an argument for the perfectibility of
the human species by way of a refutation of contradictory
theories and examination of such conditions as will perfect the
human community. In the philosophical debate over whether
man is governed by self-love, Godwin argued that man is capable of a genuinely disinterested benevolence. The turning point
in his career was the French Revolution, which spurred him to
write his major work, *Political Justice,* completed in 1793.
Though many were disillusioned after the early years of the
Revolution, Godwin's liberalism remained intact. The publication of this work gained him a far-reaching contemporary fame.

It was in 1796 that he renewed an acquaintance with Mary
Wollstonecraft. They took up residence together and, with the
approaching birth of their child and despite his attacks upon
the institution of marriage, were married in 1797. Their brief
marriage, ended by the death of his wife, was described as his
happiest period. Although Godwin wrote indefatigably, only
Political Justice is still a work of enduring fame. His *Caleb
Williams,* a novel with a social purpose, is another of his
works retaining some contemporary interest.

OF JUSTICE

From what has been said it ap-
pears that the subject of the present enquiry is strictly speaking a department of the science of morals. Morality is the
source from which its fundamental axioms must be drawn,
and they will be made somewhat clearer in the present instance if we assume the term "justice" as a general appellation for all moral duty.

That this appellation is sufficiently expressive of the subject
will appear if we consider for a moment mercy, gratitude,
temperance, or any of those duties which in looser speaking
are contradistinguished from justice. Why should I pardon
this criminal, remunerate this favor, abstain from this indulgence? If it partake of the nature of morality, it must
be either right or wrong, just or unjust. It must tend to the
benefit of the individual either without intrenching upon or

with actual advantage to the mass of individuals. Either way
it benefits the whole, because individuals are parts of the
whole. Therefore to do it is just, and to forbear it is unjust.
If justice have any meaning, it is just that I should contribute
everything in my power to the benefit of the whole.

Considerable light will probably be thrown upon our investigation if, quitting for the present the political view, we
examine justice merely as it exists among individuals. Justice
is a rule of conduct originating in the connection of one percipient being with another. A comprehensive maxim which
has been laid down upon the subject is "that we should love
our neighbor as ourselves." But this maxim, though possessing considerable merit as a popular principle, is not modeled
with the strictness of philosophical accuracy.

In a loose and general view I and my neighbor are both of
us men, and of consequence entitled to equal attention. But
in reality it is probable that one of us is a being of more worth
and importance than the other. A man is of more worth than
a beast, because, being possessed of higher faculties, he is
capable of a more refined and genuine happiness. In the same
manner the illustrious archbishop of Cambrai was of more
worth than his chambermaid, and there are few of us that
would hesitate to pronounce, if his palace were in flames and
the life of only one of them could be preserved, which of the
two ought to be preferred.

But there is another ground of preference beside the private consideration of one of them being farther removed
from the state of a mere animal. We are not connected with
one or two percipient beings, but with a society, a nation, and
in some sense with the whole family of mankind. Of consequence that life ought to be preferred which will be most conducive to the general good. In saving the life of Fénelon, suppose at the moment when he was conceiving the project of
his immortal *Telemachus,* I should be promoting the benefit
of thousands who have been cured by the perusal of it of
some error, vice and consequent unhappiness. Nay, my benefit would extend farther than this, for every individual thus
cured has become a better member of society and has contributed in his turn to the happiness, the information and improvement of others.

Supposing I had been myself the chambermaid, I ought to
have chosen to die rather than that Fénelon should have died.

The life of Fénelon was really preferable to that of the chambermaid. But understanding is the faculty that perceives the truth of this and similar propositions; and justice is the principle that regulates my conduct accordingly. It would have been just in the chambermaid to have preferred the archbishop to herself. To have done otherwise would have been a breach of justice.

Supposing the chambermaid had been my wife, my mother or my benefactor. This would not alter the truth of the proposition. The life of Fénelon would still be more valuable than that of the chambermaid; and justice—pure, unadulterated justice—would still have preferred that which was most valuable. Justice would have taught me to save the life of Fénelon at the expense of the other. What magic is there in the pronoun "my" to overturn the decisions of everlasting truth? My wife or my mother may be a fool or a prostitute, malicious, lying or dishonest. If they be, of what consequence is it that they are mine?

"But my mother endured for me the pains of child bearing, and nourished me in the helplessness of infancy." When she first subjected herself to the necessity of these cares, she was probably influenced by no particular motives of benevolence to her future offspring. Every voluntary benefit, however, entitles the bestower to some kindness and retribution. But why so? Because a voluntary benefit is an evidence of benevolent intention; that is, of virtue. It is the disposition of the mind, not the external action, that entitles to respect. But the merit of this disposition is equal whether the benefit was conferred upon me or upon another. I and another man cannot both be right in preferring our own individual benefactor, for no man can be at the same time both better and worse than his neighbor. My benefactor ought to be esteemed, not because he bestowed a benefit upon me, but because he bestowed it upon a human being. His dessert will be in exact proportion to the degree in which that human being was worthy of the distinction conferred. Thus every view of the subject brings us back to the consideration of my neighbor's moral worth and his importance to the general weal as the only standard to determine the treatment to which he is entitled. Gratitude therefore, a principle which has so often been the theme of the moralist and the poet, is no part either of justice or virtue. By gratitude I understand a sentiment which would lead me to prefer one man to another from some other consideration than that of his superior usefulness or worth; that is, which would make something true to me (for example this preferableness) which cannot be true to another man and is not true in itself.[2]

It may be objected "that my relation, my companion, or my benefactor will of course in many instances obtain an uncommon portion of my regard: for, not being universally capable of discriminating the comparative worth of different men, I shall inevitably judge most favorably of him of whose virtues I have received the most unquestionable proofs; and thus shall be compelled to prefer the man of moral worth whom I know, to another who may possess, unknown to me, an essential superiority."

This compulsion however is founded only in the present imperfection of human nature. It may serve as an apology for my error, but can never turn error into truth. It will always remain contrary to the strict and inflexible decisions of justice. The difficulty of conceiving this is owing merely to our confounding the disposition from which an action is chosen with the action itself. The disposition that would prefer virtue to vice and a greater degree of virtue to a less is undoubtedly a subject of approbation; the erroneous exercise of this disposition by which a wrong object is selected, if unavoidable, is to be deplored, but can by no coloring and under no denomination be converted into right.[3]

It may in the second place be objected "that a mutual commerce of benefits tends to increase the mass of benevolent action, and that to increase the mass of benevolent action is to contribute to the general good." Indeed! Is the general good promoted by falsehood, by treating a man of one degree of worth as if he had ten times that worth? Or as if he were in any degree different from what he really is? Would not the most beneficial consequences result from a different plan; from my constantly and carefully enquiring into the desserts of all those with whom I am connected, and from their being sure, after a certain allowance for the fallibility of human judgment, of being treated by me exactly as they deserved?

[2] This argument respecting gratitude is stated with great clearness in an Essay on the Nature of True Virtue, by the Rev. Jonathan Edwards. [Godwin's note, as are all notes in this extract unless otherwise indicated.]
[3] See this subject more copiously treated in the following chapter.

Who can tell what would be the effects of such a plan of conduct universally adopted?

There seems to be more truth in the argument, derived chiefly from the unequal distribution of property, in favor of my providing in ordinary cases for my wife and children, my brothers and relations before I provide for strangers. As long as providing for individuals belongs to individuals, it seems as if there must be a certain distribution of the class needing superintendence and supply among the class affording it, that each man may have his claim and resource. But this argument, if admitted at all, is to be admitted with great caution. It belongs only to ordinary cases; and cases of a higher order or a more urgent necessity will perpetually occur, in competition with which these will be altogether impotent. We must be severely scrupulous in measuring out the quantity of supply, and with respect to money in particular, must remember how little is yet understood of the true mode of employing it for the public benefit.

Having considered the persons with whom justice is conversant, let us next enquire into the degree in which we are obliged to consult the good of others. And here I say that it is just that I should do all the good in my power. Does any person in distress apply to me for relief? It is my duty to grant it and I commit a breach of duty in refusing. If this principle be not of universal application, it is because in conferring a benefit upon an individual I may in some instances inflict an injury of superior magnitude upon myself or society. Now the same justice that binds me to any individual of my fellowmen binds me to the whole. If, while I confer a benefit upon one man, it appear, in striking an equitable balance, that I am injuring the whole, my action ceases to be right and becomes absolutely wrong. But how much am I bound to do for the general weal; that is, for the benefit of the individuals of whom the whole is composed? Everything in my power. What, to the neglect of the means of my own existence? No; for I am myself a part of the whole. Besides, it will rarely happen but that the project of doing for others everything in my power will demand for its execution the preservation of my own existence; or in other words, it will rarely happen but that I can do more good in twenty years than in one. If the extraordinary case should occur in which I can promote the general good by my death more than by my life, justice requires that I should be content to die. In all other cases it is just that I should be careful to maintain my body and my mind in the utmost vigor and in the best condition for service.

I will suppose for example that it is right for one man to possess a greater portion of property than another, either as the fruit of his industry or the inheritance of his ancestors. Justice obliges him to regard this property as a trust and calls upon him maturely to consider in what manner it may best be employed for the increase of liberty, knowledge and virtue. He has no right to dispose of a shilling of it at the will of his caprice. So far from being entitled to well-earned applause for having employed some scanty pittance in the service of philanthropy, he is in the eye of justice a delinquent if he withhold any portion from that service. Nothing can be more incontrovertible. Could that portion have been better or more worthily employed? That it could is implied in the very terms of the proposition. Then it was just it should have been so employed.—In the same manner as my property I hold my person as a trust in behalf of mankind. I am bound to employ my talents, my understanding, my strength and my time for the production of the greatest quantity of general good. Such are the declarations of justice, so great is the extent of my duty.

But justice is reciprocal. If it be just that I should confer a benefit, it is just that another man should receive it, and if I withhold from him that to which he is entitled, he may justly complain. My neighbor is in want of ten pounds that I can spare. There is no law of political institution that has been made to reach this case and to transfer this property from me to him. But in the eye of simple justice, unless it can be shown that the money can be more beneficently employed, his claim is as complete as if he had my bond in his possession or had supplied me with goods to the amount.[4]

To this it has sometimes been answered that there is more than one person that stands in need of the money I have to spare, and of consequence I must be at liberty to bestow it as I please. I answer, if only one person offer himself to my knowledge or search, to me there is but one. Those others that I cannot find belong to other rich men to assist (rich

[4] A spirited outline of these principles is sketched in Swift's Sermon on Mutual Subjection.

men, I say, for every man is rich who has more money than his just occasions demand) and not to me. If more than one person offer, I am obliged to balance their fitness and conduct myself accordingly. It is scarcely possible to happen that two men shall be of exactly equal fitness or that I shall be equally certain of the fitness of the one as of the other.

It is therefore impossible for me to confer upon any man a favor, I can only do him a right. Whatever deviates from the law of justice, even I will suppose in the too-much done in favor of some individual or some part of the general whole, is so much subtracted from the general stock—is so much of absolute injustice.

The inference most clearly afforded by the preceding reasonings is the competence of justice as a principle of deduction in all cases of moral enquiry. The reasonings themselves are rather of the nature of illustration and example, and any error that may be imputed to them in particulars will not invalidate the general conclusion, the propriety of applying moral justice as a criterion in the investigation of political truth.

Society is nothing more than an aggregation of individuals. Its claims and its duties must be the aggregate of their claims and duties, the one no more precarious and arbitrary than the other. What has the society a right to require from me? The question is already answered: Everything that it is my duty to do. Anything more? Certainly not. Can they change eternal truth or subvert the nature of men and their actions? Can they make it my duty to commit intemperance, to maltreat or assassinate my neighbor?—Again. What is it that the society is bound to do for its members? Everything that can contribute to their welfare. But the nature of their welfare is defined by the nature of mind. That will most contribute to it which enlarges the understanding, supplies incitements to virtue, fills us with a generous consciousness of our independence, and carefully removes whatever can impede our exertions.

Should it be affirmed that it is not in the power of any political system to secure to us these advantages, the conclusion I am drawing will still be incontrovertible. It is bound to contribute everything it is able to these purposes, and no man was ever yet found hardy enough to affirm that it could do nothing. Suppose its influence in the utmost degree limited, there must be one method approaching nearer than any other to the desired object, and that method ought to be universally adopted. There is one thing that political institutions can assuredly do; they can avoid positively counteracting the true interests of their subjects. But all capricious rules and arbitrary distinctions do positively counteract them. There is scarcely any modification of society but has in it some degree of moral tendency. So far as it produces neither mischief nor benefit, it is good for nothing. So far as it tends to the improvement of the community, it ought to be universally adopted.

OF DUTY

There is a difficulty of considerable magnitude as to the subject of the preceding chapter, founded upon the difference which may exist between abstract justice and my apprehensions of justice. When I do an act wrong in itself, but which as to all the materials of judging extant to my understanding appears to be right, is my conduct virtuous or vicious?

Certain moralists have introduced a distinction upon this head between absolute and practical virtue. "There is one species of virtue," they say, "which rises out of the nature of things and is immutable, and another which rises out of the views extant to my understanding. Thus, for example, suppose I ought to worship Jesus Christ; but having been bred in the religion of Mahomet, I ought to adhere to that religion as long as its evidences shall appear to me conclusive. I am impaneled upon a jury to try a man arraigned for murder, and who is really innocent. Abstractly considered, I ought to acquit him. But I am unacquainted with his innocence, and evidence is adduced such as to form the strongest presumption of his guilt. Demonstration in such cases is not to be attained; I am obliged in every concern of human life to act upon presumption; I ought therefore to convict him."

It may be doubted however whether any good purpose is likely to be answered by employing the terms of abstract science in this versatile and uncertain manner. Morality is, if anything can be, fixed and immutable; and there must surely be some strange deception that should induce us to give to an action eternally and unchangeably wrong the epithets of rectitude, duty and virtue.

Nor have these moralists been thoroughly aware to what extent this admission would carry them. The human mind is incredibly subtle in inventing an apology for that to which its inclination leads. Nothing is so rare as pure and unmingled hypocrisy. There is no action of our lives which we were not ready at the time of adopting it to justify, unless so far as we were prevented by mere indolence and unconcern. There is scarcely any justification which we endeavor to pass upon others which we do not with tolerable success pass upon ourselves. The distinction therefore which is here set up would go near to prove that every action of every human being is entitled to the appellation of virtuous.

There is perhaps no man that cannot recollect the time when he secretly called in question the arbitrary division of property established in human society and felt inclined to appropriate to his use anything the possession of which appeared to him desirable. It is probably in some such way that men are usually influenced in the perpetration of robbery. They persuade themselves of the comparative inutility of the property to its present possessor and the inestimable advantage that would attend it in their hands. They believe that the transfer ought to be made. It is of no consequence that they are not consistent in these views, that the impressions of education speedily recur to their minds, and that in a season of adversity they readily confess the wickedness of their proceeding. It is not less true that they did what at the moment they thought to be right.

But there is another consideration that seems still more decisive of the subject before us. The worst actions, the most contrary to abstract justice and utility, have frequently been done from the most conscientious motives. Clement, Ravaillac, Damiens, and Gerard had their minds deeply penetrated with anxiety for the eternal welfare of mankind. For these objects they sacrificed their ease, and cheerfully exposed themselves to tortures and death. It was benevolence probably that contributed to light the fires of Smithfield and point the daggers of Saint Bartholomew. The inventors of the Gunpowder Treason were in general men remarkable for the sanctity of their lives and the severity of their manners. It is probable, indeed, that some ambitious views and some sentiments of hatred and abhorrence mixed with the benevolence and integrity of these persons. It is probable that no wrong action was ever committed from views entirely pure. But the deception they put upon themselves might nevertheless be complete. At all events their opinions upon the subject could not alter the real nature of the action.

The true solution of the question lies in observing that the disposition with which an action is adopted is one thing, and the action itself another. A right action may be done from a wrong disposition; in that case we approve the action but condemn the actor. A wrong action may be done from a right disposition; in that case we condemn the action but approve the actor. If the disposition by which a man is governed has a systematical tendency to the benefit of his species, he cannot fail to obtain our esteem, however mistaken he may be in his conduct.

But what shall we say to the duty of a man under these circumstances? Calvin, we will suppose, was clearly and conscientiously persuaded that he ought to burn Servetus. Ought he to have burned him or not? If he burned him, he did an action detestable in its own nature; if he refrained, he acted in opposition to the best judgment of his own understanding as to a point of moral obligation. It is absurd, however, to say that it was in any sense his duty to burn him. The most that can be admitted is that his disposition was virtuous, and that in the circumstances in which he was placed an action greatly to be deplored flowed from that disposition by invincible necessity.

Shall we say, then, that it was the duty of Calvin, who did not understand the principles of toleration, to act upon a truth of which he was ignorant? Suppose that a person is to be tried at York next week for murder and that my evidence would acquit him. Shall we say that it was my duty to go to York, though I knew nothing of the matter? Upon the same principles we might affirm that it is my duty to go from London to York in half an hour, as the trial will come on within that time, the impossibility not being more real in one case than in the other. Upon the same principles we might affirm that it is my duty to be impeccable, omniscient, and almighty.

Duty is a term the use of which seems to be to describe the mode in which any being may best be employed for the general good. It is limited in its extent by the extent of the capacity of that being. Now capacity varies in its idea in proportion as we vary the view of the subject to which it belongs. What

I am capable of if you consider me merely as a man is one thing; what I am capable of as a man of a deformed figure, of weak understanding, of superstitious prejudices, or as the case may happen is another. So much cannot be expected of me under these disadvantages as if they were absent. But if this be the true definition of duty, it is absurd to suppose in any case that an action injurious to the general welfare can be classed in the rank of duties.

To apply these observations to the cases that have been stated. Ignorance, so far as it goes, completely annihilates capacity. As I was uninformed of the trial at York, I could not be influenced by any consideration respecting it. But it is absurd to say that it was my duty to neglect a motive with which I was unacquainted. If you allege that Calvin was ignorant of the principles of toleration and had no proper opportunity to learn them, it follows that in burning Servetus he did not violate his duty, but it does not follow that it was his duty to burn him. Upon the supposition here stated duty is silent. Calvin was unacquainted with the principles of justice, and therefore could not practice them. The duty of no man can exceed his capacity; but then neither can in any case an act of injustice be of the nature of duty.

There are certain inferences that flow from this view of the subject which it may be proper to mention. Nothing is more common than for individuals and societies of men to allege that they have acted to the best of their judgment, that they have done their duty, and therefore that their conduct, even should it prove to be mistaken, is nevertheless virtuous. This appears to be an error. An action, though done with the best intention in the world, may have nothing in it of the nature of virtue. In reality the most essential part of virtue consists in the incessantly seeking to inform ourselves more accurately upon the subject of utility and right. Whoever is greatly misinformed respecting them is indebted for his error to a defect in his philanthropy and zeal.

Secondly, since absolute virtue may be out of the power of a human being, it becomes us in the meantime to lay the greatest stress upon a virtuous disposition, which is not attended with the same ambiguity. A virtuous disposition is of the utmost consequence, since it will in the majority of instances be productive of virtuous actions; since it tends, in exact proportion to the quantity of virtue, to increase our

discernment and improve our understanding; and since, if
it were universally propagated, it would immediately lead to
the great end of virtuous actions, the purest and most exquisite happiness of intelligent beings. But a virtuous disposition is principally generated by the uncontrolled exercise
of private judgment and the rigid conformity of every man to
the dictates of his conscience.

OF THE EQUALITY OF MANKIND

The equality of mankind is either physical or moral. Their
physical equality may be considered either as it relates to
the strength of the body or the faculties of the mind.

This part of the subject has been exposed to cavil and
objection. It has been said "that the reverse of this equality
is the result of our experience. Among the individuals of our
species we actually find that there are not two alike. One man
is strong and another weak. One man is wise and another
foolish. All that exists in the world of the inequality of conditions is to be traced to this as their source. The strong man
possesses power to subdue, and the weak stands in need of an
ally to protect. The consequence is inevitable: The equality
of conditions is a chimerical assumption, neither possible to
be reduced into practice nor desirable if it could be so
reduced."

Upon this statement two observations are to be made.
First, this inequality was in its origin infinitely less than it is
at present. In the uncultivated state of man diseases, effemi-
nacy and luxury were little known, and of consequence the
strength of every one much more nearly approached to the
strength of his neighbor. In the uncultivated state of man
the understandings of all were limited, their wants, their
ideas and their views nearly upon a level. It was to be expected that in their first departure from this state great
irregularities would introduce themselves, and it is the object
of subsequent wisdom and improvement to mitigate these
irregularities.

Secondly, notwithstanding the encroachments that have
been made upon the equality of mankind, a great and substantial equality remains. There is no such disparity among
the human race as to enable one man to hold several other
men in subjection, except so far as they are willing to be

subject. All government is founded in opinion. Men at present live under any particular form because they conceive it their interest to do so. One part indeed of a community or empire may be held in subjection by force; but this cannot be the personal force of their despot; it must be the force of another part of the community, who are of the opinion that it is their interest to support his authority. Destroy this opinion, and the fabric which is built upon it falls to the ground. It follows therefore that all men are essentially independent.— So much for the physical equality.

The moral equality is still less open to reasonable exception. By moral equality I understand the propriety of applying one unalterable rule of justice to every case that may arise. This cannot be questioned but upon arguments that would subvert the very nature of virtue. "Equality," it has been affirmed, "will always be an unintelligible fiction so long as the capacities of men shall be unequal and their pretended claims have neither guarantee nor sanction by which they can be enforced."[5] But surely justice is sufficiently intelligible in its own nature, abstracted from the consideration whether it be or be not reduced into practice. Justice has relation to beings endowed with perception and capable of pleasure and pain. Now it immediately results from the nature of such beings, independently of any arbitrary constitution, that pleasure is agreeable and pain odious, pleasure to be desired and pain to be obviated. It is therefore just and reasonable that such beings should contribute, so far as it lies in their power, to the pleasure and benefit of each other. Among pleasures some are more exquisite, more unalloyed and less precarious than others. It is just that these should be preferred.

From these simple principles we may deduce the moral equality of mankind. We are partakers of a common nature, and the same causes that contribute to the benefit of one contribute to the benefit of another. Our senses and faculties are of the same denomination. Our pleasures and pains will therefore be the same. We are all of us endowed with reason, able to compare, to judge and to infer. The improvement, therefore, which is to be desired for the one is to be desired for the other. We shall be provident for ourselves and useful to each other in proportion as we rise above the atmosphere

[5] Raynal, *Révolution d'Amérique*, p. 34.

of prejudice. The same independence, the same freedom from any such restraint as should prevent us from giving the reins to our own understanding or from uttering upon all occasions whatever we think to be true will conduce to the improvement of all. There are certain opportunities and a certain situation most advantageous to every human being, and it is just that these should be communicated to all, as nearly at least as the general economy will permit.

There is indeed one species of moral inequality parallel to the physical inequality that has been already described. The treatment to which men are entitled is to be measured by their merits and their virtues. That country would not be the seat of wisdom and reason where the benefactor of his species was considered in the same point of view as their enemy. But in reality this distinction, so far from being adverse to equality in any tenable sense, is friendly to it and is accordingly known by the appellation of "equity," a term derived from the same origin. Though in some sense an exception, it tends to the same purpose to which the principle itself is indebted for its value. It is calculated to infuse into every bosom an emulation of excellence. The thing really to be desired is the removing as much as possible arbitrary distinctions and leaving to talents and virtue the field of exertion unimpaired. We should endeavor to afford to all the same opportunities and the same encouragement, and to render justice the common interest and choice.

Michael Bakunin
Social and Economic Bases of Anarchism[1]

Michael Alexandrovitch Bakunin (1814–1876) The eldest son of an aristocratic family, he spent his youth on the family estate, which educated him to peasant ways through his association

[1] From "Science and the Urgent Revolutionary Task" (pamphlet in Russian; Geneva, Switzerland· Kolokol, 1870); and "The Program of the Alliance of International Revolution" (written in French and published in *Anarchichesky Vestnik,* a Russian publication in Berlin, volume V–VI [Nov., 1923], vol VII [May, 1924]) Reprinted with permission of the publisher from *The Political Philosophy of Bakunin· Scientific Anarchism.* Compiled and edited by G. P. Maximoff. Glencoe (Ill.): The Free Press, Copyright © 1953.

with the serfs. He renounced a military career to pursue philosophic studies at the Universities of Moscow and Berlin. In
1843, in Switzerland, he befriended Weitling, whose imprisonment attracted the attention of the Russian authorities, and he
was summoned to return. He refused and made his way to Paris
where he learned greatly from Marx and Proudhon, although a
dislike of Marx prevented any closeness between them. In
1849, in Dresden, he was arrested and returned to Russia as a
fugitive, where he spent eight years in solitary confinement.
After four more years in Siberia and a marriage to a young
woman strangely distant from his political concerns, he made
his way to London where he worked for a time with Herzen.
Making his way to Italy, Bakunin organized in 1864 a secret
international brotherhood known later as the "International
Alliance of Social Democracy." In 1868 he joined the First
International, where his doctrines were strongly opposed by the
Marxists. After the resulting split in 1872, the Bakuninists continued as a separate organization. He retired from the movement in 1874 after the abortive Bologna insurrection. He died
and was buried in Rome.

He had no faith in parliamentary politics and joined Proudhon in saying that universal suffrage was counterrevolution.
He believed in mass organization, collectivism, and was above
all anti-State. He held that in place of the State, there would
arise a free federation of autonomous associations enjoying the
right of secession and guaranteeing complete personal freedom.
Max Nettlau and E. H. Carr have written authoritative biographies of him. His writings were widely scattered, and he
never organized any of them into finished books. A useful
compilation is that of G. P. Maximoff, published by The Free
Press, although this is a partial collection. A project is now un-
derway for the publication of Bakunin's papers in France.

Underlying all historic problems,
national, religious, and political, there has always been the
economic problem, the most important and essential problem
not only for the drudge-people but likewise for all the estates,
for the State, and for the Church. Wealth has always been
and still is the indispensable condition for the realization of
everything human: authority, power, intelligence, knowledge, freedom. This is true to such a degree that the most
ideal church in the world—the Christian—which preaches
contempt for worldly blessings, no sooner had it succeeded in

vanquishing paganism and set up its own power upon the ruins of the latter than it directed all its energy toward acquiring wealth.

Political power and wealth are inseparable. Those who have power have the means to gain wealth and must center all their efforts upon acquiring it, for without it they will not be able to retain their power. Those who are wealthy must become strong, for, lacking power, they run the risk of being deprived of their wealth. The drudge-people have always been powerless because they were poverty-stricken, and they were poverty-stricken because they lacked organized power. In view of this, it is no wonder that among all the problems confronting them, they saw and see first and chiefly *the economic problem*—the problem of obtaining bread.

The drudge-people, the perpetual victims of civilization, the martyrs of history, did not always see and understand this problem as they do now, but they have always felt it strongly, and one may say that among all the historic problems that evoked their passive sympathy, in all their instinctive strivings and efforts in the religious and political fields, they always felt more intensely the economic problem, always aiming at solving it. Every people, taken in its totality, [is socialistic], and every toiler who is of the people, is a socialist by virtue of his position. And this manner of being a socialist is incomparably more serious than the manner of those socialists who, belonging to the ruling classes by virtue of the advantageous conditions of their lives, arrived at socialist convictions only via science and thinking.

I am by no means inclined to underestimate science or thought. I realize that it is those two factors which mainly distinguish man from other animals; I acknowledge them as the guiding stars of any human prosperity. But at the same time I realize that theirs is only a cold light, that is, whenever they do not go hand in hand with life, and that their truth becomes powerless and sterile when it does not rest upon the truth of life. Whenever they contradict life, science and thought degenerate into sophistry, into the service of untruth—or at least into shameful cowardice and inactivity.

For neither science nor thought exists in isolation, in abstraction; they manifest themselves only in the real man, and every real man is an integral being who cannot at the same time seek rigorous truth and theory and enjoy the fruits of untruth in practice. In every man, even the most sincere socialist, belonging, not by birth but through accidental circumstances in his life, to the ruling classes, that is, one who is exploiting others, you can detect this contradiction between thought and life; and this contradiction invariably paralyzes him, renders him impotent. That is why he can become a wholly sincere socialist only when he has broken *all ties* binding him to the privileged world and has renounced all its advantages.

The drudge-people have nothing to renounce and nothing to break away from; they are socialists by virtue of their position. Poverty-stricken, injured, downtrodden, the toiler becomes by instinct the representative of all indigent people, all the injured and downtrodden—and what is this social problem if not the problem of the ultimate and integral emancipation of all downtrodden people? The essential difference between the educated socialist belonging even though it be only by virtue of his education, to the ruling classes, and the unconscious socialist of the toiling people, lies in the fact that the former, while desiring to be a socialist, can never become one to the full extent, whereas the latter, while being a socialist, is not aware of it, does not know there is a social science in this world, and has never even heard the name of socialism.

One knows all about socialism, but he is not a socialist; the other is a socialist, yet does not know about it. Which is preferable? In my opinion, it is preferable to *be* a socialist. It is almost impossible to pass, so to speak, from abstract thought into life, from thought unaccompanied by life and lacking the driving power of life-necessity. But the reverse, the possibility of passing from being to thought, has been proven by the whole history of mankind. And it is now finding its additional substantiation in the history of the drudge-people.

The entire social problem is now reduced to a very simple question. The great multitudes of people have been and still are doomed to poverty and slavery. They have always constituted a vast majority in comparison to the oppressing and exploiting minority. It means that the power of numbers was always on their side. Then why have they not used it until now in order to throw off the ruinous and hateful yoke? Can one really conceive that there ever was a time when the

masses of people loved oppression, when they did not feel
that distressing yoke? That would be contrary to sound
sense, to Nature itself. Every living being strives for prosperity and freedom, and in order to hate an oppressor, it is
not necessary even to be a man, it is enough to be an animal.
So the long-suffering patience of the masses is to be accounted for by other reasons.

One of the principal causes no doubt lies in the people's
ignorance. Because of that ignorance they do not conceive of
themselves as an all-powerful mass bound by the ties of
solidarity. They are disunited in their conception of themselves as much as they are disunited in life, as a result of the
oppressing circumstances. This two-fold disunion is the
chief source of the daily impotence of the people. Because of
that, among ignorant people, or people standing on the lowest level of education or possessing a meager historic and
collective experience, every person, every community, views
the troubles and oppressions that they suffer as a personal or
particular phenomenon, and not as a general phenomenon
affecting all in the same measure and one that therefore
should bind all in one common venture, in resistance or in
work.

What happens is just the contrary: Every region, commune, family, and individual regard the others as enemies
ready to impose their yoke upon and despoil the other party;
and while this mutual alienation continues, every concerted
party, even one that is hardly organized, every caste or State
power that may represent a comparatively small number of
people, can easily bamboozle, terrorize, and oppress millions
of toilers.

The second reason—also a direct sequel of the very same
ignorance—consists in the fact that the people do not see
and do not know the principal sources of their misery, often
hating only the manifestation of the cause and not the cause
itself, just as a dog may bite the stick with which a man is
hitting it but not the man who does the hitting. Therefore
the governments, castes, and parties that until now have
based their existence upon the mental aberrations of the
people, could easily cheat the latter. Ignorant of the real
causes of their woes, the people, of course, could not have
any idea of the ways and means of their emancipation, letting
themselves be shunted from one false road to another, seek-

ing salvation where there could be none, and lending themselves as tools to be used against their own numbers by the exploiters and oppressors.

Thus the masses of the people, impelled by the same social need of improving their lives and freeing themselves of intolerable oppression, let themselves be carried from one form of religious nonsense to another, from one political form designed for the oppression of the people into another form, just as oppressive, if not even worse—like a man tormented by illness, and tossing from one side to the other, but actually feeling worse with every turn.

Such has been the history of the drudge-people in all countries, throughout the world. A hopeless, odious, horrible story capable of driving to despair anyone seeking human justice. And still one should not let himself be carried away by this feeling. Disgusting as that history has been until now, one cannot say that it was in vain or that it did not result in some benefits. What can one do if by his very nature man is condemned to work his way, through all kinds of abominations and torments, from pitch darkness to reason, from a brutish state to humanity? The historic errors, and the woes going hand in hand with them, have produced multitudes of illiterate people. And those people have paid with their sweat and blood, with poverty, hunger, slave drudgery, with torment and death—for every new movement into which they were drawn by the minorities exploiting them. Instead of books, which they could not read, history registered those lessons upon their hides. Such lessons cannot be easily forgotten. By paying dearly for every new faith, hope, and error, the masses of people attain reason via historic stupidities.

Through bitter experience they have come to realize the vanity of all religious beliefs, of all national and political movements, as a result of which the social problem came to be posed for the first time with sufficient clarity. This problem corresponds to the original and century-long instinct, but through centuries of development, from the beginning of the history of the State, it was obscured by religious, political, and patriotic mists. Those mists have now rolled away, and Europe is astir with the social problem.

Everywhere the masses are beginning to perceive the real cause of their misery, are becoming aware of the power of solidarity, and are beginning to compare their immense numbers with the insignificant number of their agelong despoilers. But if they have attained such consciousness, what prevents them from liberating themselves now?

The answer is: *Lack of organization, and the difficulty of bringing them into mutual agreement.*

We have seen that in every historically developed society, like present-day European society, for instance, the mass of people is divided into three main categories:

1) The vast majority, utterly unorganized, exploited but not exploiting others.

2) A considerable majority embracing all the estates of the realm, a minority exploiting and exploited in the same measure, oppressed and oppressing others.

3) And finally, the smallest minority of exploiters and oppressors pure and simple, conscious of their function and fully agreed as to a common plan of action among themselves: the supreme governing estate.

We have seen also that in the measure in which it grows and develops, the majority of those who make up the estates of the realm becomes in itself a semi-instinctive mass, if you like, State-organized but lacking mutual understanding or conscious direction in its mass movements and actions. In relation to the drudge-masses, who are not organized at all, they, the members of the State estates, of course, play the role of exploiters, continuing to exploit them not by means of a deliberate, mutually agreed-upon plan, but through force of habit, and traditional and juridical right, mostly believing in the lawfulness and sacredness of that right.

But at the same time, in regard to the minority in control of the government, the group that has explicit mutual understanding as to its course of action, this middle group, plays the more or less passive role of an exploited victim. And since this middle class, although insufficiently organized, still has more wealth, education, greater freedom of movement and action, and more of other means necessary to organize conspiracies and to set up an organization—more so than the drudge-people have—it frequently happens that rebellions break forth from among this middle class, rebellions often ending in victory over the government and the replacing of the latter with another government. Such has

been the nature of all the internal political upheavals of
which history tells us.

Out of these upheavals and rebellions nothing good could
come for the people. For the estate rebellions are waged
because of injuries to the estates of the realm, and not because
of injuries to the people; they have as an object the interests
of the estates, and not the interests of the people. No
matter how much the estates fight among themselves, no
matter how much they may rebel against the existing government, none of their revolutions has had, or ever could have,
for their purpose the overthrow of the economic and political foundations of the State that make possible the exploitation of the toiling masses, that is, the very existence of classes
and the class principle. No matter how revolutionary in spirit
those privileged classes might be, and much as they might
hate a particular form of the State, the State itself is sacred to
them; its integrity, power, and interests are unanimously held
up as supreme interests. Patriotism, that is, the sacrifice of
oneself, of one's person and property, for the purposes of the
State, always has been and still is deemed the highest virtue
by them.

Therefore no revolution, bold and violent though it may
be in its manifestations, has ever dared to put its sacrilegious
hand upon the holy ark of the State. And since no State is
possible without organization, administration, an army, and
a considerable number of men invested with authority—
that is, it is impossible without a government—the overthrow of one government is necessarily followed by the setting up of another, more sympathetic government, one that
is of greater use to the classes that triumphed in the struggle.

But useful though it may be, the new government, after
its honeymoon, begins to incur the indignation of the same
classes that brought it into power. Such is the nature of any
authority: it is doomed to work evil. I am not referring to
evil from the point of view of the people's interests: the
State as the fortress of the estates and the government as the
guardian of the State's interests always constitute an absolute
evil so far as the people are concerned. No, I am referring
to the evil felt as such by the estates for the exclusive benefit
of which the existence of the State and the government is
necessary. I say that notwithstanding this necessity, the State
always falls as a heavy burden upon these classes, and, while

serving their essential interests, it nevertheless fleeces and oppresses them, though to a lesser extent than it does the masses.

A government that does not abuse its power, and that is not oppressive, an impartial and honest government acting only for the interests of all classes and not ignoring such interests in exclusive concern for the persons standing at its head—such a government is, like squaring the circle, an unattainable ideal because it runs counter to human nature. And human nature, the nature of every man, is such that, given power over others, he will invariably oppress them; placed in an exceptional position and withdrawn from human equality, he becomes a scoundrel. Equality and the absence of authority are the only conditions essential to the morality of every man. Take the most radical revolutionist and place him upon the all-Russian throne or give him dictatorial power, of which so many of our green revolutionists daydream, and within a year he will have become worse than the Emperor himself.

The estates of the realm long ago convinced themselves of it, and gave currency to an adage proclaiming that *"government is a necessary evil"*—necessary of course for them but by no means for the people, to whom the State, and the government necessitated by it, is not a necessary but a fatal evil. If the ruling classes could get along without a government, retaining only the State—that is, the possibility and the right of exploiting the labor of the people—they would not set up one government instead of another. But historic experience—for instance, the sorry fate that befell the Polish gentry-ridden republic—showed them that it would be impossible to maintain a State without a government. The lack of a government begets anarchy, and anarchy leads to the destruction of the State, that is, to the enslavement of the country by another State, as was the case with the unfortunate Poland, or the full emancipation of the toiling people and the abolition of classes, which, we hope, will soon take place all over Europe.

In order to minimize the evil worked by every government, the ruling classes of the State devised various constitutional orders and forms that now have doomed the existing European States to oscillate between class anarchy and government despotism, and that have shaken the governmental edifice to such an extent that even we, though old men, may hope to become witnesses and contributing agents of its final destruction. There is no doubt that when the time of the smashup arrives, the vast majority of the persons belonging to the ruling classes in the State, will close their ranks around the latter, irrespective of their hatred toward existing governments, and will defend it against the enraged toiling people in order to save the State, save the cornerstone of their existence as a class.

But why is a government necessary for the maintenance of the State? Because no State can exist without *a permanent conspiracy,* a conspiracy directed, of course, against the masses of drudge-people, for the enslavement and fleecing of which all States exist. And in every State the government is nothing but a permanent conspiracy on the part of the minority against the majority that it enslaves and fleeces. It follows clearly from the very essence of the State that there never has been and could not be such a State organization that did not run counter to the interests of the people and that was not deeply hated by the latter.

Because of the backwardness of the people, it often happens that, far from rising against the State, they show a sort of respect and affection toward it, expecting justice from it and the avenging of the people's wrongs, and therefore they seem to be imbued with patriotic feelings. But when we look more closely into the real attitude of any of them, of even the most patriotic people, toward the State, we find that they love and revere in it only the ideal conception thereof and not the actual manifestation. The people hate the essence of the State insofar as they come in touch with it, and are always ready to destroy it insofar as they are not restrained by the organized force of the government.

We have already seen that the larger the exploiting minority in the State grows, the less it becomes capable of directly governing the State's affairs. The many-sidedness and heterogeneity of the interests of the governing classes give rise in turn to disorder, anarchy, and the weakening of the State regime necessary to keep the exploited people in requisite obedience. Therefore the interests of all the ruling classes necessarily demand that an even more compact governmental minority crystallize from their midst, one that is capable, on account of being few in number, of *agreeing between themselves* to organize their own group and all the forces of the State for the benefit of the estates and against the people.

Every government has a two-fold aim. One, the chief and avowed aim, consists in preserving and strengthening the State, civilization, and civil order, that is, the systematic and legalized dominance of the ruling class over the exploited people. The other aim is just as important in the eyes of the government, though less willingly avowed in the open, and that is the preservation of its exclusive governmental advantages and its *personnel*. The first aim is pertinent to the general interests of the ruling classes; the second to the vanity and the exceptional advantages of the individuals in the government.

By its first aim the government places itself in a hostile attitude toward the people; by its second aim toward both the people and the privileged classes, there being moments in history when the government seemingly becomes even more hostile toward the possessing classes than toward the people. This happens whenever the former, growing dissatisfied with it, try to overthrow it or curtail its power. Then the feeling of self-preservation impels the government to forget its chief aim constituting the whole meaning of its existence: the preservation of the State or class rule and class welfare as against the people. But those moments cannot last long because the government, of whatever nature it may be, cannot exist without the estates, just as the latter cannot exist without a government. For the lack of any other class, the government creates a bureaucratic class of its own, like our nobility in Russia.

The whole problem of the government consists in the following: How, by the use of the smallest possible but best organized forces taken from the people, to keep them obedient or in civil order, and at the same time preserve the independence, not of the people, which of course is out of the question, but of its State, against the ambitious designs of the neighboring powers, and, on the other hand, to increase its possessions at the expense of those same powers. In a word, war within and war without—such is the life of the government. It must be armed and ceaselessly on guard against both domestic and foreign enemies. Though itself breathing oppression and deceit, it is bound to regard all, within and outside of its borders, as enemies, and must be in a state of conspiracy against all of them.

However, the mutual enmity of the States and the governments ruling them cannot compare with the enmity of every one of them toward their own toiling people: and just as two ruling classes engaged in fierce warfare are ready to forget their most intransigent hatreds whenever a rebellion of the drudge-people looms up, so are two States and governments ready to forsake their enmities and their open warfare as soon as the threat of a social revolution appears on the horizon. The principal and most essential problem for all governments, States, and ruling classes, whatever form, name, or pretext they may use to disguise their nature, is to subdue the people and keep them in thralldom, because this is a problem of life and death for everything now called civilization or civil State.

All means are permitted to a government to attain those aims. What in private life is called infamy, vileness, crime, assumes with governments the character of valor, virtue, and duty. Machiavelli was a thousand times right in maintaining that the existence, prosperity, and power of *every* State— monarchic as well as republican—must be based upon crime. The life of every government is necessarily a series of mean, foul, and criminal acts against all alien peoples and also to a much larger extent against its own toiling people. It is a never-ending conspiracy against their prosperity and freedom.

Governmental science has been worked out and improved for centuries. I do not believe that anyone will accuse me of overstating the case if I call this science the highest form of State knavery evolved amid the constant struggle of, and by the experience of all past and present States. This is the science of fleecing the people in the way that they will feel least but that should not leave any surpluses with them—for any such surplus would give the people additional power— and that at the same time should not deprive them of the bare minimum necessary to sustain their wretched lives and for the further production of wealth.

It is the science of taking soldiers from the people and organizing them by means of skillful discipline, and of building up a regular army, the principal force of the State, a repressive force, maintained for the purpose of keeping the people in subjection. It is the science of distributing, cleverly and expeditiously, a few tens of thousands of soldiers and placing them in the most important spots of a specific region so as to keep the population in fear and obedience. It is the science of covering whole countries with the finest net of bureaucratic organization, and, by means of regulations, decrees, and other measures, shackling, disuniting, and enfeebling the working people so that they shall not be able to get together, unite, or advance, so that they shall always remain in the salutary condition of relative ignorance—that is, salutary for the government, for the State, and for the ruling classes—a condition rendering it difficult for the people to become influenced by new ideas and dynamic personalities.

This is the sole aim of any governmental organization, of the permanent conspiracy of the government against the people. And this conspiracy, openly avowed as such, embraces the entire diplomacy, the internal administration— military, civil, police, courts, finances, and education—and the Church.

And it is against this huge organization, armed with all means, mental and material, lawful and lawless, and which in an extremity can always count on the cooperation of all or nearly all the ruling classes, that the poor people have to struggle. The people, though having an overwhelming preponderance in numbers, are unarmed, ignorant, and deprived of any organization! Is victory possible? Has the struggle any chance of success?

It is not enough that the people wake up, that they finally become aware of their misery and the causes thereof. True, there is a great deal of elemental power, more power indeed than in the government, taken together with all the ruling classes; but an elemental force lacking organization is not a real power. It is upon this uncontestable advantage of organized force over the elemental force of the people that the might of the State is based.

Consequently, the question is not whether they [the people] have the capacity to rebel, but whether they are capable of building up an organization enabling them to bring the rebellion to a victorious end—not just to a casual victory but to a prolonged and ultimate triumph.

It is herein, and exclusively so, one may say, that this whole urgent problem is centered.

Therefore the first condition of victory by the people is *agreement among the people* or *organization* of the people's forces.

SUMMATION

I. *The negation of God and the principle of authority, divine and human, and also of any tutelage by a man over men*— Even when such tutelage is attempted upon adult persons wholly deprived of education, or the ignorant masses, and whether that tutelage is exercised in the name of higher considerations, or even of *scientific reasons* presented by a group of individuals of generally recognized intellectual standing, or by some other class—in either case it would lead to the formation of a sort of *intellectual aristocracy*, exceedingly odious and harmful to the cause of freedom.

Note 1. Positive and rational knowledge is the only torch lighting up man's road toward the recognition of truth and the regulation of his behavior and his relation to the society surrounding him. But this knowledge is subject to errors, and even were this not the case, it would still be presumptuous to claim to govern men in the name of such knowledge against their will. A genuinely free society can grant to knowledge only a two-fold right, enjoyment of which constitutes at the same time a duty: *first*, the upbringing and education of persons of both sexes, equally accessible to and compulsory upon children and adolescents until they become of age, after which all tutelage is to cease; and, *second*, the spreading of ideas and systems of ideas based upon exact science, and the endeavor, with the aid of absolutely free propaganda, to have those ideas deeply permeate the universal convictions of mankind.

Note 2. While definitely rejecting any tutelage (in whatever form it asserts itself) which the intellect developed by knowledge and experience—by business, worldly, and human experience—may attempt to set up over the ignorant masses, we are far from denying *the natural and beneficial influence of knowledge and experience* upon the masses, provided that that influence asserts itself very simply, by way of the natural incidence of higher intellects upon the lower intellects, and provided also that that influence is not invested with any official authority or endowed with any privileges, either political or social. For both these things necessarily produce upon one hand the enslavement of the masses, and on the other hand corruption, disintegration, and stupefaction of those who are invested and endowed with such powers.

II. *The negation of free will and the right of society to punish*—since every human individual, with no exception whatever, is but an involuntary product of natural and social environment. There are four basic causes of man's immorality: 1) *Lack of rational hygiene and upbringing;* 2) *Inequality of economic and social conditions;* 3) *The ignorance of the masses flowing naturally from this situation;* 4) *And the unavoidable consequence of those conditions—slavery.*

Rational upbringing, education, and the organization of society upon a basis of freedom and justice, are to take the place of *punishment.* During the more or less prolonged transitional period which is bound to follow the Social Revolution, society, having to defend itself against incorrigible individuals—not criminal, but dangerous—shall never apply to them any other form of punishment except that of placing them beyond the pale of its guarantees and solidarity, that is, of having them *expelled.*

III. The negation of free will does not connote the negation of freedom. *On the contrary, freedom represents the corollary, the direct result of natural and social necessity.*

Note 1. Man is not free in relation to the laws of Nature, which constitute the first basis and the necessary condition of his existence. They pervade and dominate him, just as they pervade and dominate everything that exists. Nothing is capable of saving him from their fateful omnipotence; any attempt to revolt on his part would simply lead to suicide. But thanks to the faculty inherent in his nature, by virtue of which he becomes conscious of his environment and learns to master it, *man can gradually free himself from the natural and crushing hostility of the external world—physical as well as social*—with the aid of thought, knowledge, and the application of thought to the conative instinct, that is *with the aid of his rational will.*

Note 2. Man represents the last link, the highest level in the continuous scale of beings who, beginning with the simplest elements and ending with man, constitute the world known to us. Man is an animal who, thanks to the higher development of his organism, especially the brain, possesses the faculty of thought and speech. Therein lie all the differences separating him from all other animal species—his brothers, older in point of time and younger in point of mental faculties. That difference, however, is vast. It is the sole cause of what we call our history, the meaning of which can be briefly expressed in the following words: *Man starts with animality in order to arrive at humanity, that is, the organization of society with the aid of science, conscious thought, rational work, and freedom.*

Note 3. Man is a social animal, like many other animals that appeared upon the earth before he did. *He does not create society by means of a free agreement: he is born in the midst of Nature, and apart from it he could not live as a human being—he could not even become one, nor speak, think, will, or act in a rational manner.* In view of the fact that society shapes and determines his human essence, man is dependent upon it as completely as upon physical Nature, and there is no great genius who is exempt from its domination.

IV. *Social solidarity is the first human law; freedom is the second law.* Both laws interpenetrate and are inseparable from each other, thus constituting the very essence of humanity. Thus freedom is not the negation of solidarity; on the contrary, it represents the development of, and so to speak, the humanization of the latter.

V. Freedom does not connote man's independence in relation to the immutable laws of Nature and society. It is first of all man's ability gradually to emancipate himself from the oppression *of the external physical world with the aid of knowledge and rational labor; and, further, it signifies man's right to dispose* of himself and to act in conformity with his own views and *convictions:* a right opposed to the despotic and authoritarian claims of another man, a group, or class of people, or society as a whole.

Note 1. One should not confuse sociological laws, otherwise called the laws of social physiology, and which are just as immutable and necessary for every man as the laws of physical Nature, for in substance they also are physical laws —one should not confuse those laws with political, criminal, and civil laws, which to a greater or lesser extent express the morals, customs, interests, and views dominant in a given epoch, society, or section of that society, a separate class of society. It stands to reason that, being recognized by the majority of people, or even by one ruling class, they exert a powerful influence upon every individual. That influence is beneficial or harmful, depending upon its character, but so far as society is concerned, it is neither right nor useful to have these laws imposed upon anyone by force, by the exercise of authority, and contrary to the convictions of the individual. Such a method of imposing laws would imply an attempted infringement of freedom, of personal dignity, of the very human essence of the members of society.

VI. *A natural society, in the midst of which every man is born and outside of which he could never become a rational and free being,* becomes humanized only in the measure that all men comprising it become, individually and collectively, free to an ever greater extent.

Note 1. *To be personally free* means for every man living in a social milieu not to surrender his thought or will to any authority but his own reason and his own understanding of justice; in a word, not to recognize any other truth but the one which he himself has arrived at, and not to submit to any other law but the one accepted by his own conscience. Such is the indispensable condition for the observance of human dignity, the incontestable right of man, the sign of his humanity.

To be free collectively means to live among free people and to be free by virtue of their freedom. As we have already pointed out, man cannot become a rational being, possessing a rational will, (and consequently he could not achieve individual freedom) apart from society and without its aid. Thus the freedom of everyone is the result of universal solidarity. But if we recognize this solidarity as the basis and condition of every individual freedom, it becomes evident that a man living among slaves, even in the capacity of their master, will necessarily become the slave of that state of slavery, and that only by emancipating himself from such slavery will he become free himself.

Thus, too, the freedom of all is essential to my freedom. And it follows that it would be fallacious to maintain that the freedom of all constitutes a limit for a limitation upon my freedom, for that would be tantamount to the denial of such freedom. On the contrary, universal freedom represents the necessary affirmation and boundless expansion of individual freedom.

VII. *Individual freedom of every man becomes actual and possible only through the collective freedom of society of which man constitutes a part by virtue of a natural and immutable law.*

Note 1 Like humanity, of which it is the purest expression, freedom presents not the beginning but the final moment of history Human society, as we have indicated, begins with animality. Primitive people and savages hold their humanity and their human rights in so little esteem that they begin by devouring one another, which unfortunately still continues at full speed. The second stage in the course of human development is slavery The third—in the midst of which we now live—is the period of economic exploitation, of wage labor. The fourth period, toward which we are aiming and which, it is to be hoped, we are approaching, is the epoch of *justice*, of freedom and equality, the epoch of mutual solidarity.

VIII *The primitive, natural man becomes a free man, becomes humanized, a free and moral agent, in other words, he becomes aware of his humanity and realizes within himself and for himself his own human aspect and the rights of his fellow beings.* Consequently man should wish the freedom, morality, and humanity of all men in the interest of his own humanity, his own morality, and his personal freedom.

IX. *Thus respect for the freedom of others is the highest duty of man To love this freedom and to serve it—such is the only virtue That is the basis of all morality, and there can be no other.*

X. Since freedom is the result and the clearest expression of solidarity, that is, of mutuality of interest, it can be realized only under conditions of equality. Political equality can be based only upon economic and social equality And realization of freedom through equality constitutes justice.

XI. Since labor is the only source of all values, utilities, and wealth in general, man, who is primarily a social being, must work in order to live.

XII. Only associated labor, that is, labor organized upon the principles of reciprocity and cooperation, is adequate to the task of maintaining the existence of a large and some-what civilized society. Whatever stands for civilization could be created only by labor organized and associated in this manner The whole secret of the boundless productivity of human labor consists first of all in applying to a greater or lesser extent scientifically developed reason—which in turn is the product of the already organized labor—and then in the division of that labor, but under the necessary condition of simultaneously combining or associating this divided labor.

XIII. The basis and the main content of all historic iniquities, of all political and social privileges, is the enslave-ment and exploitation of organized labor for the benefit of the strongest—for conquering nations, classes, or individuals. Such is the true historic cause of slavery, serfdom, and wage labor; and that is, by way of a summary, the basis of the so-called right of private and inherited property.

XIV. From the moment that property rights became gener-ally accepted, society had to split into two parts: on the one hand the property-owning, privileged minority, exploiting organized and forced labor, and on the other hand millions of proletarians, enthralled as slaves, serfs, or wage-workers. Some—thanks to leisure based upon the satisfaction of needs and material comfort—have at their disposal the highest blessings of civilization, education, and upbringing; and others, the millions of people, are condemned to forced labor, ignorance, and perpetual want.

XV. Thus the civilization of the minority is based upon the forced barbarism of the vast majority. Consequently the individuals who by virtue of their social position enjoy all sorts of political and social privileges, and all men of prop-erty, are in reality the natural enemies, the exploiters, and oppressors of the great masses of the people.

XVI. Because leisure—the precious advantage of the rul-ing classes—is necessary for the development of the mind, and because the development of character and personality likewise demands a certain degree of well-being and freedom in one's movements and activity, it was therefore quite natural that the ruling classes have proved to be more civilized, more intelligent, more human, and to a certain extent more moral than the great masses of people. But in view of the fact that, on the other hand, inactivity and the enjoyment of all sorts of privileges weaken the body, dry up one's affections, and misdirect the mind, it is evident that sooner or later the privileged classes are bound to sink into corruption, mental torpor, and servility. We see this happening right now.

XVII. On the other hand, forced labor and utter lack of leisure doom the great masses of the people to barbarism. By themselves they cannot foster and maintain their own mental development since, because of their inherited burden of ignorance, the rational elements of their toil—the application of science, the combining and managing of productive forces—are left exclusively to the representatives of the bourgeois class. Only the muscular, irrational, mechanical elements of work, which become even more stupefying as a result of the division of labor, have been apportioned to the masses, who are stunned, in the full sense of the word, by their daily, galley-slave drudgery.

But despite all that, thanks to the prodigious moral power inherent in labor, because in demanding justice, freedom, and equality for themselves, the workers therewith demand the same for all, there being no other social group (except women and children) who are getting a rougher deal in life than the workers; because they have enjoyed life very little and therefore have not abused it, which means that they have not become satiated with it; and also because, lacking education, they, however, possess the enormous advantage of not having been corrupted and distorted by egoistic interests and falsehoods prompted by acquisitiveness, and thus have retained their natural energy of character while the privileged classes sink ever deeper, become debilitated, and rot away—it is due to all this that only the workers believe in life, that only the workers love and desire truth, freedom, equality, and justice, and that it is only the workers to whom the future belongs.

XVIII. Our Socialist program demands and should unremittingly demand:

1) Political, economic, and social equalization of all classes and all people living on the earth.
2) Abolition of inheritance of property.

3) Appropriation of land by agricultural associations, and of capital and all the means of production by the industrial associations.

4) Abolition of the patriarchal family law, based exclusively upon the right to inherit property and also upon the equalization of man and woman in point of political, economic, and social rights.

5) The upkeep, upbringing, and educating of the children of both sexes until they become of age, it being understood that scientific and technical training, including the branches of higher teaching, is to be both equal for and compulsory for all.

The school is to replace the church and to render unnecessary criminal codes, gendarmes, punishments, prisons, and executioners.

Children do not constitute anyone's property; they are not the property of their parents nor even of society. They belong only to their own future freedom.

But in children this freedom is not yet real. It is only potential; for real freedom, that is, the full awareness and the realization thereof in every individual, preeminently based upon the feeling of one's dignity and upon genuine respect for the freedom and dignity of others, that is, upon justice— such freedom can develop in children only by virtue of the rational development of their minds, character, and rational will.

Hence it follows that society, the whole future of which depends upon the adequate education and upbringing of children, and which therefore has not only the right but also the duty to watch over them, is the only natural guardian of children of both sexes. And since, as a result of the forthcoming abolition of the right of inheritance, society is to become the only heir, it will then deem it as one of its primary duties to furnish all the necessary means for the upkeep, upbringing, and education of children of both sexes, irrespective of their origin and of their parents.

The rights of the parents shall reduce themselves to loving their children and exercising over them the only authority compatible with that, inasmuch as such authority does not run counter to their morality, their mental development, and their future freedom.

Marriage, in the sense of being a civil and political act, like any intervention of society in questions of love, is bound to disappear. The children will be *entrusted*—naturally and not by right—*to the mother,* as her prerogative under rational supervision of society.

In view of the fact that minors, especially children, are largely incapable of reasoning and consciously governing their acts, *the principle of tutelage and authority,* which is to be eliminated from the life of society, will still find a natural sphere of application in the upbringing and education of children. However, such authority and tutelage should be *truly humane and rational,* and altogether alien to all the refrains of theology, metaphysics, and jurisprudence. They should start from the premise that from his birth not a single human being is either bad or good, and that *good,* that is, the love of freedom, the consciousness of justice and solidarity, the cult of or rather the respect for truth, reason, and labor, can be developed in men only through rational upbringing and education. Thus, we emphasize here, the sole aim of this *authority* should be to prepare all children for the utmost freedom. This aim can be achieved only by gradual self-effacement on the part of authority, and its giving place to self-activity on the part of the children, in the measure that they approach maturity.

Education should embrace all the branches of science, technique, and knowledge of crafts. It should be at once scientific and professional, general, compulsory for all children, and special—conforming to the tastes and proclivities of every one of them, so that every young boy and girl, upon leaving school and becoming of age, would be fit for either mental or manual work.

Freed from the tutelage of society, they are at liberty to enter or not to enter any of the labor associations. However, they will necessarily want to enter such associations, for with the abolition of the right of inheritance and the passing of all the land, capital, and means of production into the hands of the international federation of free workers' associations, there will be no more room nor opportunity for competition, that is, for the existence of isolated labor.

No one will be able to exploit the labor of others; everyone will have to work in order to live. And anyone who does not want to work will have the alternative of starving if he

cannot find an association or commune that will feed him
out of considerations of pity. But then it also will be found
just not to grant him any political rights, since, though being
an able-bodied man, he prefers the shameful state of living
at the expense of someone else; for social and political rights
will have only one basis—the labor contributed by everyone.

During the transitional period, however, society will be
confronted with the problem of individuals (and unfortunately there will be many of them) who grew up under the
prevailing system of organized injustice and special privileges
and who were not brought up with a realization of the need
for justice and true human dignity and likewise with respect
for and the habit of work. In regard to those individuals revolutionary or revolutionized society will find itself facing a
distressing dilemma: It will either have to force them to work,
which would be despotism, or let itself be exploited by idlers;
and that would be a new slavery and the source of a new corruption of society.

In a society organized upon the principles of equality and
justice, which serve as the basis of true freedom, given a
rational organization of education and upbringing and likewise the pressure of public opinion, which, being based upon
respect for labor, must despise idlers—in such a society idleness and parasites will be impossible. Having become exceedingly rare exceptions, those cases of idleness shall be regarded
as special maladies to be subjected to clinical treatment. Only
children—until they reach a certain degree of strength, and
afterward only inasmuch as it is necessary to give them time
to acquire knowledge and not to overload them with work
—invalids, old people, and sick persons can be exempted
from labor without resulting in the loss of anyone's dignity
or the impairment of the rights of free men.

XIX. *In the interests of their radical and full economic
emancipation, workers should demand the complete and
resolute abolition of the State with all of its institutions.*

Note 1. What is the State? It is the historic organization of
authority and tutelage, divine and human, extended to the
masses of people in the name of some religion, or in the name
of the alleged exceptional and privileged ability of one or
sundry property-owning classes, to the detriment of the great
mass of workers whose forced labor is cruelly exploited by
those classes.

Conquest, which became the foundation of property right and of the right of inheritance, is also the basis of every State. The legitimized exploitation of the labor of the masses for the benefit of a certain number of property-owners (most of whom are fictitious, there being only a very small number of those who exist in reality) consecrated by *the Church* in the name of a fictitious Divinity that has always been made to side with the strongest and cleverest—that is what is called "right." The development of prosperity, comfort, luxury, and the subtle and distorted intellect of the privileged classes—a development necessarily rooted in the misery and ignorance of the vast majority of the population—is called "civilization"; and the organization guaranteeing the existence of this complex of historic iniquities is called "the State."

So the workers must wish for the destruction of the State.

Note 2. The State, necessarily reposing upon the exploitation and enslavement of the masses, and as such oppressing and trampling upon all the liberties of the people, and upon any form of justice, is bound to be brutal, conquering, predatory, and rapacious in its foreign relations. The State—any State, whether monarchy or republic—is the negation of humanity. It is the negation of humanity because, while setting as its highest or absolute aim *the patriotism of its citizens,* and placing, in accordance with its principles, above all other interests in the world the interests of its own self-preservation, of its own might within its own borders and its outward expansion, the State negates all particular interests and the human rights of its subjects as well as the rights of aliens. And thereby the State violates international solidarity among peoples and individuals, placing them outside of justice, and outside of humanity.

Note 3. The State is the younger brother of the Church. It can find no other reason for its existence apart from the theological or metaphysical idea. Being by its nature contrary to human justice, it has to seek its rationale in the theological or metaphysical fiction of divine justice. The ancient world lacked entirely the concept of nation or society, that is, the latter was completely enslaved and absorbed by the State, and every State deduced its origin and its special right of existence and domination from some god or system of gods deemed to be the exclusive patron of that State. In the ancient world man as an individual was unknown; the very idea of humanity was lacking. There were only citizens. That is why in that civilization slavery was a natural phenomenon and the necessary basis for the fruits of citizens.

When Christianity destroyed polytheism and proclaimed the only God, the States had to revert to the saints from the Christian paradise; and every Catholic State had one or several patron saints, its defenders and intercessors before the Lord God, who on that occasion may well have found himself in an embarrassing position. Besides, every State still finds it necessary to declare that the Lord God patronizes it in some special manner.

Metaphysics and the science of law, based in its idea upon metaphysics but in reality upon the class interests of the propertied classes, also sought to discover a rational basis for the fact of the existence of the State. They reverted to the fiction of the general and tacit agreement or contract, or to the fiction of objective justice and the general good of the people allegedly represented by the State.

According to the Jacobin democrats, the State has the task of making possible the triumph of the general and collective interests of all citizens over the egoistic interests of separate individuals, communes, and regions. The State is universal justice and collective reason triumphing over the egoism and stupidity of individuals. It is the declaration of the worthlessness and the unreasonableness of every individual in the name of the wisdom and the virtue of all. It is the negation of fact, or, which is the same thing, infinite limitation of all particular liberties, individual and collective, in the name of freedom for all—the collective and general freedom that in reality is only a depressing abstraction, deduced from the negation or the limitation of the rights of separate individuals and based upon the factual slavery of everyone.

In view of the fact that every abstraction can exist only inasmuch as it is backed up by the positive interests of a real being, the abstraction *State* in reality represents the positive interests of the ruling and property-owning, exploiting, and so-called intelligent classes, and also the systematic immolation for their benefit of the interests and freedom of the enslaved masses.[2]

[2] According to Max Nettlau, this summation by Bakunin was written March 25-30, 1871.

Peter Kropotkin
Modern Science and Anarchism[1]

Peter Alexeyevich Kropotkin (1842–1921) Born in Moscow to an aristocratic family, Kropotkin was originally destined for a military career. After his education at a select military school where his interests in Russian politics and natural science became firm, he chose service with a Siberian regiment where his experiences in studying reform were to shape his thought. As an official in Siberia, in 1862, he made important geographical and anthropological investigations that yielded valuable results in correcting distortions in map representation. At the social level, he concluded that State action was ineffective while mutual aid was of great importance in the struggle for existence. He made a reputation in science and in his thirtieth year was faced with the decision of proceeding with his career or indulging political impulses. He renounced a scientific career. He joined the International in 1872 but was soon disappointed with its limitations. The well-known events that led to a split brought the International to two opposite paths. The federative and libertarian wing drew Kropotkin's loyalties. Returning to Russia, after having fully worked out his theories and in order to propagate them, he was there arrested. After a dramatic escape in 1876 he made his way to England and then to Switzerland to rejoin the Jura Federation, to Paris and back to Switzerland to edit *Le Révolte*. The assassination of the Czar led to his expulsion. He fled to England and resumed his researches on the French Revolution. Discouraged by the political atmosphere, he and his wife returned to Paris. With others they were arrested in 1882 and tried in a spectacular public trial in which the accused conducted a brilliant defense enabling them to preach anarchism to Europe. Returning to Russia after the 1905 Revolution, the remainder of his life was devoted to his writings. Among the best known of his works are, *The Conquest of Bread; Fields, Factories and Workshops; Mutual Aid;* and the unfinished *Ethics*.

THE ORIGIN OF ANARCHISM

Anarchy does not draw its origin from any scientific researcher, or from any system of phil-

[1] From *Modern Science and Anarchism*, by Peter Kropotkin. London: Freedom Press, 1912.

osophy. Sociological sciences are still far from having acquired the same degree of accuracy as physics or chemistry. Even in the study of climate and weather (in Meteorology), we are not yet able to predict a month or even a week beforehand what weather we are going to have; consequently, it would be foolish to pretend that with the aid of such a young science as Sociology is, dealing moreover with infinitely more complicated things than wind and rain, we could scientifically predict events. We must not forget either that scientific men are but ordinary men, and that the majority of them belong to the leisured class and consequently share the prejudices of this class; most of them are even in the pay of the State. It is, therefore, quite evident that anarchy does not come from universities.

Like socialism in general, and like all other social movements, anarchism originated among the people, and it will preserve its vitality and creative force so long only as it remains a movement of the people.

From all times two currents of thought and action have been in conflict in the midst of human societies. On the one hand, the masses, the people, worked out, by their way of life, a number of necessary institutions in order to make social existence possible, to maintain peace, to settle quarrels, and to practice mutual aid in all circumstances that required combined effort. Tribal customs among savages, the village communities, later on industrial guilds in the cities of the Middle Ages, the first elements of international law that these cities elaborated to settle their mutual relations; these and many other institutions were developed and worked out, not by legislation, but by the creative spirit of the masses.

On the other hand, there have always flourished among men, magi, shamans, wizards, rain makers, oracles, and priests, who were the founders and the keepers of a rudimentary knowledge of Nature, and of the first elements of worship (worship of the sun, the moon, the forces of Nature, ancestor worship). Knowledge and superstition went then hand in hand—the first rudiments of science and the beginnings of all arts and crafts being thoroughly interwoven with magic, the formula and rites of which were carefully concealed from the uninitiated. By the side of these earliest representatives of religion and science, there were also the experts in ancient customs—those men, like the *brehons* of

Ireland, who kept in their memories the precedents of law. And there were also the chiefs of the military bands, who were supposed to possess the magic secrets of success in warfare.

These three groups of men formed among themselves secret societies for the keeping and transmission (after a long and painful initiation) of the secrets of their knowledge and crafts; and if at times they opposed each other, they generally agreed in the long run; they leagued together and upheld one another in different ways, in order to be able to command the masses, to reduce them to obedience, to govern them, and to make them work for them.

It is evident that anarchy represents the first of these two currents, that is to say, the creative constructive force of the masses, who elaborated common-law institutions in order to defend themselves against a domineering minority. It is also by the creative and constructive force of the people, aided by the whole strength of modern science and technique, that to-day anarchy strives to set up institutions that are indispensable to the free development of society, in opposition to those who put their hope in laws made by governing minorities.

We can therefore say that from all times there have been Anarchists and Statists.

Moreover, we always find that institutions, even the best of them, that were built up to maintain equality, peace, and mutual aid, become petrified as they grow old. They lose their original purpose, they fall under the domination of an ambitious minority, and gradually they become an obstacle to the ulterior development of society. Then individuals, more or less isolated, rebel against these institutions. But while some of these discontented, who rebel against an institution that has become irksome, strive to modify it for the common welfare, and above all to overthrow an authority not only alien to the institution, but grown to be more powerful even than the institution itself—others endeavor to emancipate themselves from the mutual aid institutions altogether. They reject the tribal customs, the village community, the guilds, etc., only to set themselves outside and above the social institutions altogether, in order to dominate the other members of society and to enrich themselves at society's expense.

All really serious political, religious, economic reformers

have belonged to the first of the two categories; and among
them there have always been individuals who, without waiting for all their fellow citizens, or even a minority of them,
to be imbued with similar ideas, strove to incite more or less
numerous groups against oppression, or advanced alone if
they had no following. There were revolutionists in all times
known to history.

However, these revolutionists appeared under two different
aspects. Some of them, while rebelling against the authority
that oppressed society, in nowise tried to destroy this authority; they simply strove to secure it for themselves. Instead of
a power that had grown oppressive, they sought to constitute
a new power, of which they would be the holders; and they
promised, often in good faith, that the new authority handed
over to them would have the welfare of the people at heart
and would be their true representative—a promise that later
on was inevitably forgotten or betrayed. Thus were constituted imperial authority in the Rome of the Caesars, ecclesiastical authority in the first centuries of our era, dictatorial
power in the decaying cities of the Middle Ages, and so forth.
The same line of thought brought about royal authority in
Europe at the end of feudal times. Faith in an emperor "for
the people," a Caesar, is not yet dead, even in the present day.

But side by side with this authoritarian current, another
current asserted itself every time the necessity was felt of re-
vising the established institutions. At all times, from ancient
Greece till nowadays, there were individuals and currents of
thought and action that sought, not to replace any particular
authority by another, but to destroy the authority that had
grafted itself on popular institutions, without creating a new
one to take its place. They proclaimed the sovereignty of both
the individual and the people, and they tried to free the popular institutions from authoritarian overgrowths; they worked
to give back full liberty to the collective spirit of the masses,
so that popular genius might freely reconstruct institutions of
mutual aid and protection, in harmony with new needs and
new conditions of existence. In the cities of ancient Greece,
and especially in those of the Middle Ages—Florence, Pskov,
etc.—we find many examples of this kind of conflict.

We may therefore say that Jacobins and anarchists have
existed at all times among reformers and revolutionists.

Formidable popular movements, stamped with the character of anarchism, took place several times in the past. Villages and cities rose against the principle of government, against the supporters of the State, its tribunals, its laws, and they proclaimed the sovereignty of the rights of man. They denied all written law, and asserted that every man should govern himself according to his conscience. They thus tried to found a new society, based on the principles of equality, full liberty, and work. In the Christian movement in Judea, under Augustus, against the Roman law, the Roman State, and the morality, or rather the immorality, of that epoch, there was unquestionably much anarchism. Little by little this movement degenerated into a Church movement, fashioned after the Hebrew Church and Imperial Rome itself, which naturally killed all that Christanity possessed of anarchism at its outset, gave the Christian teachings a Roman form, and soon made of it the mainstay of authority, State, slavery, and oppression. The first seeds of "opportunism" introduced into Christianity are already strong in the four Gospels and the Acts of the Apostles—or, at least, in the versions of the same that are incorporated in the New Testament.

The Anabaptist movement of the sixteenth century, which in the main inaugurated and brought about the Reformation, also had an anarchist basis. But, crushed by those reformers who, under Luther's rule, leagued with princes against the rebellious peasants, the movement was suppressed by a great massacre of peasants and the poorer citizens of the towns. Then the right wing of the reformers degenerated little by little, till it became the compromise between its own conscience and the State that exists today under the name of Protestantism.

Thus, to summarize: Anarchism had its origin in the same creative, constructive activity of the masses that has worked out in times past all the social institutions of mankind—and in the revolts of both the individuals and the nations against the representatives of force, external to these social institutions, who had laid their hands upon these institutions and used them for their own advantage. Those of the rebels whose aim was to restore to the creative genius of the masses the necessary freedom for its creative activity, so that it might

work out the required new institutions, were imbued with the
anarchist spirit.

In our times, anarchy was brought forth by the same critical and revolutionary protest which gave rise to socialism in
general. However, one portion of the socialists, after having
reached the negation of capitalism and of society based on
the subjection of labor to capital, stopped in its development
at this point. They did not declare themselves against what
constitutes the real strength of capitalism: the State and its
principal supports— centralization of authority, law, always
made by a minority for its own profit, and a form of justice
whose chief aim is to protect Authority and capitalism. As to
anarchism, it did not stop in its criticism before these institutions. It lifted its sacrilegious arm not only against capitalism, but also against these pillars of capitalism: Law, Authority, and the State.

A FEW CONCLUSIONS OF ANARCHISM

Such being the leading ideas of anarchism, let us take now
a few concrete illustrations, to show the place that our ideas
occupy in the scientific and social movement of our own
times.

When we are told that we must respect Law (written with
a capital letter), because "Law is Truth expressed in an objective form," or because "the leading steps in the evolution
of Law are the same as those of the evolution of Mind," or
again, because "Law and Morality are identical, and only
differ from each other in form"—we listen to such high-
flown assertions with as little reverence as Mephistopheles
did in Goethe's *Faust*. We know, of course, that those who
wrote them spent much effort of mind before they thus
worded their thoughts, imagining them to be extremely deep;
but we know also that these were nothing but unconscious
attempts at broad generalizations, founded, however, on an
altogether insufficient basis and obscured by words so chosen
as to hypnotize men by their high-style obscurity.

In fact, in ancient times men endeavored to give a divine
origin to Law; later on, they strove to give it a metaphysical
basis; but today we are able to study the origin of the conceptions of Law, and their anthropological development, just
as we are able to study the evolution of weaving or of the

ways of honey-making by the bees. Having now at our disposal the work of the anthropological school, we study the appearance of social customs and conceptions of Law amongst the most primitive savages, and we follow their gradual-development through the codes of different historical periods, down to our own times.

In so doing, we come to the conclusion, already mentioned on one of the preceding pages:—All laws have *a double origin,* and it is precisely this double origin which distinguishes them from customs established by usage and representing the principles of morality existing in a particular society at a particular epoch. Law confirms these customs: it crystallizes them; but at the same time it takes advantage of these generally approved customs, in order to introduce in disguise, under their sanction, some new institution that is entirely to the advantage of the military and governing minorities. For instance, Law introduces, or gives sanction to, slavery, caste, paternal, priestly, and military authority; or else it smuggles in serfdom, and, later on, subjection to the State. By this means, Law has always succeeded in imposing a yoke on man without his perceiving it, a yoke that he has never been able to throw off save by means of revolutions.

Things came to pass in this way from the earliest time till our own; and we see the same going on now, even in the advanced legislation of our own days—in the so-called Labor legislation; because, side by side with the "protection of the worker," which represents their acknowledged aim, these laws surreptitiously insert the idea of *compulsory* arbitration by the State in case of a strike (compulsory arbitration—what a contradiction!); or they interpolate the principle of a compulsory working day of so many hours. They open the door to the military working of railways in case of a strike; they give legal sanction to the oppression of peasants in Ireland, by imposing high prices for the redemption of the land; and so on. And such a system will flourish as long as *part* of society will make laws for the *whole* of society; and by this means they further extend the power of the State, which constitutes the principal prop of capitalism.

As long as laws are made and enforced, the result necessarily will be the same.

We understand, therefore, why anarchism, since Godwin, has disowned all written laws, although the anarchists, more

than any legislators, aspire to justice, which—let us repeat it
—is equivalent to *Equality,* and impossible without it.

When the objection is raised against us that in repudiating
Law we repudiate *Morality,* as we do not recognize the "categorical imperative" about which Kant spoke to us, we answer that the language of this objection is in itself strange and
incomprehensible to our mind.[2] It is just as strange and incomprehensible as it would be to a naturalist who studied
Morality. Before entering into the discussion, we therefore
ask our interlocutors this question: "What do you mean by
this 'categorical imperative'? Cannot you translate your assertion into comprehensible language, as, for example, La-
place used to do when he found the means of expressing the
formulae of higher mathematics in words that every one
understood? All great scientists do that; why do not you do
as much?"

In fact, what is meant when the words "universal law" or
"categorical imperative" are used? Is it that all men accept the
idea: "Do not do to others what you do not want them to do
to you"? If so, very well. Let us begin to study (as Hutchinson
and Adam Smith have done before us) whence came this
moral conception, and how did it develop? Let us then study
in what degree this idea of Justice implies Equality. A very
important question, because only those who consider *others*
as their *equals* can obey the rule: "Do not do to *others* what
you do not wish them to do to you." A serf-owner and a slave
merchant can evidently not recognize the "universal law" or
the "categorical imperative" as regards serfs and negroes,
because they do not look upon them as equals. And if our
remark be correct, let us see whether it is possible to in-
culcate morality while inculcating ideas of inequality.

Let us analyze next, as Guyau did, the "sacrifice of self,"
and, having done that, let us see what were the causes and the
conditions that have most contributed in history to the development of moral sentiment—both of that sentiment which
is expressed in the commandment concerning our neighbor,
and of that other feeling which leads to self-sacrifice. Then
we shall be able to deduce which social conditions and insti-

[2] I am mentioning here an objection that I borrow from a recent correspondence with a German doctor. [Kropotkin's note, as are others in this
extract.]

tutions promise the best results in the future. We shall learn how much religion contributed to it, and how far the economic and political inequalities established by Law hamper it: What is the part contributed towards the development of these feelings by Law, punishments, prisons, judges, jailers, and executioners.

Let us study all this in detail, separately, and then we shall be able to talk, with some practical result, of social morality and of moralization by Law, by tribunals, and by superintendents of police. But high-flown words, which only serve to hide from us the superficiality of our would-be knowledge, had better be left alone. They may have been unavoidable at a certain period of history, though even then their having been useful is very doubtful; but now, fit as we are to undertake the study of the most arduous social questions in exactly the same way as the gardener on the one hand and the physiologist on the other hand, study the most favorable conditions for the growth of a plant—let us do so!

Again, when an economist comes and says to us: "In an absolutely open market the value of goods is measured by the quantity of work socially necessary to produce those goods" (see Ricardo, Proudhon, Marx, and so many others), we do *not* accept this assertion as an article of faith for the reason that it was put forth by a particular authority, or that it may seem to us "devilishly socialistic." "It is possible," we say, "that it is true. But do you not see that, in making this assertion, you maintain that the value and quantity of work necessary are *proportional*, just as the rapidity of a falling body is proportional to the number of seconds that the fall lasts? You thus affirm a certain *quantitative relation* between labor and market value. Very well; but have you, then, made mensurations, observations—*quantitative measures* that alone could confirm a *quantitative* assertion?

You can say that, *broadly speaking*, the exchange value of goods grows if the quantity of necessary work is greater. *This is how Adam Smith expressed himself;* but then he was wise enough to add that under capitalist production the proportionality between exchange value and the amount of necessary labor exists no more. But to jump to the conclusion that *consequently* the two quantities are *proportional*, that one is the measure of the other, and that this is a law of Economics,

is a gross error. As gross as to affirm, for example, that the
quantity of rain that is going to fall tomorrow will be proportional to the quantity of millimeters that the barometer
will have fallen below the average established at a certain
place in a certain season.

The man who first remarked that there was a correlation
between the lower level of the barometer and the quantity of
rain that falls—the man who first remarked that a stone falling from a great height has acquired a greater velocity than a
stone that has only fallen one yard, made scientific discoveries. That is what Adam Smith did as regards Value. But the
man who would come after such a general remark has been
made, and affirm that the quantity of rain fallen *is measured* by the quantity the barometer has fallen below the
average, or else, that the space traversed by a falling stone is
proportional to the duration of the fall and is measured by
it, would be talking nonsense. Besides, he would prove that
scientific methods of research are absolutely strange to him.
He would prove that his writings are *not scientific,* however
full of words borrowed from scientific jargon. But this was
exactly what was done by those who made the above-
mentioned affirmation about Value.

It must be noticed that if the absence of exact numerical
data be alleged as an excuse for the superficial dealing with
economic matters of which we spoke previously—this is no
excuse at all.

In the domain of exact sciences we know very many cases
where two quantities depend upon each other, so that if one
of them increases, the other increases as well—and yet we
know that they are *not* proportional to each other. The
rapidity of growth of a plant certainly depends, among other
causes, upon the quantity of heat it obtains. Both the height
of the sun above the horizon and the average temperature of
every separate day (deduced from many years' observations)
increase every day after March 22. The recoil of a gun increases when we increase the quantity of powder in the
cartridge. And so on.

But where is the man of science who, after having noticed
these relations, would conclude that *consequently* the rapidity
of growth of the plant and the quantity of heat it receives,
the height of the sun above the horizon and the average daily

temperature, the recoil of the gun and the quantity of powder in the cartridge are *proportional?* that, if one of the two increases twice, or thrice, the other will increase at the same ratio? in other words, that *the one is the measure of the other?* A man of science knows that thousands of other relations, besides that of proportionality, may exist between the two quantities; and unless he has made *a number of measurements* that prove that *such* a relation of simple proportionality exists, nobody will ever dare to make such an affirmation.

Yet this is what economists do, when they say that labor *is* the measure of value! Worse than that, they even do not see that they only make a mere *suggestion, a guess.* They boldly affirm that their affirmation is a Law; they even do not understand the need of verifying it by measurements.

In reality, the relations between such quantities as the growth of a plant and the heat it receives, the quantity of powder burned and the recoil of a gun, etc., are too complicated to be expressed by a mere arithmetical proportion. And this is also the case with the relation between Labor and Value. Value in exchange and the necessary Labor are *not proportional to each other;* Labor is *not the measure* of Value, and Adam Smith had already noticed it. After having begun by stating it *was,* he soon noticed that this was true only in the tribal stage of mankind. Under the capitalist system, value in exchange is measured *no more* by the amount of necessary labor. Many other factors come in in a capitalist society, so as to alter the simple relation that may have existed once between labor and exchange value. But modern economists take no heed of that: they go on repeating what Ricardo wrote in the first half of the nineteenth century.

The same remark which we make concerning Value applies to most of the assertions that are made by the economists and the so-called scientific socialists, who continually represent their guesses as "natural laws." Not only do we maintain that most of these would-be "laws" are not correct, but we are certain that those who believe in such "laws" would themselves recognize their mistake as soon as they would realize, as naturalists do, the necessity of submitting every numerical, quantitative statement to a numerical, quantitative test.

All political economy takes, in an anarchist's view, an aspect quite different from the aspect given to it by the economists, who, being unaccustomed to use the scientific, inductive method, even do not realize what a "natural law" is, although they very much like to use this expression. They even do not notice the *conditional* character of all so-called natural laws.

In fact, every natural law always means this:—"*If* such and such conditions are at work, the result will be this and that.—*If* a straight line crosses another line, so as to make equal angles on both its sides at the crossing point, the consequences will be such and such.—*If* those movements only which go on in the interstellar space act upon two bodies, and there is not, at a distance that is not infinitely great, a third, or a fourth body acting upon the two, then the centers of gravity of these two bodies will begin to move towards each other at such a speed" (this is the law of gravitation). And so on.

Always, there is an *if*—a condition to be fulfilled.

Consequently, all the so-called *laws* and theories of political economy are nothing but assertions of the following kind:—

"Supposing that there always are in a given country a considerable number of people who cannot exist one month, or even one fortnight, without earning a salary and accepting for that purpose the conditions that the State will impose upon them (in the shape of taxes, land rent, and so on), or those which will be offered to them by those whom the State recognizes as owners of the soil, the factories, the railways, etc.—such and such consequences will follow."

Up till now, the academic economists have always simply enumerated what happens under such conditions, without specifying and analyzing the conditions themselves. Even if they were mentioned, they were forgotten immediately, to be spoken of no more.

This is bad enough, but there is in their teachings something worse than that. The economists represent *the facts that result from these conditions as laws—as fatal, immutable laws*. And they call that "Science."

As to the socialist political economists, they criticize, it is true, some of the conclusions of the academical economists, or they explain differently certain facts; but all the time they also forget the just-mentioned conditions and give to the economic *facts* of a given epoch too much stability, by representing them as natural *laws*. None of them has yet traced his own way in economic science. The most that was done (by Marx in his *Capital*) was to take the metaphysical definitions of the academical economists, like Ricardo, and to say: "You see, even if we take your own definitions, we can prove that the capitalist exploits the worker!" Which sounds very nice in a pamphlet, but is very far from being Economic Science.

Altogether, we think that to become a science, political economy has to be built up in a different way. It must be treated as a natural science and use the methods used in all exact, empirical sciences; and it must trace for itself a different aim. It must take, with regard to human societies, a position analogous to that which is occupied by Physiology with regard to plants and animals. It must be a Physiology of Society.

Its aim must be the study of the ever-growing sum of *needs* of society, and the *means* used—both formerly and nowadays—for satisfying them. It must see how far these means were, and are now, suitable for the aims that are kept in view. And then—the purpose of each science being prediction and application to the demands of practical life (Bacon said so long since)—Political Economy must study the means of best satisfying the present and future needs with *the least expenditure of energy* (with *economy*), and with the best results for mankind altogether.

It is thus evident why our conclusions are so different in many respects from those arrived at by the economists, both academic and social democratic; why we do not consider as "laws" certain "correlations" indicated by them; why our exposition of socialism is so different from theirs; and why we draw from the study of the tendencies of modern economic life conclusions so different from their conclusions as regards what is desirable and possible; in other words, why we come to free communism, while they come to state capitalism and the collectivist wage system.

It is possible that we are wrong and they are right. But the question as to which of us is right, and which wrong, cannot be settled by means of Byzantine commentaries as to what such or such a writer intended to say, or by talking about what agrees with the "trilogy" of Hegel; most certainly not by continuing to use the dialectic method.

It can be done *only by studying the facts of Economics in the same way and by the same methods as we study natural sciences.*[3]

By using still the same method, the anarchist comes to his own conclusions as regards the different political forms of society, and especially the State. We are not impressed in the least by assertions such as the following: "The State is the affirmation of the idea of supreme Justice in Society," or

[3] The following few abstracts from the letter of a well-known biologist, a Belgian professor, which I received while I was reading the proofs of the French edition of this work, will better explain what is meant by the above lines; the passages in straight brackets [. . .] are added by me:—

"In proportion as I advance in the reading of 'Fields, Factories, and Workshops,' I become more and more convinced that henceforward the study of economic and social questions will only be accessible to those who have studied natural sciences and *are imbued with the spirit of these sciences.* Those who have received the so-called classical education only are incapable of understanding the present movement of ideas, and are equally incapable of studying quite a number of special questions.

". . . The idea of integration of labor, and of *the division of labor in time* [that is, the idea that it would be advantageous for society if every one could work alternately in agriculture, industry, and intellectual pursuits, in order to vary his work and to develop his individuality in all directions], is sure to become one of the cornerstones of economic science. There is a mass of biological facts which are in accordance with the above underlined idea, which show that this is a law of Nature [in other words, that in Nature an economy of energy is often obtained by this means]. If we examine the vital functions of a living being during the different stages of its existence, or even during different seasons, and in some cases during different hours of the day, we find an application of that division of labor in time, which is intimately connected with division of labor between the organs (Adam Smith's law).

"Men of science unacquainted with natural sciences are incapable of understanding the real scope of a Law in Nature; they are blinded by the mere word *law,* and they imagine that a law, like that of Adam Smith, has a fatal force from which it is impossible to escape. When they are shown the other side of this law—i.e., its deplorable results from the point of view of individual development and happiness—they reply: *'This law is inexorable,'* and very often this reply is given with a sharp intonation which shows a feeling of infallibility. But the naturalist knows very well that science knows how to annul the bad effects of a natural *law:* that very often the man who tries to go against Nature achieves his aim.

"Gravity makes physical bodies fall, but the same gravity makes a balloon *rise* [aviation with machines heavier than air is another recent example in point]. For *us* it is so simple; but the economists of the classical school seem to have the greatest trouble in understanding the scope of such an observation.

"The law of *division of labor in time* will be some day the counterpart of the law of Adam Smith, and it will permit us to obtain the integration of work in the individual."

"The State is the Instrument and the Bearer of Progress," or "Without State—no Society."

True to our method, we study the State with the same disposition of mind as if we studied a society of ants or bees, or of birds which have come to nest on the shores of an Arctic lake or sea. To repeat here the conclusions we have come to in consequence of such studies, would be needless. We would have to repeat what has been said by anarchists from the times of Godwin till the present day, and which can be found with all necessary developments in a number of books and pamphlets.

Suffice it for our purpose to say that for *our* European civilization (the civilization of the last fifteen hundred years, to which civilization we belong) the State is a form of society that was developed only since the sixteenth century, and this under the influence of a series of causes that one will find mentioned, for instance, in my essay, "The State: Its Historic Role." Before that, and since the fall of the Roman Empire, the State—in its Roman form—did not exist. If we find it, nevertheless, in historical schoolbooks, even at the outset of the barbarian period, it is a product of the imagination of historians who will draw the genealogical trees of kings—in France, up to the heads of the Merovingian bands, and in Russia, up to Rurik in 862. *Real* historians know that the State was constituted only upon the ruins of the medieval free cities.

On the other side, the State, considered as a political power, State Justice, the Church, and capitalism are facts and conceptions that we cannot separate from each other. In the course of history these institutions have developed, supporting and reinforcing each other.

They are connected with each other—not as mere accidental coincidences. They are linked together by the links of cause and effect.

The State is, for us, a society of mutual insurance between the landlord, the military commander, the judge, the priest, and later on the capitalist, in order to support each other's authority over the people, and for exploiting the poverty of the masses and getting rich themselves.

Such was the origin of the State; such was its history; and such is its present essence.

Consequently, to imagine that capitalism may be abolished
while the State is maintained, and with the aid of the State—
while the latter was founded for forwarding the development
of capitalism and was always growing in power and solidity,
in proportion as the power of capitalism grew up—to cherish
such an illusion is as unreasonable, in our opinion, as it was
to expect the emancipation of Labor from the Church, or
from Cæsarism or imperialism. Certainly, in the first half of
the nineteenth century, there have been many socialists who
had such dreams; but to live in the same dreamland now that
we enter in the twentieth century, is really too childish.

A new form of economic organization will necessarily require a new form or political structure. And, whether the
change be accomplished suddenly, by a revolution, or slowly,
by the way of a gradual evolution, the two changes, political
and economic, must go on abreast, hand in hand.

Each step towards economic freedom, each victory won
over capitalism will be at the same time a step towards political liberty—towards liberation from the yoke of the State by
means of free agreement, territorial, professional, and functional. And each step made towards taking from the State
any one of its powers and attributes will be helping the
masses to win a victory over capitalism.

THE MEANS OF ACTION

It is self-evident that if the anarchists differ so much in their
methods of investigation and in their fundamental principles,
both from the academic men of science and from their social
democratic colleagues, they must equally differ from them
in their means of action.

Holding the opinions we do about Law and the State, we
evidently cannot see a source of progress, and still less an
approach to the required social changes, in an ever-growing
submission of the individual to the State.

We cannot either go on saying, as superficial critics of present society often say when they require the State management of industries, that modern capitalism has its origin in
an "anarchy of production" due to the "non-intervention of
the State" and to the liberal doctrine of "let things alone"
(laissez faire, laissez passer). This would amount to saying

that the State *has* practiced this doctrine, while in reality it never has practiced it. We know, on the contrary, that while all governments have given the capitalists and monopolists full liberty to enrich themselves with the underpaid labor of working men reduced to misery, they have *never, nowhere* given the working men the liberty of opposing that exploitation. Never has any government applied the "leave things alone" principle to the exploited masses. It reserved it for the exploiters only.

In France, even under the terrible "revolutionary" (i.e., Jacobinist) Convention, strikes were treated as a "coalition" —as "a conspiracy to form a State within the State"—and punished with death. So we need not speak after that of the anti-labor legislation of the Napoleonic Empire, the monarchic Restoration, or even the present middle-class Republic.

In England, workingmen were hanged for striking, under the pretext of "intimidation," as late as in 1813; and in 1834 workingmen were transported to Australia for having dared to found, with Robert Owen, a "National Trades' Union." In the "sixties" strikers were sent to hard labor for picketing, under the pretext of thus defending "freedom of labor"; and not further back than 1903, as a result of the Taff Vale decision, the Amalgamated Society of Railway Servants had to pay £26,000 to a railway company for having declared a strike.

Need we speak after that of France, where the right of constituting labor unions and peasant syndicates was obtained only in 1884, after the anarchist agitation that broke out at Lyons and among the miners in 1883; or of Switzerland, where strikers were shot at Airolo during the boring of the St. Gothard tunnel; to say nothing of Germany, Spain, Russia, and the United States, where State intervention in favor of capitalist misrule was still worse?

On the other side, we have only to remember how every State reduces the peasants and the industrial workers to a life of misery, by means of taxes and through the monopolies it creates in favor of the landlords, the cotton lords, the railway magnates, the publicans, and the like. We have only to think how the communal possession of the land was destroyed in this country by enclosure acts, or how at this very moment it is destroyed in Russia, in order to supply "hands" to the landlords and the great factories.

And we need only to look round, to see how everywhere in Europe and America the States are constituting monopolies in favor of capitalists at home, and still more in conquered lands, such as Egypt, Tonkin, the Transvaal, and so on.

What, then, is the use of talking, with Marx, about the "primitive accumulation"—as if this "push" given to capitalists were a thing of the past? In reality, new monopolies have been granted every year till now by the parliaments of all nations to railway, tramway, gas, water, and maritime transport companies, schools, institutions, and so on. The State's "push" is, and has ever been, the first foundation of all great capitalist fortunes.

In short, nowhere has the system of "nonintervention of the State" ever existed. Everywhere the State has been, and still is, the main pillar and the creator, direct and indirect, of capitalism and its powers over the masses. Nowhere, since States have grown up, have the masses had the freedom of resisting the oppression by capitalists. The few rights they have now they have gained only by determination and endless sacrifice.

To speak therefore of "nonintervention of the State" may be all right for middle-class economists, who try to persuade the workers that their misery is "a law of Nature." But—how can socialists use such language? The State has *always* interfered in the economic life in favor of the capitalist exploiter. It has always granted him protection in robbery, given aid and support for further enrichment. *And it could not be otherwise*. To do so was one of the functions—the chief mission—of the State.

The State was established for the precise purpose of imposing the rule of the landowners, the employers of industry, the warrior class, and the clergy upon the peasants on the land and the artisans in the city. And the rich perfectly well know that if the machinery of the State ceased to protect them, their power over the laboring classes would be gone immediately.

Socialism, we have said—whatever form it may take in its evolution towards communism—must find *its own form* of political organization. Serfdom and absolute monarchy have always marched hand in hand. The one rendered the other a necessity. The same is true of capitalist rule, whose political form is representative government, either in a republic or in a monarchy. This is why socialism *cannot* utilize representative government as a weapon for liberating labor, just as it cannot utilize the Church and its theory of divine right, or imperialism and Caesarism, with its theory of hierarchy of functionaries, for the same purpose.

A new form of political organization has to be worked out the moment that socialist principles shall enter into our life. And it is self-evident that this new form will have to be *more popular, more decentralized, and nearer to the folkmote self-government* than representative government can ever be.

This is also the tendency which begins to prevail in the conception of men, the moment they free themselves from the prejudice of authority. If we carefully observe life in this country, in France, and in the States, we see, indeed, a decided tendency towards constituting independent communes, municipal and rural, associations, societies, federations, etc., assuming wide social and economic functions, and connected with each other by free agreement, independent of State intervention. Of course, it is not the German emperor, or the English imperialists, or even the Swiss Jacobin radicals who pursue such aims. These people have their eyes turned backwards. But there is a progressive fraction of society, chiefly among the working men, both in Europe and America, who work hard to create such new channels of common life and work, independent of and quite outside the State.

Knowing all this, we obviously cannot see an element of progress in an ever-increasing submission to the State. On the contrary, we represent ourselves a forward movement of society as an approach to *the abolition of all the authority of government,* as a *development of free agreement* for all that formerly was a function of Church and State, and as a *development of free initiative* in every individual and every group. And these are the tendencies which determine the tactics of the anarchists in the life of both the individual and our circles.

Finally, being a revolutionary party, what we study in history is chiefly the genesis and the gradual development of

previous revolutions. In these studies we try to free history
from the State interpretation which has been given to it by
State historians. We try to reconstitute in it the true role of
of the people, the advantages it obtained from a revolution,
the ideas it launched into circulation, and the faults of tactics
it committed.

Studying the beginnings of a revolution, we are not yet
satisfied when we have read how miserable were the masses
before the revolution. We want to know: how did they pass
from their condition of inactivity and despair to their revolutionary activity? How did they wake up? What did they do
after the awakening?

We understand, for instance, the great French Revolution
quite differently from a Louis Blanc, who saw in it a political
movement directed by the Jacobinist Club. We see in it a
great *popular* movement, which took place especially in the
villages, among the peasants, for the abolition of feudal
servitude and the return to the villages of the lands seized
since 1669 in virtue of enclosure acts; and in the towns—for
getting rid of the misery of the town proletariat by means
of a national organization of exchange and socialization of
production. (See my "Great French Revolution.")

We study the movement towards communism that began
to develop amongst the poorest part of the population in
1793–94, and the admirable forms of voluntary popular
organization for a variety of functions, economic and political, that they worked out in the "Sections" of the great cities
and some of the small municipalities. On the other side, we
carefully study the growth of the power of the middle
classes, who worked with energy and knowledge at constituting their own authority, in lieu of the broken authority of the
king and his *camarilla*. We see how they labored to build up a
powerful centralized State, and thus to consolidate the property they acquired during or through the Revolution, as well
as their full right to enrich themselves with the underpaid
work of the poorer classes. We study the development and
the struggle of these two powers, and try to find out why the
latter gained the upper hand over the former.

And then we see how the centralized State, created by the
Jacobinist middle classes, prepared the way for the autocratic empire of Napoleon I. We see how, half a century
later, Napoleon III found in the dreams of those who meant

to create a centralized republic the necessary elements for his Second Empire. And we understand how this centralized authority, which for seventy years in succession killed in France every local effort and every personal effort made outside the State hierarchy, remains till now the curse of the country. The first effort to be free from it was only made in 1871 by the Paris Communalist proletarians.

It is thus seen how in this domain, too, our comprehension of history and the conclusions we draw therefrom are quite different from the comprehension and the historical conclusions of both the middle-class and the socialist political parties.

Without entering here into an analysis of the different revolutionary movements, it is sufficient to say that our conception of the coming social revolution is quite different from that of a Jacobin dictatorship, or the transformation of social institutions effected by a convention, a parliament, or a dictator. Never has a revolution been brought about on those lines; and if the present working-class movement takes this form, it will be doomed to have no lasting result.

On the contrary, we believe that if a revolution begins, it must take the form of a widely spread popular movement, during which movement, in every town and village invaded by the insurrectionary spirit, the masses set themselves to the work of reconstructing society on new lines. The people—both the peasants and the town workers—must themselves begin the constructive work, on more or less communist principles, without waiting for schemes and orders from above. From the very beginning of the movement they must contrive to house and to feed everyone, and then set to work to produce what is necessary to feed, house, and clothe all of them.

They may not be—they are sure not to be—the *majority* of the nation. But if they are a respectably numerous minority of cities and villages scattered over the country, starting life on their own new socialist lines, they will be able to win the right to pursue their own course. In all probability they will draw towards them a notable portion of the land, as was the case in France in 1793–94.

As to the government, whether it be constituted by force only or by election; be it "the dictatorship of the proletariat," as they used to say in France in the forties, and as they still say in Germany, or else an elected "provisional government," or a "convention"; we put no faith in it. We know beforehand that it will be able to do nothing to accomplish the revolution, so long as the people themselves do not accomplish the change by working out on the spot the necessary new institutions.

We say so, not because we have a personal dislike of governments, but because the whole of history shows us that men thrown into a government by a revolutionary wave have never been able to accomplish what was expected from them. And this is *unavoidable*. Because in the task of reconstructing society on new principles, separate men, however intelligent and devoted they may be, are sure to fail. The collective spirit of the masses is necessary for this purpose. Isolated men can sometimes find the legal expression to sum up the destruction of old social forms—when the destruction is already proceeding. At the utmost, they may widen, perhaps, the sphere of the reconstructive work, extending what is being done in a part of the country, over a larger part of the territory. But to impose the reconstruction by law is absolutely impossible, as was proved, among other examples, by the whole history of the French Revolution. Many thousands of the *laws* passed by the revolutionary Convention had not even been put into force when reaction came and flung those laws into the wastepaper basket.

During a revolution new forms of life will always germinate on the ruins of the old forms, but no government will ever be able to find their expression *so long as these forms will not have taken a definite shape during the work itself of reconstruction*, which must be going on in thousands of spots at the same time. Who guessed—who, in fact, could have guessed—before 1789 the role going to be played by the municipalities and the Commune of Paris in the revolutionary events of 1789–93? It is impossible to legislate for *the future*. All we can do is to vaguely guess its essential tendencies and clear the road for it.

It is evident that in understanding the problem of the social revolution in this way, anarchism cannot let itself be seduced by a program that offers as its aim: "The conquest of the power now in the hands of the State."

We know that this conquest is not possible by peaceful means. The middle class will not give up its power without a struggle. It will resist. And in proportion as socialists will become part of the government, and share power with the middle class, their socialism will grow paler and paler. This is, indeed, what socialism is rapidly doing. Were this not so, the middle classes, who are very much more powerful numerically and intellectually than most socialists imagine them to be, would not share their power with the socialists.

On the other hand, we also know that if an insurrection succeeded in giving to France, to England, or to Germany a provisional socialist government, such a government, without the spontaneous constructive-activity of the people, would be absolutely powerless; and it would soon become a hindrance and a check to the revolution.

In studying the preparatory periods of revolutions, we come to the conclusion that no revolution has had its origin in the power of resistance or the power of attack of a parliament or any other representative body. *All resolutions began among the people.* None has ever appeared armed from head to foot, like Minerva rising from the brain of Jupiter. All had, besides their period of incubation, their period of evolution, during which the masses, after having formulated very modest demands in the beginning, gradually began to conceive the necessity of more and more thorough and deeper changes: they grew more bold and daring in their conceptions of the problems of the moment, they gained confidence, and, having emerged from the lethargy of despair, they widened their program. The "humble remonstrances" they formulated at the outset, grew step by step to be truly revolutionary demands.

In fact, it took France four years, from 1789 to 1793, to create a republican minority that would be strong enough to impose itself.

As to the period of incubation, this is how we understand it. To begin with, isolated individuals, profoundly disgusted by what they saw around them, rebelled separately. Many of them perished without any apparent result; but the indifference of society was shaken. Even those who were most satisfied with existing conditions and the most ignorant were brought by these separate acts of rebellion to ask themselves:

"For what cause did these people, honest and full of energy, rebel and prove ready to give their lives?" Gradually it became impossible to remain indifferent: people were compelled to declare themselves for or against the aims pursued by these individuals. Social thought woke up.

Little by little, small groups of men were imbued with the same spirit of revolt. They also rebelled—sometimes with the hope of a partial success; for example, that of winning a strike and of obtaining bread for their children, or of getting rid of some hated functionary; but very often also without any hope of success: they broke into revolt simply because they could not remain patient any longer. Not one or two such revolts, but hundreds of small insurrections in France and in England preceded the Revolution. *This again was unavoidable.* Without such insurrections, no revolution has ever broken out. Without the menace contained in such revolts, no serious concession has ever been wrung by the people from the governing classes. Without such risings, the social mind was never able to get rid of its deep-rooted prejudices, nor to embolden itself sufficiently to conceive *hope.* And *hope*—the hope of an improvement—was always the mainspring of revolutions.

The *pacific* abolition of serfdom in Russia is often mentioned as a proof of the possibility of a deep change being accomplished without a revolution. But it is forgotten, or ignored, that a long series of peasant insurrections preceded and brought about the abolition of serfdom. These revolts began as early as the fifties, perhaps as an echo of 1848, and every year they spread more and more over Russia, while at the same time they became more and more serious and took a violent character, up till then unknown. This lasted till 1857, when Alexander II at last issued his letter to the nobility of the Lithuanian provinces, containing a promise of liberation to the serfs. The words of Herzen: "Better give liberty from above, than wait till it comes from below"— words repeated by Alexander II before the nobility of Moscow, in 1856—were not a mere menace: *they expressed the real state of affairs.* It was the dread of a peasant uprising, perhaps even more terrible than that of Pugachen in 1773, which induced the serf-owners to yield.

The same has occurred whenever a revolution drew near, and we can safely say that as a general rule the character of each revolution was determined by the character and the purpose of the insurrections that preceded it.

Consequently, to expect a *social* revolution to come like a Christmas box, without being heralded by small acts of revolt and insurrections, is to cherish a vain hope. It would be shutting one's eyes to what *is* going on all round, in Europe and America, and taking no notice of the hundreds of strikes and small uprisings occurring everywhere, and gradually assuming a more widespread and a deeper character.

Benjamin R. Tucker

State Socialism and Libertarianism[1]

Benjamin R. Tucker (1854–1939)   Tucker was born in South Dartmouth, Massachusetts. His interest in anarchist thought came about as a result of early political activity on behalf of Horace Greeley in the 1872 presidential campaign in Boston. There he met Josiah Warren and William B. Greene, individualist anarchists. He studied the anarchist literature and became associate editor of *The Word* in 1874. Shortly after, he was imprisoned for refusing to pay his taxes, and then tried another publishing venture, the *Radical Review,* which lasted only two years. He started the weekly *Liberty.* He published and translated a wide variety of anarchist and libertarian books.

Probably no agitation has ever attained the magnitude, either in the number of its recruits or the area of its influence, which has been attained by modern socialism, and at the same time been so little understood and so misunderstood, not only by the hostile and the indifferent, but by the friendly, and even by the great mass of its adherents themselves. This unfortunate and highly dangerous state of things is due partly to the fact that the human relationships which this movement—if anything so chaotic can be called a movement—aims to transform, involve no special class or classes, but literally all mankind; partly to the fact that these relationships are infinitely more

[1] From Benjamin R. Tucker, *Instead of a Book: A Fragmentary Exposition of Philosophical Anarchism.* New York: B. R. Tucker, Publisher, 1897.

varied and complex in their nature than those with which
any special reform has ever been called upon to deal; and
partly to the fact that the great moulding forces of society,
the channels of information and enlightenment, are well-
nigh exclusively under the control of those whose immediate
pecuniary interests are antagonistic to the bottom claim of
socialism that labor should be put in possession of its own.

Almost the only persons who may be said to comprehend
even approximately the significance, principles, and purposes
of socialism are the chief leaders of the extreme wings of the
socialistic forces, and perhaps a few of the money kings
themselves. It is a subject of which it has lately become quite
the fashion for preacher, professor, and penny-a-liner to
treat, and, for the most part, woeful work they have made
with it, exciting the derision and pity of those competent to
judge. That those prominent in the intermediate socialistic
divisions do not fully understand what they are about is
evident from the positions they occupy. If they did; if they
were consistent, logical thinkers; if they were what the
French call *consequent* men—their reasoning faculties would
long since have driven them to one extreme or the other.

For it is a curious fact that the two extremes of the vast
army now under consideration, though united, as has been
hinted above, by the common claim that labor shall be put in
possession of its own, are more diametrically opposed to
each other in their fundamental principles of social action
and their methods of reaching the ends aimed at than either
is to their common enemy, the existing society. They are
based on two principles the history of whose conflict is almost equivalent to the history of the world since man came
into it; and all intermediate parties, including that of the
upholders of the existing society, are based upon a compromise between them. It is clear, then, that any intelligent,
deep-rooted opposition to the prevailing order of things must
come from one or the other of these extremes, for anything
from any other source, far from being revolutionary in character, could be only in the nature of such superficial modification as would be utterly unable to concentrate upon itself
the degree of attention and interest now bestowed upon
modern socialism.

The two principles referred to are *Authority* and *Liberty*,
and the names of the two schools of socialistic thought which

fully and unreservedly represent one or the other of them are, respectively, State socialism and anarchism. Whoso knows what these two schools want and how they propose to get it understands the socialistic movement. For, just as it has been said that there is no halfway house between Rome and Reason, so it may be said that there is no halfway house between State socialism and anarchism. There are, in fact, two currents steadily flowing from the center of the socialistic forces, which are concentrating them on the left and on the right; and, if socialism is to prevail, it is among the possibilities that, after this movement of separation has been completed and the existing order has been crushed out between the two camps, the ultimate and bitterer conflict will be still to come. In that case all the eight-hour men, all the trades unionists, all the Knights of Labor, all the land nationalizationists, all the greenbackers, and, in short, all the members of the thousand and one different battalions belonging to the great army of labor, will have deserted their old posts, and, these being arrayed on the one side and the other, the great battle will begin. What a final victory for the State socialists will mean, and what a final victory for the anarchists will mean, it is the purpose of this paper to briefly state.

To do this intelligently, however, I must first describe the ground common to both, the features that make socialists of each of them.

The economic principles of modern socialism are a logical deduction from the principle laid down by Adam Smith in the early chapters of his *Wealth of Nations*—namely, that labor is the true measure of price. But Adam Smith, after stating this principle most clearly and concisely, immediately abandoned all further consideration of it to devote himself to showing what actually does measure price, and how, therefore, wealth is at present distributed. Since his day nearly all the political economists have followed his example by confining their function to the description of society as it is in its industrial and commercial phases. Socialism, on the contrary, extends its function to the description of society as it should be, and the discovery of the means of making it what it should be. Half a century or more after Smith enunciated the principle above stated, socialism picked it up where he had dropped it, and, in following it to its logical conclusions, made it the basis of a new economic philosophy.

This seems to have been done independently by three different men, of three different nationalities, in three different languages: Josiah Warren, an American; Pierre J. Proudhon, a Frenchman; Karl Marx, a German Jew. That Warren and Proudhon arrived at their conclusions singly and unaided is certain; but whether Marx was not largely indebted to Proudhon for his economic ideas is questionable. However this may be, Marx's presentation of the ideas was in so many respects peculiarly his own that he is fairly entitled to the credit of orginality. That the work of this interesting trio should have been done so nearly simultaneously would seem to indicate that socialism was in the air, and that the time was ripe and the conditions favorable for the appearance of this new school of thought. So far as priority of time is concerned, the credit seems to belong to Warren, the American—a fact that should be noted by the stump orators who are so fond of declaiming against socialism as an imported article. Of the purest revolutionary blood, too, this Warren, for he descends from the Warren who fell at Bunker Hill.

From Smith's principle that labor is the true measure of price—or, as Warren phrased it, that cost is the proper limit of price—these three men made the following deductions: that the natural wage of labor is its product; that this wage, or product, is the only just source of income (leaving out, of course, gift, inheritance, etc.); that all who derive income from any other source abstract it directly or indirectly from the natural and just wage of labor; that this abstracting process generally takes one of three forms—interest, rent, and profit; that these three constitute the trinity of usury, and are simply different methods of levying tribute for the use of capital; that, capital being simply stored-up labor that has already received its pay in full, its use ought to be gratuitous, on the principle that labor is the only basis of price; that the lender of capital is entitled to its return intact, and nothing more; that the only reason that the banker, the stockholder, the landlord, the manufacturer, and the merchant are able to exact usury from labor lies in the fact that they are backed by legal privilege, or monopoly; and that the only way to secure to labor the enjoyment of its entire product, or natural wage, is to strike down monopoly.

It must not be inferred that either Warren, Proudhon, or

Marx used exactly this phraseology, or followed exactly this line of thought, but it indicates definitely enough the fundamental ground taken by all three, and their substantial thought up to the limit to which they went in common. And, lest I may be accused of stating the positions and arguments of these men incorrectly, it may be well to say in advance that I have viewed them broadly, and that, for the purpose of sharp, vivid, and emphatic comparison and contrast, I have taken considerable liberty with their thought by rearranging it in an order, and often in a phraseology, of my own, but, I am satisfied, without, in so doing, misrepresenting them in any essential particular.

It was at this point—the necessity of striking down monopoly—that came the parting of their ways. Here the road forked. They found that they must turn either to the right or to the left—follow either the path of authority or the path of liberty. Marx went one way; Warren and Proudhon the other. Thus were born State socialism and anarchism.

First, then, State socialism, which may be described as *the doctrine that all the affairs of men should be managed by the government, regardless of individual choice.*

Marx, its founder, concluded that the only way to abolish the class monopolies was to centralize and consolidate all industrial and commercial interests, all productive and distributive agencies, in one vast monopoly in the hands of the State. The government must become banker, manufacturer, farmer, carrier, and merchant, and in these capacities must suffer no competition. Land, tools, and all instruments of production must be wrested from individual hands, and made the property of the collectivity. To the individual can belong only the products to be consumed, not the means of producing them. A man may own his clothes and his food, but not the sewing machine that makes his shirts or the spade that digs his potatoes. Product and capital are essentially different things; the former belongs to individuals, the latter to society. Society must seize the capital that belongs to it, by the ballot if it can, by revolution if it must. Once in possession of it, it must administer it on the majority principle, through its organ, the State, utilize it in production and distribution, fix all prices by the amount of labor involved, and employ the whole people in its workshops, farms, stores, etc. The nation must be transformed into a vast bureaucracy, and every individual into a State official. Everything must be done on the cost principle, the people having no motive to make a profit out of themselves. Individuals not being allowed to own capital, no one can employ another, or even himself. Every man will be a wage-receiver, and the State the only wage-payer. He who will not work for the State must starve, or, more likely, go to prison. All freedom of trade must disappear. Competition must be utterly wiped out. All industrial and commercial activity must be centered in one vast, enormous, all-inclusive monopoly. The remedy for *monopolies* is MONOPOLY.

Such is the economic program of State socialism as adopted from Karl Marx. The history of its growth and progress cannot be told here. In this country the parties that uphold it are known as the Socialistic Labor Party, which pretends to follow Karl Marx; the Nationalists, who follow Karl Marx filtered through Edward Bellamy; and the Christian Socialists, who follow Karl Marx filtered through Jesus Christ.

What other applications this principle of authority, once adopted in the economic sphere, will develop is very evident. It means the absolute control by the majority of all individual conduct. The right of such control is already admitted by the State socialists, though they maintain that, as a matter of fact, the individual would be allowed a much larger liberty than he now enjoys. But he would only be allowed it; he could not claim it as his own. There would be no foundation of society upon a guaranteed equality of the largest possible liberty. Such liberty as might exist would exist by sufferance and could be taken away at any moment. Constitutional guarantees would be of no avail. There would be but one article in the constitution of a State socialistic country: "The right of the majority is absolute."

The claim of the State socialists, however, that this right would not be exercised in matters pertaining to the individual in the more intimate and private relations of his life is not borne out by the history of governments. It has ever been the tendency of power to add to itself, to enlarge its sphere, to encroach beyond the limits set for it; and where the habit of resisting such encroachment is not fostered, and the individual is not taught to be jealous of his rights, individuality gradually disappears and the government or State becomes the all in all. Control naturally accompanies responsibility. Under the system of State socialism, therefore, which holds the community responsible for the health, wealth, and wisdom of the individual, it is evident that the community, through its majority expression, will insist more and more on prescribing the conditions of health, wealth, and wisdom, thus impairing and finally destroying individual independence and with it all sense of individual responsibility.

Whatever, then, the State socialists may claim or disclaim, their system, if adopted, is doomed to end in a State religion, to the expense of which all must contribute and at the altar of which all must kneel; a State school of medicine, by whose practitioners the sick must invariably be treated; a State system of hygiene, prescribing what all must and must not eat, drink, wear, and do; a State code of morals, which will not content itself with punishing crime, but will prohibit what the majority decide to be vice; a State system of instruction, which will do away with all private schools, academies, and colleges; a State nursery, in which all children must be brought up in common at the public expense; and, finally, a State family, with an attempt at stirpiculture, or scientific breeding, in which no man and woman will be allowed to have children if the State prohibits them and no man and woman can refuse to have children if the State orders them. Thus will authority achieve its acme and monopoly be carried to its highest power.

Such is the ideal of the logical State socialist, such is the goal which lies at the end of the road that Karl Marx took. Let us now follow the fortunes of Warren and Proudhon, who took the other road—the road of liberty.

This brings us to anarchism, which may be described as *the doctrine that all the affairs of men should be managed by individuals or voluntary associations, and that the State should be abolished.*

When Warren and Proudhon, in prosecuting their search for justice to labor, came face to face with the obstacle of class monopolies, they saw that these monopolies rested upon authority, and concluded that the thing to be done was, not to strengthen this authority and thus make monopoly universal, but to utterly uproot authority and give full sway to the opposite principle, liberty, by making competition, the antithesis of monopoly, universal. They saw in competition

the great leveller of prices to the labor cost of production.
In this they agreed with the political economists. The query
then naturally presented itself why all prices do not fall to
labor cost; where there is any room for incomes acquired
otherwise than by labor; in a word, why the usurer, the
receiver of interest, rent, and profit, exists. The answer was
found in the present one-sidedness of competition. It was
discovered that capital had so manipulated legislation that
unlimited competition is allowed in supplying productive
labor, thus keeping wages down to the starvation point, or as
near it as practicable; that a great deal of competition is
allowed in supplying distributive labor, or the labor of the
mercantile classes, thus keeping, not the prices of goods, but
the merchants' actual profits on them, down to a point somewhat approximating equitable wages for the merchants'
work; but that almost no competition at all is allowed in
supplying capital, upon the aid of which both productive and
distributive labor are dependent for their power of achievement, thus keeping the rate of interest on money and of
house-rent and ground-rent at as high a point as the necessities of the people will bear.

On discovering this, Warren and Proudhon charged the
political economists with being afraid of their own doctrine.
The Manchester men were accused of being inconsistent.
They believed in liberty to compete with the laborer in order
to reduce his wages, but not in liberty to compete with the
capitalist in order to reduce his usury. *Laissez faire* was very
good sauce for the goose, labor, but very poor sauce for the
gander, capital. But how to correct this inconsistency, how
to serve this gander with this sauce, how to put capital at the
service of business men and laborers at cost, or free of usury,
—that was the problem.

Marx, as we have seen, solved it by declaring capital to be
a different thing from product, and maintaining that it
belonged to society and should be seized by society and
employed for the benefit of all alike. Proudhon scoffed at this
distinction between capital and product. He maintained that
capital and product are not different kinds of wealth, but
simply alternate conditions or functions of the same wealth;
that all wealth undergoes an incessant transformation from
capital into product and from product back into capital, the
process repeating itelf interminably; that capital and product

are purely social terms; that what is product to one man immediately becomes capital to another, and vice versa; that, if there were but one person in the world, all wealth would be to him at once capital and product; that the fruit of A's toil is his product, which when sold to B, becomes B's capital (unless B is an unproductive consumer, in which case it is merely wasted wealth, outside the view of social economy); that a steam engine is just as much product as a coat, and that a coat is just as much capital as a steam engine; and that the same laws of equity govern the possession of the one that govern the possession of the other.

For these and other reasons Proudhon and Warren found themselves unable to sanction any such plan as the seizure of capital by society. But, though opposed to socializing the ownership of capital, they aimed nevertheless to socialize its effects by making its use beneficial to all instead of a means of impoverishing the many to enrich the few. And when the light burst in upon them, they saw that this could be done by subjecting capital to the natural law of competition, thus bringing the price of its use down to cost—that is, to nothing beyond the expenses incidental to handling and transferring it. So they raised the banner of Absolute Free Trade; free trade at home, as well as with foreign countries; the logical carrying out of the Manchester doctrine; *laissez faire* the universal rule. Under this banner they began their fight upon monopolies, whether the all-inclusive monopoly of the State socialists, or the various class monopolies that now prevail.

Of the latter they distinguished four of principal importance: the money monopoly, the land monopoly, the tariff monopoly, and the patent monopoly.

First in the importance of its evil influence they considered the money monopoly, which consists of the privilege given by the government to certain individuals, or to individuals holding certain kinds of property, of issuing the circulating medium, a privilege that is now enforced in this country by a national tax of ten percent upon all other persons who attempt to furnish a circulating medium, and by State laws making it a criminal offence to issue as currency. It is claimed that the holders of this privilege control the rate of interest, the rate of rent of houses and buildings, and the prices of goods—the first directly, and the second and third indirectly.

For, say Proudhon and Warren, if the business of banking were made free to all, more and more persons would enter into it until the competition should become sharp enough to reduce the price of lending money to the labor cost, which statistics show to be less than three-fourths of one percent. In that case the thousands of people who are now deterred from going into business by the ruinously high rates which they must pay for capital with which to start and carry on business will find their difficulties removed. If they have property which they do not desire to convert into money by sale, a bank will take it as collateral for a loan of a certain proportion of its market value at less than one percent discount. If they have no property, but are industrious, honest, and capable, they will generally be able to get their individual notes endorsed by a sufficient number of known and solvent parties; and on such business paper they will be able to get a loan at a bank on similarly favorable terms. Thus interest will fall at a blow. The banks will really not be lending capital at all, but will be doing business on the capital of their customers, the business consisting in an exchange of the known and widely available credits of the banks for the unknown and unavailable, but equally good, credits of the customers, and a charge therefore of less than one percent, not as interest for the use of capital, but as pay for the labor of running the banks. This facility of acquiring capital will give an unheard-of impetus to business, and consequently create an unprecedented demand for labor—a demand that will always be in excess of the supply, directly the contrary of the present condition of the labor market. Then will be seen an exemplification of the words of Richard Cobden that, when two laborers are after one employer, wages fall, but when two employers are after one laborer wages rise. Labor will then be in a position to dictate its wages, and will thus secure its natural wage, its entire product. Thus the same blow that strikes interest down will send wages up. But this is not all. Down will go profits also. For merchants, instead of buying at high prices on credit, will borrow money of the banks at less than one percent, buy at low prices for cash, and correspondingly reduce the prices of their goods to their customers. And with the rest will go house-rent. For no one who can borrow capital at one percent with which to build a house of his own will consent to pay rent to a landlord at a higher rate than that. Such is the vast claim made by Proudhon and Warren as to the results of the simple abolition of the money monopoly.

Second in importance comes the land monopoly, the evil effects of which are seen principally in exclusively agricultural countries, like Ireland. This monopoly consists in the enforcement by government of land titles which do not rest upon personal occupancy and cultivation. It was obvious to Warren and Proudhon that, as soon as individuals should no longer be protected by their fellows in anything but personal occupancy and cultivation of land, ground-rent would disappear, and so usury have one less leg to stand on. Their followers of today are disposed to modify this claim to the extent of admitting that the very small fraction of ground-rent which rests, not on monopoly, but on superiority of soil or site, will continue to exist for a time and perhaps forever, though tending constantly to a minimum under conditions of freedom. But the inequality of soils which gives rise to the economic rent of land, like the inequality of human skill which gives rise to the economic rent of ability, is not a cause for serious alarm even to the most thorough opponent of usury, as its nature is not that of a germ from which other and graver inequalities may spring, but rather that of a decaying branch which may finally wither and fall.

Third, the tariff monopoly, which consists in fostering production at high prices and under unfavorable conditions by visiting with the penalty of taxation those who patronize production at low prices and under favorable conditions. The evil to which this monopoly gives rise might more properly be called *mis*usury than usury, because it compels labor to pay, not exactly for the use of capital, but rather for the misuse of capital. The abolition of this monopoly would result in a great reduction in the prices of all articles taxed, and this saving to the laborers who consume these articles would be another step toward securing to the laborer his natural wage, his entire product. Proudhon admitted, however, that to abolish this monopoly before abolishing the money monopoly would be a cruel and disastrous policy, first, because the evil of scarcity of money, created by the money monopoly, would be intensified by the flow of money out of the country that would be involved in an excess of imports over exports, and, second, because that fraction of the laborers of the country which is now employed in the protected industries would be turned adrift to face starvation without the benefit of the insatiable demand for labor which a competitive money system would create. Free trade in money at home, making money and work abundant, was insisted upon by Proudhon as a prior condition of free trade in goods with foreign countries.

Fourth, the patent monopoly, which consists in protecting inventors and authors against competition for a period long enough to enable them to extort from the people a reward enormously in excess of the labor measure of their services— in other words, in giving certain people a right of property for a term of years in laws and facts of Nature, and the power to exact tribute from others for the use of this natural wealth, which should be open to all. The abolition of this monopoly would fill its beneficiaries with a wholesome fear of competition that would cause them to be satisfied with pay for their services equal to that which other laborers get for theirs, and to secure it by placing their products and works on the market at the outset at prices so low that their lines of business would be no more tempting to competitors than any other lines.

The development of the economic program that consists in the destruction of these monopolies and the substitution for them of the freest competition led its authors to a perception of the fact that all their thought rested upon a very fundamental principle, the freedom of the individual, his right of sovereignty over himself, his products, and his affairs, and of rebellion against the dictation of external authority. Just as the idea of taking capital away from individuals and giving it to the government started Marx in a path that ends in making the government everything and the individual nothing, so the idea of taking capital away from government-protected monopolies and putting it within easy reach of all individuals started Warren and Proudhon in a path that ends in making the individual everything and the government nothing. If the individual has a right to govern himself, all external government is tyranny. Hence the necessity of abolishing the State. This was the logical conclusion to which Warren and Proudhon were forced, and it became the fundamental article of their political philosophy. It is the doctrine that Proudhon named "an-archism," a word derived from the Greek, and meaning not necessarily absence of order, as it generally sup-

posed, but absence of rule. The anarchists are simply unter-
rified Jeffersonian Democrats. They believe that "the best
government is that which governs least," and that that which
governs least is no government at all. Even the simple police
function of protecting person and property they deny to
governments supported by compulsory taxation. Protection
they look upon as a thing to be secured, as long as it is necessary, by voluntary association and cooperation for self-
defence, or as a commodity to be purchased, like any other
commodity, of those who offer the best article at the lowest
price. In their view it is in itself an invasion of the individual
to compel him to pay for or suffer a protection against
invasion that he has not asked for and does not desire.
And they further claim that protection will become a drug in
the market, after poverty and consequently crime have disappeared through the realization of their economic program. Compulsory taxation is to them the life-principle of
all the monopolies, and passive, but organized, resistance to
the tax collector they contemplate, when the proper time
comes, as one of the most effective methods of accomplishing
their purposes.

Their attitude on this is a key to their attitude on all other
questions of a political or social nature. In religion they are
atheistic as far as their own opinions are concerned, for they
look upon divine authority and the religious sanction of
morality as the chief pretexts put forward by the privileged
classes for the exercise of human authority. "If God exists,"
said Proudhon, "he is man's enemy." And, in contrast to
Voltaire's famous epigram, "If God did not exist, it would be
necessary to invent him," the great Russian Nihilist, Michael
Bakounine, placed this antithetical proposition: "If God existed, it would be necessary to abolish him." But although,
viewing the devine hierarchy as a contradiction of anarchy,
they do not believe in it, the anarchists nonetheless firmly
believe in the liberty to believe in it. Any denial of religious
freedom they squarely oppose.

Upholding thus the right of every individual to be or select
his own priest, they likewise uphold his right to be or select
his own doctor. No monopoly in theology, no monopoly in
medicine. Competition everywhere and always; spiritual advice and medical advice alike to stand or fall on their own
merits. And not only in medicine, but in hygiene, must this

principle of liberty be followed. The individual may decide for himself not only what to do to get well, but what to do to keep well. No external power must dictate to him what he must and must not eat, drink, wear, or do.

Nor does the anarchistic scheme furnish any code of morals to be imposed upon the individual. "Mind your own business" is its only moral law. Interference with another's business is a crime and the only crime, and as such may properly be resisted. In accordance with this view the anarchists look upon attempts to arbitrarily suppress vice as in themselves crimes. They believe liberty and the resultant social well-being to be a sure cure for all the vices. But they recognize the right of the drunkard, the gambler, the rake, and the harlot to live their lives until they shall freely choose to abandon them.

In the matter of the maintenance and rearing of children the anarchists would neither institute the communistic nursery which the State socialists favor nor keep the communistic school system which now prevails. The nurse and the teacher, like the doctor and the preacher, must be selected voluntarily, and their services must be paid for by those who patronize them. Parental rights must not be taken away, and parental responsibilities must not be foisted upon others.

Even in so delicate a matter as that of the relations of the sexes the anarchists do not shrink from the application of their principle. They acknowledge and defend the right of any man and woman, or any men and women, to love each other for as long or as short a time as they can, will, or may. To them legal marriage and legal divorce are equal absurdities. They look forward to a time when every individual, whether man or woman, shall be self-supporting, and when each shall have an independent home of his or her own, whether it be a separate house or rooms in a house with others; when the love relations between these independent individuals shall be as varied as are individual inclinations and attractions; and when the children born of these relations shall belong exclusively to the mothers until old enough to belong to themselves.

Such are the main features of the Anarchistic social ideal.

Rudolf Rocker The Ideology of Anarchism[1]

Rudolf Rocker (1873–1958)   Rocker was born in Mainz, Germany, son of a workingman who died when the boy was five years of age. It was an uncle who introduced him to the German Social Democratic movement, but he was soon disappointed by the rigidities of German socialism. As a bookbinder, he wandered from one employment to another, and, from the contacts he made in this occupation, he became interested in anarchism. He lived in Paris and in London until after World War I. Although of Christian background, he identified himself with the Jewish and Slavic immigrants who settled in East London. He edited a Yiddish newspaper, *Arbeiter Freund,* and a Yiddish literary monthly, *Germinal.* He contributed his organizing efforts to the Jewish labor unions in England. Interned as an enemy alien in England in 1914, Rocker and his wife left England upon their release. In 1919 he returned to Germany. With the rise of Nazism he fled to the United States. He is the author of a biography of Johann Most. His most widely read book was *Nationalism and Culture,* published in 1937.

Anarchism is a definite intellectual current of social thought, whose adherents advocate the abolition of economic monopolies and of all political and social coercive institutions within society. In place of the capitalist economic order, anarchists would have a free association of all productive forces based upon co-operative labor, which would have for its sole purpose the satisfying of the necessary requirements of every member of society. In place of the present national states with their lifeless machinery of political and bureaucratic institutions, anarchists desire a federation of free communities that shall be bound to one another by their common economic and social interests and arrange their affairs by mutual agreement and free contract.

[1] From "Anarchism and Anarcho-Syndicalism" by Rudolf Rocker, in *European Ideologies: A Survey of Twentieth-Century Political Ideas.* Edited by Feliks Gross. N.Y.: Philosophical Library, Copyright © 1961. Reprinted by permission of the publisher.

Anyone who studies profoundly the economic and political development of the present social system will recognize that these objectives do not spring from the utopian ideas of a few imaginative innovators, but that they are the logical outcome of a thorough examination of existing social maladjustments, which, with every new phase of the present social conditions, manifest themselves more plainly and more unwholesomely. Modern monopoly-capitalism and the totalitarian state are merely the last stages in a development which could culminate in no other end.

The portentous development of our present economic system, leading to a mighty accumulation of social wealth in the hands of privileged minorities and to a constant repression of the great masses of the people, prepared the way for the present political and social reaction and befriended it in every way. It sacrificed the general interests of human society to the private interests of individuals, and thus systematically undermined a true relationship between men. People forgot that industry is not an end in itself, but should be only a means to insure to man his material subsistence and to make accessible to him the blessings of a higher intellectual culture. Where industry is everything, where labor loses its ethical importance and man is nothing, there begins the realm of ruthless economic despotism, whose workings are no less disastrous than those of any political despotism. The two mutually augment one another; they are fed from the same source.

Our modern social system has internally split the social organism of every country into hostile classes, and externally it has broken up the common cultural circle into hostile nations; both classes and nations confront one another with open antagonism, and by their ceaseless warfare keep the communal social life in continual convulsions. Two world wars within half a century and their terrible after effects, and the constant danger of new wars, which today dominates all peoples, are only the logical consequences of this unendurable condition which can only lead to further universal catastrophes. The mere fact that most states are obliged today to spend the better part of their annual income for so-called national defense and the liquidation of old war debts is proof of the untenability of the present status; it should make clear to everybody that the alleged protection that the state affords the individual is certainly purchased too dearly.

The ever-growing power of a soulless political bureaucracy that supervises and safeguards the life of man from the cradle to the grave is putting ever-greater obstacles in the way of cooperation among human beings. A system that in every act of its life sacrifices the welfare of large sections òf the people, of whole nations, to the selfish lust for power and the economic interests of small minorities must necessarily dissolve the social ties and lead to a constant war of each against all. This system has merely been the pacemaker for the great intellectual and social reaction that finds its expression today in modern fascism and the idea of the totalitarian State, far surpassing the obsession for power of the absolute monarchy of past centuries and seeking to bring every sphere of human activity under the control of the State. "All for the State; all through the State; nothing without the State!" became the *leitmotif* of a new political theology. As in various systems of ecclesiastical theology God is everything and man nothing, so for this modern political creed the State is everything and the citizen nothing. And just as the words the *"will of God"* were used to justify the will of privileged castes, so today there hides behind the *will of the State* only the selfish interests of those who feel called upon to interpret this will in their own sense and to force it upon the people.

In modern anarchism we have the confluence of the two great currents that before and since the French Revolution have found such characteristic expression in the intellectual life of Europe: socialism and liberalism. Modern socialism developed when profound observers of social life came to see more and more clearly that political constitutions and changes in the form of government could never get to the root of the great problem that we call the "social question." Its supporters recognized that an equalizing of social and economic conditions for the benefit of all, despite the loveliest of theoretical assumptions, is not possible so long as people are separated into classes on the basis of their owning or not owning property, classes whose mere existence excludes in advance any thought of a genuine community. And so there developed the conviction that only by the elimination of economic monopolies and by common ownership of the means of production does a condition of social justice become feasible, a condition in which society shall become a real

community, and human labor shall no longer serve the ends
of exploitation but assure the well-being of everyone. But as
soon as socialism began to assemble its forces and become a
movement, there at once came to light certain differences of
opinion due to the influence of the social environment in
different countries. It is a fact that every political concept
from theocracy to Caesarism and dictatorship have affected
certain factions of the socialist movement.

Meanwhile, two other great currents in political thought
had a decisive significance on the development of socialist
ideas: liberalism, which had powerfully stimulated advanced
minds in the Anglo-Saxon countries, Holland and Spain in
particular, and Democracy in the sense, to which Rousseau
gave expression in his *Social Contract*, and which found its
most influential representatives in the leaders of French
Jacobinìsm. While liberalism in its social theories started off
from the individual and wished to limit the State's activities
to a minimum, democracy took its stand on an abstract collective concept, Rousseau's *general will*, which it sought to
fix in the national state. Liberalism and democracy were preeminently political concepts, and since most of the original
adherents of both did scarcely consider the economic conditions of society, the further development of these conditions
could not be practically reconciled with the original principles of democracy, and still less with those of liberalism.
Democracy with its motto of *equality of all citizens before
the law,* and liberalism with its *right of man over his own
person,* both were wrecked on the realities of capitalist economy. As long as millions of human beings in every country
have to sell their labor to a small minority of owners, and
sink into the most wretched misery if they can find no
buyers, the so-called equality before the law remains merely
a pious fraud, since the laws are made by those who find
themselves in possession of the social wealth. But in the same
way there can be no talk of a right over one's own person,
for that right ends when one is compelled to submit to the
economic dictation of another if one does not want to starve.

In common with liberalism, anarchism represents the idea
that the happiness and prosperity of the individual must be
the standard in all social matters. And, in common with the
great representatives of liberal thought, it has also the idea of
limiting the functions of government to a minimum. Its ad-

herents have followed this thought to its ultimate consequences, and wish to eliminate every institution of political power from the life of society. When Jefferson clothes the basic concept of liberalism in the words: "That government is best which governs least," then anarchists say with Thoreau: "That government is best which governs not at all."

In common with the founders of socialism, anarchists demand the abolition of economic monopoly in every form and shape and uphold common ownership of the soil and all other means of production, the use of which must be available to all without distinction; for personal and social freedom is conceivable only on the basis of equal economic conditions for everybody. Within the socialist movement itself the anarchists represent the viewpoint that the struggle against capitalism must be at the same time a struggle against all coercive institutions of political power, for in history economic exploitation has always gone hand in hand with political and social oppression. The exploitation of man by man and the domination of man over man are inseparable, and each is the condition of the other.

As long as a possessing and a nonpossessing group of human beings face one another in enmity within society, the State will be indispensible to the possessing minority for the protection of its privileges. When this condition of social injustice vanishes to give place to a higher order of things, which shall recognize no special rights and shall have as its basic assumption the community of social interests, government over men must yield the field to the administration of economic and social affairs, or, to speak with Saint-Simon: "The time will come when the art of governing men will disappear. A new art will take its place, the art of administering things." In this respect anarchism has to be regarded as a kind of voluntary socialism.

This disposes also of the theory maintained by Marx and his followers that the State, in the form of a proletarian dictatorship, is a necessary transitional stage to a classless society, in which the State, after the elimination of all class conflicts and then the classes themselves, will dissolve itself and vanish from the canvas. For this concept, which completely mistakes the real nature of the State and the significance in history of the factor of political power, is only the logical outcome of so-called economic materialism, which sees in all the phenomena of history merely the inevitable effects of the methods of production of the time. Under the influence of this theory people came to regard the different forms of the State and all other social institutions as a "juridical and political superstructure on the economic edifice" of society, and thought that they had found in it the key to every historic process. In reality every section of history affords us thousands of examples of the way in which the economic development of countries was set back for centuries by the State and its power policy.

Before the rise of the ecclesiastical monarchy, Spain, industrially, was the most advanced country in Europe and held the first place in economic production in almost every field. But a century after the triumph of the Christian monarchy most of its industries had disappeared; what was left of them survived only in the most wretched condition. In most industries they had reverted to the most primitive methods of production. Agriculture collapsed, canals and waterways fell into ruin, and vast stretches of the country were transformed into deserts. Princely absolutism in Europe, with its silly "economic ordinances" and "industrial legislation," which severely punished any deviation from the prescribed methods of production and permitted no new inventions, blocked industrial progress in European countries for centuries, and prevented its natural development. And even now after the horrible experiences of two world wars, the power policy of the larger national states proves to be the greatest obstacle to the reconstruction of European economy.

In Russia, however, where the so-called dictatorship of the proletariat has ripened into reality, the aspirations of a particular party for political power have prevented any truly socialistic reorganization of economic life and have forced the country into the slavery of a grinding State Capitalism. The proletarian dictatorship, which naïve souls believe is an inevitable transition stage to real socialism, has today grown into a frightful despotism and a new imperialism, which lags behind the tyranny of fascist states in nothing. The assertion that the State must continue to exist until society is no longer divided into hostile classes almost sounds, in the light of all historical experience, like a bad joke.

Every type of political power presupposes some particular form of human slavery, for the maintenance of which it is

called into being. Just as outwardly, that is, in relation to
other states, the State has to create certain artificial antagonisms in order to justify its existence, so also internally the
cleavage of society into castes, ranks and classes is an essential condition of its continuance. The development of the
Bolshevist bureaucracy in Russia under the alleged dictatorship of the proletariat—which has never been anything but
the dictatorship of a small clique *over* the proletariat and the
whole Russian people—is merely a new instance of an old
historical experience that has repeated itself countless times.
This new ruling class, which today is rapidly growing into a
new aristocracy, is set apart from the great masses of the
Russian peasants and workers just as clearly as are the privileged castes and classes in other countries from the mass of
the people. And this situation becomes still more unbearable
when a despotic State denies to the lower classes the right to
complain of existing conditions, so that any protest is made
at the risk of their lives.

But even a far greater degree of economic equality than
that which exists in Russia would be no guarantee against
political and social oppression. Economic equality alone is
not social liberation. It is precisely this which all the schools
of authoritarian socialism have never understood. In the
prison, in the cloister, or in the barracks one finds a fairly
high degree of economic equality, as all the inmates are provided with the same dwelling, the same food, the same uniform, and the same tasks. The ancient Inca state in Peru and
the Jesuit state in Paraguay had brought equal economic
provision for every inhabitant to a fixed system, but in spite
of this the vilest despotism prevailed there, and the human
being was merely the automation of a higher will on whose
decisions he had not the slightest influence. It was not without reason that Proudhon saw in a "socialism" without freedom the worst form of slavery. The urge for social justice
can only develop properly and be effective when it grows out
of man's sense of freedom and responsibility, and is based
upon it. In other words, *socialism will be free or it will not be
at all*. In its recognition of this fact lies the genuine and profound justification of anarchism.

Institutions serve the same purpose in the life of society
as physical organs do in plants and animals; they are the organs of the social body. Organs do not develop arbitrarily,

but owe their origin to definite necessities of the physical and social environment. Changed conditions of life produce changed organs. But an organ always performs the function it was evolved to perform, or a related one. And it gradually disappears or becomes rudimentary as soon as its function is no longer necessary to the organism.

The same is true of social institutions. They, too, do not arise arbitrarily, but are called into being by special social needs to serve definite purposes. In this way the modern State was evolved, after economic privileges and class divisions associated with them had begun to make themselves more and more conspicuous in the framework of the old social order. The newly-arisen possessing classes had need of a political instrument of power to maintain their economic and social privileges over the masses of their own people, and to impose them from without on other groups of human beings. Thus arose the appropriate social conditions for the evolution of the modern State as the organ of political power for the forcible subjugation and oppression of the non-possessing classes. This task is the essential reason for its existence. Its external forms have altered in the course of its historical development, but its functions have always re-mained the same. They have even constantly broadened in just the measure in which its supporters have succeeded in making further fields of social activities subservient to their ends. And, just as the functions of a physical organ cannot be arbitrarily altered so that, for example, one cannot, at will, hear with one's eyes or see with one's ears, so also one cannot, at pleasure, transform an organ of social oppression into an instrument for the liberation of the oppressed.

Anarchism is no patent solution for all human problems, no Utopia of a perfect social order (as it has so often been called), since, on principle, it rejects all absolute schemes and concepts. It does not believe in any absolute truth, or in any definite final goals for human development, but in an un-limited perfectibility of social patterns and human living conditions, which are always straining after higher forms of expression, and to which, for this reason, one cannot assign any definite terminus nor set any fixed goal. The greatest evil of any form of power is just that it always tries to force the rich diversity of social life into definite forms and adjust it to particular norms. The stronger its supporters feel them-

selves, the more completely they succeed in bringing every
field of social life into their service, the more crippling is their
influence on the operation of all creative cultural forces, the
more unwholesomely does it affect the intellectual and social
development of power and a dire omen for our times, for it
shows with frightful clarity to what a monstrosity Hobbes'
Leviathan can be developed. It is the perfect triumph of the
political machine over mind and body, the rationalization
of human thought, feeling and behavior according to the established rules of the officials and, consequently, the end of
all true intellectual culture.

Anarchism recognizes only the relative significance of
ideas, institutions, and social conditions. It is, therefore not
a fixed, self-enclosed social system, but rather a definite trend
in the historical development of mankind, which, in contrast
with the intellectual guardianship of all clerical and governmental institutions, strives for the free unhindered unfolding
of all the individual and social forces in life. Even freedom is
only a relative, not an absolute concept, since it tends constantly to broaden its scope and to affect wider circles in
manifold ways. For the anarchist, freedom is not an abstract
philosophical concept, but the vital concrete possibility for
every human being to bring to full development all capacities
and talents with which nature has endowed him, and turn
them to social account. The less this natural development of
man is interfered with by ecclesiastical or political guardianship, the more efficient and harmonious will human personality become, the more will it become the measure of the
intellectual culture of the society in which it has grown. This
is the reason that all great culture periods in history have
been periods of political weakness, for political systems are
always set upon the mechanizing and not the organic development of social forces. State and Culture are irreconcilable opposites. Nietzsche, who was not an anarchist,
recognized this very clearly when he wrote: "No one can
finally spend more than he has. That holds good for individuals; it holds good for peoples. If one spends oneself for
power, for higher politics, for husbandry, for commerce,
parliamentarism, military interests—if one gives away that
amount of reason, earnestness, will, self-mastery which constitutes one's real self for one thing—he will not have it for
the other. Culture and the State—let no one be deceived

about this—are antagonists: the *Culture State* is merely a modern idea. The one lives on the other, the one prospers at the expense of the other. All great periods of culture are periods of political decline. Whatever is great in a cultured sense is nonpolitical, is even antipolitical."

Where the influence of political power on the creative forces in society is reduced to a minimum, there culture thrives the best, for political rulership always strives for uniformity and tends to subject every aspect of social life to its guardianship. And, in this, it finds itself in inescapable contradiction to the creative aspirations of cultural development, which is always on the quest for new forms and fields of social activity, and for which freedom of expression, the many-sidedness and the continual changing of things, are just as vitally necessary as rigid forms, dead rules, and the forcible suppression of ideas are for the conservation of political power. Every successful piece of work stirs the desire for greater perfection and deeper inspiration; each new form becomes the herald of new possibilities of development. But power always tries to keep things as they are, safely anchored to stereotypes. That has been the reason for all revolutions in history. Power operates only destructively, bent always on forcing every manifestation of social life into the straitjacket of its rules. Its intellectual expression is dead dogma, its physical form brute force. And this unintelligence of its objectives sets its stamp on its representatives also, and renders them often stupid and brutal, even when they were originally endowed with the best talents. One who is constantly striving to force everything into a mechanical order at last becomes a machine himself and loses all human feelings.

It was from this understanding that modern anarchism was born and draws its moral force. Only freedom can inspire men to great things and bring about intellectual and social transformations. The art of ruling men has never been the art of educating and inspiring them to a new shaping of their lives. Dreary compulsion has at its command only lifeless drill, which smothers any vital initiative at its birth and brings forth only subjects, not free men. Freedom is the very essence of life, the impelling force in all intellectual and social development, the creator of every new outlook for the future of mankind. The liberation of man from economic

exploitation and from intellectual, social, and political oppression, which finds its highest expression in the philosophy
of anarchism, is the first prerequisite for the evolution of a
higher social culture and a new humanity.

section two

Anarchism
as a Style
of Life

Joseph Conrad
The Inspector and the Professor[1]

Joseph Conrad (1857–1924) Conrad's biography is a remarkable
one for a writer. He was born in the Ukraine in 1857 and was
the son of a poet and revolutionist. He spent most of his youth
at sea. He first learned English at the age of twenty, laboriously
from newspapers. He lived to become a great novelist and a
master stylist of the English language, spending most of his
adult life in England. He wrote nothing until the age of thirty-
two. As a personality, he was a nervous, abrupt, introverted
man with few friends. Writing was a painful and agonizing
process for him. He has never been a popular writer, but he
was a master. There are a great many studies on his life and
work. Some of his best known works are: *An Outcast of the
Islands, The Nigger of the "Narcissus," Lord Jim, Nostromo,
The Rover, The Secret Agent.*

The Professor had turned into a
street to the left, and walked along, with his head carried
rigidly erect, in a crowd whose every individual almost overtopped his stunted stature. It was vain to pretend to himself
that he was not disappointed. But that was mere feeling; the
stoicism of his thought could not be disturbed by this or any

---

[1] From *The Secret Agent* by Joseph Conrad. Copyright 1907 by J. M. Dent
& Sons Ltd. Reprinted by permission of the publishers.

other failure. Next time, or the time after next, a telling
stroke would be delivered—something really startling—a
blow fit to open the first crack in the imposing front of the
great edifice of legal conceptions sheltering the atrocious injustice of society. Of humble origin, and with an appearance
really so mean as to stand in the way of his considerable
natural abilities, his imagination had been fired early by the
tales of men rising from the depths of poverty to positions
of authority and affluence. The extreme, almost ascetic purity of his thought, combined with an astounding ignorance
of worldly conditions, had set before him a goal of power
and prestige to be attained without the medium of arts,
graces, tact, wealth—by sheer weight of merit alone. On that
view he considered himself entitled to undisputed success.
His father, a delicate dark enthusiast with a sloping forehead, had been an itinerant and rousing preacher of some
obscure but rigid Christian sect—a man supremely confident
in the privileges of his righteousness. In the son, individualist
by temperament, once the science of colleges had replaced
thoroughly the faith of conventicles, this moral attitude
translated itself into a frenzied puritanism of ambition. He
nursed it as something secularly holy. To see it thwarted
opened his eyes to the true nature of the world, whose morality was artificial, corrupt, and blasphemous. The way of
even the most justifiable revolutions is prepared by personal
impulses disguised into creeds. The Professor's indignation
found in itself a final cause that absolved him from turning
to destruction as the agent of his ambition. To destroy public
faith in legality was the imperfect formula of his pedantic
fanaticism; but the subconscious conviction that the framework of an established social order cannot be effectually
shattered except by some form of collective or individual
violence was precise and correct. He was a moral agent—
that was settled in his mind. By exercising his agency with
ruthless defiance he procured for himself the appearances
of power and personal prestige. That was undeniable to his
vengeful bitterness. It pacified its unrest; and in their own
way the most ardent of revolutionaries are, perhaps, doing
no more but seeking for peace in common with the rest of
mankind—the peace of soothed vanity, of satisfied appetites,
or, perhaps, of appeased conscience.

Lost in the crowd, miserable and undersized, he medi-

tated confidently on his power, keeping his hand in the left
pocket of his trousers, grasping lightly the india-rubber ball,
the supreme guarantee of his sinister freedom; but after a
while he became disagreeably affected by the sight of the
roadway thronged with vehicles and of the pavement
crowded with men and women. He was in a long, straight
street, peopled by a mere fraction of an immense multitude;
but all round him, on and on, even to the limits of the horizon hidden by the enormous piles of bricks, he felt the mass
of mankind mighty in its numbers. They swarmed numerous
like locusts, industrious like ants, thoughtless like a natural
force, pushing on blind and orderly and absorbed, impervious to sentiment, to logic—to terror, too, perhaps.

That was the form of doubt he feared most. Impervious
to fear! Often while walking abroad, when he happened also
to come out of himself, he had such moments of dreadful
and sane mistrust of mankind. What if nothing could move
them? Such moments come to all men whose ambition aims
at a direct grasp upon humanity—to artists, politicians,
thinkers, reformers, or saints. A despicable emotional state
this, against which solitude fortifies a superior character; and
with severe exultation the Professor thought of the refuge of
his room, with its padlocked cupboard, lost in a wilderness of
poor houses, the hermitage of the perfect anarchist. In order
to reach sooner the point where he could take his omnibus,
he turned brusquely out of the populous street into a narrow
and dusky alley paved with flagstones. On one side the low
brick houses had in their dusty windows the sightless, mori-
bund look of incurable decay—empty shells awaiting demo-
lition. From the other side life had not departed wholly as
yet. Facing the only gas lamp yawned the cavern of a
second-hand furniture dealer, where, deep in the gloom of a
sort of narrow avenue winding through a bizarre forest of
wardrobes, with an undergrowth tangle of table legs, a tall
pier-glass glimmered, like a pool of water in a wood. An
unhappy, homeless couch, accompanied by two unrelated
chairs, stood in the open. The only human being making use
of the alley, besides the Professor, coming stalwart and erect
from the opposite direction checked his swinging pace
suddenly.

"Halloo!" he said, and stood a little on one side watchfully.

The Professor had already stopped, with a ready half-turn

which brought his shoulders very near the other wall. His
right hand fell lightly on the back of the outcast couch, the
left remained purposefully plunged deep in the trousers-
pocket, and the roundness of the heavy rimmed spectacles
imparted an owlish character to his moody, unperturbed
face.

It was like a meeting in a side corridor of a mansion full
of life. The stalwart man was buttoned up in a dark overcoat, and carried an umbrella. His hat, tilted back, uncovered a good deal of forehead, which appeared very white
in the dusk. In the dark patches of the orbits the eyeballs
glimmered piercingly. A long, drooping mustache, the color
of ripe corn, framed with its points the square block of his
shaved chin.

"I am not looking for you," he said, curtly.

The Professor did not stir an inch. The blended noises of
the enormous town sank down to an inarticulate, low murmur. Chief Inspector Heat, of the Special Crimes Department, changed his tone.

"Not in a hurry to get home?" he asked, with mocking
simplicity.

The unwholesome-looking little moral agent of destruction
exulted silently in the possession of personal prestige, keeping in check this man armed with the defensive mandate of a
menaced society. More fortunate than Caligula, who wished
that the Roman Senate had only one head for the better satisfaction of his cruel lust, he beheld in that one man all the
forces he had set at defiance: the force of law, property, oppression, and injustice. He beheld all his enemies, and fear-
lessly confronted them all in a supreme satisfaction of his
vanity. They stood perplexed before him as if before a
dreadful portent. He gloated inwardly over the chance of this
meeting affirming his superiority to the multitude of
mankind.

It was in reality a chance meeting. Chief Inspector Heat
had had a disagreeably busy day since his department received the first telegram from Greenwich a little after eleven
in the morning. First of all, the fact of the outrage being
attempted less than a week after he had assured a high
official that no outbreak of anarchist activity was to be apprehended was sufficiently annoying. If he ever thought himself safe in making a statement, it was then. He had made

that statement with infinite satisfaction to himself, because
it was clear that the high official desired greatly to hear that
very thing. He had affirmed that nothing of the sort could
even be thought of without the department being aware of it
within twenty-four hours; and he had spoken thus in his consciousness of being the great expert of his department. He
had gone even so far as to utter words which true wisdom
would have kept back. But Chief Inspector Heat was not
very wise—at least, not truly so. True wisdom, which is not
certain of anything in this world of contradictions, would
have prevented him from attaining his present position. It
would have alarmed his superiors, and done away with his
chances of promotion. His promotion had been very rapid.

"There isn't one of them, sir, that we couldn't lay our
hands on at any time of night and day. We know what each
of them is doing hour by hour," he had declared. And the
high official had deigned to smile. This was so obviously the
right thing to say for an officer of Chief Inspector Heat's
reputation that it was perfectly delightful. The high official
believed the declaration, which chimed in with his idea of
the fitness of things. His wisdom was of an official kind,
or else he might have reflected upon a matter not of theory
but of experience, that in the close-woven stuff of relations
between conspirator and police there occur unexpected
solutions of continuity, sudden holes in space and time. A
given anarchist may be watched inch by inch and minute by
minute, but a moment always comes when somehow all
sight and touch of him are lost for a few hours, during which
something (generally an explosion) more or less deplorable
does happen. But the high official, carried away by his sense
of the fitness of things, had smiled, and now the recollection
of that smile was very annoying to Chief Inspector Heat,
principal expert in anarchist procedure.

This was not the only circumstance whose recollection
depressed the usual serenity of the eminent specialist. There
was another dating back only to that very morning. The
thought that when called urgently to his Assistant Commissioner's private room he had been unable to conceal his
astonishment was distinctly vexing. His instinct of a successful man had taught him long ago that, as a general rule, a
reputation is built on manner as much as on achievement.
And he felt that his manner, when confronted with the tele-

gram, had not been impressive. He had opened his eyes widely, and had exclaimed "Impossible!" exposing himself thereby to the unanswerable retort of a fingertip laid forcibly on the telegram which the Assistant Commissioner, after reading it aloud, had flung on the desk. To be crushed, as it were, under the tip of a forefinger, was an unpleasant experience. Very damaging, too! Furthermore, Chief Inspector Heat was conscious of not having mended matters by allowing himself to express a conviction.

"One thing I can tell you at once: none of our lot had anything to do with this."

He was strong in his integrity of a good detective, but he saw now that an impenetrably attentive reserve towards this incident would have served his reputation better. On the other hand, he admitted to himself that it was difficult to preserve one's reputation if rank outsiders were going to take a hand in the business. Outsiders are the bane of the police as of other professions. The tone of the Assistant Commissioner's remarks had been sour enough to set one's teeth on edge.

And since breakfast Chief Inspector Heat had not managed to get anything to eat.

Starting immediately to begin his investigation on the spot, he had swallowed a good deal of raw, unwholesome fog in the park. Then he had walked over to the hospital; and, when the investigation in Greenwich was concluded at last, he had lost his inclination for food. Not accustomed, as the doctors are, to examine closely the mangled remains of human beings, he had been shocked by the sight disclosed to his view when a waterproof sheet had been lifted off a table in a certain apartment of the hospital.

Another waterproof sheet was spread over that table in the manner of a tablecloth, with the corners turned up over a sort of mound—a heap of rags, scorched and bloodstained, half concealing what might have been an accumulation of raw material for a cannibal feast. It required considerable firmness of mind not to recoil before that sight. Chief Inspector Heat, an efficient officer of his department, stood his ground, but for a whole minute he did not advance. A local constable in uniform cast a sidelong glance, and said, with stolid simplicity:

"He's all there. Every bit of him. It was a job."

He had been the first man on the spot after the explosion. He mentioned the fact again. He had seen something like a heavy flash of lightning in the fog. At that time he was standing at the door of the King William Street Lodge, talking to the keeper. The concussion made him tingle all over. He ran between the trees towards the Observatory. "As fast as my legs would carry me," he repeated twice.

Chief Inspector Heat, bending forward over the table in a gingerly and horrified manner, let him run on. The hospital porter and another man turned down the corners of the cloth, and stepped aside. The Chief Inspector's eyes searched the gruesome detail of that heap of mixed things, which seemed to have been collected in shambles and rag shops.

"You used a shovel," he remarked, observing a sprinkling of small gravel, tiny brown bits of bark, and particles of splintered wood as fine as needles.

"Had to in one place," said the stolid constable. "I sent a keeper to fetch a spade. When he heard me scraping the ground with it, he leaned his forehead against a tree, and was as sick as a dog."

The Chief Inspector, stooping guardedly over the table, fought down the unpleasant sensation in his throat. The shattering violence of destruction, which had made of that body a heap of nameless fragments, affected his feelings with a sense of ruthless cruelty, though his reason told him the effect must have been as swift as a flash of lightning. The man, whoever he was, had died instantaneously; and yet it seemed impossible to believe that a human body could have reached that state of disintegration without passing through the pangs of inconceivable agony. No physiologist, and still less of a metaphysician, Chief Inspector Heat rose by the force of sympathy, which is a form of fear, above the vulgar conception of time. Instantaneous! He remembered all he had ever read in popular publications of long and terrifying dreams dreamed in the instant of waking; of the whole past life lived with frightful intensity by a drowning man as his doomed head bobs up, streaming, for the last time. The inexplicable mysteries of conscious existence beset Chief Inspector Heat till he evolved a horrible notion that ages of atrocious pain and mental torture could be contained between two successive winks of an eye. And meantime the Chief Inspector went on peering at the table with a calm face

and the slightly anxious attention of an indigent customer
bending over what may be called the by-product of a
butcher's shop with a view to an inexpensive Sunday dinner.
All the time his trained faculties of an excellent investigator,
who scorns no chance of information, followed the self-
satisfied, disjointed loquacity of the constable.

"A fair-haired fellow," the last observed, in a placid tone,
and paused. "The old woman who spoke to the sergeant
noticed a fair-haired fellow coming out of Maze Hill Station." He paused. "And he was a fair-haired fellow. She
noticed two men coming out of the station after the up-train
had gone on," he continued, slowly. "She couldn't tell if
they were together. She took no particular notice of the big
one, but the other was a fair, slight chap, carrying a tin
varnish can in one hand." The constable ceased.

"Know the woman?" muttered the Chief Inspector, with
his eyes fixed on the table, and a vague notion in his mind of
an inquest to be held presently upon a person likely to remain
forever unknown.

"Yes. She's housekeeper to a retired publican, and attends
the chapel in Park Place sometimes," the constable uttered
weightily, and paused, with another oblique glance at the
table. Then suddenly: "Well, here he is—all of him I could
see. Fair. Slight—slight enough. Look at that foot there. I
picked up the legs first, one after another. He was that
scattered you didn't know where to begin."

The constable paused; the least flicker of an innocent,
self-laudatory smile invested his round face with an infantile
expression.

"Stumbled," he announced, positively—"I stumbled once
myself, and pitched on my head, too, while running up.
Them roots do stick out all about the place. Stumbled against
the root of a tree and fell, and that thing he was carrying
must have gone off right under his chest, I expect."

The echo of the words "Person unknown" repeating itself
in his inner consciousness bothered the Chief Inspector
considerably. He would have liked to trace this affair back to
its mysterious origin for his own information. He was pro-
fessionally curious. Before the public he would have liked
to vindicate the efficiency of his department by establishing
the identity of that man. He was a loyal servant. That, however, appeared impossible. The first term of the problem

was unreadable—lacked all suggestion but that of atrocious cruelty.

Overcoming his physical repugnance, Chief Inspector Heat stretched out his hand without conviction for the salving of his conscience, and took up the least soiled of the rags. It was a narrow strip of velvet with a larger triangular piece of dark-blue cloth hanging from it. He held it up to his eyes, and the police-constable spoke.

"Velvet collar. Funny the old woman should have noticed the velvet collar. Dark-blue overcoat with a velvet collar, she has told us. He was the chap she saw, and no mistake. And here he is all complete, velvet collar and all. I don't think I missed a single piece as big as a postage stamp."

At this point the trained faculties of the Chief Inspector ceased to hear the voice of the constable. He moved to one of the windows for better light. His face, averted from the room, expressed a startled, intense interest while he examined closely the triangular piece of broadcloth. By a sudden jerk he detached it, and, only after stuffing it into his pocket, turned round to the room, and flung the velvet collar back on the table.

"Cover up," he directed the attendants curtly, without another look, and, saluted by the constable, carried off his spoil hastily.

A convenient train whirled him up to town, alone and pondering deeply, in a third-class compartment. That singed piece of pilot cloth was incredibly valuable, and he could not defend himself from astonishment at the casual manner it had come into his possession. It was as if Fate had thrust that clue into his hands. And, after the manner of the average man, whose ambition is to command events, he began to mistrust such a gratuitous and accidental success—just because it seemed forced upon him. The practical value of success depends not a little on the way you look at it. But Fate looks at nothing. It has no discretion. He no longer considered it eminently desirable all round to establish publicly the identity of the man who had blown himself up that morning with such horrible completeness. But he was not certain of the view his department would take. A department is to those it employs a complex personality with ideas and even fads of its own. It depends on the loyal devotion of its servants, and the devoted loyalty of trusted servants is associated with a certain amount of affectionate contempt, which keeps it sweet, as it were. By a benevolent provision of nature no man is a hero to his valet, or else the heroes would have to brush their own clothes. Likewise no department appears perfectly wise to the intimacy of its workers. A department does not know so much as some of its servants. Being a dispassionate organism, it can never be perfectly informed. It would not be good for its efficiency to know too much. Chief Inspector Heat got out of the train in a state of thoughtfulness entirely untainted with disloyalty, but not quite free of that jealous mistrust which so often springs on the ground of perfect devotion, whether to women or to institutions.

It was in this mental disposition, physically very empty, but still nauseated by what he had seen, that he had come upon the Professor. Under these conditions which make for irascibility in a sound, normal man, this meeting was specially unwelcome to Chief Inspector Heat. He had not been thinking of the Professor; he had not been thinking of any individual anarchist at all. The complexion of that case had somehow forced upon him the general idea of the absurdity of things human, which in the abstract is sufficiently annoying to an unphilosophical temperament, and in concrete instances becomes exasperating beyond endurance. At the beginning of his career Chief Inspector Heat had been concerned with the more violent forms of thieving. He had gained his spurs in that sphere, and naturally enough had kept for it, after his promotion to another department, a feeling not very far removed from affection. Thieving was not a sheer absurdity. It was a form of human industry, perverse indeed, but still an industry exercised in an industrious world; it was work undertaken for the same reason as the work in potteries, in coal mines, in fields, in tool-grinding shops. It was labor, whose practical difference from the other forms of labor consisted in the nature of its risk, which did not lie in ankylosis, or lead poisoning, or fire-damp, or gritty dust, but in what may be briefly defined in its own special phraseology as "Seven years hard." Chief Inspector Heat was, of course, not insensible to the gravity of moral differences. But neither were the thieves he had been looking after. They submitted to the severe sanctions of a morality familiar to Chief Inspector Heat with a certain resignation. They were his fellow citizens gone wrong because of imperfect education, Chief Inspector Heat believed; but allowing for that difference, he could understand the mind of a burglar, because, as a matter of fact, the mind and the instincts of a burglar are of the same kind as the mind and the instincts of a police officer. Both recognize the same conventions, and have a working knowledge of each other's methods and of. the routine of their respective trades. They understand each other, which is advantageous to both, and establishes a sort of amenity in their relations. Products of the same machine, one classed as useful and the other as noxious, they take the machine for granted in different ways, but with a seriousness essentially the same. The mind of Chief Inspector Heat was inaccessible to ideas of revolt. But his thieves were not rebels. His bodily vigor, his cool, inflexible manner, his courage and his fairness, had secured for him much respect and some adulation in the sphere of his early successes. He had felt himself revered and admired. And Chief Inspector Heat, arrested within six paces of the anarchist nicknamed "The Professor," gave a thought of regret to the world of thieves sane, without morbid ideals, working by routine, respectful of constituted authorities, free from all taint of hate and despair.

After paying this tribute to what is normal in the constitution of society (for the idea of thieving appeared to his instinct as normal as the idea of property), Chief Inspector Heat felt very angry with himself for having stopped, for having spoken, for having taken that way at all on the ground of it being a short cut from the station to the headquarters. And he spoke again in his big authoritative voice, which, being moderated, had a threatening character.

"You are not wanted, I tell you," he repeated.

The anarchist did not stir. An inward laugh of derision, uncovering not only his teeth but his gums as well, shook him all over, without the slightest sound. Chief Inspector Heat was led to add, against his better judgment:

"Not yet. When I want you, I will know where to find you."

Those were perfectly proper words, he felt, within the tradition and suitable to his character of a police officer addressing one of his special flock. But the reception they

got departed from tradition and propriety. It was outrageous.
The stunted, weakly figure before him spoke at last.

"I've no doubt the papers would give you an obituary notice then. You know best what that would be worth to you.
I should think you can imagine easily the sort of stuff that
would be printed. But you may be exposed to the unpleasant-
ness of being buried together with me, though I suppose
your friends would make an effort to sort us out as much
as possible."

With all his healthy contempt for the spirit dictating such
speeches, the atrocious allusiveness of the words had its
effect on Chief Inspector Heat. He had too much insight, and
too much exact information as well, to dismiss them as rot.
The dusk of this narrow lane took on a sinister tint from the
dark, frail little figure, its back to the wall, and speaking with
a weak, self-confident voice. To the vigorous, tenacious
vitality of the Chief Inspector, the physical wretchedness of
that being, so obviously not fit to live, was ominous; for it
seemed to him that if he had the misfortune to be such a
miserable object he would not have cared how soon he died.
Life had such a strong hold upon him that a fresh wave of
nausea broke out in slight perspiration upon his brow. The
murmur of town life, the subdued rumble of wheels in the
two invisible streets to the right and left, came through the
curve of the sordid lane to his ears with a precious familiarity
and an appealing sweetness. He was human. But Chief Inspector Heat was also a man, and he could not let such words
pass.

"All this is good to frighten children with," he said. "I'll
have you yet."

It was very well said, without scorn, with an almost austere
quietness.

"Doubtless," was the answer; "but there's no time like the
present, believe me. For a man of real convictions this is a
fine opportunity of self-sacrifice. You may not find another
so favorable, so humane. There isn't even a cat near us, and
these condemned old houses would make a good heap of
bricks where you stand. You'll never get me at so little cost
to life and property, which you are paid to protect."

"You don't know who you're speaking to," said Chief
Inspector Heat, firmly. "If I were to lay my hands on you
now I would be no better than yourself."

"Ah! The game!"

"You may be sure our side will win in the end. It may yet be necessary to make people believe that some of you ought to be shot at sight like mad dogs. Then that will be the game. But I'll be damned if I know what yours is. I don't believe you know yourselves. You'll never get anything by it."

"Meantime it's you who get something from it—so far. And you get it easily, too. I won't speak of your salary, but haven't you made your name simply by not understanding what we are after?"

"What are you after, then?" asked Chief Inspector Heat, with scornful haste, like a man in a hurry who perceives he is wasting his time.

The perfect anarchist answered by a smile which did not part his thin, colorless lips; and the celebrated Chief Inspector felt a sense of superiority which induced him to raise a warning finger.

"Give it up—whatever it is," he said, in an admonishing tone, but not so kindly, as if he were condescending to give good advice to a cracksman of repute. "Give it up. You'll find we are too many for you."

The fixed smile on the Professor's lips wavered as if the mocking spirit within had lost its assurance. Chief Inspector Heat went on:

"Don't you believe me—eh? Well, you've only got to look about you. We are. And, anyway, you're not doing it well. You're always making a mess of it. Why, if the thieves didn't know their work better, they would starve."

The hint of an invisible multitude behind that man's back roused a sombre indignation in the breast of the Professor. He smiled no longer his enigmatic and mocking smile. The resisting power of numbers, the unattackable stolidity of a great multitude, was the haunting fear of his sinister loneliness. His lips trembled for some time before he managed to say in a strangled voice:

"I am doing my work better than you're doing yours."

"That'll do now," interrupted Chief Inspector Heat hurriedly; and the Professor laughed right out this time. While still laughing he moved on; but he did not laugh long. It was a sad-faced, miserable little man who emerged from the narrow passage into the bustle of the broad throughfare. He walked with the nerveless gait of a tramp going on, still

going on, indifferent to rain or sun in a sinister detachment
from the aspects of sky and earth. Chief Inspector Heat, on
the other hand, after watching him for a while, stepped out
with the purposeful briskness of a man disregarding indeed
the inclemencies of the weather, but conscious of having an
authorized mission on this earth and the moral support of
his kind. All the inhabitants of the immense town, the population of the whole country, and even the teeming millions
struggling upon the planet, were with him—down to the
very thieves and mendicants. Yes, the thieves themselves
were sure to be with him in his present work. The consciousness of universal support in his general activity heartened
him to grapple with the particular problem.

The problem immediately before the Chief Inspector was
that of managing the Assistant Commissioner of his department. This is the perennial problem of trusty and loyal servants; anarchism gave it its particular complexion, but nothing
more. Truth to say, Chief Inspector Heat thought but little of
anarchism. He did not attach undue importance to it, and
could never bring himself to consider it seriously. It had more
the character of disorderly conduct; disorderly without the
human excuse of drunkenness, which at any rate implies
good feeling and an amiable leaning towards festivity. As
criminals, anarchists were distinctly no class—no class at
all. And recalling the Professor, Chief Inspector Heat, without checking his swinging pace, muttered through his teeth:
"Lunatic."

Catching thieves was another matter altogether. It had
that quality of seriousness, belonging to every form of open
sport, where the best man wins under perfectly comprehensible rules. There were no rules for dealing with anarchists.
And that was distasteful to the Chief Inspector. It was all
foolishness, but that foolishness excited the public mind,
affected persons in high places, and touched upon international relations. A hard, merciless contempt settled rigidly on
the Chief Inspector's face as he walked on. His mind ran
over all the anarchists of his flock. Not one of them had half
the spunk of this or that burglar he had known. Not half—
not one-tenth.

At headquarters the Chief Inspector was admitted at once
to the Assistant Commissioner's private room. He found
him, pen in hand, bent over a great table bestrewn with

papers, as if worshipping an enormous double inkstand of bronze and crystal. Speaking tubes resembling snakes were tied by the heads to the back of the Assistant Commissioner's wooden arm-chair, and their gaping mouths seemed ready to bite his elbows. And in this attitude he raised only his eyes, whose lids were darker than his face and very much creased. The reports had come in: every anarchist had been exactly accounted for.

After saying this he lowered his eyes, signed rapidly two single sheets of paper, and only then laid down his pen, and sat well back, directing an inquiring gaze at his renowned subordinate. The Chief Inspector stood it well, deferential but inscrutable.

"I dare say you were right," said the Assistant Commissioner, "in telling me at first that the London anarchists had nothing to do with this. I quite appreciate the excellent watch kept on them by your men. On the other hand, this, for the public, does not amount to more than a confession of ignorance."

The Assistant Commissioner's delivery was leisurely as it were cautious. His thought seemed to rest poised on a word before passing to another, as though words had been the stepping-stones for his intellect, picking its way across the waters of error. "Unless you have brought something useful from Greenwich," he added.

The Chief Inspector began at once the account of his investigation in a clear, matter-of-fact manner. His superior, turning his chair a little, and crossing his thin legs, leaned sideways on his elbow, with one hand shading his eyes. His listening attitude had a sort of angular and sorrowful grace. Gleams, as of highly burnished silver, played on the sides of his ebony black head when he inclined it slowly at the end.

Chief Inspector Heat waited with the appearance of turning over in his mind all he had just said, but, as a matter of fact, considering the advisability of saving something more. The Assistant Commissioner cut his hesitation short.

"You believe there were two men?" he asked, without uncovering his eyes.

The Chief Inspector thought it more than probable. In his opinion, the two men had parted from each other within a hundred yards from the Observatory walls. He explained also how the other man could have got out of the park speedily without being observed. The fog, though not very dense, was in his favor. He seemed to have escorted the other to the spot, and then to have left him there to do the job single-handed. Taking the time those two were seen coming out of Maze Hill Station by the old woman, and the time when the explosion was heard, the Chief Inspector thought that the other man might have been actually at the Greenwich Park Station, ready to catch the next train up, at the moment his comrade was destroying himself so thoroughly.

"Very thoroughly—eh?" murmured the Assistant Commissioner from under the shadow of his hand.

The Chief Inspector, in a few vigorous words, described the aspect of the remains. "The coroner's jury will have a treat," he added, grimly.

The Assistant Commissioner uncovered his eyes.

"We shall have nothing to tell them," he remarked, languidly.

He looked up, and for a time watched the markedly noncommittal attitude of his Chief Inspector. His nature was one that is not easily accessible to illusions. He knew that a department is at the mercy of its subordinate officers, who have their own conceptions of loyalty. His career had begun in a tropical colony. He had liked his work there. It was police work. He had been very successful in tracking and breaking up certain nefarious secret societies among the natives. Then he took his long leave, and got married rather impulsively. It was a good match from a worldly point of view, but his wife formed an unfavorable opinion of the colonial climate on hearsay evidence. On the other hand, she had influential connections. It was an excellent match. But he did not like the work he had to do now. He felt himself dependent on too many subordinates and too many masters. The near presence of that strange, emotional phenomenon called public opinion weighed upon his spirits, and alarmed him by its irrational nature. No doubt that from ignorance he exaggerated to himself its power for good and evil—especially for evil; and the rough east winds of the English spring (which agreed with his wife) augmented his general mistrust of men's motives and of the efficiency of their organization. The futility of office work especially appalled him on those days so trying to his sensitive liver.

He got up, unfolding himself to his full height, and with a

heaviness of step remarkable in so slender a man, moved across the room to the window. The panes streamed with rain, and the short street he looked down into lay wet and empty, as if swept clear suddenly by a great flood. It was a very trying day, choked in raw fog to begin with, and now drowned in cold rain. The flickering, blurred flames of gas lamps seemed to be dissolving in a watery atmosphere. And the lofty pretensions of a mankind oppressed by the miserable indignities of the weather appeared as a colossal and hopeless vanity deserving of scorn, wonder, and compassion.

"Horrible, horrible!" thought the Assistant Commissioner to himself, with his face near the windowpane. "We have been having this sort of thing now for ten days; no, a fortnight—a fortnight." He ceased to think completely for a time. That utter stillness of his brain lasted about three seconds. Then he said, perfunctorily: "You have set inquiries on foot for tracing that other man up and down the line?"

He had no doubt that everything needful had been done. Chief Inspector Heat knew, of course, thoroughly, the business of manhunting. And these were the routine steps, too, that would be taken as a matter of course by the merest beginner. A few inquiries among the ticket collectors and the porters of the two small railway stations would give additional details as to the appearance of the two men; the inspection of the collected tickets would show at once where they came from that morning. It was elementary, and could not have been neglected. Accordingly the Chief Inspector answered that all this had been done directly the old woman had come forward with her deposition. And he mentioned the name of a station. "That's where they came from, sir," he went on. "The porter who took the tickets at Maze Hill remembers two chaps answering to the description passing the barrier. They seemed to him two respectable workingmen of a superior sort—sign painters or house decorators. The big man got out of a third-class compartment backward, with a bright tin can in his hand. On the platform he gave it to carry to the fair young fellow who followed him. All this agrees exactly with what the old woman told the police sergeant in Greenwich."

The Assistant Commissioner, still with his face turned to the window, expressed his doubt as to these two men having had anything to do with the outrage. All this theory rested upon the utterances of an old charwoman who had been nearly knocked down by a man in a hurry. Not a very substantial authority, indeed, unless on the ground of sudden inspiration, which was hardly tenable.

"Frankly, now, could she have been really inspired?" he queried, with grave irony, keeping his back to the room, as if entranced by the contemplation of the town's colossal forms half lost in the night. He did not even look round when he heard the mutter of the word "Providential" from the principal subordinate of his department, whose name, printed sometimes in the papers, was familiar to the great public as that of one of its zealous and hard-working protectors. Chief Inspector Heat raised his voice a little.

"Strips and bits of bright tin were quite visible to me," he said. "That's a pretty good corroboration."

"And these men came from that little country station," the Assistant Commissioner mused aloud, wondering. He was told that such was the name on two tickets out of three given up out of that train at Maze Hill. The third person who got out was a hawker from Gravesend well known to the porters. The Chief Inspector imparted that information in a tone of finality with some ill humor, as loyal servants will do in the consciousness of their fidelity and with the sense of the value of their loyal exertions. And still the Assistant Commissioner did not turn away from the darkness outside, as vast as a sea.

"Two foreign anarchists coming from that place," he said, apparently to the windowpane. "It's rather unaccountable."

"Yes, sir. But it would be still more unaccountable if that Michaelis weren't staying in a cottage in the neighborhood."

At the sound of that name, falling unexpectedly into this annoying affair, the Assistant Commissioner dismissed brusquely the vague remembrance of his daily whist party at his club. It was the most comforting habit of his life, in a mainly successful display of his skill without the assistance of any subordinate. He entered his club to play from five to seven, before going home to dinner, forgetting for those two hours whatever was distasteful in his life, as though the game were a beneficent drug for allaying the pangs of moral discontent. His partners were the gloomily humorous editor of a celebrated magazine; a silent, elderly barrister with malicious little eyes; and a highly martial, simpleminded old Colonel with nervous brown hands. They were his club acquaintances merely. He never met them elsewhere except at the card table. But they all seemed to approach the game in the spirit of co-sufferers, as if it were indeed a drug against the secret ills of existence; and every day as the sun declined over the countless roofs of the town, a mellow, pleasurable impatience, resembling the impulse of a sure and profound friendship, lightened his professional labors. And now this pleasurable sensation went out of him with something resembling a physical shock, and was replaced by a special kind of interest in his work of social protection—an improper sort of interest, which may be defined best as a sudden and alert mistrust of the weapon in his hand.

Fyodor Dostoyevsky   Underground Man[1]

Fyodor Mikhailovich Dostoyevsky (1821–1881) All of his life he had endured poverty and epilepsy—the former more than a little aggravated by a penchant for gambling. He was the son of a doctor who was attached to a hospital for the poor in Moscow. He acquired a considerable reputation as an author by the time he was arrested in St. Petersburg in 1849 for his radical political involvements. He was sentenced to death. In a dramatic last-minute reprieve his sentence was commuted to exile in Siberia, where he spent some ten years as a convict, and then in military service. Returning to St. Petersburg, where, after the events of a tragic first marriage, he remarried and devoted the rest of his life to the writing of his major novels. In his youth a revolutionary, he returned from exile greatly embittered. He was suspicious of West European liberalism and espoused a form of Russian nationalism that saw Russia uniting the nations of Europe in the name of Christ as a resolution of social problems. He rejected the socialism of the West as well as its capitalism as inimical to spiritual values. His work is a constant engagement in the moral dialogue on the question of how the demands of the individual and the social order mitigate each other. He created a literature rich in Russian types but his chief characteristics reveal people whose sufferings emanate from within rather than stemming from oppressive social conditions. They live on an emotional precipice exposing the danger-

[1] From *Notes from Underground*, by Fyodor Dostoyevsky, Translated by Constance Garnett. New York: Macmillan Co., Part One, Sections I–VII.

ous consequences for the personality when it is lived as a law
unto itself. His prison reminiscences, *The House of the Dead*,
constitutes a document of social importance. His earliest successful work, *Poor Folk*, was acclaimed as the first attempt at a
social novel in Russia. His major works are widely known
classics, some of which are *The Brothers Karamazov, Crime
and Punishment, The Idiot, The Possessed,* and *Raw Youth.*

1

                 I am a sick man—I am a spiteful
man. I am an unattractive man. I believe my liver is diseased.
However, I know nothing at all about my disease, and do not
know for certain whàt ails me. I don't consult a doctor for
it, and never have, though I have a respect for medicine and
doctors. Besides, I am extremely superstitious, sufficiently
so to respect medicine, anyway (I am well-educated enough
not to be superstitious, but I am superstitious). No, I refuse
to consult a doctor from spite. That you probably will not
understand. Well, I understand it, though. Of course, I
can't explain who it is precisely that I am mortifying in this
case by my spite: I am perfectly well aware that I cannot
"pay out" the doctors by not consulting them; I know better
than any one that by all this I am only injuring myself and
no one else. But still, if I don't consult a doctor it is from
spite. My liver is bad, well—let it get worse!

I have been going on like that for a long time—twenty
years. Now I am forty. I used to be in the government service, but am no longer. I was a spiteful official. I was rude and
took pleasure in being so. I did not take bribes, you see, so
I was bound to find a recompense in that, at least. (A poor
jest, but I will not scratch it out. I wrote it thinking it would
sound very witty; but now that I have seen myself that I only
wanted to show off in a despicable way, I will not scratch it
out on purpose!)

When petitioners used to come for information to the
table at which I sat, I used to grind my teeth at them, and felt
intense enjoyment when I succeeded in making anybody
unhappy. I almost did succeed. For the most part they were
all timid people—of course, they were petitioners. But of the
uppish ones there was one officer in particular I could not
endure. He simply would not be humble, and clanked his

sword in a disgusting way. I carried on a feud with him for eighteen months over that sword. At last I got the better of him. He left off clanking it. That happened in my youth, though.

But do you know, gentlemen, what was the chief point about my spite? Why, the whole point, the real sting of it lay in the fact that continually, even in the moment of the acutest spleen, I was inwardly conscious with shame that I was not only not a spiteful but not even an embittered man, that I was simply scaring sparrows at random and amusing myself by it. I might foam at the mouth, but bring me a doll to play with, give me a cup of tea with sugar in it, and maybe I should be appeased. I might even be genuinely touched, though probably I should grind my teeth at myself afterwards and lie awake at night with shame for months after. That was my way.

I was lying when I said just now that I was a spiteful official. I was lying from spite. I was simply amusing myself with the petitioners and with the officer, and in reality I never could become spiteful. I was conscious every moment in myself of many, very many elements absolutely opposite to that. I felt them positively swarming in me, these opposite elements. I knew that they had been swarming in me all my life and craving some outlet from me, but I would not let them, would not let them, purposely would not let them come out. They tormented me till I was ashamed: they drove me to convulsions and—sickened me, at last, how they sickened me! Now, are not you fancying, gentlemen, that I am expressing remorse for something now, that I am asking your forgiveness for something? I am sure you are fancying that —However, I assure you I do not care if you are—

It was not only that I could not become spiteful, I did not know how to become anything: neither spiteful nor kind, neither a rascal nor an honest man, neither a hero nor an insect. Now, I am living out my life in my corner, taunting myself with the spiteful and useless consolation that an intelligent man cannot become anything seriously, and it is only the fool who becomes anything. Yes, a man in the nineteenth century must and morally ought to be preeminently a characterless creature; a man of character, an active man is preeminently a limited creature. That is my conviction of forty years. I am forty years old now, and you know forty years is a whole lifetime; you know it is extreme old age. To live longer than forty years is bad manners, is vulgar, immoral. Who does live beyond forty? Answer that, sincerely and honestly. I will tell you who do: fools and worthless fellows. I tell all old men that to their face, all these venerable old men, all these silver-haired and reverend seniors! I tell the whole world that to its face! I have a right to say so, for I shall go on living to sixty myself. To seventy! To eighty!—Stay, let me take breath—

You imagine no doubt, gentlemen, that I want to amuse you. You are mistaken in that, too. I am by no means such a mirthful person as you imagine, or as you may imagine; however, irritated by all this babble (and I feel that you are irritated) you think fit to ask me who am I—then my answer is, I am a collegiate assessor. I was in the service that I might have something to eat (and solely for that reason), and when last year a distant relation left me six thousand rubles in his will I immediately retired from the service and settled down in my corner. I used to live in this corner before, but now I have settled down in it. My room is a wretched, horrid one in the outskirts of the town. My servant is an old country woman, ill-natured from stupidity, and, moreover, there is always a nasty smell about her. I am told that the Petersburg climate is bad for me, and that with my small means it is very expensive to live in Petersburg. I know all that better than all these sage and experienced counsellors and monitors.—But I am remaining in Petersburg; I am not going away from Petersburg! I am not going away because— ech! Why, it is absolutely no matter whether I am going away or not going away.

But what can a decent man speak of with most pleasure? Answer: Of himself.

Well, so I will talk about myself.

2

I want now to tell you, gentlemen, whether you care to hear it or not, why I could not even become an insect. I tell you solemnly, that I have many times tried to become an insect. But I was not equal even to that. I swear, gentlemen, that to be too conscious is an illness—a real thoroughgoing illness. For man's everyday needs, it would have been quite enough to have the ordinary human consciousness, that is, half or a quarter of the amount which falls to the lot of a cultivated man of our unhappy nineteenth century, especially one who has the fatal ill-luck to inhabit Petersburg, the most theoretical and intentional town on the whole terrestrial globe. (There are intentional and unintentional towns.) It would have been quite enough, for instance, to have the consciousness by which all so-called direct persons and men of action live. I bet you think I am writing all this from affectation, to be witty at the expense of men of action; and what is more, that from ill-bred affectation, I am clanking a sword like my officer. But, gentlemen, whoever can pride himself on his diseases and even swagger over them?

Though, after all, every one does do that; people do pride themselves on their diseases, and I do, maybe, more than any one. We will not dispute it; my contention was absurd. But yet I am firmly persuaded that a great deal of consciousness, every sort of consciousness, in fact, is a disease. I stick to that. Let us leave that, too, for a minute. Tell me this: why does it happen that at the very, yes, at the very moments when I am most capable of feeling every refinement of all that is "good and beautiful," as they used to say at one time, it would, as though of design, happen to me not only to feel but to do such ugly things, such that—Well, in short, actions that all, perhaps, commit; but which, as though purposely, occurred to me at the very time when I was most conscious that they ought not to be committed. The more conscious I was of goodness and of all that was "good and beautiful," the more deeply I sank into my mire and the more ready I was to sink in it altogether. But the chief point was that all this was, as it were, not accidental in me, but as though it were bound to be so. It was as though it were my most normal condition, and not in the least disease or depravity, so that at last all desire in me to struggle against this depravity passed. It ended by my almost believing (perhaps actually believing) that this was perhaps my normal condition. But at first, in the beginning, what agonies I endured in that struggle! I did not believe it was the same with other people, and all my life I hid this fact about myself as a secret. I was ashamed (even now, perhaps, I am ashamed): I got to the point of feeling a sort of secret abnormal, despicable enjoyment in returning home to my corner on some

disgusting Petersburg night, acutely conscious that that day
I had committed a loathsome action again, that what was
done could never be undone, and secretly, inwardly gnawing, gnawing at myself for it, tearing and consuming myself
till at last the bitterness turned into a sort of shameful accursed sweetness, and at last—into positive real enjoyment!
Yes, into enjoyment, into enjoyment! I insist upon that. I
have spoken of this because I keep wanting to know for a
fact whether other people feel such enjoyment? I will explain; the enjoyment was just from the too intense consciousness of one's own degradation; it was from feeling oneself
that one had reached the last barrier, that it was horrible, but
that it could not be otherwise; that there was no escape for
you; that you never could become a different man; that even
if time and faith were still left you to change into something
different you would most likely not wish to change; or if you
did wish to, even then you would do nothing; because perhaps in reality there was nothing for you to change into.

And the worst of it was, and the root of it all, that it was
all in accord with the normal fundamental laws of overacute
consciousness, and with the inertia that was the direct result of those laws, and that consequently one was not only
unable to change but could do absolutely nothing. Thus it
would follow, as the result of acute consciousness, that one
is not to blame in being a scoundrel; as though that were any
consolation to the scoundrel once he has come to realize
that he actually is a scoundrel. But enough—Ech, I have
talked a lot of nonsense, but what have I explained? How is
enjoyment in this to be explained? But I will explain it. I
will get to the bottom of it! That is why I have taken up my
pen—

I, for instance, have a great deal of *amour propre*. I am as
suspicious and prone to take offence as a humpback or a
dwarf. But upon my word I sometimes have had moments
when if I had happened to be slapped in the face I should,
perhaps, have been positively glad of it. I say, in earnest,
that I should probably have been able to discover even in
that a peculiar sort of enjoyment—the enjoyment, of course,
of despair; but in despair there are the most intense enjoyments, especially when one is very acutely conscious of the
hopelessness of one's position. And when one is slapped in
the face—why then the consciousness of being rubbed into a

pulp would positively overwhelm one. The worst of it is, look at it which way one will, it still turns out that I was always the most to blame in everything. And what is most humiliating of all, to blame for no fault of my own but, so to say, through the laws of nature. In the first place, to blame because I am cleverer than any of the people surrounding me. (I have always considered myself cleverer than any of the people surrounding me, and sometimes, would you believe it, have been positively ashamed of it. At any rate, I have all my life, as it were, turned my eyes away and never could look people straight in the face.) To blame, finally, because even if I had had magnanimity, I should only have had more suffering from the sense of its uselessness. I should certainly have never been able to do anything from being magnanimous—neither to forgive, for my assailant would perhaps have slapped me from the laws of nature, and one cannot forgive the laws of nature; nor to forget, for even if it were owing to the laws of nature, it is insulting all the same. Finally, even if I had wanted to be anything but magnanimous, had desired on the contrary to revenge myself on my assailant, I could not have revenged myself on any one for anything because I should certainly never have made up my mind to do anything, even if I had been able to. Why should I not have made up my mind? About that in particular I want to say a few words.

3

With people who know how to revenge themselves and to stand up for themselves in general, how is it done? Why, when they are possessed, let us suppose, by the feeling of revenge, then for the time there is nothing else but that feeling left in their whole being. Such a gentleman simply dashes straight for his object like an infuriated bull with its horns down, and nothing but a wall will stop him. (By the way: facing the wall, such gentlemen—that is, the "direct" persons and men of action—are genuinely nonplussed. For them a wall is not an evasion, as for us people who think and consequently do nothing; it is not an excuse for turning aside, an excuse for which we are always very glad, though we scarcely believe in it ourselves, as a rule. No, they are nonplussed in all sincerity. The wall has for them something tranquillizing, morally soothing, final—maybe even something mysterious—but of the wall later.)

Well, such a direct person I regard as the real normal man, as his tender mother nature wished to see him when she graciously brought him into being on the earth. I envy such a man till I am green in the face. He is stupid. I am not disputing that, but perhaps the normal man should be stupid, how do you know? Perhaps it is very beautiful, in fact. And I am the more persuaded of that suspicion, if one can call it so, by the fact that if you take, for instance, the antithesis of the normal man, that is, the man of acute consciousness, who has come, of course, not out of the lap of nature but out of a retort (this is almost mysticism, gentlemen, but I suspect this, too), this retort-made man is sometimes so nonplussed in the presence of his antithesis that with all his exaggerated consciousness he genuinely thinks of himself as a mouse and not a man. It may be an acutely conscious mouse, yet it is a mouse, while the other is a man, and therefore, et cetera, et cetera. And the worst of it is, he himself, his very own self, looks on himself as a mouse; no one asks him to do so; and that is an important point. Now let us look at this mouse in action. Let us suppose, for instance, that it feels insulted, too (and it almost always does feel insulted), and wants to revenge itself, too. There may even be a greater accumulation of spite in it than in *l'homme de la nature et de la vérité*. The base and nasty desire to vent that spite on its assailant rankles perhaps even more nastily in it than in *l'homme de la nature et de la vérité*. For through his innate stupidity the latter looks upon his revenge as justice pure and simple; while in consequence of his acute consciousness the mouse does not believe in the justice of it. To come at last to the deed itself, to the very act of revenge. Apart from the one fundamental nastiness the luckless mouse succeeds in creating around it so many other nastinesses in the form of doubts and questions, adds to the one question so many unsettled questions that there inevitably works up around it a sort of fatal brew, a stinking mess, made up of its doubts, emotions, and of the contempt spat upon it by the direct men of action who stand solemnly about it as judges and arbitrators, laughing at it till their healthy sides ache. Of course the only thing left for it is to dismiss all that with a wave of its paw, and, with a smile of assumed contempt in

which it does not even itself believe, creep ignominiously
into its mousehole. There in its nasty, stinking, underground
home our insulted, crushed and ridiculed mouse promptly
becomes absorbed in cold, malignant and, above all, everlasting spite. For forty years together it will remember its
injury down to the smallest, most ignominious details, and
every time will add, of itself, details still more ignominious,
spitefully teasing and tormenting itself with its own imagination. It will itself be ashamed of its imaginings, but yet it
will recall it all, it will go over and over every detail, it will
invent unheard of things against itself, pretending that those
things might happen, and will forgive nothing. Maybe it will
begin to revenge itself, too, but, as it were, piecemeal, in
trivial ways, from behind the stove, incognito, without believing either in its own right to vengeance, or in the success
of its revenge knowing that from all its efforts at revenge it
will suffer a hundred times more than he on whom it
revenges itself, while he, I daresay, will not even scratch
himself. On its deathbed it will recall it all over again, with
interest accumulated over all the years and—

But it is just in that cold, abominable half despair, half
belief, in that conscious burying oneself alive for grief in
the underworld for forty years, in that acutely recognized
and yet partly doubtful hopelessness of one's position, in
that hell of unsatisfied desires turned inward, in that fever
of oscillations, of resolutions determined forever and re-
pented of again a minute later—that the savor of that strange
enjoyment of which I have spoken lies. It is so subtle, so difficult of analysis, that persons who are a little limited, or even
simply persons of strong nerves, will not understand a single
atom of it. "Possibly," you will add on your own account
with a grin, "people will not understand it either who have
never received a slap in the face," and in that way you will
politely hint to me that I, too, perhaps, have had the experience of a slap in the face in my life, and so I speak as one
who knows. I bet that you are thinking that. But set your
minds at rest, gentlemen, I have not received a slap in the
face, though it is absolutely a matter of indifference to me
what you may think about it. Possibly, I even regret, myself,
that I have given so few slaps in the face during my life. But
enough—not another word on that subject of such extreme
interest to you.

I will continue calmly concerning persons with strong nerves who do not understand a certain refinement of enjoyment. Though in certain circumstances these gentlemen bellow their loudest like bulls, though this, let us suppose, does them the greatest credit, yet, as I have said already, confronted with the impossible they subside at once. The impossible means the stone wall! What stone wall? Why, of course, the laws of nature, the deductions of natural science, mathematics. As soon as they prove to you, for instance, that you are descended from a monkey, then it is no use scowling, accept it for a fact. When they prove to you that in reality one drop of your own fat must be dearer to you than a hundred thousand of your fellow creatures, and that this conclusion is the final solution of all so-called virtues and duties and all such prejudices and fancies, then you have just to accept it, there is no help for it, for twice two is a law of mathematics. Just try refuting it.

"Upon my word," they will shout at you, "it is no use protesting: it is a case of twice two makes four! Nature does not ask your permission, she has nothing to do with your wishes, and whether you like her laws or dislike them, you are bound to accept her as she is, and consequently all her conclusions. A wall, you see, is a wall—and so on, and so on."

Merciful Heavens! but what do I care for the laws of nature and arithmetic, when, for some reason, I dislike those laws and the fact that twice two makes four? Of course I cannot break through the wall by battering my head against it if I really have not the strength to knock it down, but I am not going to be reconciled to it simply because it is a stone wall and I have not the strength.

As though such a stone wall really were a consolation, and really did contain some word of conciliation, simply because it is as true as twice two makes four. Oh, absurdity of absurdities! How much better it is to understand it all, to recognize it all, all the impossibilities and the stone wall; not to be reconciled to one of those impossibilities and stone walls if it disgusts you to be reconciled to it; by the way of the most inevitable, logical combinations to reach the most revolting conclusion on the everlasting theme, that even for the stone wall you are yourself somehow to blame, though again it is as clear as day you are not to blame in the least, and there-

fore grinding your teeth in silent impotence to sink into luxu-
rious inertia, brooding on the fact that there is no one even
for you to feel vindictive against, that you have not, and
perhaps never will have, an object for your spite, that it is a
sleight of hand, a bit of juggling, a cardsharper's trick, that
it is simply a mess, no knowing what and no knowing who,
but in spite of all these uncertainties and jugglings, still there
is an ache in you, and the more you do not know, the worse
the ache.

4

"Ha, ha, ha! You will be finding enjoyment in toothache
next," you cry, with a laugh.

"Well? Even in toothache there is enjoyment," I answer.
I had toothache for a whole month and I know there is. In
that case, of course, people are not spiteful in silence, but
moan; but they are not candid moans, they are malignant
moans, and the malignancy is the whole point. The enjoyment of the sufferer finds expression in those moans; if he
did not feel enjoyment in them he would not moan. It is a
good example, gentlemen, and I will develop it. Those moans
express in the first place all the aimlessness of your pain,
which is so humiliating to your consciousness; the whole
legal system of nature on which you spit disdainfully, of
course, but from which you suffer all the same while she does
not. They express the consciousness that you have no enemy
to punish, but that you have pain; the consciousness that in
spite of all possible Vagenheims you are in complete slavery
to your teeth; that if some one wishes it, your teeth will leave
off aching, and if he does not, they will go on aching another
three months; and that finally if you are still contumacious
and still protest, all that is left you for your own gratification
is to thrash yourself or beat your wall with your first as hard
as you can, and absolutely nothing more. Well, these mortal
insults, these jeers on the part of some one unknown, end at
last in an enjoyment which sometimes reaches the highest
degree of voluptuousness. I ask you, gentlemen, listen sometimes to the moans of an educated man of the nineteenth
century suffering from toothache, on the second or third day
of the attack, when he is beginning to moan, not as he
moaned on the first day, that is, not simply because he has

toothache, not just as any coarse peasant, but as a man affected by progress and European civilization, a man who is
"divorced from the soil and the national elements," as they
express it nowadays. His moans become nasty, disgustingly
malignant, and go on for whole days and nights. And of
course he knows himself that he is doing himself no sort of
good with his moans; he knows better than anyone that he
is only lacerating and harassing himself and others for nothing; he knows that even the audience before whom he is
making his efforts, and his whole family, listen to him with
loathing, do not put a ha'porth of faith in him, and inwardly
understand that he might moan differently, more simply,
without trills and flourishes, and that he is only amusing himself like that from ill-humor, from malignancy. Well, in all
these recognitions and disgraces it is that there lies a voluptuous pleasure. As though he would say: "I am worrying
you, I am lacerating your hearts, I am keeping everyone in
the house awake. Well, stay awake then, you, too, feel every
minute that I have toothache. I am not a hero to you now, as
I tried to seem before, but simply a nasty person, an im-
postor. Well, so be it, then! I am very glad that you see
through me. It is nasty for you to hear my despicable moans:
well, let it be nasty; here I will let you have a nastier flourish
in a minute—" You do not understand even now, gentlemen?
No, it seems our development and our consciousness must
go further to understand all the intricacies of this pleasure.
You laugh? Delighted. My jests, gentlemen, are of course in
bad taste, jerky, involved, lacking self-confidence. But of
course that is because I do not respect myself. Can a man of
perception respect himself at all?

5

Come, can a man who attempts to find enjoyment in the very
feeling of his own degradation possibly have a spark of respect for himself? I am not saying this now from any mawk-
ish kind of remorse. And, indeed, I could never endure saying, "Forgive me, Papa, I won't do it again," not because I
am incapable of saying that—on the contrary, perhaps just
because I have been too capable of it, and in what a way, too!
As though of design I used to get into trouble in cases when
I was not to blame in any way. That was the nastiest part of

it. At the same time I was genuinely touched and penitent, I used to shed tears and, of course, deceived myself, though I was not acting in the least and there was a sick feeling in my heart at the time—For that one could not blame even the laws of nature, though the laws of nature have continually all my life offended me more than anything. It is loathsome to remember it all, but it was loathsome even then. Of course, a minute or so later I would realize wrathfully that it was all a lie, a revolting lie, an affected lie, that is, all this penitence, this emotion, these vows of reform. You will ask why did I worry myself with such antics: answer, because it was very dull to sit with one's hands folded, and so one began cutting capers. That is really it. Observe yourselves more carefully, gentlemen, then you will understand that it is so. I invented adventures for myself and made up a life, so as at least to live in some way. How many times it has happened to me— well, for instance, to take offence simply on purpose, for nothing; and one knows oneself, of course, that one is offended at nothing, that one is putting it on, but yet one brings oneself, at last to the point of being really offended. All my life I have had an impulse to play such pranks, so that in the end I could not control it in myself. Another time, twice, in fact, I tried hard to be in love. I suffered, too, gentlemen, I assure you. In the depth of my heart there was no faith in my suffering, only a faint stir of mockery, but yet I did suffer, and in the real, orthodox way; I was jealous, beside myself—and it was all from *ennui*, gentlemen, all from *ennui;* inertia overcame me. You know the direct, legitimate fruit of consciousness is inertia, that is, conscious sitting-with-the-hands-folded. I have referred to this already. I repeat, I repeat with emphasis: all "direct" persons and men of action are active just because they are stupid and limited. How explain that? I will tell you: in consequence of their limitation they take immediate and secondary causes for primary ones, and in that way persuade themselves more quickly and easily than other people do that they have found an infallible foundation for their activity, and their minds are at ease and you know that is the chief thing. To begin to act, you know, you must first have your mind completely at ease and no trace of doubt left in it. Why, how am I, for example to set my mind at rest? Where are the primary causes

on which I am to build? Where are my foundations? Where
am I to get them from? I exercise myself in reflection, and
consequently with me every primary cause at once draws
after itself another still more primary, and so on to infinity.
That is just the essence of every sort of consciousness and
reflection. It must be a case of the laws of nature again. What
is the result of it in the end? Why, just the same. Remember
I spoke just now of vengeance. (I am sure you did not take
it in.) I said that a man revenges himself because he sees
justice in it. Therefore he has found a primary cause, that is,
justice. And so he is at rest on all sides, and consequently he
carries out his revenge calmly and successfully, being persuaded that he is doing a just and honest thing. But I see no
justice in it, I find no sort of virtue in it either, and consequently if I attempt to revenge myself, it is only out of spite.
Spite, of course, might overcome everything, all my doubts,
and so might serve quite successfully in place of a primary
cause, precisely because it is not a cause. But what is to be
done if I have not even spite (I began with that just now, you
know). In consequence again of those accursed laws of consciousness, anger in me is subject to chemical disintegration.
You look into it, the object flies off into air, your reasons
evaporate, the criminal is not to be found, the wrong becomes not a wrong but a phantom, something like the toothache, for which no one is to blame, and consequently there
is only the same outlet left again—that is, to beat the wall as
hard as you can. So you give it up with a wave of the hand
because you have not found a fundamental cause. And try
letting yourself be carried away by your feelings, blindly,
without reflection, without a primary cause, repelling consciousness at least for a time; hate or love, if only not to sit
with your hands folded. The day after tomorrow, at the
latest, you will begin despising yourself for having knowingly deceived yourself. Result: a soap bubble and inertia.
Oh, gentlemen, do you know, perhaps I consider myself an
intelligent man, only because all my life I have been able
neither to begin nor to finish anything. Granted I am a babbler, a harmless vexatious babbler, like all of us. But what is
to be done if the direct and sole vocation of every intelligent
man is babble, that is, the intentional pouring of water
through a sieve?

6

Oh, if I had done nothing simply from laziness! Heavens, how I should have respected myself, then. I should have respected myself because I should at least have been capable of being lazy; there would at least have been one quality, as it were, positive in me, in which I could have believed myself. Question: What is he? Answer: A sluggard; how very pleasant it would have been to hear that of oneself! It would mean that I was positively defined, it would mean that there was something to say about me. "Sluggard"—why, it is a calling and vocation, it is a career. Do not jest, it is so. I should then be a member of the best club by right, and should find my occupation in continually respecting myself. I knew a gentleman who prided himself all his life on being a connoisseur of Lafitte. He considered this as his positive virtue, and never doubted himself. He died, not simply with a tranquil, but with a triumphant, conscience, and he was quite right, too. Then I should have chosen a career for myself, I should have been a sluggard and a glutton, not a simple one, but, for instance, one with sympathies for everything good and beautiful. How do you like that? I have long had visions of it. That "good and beautiful" weighs heavily on my mind at forty. But that is at forty; then—oh, then it would have been different! I should have found for myself a form of activity in keeping with it, to be precise, drinking to the health of everything "good and beautiful." I should have snatched at every opportunity to drop a tear into my glass and then to drain it to all that is "good and beautiful." I should then have turned everything into the good and the beautiful; in the nastiest, unquestionable trash, I should have sought out the good and the beautiful. I should have exuded tears like a wet sponge. An artist, for instance, paints a picture worthy of Gay. At once I drink to the health of the artist who painted the picture worthy of Gay, because I love all that is "good and beautiful." An author has written *As you will:* at once I drink to the health of "anyone you will" because I love all that is "good and beautiful."

I should claim respect for doing so. I should persecute any one who would not show me respect. I should live at ease, I should die with dignity, why, it is charming, perfectly charming! And what a good round belly I should have grown, what a treble chin I should have established, what a ruby nose I should have colored for myself, so that every one would have said, looking at me: "Here is an asset! Here is something real and solid!" And, say what you like, it is very agreeable to hear such remarks about oneself in this negative age.

7

But these are all golden dreams. Oh, tell me, who was it first announced, who was it first proclaimed, that man only does nasty things because he does not know his own interests; and that if he were enlightened, if his eyes were opened to his real normal interests, man would at once cease to do nasty things, would at once become good and noble because, being enlightened and understanding his real advantage, he would see his own advantage in the good and nothing else, and we all know that not one man can, consciously, act against his own interests, consequently, so to say, through necessity, he would begin doing good? Oh, the babe! Oh, the pure, innocent child! Why, in the first place, when in all these thousands of years has there been a time when man has acted only from his own interest? What is to be done with the millions of facts that bear witness that men, *consciously,* that is fully understanding their real interests, have left them in the background and have rushed headlong on another path, to meet peril and danger, compelled to this course by nobody and by nothing, but, as it were, simply disliking the beaten track, and have obstinately, wilfully, struck out another difficult, absurd way, seeking it almost in the darkness. So, I suppose, this obstinacy and perversity were pleasanter to them than any advantage—Advantage! What is advantage? And will you take it upon yourself to define with perfect accuracy in what the advantage of man consists? And what if it so happens that a man's advantage, *sometimes,* not only may, but even must, consist in his desiring in certain cases what is harmful to himself and not advantageous. And if so, if there can be such a case, the whole principle falls into dust. What do you think—are there such cases? You laugh; laugh away, gentlemen, but only answer me: have man's advantages been reckoned up with perfect certainty? Are there not some which not only have not been included but cannot possibly be included under any classification? You see, you gentlemen have, to the best of my knowledge, taken your whole register of human advantages from the averages of statistical figures and politico-economical formulas. Your advantages are prosperity, wealth, freedom, peace—and so on, and so on. So that the man who should, for instance, go openly and knowingly in opposition to all that list would, to your thinking, and indeed mine, too, of course, be an obscurantist or an absolute madman: would not he? But, you know, this is what is surprising: why does it so happen that all these statisticians, sages and lovers of humanity, when they reckon up human advantages invariably leave out one? They don't even take it into their reckoning in the form in which it should be taken, and the whole reckoning depends upon that. It would be no great matter, they would simply have to take it, this advantage, and add it to the list. But the trouble is, that this strange advantage does not fall under any classification and is not in place in any list. I have a friend for instance—Ech! gentlemen, but of course he is your friend, too; and indeed there is no one, no one, to whom he is not a friend! When he prepares for any undertaking this gentleman immediately explains to you, elegantly and clearly, exactly how he must act in accordance with the laws of reason and truth. What is more, he will talk to you with excitement and passion of the true normal interests of man; with irony he will upbraid the shortsighted fools who do not understand their own interests, nor the true significance of virtue; and, within a quarter of an hour, without any sudden outside provocation, but simply through something inside him which is stronger than all his interests, he will go off on quite a different task—that is, act in direct opposition to what he has just been saying about himself, in opposition to the laws of reason, in opposition to his own advantage, in fact in opposition to everything—I warn you that my friend is a compound personality, and therefore it is difficult to blame him as an individual. The fact is, gentlemen, it seems there must really exist something that is dearer to almost every man than his greatest advantages, or (not to be illogical) there is a most advantageous advantage (the very one omitted of which we spoke just now) which is more important and more advantageous than all other advantages, for the sake of which a man if necessary is ready to act in opposition to all laws; that

is, in opposition to reason, honor, peace, prosperity—in
fact, in opposition to all those excellent and useful things if
only he can attain that fundamental, most advantageous advantage which is dearer to him than all. "Yes, but it's advantage all the same" you will retort. But excuse me, I'll
make the point clear, and it is not a case of playing upon
words. What matters is, that this advantage is remarkable
from the very fact that it breaks down all our classifications,
and continually shatters every system constructed by lovers
of mankind for the benefit of mankind. In fact, it upsets
everything. But before I mention this advantage to you, I
want to compromise myself personally, and therefore I
boldly declare that all these fine systems, all these theories
for explaining to mankind their real normal interests, in
order that inevitably striving to pursue these interests they
may at once become good and noble—are, in my opinion,
so far, mere logical exercises! Yes, logical exercises. Why, to
maintain this theory of the regeneration of mankind by means
of the pursuit of his own advantage is to my mind almost the
same thing as—as to affirm, for instance, following Buckle,
that through civilization mankind becomes softer, and consequently less bloodthirsty and less fitted for warfare. Logically
it does seem to follow from his arguments. But man has such
a predilection for systems and abstract deductions that he is
ready to distort the truth intentionally, he is ready to deny
the evidence of his senses only to justify his logic. I take this
example because it is the most glaring instance of it. Only
look about you: blood is being spilt in streams, and in the
merriest way, as though it were champagne. Take the whole
of the nineteenth century in which Buckle lived. Take
Napoleon—the Great and also the present one. Take North
America—the eternal union. Take the farce of Schleswig-
Holstein—And what is it that civilization softens in us? The
only gain of civilization for mankind is the greater capacity
for variety of sensations—and absolutely nothing more. And
through the development of this many-sidedness man may
come to find enjoyment in bloodshed. In fact, this has already
happened to him. Have you noticed that it is the most civilized gentlemen who have been the subtlest slaughterers, to
whom the Attilas and Stenka Razins could not hold a candle,
and if they are not so conspicuous as the Attilas and Stenka
Razins it is simply because they are so often met with, are so

ordinary and have become so familiar to us. In any case civilization has made mankind if not more bloodthirsty, at least more vilely, more loathsomely bloodthirsty. In old days he saw justice in bloodshed and with his conscience at peace exterminated those he thought proper. Now we do think bloodshed abominable and yet we engage in this abomination, and with more energy than ever. Which is worse? Decide that for yourselves. They say that Cleopatra (excuse an instance from Roman history) was fond of sticking gold pins into her slave girls' breasts and derived gratification from their screams and writhings. You will say that that was in the comparatively barbarous times; that these are barbarous times too, because also, comparatively speaking, pins are stuck in even now; that though man has now learned to see more clearly than in barbarous ages, he is still far from having learnt to act as reason and science would dictate. But yet you are fully convinced that he will be sure to learn when he gets rid of certain old bad habits, and when common sense and science have completely re-educated human nature and turned it in a normal direction. You are confident that then man will cease from *intentional* error and will, so to say, be compelled not to want to set his will against his normal interests. That is not all; then, you say, science itself will teach man (though to my mind it's a superfluous luxury) that he never has really had any caprice or will of his own, and that he himself is something of the nature of a piano key or the stop of an organ, and that there are, besides, things called the laws of nature; so that everything he does is not done by his willing it, but is done of itself, by the laws of nature. Consequently we have only to discover these laws of nature, and man will no longer have to answer for his actions and life will become exceedingly easy for him. All human actions will then, of course, be tabulated according to these laws, mathematically, like tables of logarithms up to 108,000, and entered in an index; or, better still, there would be published certain edifying works of the nature of encyclopaedic lexicons, in which everything will be so clearly calculated and explained that there will be no more incidents or adventures in the world.

Then—this is all what you say—new economic relations will be established, all ready-made and worked out with mathematical exactitude, so that every possible question will vanish in the twinkling of an eye, simply because every possible answer to it will be provided. Then the "Palace of Crystal" will be built. Then—In fact, those will be halcyon days. Of course there is no guaranteeing (this is my comment) that it will not be, for instance, frightfully dull then (for what will one have to do when everything will be calculated and tabulated), but on the other hand everything will be extraordinarily rational. Of course boredom may lead you to anything. It is boredom sets one sticking golden pins into people, but all that would not matter. What is bad (this is my comment again) is that I dare say people will be thankful for the gold pins then. Man is stupid, you know, phenomenally stupid; or rather he is not at all stupid, but he is so ungrateful that you could not find another like him in all creation. I, for instance, would not be in the least surprised if all of a sudden, *à propos* of nothing, in the midst of general prosperity a gentleman with an ignoble, or rather with a reactionary and ironical, countenance were to arise and, putting his arms akimbo, say to us all: "I say, gentlemen, hadn't we better kick over the whole show and scatter rationalism to the winds, simply to send these logarithms to the devil, and to enable us to live once more at our own sweet foolish will!" That again would not matter, but what is annoying is that he would be sure to find followers—such is the nature of man. And all that for the most foolish reason, which, one would think, was hardly worth mentioning: that is, that man everywhere and at all times, whoever he may be, has preferred to act as he chose and not in the least as his reason and advantage dictated. And one may choose what is contrary to one's own interests, and sometimes one *positively ought* (that is my idea). One's own free unfettered choice, one's own caprice, however wild it may be, one's own fancy worked up at times to frenzy—is that very "most advantageous advantage" which we have overlooked, which comes under no classification and against which all systems and theories are continually being shattered to atoms. And how do these wiseacres know that man wants a normal, a virtuous choice? What has made them conceive that man must want a rationally advantageous choice? What man wants is simply *independent* choice, whatever that independence may cost and wherever it may lead. And choice, of course, the devil only knows what choice.

Leo Tolstoy   What Is To Be Done?[1]

Leo Tolstoy (1828–1910)   Tolstoy was born into the aristocracy
and, until his later years, lived the life of a comfortable gentleman and a man of letters. In his youth and middle years he
wrote chiefly fiction, much of which is widely known to English-
speaking readers. He traveled widely throughout Europe, returning home in 1861, the year of the emancipation of the serfs.
The atmosphere of reform drove him into a number of unsuccessful education experiments. During the writing of *Anna
Karenina,* in the 1870s, he experienced a spiritual crisis from
which he emerged with a rationalistic variety of evangelic Christianity, the primary tenets of which were brotherly love and
nonresistance to evil. The achievement of inner freedom and
personal righteousness through his doctrine led him to seek
social applications of it. He rejected the Church as the cor-
ruptor of Christ's teachings and opposed the State because it
rested on force. In the period dating from 1880, out of an
exaltation of asceticism, he repudiated his hereditary property
and took up the peasant's life. Tolstoy's writings on law, the
State, property, religion, that best express his anarchism are
contained in *My Confession, The Gospel in Brief, My Religion,
What Shall We Do Then? On Life,* and *The Kingdom of God
Is Within You.*

The division of labor in human
society has always existed, and I dare say always will exist;
but the question for us is not whether or not it has been and
will still continue, but what should guide us to arrange that
this division may be a right one.

If we take the facts of observation for our standard, we
must refuse to have any standard at all: every division of
labor that we see among men, and that may seem to us to be
a right one, we shall consider right; and this is what the ruling scientific science is leading us to.

Division of labor!

[1] From *What Is To Be Done?*, by Leo Tolstoy, New York: Thomas Y.
Crowell & Co., 1899.

Some are occupied with mental and spiritual, others with muscular and physical, labor.

With what an assurance do men express this! They wish to think so, and that seems to them in reality a correct exchange of services which is only the very apparent ancient violence.

Thou, or rather you (because it is always many who have to feed one)—you feed me, dress me, do for me all this rough labor, which I require of you, to which you are accustomed from your infancy, and I do for you that mental work to which I have already become accustomed. Give me bodily food, and I will give you in return the spiritual.

The statement seems to be a correct one; and it would really be so if only such exchange of services were free, if those who supply the bodily food were not obliged to supply it before they get the spiritual. The producer of the spiritual food says, "In order that I may be able to give you this food, you must feed me, clothe me, and remove all filth from my house."

But as for the producer of bodily food, he must do it without making any claims of his own, and he has to give bodily food whether he receive spiritual food or not. If the exchange were a free one, the conditions on both sides would be equal. We agree that spiritual food is as necessary to man as bodily. The learned man, the artist, says, "Before we can begin to serve men by giving them spiritual food, we want men to provide us with bodily food."

But why should not the producers of this latter say, "Before we begin to serve you with bodily food, we want spiritual food; and until we receive it, we cannot labor"?

You say, "I require the labor of a plowman, a smith, a bootmaker, a carpenter, masons, and others, in order that I may prepare the spiritual food I have to offer."

Every workman might say, too, "Before I go to work, to prepare bodily food for you, I want the fruits of the spirit. In order to have strength for laboring, I require a religious teaching, the social order of common life, application of knowledge to labor, and the joys and comforts which art gives. I have no time to work out for myself a teaching concerning the meaning of life—give it to me.

"I have no time to think out statutes of common life that would prevent the violation of justice—give me this too. I have no time to study mechanics, natural philosophy, chemistry, technology; give me books with information as to how I am to improve my tools, my ways of working, my dwelling, the heating and lighting of it. I have no time to occupy myself with poetry, with plastic art, or music; give me those excitements and comforts necessary for life; give me these productions of the arts."

You say it is impossible for you to do your important and necessary business if you were to be deprived of the labor working people do for you; and I say, a workman may declare, "It is impossible for me to do my important and necessary business, not less important than yours—to plow, to cart away refuse, and clean *your* houses—if I be deprived of a religious guidance corresponding to the wants of my intellect and my conscience, of a reasonable government that would secure my labor, of information for easing my labor, and the enjoyment of art to ennoble it. All you have offered me in the shape of spiritual food is not only of no use to me whatever, but I cannot even understand to whom it could be of any use. And until I receive this nourishment, proper for me as for every man, I cannot produce bodily food to feed you with."

What if the working people should speak thus? And if they said so, it would be no jest, but the simplest justice. If a workingman said this, he would be far more in the right than a man of intellectual labor; because the labor produced by the workingman is more urgent and more necessary than that done by the producer of intellectual work, and because a man of intellect is hindered by nothing from giving that spiritual food which he promised to give, but the workingman is hindered in giving the bodily food by the fact that he himself is short of it.

What, then, should we, men of intellectual labor, answer, if such simple and lawful claims were made upon us? How should we satisfy these claims? Should we satisfy the religious wants of the people by the catechism of Philaret, by sacred histories of Sokolof, by the literature sent out by various monasteries and St. Isaak's cathedral? And should we satisfy their demand for order by the Code of Laws, and cassation verdicts of different departments, or by statutes of committees and commissions? And should we satisfy their want of knowledge by giving them spectrum analysis, a survey of the Milky Way, speculative geometry, microscopic investigations, controversies concerning spiritualism and mediumism, the activity of academies of science? How should we satisfy their artistic wants? By Pushkin, Dostoyevsky, Turgenev, L. Tolstoy, by pictures of French *salons,* and of those of our artists who represent naked women, satin, velvet, and landscapes, and pictures of domestic life, by the music of Wagner, and that of our own musicians?

All this is of no use, and cannot be of any use, because we, with our right to utilize the labor of the people, and absence of all duties in our preparation of their spiritual food, have quite lost from sight the single destination our activity should have.

We do not even know what is required by the workingman; we have even forgotten his mode of life, his views of things, his language; we have even lost sight of the very working people themselves, and we study them like some ethnographical rarity or newly discovered continent. Now, we, demanding for ourselves bodily food, have taken upon ourselves to provide the spiritual; but in consequence of the imaginary division of labor, according to which we may not only first take our dinner and afterward do our work, but may during many generations dine luxuriously, and do no work—in the way of compensation for our food we have prepared something that is of use, as it seems to us, for ourselves and for science and art, but of no use whatever for those very people whose labor we consume under the pretext of providing them in return with intellectual food, and not only of no use, but quite unintelligible and distasteful to them.

In our blindness we have to such a degree left out of sight the duty that we took upon us, that we have even forgotten for what our labor is being done; and the very people whom we undertook to serve, we have made an object of our scientific and artistic activities. We study them and represent them for our own pleasure and amusement: we have quite forgotten that it is our duty, not to study and depict, but to serve them.

We have to such a degree left out of sight the duty that we assumed, that we have not even noticed that other people do what we undertook in the departments of science and art, and that our place turns out to be occupied.

It appears that, while we have been in controversy, now about the Immaculate Conception, and now about spontaneous generation of organisms; now about spiritualism, and now about the forms of atoms; now about pangenesis, now about protoplasms, and so on—the rest of the world nonetheless required intellectual food, and the abortive outcasts of science and art began to provide for the people this spiritual food by order of various speculators who had in view exclusively their own profit and gain.

Now, for some forty years in Europe and ten years in Russia, millions of books and pictures and songs have been circulating; shows have been opened; and the people look and sing and receive intellectual food, though not from those who promised to provide it for them; and we, who justify our idleness by the need for that intellectual food which we pretend to provide for the people, are sitting still, and taking no notice.

But we cannot do so, because our final justification has vanished from under our feet. We have taken upon ourselves a peculiar department: we have a peculiar functional activity of our own. We are the brain of the people. They feed us, and we have undertaken to teach them. Only for the sake of this have we freed ourselves from labor. What, then, have we been teaching them? They have waited years, tens of years, hundreds of years. And we are still conversing among ourselves, and teaching each other, and amusing ourselves, and have quite forgotten them; we have so totally forgotten them that others have taken upon themselves to teach and amuse them, and we have not even become aware of this in our flippant talk about division of labor: and it is very obvious that all our talk about the utility we offer to the people was only a shameful excuse.

It is only to us, with our perverted ideas, that it seems, when the master sends his clerk to be a peasant, or government sentences one of its ministers to deportation, that they are punished and have been dealt with hardly. But in reality they have had a great good done to them—that is, they have exchanged their heavy special work for a pleasant alternation of labor.

In a natural society all is quite different. I know a commune where the people earn their living themselves. One of the members of this community was more educated than the rest; and they required him to deliver lectures, for which he had to prepare himself during the day, in order to be able to deliver them in the evening. He did it joyfully, feeling that he was useful to others, and that he could do it well. But he got tired of the exclusive mental labor, and his health suffered accordingly. The members of the community therefore pitied him, and asked him to come again and labor in the field.

For men who consider labor to be the essential thing and the joy of life, the ground, the basis, of it will always be the struggle with nature—not only agricultural labor, but also that of handicraft, mental work, and intercourse with men.

The divergence from one or many of these kinds of labor and specialties of labor will be performed only when a man of special gifts, being fond of this work, and knowing that he performs it better than anybody else, will sacrifice his own advantage in order to fulfill the demands of others put directly to him.

Only with such a view of labor, and the natural division of labor resulting from it, will the curse disappear that we in our imagination have put upon labor; and every labor will always be a joy, because man will do either an unquestionably useful, pleasant, and easy work, or will be conscious that he makes a sacrifice in performing a more difficult special labor for the good of others.

But the division of labor is, it is said, more advantageous. Advantageous for whom? Is it more advantageous to make as quickly as possible as many boots and cotton prints as possible? But who will make these boots and cotton prints? Men who from generation to generation have been making only pinheads? How, then, can it be more advantageous for people? If the question were to make as many cotton prints and pins as possible, it would be so; but the question is, how to make people happy?

The happiness of men consists in life. And life is in labor.

How, then, can the necessity of a painful, oppressing work be advantageous for men? If the question were only for the advantage of some men without any consideration of the welfare of all, then it would be most advantageous for some men to eat others.

The thing most advantageous for all men is that which I wish for myself—the greatest welfare and the satisfying of

all my wants, those of body as well as those of soul, of conscience, and of reason, which are ingrafted in me.

And now, for myself, I have found that for my welfare
and for the satisfying of these wants, I need only to be cured
of the folly in which I, as well as the Krapivensky madman,
have lived, which consisted in the idea that gentlefolk need
not work, and that all must be done for them by others, and
that, producing nothing, I have to do only what is proper to
man—satisfy my own wants.

And having discovered this, I became persuaded that this
labor for the satisfying of my own wants is divisible into
various kinds of labor, each of which has its own charm, and
is not only not a burden, but serves as rest after some other.

I have divided my labor into four parts parallel to the
four parts of the laborer's day's work, which are divided by
his meals; and thus I try to satisfy my wants.

These are, then, the answers to the question, "What is to
be done?" which I have found for myself.

First, To avoid deceiving myself. However far I have gone
astray from that road of life which my reason shows to me,
I must not be afraid of the truth.

Secondly, To renounce my own righteousness, my own
advantages, peculiarities, distinguishing me from others, and
to confess the guilt of such.

Thirdly, To fulfill that eternal, unquestionable law of
man—by laboring with all my being to struggle with nature,
to sustain my own life, and the lives of others.

I have now finished, having said all that concerns myself;
but I cannot restrain my desire to say that which concerns
everyone, and to verify by several considerations my own
deductions.

I wish to explain why it is I think that a great many of my
own class must arrive where I myself am, and I must also
speak of what will result if even some few men arrive there;
and in the first place, if only men of our circle, our caste,
will seriously think the matter out themselves, the younger
generation, who seek their own personal happiness, will
become afraid of the ever increasing misery of lives, which
obviously leads them to ruin; scrupulous persons among us

(if they would examine themselves more closely) will be terrified at the cruelty and unlawfulness of their own lives, and timid persons will be frightened at the danger of their mode of life.

The misery of our lives! However we, rich men, may try to mend and to support, with the assistance of our science and art, this our false life, it must become weaker every day, unhealthier, and more and more painful: with each year suicide, and the sin against the unborn babe, increase; with each year the new generations of our class grow weaker, with each year we more and more feel the increasing dullness of our lives.

It is obvious that on this road, with an increase of the comforts and delights of life, of cures, artificial teeth and hair, and so on, there can be no salvation.

This truth has become such a truism that in newspapers advertisements are printed about stomach powder for rich people, under the title "Blessings of the poor," where they say that only poor people have a good digestion, and the rich need help, and among other things this powder. You cannot ameliorate this matter by any kind of amusements, comforts, powders, but only by turning over a new leaf.

Our lives are in contradiction to our consciences. However much we may try to justify to ourselves our treason against mankind, all our justification falls to pieces before evidence: around us people are dying from overwork and want; and we destroy the food, clothes, labor of men merely in order to amuse ourselves. And therefore the conscience of a man of our circle, though he may have but a small remainder of it in his breast, cannot be stifled, and poisons all these comforts and charms of life which our suffering and perishing brethren procure for us. But not only does every scrupulous man feel this himself, but he must feel it more acutely at present, because the best part of art and science, that part in which there still remains a sense of its high calling, constantly reminds him of his cruelty, and the unlawfulness of his position.

The old secure justifications are all destroyed; and the new ephemeral justifications of the progress of science for science's sake, and art for art's sake, will not bear the light of plain common sense.

The conscience of men cannot be calmed by new ideas: it can be calmed only by turning over a new leaf, when there will no longer be any necessity for justification.

The danger to our lives! However much we may try to hide from ourselves the plain and most obvious danger of exhausting the patience of those men whom we oppress; however much we may try to counteract this danger by all sorts of deceit, violence, and flattery—it is still growing with each day, with each hour, and it has long been threatening us; but now it is so ripe that we are scarcely able to hold our course in a vessel tossed by a roaring and overflowing sea— a sea that will presently swallow us up in wrath.

The workman's revolution, with the terrors of destruction and murder, not only threatens us, but we have been already living upon its verge during the last thirty years, and it is only by various cunning devices that we have been postponing the crisis.

Such is the state in Europe; such is the state in Russia, because we have no safety valves. The classes who oppress the people, with the exception of the Czar, have no longer in the eyes of our people any justification; they all keep up their position merely by violence, cunning, and expediency; but the hatred toward us of the worst representatives of the people, and the contempt of us from the best, is increasing with every hour.

Among the Russian people during the last three or four years, a new word, full of significance, has been circulating: by this word, which I never heard before, people are swearing in the streets, and calling us parasites.

The hatred and contempt of the oppressed people are increasing, and the physical and moral strength of the richer classes are decreasing: the deceit that supports all this is wearing out, and the rich classes have nothing wherewith to comfort themselves. To return to the old order of things is impossible: one thing only remains for those who are not willing to change the course of their lives, and to turn over a new leaf—to hope that, during their lives, they will fare well enough, after which the people may do as they like. So think the blind crowd of the rich; but the danger is ever increasing, and the awful catastrophe is coming nearer and nearer.

There are three reasons that prove to rich people the

necessity of turning over a new leaf: First, the desire for their own personal welfare and that of their families, which is not secured by the way in which rich people are living; secondly, the inability to satisfy the voice of conscience, which is obviously impossible in the present condition of things; and thirdly, the threatening and constantly increasing danger to life, which cannot be met by any outward means. All these together ought to induce rich people to change their mode of life. This change alone would satisfy the desire of welfare and conscience, and would remove the danger. And there is but one means of making such change —to leave off deceiving ourselves, to repent, and to acknowledge labor to be, not a curse, but the joyful business of life.

To this it is replied, "What will come from the fact of my physical labor during ten, eight, or five hours, which thousands of peasants would gladly do for the money which I have?"

The first good would be, that you will become livelier, healthier, sounder, kinder; and you will learn that real life from which you have been hiding yourself, or which was hidden from you.

The second good will be that, if you have a conscience, it will not only not suffer as it suffers now looking at the labor of men, the importance of which we always, from our ignorance, either increase or diminish, but you will constantly experience a joyful acknowledgment that with each day you are more and more satisfying the demands of your conscience, and are leaving behind you that awful state in which so much evil is accumulated in our lives that we feel that we cannot possibly do any good in the world; you will experience the joy of free life, with the possibility of doing good to others; you will open for yourself a way into the regions of the world of morality which has hitherto been shut to you.

The third good will be this, that, instead of constant fear of revenge for your evil deeds, you will feel that you are saving others from this revenge, and are principally saving the oppressed from the cruel feeling of rancor and resentment.

But it is usually said that it would be ridiculous if we, men of our stamp, with deep philosophical, scientific, political, artistic, ecclesiastical, social questions before us, we state ministers, senators, academists, professors, artists, singers, we whose quarter-hours are valued so highly by men, should spend our time in doing—what? Cleaning our boots, washing our shirts, digging, planting potatoes, or feeding our chickens and cows, and so on—in such business which not only our house porter, our cook, but thousands of men besides who value our time, would be very glad to do for us.

But why do we dress, wash, and comb our hair ourselves? Why do we walk, hand chairs to ladies, to our guests, open and shut the door, help people into carriages, and perform hundreds of such actions that were formerly performed for us by our slaves?

Because we consider that such may be done by ourselves; that it is compatible with human dignity, that is, human duty. The same holds good with physical labor. Man's dignity, his sacred duty, is to use his hands, his feet, for that purpose for which they were given him, and not to be wasted by disuse, not that he may wash and clean them and use them only for the purpose of stuffing food and cigarettes into his mouth.

Such is the meaning of physical labor for every man in every society. But in our class, with the divergence from this law of nature came the misery of a whole circle of men; and for us, physical labor receives another meaning—the meaning of a preaching and a propaganda that divert the terrible evil that threatens mankind.

To say that for an educated man physical labor is a useless occupation is the same as to say, in the building of a temple, "What importance can there be in putting each stone exactly in its place?" Every great act is done under the conditions of imperceptibility, modesty, and simplicity. One can neither plow, nor feed cattle, nor think, during a great illumination, or thundering of guns, or while in uniform.

Illumination, the roar of cannon, music, uniforms, cleanliness, brilliancy, which we usually connect with the idea of the importance of any act, are, on the contrary, tokens of the absence of importance in the same. Great, true deeds are always simple and modest. And such is also the greatest deed that is left to us to do—the solution of those awful contradictions in which we are living. And the acts that solve those contradictions are those modest, imperceptible, seemingly ridiculous acts, such as helping ourselves by physical labor and, if possible, helping others too: this is what we rich people have to do, if we understand the misery, wrong, and danger of the position in which we are living.

What will come out of the circumstance that I, and another, and a third, and a tenth man, do not despise physical labor, but consider it necessary for our happiness, for the calming of our consciences, and for our safety? This will come of it—that one, two, three, ten men, coming into conflict with no one, without the violence either of the government or of revolution, will solve for themselves the problem that is before all the world, and which has appeared insolvable; and they will solve it in such a way that life will become for them a good thing: their consciences will be calm, and the evil that oppresses them will cease to be dreadful to them.

Another effect will be this: that other men, too, will see that the welfare, which they have been looking for everywhere, is quite close by them, that seemingly insolvable contradictions of conscience and the order of the world are solved in the easiest and pleasantest way, and that, instead of being afraid of men surrounding them, they must have intercourse with them and love them.

The seemingly insolvable economical and social questions are like the problem of Krilof's casket. The casket opened of itself, without any difficulty: but it will not open until men do the very simplest and most natural thing—that is, open it. The seemingly insolvable question is the old question of utilizing some men's labor by others: this question in our time has found its expression in property.

Formerly, other men's labor was used simply by violence, by slavery: in our time, it is being done by the means of property. In our time, property is the root of all evil and of the sufferings of men who possess it, or are without it, and of all the remorse of conscience of those who misuse it, and of the danger from the collision between those who have it and those who have it not.

Property is the root of all evil; and, at the same time, property is that toward which all the activity of our modern society is directed, and that which directs the activity of the world. States and governments intrigue, make wars, for the sake of property, for the possession of the banks of the Rhine, of land in Africa, China, the Balkan Peninsula.

Bankers, merchants, manufacturers, landowners, labor, use cunning, torment themselves, torment others, for the sake of property; government functionaries, tradesmen, landlords, struggle, deceive, oppress, suffer, for the sake of property; courts of justice and police protect property; penal servitude, prisons, all the terrors of so-called punishments—all is done for the sake of property.

Property is the root of all evil; and now all the world is busy with the distribution and protection of wealth.

What, then, is property? Men are accustomed to think that property is something really belonging to man, and for this reason they have called it "property." We speak indiscriminately of our own house and our own land. But this is obviously an error and a superstition. We know, and if we do not it is easy to perceive, that property is only the means of utilizing other men's labor. And another's labor can by no means belong to me.

Man has been always calling his own that which is subject to his own will and joined with his own consciousness. As soon as man calls his own something that is not his body, but which he should like to be subject to his will as his body is, then he makes a mistake, and gets disappointment, suffering, and compels other people to suffer as well. Man calls his wife his own—his children, his slaves, his belongings, his own too; but the reality always shows him his error, and he must either get rid of this superstition, or suffer and make others suffer.

Now we, having nominally renounced the possessing of slaves, owing to money (and to its exactment by the government), claim our right also to money; that is, to the labor of other men.

But as to our claiming our wives as our property, or our sons, our slaves, our horses—this is pure fiction contradicted by reality, and which only makes those suffer who believe in it; because a wife or a son will never be so subject to my will as my body is; therefore my own body will always remain the only thing I can call my true property; so also money—property will never be real property, but only a deception and a source of suffering, and it is only my own body that will be my property, that which always obeys me, and is connected with my consciousness.

It is only to us, who are so accustomed to call other things than our body our own, that such a wild superstition may appear useful for us, and be without evil results; but we have only to reflect upon the nature of the matter in order to see how this, like every other superstition, brings with it only dreadful consequences.

Let us take the most simple example. I consider myself my own, and another man like myself I consider my own, too. I must understand how to cook my dinner: if I were free from the superstition of considering another man as my property, I should have been taught this art as well as every other necessary to my real property (that is, my body); but now I have it taught to my imaginary property, and the result is that my cook does not obey me, does not wish to humor me, and even runs away from me, or dies, and I remain with an unsatisfied want, and have lost the habit of learning, and recognize that I have spent as much time in cares about this cook as I should have spent in learning the art of cooking myself.

The same is the case with the property of buildings, clothes, wares; with the property of the land; with the property of money. Every imaginary property calls forth in me a noncorresponding want that cannot always be gratified, and deprives me of the possibility of acquiring for my true and sure property—my own body—that information, that skill, those habits, improvements, which I might have acquired.

The result is always that I have spent (without gain to myself—to my true property) strength, sometimes my whole life, on that which never has been and never could be my property.

I provide myself with an imaginary "private" library, a "private" picture gallery, "private" apartments, clothes; acquire my "own" money in order to purchase with it everything I want, and the matter stands thus—that I, being busy about this imaginary property, as if it were real, leave quite out of sight that which is my true property, upon which I may really labor, and which really may serve me, and which always remains in my power.

Words have always a definite meaning until we purposely give them a false signification.

What does property mean?

Property means that which is given to me alone, which belongs to me alone, exclusively; that with which I may always do everything I like, which nobody can take away from me, which remains mine to the end of my life, and that I ought to use in order to increase and to improve it. Such property for every man is only himself.

And it is in this very sense that imaginary property is understood, that very property for the sake of which (in order to make it impossible for this imaginary property to become a real one) all the sufferings of this world exist— wars, executions, judgments, prisons, luxury, depravity, murders, and the ruin of mankind.

What, then, will come out of the circumstance that ten men plow, hew wood, make boots, not from want, but from the acknowledgment that man needs work, and that the more he works, the better it will be for him?

This will come out of it: that ten men, or even one single man, in thought and in deed, will show men that this fearful evil from which they are suffering is not the law of their destiny, nor the will of God, nor any historical necessity, but a superstition; not at all a strong or overpowering one, but weak and null, in which it is only necessary to leave off believing, as in idols, in order to get rid of it, and to destroy it as a frail cobweb is swept away.

Men who begin to work in order to fulfill the pleasant law of their lives, who work for the fulfillment of the law of labor, will free themselves from the superstition of property which is so full of misery, and then all these worldly establishments that exist in order to protect this imaginary property outside of one's own body will become not only unnecessary for them but burdensome; and it will become plain to all that these institutions are not necessary, but pernicious, imaginary, and false conditions of life.

For a man who considers labor not a curse, but a joy, property outside his own body—that is, the right or possibility of utilizing other men's labor—will be not only useless, but an impediment. If I am fond of cooking my dinner, and accustomed to do it, then the fact that another man will do it for me will deprive me of my usual business, and will not satisfy me so well as I have satisfied myself; besides, the acquirement of an imaginary property will not be necessary for such a man: a man who considers labor to be his very life fills up with it all his life and therefore requires less and

less the labor of others—in other words, property in order
to fill up his unoccupied time and to embellish his life.

If the life of a man is occupied by labor, he does not
require many rooms, much furniture, various fine clothes;
he does not require expensive food, carriages, amusements.
But particularly a man who considers labor to be the business
and the joy of his life will not seek to ease his own labor by
utilizing that of others.

A man who considers life to consist in labor, in proportion
as he acquires more skill, craft, and endurance, will aim at
having more and more work to do, which should occupy all
his time. For such a man, who sees the object of his life in
labor and not in the results of this labor for the acquirement
of property, there cannot be even a question about the instruments of labor. Though such a man will always choose the
most productive instrument of labor, he will have the same
satisfaction in working with the most unproductive.

If he has a steam plow, he will plow with it; if he has not
such, he will plow with a horse plow; if he has not this, he
will plow with the plain Russian *sokha;* if he has not even
this, he will use a spade: and under any circumstances, he
will attain his aim; that is, will pass his life in a labor useful
to man, and therefore he will have fullest satisfaction; and
the position of such a man, according to exterior and interior
circumstances, will be happier than the condition of a man
who gives his life away to acquire property.

According to exterior circumstances, he will never want,
because men, seeing that he does not mind work, will always
try to make his labor most productive to them, as they
arrange a mill by running water; and in order that his labor
may be more productive, they will provide for his material
existence, which they will never do for men who aim at
acquiring property.

And the providing for material wants is all that a man
requires. According to interior conditions, such a man will
be always happier than he who seeks for property, because
the latter will never receive what he is aiming at, and the former always in proportion to his strength: even the weak, old,
dying (according to the proverb, with a *Kored* in his hands),
will receive full satisfaction, and the love and sympathy of
men.

One of the consequences of this will be that some odd, half-insane persons will plow, make boots, and so on, instead of smoking, playing cards, and riding about, carrying with them, from one place to another, their dullness during the ten hours that every man of letters has at his command.

Another result will be that those silly people will demonstrate, in deed, that that imaginary property for the sake of which men suffer, torment themselves and others, is not necessary for happiness, and even impedes it, and is only a superstition; and that true property is only one's own head, hands, feet; and that in order to utilize this true property usefully and joyfully, it is necessary to get rid of the false idea of property outside one's own body, on which we waste the best powers of our life.

Another result will be that these men will show that, when a man leaves off believing in imaginary property, then only will he make real use of his true property—his own body, which will yield him fruit a hundredfold, and such happiness of which we have no idea as yet; and he will be a useful, strong, kind man, who will everywhere stand on his own feet, will always be a brother to everybody, will be intelligible to all, desired by all, and dear to all.

And men, looking at one, at ten, such silly men will understand what they have all to do in order to undo that dreadful knot in which they have all been tied by the superstition respecting property, in order to get rid of the miserable condition from which they are groaning now, and from which they do not know how to free themselves.

But what can a man do in a crowd who do not agree with him? There is no reasoning that could more obviously demonstrate the unrighteousness of those who employ it as does this. The boatmen are dragging vessels against the stream. Is it possible that there could be found such a stupid boatman who would refuse to do his part in dragging because he alone cannot drag the boat up against the stream? He who, besides his rights of animal life—to eat and to sleep—acknowledges any human duty, knows very well wherein such duty consists: just in the same way as a boatman knows that he has only to get into his breast collar, and to walk in the given direction, to find out what he has to do and how to do it.

And so with the boatmen, and with all men who do any labor in common, so with the labor of all mankind; each man need only keep on his breast collar, and go in the given direction. And for this purpose one and the same reason is given to all men, that this direction may always be the same.

And that this direction *is* given to us is obvious and certain from the lives of those who surround us, as well as in the conscience of every man, and in all the previous expressions of human wisdom; so that only he who does not want work may say that he does not see it.

What will, then, come out of this?

This: that first one man, then another, will drag; looking at them, a third will join; and so one by one the best men will join, until the business will be set a-going, and will move as of itself, inducing those also to join who do not yet understand why and wherefore it is being done.

First, to the number of men who conscientiously work in order to fulfill the law of God, will be added those who will accept half conscientiously and half upon faith; then to these a still greater number of men, only upon the faith in the foremost men; and lastly the majority of people: and then it will come to pass that men will cease to ruin themselves, and will find out happiness.

This will happen soon when men of our circle, and after them all the great majority of working people, will no longer consider it shameful to clean sewers, but will consider it shameful to fill them up in order that other men, *our brethren,* may carry their contents away; they will not consider it shameful to go visiting in common boots, but they will consider it shameful to walk in goloshes by barefooted people; they will not think it shameful not to know French, or about the last novel, but they will consider it shameful to eat bread, and not to know how it is prepared; they will not consider it shameful not to have a starched shirt or a clean dress, but that it is shameful to wear a clean coat as a token of one's idleness; they will not consider it shameful to have dirty hands, but not to have callouses on their hands.

Within my memory, still more striking changes have taken place. I remember that at table, behind each chair, a servant stood with a plate. Men made visits accompanied by two footmen. A Cossack boy and a girl stood in a room to give people their pipes, and to clean them, and so on. Now this seems to us strange and remarkable. But is it not equally strange that a young man or woman, or even an elderly man, in order to visit a friend, should order his horses to be harnessed, and that well-fed horses are only kept for this purpose? Is it not as strange that one man lives in five rooms, or that a women spends tens, hundreds, thousands of rubles for her dress when she only needs some flax and wool in order to spin dresses for herself and clothes for her husband and children?

Is it not strange that men live doing nothing, riding to and fro, smoking and playing, and that a battalion of people are busy feeding and warming them?

Is it not strange that old people quite gravely talk and write in newspapers about theaters, music, and other insane people drive to look at musicians or actors?

Is it not strange that tens of thousands of boys and girls are brought up so as to make them unfit for every work (they return home from school, and their two books are carried for them by a servant)?

There will soon come a time, and it is already drawing near, when it will be shameful to dine on five courses served by footmen, and cooked by any but the masters themselves; it will be shameful not only to ride thoroughbreds or in a coach when one has feet to walk on; to wear on weekdays such dress, shoes, gloves, in which it is impossible to work; it will be shameful to play on a piano that costs one hundred and fifty pounds, or even ten pounds, while others work for one; to feed dogs upon milk and white bread, and to burn lamps and candles without working by their light; to heat stoves in which the meal is not cooked. Then it would be impossible to think about giving openly not merely one pound, but sixpence, for a place in a concert or in a theater. All this will be when the law of labor becomes public opinion.

Albert Camus   Rebellious Man[1]

Albert Camus (1913–1960)   Camus was born in Algeria. For a short period of time he was a communist. Then his association

[1] From *The Rebel* by Albert Camus, translated by Anthony Bower, Copyright 1956 by Alfred A. Knopf, Inc. Published in London by Hamish Hamilton Ltd. Reprinted by permission of the publishers.

with Sartre earned him the reputation of being an existentialist,
although the two men severed their relationship after a profound political disagreement. In recoiling from communist
rigidity, he also rejected a nihilism that felt little commitment
about man's behavior. He clung to faith in individual man
whose assertion of life as a value might save him from utter
despair and from collectivist extremities. He perished in a tragic
car accident at the age of 46. He published a considerable number of plays. His two most widely known novels are *The
Stranger* and *The Plague*. His two philosophic volumes are *The
Myth of Sisyphus* and *The Rebel*.

HISTORICAL REBELLION

Freedom, "that terrible word in-
scribed on the chariot of the storm," is the motivating
principle of all revolutions. Without it, justice seems inconceivable to the rebel's mind. There comes a time, however,
when justice demands the suspension of freedom. Then
terror, on a grand or small scale, makes its appearance to
consummate the revolution. Every act of rebellion expresses
a nostalgia for innocence and an appeal to the essence of
being. But, one day, nostalgia takes up arms and assumes the
responsibility of total guilt; in other words, adopts murder
and violence. The servile rebellions, the regicide revolutions,
and the twentieth-century revolutions have thus, consciously,
accepted a burden of guilt that increased in proportion to the
degree of liberation they proposed to introduce. This contradiction, which has become only too obvious, prevents our
contemporary revolutionaries from displaying that aspect of
happiness and optimism that shone forth from the faces and
the speeches of the members of the Constituent Assembly in
1789. Is this contradiction inevitable? Does it characterize or
betray the value of rebellion? These questions are bound to
arise about revolution as they are bound to arise about metaphysical rebellion. Actually, revolution is only the logical
consequence of metaphysical rebellion, and we shall discover, in our analysis of the revolutionary movement, the
same desperate and bloody effort to affirm the dignity of man
in defiance of the things that deny its existence. The revolutionary spirit thus undertakes the defence of that part of
man which refuses to submit. In other words, it tries to
assure him his crown in the realm of time, and, rejecting

God, it chooses history with an apparently inevitable logic.

In theory, the word revolution retains the meaning that it has in astronomy. It is a movement that describes a complete circle, that leads from one form of government to another after a total transition. A change of regulations concerning property without a corresponding change of government is not a revolution, but a reform. There is no kind of economic revolution, whether its methods are violent or pacific, that is not, at the same time, manifestly political. Revolution can already be distinguished, in this way, from rebellion. The warning given to Louis XVI—"No, sire, this is not a rebellion, it is a revolution"—accents the essential difference. It means precisely that "it is the absolute certainty of a new form of government." Rebellion is, by nature, limited in scope. It is no more than an incoherent pronouncement. Revolution, on the contrary, originates in the realm of ideas. Specifically, it is the injection of ideas into historic experience while rebellion is only the movement that leads from individual experience into the realm of ideas. While even the collective history of a movement of rebellion is always that of a fruitless struggle with facts, of an obscure protest that involves neither methods nor reasons, a revolution is an attempt to shape actions to ideas, to fit the world into a theoretic frame. That is why rebellion kills men while revolution destroys both men and principles. But, for the same reasons, it can be said that there has not yet been a revolution in the course of history. There could only be one and that would be the definitive revolution. The movement that seems to complete the circle already begins to describe another, at the precise moment when the new government is formed. The anarchists, with Varlet as their leader, were made well aware of the fact that government and revolution are incompatible in the direct sense. "It implies a contradiction," says Proudhon, "that a government could ever be called revolutionary, for the very simple reason that it is the government." Now that the experiment has been made, let us qualify that statement by adding that a government can only be revolutionary in opposition to other governments. Revolutionary governments are, most of the time, obliged to be war governments. The more extensive the revolution the more considerable the chances of the war that it implies. The society born of the revolution of 1789 wanted to fight for

Europe. The society born of the 1917 revolution is fighting
for universal dominion. Total revolution ends by demanding
—we shall see why—the control of the world.

While waiting for this to happen, if happen it must, the
history of man, in one sense, is the sum total of his successive
rebellions. In other words, the movement of transition that
can be clearly expressed in terms of space is only an approxi-
mation in terms of time. What was devoutly called, in the
nineteenth century, the progressive emancipation of the
human race appears, from the outside, like an uninterrupted
series of rebellions that overreach themselves and try to find
their formulation in ideas, but that have not yet reached the
point of definitive revolution where everything on heaven
and earth would be stablized. A superficial examination
seems to infer, rather than any real emancipation, an affirmation of mankind by man, an affirmation increasingly broad
in scope but that is always unrealized. In fact, if there had
ever been one real revolution, there would be no more history. Unity would have been achieved and death would
have been satiated. That is why all revolutionaries finally
aspire to world unity and act as though they believed that
history were dead. The originality of twentieth-century revolution lies in the fact that, for the first time, it openly claims
to realize the ancient dream of unity of the human race
and, at the same time, the definitive consummation of history. Just as rebel movements led to the point of "All or
Nothing" and just as metaphysical rebellion demanded the
unity of the world, the twentieth-century revolutionary movement, when it arrived at the most obvious conclusions of its
logic, insisted with threats of force on arrogating to itself the
whole of history. Rebellion is therefore compelled, on pain
of appearing futile or being out of date, to become revolutionary. It no longer suffices for the rebel to declare himself
God or to look to his own salvation by adopting a certain
attitude of mind. The species must be deified, as Nietzsche
attempted to do, and his ideal of the superman must be
adopted so as to assure salvation for all—as Ivan Karamazov
wanted. For the first time, the Possessed appear on the scene
and proceed to give the answer to one of the secrets of the
times: the identity of reason and of the will to power. Now
that God is dead, the world must be changed and organized
by the forces at man's disposal. The force of imprecation

alone is not enough, and weapons are needed for the conquest of totality. Revolution, even, and above all, revolution that claims to be materialist, is only a limitless metaphysical crusade. But can totality claim to be unity? That is the question that this book must answer. So far we can only say that the purpose of this analysis is not to give, for the hundredth time, a description of the revolutionary phenomenon, nor once more to examine the historic or economic causes of great revolutions. Its purpose is to discover in certain revolutionary data the logical sequence, the explanations, and the invariable themes of metaphysical rebellion.

The majority of revolutions are shaped by, and derive their originality from, murder. All, or almost all, have been homicidal. But some, in addition, have practiced regicide and deicide. Just as the history of metaphysical rebellion began with Sade, so our real inquiry only begins with his contemporaries, the regicides, who attack the incarnation of divinity without yet daring to kill the principle of eternity.

When a slave rebels against his master the situation presented is of one man pitted against another, under a cruel sky, far from the exalted realms of principles. The final result is merely the murder of a man. The servile rebellions, peasant risings, beggar tumults, rustic outbreaks, all advance the concept of a principle of equality, life for life, which despite every kind of mystification and audacity will always be found in the purest manifestations of the revolutionary spirit: Russian terrorism in 1905, for example.

Spartacus' rebellion, which took place as the ancient world was coming to an end, a few decades before the Christian era, is an excellent illustration of this point. First we note that this is a rebellion of gladiators, that is to say, of slaves consecrated to single combat and condemned, for the delectation of their masters, to kill or be killed. Beginning with seventy men, this rebellion ended with an army of seventy thousand insurgents, which crushed the best Roman legions and advanced through Italy to march on the Eternal City itself. However, as André Prudhommeaux remarks, this rebellion introduced no new principle to Roman life. The proclamation issued by Spartacus goes no further than to offer "equal rights" to the slaves. The transition from fact to right that we analyzed in the first stage of rebellion is, in fact, the only logical acquisition that one can find on this level of rebellion. The insurgent rejects slavery and affirms his equality with his master. He wants to be master in his turn.

Spartacus' rebellion is a constant illustration of this principle of positive claims. The slave army liberates the slaves and immediately hands over their former masters to them in bondage. According to one tradition, of doubtful veracity it is true, gladiatorial combats were even organized between several hundred Roman citizens while the slaves sat in the grandstands delirious with joy and excitement. But to kill men only leads to killing more men. To allow a principle to triumph, another principle must be overthrown. The city of light of which Spartacus dreamed could only have been built on the ruins of eternal Rome, of its institutions and of its gods. Spartacus' army marches to lay siege to a Rome paralyzed with fear at the prospect of having to pay for its crimes. However, at the decisive moment, within sight of the sacred walls, the army halts and wavers, as if it were retreating before the principles, the institutions, the city of the gods. When these had been destroyed, what could he put in their place, except the brutal desire for justice, the wounded and exacerbated love that until this moment, had kept these wretches on their feet.[2] In any case, the army retreated without having fought, and then made the curious move of deciding to return to the place where the slave rebellion originated, to retrace the long road of its victories and to return to Sicily. It was as though these outcasts, forever alone and helpless before the great tasks that awaited them and too daunted to assail the heavens, returned to what was purest and most heartening in their history, to the land of their first awakening, where it was easy and right to die.

Then began their defeat and martyrdom. Before the last battle, Spartacus crucified a Roman citizen to show his men the fate that was in store for them. During the battle, Spartacus himself tried with frenzied determination, the symbolism of which is obvious, to reach Crassus, who was commanding the Roman legions. He wanted to perish, but in single combat

---

[2] Spartacus' rebellion recapitulates the program of the servile rebellions that preceded it. But this program is limited to the distribution of land and the abolition of slavery. It is not directly concerned with the gods of the city. [Camus' note, as are others in this extract.]

with the man who symbolized, at that moment, every Roman master; it was his dearest wish to die, but in absolute equality. He did not reach Crassus: principles wage war at a distance and the Roman general kept himself apart. Spartacus died as he wished, but at the hands of mercenaries, slaves like himself, who killed their own freedom with his. In revenge for the one crucified citizen, Crassus crucified thousands of slaves. The six thousand crosses that, after such a just rebellion, staked out the road from Capua to Rome, demonstrated to the servile crowd that there is no equality in the world of power and that the masters calculate, at a usurious rate, the price of their own blood.

The Cross is also Christ's punishment. One can imagine that He only chose a slave's punishment, a few years later, so as to reduce the enormous distance that henceforth would separate humiliated humanity from the implacable face of the Master. He intercedes, He submits to the most extreme injustice so that rebellion shall not divide the world in two, so that suffering will also light the way to heaven and preserve it from the curses of mankind. What is astonishing in, the fact that the revolutionary spirit, when it wanted to affirm the separation of heaven and earth, should begin by disembodying the divinity by killing His representatives on earth? In certain aspects, the period of rebellions comes to an end in 1793 and revolutionary times begin—on a scaffold.[3]

STATE TERRORISM AND IRRATIONAL TERROR

All modern revolutions have ended in a reinforcement of the power of the State. Seventeen eighty-nine brings Napoleon; 1848 Napoleon III; 1917 Stalin; the Italian disturbances of the twenties, Mussolini; the Weimar Republic, Hitler. These revolutions, particularly after the First World War had liquidated the vestiges of divine right, still proposed, with increasing audacity, to build the city of humanity and of authentic freedom. The growing omnipotence of the State sanctioned this ambition on every occasion. It would be erroneous to say that this was bound to happen. But it is possible to

[3] In that this book is not concerned with the spirit of rebellion inside Christianity, the Reformation has no place here, nor the numerous rebellions against ecclesiastical authority that preceded it. But we can say, at least, that the Reformation prepares the way for Jacobinism and in one sense initiates the reforms that 1789 carries out.

examine how it did happen; and perhaps the lesson will automatically follow.

Apart from a few explanations, which are not the subject of this essay, the strange and terrifying growth of the modern State can be considered as the logical conclusion of inordinate technical and philosophical ambitions, foreign to the true spirit of rebellion, but which, nevertheless, gave birth to the revolutionary spirit of our time. The prophetic dream of Marx and the overinspired predictions of Hegel or of Nietzsche ended by conjuring up, after the city of God had been razed to the ground, either a rational or an irrational State, but one that in both cases was founded on terror.

In actual fact, the fascist revolutions of the twentieth century do not merit the title of revolution. They lacked the ambition of universality. Mussolini and Hitler, of course, tried to build an empire and the National-Socialist ideologists were bent, explicitly, on world domination. But the difference between them and the classic revolutionary movement is that, of the nihilist inheritance, they chose to deify the irrational, and the irrational alone, instead of deifying reason. In this way they renounced their claim to universality. And yet Mussolini is a disciple of Hegel and Hitler of Nietzsche; and both illustrate, historically, some of the prophecies of German ideology. In this respect they belong to the history of rebellion and of nihilism. They were the first to construct a State on the concept that everything was meaningless and that history was only written in terms of the hazards of force. The consequences were not long in appearing.

As early as 1914 Mussolini proclaimed the "holy religion of anarchy," and declared himself the enemy of every form of Christianity. As for Hitler, his professed religion unhesitatingly juxtaposed the God-Providence and Valhalla. Actually his god was an argument at a political meeting and a manner of reaching an impressive climax at the end of speeches. As long as he was successful, he chose to believe that he was inspired. In the hour of defeat, he considered himself betrayed by his people. Between the two nothing intervened to announce to the world that he would ever have been capable of thinking himself guilty in regard to any principle. The only man of superior culture who gave Nazism even an appearance of being a philosophy, Ernst Junger, even went so far as to choose the actual formulae of nihilism:

"The best answer to the betrayal of life by the spirit, is the betrayal of the spirit by the spirit, and one of the great and cruel pleasures of our times is to participate in the work of destruction."

Men of action, when they are without faith, have never believed in anything but action. For Hitler, the insupportable paradox lay precisely in wanting to found a stable order on perpetual change and on negation. Rauschning, in his *The Revolution of Nihilism,* was right in saying that the Hitlerian revolution was dynamic to the utmost degree. In Germany, shaken to its foundations by a war without precedent, by defeat and by economic distress, values no longer existed. Although one must take into consideration what Goethe called "the German destiny of making everything difficult," the epidemic of suicides that affected the entire country, between the two wars, indicates a great deal about the state of mental confusion. To those who despair of everything, reason cannot provide a faith, but only passion, and in this case it must be the same passion that lay at the root of the despair, namely, humiliation and hatred. There was no longer any standard of values, both common to and superior to the German people, in the name of which it would have been possible for them to judge one another. The Germany of 1933 thus agreed to adopt the degraded values of a mere handful of men and tried to impose them on an entire civilization. Deprived of the morality of Goethe, Germany chose, and submitted to, the ethics of the gang.

Gangster morality is an inexhaustible round of triumph and revenge, defeat and resentment. When Mussolini extolled "the elementary forces of the individual," he announced the exaltation of the dark powers of blood and instinct, the biological justification of all the worst things produced by the instinct of domination. At the Nuremberg trials, Frank emphasized "the hatred of form" that animated Hitler. It is true that this man was nothing but an elemental force in motion, directed and rendered more effective by extreme cunning and by a relentless tactical clairvoyance. Even his physical appearance, which was thoroughly mediocre and commonplace, was no limitation: it established him firmly with the masses. Action alone kept him alive. For him, to exist was to act. That is why Hitler and his regime could not dispense with enemies. They could

only define themselves, frenetic dandies[4] that they were, in
relation to their enemies and only assume their final form in
the bloody battle that was to be their downfall. The Jews,
the Freemasons, the plutocrats, the Anglo-Saxons, the bestial
Slavs succeeded one another in their propaganda and their
history as a means of bolstering up, each time a little higher,
the blind force that was stumbling headlong towards its end.
Perpetual strife demanded perpetual stimulants.

Hitler was history in its purest form. "Evolution," said
Junger, "is far more important than living." Thus he preaches
complete identification with the stream of life, on the lowest
level and in defiance of all superior reality. A regime that
invented a biological foreign policy was obviously acting
against its own best interests. But at least it obeyed its own
particular logic. Rosenberg speaks pompously of life in the
following terms: "The style of a column on the march, and it
is of little importance towards what destination and for what
ends this column is marching." Though later the column will
strew ruins over the pages of history and will devastate its
own country, it will at least have had the gratification of living. The real logic of this dynamism was either total defeat
or a progress from conquest to conquest and from enemy to
enemy, until the eventual establishment of the empire of
blood and action. It is very unlikely that Hitler ever had any
conception, except in the most elementary fashion, of this
empire. Neither by culture, nor even by instinct or tactical
intelligence, was he equal to his destiny. Germany collapsed
as a result of having engaged in a struggle for empire with
the concepts of provincial politics. But Junger had grasped
the import of this logic and had formulated it in definite
terms. He had a vision of "a technological world empire,"
of a "religion of anti-Christian technology," of which the
faithful and the militants would have themselves been the
priests because (and here Junger rejoins Marx), by his
human structure, the worker is universal. "The Statutes of
a new authoritarian regime take the place of a change in the
social contract. The worker is removed from the sphere of
negotiation, from pity and from literature and elevated to
the sphere of action. Legal obligations are transformed into
military obligations." It can be seen that the empire is simul-

---

[4] It is well known that Goering sometimes entertained dressed as Nero and
with his face made up.

taneously the factory and the barracks of the world, where
Hegel's soldier-worker reigns as a slave. Hitler was halted
relatively soon on the way to the realization of this empire.
But even if he had gone still further, we would only have
witnessed the more and more extensive deployment of an
irresistible dynamism and the increasingly violent enforcement of cynical principles which alone would be capable of
serving this dynamism.

Speaking of such a revolution, Rauschning says that it has
nothing to do with liberation, justice, and inspiration: it is
"the death of freedom, the triumph of violence, and the enslavement of the mind." Fascism is an act of contempt, in
fact. Inversely, every form of contempt, if it intervenes in
politics, prepares the way for, or establishes, fascism. It must
be added that fascism cannot be anything else but an expression of contempt without denying itself. Junger drew the
conclusion from his own principles that it was better to be
criminal than bourgeois. Hitler, who was endowed with less
literary talent but, on this occasion, with more coherence,
knew that to be either one or the other was a matter of complete indifference, from the moment that one ceased to believe in anything but success. Thus he authorized himself to
be both at the same time. "Fact is all," said Mussolini. And
Hitler added: "When the race is in danger of being oppressed
. . . the question of legality only plays a secondary role."
Moreover, in that the race must always be menaced in order
to exist, there is never any legality. "I am ready to sign anything, to agree to anything. . . . As far as I am concerned,
I am capable, in complete good faith, of signing treaties today and of dispassionately tearing them up tomorrow if the
future of the German people is at stake." Before he declared
war, moreover, Hitler made the statement to his generals that
no one was going to ask the victor if he had told the truth or
not. The *leitmotif* of Goering's defence at the Nuremberg
trials returned time and again to this theme, "the victor will
always be the judge and the vanquished will always be the
accused." That is a point that can certainly be argued. But
then it is hard to understand Rosenberg when he said during
the Nuremberg trials that he had not foreseen that the Nazi
myth would lead to murder. When the English prosecuting
counsel observes that "from *Mein Kampf* the road led
straight to the gas chambers at Maidanek," he touches on the

real subject of the trial, the historic responsibilities of Western nihilism and the only one that, nevertheless, was not really discussed at Nuremberg, for reasons only too apparent. A trial cannot be conducted by announcing the general culpability of a civilization. Only the actual deeds that, at least, stank in the nostrils of the entire world were brought to judgment.

Hitler, in any event, invented the perpetual motion of conquest without which he would have been nothing at all. But the perpetual enemy is perpetual terror, this time on the level of the State. The State is identified with the "apparatus," that is to say with the sum total of mechanisms of conquest and repression. Conquest directed towards the interior of the country is called repression or propaganda ("the first step on the road to hell," according to Frank)—directed towards the exterior, it creates the army. All problems are thus military, posed in terms of power and efficiency. The supreme commander determines policy and also deals with all the main problems of administration. This principle, axiomatic as far as strategy is concerned, is applied to civil life in general. One leader, one people, signifies one master and millions of slaves. The political intermediaries who are, in all societies, the guarantors of freedom, disappear to make way for a booted and spurred Jehovah who rules over the silent masses or, which comes to the same thing, over masses who shout words of command at the top of their lungs. There is no organ of conciliation or mediation interposed between the leader and the people, nothing in fact but the apparatus, in other words the party, which is the emanation of the leader and the tool of his will to oppress. In this way the first and sole principle of this degraded form of mysticism is born, the *Führerprinzip*, which restores idolatry and a debased deity to the world of nihilism.

Mussolini, who was a Latin and, therefore, by nature a jurist, contented himself with reasons of State, which he transformed, with a great deal of rhetoric, into the absolute. "Nothing beyond the State, above the State, against the State. Everything to the State, for the State, in the State." The Germany of Hitler gave his false reasoning its real expression, which was that of a religion. "Our divine mission," a Nazi newspaper says during a party congress, "was to lead everyone back to his origins, back to the common Mother.

It was truly a divine mission." The origins of this are to be found in a primitive baying to the moon. Who is the god in question? An official party declaration answers that "all of us, here below, believe in Adolf Hitler, our Führer . . . and [we confess] that National Socialism is the only faith which can lead our people to salvation." The command-ments of the leader, standing in the burning bush of search-lights, on a Sinai of planks and flags, therefore comprise both law and virtue. If the superhuman microphones give orders only once for a crime to be committed, then the crime is handed down from chief to subchief until it reaches the slave who receives orders without being able to pass them on to anybody. One of the Dachau executioners weeps in prison and says, "I only obeyed orders. The Führer and the Reichsführer, alone, planned all this and then they ran away. Gluecks received orders from Kaltenbrunner and, finally, I received orders to carry out the shootings. I have been left holding the bag because I was only a little *Hauptscharführer* and because I couldn't hand it on any lower down the line. Now they say I am the assassin." Goering, during the trial, proclaimed his loyalty to the Führer and said that "there was still a code of honor in that accursed life." Honor lay in obedience, which was often confused with crime. Military law punishes disobedience by death and its honor is servi-tude. When all the world has become military, then crime consists in not killing if military orders insist on it.

Orders, unfortunately, seldom insist on good deeds. Pure doctrinal dynamism cannot be directed towards good, but only towards efficaciousness. As long as enemies exist, terror will exist; and there will be enemies as long as dynamism exists to insure that "all the influences liable to undermine the sovereignty of the people, as exercised by the Führer with the assistance of the party . . . must be eliminated." Enemies are heretics, they must be converted by preaching or propaganda; they must be exterminated by Inquisition or Gestapo. The result is that man, if he is a member of the party, is no more than a tool in the hands of the Führer, a cog in the apparatus, or, if he is the enemy of the Führer, a waste product of the machine. The impetus towards irration-ality of this movement, born of rebellion, now even goes so far as to propose subjugating all that makes man more than a cog in the machine; in other words, rebellion itself. The romantic individualism of the German revolution finally peters out in the world of inanimate objects. Irrational terror transforms men into matter, "planetary bacilli," according to Hitler's formula. This formula proposes the destruction, not only of the individual, but of the universal possibilities of the individual, of reflection, solidarity, and the urge to absolute love. Propaganda and torture are the direct means of bringing about disintegration; more destructive still are systematic degradation, joint culpability with the cynical criminal and forced complicity. He who kills or tortures will only experience the shadow of victory: he will be unable to feel that he is innocent. Thus, he must create guilt in his victim so that, in a world that has no direction, universal guilt will authorize no other course of action but the use of force and give its blessing to nothing but success. When the concept of innocence disappears from the mind of the innocent victim himself, the value of power establishes a definitive rule over a world in despair. That is why an unworthy and cruel condemnation to penitence reigns in this world where only the stones are innocent. The condemned are compelled to hang one another. Even the innocent cry of maternity is stifled, as in the case of the Greek mother who was forced by an officer to choose which of her three sons was to be shot. This is the final realization of freedom: the power to kill and degrade saves the servile soul from utter emptiness. The hymn of German freedom is sung, to the music of a prisoners' orchestra, in the camps of death.

The crimes of the Hitler regime, among them the massacre of the Jews, are without precedent in history because history gives no other example of a doctrine of such total destruction being able to seize the levers of command of a civilized nation. But above all, for the first time in history, the rulers of a country have used their immense power to establish a mystique beyond the bounds of any ethical considerations. This first attempt to found a Church on nothingness was paid for by complete annihilation. The destruction of Lidice demonstrates clearly that the systematic and scientific aspect of the Nazi movement really hides an irrational drive that can be interpreted only as a drive of despair and arrogance. Until then, there were supposedly only two possible attitudes towards a village that was considered rebellious. Either calculated repression and cold-blooded execution of hostages, or a savage and necessarily brief sack by enraged soldiers. Lidice was destroyed by both methods simultaneously. It illustrates the ravages of that irrational form of reason which is the only value that can be found in the whole story. Not only were all the houses burned to the ground, the hundred and seventy-four men of the village shot, the two hundred and three women deported, and the three hundred children transferred elsewhere to be educated in the religion of the Führer, but special teams spent months at work levelling the terrain with dynamite, destroying the very stones, filling in the village pond and, finally, diverting the course of the river. After that, Lidice was really nothing more than a mere possibility according to the logic of the movement. To make assurance doubly sure, the cemetery was emptied of its dead who might have been a perpetual reminder that once something existed in this place.

The nihilist revolution, which is expressed historically in the Hitlerian religion, thus only aroused an insensate passion for nothingness that ended by turning against itself. Negation, this time without and despite Hegel, has not been creative. Hitler presents the example that is perhaps unique in history of a tyrant who has left absolutely no trace of his activities. For himself, for his people, and for the world, he was nothing but the epitome of suicide and murder. Seven million Jews assassinated, seven million Europeans deported or killed, ten million war victims are, perhaps, not sufficient to allow history to pass judgment: history is accustomed to murderers. But the very destruction of Hitler's final justification, by which we mean the German nation, henceforth makes this man, whose presence in history for years on end haunted the minds of millions of men, into an inconsistent and contemptible phantom. Speer's deposition at the Nuremberg trials showed that Hitler, although he could have stopped the war before the point of total disaster, really wanted universal suicide and the material and political destruction of the German nation. The only value for him remained, until the bitter end, success. Since Germany had lost the war, she was cowardly and treacherous and she deserved to die. "If the German people are incapable of victory, they are unworthy to live." Hitler, therefore, decided to drag them with him to the grave and to make his death an apotheosis, when the Russian cannons were already splitting apart the walls of his palace in Berlin. Hitler, Goering, who wanted to see his bones placed in a marble tomb, Goebbels, Himmler, Ley, killed themselves in dugouts or in cells. But their deaths were deaths for nothing, and they themselves were like a bad dream, a puff of smoke that vanishes. Neither efficacious nor exemplary, they consecrate the bloodthirsty vanity of nihilism. "They thought they were free," Frank cries hysterically; "didn't they know that no one escapes from Hitlerism?" They did not know: nor did they know that the negation of everything is in itself a form of servitude and that real freedom is an inner submission to a value that defies history and its successes.

But the fascist mystics, even though they aimed at gradually dominating the world, really never had pretensions to a universal empire. At the very most, Hitler, astonished at his own victories, was diverted from the provincial origins of his movement towards the indefinite dream of an empire of the Germans that had nothing to do with the universal city. Russian communism, on the contrary, by its very origins, openly aspires to world empire. That is its strength, its deliberate significance and its importance in our history. Despite appearances, the German revolution had no hope of a future. It was only a primitive impulse whose ravages have been greater than its real ambitions. Russian communism, on the contrary, has appropriated the metaphysical ambition that this book describes, the erection, after the death of God, of a city of man finally deified. The name "revolution," to which Hitler's adventure had no claim, was once deserved by Russian communism, and although it apparently deserves it no longer, it claims that one day it will deserve it forever. For the first time in history, a doctrine and a movement supported by an empire in arms has, as its purpose, definitive revolution and the unification of the world. It remains for us to examine this intention in detail. Hitler, at the height of his madness, wanted to fix the course of history for a thousand years. He thought himself on the point of doing so, and the realist philosophers of the conquered nations were preparing to acknowledge this and to excuse it, when the battle of Britain and Stalingrad threw him back on the path of death and set history once more on the march. But, as indefatigable as history itself, the claim of the human race to divinity is once more brought to life with more serious-

ness, more efficiency, and more reason under the auspices of
the rational state as it is to be found in Russia.

Emma Goldman Love Among the Free [1]

Emma Goldman (1869–1940)   Born in Kovno, Russia, Emma Goldman came to the United States in 1886. Her early schooling
consisted of a wretchedly oppressive religious education, which
was mercifully shortlived. As a girl she witnessed the cruel
beating of a peasant that was to leave its mark upon her. In her
last few months of school, she came into contact with radical
students, which also left an important influence. On arriving in
the United States, she settled in Rochester, where exhausting
factory work and an unhappy marriage ending in divorce made
her decide to resettle in New York. In New York she came
into contact with anarchist circles and expanded her great oratorical talents on behalf of the movement. She was a great
champion of women's rights and fought for birth-control methods with Margaret Sanger. She wrote a great number of articles, traveled widely on behalf of the anarchist movement, suffered deportation to Russia with Berkman, made her way back
to the U. S. She spent a number of years in England, Canada,
and Spain, agitating, sometimes enduring imprisonment and
always giving her life and energies to her ideals. She was described as a highly dynamic and attractive personality with an
impressive and untainted crusading zeal. Some of her books
are: *Anarchism and Other Essays, The Social Significance of
the Modern Drama, My Disillusionment in Russia, Living My
Life,* and numerous pamphlets.

THE TRAGEDY OF WOMAN'S EMANCIPATION

I begin with an admission: Re-
gardless of all political and economic theories, treating of
the fundamental differences between various groups within
the human race, regardless of class and race distinctions,
regardless of all artificial boundary lines between woman's

[1] From *Anarchism and Other Essays* by Emma Goldman. Copyright 1917,
Emma Goldman. Originally published by the Mother Earth Publishing Association.

rights and man's rights, I hold that there is a point where these differentiations may meet and grow into one perfect whole.

With this I do not mean to propose a peace treaty. The general social antagonism that has taken hold of our entire public life today, brought about through the force of opposing and contradictory interests, will crumble to pieces when the reorganization of our social life, based upon the principles of economic justice, shall have become a reality.

Peace or harmony between the sexes and individuals does not necessarily depend on a superficial equalization of human beings; nor does it call for the elimination of individual traits and peculiarities. The problem that confronts us today, and that the nearest future is to solve, is how to be one's self and yet in oneness with others, to feel deeply with all human beings and still retain one's own characteristic qualities. This seems to me to be the basis upon which the mass and the individual, the true democrat and the true individuality, man and woman, can meet without antagonism and opposition. The motto should not be: Forgive one another; rather, Understand one another. The oft-quoted sentence of Madame de Staël—"To understand everything means to forgive everything"—has never particularly appealed to me; it has the odor of the confessional; to forgive one's fellow being conveys the idea of pharisaical superiority. To understand one's fellow being suffices. The admission partly represents the fundamental aspect of my views on the emancipation of woman and its effect upon the entire sex.

Emancipation should make it possible for woman to be human in the truest sense. Everything within her that craves assertion and activity should reach its fullest expression; all artificial barriers should be broken, and the road towards greater freedom cleared of every trace of centuries of submission and slavery.

This was the original aim of the movement for woman's emancipation. But the results so far achieved have isolated woman and have robbed her of the fountain springs of that happiness which is so essential to her. Merely external emancipation has made of the modern woman an artificial being, who reminds one of the products of French arboriculture with its arabesque trees and shrubs, pyramids, wheels, and wreaths; anything, except the forms that would be

reached by the expression of her own inner qualities. Such
artificially grown plants of the female sex are to be found
in large numbers, especially in the so-called intellectual
sphere of our life.

Liberty and equality for woman! What hopes and aspirations these words awakened when they were first uttered by
some of the noblest and bravest souls of those days. The sun
in all his light and glory was to rise upon a new world; in
this world woman was to be free to direct her own destiny—
an aim certainly worthy of the great enthusiasm, courage,
perserverance, and ceaseless effort of the tremendous host
of pioneer men and women, who staked everything against
a world of prejudice and ignorance.

My hopes also move towards that goal, but I hold that the
emancipation of woman, as interpreted and practically applied today, has failed to reach that great end. Now, woman
is confronted with the necessity of emancipating herself
from emancipation, if she really desires to be free. This may
sound paradoxical, but is, nevertheless, only too true.

What has she achieved through her emancipation? Equal
suffrage in a few States. Has that purified our political life,
as many well-meaning advocates predicted? Certainly not.
Incidentally, it is really time that persons with plain, sound
judgment should cease to talk about corruption in politics in
a boarding school tone. Corruption of politics has nothing to
do with the morals, or the laxity of morals, of various political personalities. Its cause is altogether a material one. Politics is the reflex of the business and industrial world, the
mottos of which are: "To take is more blessed than to give";
"buy cheap and sell dear"; "one soiled hand washes the
other." There is no hope even that woman, with her right to
vote, will ever purify politics.

Emancipation has brought woman economic equality with
man; that is, she can choose her own profession and trade;
but as her past and present physical training has not equipped
her with the necessary strength to compete with man, she is
often compelled to exhaust all her energy, use up her vitality,
and strain every nerve in order to reach the market value.
Very few ever succeed, for it is a fact that women teachers,
doctors, lawyers, architects, and engineers are neither met
with the same confidence as their male colleagues, nor
receive equal remuneration. And those that do reach that

enticing equality generally do so at the expense of their physical and psychical well-being. As to the great mass of working girls and women, how much independence is gained if the narrowness and lack of freedom of the home is exchanged for the narrowness and lack of freedom of the factory, sweatshop, department store, or office? In addition is the burden that is laid on many women of looking after a "home, sweet home"—cold, dreary, disorderly, uninviting—after a day's hard work. Glorious independence! No wonder that hundreds of girls are so willing to accept the first offer of marriage, sick and tired of their "independence" behind the counter, at the sewing or typewriting machine. They are just as ready to marry as girls of the middle class, who long to throw off the yoke of parental supremacy. A so-called independence that leads only to earning the merest subsistence is not so enticing, not so ideal, that one could expect woman to sacrifice everything for it. Our highly praised independence is, after all, but a slow process of dulling and stifling woman's nature, her love instinct, and her mother instinct.

Nevertheless, the position of the working girl is far more natural and human than that of her seemingly more fortunate sister in the more cultured professional walks of life—teachers, physicians, lawyers, engineers, etc., who have to make a dignified, proper appearance, while the inner life is growing empty and dead.

The narrowness of the existing conception of woman's independence and emancipation; the dread of love for a man who is not her social equal; the fear that love will rob her of her freedom and independence; the horror that love or the joy of motherhood will only hinder her in the full exercise of her profession—all these together make of the emancipated modern woman a compulsory vestal, before whom life, with its great clarifying sorrows and its deep, entrancing joys, rolls on without touching or gripping her soul.

Emancipation, as understood by the majority of its adherents and exponents, is of too narrow a scope to permit the boundless love and ecstacy contained in the deep emotion of the true woman, sweetheart, mother, in freedom.

The tragedy of the self-supporting or economically free woman does not lie in too many, but in too few experiences. True, she surpasses her sister of past generations in knowledge of the world and human nature; it is just because of this that she feels deeply the lack of life's essence, which alone can enrich the human soul, and without which the majority of women have become mere professional automatons.

That such a state of affairs was bound to come was foreseen by those who realized that, in the domain of ethics, there still remained many decaying ruins of the time of the undisputed superiority of man; ruins that are still considered useful. And, what is more important, a goodly number of the emancipated are unable to get along without them. Every movement that aims at the destruction of existing institutions and the replacement thereof with something more advanced, more perfect, has followers who in theory stand for the most radical ideas, but who, nevertheless, in their everyday practice, are like the average Philistine, feigning respectability and clamoring for the good opinion of their opponents. There are, for example, socialists, and anarchists, who stand for the idea that property is robbery, yet who will grow indignant if anyone owe them the value of a half-dozen pins.

The same Philistine can be found in the movement for woman's emancipation. Yellow journalists and milk-and-water litterateurs have painted pictures of the emancipated woman that make the hair of the good citizen and his dull companion stand up on end. Every member of the woman's-rights movement was pictured as a Georges Sand in her absolute disregard of morality. Nothing was sacred to her. She had no respect for the ideal relation between man and woman. In short, emancipation stood only for a reckless life of lust and sin; regardless of society, religion, and morality. The exponents of woman's rights were highly indignant at such misrepresentation, and, lacking humor, they exerted all their energy to prove that they were not at all so bad as they were painted, but the very reverse. Of course, as long as woman was the slave of man, she could not be good and pure, but now that she was free and independent she would prove how good she could be and that her influence would have a purifying effect on all institutions in society. True, the movement for woman's rights has broken many old fetters, but it has also forged new ones. The great movement of *true* emancipation has not met with a great race of women who could look liberty in the face. Their narrow, Puritanical vision banished man, as a disturber and doubtful character,

out of their emotional life. Man was not to be tolerated at
any price, except perhaps as the father of a child, since a
child could not very well come to life without a father.
Fortunately, the most rigid Puritans never will be strong
enough to kill the innate craving for motherhood. But
woman's freedom is closely allied with man's freedom, and
many of my so-called emancipated sisters seem to overlook
the fact that a child born in freedom needs the love and
devotion of each human being about him, man as well as
woman. Unfortunately, it is this narrow conception of human
relations that has brought about a great tragedy in the lives
of the modern man and woman.

About fifteen years ago appeared a work from the pen of
the brilliant Norwegian Laura Marholm, called *Woman, a
Character Study*. She was one of the first to call attention to
the emptiness and narrowness of the exising conception of
woman's emancipation, and its tragic effect upon the inner
life of woman. In her work Laura Marholm speaks of the
fate of several gifted women of international fame: the genius
Eleonora Duse; the great mathematician and writer Sonya
Kovalevsky; the artist and poet-nature Marie Bashkirtseff,
who died so young. Through each description of the lives of
these women of such extraordinary mentality runs a marked
trail of unsatisfied craving for a full, rounded, complete, and
beautiful life, and the unrest and loneliness resulting from the
lack of it. Through these masterly psychological sketches
one cannot help but see that the higher the mental development of woman, the less possible it is for her to meet a con-
genial mate who will see in her not only sex, but also the
human being, the friend, the comrade and strong individuality, who cannot and ought not lose a single trait of her
character.

The average man with his self-sufficiency, his ridiculously
superior airs of patronage towards the female sex, is an
impossibility for woman as depicted in the *Character Study*
by Laura Marholm. Equally impossible for her is the man
who can see in her nothing more than her mentality and her
genius, and who fails to awaken her woman nature.

A rich intellect and a fine soul are usually considered necessary attributes of a deep and beautiful personality. In the
case of the modern woman, these attributes serve as a hindrance to the complete assertion of her being. For over a

hundred years the old form of marriage, based on the
Bible, "till death doth part," has been denounced as an
institution that stands for the sovereignty of the man over
the woman, of her complete submission to his whims and
commands, and absolute dependence on his name and support. Time and again it has been conclusively proved that
the old matrimonial relation restricted woman to the function of man's servant and the bearer of his children. And yet
we find many emancipated women who prefer marriage,
with all its deficiencies, to the narrowness of an unmarried
life, narrow and unendurable because of the chains of moral
and social prejudice that cramp and bind her nature.

The explanation of such inconsistency on the part of many
advanced women is to be found in the fact that they never
truly understood the meaning of emancipation. They thought
that all that was needed was independence from external
tyrannies; the internal tyrants, far more harmful to life and
growth—ethical and social conventions—were left to take
care of themselves; and they have taken care of themselves.
They seem to get along as beautifully in the heads and hearts
of the most active exponents of woman's emancipation, as in
the heads and hearts of our grandmothers.

These internal tyrants, whether they be in the form of
public opinion or what will mother say, or brother, father,
aunt, or relative of any sort; what will Mrs. Grundy, Mr.
Comstock, the employer, the Board of Education say? All
these busybodies, moral detectives, jailers of the human
spirit, what will they say? Until woman has learned to defy
them all, to stand firmly on her own ground and to insist
upon her own unrestricted freedom, to listen to the voice of
her nature, whether it call for life's greatest treasure, love for
a man, or her most glorious privilege, the right to give birth
to a child, she cannot call herself emancipated. How many
emancipated women are brave enough to acknowledge that
the voice of love is calling, wildly beating against their
breasts, demanding to be heard, to be satisfied.

The French writer Jean Reibrach, in one of his novels,
New Beauty, attempts to picture the ideal, beautiful, emancipated woman. This ideal is embodied in a young girl, a
physician. She talks very cleverly and wisely of how to feed
infants; she is kind, and administers medicines free to poor
mothers. She converses with a young man of her acquaint-

ance about the sanitary conditions of the future, and how various bacilli and germs shall be exterminated by the use of stone walls and floors, and by the doing away with rugs and hangings. She is, of course, very plainly and practically dressed, mostly in black. The young man, who, at their first meeting, was overawed by the wisdom of his emancipated friend, gradually learns to understand her, and recognizes one fine day that he loves her. They are young, and she is kind and beautiful, and though always in rigid attire, her appearance is softened by a spotlessly clean white collar and cuffs. One would expect that he would tell her of his love, but he is not one to commit romantic absurdities. Poetry and the enthusiasm of love cover their blushing faces before the pure beauty of the lady. He silences the voice of his nature, and remains correct. She, too, is always exact, always rational, always well-behaved. I fear if they had formed a union, the young man would have risked freezing to death. I must confess that I can see nothing beautiful in this new beauty, who is as cold as the stone walls and floors she dreams of. Rather would I have the love songs of romantic ages, rather Don Juan and Madame Venus, rather an elopement by ladder and rope on a moonlight night, followed by the father's curse, mother's moans, and the moral comments of neighbors, than correctness and propriety measured by yardsticks. If love does not know how to give and take without restrictions, it is not love, but a transaction that never fails to lay stress on a plus and a minus.

The greatest shortcoming of the emancipation of the present day lies in its artificial stiffness and its narrow respectabilities, which produce an emptiness in woman's soul that will not let her drink from the fountain of life. I once remarked that there seemed to be a deeper relationship between the old-fashioned mother and hostess, ever on the alert for the happiness of her little ones and the comfort of those she loved, and the truly new woman, than between the latter and her average emancipated sister. The disciples of emancipation pure and simple declared me a heathen, fit only for the stake. Their blind zeal did not let them see that my comparison between the old and the new was merely to prove that a goodly number of our grandmothers had more blood in their veins, far more humor and wit, and certainly a greater amount of naturalness, kind heartedness, and sim-

plicity, than the majority of our emancipated professional
women who fill the colleges, halls of learning, and various
offices. This does not mean a wish to return to the past, nor
does it condemn woman to her old sphere, the kitchen and
the nursery.

Salvation lies in an energetic march onward towards a
brighter and clearer future. We are in need of unhampered
growth out of old traditions and habits. The movement for
woman's emancipation has so far made but the first step in
that direction. It is to be hoped that it will gather strength to
make another. The right to vote, or equal civil rights, may be
good demands, but true emancipation begins neither at the
polls nor in courts. It begins in woman's soul. History tells us
that every oppressed class gained true liberation from its
masters through its own efforts. It is necessary that woman
learn that lesson, that she realize that her freedom will reach
as far as her power to achieve her freedom reaches. It is,
therefore, far more important for her to begin with her inner
regeneration, to cut loose from the weight of prejudices,
traditions, and customs. The demand for equal rights in
every vocation of life is just and fair; but, after all, the most
vital right is the right to love and be loved. Indeed, if partial
emancipation is to become a complete and true emancipation
of woman, it will have to do away with the ridiculous notion
that to be loved, to be sweetheart and mother, is synonymous
with being slave or subordinate. It will have to do away with
the absurd notion of the dualism of the sexes, or that man
and woman represent two antagonistic worlds.

Pettiness separates; breadth unites. Let us be broad and
big. Let us not overlook vital things because of the bulk of
trifles confronting us. A true conception of the relation of
the sexes will not admit of conqueror and conquered; it
knows of but one great thing: to give of one's self bound-
lessly, in order to find one's self richer, deeper, better. That
alone can fill the emptiness, and transform the tragedy of
woman's emancipation into joy, limitless joy.

MARRIAGE AND LOVE

The popular notion about marriage and love is that they
are synonymous, that they spring from the same motives,

and cover the same human needs. Like most popular notions this also rests not on actual facts, but on superstition.

Marriage and love have nothing in common; they are as far apart as the poles; are, in fact, antagonistic to each other. No doubt some marriages have been the result of love. Not, however, because love could assert itself only in marriage; much rather is it because few people can completely outgrow a convention. There are today large numbers of men and women to whom marriage is naught but a farce, but who submit to it for the sake of public opinion. At any rate, while it is true that some marriages are based on love, and while it is equally true that in some cases love continues in married life, I maintain that it does so regardless of marriage, and not because of it.

On the other hand, it is utterly false that love results from marriage. On rare occasions one does hear of a miraculous case of a married couple falling in love after marriage, but on close examination it will be found that it is a mere adjustment to the inevitable. Certainly the growing-used to each other is far away from the spontaneity, the intensity, ånd beauty of love, without which the intimacy of marriage must prove degrading to both the woman and the man.

Marriage is primarily an economic arrangement, an insurance pact. It differs from the ordinary life-insurance agreement only in that it is more binding, more exacting. Its returns are insignificantly small compared with the investments. In taking out an insurance policy one pays for it in dollars and cents, always at liberty to discontinue payments. If, however, woman's premium is a husband, she pays for it with her name, her privacy, her self-respect, her very life, "until death doth part." Moreover, the marriage insurance condemns her to lifelong dependency, to parasitism, to complete uselessness, individual as well as social. Man, too, pays his toll, but as his sphere is wider, marriage does not limit him as much as woman. He feels his chains more in an economic sense.

Thus Dante's motto over Inferno applies with equal force to marriage: "Ye who enter here leave all hope behind."

That marriage is a failure none but the very stupid will deny. One has but to glance over the statistics of divorce to realize how bitter a failure marriage really is. Nor will the

stereotyped Philistine argument that the laxity of divorce
laws and the growing looseness of woman account for the
fact that first, every twelfth marriage ends in divorce; second, that since 1870 divorces have increased from 28 to 73
for every hundred thousand population; third, that adultery,
since 1867, as ground for divorce, has increased 270.8 percent; fourth, that desertion increased 369.8 percent.

Added to these startling figures is a vast amount of material, dramatic and literary, further elucidating this subject.
Robert Herrick, in *Together;* Pinero, in *Mid-Channel;* Eugene Walter, in *Paid in Full,* and scores of other writers are
discussing the barrenness, the monotony, the sordidness, the
inadequacy of marriage as a factor for harmony and
understanding.

The thoughtful social student will not content himself
with the popular superficial excuse for this phenomenon. He
will have to dig down deeper into the very life of the sexes to
know why marriage proves so disastrous.

Edward Carpenter says that behind every marriage stands
the lifelong environment of the two sexes; an environment
so different from each other that man and woman must
remain strangers. Separated by an insurmountable wall of
superstition, custom, and habit, marriage has not the poten-
tiality of developing knowledge of, and respect for, each
other, without which every union is doomed to failure.

Henrik Ibsen, the hater of all social shams, was probably
the first to realize this great truth. Nora leaves her husband,
not—as the stupid critic would have it—because she is tired
of her responsibilities or feels the need of woman's rights,
but because she has come to know that for eight years she
had lived with a stranger and borne him children. Can there
be anything more humiliating, more degrading than a lifelong
proximity between two strangers? No need for the woman
to know anything of the man, save his income. As to the
knowledge of the woman—what is there to know except
that she has a pleasing appearance? We have not yet outgrown the theologic myth that woman has no soul, that she
is a mere appendix to man, made out of his rib just for the
convenience of the gentleman who was so strong that he was
afraid of his own shadow.

Perchance the poor quality of the material whence woman
comes is responsible for her inferiority. At any rate, woman

has no soul—what is there to know about her? Besides, the less soul a woman has the greater her asset as a wife, the more readily will she absorb herself in her husband. It is this slavish acquiescence to man's superiority that has kept the marriage institution seemingly intact for so long a period. Now that woman is coming into her own, now that she is actually growing aware of herself as a being outside of the master's grace, the sacred institution of marriage is gradually being undermined, and no amount of sentimental lamentation can stay it.

From infancy, almost, the average girl is told that marriage is her ultimate goal; therefore her training and education must be directed towards that end. Like the mute beast fattened for slaughter, she is prepared for that. Yet, strange to say, she is allowed to know much less about her function as wife and mother than the ordinary artisan of his trade. It is indecent and filthy for a respectable girl to know anything of the marital relation. Oh, for the inconsistency of respectability, that needs the marriage vow to turn something that is filthy into the purest and most sacred arrangement that none dare question or criticize. Yet that is exactly the attitude of the average upholder of marriage. The prospective wife and mother is kept in complete ignorance of her only asset in the competitive field—sex. Thus she enters into lifelong relations with a man only to find herself shocked, repelled, outraged beyond measure by the most natural and healthy instinct, sex. It is safe to say that a large percentage of the unhappiness, misery, distress, and physical suffering of matrimony is due to the criminal ignorance in sex matters that is being extolled as a great virtue. Nor is it at all an exaggeration when I say that more than one home has been broken up because of this deplorable fact.

If, however, woman is free and big enough to learn the mystery of sex without the sanction of State or Church, she will stand condemned as utterly unfit to become the wife of a "good" man, his goodness consisting of an empty head and plenty of money. Can there be anything more outrageous than the idea that a healthy, grown woman, full of life and passion, must deny nature's demand, must subdue her most intense craving, undermine her health, and break her spirit, must stunt her vision, abstain from the depth and glory of sex experience until a "good" man comes along to take her unto himself as a wife? That is precisely what marriage means. How can such an arrangement end except in failure? This is one, though not the least important, factor of marriage, which differentiates it from love.

Ours is a practical age. The time when Romeo and Juliet risked the wrath of their fathers for love, when Gretchen exposed herself to the gossip of her neighbors for love, is no more. If, on rare occasions, young people allow themselves the luxury of romance, they are taken in care by the elders, drilled and pounded until they become "sensible."

The moral lesson instilled in the girl is not whether the man has aroused her love, but rather is it, "How much?" The important and only God of practical American life: Can the man make a living? Can he support a wife? That is the only thing that justifies marriage. Gradually this saturates every thought of the girl; her dreams are not of moonlight and kisses, of laughter and tears; she dreams of shopping tours and bargain counters. This soul poverty and sordidness are the elements inherent in the marriage institution. The State and the Church approve of no other ideal, simply because it is the one that necessitates the State and Church control of men and women.

Doubtless there are people who continue to consider love above dollars and cents. Particularly is this true of that class whom economic necessity has forced to become self-supporting. The tremendous change in woman's position, wrought by that mighty factor, is indeed phenomenal when we reflect that it is but a short time since she has entered the industrial arena. Six million women wage earners; six million women, who have the equal right with men to be exploited, to be robbed, to go on strike; aye, to starve even. Anything more, my lord? Yes, six million wage workers in every walk of life, from the highest brain work to the most difficult menial labor in the mines and on the railroad tracks; yes, even detectives and policemen. Surely the emancipation is complete.

Yet with all that, but a very small number of the vast army of women wage workers look upon work as a permanent issue, in the same light as does man. No matter how decrepit the latter, he has been taught to be independent, self-supporting. Oh, I know that no one is really independent

in our economic treadmill; still, the poorest specimen of a
man hates to be a parasite; to be known as such, at any rate.

The woman considers her position as worker transitory, to
be thrown aside for the first bidder. That is why it is infinitely
harder to organize women than men. "Why should I join a
union? I am going to get married, to have a home." Has she
not been taught from infancy to look upon that as her ultimate calling? She learns soon enough that the home, though
not so large a prison as the factory, has more solid doors and
bars. It has a keeper so faithful that naught can escape him.
The most tragic part, however, is that the home no longer
frees her from wage slavery; it only increases her task.

According to the latest statistics submitted before a committee "on labor and wages, and congestion of population,"
ten percent of the wage workers in New York City alone are
married, yet they must continue to work at the most poorly
paid labor in the world. Add to this horrible aspect the
drudgery of housework, and what remains of the protection
and glory of the home? As a matter of fact, even the middle-
class girl in marriage cannot speak of her home, since it
is the man who creates her sphere. It is not important whether
the husband is a brute or a darling. What I wish to prove is
that marriage guarantees woman a home only by the grace
of her husband. There she moves about in *his* home, year
after year, until her aspect of life and human affairs becomes
as flat, narrow, and drab as her surroundings. Small wonder
if she becomes a nag, petty, quarrelsome, gossipy, unbearable, thus driving the man from the house. She could not go
if she wanted to; there is no place to go. Besides, a short
period of married life, of complete surrender of all faculties,
absolutely incapacitates the average woman for the outside
world. She becomes reckless in appearance, clumsy in her
movements, dependent in her decisions, cowardly in her
judgment, a weight and a bore, which most men grow to
hate and despise. Wonderfully inspiring atmosphere for the
bearing of life, is it not?

But the child, how is it to be protected, if not for marriage?
After all, is not that the most important consideration? The
sham, the hypocrisy of it! Marriage protecting the child, yet
thousands of children destitute and homeless. Marriage protecting the child, yet orphan asylums and reformatories over-
crowded, the Society for the Prevention of Cruelty to Chil-

dren keeping busy in rescuing the little victims from "loving" parents, to place them under more loving care, the Gerry Society. Oh, the mockery of it!

Marriage may have the power to "bring the horse to water," but has it ever made him drink? The law will place the father under arrest, and put him in convict's clothes; but has that ever stilled the hunger of the child? If the parent has no work, or if he hides his identity, what does marriage do then? It invokes the law to bring the man to "justice," to put him safely behind closed doors; his labor, however, goes not to the child, but to the State. The child receives but a blighted memory of its father's stripes.

As to the protection of the woman—therein lies the curse of marriage. Not that it really protects her, but the very idea is so revolting, such an outrage and insult on life, so degrading to human dignity, as to forever condemn this parasitic institution.

It is like that other paternal arrangement—capitalism. It robs man of his birthright, stunts his growth, poisons his body, keeps him in ignorance, in poverty and dependence, and then institutes charities that thrive on the last vestige of man's self-respect.

The institution of marriage makes a parasite of woman, an absolute dependent. It incapacitates her for life's struggle, annihilates her social consciousness, paralyzes her imagination, and then imposes its gracious protection, which is in reality a snare, a travesty on human character.

If motherhood is the highest fulfillment of woman's nature, what other protection does it need save love and freedom? Marriage but defiles, outrages, and corrupts her fulfillment. Does it not say to woman, Only when you follow me shall you bring forth life? Does it not condemn her to the block, does it not degrade and shame her if she refuses to buy her right to motherhood by selling herself? Does not marriage only sanction motherhood, even though conceived in hatred, in compulsion? Yet, if motherhood be of free choice, of love, of ecstasy, of defiant passion, does it not place a crown of thorns upon an innocent head and carve in letters of blood the hideous epithet, "Bastard"? Were marriage to contain all the virtues claimed for it, its crimes against motherhood would exclude it forever from the realm of love.

Love, the strongest and deepest element in all life, the

harbinger of hope, of joy, of ecstasy; love, the defier of all
laws, of all conventions; love, the freest, the most powerful
molder of human destiny; how can such an all-compelling
force be synonymous with that poor little State and Church-
begotten weed, marriage?

Free love? As if love is anything but free! Man has bought
brains, but all the millions in the world have failed to buy
love. Man has subdued bodies, but all the power on earth
has been unable to subdue love. Man has conquered whole
nations, but all his armies could not conquer love. Man has
chained and fettered the spirit, but he has been utterly helpless before love. High on a throne, with all the splendor and
pomp his gold can command, man is yet poor and desolate,
if love passes him by. And if it stays, the poorest hovel is
radiant with warmth, with life and color. Thus love has the
magic power to make of a beggar a king. Yes, love is free;
it can dwell in no other atmosphere. In freedom it gives itself
unreservedly, abundantly, completely. All the laws on the
statutes, all the courts in the universe, cannot tear it from the
soil, once love has taken root. If, however, the soil is sterile,
how can marriage make it bear fruit? It is like the last desperate struggle of fleeting life against death.

Love needs no protection; it is its own protection. So long
as love begets life no child is deserted, or hungry, or famished
for the want of affection. I know this to be true. I know
women who became mothers in freedom by the men they
loved. Few children in wedlock enjoy the care, the protection,
the devotion free motherhood is capable of bestowing.

The defenders of authority dread the advent of a free
motherhood, lest it will rob them of their prey. Who would
fight wars? Who would create wealth? Who would make the
policeman, the jailer, if woman were to refuse the indis-
criminate breeding of children? "The race, the race!" shouts
the king, the president, the capitalist, the priest. The race
must be preserved, though woman be degraded to a mere
machine,—and the marriage institution is our only safety
valve against the pernicious sex-awakening of woman. But
in vain these frantic efforts to maintain a state of bondage.
In vain, too, the edicts of the Church, the mad attacks of
rulers, in vain even the arm of the law. Woman no longer
wants to be a party to the production of a race of sickly,
feeble, decrepit, wretched human beings, who have neither

the strength nor moral courage to throw off the yoke of poverty and slavery. Instead she desires fewer and better children, begotten and reared in love and through free choice; not by compulsion, as marriage imposes. Our pseudo moralists have yet to learn the deep sense of responsibility toward the child, that love in freedom has awakened in the breast of woman. Rather would she forego forever the glory of motherhood than bring forth life in an atmosphere that breathes only destruction and death. And if she does become a mother, it is to give to the child the deepest and best her being can yield. To grow with the child is her motto; she knows that in that manner alone can she help build true manhood and womanhood.

Ibsen must have had a vision of a free mother, when, with a master stroke, he portrayed Mrs. Alving. She was the ideal mother because she had outgrown marriage and all its horrors, because she had broken her chains, and set her spirit free to soar until it returned a personality, regenerated and strong. Alas, it was too late to rescue her life's joy, her Oswald; but not too late to realize that love in freedom is the only condition of a beautiful life. Those who, like Mrs. Alving, have paid with blood and tears for their spiritual awakening, repudiate marriage as an imposition, a shallow, empty mockery. They know, whether love lasts but one brief span of time or for eternity, it is the only creative, inspiring, elevating basis for a new race, a new world.

In our present pygmy state, love is indeed a stranger to most people. Misunderstood and shunned, it rarely takes root; or if it does, it soon withers and dies. Its delicate fiber can not endure the stress and strain of the daily grind. Its soul is too complex to adjust itself to the slimy woof of our social fabric. It weeps and moans and suffers with those who have need of it, yet lack the capacity to rise to love's summit. Some day, some day men and women will rise, they will reach the mountain peak, they will meet big and strong and free, ready to receive, to partake, and to bask in the golden rays of love. What fancy, what imagination, what poetic genius can foresee even approximately the potentialities of such a force in the life of men and women. If the world is ever to give birth to true companionship and oneness, not marriage, but love will be the parent.

Sacco and Vanzetti
". . . we will fight until the last moment" [1]

Nicola Sacco (1891–1927)   Sacco was born in Italy and emigrated to the United States in 1908. With Bartolomeo Vanzetti he was arrested on charges of murdering a shoe factory paymaster and guard at South Braintree, Massachusetts. They were tried and convicted in an atmosphere of antiradical hysteria. The trial ended July 14, 1921, and they were electrocuted August 23, 1927. During the years of their incarceration, widespread doubt of their guilt reached worldwide proportions resulting in protest. Many books and articles, written by those in and out of the legal profession, have left detailed accounts of one of the most controversial and best known cases in United States history.

Bartolomeo Vanzetti (1888–1927)   Arrested with Nicola Sacco on charges of murdering a shoe factory paymaster and guard in South Braintree, Massachusetts, and convicted on July 14, 1921, Vanzetti left a most moving and articulate statement of the vindication of Sacco and himself. In an atmosphere of hysteria the two were sentenced to die and were electrocuted on August 23, 1927. With the encouragement of supporters, Vanzetti issued letters and articles from his prison cell and displayed a highly sensitive intelligence despite the fact that he was largely self-educated. The Sacco-Vanzetti case inspired controversy reaching worldwide proportions. Belief in their innocence became widespread as they were seen to be victims of antianarchist hatred. Neither has been officially cleared of the charges against them in the State of Massachusetts although considerable pressure has periodically mounted to bring this about.

"If it had not been for these thing, I might have live out my life talking at street corners to scorning men. I

[1] From *The Letters of Sacco and Vanzetti.* Edited by Denman Frankfurter and Gardner Jackson. N.Y.: by The Viking Press, Inc., Copyright 1955. Reprinted with the publisher's permission.

might have die, unmarked, unknown, a failure. Now we
are not a failure. This is our career and our triumph.
Never in our full life could we hope to do such work
for tolerance, for joostice, for man's onderstanding of
man as now we do by accident. Our words—our lives—
our pains—nothing! The taking of our lives—lives of
a good shoemaker and a poor fish-peddler—all! That
last moment belongs to us—that agony is our triumph."

FROM A STATEMENT MADE BY VANZETTI
AFTER RECEIVING SENTENCE, APRIL 9, 1927.

July 19, 1927. Charlestown State Prison

MY DEAR INES:

I would like that you should understand what I am going to
say to you, and I wish I could write you so plain, for I long
so much to have you hear all the heart-beat eagerness of
your father, for I love you so much as you are the dearest
little beloved one.

It is quite hard indeed to make you understand in your
young age, but I am going to try from the bottom of my
heart to make you understand how dear you are to your
father's soul. If I cannot succeed in doing that, I know that
you will save this letter and read it over in future years to
come and you will see and feel the same heart-beat affection
as your father feels in writing it to you.

I will bring with me your little and so dearest letter and
carry it right under my heart to the last day of my life. When
I die, it will be buried with your father who loves you so
much, as I do also your brother Dante and holy dear mother.

You don't know Ines, how dear and great your letter was
to your father. It is the most golden present that you could
have given to me or that I could have wished for in these
sad days.

It was the greatest treasure and sweetness in my struggling
life that I could have lived with you and your brother Dante
and your mother in a neat little farm, and learn all your
sincere words and tender affection. Then in the summertime to be sitting with you in the home nest under the oak
tree shade—beginning to teach you of life and how to read

and write, to see you running, laughing, crying and singing through the verdant fields picking the wild flowers here and there from one tree to another, and from the clear, vivid stream to your mother's embrace.

The same I have wished to see for other poor girls, and their brothers, happy with their mother and father as I dreamed for us—but it was not so and the nightmare of the lower classes saddened very badly your father's soul.

For the things of beauty and of good in this life, mother nature gave to us all, for the conquest and the joy of liberty. The men of this dying old society, they brutally have pulled me away from the embrace of your brother and your poor mother. But, in spite of all, the free spirit of your father's faith still survives, and I have lived for it and for the dream that some day I would have come back to life, to the embrace of your dear mother, among our friends and comrades again, but woe is me!

I know that you are good and surely you love your mother, Dante and all the beloved ones—and I am sure that you love me also a little, for I love you much and then so much. You do not know Ines, how often I think of you every day. You are in my heart, in my vision, in every angle of this sad walled cell, in the sky and everywhere my gaze rests.

Meantime, give my best paternal greetings to all the friends and comrades, and doubly so to our beloved ones. Love and kisses to your brother and mother.

With the most affectionate kiss and ineffable caress from him who loves you so much that he constantly thinks of you. Best warm greetings from Bartolo to you all.

[*From Sacco to his daughter*]   YOUR FATHER

August 18, 1927. Charlestown State Prison

MY DEAR SON AND COMPANION:

Since the day I saw you last I had always the idea to write you this letter, but the length of my hunger strike and the thought I might not be able to explain myself, made me put it off all this time.

The other day, I ended my hunger strike and just as soon as I did that I thought of you to write to you, but I find that I did not have enough strength and I cannot finish it at one time. However, I want to get it down in any way before they take us again to the death-house, because it is my conviction that just as soon as the court refuses a new trial to us they will take us there. And between Friday and Monday, if nothing happens, they will electrocute us right after midnight, on August 22nd. Therefore, here I am, right with you with love and with open heart as ever I was yesterday.

I never thought that our inseparable life could be separated, but the thought of seven dolorous years makes it seem it did come, but then it has not changed really the unrest and the heart-beat of affection. That has remained as it was. More. I say that our ineffable affection reciprocal, is today more than any other time, of course. That is not only a great deal but it is grand because you can see the real brotherly love, not only in joy but also and more in the struggle of suffering. Remember this, Dante. We have demonstrated this, and modesty apart, we are proud of it.

Much we have suffered during this long Calvary. We protest today as we protested yesterday. We protest always for our freedom.

If I stopped hunger strike the other day, it was because there was no more sign of life in me. Because I protested with my hunger strike yesterday as today I protest for life and not for death.

I sacrificed because I wanted to come back to the embrace of your dear little sister Ines and your mother and all the beloved friends and comrades of life and not death. So Son, today life begins to revive slow and calm, but yet without horizon and always with sadness and visions of death.

Well, my dear boy, after your mother had talked to me so much and I had dreamed of you day and night, how joyful it was to see you at last. To have talked with you like we used to in the days—in those days. Much I told you on that visit and more I wanted to say, but I saw that you will remain the same affectionate boy, faithful to your mother who loves you so much, and I did not want to hurt your sensibilities any longer, because I am sure that you will continue to be the same boy and remember what I have told you. I knew that and what here I am going to tell you will touch your sensibilities, but don't cry Dante, because many tears have been wasted, as your mother's have been wasted for seven years, and never did any good. So, Son, instead of crying, be strong, so as to be able to comfort your mother, and when you want to distract your mother from the discouraging soulness, I will tell you what I used to do. To take her for a long walk in the quiet country, gathering wild flowers here and there, resting under the shade of trees, between the harmony of the vivid stream and the gentle tranquility of the mothernature, and I am sure that she will enjoy this very much, as you surely would be happy for it. But remember always, Dante, in the play of happiness, don't you use all for yourself only, but down yourself just one step, at your side and help the weak ones that cry for help, help the prosecuted and the victim, because that are your better friends; they are the comrades that fight and fall as your father and Bartolo fought and fell yesterday for the conquest of the joy of freedom for all and the poor workers. In this struggle of life you will find more love and you will be loved.

I am sure that from what your mother told me about what you said during these last terrible days when I was lying in the iniquitous death-house—that description gave me happiness because it showed you will be the beloved boy I had always dreamed.

Therefore whatever should happen tomorrow, nobody knows, but if they should kill us, you must not forget to look at your friends and comrades with the smiling gaze of gratitude as you look at your beloved ones, because they love you as they love every one of the fallen persecuted comrades. I tell you, your father that is all the life to you, your father that loved you and saw them, and knows their noble faith (that is mine) their supreme sacrifice that they are still doing for our freedom, for I have fought with them, and they are the ones that still hold the last of our hope that today they can still save us from electrocution, it is the struggle and fight between the rich and the poor for safety and freedom, Son, which you will understand in the future of your years to come, of this unrest and struggle of life's death.

Much I thought of you when I was lying in the death-house—the singing, the kind tender voices of the children from the playground, where there was all the life and the joy of liberty—just one step from the wall which contains the buried agony of three buried souls. It would remind me so often of you and your sister Ines, and I wish I could see you every moment. But I feel better that you did not come to the death-house so that you could not see the horrible picture of three lying in agony waiting to be electrocuted, because I do not know what effect it would have on your young age. But then, in another way if you were not so sensitive it would be very useful to you tomorrow when you could use this horrible memory to hold up to the world the shame of the country in this cruel persecution and unjust death. Yes, Dante, they can crucify our bodies today as they are doing, but they cannot destroy our ideas, that will remain for the youth of the future to come.

Dante, when I said three human lives buried, I meant to say that with us there is another young man by the name of Celestino Maderios that is to be electrocuted at the same time with us. He has been twice before in that horrible death-house, that should be destroyed with the hammers of real progress—that horrible house that will shame forever the future of the citizens of Massachusetts. They should destroy that house and put up a factory or school, to teach many of the hundreds of the poor orphan boys of the world.

Dante, I say once more to love and be nearest to your mother and the beloved ones in these sad days, and I am sure that with your brave heart and kind goodness they will feel less discomfort. And you will also not forget to love me a little for I do—O, Sonny! thinking so much and so often of you.

Best fraternal greetings to all the beloved ones, love and kisses to your little Ines and mother. Most hearty affectionate embrace,

YOUR FATHER AND COMPANION

P.S. Bartolo send you the most affectionate greetings. I hope that your mother will help you to understand this letter because I could have written much better and more simple, if I was feeling good. But I am so weak.
[*From Sacco to his son*]

*August 21, 1927. From the Death House
of Massachusetts State Prison*

MY DEAR DANTE:

I still hope, and we will fight until the last moment, to

revindicate our right to live and to be free, but all the forces of the State and of the money and reaction are deadly against us because we are libertarians or anarchists.

I write little of this because you are now and yet too young to understand these things and other things of which I would like to reason with you.

But, if you do well, you will grow and understand your father's and my case and your father's and my principles, for which we will soon be put to death.

I tell you now that all that I know of your father, he is not a criminal, but one of the bravest men I ever knew. Some day you will understand what I am about to tell you. That your father has sacrificed everything dear and sacred to the human heart and soul for his fate in liberty and justice for all. That day you will be proud of your father, and if you come brave enough, you will take his place in the struggle between tyranny and liberty and you will vindicate his (our) names and our blood.

If we have to die now, you shall know, when you will be able to understand this tragedy in its fullest, how good and brave your father has been with you, you father and I, during these eight years of struggle, sorrow, passion, anguish and agony.

Even from now you shall be good, brave with your mother, with Ines, and with Susie—brave, good Susie[2]—and do all you can to console and help them.

I would like you to also remember me as a comrade and friend to your father, your mother and Ines, Susie and you, and I assure you that neither have I been a criminal, that I have committed no robbery and no murder, but only fought modestly to abolish crimes from among mankind and for the liberty of all.

Remember Dante, each one who will say otherwise of your father and I, is a liar, insulting innocent dead men who have been brave in their life. Remember and know also, Dante, that if your father and I would have been cowards and hypocrits and rinnegetors of our faith, we would not have been put to death. They would not even have convicted a lebbrous dog; not even executed a deadly poisoned scorpion on such evidence as that they framed against us. They

---

[2] Faithful friend of Mrs. Sacco, with whom she and her children lived during the last years of the case.

would have given a new trial to a matricide and abitual felon
on the evidence we presented for a new trial.

Remember, Dante, remember always these things; we are
not criminals; they convicted us on a frame-up; they denied
us a new trial; and if we will be executed after seven years,
four months and seventeen days of unspeakable tortures and
wrong, it is for what I have already told you; because we
were for the poor and against the exploitation and oppression of the man by the man.

The documents of our case, which you and other ones
will collect and preserve, will prove to you that your father,
your mother, Ines, my family and I have sacrificed by and
to a State Reason of the American Plutocratic reaction.

The day will come when you will understand the atrocious
cause of the above written words, in all its fullness. Then
you will honor us.

Now Dante, be brave and good always. I embrace you.

P.S. I left the copy of *An American Bible* to your mother
now, for she will like to read it, and she will give it to you
when you will be bigger and able to understand it. Keep it
for remembrance. It will also testify to you how good and
generous Mrs. Gertrude Winslow has been with us all. Good-
bye Dante.

BARTOLOMEO

section three
Anarchism as a System of Philosophy

Max Stirner **The Ego and His Own**[1]

Max Stirner (1806–1856) Stirner was a German social philosopher. He supported himself first as a teacher and then as a translator. It was through the anarchist John Henry Mackay that an interest in Stirner's work was stimulated in England and the United States. Mackay presented Stirner to the public as the spiritual forefather of individualistic anarchism. The impression that Stirner was an anarchist arises from his rejection of all political and moral ties of the individual and his attack on all general concepts, such as right, virtue, duty, etc. The individual himself is the overriding reality, these concepts being mere ghosts. Egotism determines everything. He sets his own tasks against these "ghosts," thereby rising above them by mastering himself. All relations in which the individual enters are now freely chosen, as among possessions, and exist solely for the ego. The ego is not an antimoral force for Stirner. It is merely a fact. Stirner's individualistic egotism was highly democratic. He wrote *The Ego and Its Own* for proletarians and hoped for everyman to emerge as this liberated individualist.

A HUMAN LIFE

From the moment when he catches sight of the light of the world a man seeks to find out

[1] From *The Ego and His Own*, by Max Stirner (Johann Kaspar Schmidt). Translated by Steven T. Byington. New York: E. C. Walker, 1907.

himself and get hold of *himself* out of its confusion, in which he, with everything else, is tossed about in motley mixture.

But everything that comes in contact with the child defends itself in turn against his attacks, and asserts its own persistence.

Accordingly, because each thing *cares for itself* and at the same time comes into constant collision with other things, the *combat* of self-assertion is unavoidable.

Victory or *defeat*—between the two alternatives the fate of the combat wavers. The victor becomes the *lord,* the vanquished one the *subject:* the former exercises *supremacy* and "rights of supremacy," the latter fulfills in awe and deference the "duties of a subject."

But both remain *enemies,* and always lie in wait: they watch for each other's *weaknesses*—children for those of their parents and parents for those of their children (e.g., their fear); either the stick conquers the man, or the man conquers the stick.

In childhood liberation takes the direction of trying to get to the bottom of things, to get at what is "back of" things; therefore we spy out the weak points of everybody, for which, it is well known, children have a sure instinct; therefore we like to smash things, like to rummage through hidden corners, pry after what is covered up or out of the way, and try what we can do with everything. When we once get at what is back of the things, we know we are safe; when, e.g., we have got at the fact that the rod is too weak against our obduracy, then we no longer fear it, "have outgrown it."

Back of the rod, mightier than it, stands our—obduracy, our obdurate courage. By degrees we get at what is back of everything that was mysterious and uncanny to us, the mysteriously dreaded might of the rod, the father's stern look, etc., and back of all we find our—ataraxy, i.e., imperturbability, intrepidity, our counter force, our odds of strength, our invincibility. Before that which formerly inspired in us fear and deference we no longer retreat shyly, but take *courage.* Back of everything we find our *courage,* our superiority; back of the sharp command of parents and authorities stands, after all, our courageous choice or our outwitting shrewdness. And the more we feel ourselves, the smaller appears that which before seemed invincible. And

what is our trickery, shrewdness, courage, obduracy? What
else but—*mind!*[2]

Through a considerable time we are spared a fight that is
so exhausting later—the fight against *reason.* The fairest part
of childhood passes without the necessity of coming to blows
with reason. We care nothing at all about it, do not meddle
with it, admit no reason. We are not to be persuaded to anything by *conviction,* and are deaf to good arguments, principles, etc.; on the other hand, coaxing, punishment, and the
like are hard for us to resist.

This stern life-and-death combat with *reason* enters later,
and begins a new phase; in childhood we scamper about without racking our brains much.

Mind is the name of the *first* self-discovery, the first un-
deification of the divine, i.e., of the uncanny, the spooks, the
"powers above." Our fresh feeling of youth, this feeling of
self, now defers to nothing; the world is discredited, for we
are above it, we are *mind.*

Now for the first time we see that hitherto we have not
looked at the world *intelligently* at all, but only stared at it.

We exercise the beginnings of our strength on *natural
powers.* We defer to parents as a natural power; later we say:
Father and mother are to be forsaken, all natural power to
be counted as riven. They are vanquished. For the rational,
i.e., "intellectual" man there is no family as a natural power;
a renunciation of parents, brothers, etc., makes its appearance. If these are "born again" as *intellectual, rational powers,* they are no longer at all what they were before.

And not only parents, but *men in general,* are conquered
by the young man; they are no hindrance to him, and are no
longer regarded; for now he says: One must obey God rather
than men.

From this high standpoint everything *"earthly"* recedes
into contemptible remoteness; for the standpoint is—the
heavenly.

The attitude is now altogether reversed; the youth takes
up an *intellectual* position, while the boy, who did not yet
feel himself as mind, grew up in mindless learning. The
former does not try to get hold of *things* (e.g., to get into his

2 [*Geist.* This word will be translated sometimes "mind" and sometimes
"spirit" in the following pages.–Translator's note.]

head the *data* of history), but of the *thoughts* that lie hidden
in things, and so, e.g., of the *spirit* of history. On the other
hand, the boy understands *connections* no doubt, but not
ideas, the spirit; therefore he strings together whatever can
be learned, without proceeding a priori and theoretically,
i.e., without looking for ideas.

As in childhood one had to overcome the resistance of
the *laws of the world,* so now in everything that he proposes
he is met by an objection of the mind, of reason, of his *own
conscience.* "That is unreasonable, unchristian, unpatriotic,"
and the like, cries conscience to us, and—frightens us away
from it. Not the might of the avenging Eumenides, not
Poseidon's wrath, not God, far as he sees the hidden, not the
father's rod of punishment, do we fear, but—*conscience.*

We "run after our thoughts" now, and follow their commands just as before we followed parental, human ones. Our
course of action is determined by our thoughts (ideas, conceptions, *faith)* as it is in childhood by the commands of our
parents.

For all that, we were already thinking when we were children, only our thoughts were not fleshless, abstract, *absolute,*
i.e., NOTHING BUT THOUGHTS, a heaven in themselves, a pure
world of thought, *logical* thoughts.

On the contrary, they had been only thoughts that we had
about a *thing;* we thought of the thing so or so. Thus we may
have thought "God made the world that we see there," but
we did not think of ("search") the "depths of the Godhead
itself"; we may have thought "that is the truth about the
matter," but we did not think of Truth itself, nor unite into
one sentence "God is truth." The "depths of the Godhead,
who is truth," we did not touch. Over such purely logical,
i.e., theological questions, "What is truth?" Pilate does not
stop, though he does not therefore hesitate to ascertain in an
individual case "what truth there is in the thing," i.e., whether
the *thing* is true.

Any thought bound to a *thing* is not yet *nothing but a
thought,* absolute thought.

To bring to light *the pure thought,* or to be of its party, is
the delight of youth; and all the shapes of light in the world
of thought, like truth, freedom, humanity, Man, etc., illumine
and inspire the youthful soul.

But, when the spirit is recognized as the essential thing,

it still makes a difference whether the spirit is poor or rich, and therefore one seeks to become rich in spirit; the spirit wants to spread out so as to found its empire—an empire that is not of this world, the world just conquered. Thus, then, it longs to become all in all to itself; i.e., although I am spirit, I am not yet *perfected* spirit, and must first seek the complete spirit.

But with that I, who had just now found myself as spirit, lose myself again at once, bowing before the complete spirit as one not my own but *supernal,* and feeling my emptiness.

Spirit is the essential point for everything, to be sure; but then is every spirit the "right" spirit? The right and true spirit is the ideal of spirit, the "Holy Spirit." It is not my or your spirit, but just—an ideal, supernal one, it is "God." "God is spirit." And this supernal "Father in heaven gives it to those that pray to him."[3]

The man is distinguished from the youth by the fact that he takes the world as it is, instead of everywhere fancying it amiss and wanting to improve it, i.e., model it after his ideal; in him the view that one must deal with the world according to his *interest,* not according to his *ideals,* becomes confirmed.

So long as one knows himself only as *spirit,* and feels that all the value of his existence consists in being spirit (it becomes easy for the youth to give his life, the "bodily life," for a nothing, for the silliest point of honor), so long it is only *thoughts* that one has, ideas that he hopes to be able to realize some day when he has found a sphere of action; thus one has meanwhile only *ideals,* unexecuted ideas or thoughts.

Not till one has fallen in love with his *corporeal* self, and takes a pleasure in himself as a living flesh-and-blood person —but it is in mature years, in the man, that we find it so— not till then has one a personal or *egoistic* interest, i.e., an interest not only of our spirit, for instance, but of total satisfaction, satisfaction of the whole chap, a *selfish* interest. Just compare a man with a youth, and see if he will not appear to you harder, less magnanimous, more selfish. Is he therefore worse? No, you say; he has only become more definite, or, as you also call it, more "practical." But the main point is this, that he makes *himself* more the center than does the

[3] [Luke 11. 13—Translator's note.]

youth, who is infatuated about other things, e.g., God, fatherland, and so on.

Therefore the man shows a *second* self-discovery. The
youth found himself as *spirit* and lost himself again in the
general spirit, the complete, holy spirit, Man, mankind—in
short, all ideals; the man finds himself as *embodied* spirit.

Boys had only *unintellectual* interests (i.e., interests devoid of thoughts and ideas), youths only *intellectual* ones;
the man has bodily, personal, egoistic interests.

If the child has not an *object* that it can occupy itself with,
it feels *ennui;* for it does not yet know how to occupy itself
with *itself.* The youth, on the contrary, throws the object
aside, because for him *thoughts* arose out of the object; he
occupies himself with his *thoughts,* his dreams, occupies
himself intellectually, or "his mind is occupied."

The young man includes everything not intellectual under
the contemptuous name of "externalities." If he nevertheless
sticks to the most trivial externalities (e.g., the customs of
students' clubs and other formalities), it is because, and
when, he discovers *mind* in them, i.e., when they are *symbols*
to him.

As I find myself back of things, and that as mind, so I
must later find *myself* also back of *thoughts*—to wit, as
their creator and *owner.* In the time of spirits thoughts grew
till they overtopped my head, whose offspring they yet were;
they hovered about me and convulsed me like fever-phan-
tasies—an awful power. The thoughts had become *corporeal*
on their own account, were ghosts, such as God, Emperor,
Pope, Fatherland, etc. If I destroy their corporeity, then I
take them back into mine, and say: "I alone am corporeal."
And now I take the world as what it is to me, as *mine,* as my
property; I refer all to myself.

If as spirit I had thrust away the world in the deepest contempt, so as owner I thrust spirits or ideas away into their
"vanity." They have no longer any power over me, as no
"earthly might" has power over the spirit.

The child was realistic, taken up with the things of this
world, till little by little he succeeded in getting at what was
back of these very things; the youth was idealistic, inspired
by thoughts, till he worked his way up to where he became
the man, the egoistic man, who deals with things and
thoughts according to his heart's pleasure, and sets his per-

sonal interest above everything. Finally, the old man? When
I become one, there will still be time enough to speak of that.

ʷ °

THE OWNER

To the chapter of society belongs also "the party," whose
praise has of late been sung.

In the State the *party* is current. "Party, party, who should
not join one!" But the individual is *unique*,[4] not a member of
the party. He unites freely, and separates freely again. The
party is nothing but a State in the State, and in this smaller
bee-State "peace" is also to rule just as in the greater. The
very people who cry loudest that there must be an *opposition*
in the State inveigh against every discord in the party. A
proof that they too want only a—State. All parties are shattered not against the State, but against the ego.[5]

One hears nothing oftener now than the admonition to
remain true to his party; party men despise nothing so much
as a mugwump. One must run with his party through thick
and thin, and unconditionally approve and represent its chief
principles. It does not indeed go quite so badly here as with
closed societies, because these bind their members to fixed
laws or statutes (e.g., the orders, the Society of Jesus, etc.).
But yet the party ceases to be a union at the same moment at
which it makes certain principles *binding* and wants to have
them assured against attacks; but this moment is the very
birth-act of the party. As party it is already a *born society*,
a dead union, an idea that has become fixed. As party of absolutism it cannot will that its members should doubt the irre-
fragable truth of this principle; they could cherish this doubt
only if they were egoistic enough to want still to be something outside their party, i.e., nonpartisans. Nonpartisan
they cannot be as party men, but only as egoists. If you are a
Protestant and belong to that party, you must only justify
Protestantism, at most "purge" it, not reject it; if you are a
Christian and belong among men to the Christian party, you
cannot go beyond this as a member of this party, but only
when your egoism, i.e., nonpartisanship, impels you to it.
What exertions the Christians, down to Hegel and the Com-

4 [*einzig.*—Translator's note.]
5 [*am Einzigen.*—Translator's note.]

munists, have put forth to make their party strong! They stuck to it that Christianity must contain the eternal truth, and that one needs only to get at it, make sure of it, and justify it.

In short, the party cannot bear nonpartisanship, and it is in this that egoism appears. What matters the party to me? I shall find enough anyhow who *unite* with me without swearing allegiance to my flag.

He who passes over from one party to another is at once abused as a "turncoat." Certainly *morality* demands that one stand by his party, and to become apostate from it is to spot oneself with the stain of "faithlessness"; but ownness knows no commandment of "faithfulness, adhesion, etc.," ownness permits everything, even apostasy, defection. Unconsciously even the moral themselves let themselves be led by this principle when they have to judge one who passes over to *their* party—nay, they are likely to be making proselytes; they should only at the same time acquire a consciousness of the fact that one must commit *immoral* actions in order to commit his own—i.e., here, that one must break faith, yes, even his oath, in order to determine himself instead of being determined by moral considerations. In the eyes of people of strict moral judgment an apostate always shimmers in equivocal colors, and will not easily obtain their confidence; for there sticks to him the taint of "faithlessness," i.e., of an immorality. In the lower man this view is found almost generally; advanced thinkers fall here too, as always, into an uncertainty and bewilderment, and the contradiction necessarily founded in the principle of morality does not, on account of the confusion of their concepts, come clearly to their consciousness. They do not venture to call the apostate immoral downright, because they themselves entice to apostasy, to defection from one religion to another, etc.; still, they cannot give up the standpoint of morality either. And yet here the occasion was to be seized to step outside of morality.

Are the Own or Unique[6] perchance a party? How could they be *own* if they were such as *belonged* to a party?

Or is one to hold with no party? In the very act of joining them and entering their circle one forms a *union* with them

6 [*Einzigen*—Translator's note.]

that lasts as long as party and I pursue one and the same goal. But today I still share the party's tendency, and by tomorrow I can do so no longer and I become "untrue" to it. The party has nothing *binding* (obligatory) for me, and I do not have respect for it; if it no longer pleases me, I become its foe.

In every party that cares for itself and its persistence, the members are unfree (or better, unown) in that degree, they lack egoism in that degree, in which they serve this desire of the party. The independence of the party conditions the lack of independence in the party members.

A party, of whatever kind it may be, can never do without a *confession of faith.* For those who belong to the party must *believe* in its principle, it must not be brought in doubt or put in question by them, it must be the certain, indubitable thing for the party member. That is: One must belong to a party body and soul, else one is not truly a party man, but more or less—an egoist. Harbor a doubt of Christianity, and you are already no longer a true Christian, you have lifted yourself to the "effrontery" of putting a question beyond it and haling Christianity before your egoistic judgment seat. You have—*sinned* against Christianity, this party cause (for it is surely not e.g., a cause for the Jews, another party). But well for you if you do not let yourself be affrighted: your effrontery helps you to ownness.

So then an egoist could never embrace a party or take up with a party? Oh, yes, only he cannot let himself be embraced and taken up by the party. For him the party remains all the time nothing but a *gathering:* he is one of the party, he takes part.

The best State will clearly be that which has the most loyal citizens, and the more the devoted mind for *legality* is lost, so much the more will the State, this system of morality, this moral life itself, be diminished in force and quality. With the "good citizens" the good State too perishes and dissolves into anarchy and lawlessness. "Respect for the law!" By this cement the total of the State is held together. "The law is *sacred,* and he who affronts it a *criminal.*" Without crime no State: the moral world—and this the State is—is crammed full of scamps, cheats, liars, thieves, etc. Since the State is the "lordship of law," its hierarchy, it follows that the egoist, in all cases where *his* advantage runs against the State's, can satisfy himself only by crime.

The State cannot give up the claim that its *laws* and ordinances are *sacred.*[7] At this the individual ranks as the *unholy*[8] (barbarian, natural man, "egoist") over against the State, exactly as he was once regarded by the Church; before the individual the State takes on the nimbus of a saint.[9] Thus it issues a law against dueling. Two men who are both at one in this, that they are willing to stake their life for a cause (no matter what), are not to be allowed this, because the State will not have it: it imposes a penalty on it. Where is the liberty of self-determination then? It is at once quite another situation if, as, e.g., in North America, society determines to let the duelists bear certain evil *consequences* of their act, e.g., withdrawal of the credit hitherto enjoyed. To refuse credit is everybody's affair, and, if a society wants to withdraw it for this or that reason, the man who is hit cannot therefore complain of encroachment on his liberty: the society is simply availing itself of its own liberty. That is no penalty for sin, no penalty for a *crime.* The duel is no crime there, but only an act against which the society adopts countermeasures, resolves on a *defence.* The State, on the contrary, stamps the duel as a crime, i.e., as an injury to its sacred law: it makes it a *criminal case.* The society leaves it to the individual's decision whether he will draw upon himself evil consequences and inconveniences by his mode of action, and hereby recognizes his free decision; the State behaves in exactly the reverse way, denying all right to the individual's decision and, instead, ascribing the sole right to its own decision, the law of the State, so that he who transgresses the State's commandment is looked upon as if he were acting against God's commandment—a view which likewise was once maintained by the Church. Here God is the Holy in and of himself, and the commandments of the Church, as of the State, are the commandments of this Holy One, which he transmits to the world through his anointed and Lords-by-the-Grace-of-God. If the Church had *deadly sins,* the State has *capital crimes;* if the one had *heretics,* the

---

[7] [*heilig*–Translator's note.]
[8] [*unheilig*–Translator's note.]
[9] [*Heiliger*–Translator's note.]

other had *traitors;* the one *ecclesiastical penalties,* the other *criminal penalities;* the one *inquisitorial* processes, the other *fiscal;* in short, there sins, here crimes, there sinners, here criminals, there inquisition and here—inquisition. Will the sanctity of the State not fall like the Church's? The awe of its laws, the reverence for its highness, the humility of its "subjects," will this remain? Will the "saint's" face not be stripped of its adornment?

What a folly, to ask of the State's authority that it should enter into an honorable fight with the individual, and, as they express themselves in the matter of freedom of the press, share sun and wind equally! If the State, this thought, is to be a *de facto* power, it simply must be a superior power against the individual. The State is "sacred" and must not expose itself to the "impudent attacks" of individuals. If the State is *sacred,* there must be censorship. The political liberals admit the former and dispute the inference. But in any case they concede repressive measures to it, for—they stick to this, that State is *more* than the individual and exercises a justified revenge, called punishment.

Punishment has a meaning only when it is to afford expiation for the injuring of a *sacred thing.* If something is sacred to any one, he certainly deserves punishment when he acts as its enemy. A man who lets a man's life continue in existence *because* to him it is sacred and he has a *dread* of touching it is simply a—*religious* man.

Weitling lays crime at the door of "social disorder," and lives in the expectation that under communistic arrangements crimes will become impossible, because the temptations to them, e.g., money, fall away. As, however, his organized society is also exalted into a sacred and inviolable one, he miscalculates in that good-hearted opinion. Such as with their mouth professed allegiance to the communistic society, but worked underhand for its ruin, would not be lacking. Besides, Weitling has to keep on with "curative means against the natural remainder of human diseases and weaknesses," and "curative means" always announce to begin with that individuals will be looked upon as "called" to a particular "salvation" and hence treated according to the requirements of this "human calling." *Curative means* or *healing* is only the reverse side of *punishment,* the *theory of cure* runs parallel with the *theory of punishment;* if the latter sees in an action a sin against right, the former takes it for a sin of the man *against himself,* as a decadence from his health. But the correct thing is that I regard it either as an action that *suits me* or as one that *does not suit me,* as hostile or friendly to *me,* i.e., that I treat it as my *property,* which I cherish or demolish. "Crime" or "disease" are not either of them an *egoistic* view of the matter, i.e., a judgment *starting from me,* but starting from *another*—to wit, whether it injures *right,* general right, or the *health* partly of the individual (the sick one), partly of the generality *(society).* "Crime" is treated inexorably, "disease" with "loving gentleness, compassion," and the like.

Punishment follows crime. If crime falls because the sacred vanishes, punishment must not less be drawn into its fall; for it too has significance only over against something sacred. Ecclesiastical punishments have been abolished. Why? Because how one behaves toward the "holy God" is his own affair. But, as this one punishment, *ecclesiastical punishment,* has fallen, so all *punishments* must fall. As sin against the so-called God is a man's own affair, so that against every kind of the so-called sacred. According to our theories of penal law, with whose "improvement in conformity to the times" people are tormenting themselves in vain, they want to *punish* men for this or that "inhumanity"; and therein they make the silliness of these theories especially plain by their consistency, hanging the little thieves and letting the big ones run. For injury to property they have the house of correction, and for "violence to thought," suppression of "natural rights of man," only—representations and petitions.

The criminal code has continued existence only through the sacred, and perishes of itself if punishment is given up. Now they want to create everywhere a new penal law, without indulging in a misgiving about punishment itself. But it is exactly punishment that must make room for satisfaction, which, again, cannot aim at satisfying right or justice, but at procuring *us* a satisfactory outcome. If one does to us what we *will not put up with,* we break his power and bring our own to bear: we satisfy *ourselves* on him, and do not fall into the folly of wanting to satisfy right (the spook). It is not the *sacred* that is to defend itself against man, but man against man; as *God* too, you know, no longer defends himself against man, God to whom formerly (and in part, indeed, even now) all the "servants of God" offered their hands to punish the blasphemer, as they still at this very day lend their hands to the sacred. This devotion to the sacred brings it to pass also that, without lively participation of one's own, one only delivers misdoers into the hands of the police and courts: a nonparticipating making over to the authorities, "who, of course, will best administer sacred matters." The people are quite crazy for hounding the police on against everything that seems to it to be immoral, often only unseemly, and this popular rage for the moral protects the police institution more than the government could in any way protect it.

In crime the egoist has hitherto asserted himself and mocked at the sacred; the break with the sacred, or rather of the sacred, may become general. A revolution never returns, but a mighty, reckless, shameless, conscienceless, proud—*crime,* does it not rumble in distant thunders, and do you not see how the sky grows presciently silent and gloomy?

He who refuses to spend his powers for such limited societies as family, party, nation, is still always longing for a worthier society, and thinks he has found the true object of love, perhaps, in "human society" or "mankind," to sacrifice himself to which constitutes his honor; from now on he "lives for and serves *mankind.*"

People is the name of the body, *State* of the spirit, of that *ruling person* that has hitherto suppressed me. Some have wanted to transfigure peoples and States by broadening them out to "mankind" and "general reason"; but servitude would only become still more intense with this widening, and philanthropists and humanitarians are as absolute masters as politicians and diplomats.

Modern critics inveigh against religion because it sets God, the divine, moral, etc., *outside* of man, or makes them something objective, in opposition to which the critics rather transfer these very subjects *into* man. But those critics nonetheless fall into the proper error of religion, to give man a "destiny," in that they too want to have him divine, human, and the like: morality, freedom and humanity, etc., are his essence. And, like religion, politics too wanted to *"educate"* man, to bring him to the realization of his "essence," his "destiny," to *make* something out of him—to wit, a "true man," the one in the form of the "true believer," the other in that of the "true citizen or subject." In fact, it comes to the same whether one calls the destiny the divine or human.

Under religion and politics man finds himself at the standpoint of *should:* he *should* become this and that, should be so and so. With this postulate, this commandment, every one steps not only in front of another but also in front of himself. Those critics say: You should be a whole, free man. Thus they too stand in the temptation to proclaim a new *religion,* to set up a new absolute, an ideal—to wit, freedom. Men *should* be free. Then there might even arise *missionaries* of freedom, as Christianity, in the conviction that all were properly destined to become Christians, sent out missionaries of the faith. Freedom would then (as have hitherto faith as Church, morality as State) constitute itself as a new *community* and carry on a like "propaganda" therefrom. Certainly no objection can be raised against a getting together; but so much the more must one oppose every renewal of the old *care* for us, of culture directed toward an end—in short, the principle of *making something* out of us, no matter whether Christians, subjects, or freemen and men.

One may well say with Feuerbach and others that religion has displaced the human from man, and has transferred it so into another world that, unattainable, it went on with its own existence there as something personal in itself, as a "God": but the error of religion is by no means exhausted with this. One might very well let fall the personality of the displaced human, might transform God into the divine, and still remain religious. For the religious consists in discontent with the *present* man, i.e., in the setting up of a "perfection" to be striven for, in "man wrestling for his completion." ("Ye therefore *should* be perfect as your father in heaven is perfect." Matt. 5: 48): it consists in the fixation of an *ideal,* an absolute. Perfection is the "supreme good," the *finis bonorum;* everyone's ideal is the perfect man, the true, the free man, etc.

The efforts of modern times aim to set up the ideal of the "free man." If one could find it, there would be a new— religion, because a new ideal; there would be a new longing, a new torment, a new devotion, a new deity, a new contrition.

With the ideal of "absolute liberty," the same turmoil is

made as with everything absolute, and according to Hess, e.g., it is said to "be realizable in absolute human society." Nay, this realization is immediately afterward styled a "vocation"; just so he then defines liberty as "morality": the kingdom of "justice" (i.e., equality) and "morality" (i.e., liberty) is to begin, etc.

Ridiculous is he who, while fellows of his tribe, family, nation, etc., rank high, is—nothing but "puffed up" over the merit of his fellows; but blinded too is he who wants only to be "man." Neither of them puts his worth in *exclusiveness*, but in *connectedness*, or in the "tie" that conjoins him with others, in the ties of blood, of nationality, of humanity.

Through the "Nationals" of today the conflict has again been stirred up between those who think themselves to have merely human blood and human ties of blood, and the others who brag of their special blood and the special ties of blood.

If we disregard the fact that pride may mean conceit, and take it for consciousness alone, there is found to be a vast difference between pride in "belonging to" a nation and therefore being its property, and that in calling a nationality one's property. Nationality is my quality, but the nation my owner and mistress. If you have bodily strength, you can apply it at a suitable place and have a self-consciousness or pride of it; if, on the contrary, your strong body has you, then it pricks you everywhere, and at the most unsuitable place, to show its strength: you can give nobody your hand without squeezing his.

The perception that one is more than a member of the family, more than a fellow of the tribe, more than an individual of the people, etc., has finally led to saying, one is more than all this because one is man, or, the man is more than the Jew, German, etc. "Therefore be everyone wholly and solely—man!" Could one not rather say: Because we are more than what has been stated, therefore we will be this, as well as that "more" also? Man and German, then, man and Guelph, etc.? The Nationals are in the right; one cannot deny his nationality: and the humanitarians are in the right; one must not remain in the narrowness of the national. In *uniqueness*[10] the contradiction is solved; the national is my quality. But I am not swallowed up in my

---

10 [*Einzigkeit*–Translator's note.]

quality—as the human too is my quality, but I give to man his existence first through my uniqueness.

History seeks for Man: but he is I, you, we. Sought as a mysterious *essence,* as the divine, first as *God,* then as *Man* (humanity, humaneness, and mankind), he is found as the individual, the finite, the unique one.

I am owner of humanity, am humanity, and do nothing for the good of another humanity. Fool, you who are a unique humanity, that you make a merit of wanting to live for another than you are.

The hitherto-considered relation of me to the *world of men* offers such a wealth of phenomena that it will have to be taken up again and again on other occasions, but here, where it was only to have its chief outlines made clear to the eye, it must be broken off to make place for an apprehension of two other sides toward which it radiates. For, as I find myself in relation not merely to men so far as they present in themselves the concept "man" or are children of men (children of *Man,* as children of God are spoken of), but also to that which they have of man and call their own, and as therefore I relate myself not only to that which they *are* through man, but also to their human *possessions:* so, besides the world of men, the world of the senses and of ideas will have to be included in our survey, and somewhat said of what men call their own of sensuous goods, and of spiritual as well.

According as one had developed and clearly grasped the concept of man, he gave it to us to respect as this or that *person of respect,* and from the broadest understanding of this concept there proceeded at last the command "to respect Man in everyone." But, if I respect Man, my respect must likewise extend to the human, or what is Man's.

Men have somewhat of their *own,* and *I* am to recognize this own and hold it sacred. Their own consists partly in outward, partly in inward *possessions.* The former are things, the latter spiritualities, thoughts, convictions, noble feelings, etc. But I am always to respect only *rightful* or *human* possessions; the wrongful and unhuman I need not spare, for only *Man's* own is men's real own. An inward possession of this sort is, e.g., religion; because *religion* is free, i.e., is Man's, *I* must not strike at it. Just so *honor* is an inward possession; it is free and must not be struck at by me (action for insult, caricatures, etc.). Religion and honor are "spiritual property." In tangible property the person stands foremost: my person is my property. Hence freedom of the person; but only the *rightful* or human person is free, the other is locked up. Your life is your property; but it is sacred for men only if it is not that of an inhuman monster.

What a man as such cannot defend of bodily goods, we may take from him: this is the meaning of competition, of freedom of occupation. What he cannot defend of spiritual goods falls a prey to us likewise: so far goes the liberty of discussion, of science, of criticism.

But *consecrated* goods are inviolable. Consecrated and guaranteed by whom? Proximately by the State, society, but properly by man or the "concept," the "concept of the thing": for the concept of consecrated goods is this, that they are truly human, or rather that the holder possesses them as man and not as un-man.

On the spiritual side man's faith is such goods, his honor, his moral feeling—yes, his feeling of decency, modesty, etc. Actions (speeches, writings) that touch honor are punishable; attacks on "the foundation of all religion"; attacks on political faith; in short, attacks on everything that a man "rightly" has.

How far critical liberalism would extend the sanctity of goods—on this point it has not yet made any pronouncement, and doubtless fancies itself to be ill-disposed toward all sanctity; but, as it combats egoism, it must set limits to it, and must not let the un-man pounce on the human. To its theoretical contempt for the "masses" there must correspond a practical snub if it should get into power.

What extension the concept "man" receives, and what comes to the individual man through it—what, therefore, man and the human are—on this point the various grades of liberalism differ, and the political, the social, the humane man are each always claiming more than the other for "man." He who has best grasped this concept knows best what is "man's." The State still grasps this concept in political restriction, society in social; mankind, so it is said, is the first to comprehend it entirely, or "the history of mankind develops it." But, if "man is discovered," then we know also what pertains to man as his own, man's property, the human.

But let the individual man lay claim to ever so many rights because Man or the concept man "entitles" him to them, i.e., because his being man does it: what do *I* care for his right and his claim? If he has his right only from Man and does not have it from *me*, then for *me* he has no right. His life, e.g., counts to *me* only for what it is *worth to me*. I respect neither a so-called right of property (or his claim to tangible goods) nor yet his right to the "sanctuary of his inner nature" (or his right to have the spiritual goods and divinities, his gods, remain unaggrieved). His goods, the sensuous as well as the spiritual, are *mine,* and I dispose of them as proprietor, in the measure of my—might.

In the *property question* lies a broader meaning than the limited statement of the question allows to be brought out. Referred solely to what men call our possessions, it is capable of no solution; the decision is to be found only in him "from whom we have everything." Property depends on the *owner.*

The Revolution directed its weapons against everything which came "from the grace of God," e.g., against divine right, in whose place the human was confirmed. To that which is granted by the grace of God, there is opposed that which is derived "from the essence of man."

Now, as men's relation to each other, in opposition to the religious dogma that commands a "Love one another for God's sake," had to receive its human position by a "Love each other for man's sake," so the revolutionary teaching could not do otherwise than, first as to what concerns the relation of men to the things of this world, settle it that the world, which hitherto was arranged according to God's ordinance, henceforth belongs to "Man."

The world belongs to "Man," and is to be respected by me as his property.

Property is what is mine!

Property in the civic sense means *sacred* property, such that I must *respect* your property. "Respect for property!" Hence the politicians would like to have everyone possess his little bit of property, and they have in part brought about

an incredible parcellation by this effort. Each must have his
bone on which he may find something to bite.

The position of affairs is different in the egoistic sense. I
do not step shyly back from your property, but look upon it
always as *my* property, in which I need to "respect" nothing.
Pray do the like with what you call my property!

With this view we shall most easily come to an understanding with each other.

The political liberals are anxious that, if possible, all
servitudes be dissolved, and everyone be free lord on his
ground, even if this ground has only so much area as can
have its requirements adequately filled by the manure of one
person. (The farmer in the story married even in his old age
"that he might profit by his wife's dung.") Be it ever so little,
if one only has somewhat of his own—to wit, a *respected*
property! The more such owners, such cotters,[11] the more
"free people and good patriots" has the State.

Political liberalism, like everything religious, counts on
respect, humaneness, the virtues of love. Therefore does it
live in incessant vexation. For in practice people respect
nothing, and every day the small possessions are brought up
again by greater proprietors, and the "free people" change
into day laborers.

If, on the contrary, the "small proprietors" had reflected
that the great property was also theirs, they would not have
respectfully shut themselves out from it, and would not have
been shut out.

Property as the civic liberals understand it deserves the
attacks of the Communists and Proudhon: it is untenable,
because the civic proprietor is in truth nothing but a propertyless man, one who is everywhere *shut out.* Instead of
owning the world, as he might, he does not own even the
paltry point on which he turns around.

Proudhon wants not the *propriétaire* but the *possesseur*
or *usufruitier.*[12] What does that mean? He wants no one to
own the land; but the benefit of it—even though one were
allowed only the hundredth part of this benefit, this fruit—
is at any rate one's property, which he can dispose of at will.
He who has only the benefit of a field is assuredly not the

---

11 [The words "cot" and "dung" are alike in German.–Translator's note.]
12 E.g., *"Qu'est-ce que la Propriété."* [Stirner's note.]

proprietor of it; still less he who, as Proudhon would have it, must give up so much of this benefit as is not required for his wants; but he is the proprietor of the share that is left him. Proudhon, therefore, denies only such and such property, not *property* itself. If we want no longer to leave the land to the landed proprietors, but to appropriate it to ourselves, we unite ourselves to this end, form a union, a *société,* that makes *itself* proprietor; if we have good luck in this, then those persons cease to be landed proprietors. And, as from the land, so we can drive them out of many another property yet, in order to make it *our* property, the property of the —*conquerors.* The conquerors form a society which one may imagine so great that it by degrees embraces all humanity; but so-called humanity too is as such only a thought (spook); the individuals are its reality. And these individuals as a collective mass will treat land and earth not less arbitrarily than an isolated individual or so-called *propriétaire.* Even so, therefore, *property* remains standing, and that as "exclusive" too, in that *humanity,* this great society, excludes the *individual* from its property (perhaps only leases to him, gives him as a fief, a piece of it) as it besides excludes everything that is not humanity, e.g., does not allow animals to have property.—So too it will remain, and will grow to be. That in which *all* want to have a *share* will be withdrawn from that individual who wants to have it for himself alone: it is made a *common estate.* As a *common estate* everyone has his *share* in it, and this share is his *property.* Why, so in our old relations a house that belongs to five heirs is their common estate; but the fifth part of the revenue is each one's property. Proudhon might spare his prolix pathos if he said: "There are some things that belong only to a few, and to which we others will from now on lay claim or—siege. Let us take them, because one comes to property by taking, and the property of which for the present we are still deprived came to the proprietors likewise only by taking. It can be utilized better if it is in the hands of *us all* than if the few control it. Let us therefore associate ourselves for the purpose of this robbery *(vol).*"—Instead of this, he tries to get us to believe that society is the original possessor and the sole proprietor, of imprescriptible right; against it the so-called proprietors have become thieves *(La propriété c'est le vol);* if it now deprives of his property the present proprietor, it robs him of nothing, as it is only availing itself of its imprescriptible right.—So far one comes with the spook of society as a *moral person*. On the contrary, what man can obtain belongs to him: the world belongs to *me*. Do you say anything else by your opposite proposition, "The world belongs to *all*"? All are I and again I, etc. But you make out of the "all" a spook, and make it sacred, so that then the "all" become the individual's fearful *master*. Then the ghost of "right" places itself on their side.

Proudhon, like the communists, fights against *egoism*. Therefore they are continuations and consistent carryings-out of the Christian principle, the principle of love, of sacrifice for something general, something alien. They complete in property, e.g., only what has long been extant as a matter of fact—viz. the propertylessness of the individual. When the law says, *Ad reges potestas omnium pertinet, ad singulos proprietas; omnia rex imperio possidet, singuli dominio*, this means: The king is proprietor, for he alone can control and dispose of "everything," he has *potestas* and *imperium* over it. The communists make this clearer, transferring that *imperium* to the "society of all." Therefore: Because enemies of egoism, they are on that account—Christians, or, more generally speaking, religious men, believers in ghosts, dependents, servants of some generality (God, society, etc.). In this too Proudhon is like the Christians, that he ascribes to God that which he denies to men. He names him the *Propriétaire* of the earth. Herewith he proves that he cannot think away the *proprietor as such; he* comes to a proprietor at last, but removes him to the other world.

Neither God nor Man ("human society") is proprietor, but the individual.

Henry David Thoreau   **Civil Disobedience**[1]

Henry David Thoreau (1817–1862)   Thoreau was an American writer born in Concord, Massachusetts. He was graduated from Harvard University in 1837 and taught school in Concord from

[1] From "Civil Disobedience," Vol. 10 *(Miscellanies)* of *The Writings of Henry David Thoreau*. Boston and New York: Houghton Mifflin Co., 1863.

1839 to 1841. He lived at the home of Ralph W. Emerson from 1841 to 1843, where he was associated with the Transcendentalists. In 1845 he retired to a small dwelling beside Walden Pond until 1847. Here he wrote the well-known *Walden or Life in the Woods* (1854). He lived alternately at the home of his father and Emerson, making occasional excursions to Maine and Cape Cod.

He published only two books in his lifetime, the above mentioned *Walden* and *A Week on the Concord and Merrimack Rivers* (1849) in addition to a few magazine articles. From his journals, manuscripts and letters, twenty volumes of *The Writings of Henry David Thoreau* were culled and published in 1906. His essay on civil disobedience strongly influenced pacifist politics in the United States during the nineteenth century.

A highly competent biography of him was written by Henry Seidel Canby, which appeared in 1939.

I heartily accept the motto—"That government is best which governs least"; and I should like to see it acted up to more rapidly and systematically. Carried out, it finally amounts to this, which also I believe—"That government is best which governs not at all"; and when men are prepared for it, that will be the kind of government which they will have. Government is at best but an expedient; but most governments are usually, and all governments are sometimes, inexpedient. The objections which have been brought against a standing army, and they are many and weighty, and deserve to prevail, may also at last be brought against a standing government. The standing army is only an arm of the standing government. The government itself, which is only the mode which the people have chosen to execute their will, is equally liable to be abused and perverted before the people can act through it. Witness the present Mexican war, the work of comparatively a few individuals using the standing government as their tool; for, in the outset, the people would not have consented to this measure.

This American government—what is it but a tradition, though a recent one, endeavoring to transmit itself unimpaired to posterity, but each instant losing some of its integrity? It has not the vitality and force of a single living man; for a single man can bend it to his will. It is a sort of wooden gun to the people themselves. But it is not the less necessary for this; for the people must have some complicated machinery or other, and hear its din, to satisfy that idea of government which they have. Governments show thus how successfully men can be imposed on, even impose on themselves, for their own advantage. It is excellent, we must all allow. Yet this government never of itself furthered any enterprise, but by the alacrity with which it got out of its way. *It* does not keep the country free. *It* does not settle the West. *It* does not educate. The character inherent in the American people has done all that has been accomplished; and it would have done somewhat more, if the government had not sometimes got in its way. For government is an expedient by which men would fain succeed in letting one another alone; and, as has been said, when it is most expedient, the governed are most let alone by it. Trade and commerce, if they were not made of India-rubber, would never manage to bounce over the obstacles which legislators are continually putting in their way; and, if one were to judge these men wholly by the effects of their actions and not partly by their intentions, they would deserve to be classed and punished with those mischievous persons who put obstructions on the railroads.

But, to speak practically and as a citizen, unlike those who call themselves no-government men, I ask for, not at once no government, but *at once* a better government. Let every man make known what kind of government would command his respect, and that will be one step toward obtaining it.

After all, the practical reason why, when the power is once in the hands of the people, a majority are permitted, and for a long period continue, to rule is not because they are most likely to be in the right, nor because this seems fairest to the minority, but because they are physically the strongest. But a government in which the majority rule in all cases cannot be based on justice, even as far as men understand it. Can there not be a government in which majorities do not virtually decide right and wrong, but conscience?—in which majorities decide only those questions to which the rule of expediency is applicable? Must the citizen ever for a moment, or in the least degree, resign his conscience to the legislator? Why has every man a conscience, then? I think that we should be men first, and sub-

jects afterward. It is not desirable to cultivate a respect for
the law, so much as for the right. The only obligation which
I have a right to assume is to do at any time what I think
right. It is truly enough said, that a corporation has no conscience; but a corporation of conscientious men is a corporation *with* a conscience. Law never made men a whit more
just; and, by means of their respect for it, even the well-
disposed are daily made the agents of injustice. A common
and natural result of an undue respect for law is, that you
may see a file of soldiers, colonel, captain, corporal, privates,
powder-monkeys, and all, marching in admirable order over
hill and dale to the wars, against their wills, ay, against their
common sense and consciences, which makes it very steep
marching indeed, and produces a palpitation of the heart.
They have no doubt that it is a damnable business in which
they are concerned; they are all peaceably inclined. Now,
what are they? Men at all? or small movable forts and magazines, at the service of some unscrupulous man in power?
Visit the Navy-Yard, and behold a marine, such a man as an
American government can make, or such as it can make a
man with its black arts,—a mere shadow and reminiscence
of humanity, a man laid out alive and standing, and already,
as one may say, buried under arms with funeral accompaniments, though it may be—

> "Not a drum was heard, not a funeral note,
>   As his corse to the rampart we hurried;
> Not a soldier discharged his farewell shot
>   O'er the grave where our hero we buried."

The mass of men serve the state thus, not as men mainly,
but as machines, with their bodies. They are the standing
army, and the militia, jailers, constables, posse comitatus,
etc. In most cases there is no free exercise whatever of the
judgment or of the moral sense; but they put themselves on
a level with wood and earth and stones; and wooden men
can perhaps be manufactured that will serve the purpose as
well. Such command no more respect than men of straw
or a lump of dirt. They have the same sort of worth only as
horses and dogs. Yet such as these even are commonly
esteemed good citizens. Others—as most legislators, politicians, lawyers, ministers, and office-holders—serve the

state chiefly with their heads; and, as they rarely make any moral distinctions, they are as likely to serve the Devil, without *intending* it, as God. A very few, as heroes, patriots, martyrs, reformers in the great sense, and *men,* serve the state with their consciences also, and so necessarily resist it for the most part; and they are commonly treated as enemies by it. A wise man will only be useful as a man, and will not submit to be "clay," and "stop a hole to keep the wind away," but leave that office to his dust at least:—

> "I am too high-born to be propertied,
>   To be a secondary at control,
>   Or useful serving-man and instrument
>   To any sovereign state throughout the world."

He who gives himself entirely to his fellowmen appears to them useless and selfish; but he who gives himself partially to them is pronounced a benefactor and philanthropist.

How does it become a man to behave toward this American government today? I answer, that he cannot without disgrace be associated with it. I cannot for an instant recognize that political organization as *my* government which is the *slave's* government also.

All men recognize the right of revolution; that is, the right to refuse allegiance to, and to resist, the government, when its tyranny or its inefficiency are great and unendurable. But almost all say that such is not the case now. But such was the case, they think, in the Revolution of '75. If one were to tell me that this was a bad government because it taxed certain foreign commodities brought to its ports, it is most probable that I should not make an ado about it, for I can do without them. All machines have their friction; and possibly this does enough good to counterbalance the evil. At any rate, it is a great evil to make a stir about it. But when the friction comes to have its machine, and oppression and robbery are organized, I say, let us not have such a machine any longer. In other words, when a sixth of the population of a nation which has undertaken to be the refuge of liberty are slaves, and a whole country is unjustly overrun and conquered by a foreign army, and subjected to military law, I think that it is not too soon for honest men to rebel and revolutionize. What makes this duty the more urgent is the fact that the country so overrun is not our own, but ours is the invading army.

Paley, a common authority with many on moral questions, in his chapter on the "Duty of Submission to Civil Government," resolves all civil obligation into expediency; and he proceeds to say, "that so long as the interest of the whole society requires it, that is, so long as the established government cannot be resisted or changed without public inconveniency, it is the will of God that the established government be obeyed, and no longer. . . . This principle being admitted, the justice of every particular case of resistance is reduced to a computation of the quantity of the danger and grievance on the one side, and of the probability and expense of redressing it on the other." Of this, he says, every man shall judge for himself. But Paley appears never to have contemplated those cases to which the rule of expediency does not apply, in which a people, as well as an individual, must do justice, cost what it may. If I have unjustly wrested a plank from a drowning man, I must restore it to him though I drown myself. This, according to Paley, would be inconvenient. But he that would save his life, in such a case, shall lose it. This people must cease to hold slaves, and to make war on Mexico, though it cost them their existence as a people.

In their practice, nations agree with Paley; but does any one think that Massachusetts does exactly what is right at the present crisis?

> "A drab of state, a cloth-o'-silver slut,
>   To have her train borne up, and her soul trail
>   in the dirt."

Practically speaking, the opponents to a reform in Massachusetts are not a hundred thousand politicians at the South, but a hundred thousand merchants and farmers here, who are more interested in commerce and agriculture than they are in humanity, and are not prepared to do justice to the slave and to Mexico, *cost what it may*. I quarrel not with far-off foes, but with those who, near at home, cooperate with, and do the bidding of, those far away, and without whom the latter would be harmless. We are accustomed to say, that the mass of men are unprepared; but improvement is slow, because the few are not materially wiser or better

than the many. It is not so important that many should be as
good as you, as that there be some absolute goodness somewhere; for that will leave the whole lump. There are
thousands who are *in opinion* opposed to slavery and to the
war, who yet in effect do nothing to put an end to them; who,
esteeming themselves children of Washington and Franklin,
sit down with their hands in their pockets, and say that they
know not what to do, and do nothing; who even postpone the
question of freedom to the question of free trade, and quietly
read the prices-current along with the latest advices from
Mexico, after dinner, and, it may be, fall asleep over them
both. What is the price-current of an honest man and patriot
today? They hesitate, and they regret, and sometimes they
petition; but they do nothing in earnest and with effect. They
will wait, well disposed, for others to remedy the evil, that
they may no longer have it to regret. At most, they give only
a cheap vote, and a feeble countenance and Godspeed, to
the right, as it goes by them. There are nine hundred and
ninety-nine patrons of virtue to one virtuous man. But it is
easier to deal with the real possessor of a thing than with the
temporary guardian of it.

All voting is a sort of gaming, like checkers or back-
gammon, with a slight moral tinge to it, a playing with right
and wrong, with moral questions; and betting naturally
accompanies it. The character of the voters is not staked. I
cast my vote, perchance, as I think right; but I am not vitally
concerned that that right should prevail. I am willing to leave
it to the majority. Its obligation, therefore, never exceeds that
of expediency. Even voting *for the right* is *doing* nothing for
it. It is only expressing to men feebly your desire that it
should prevail. A wise man will not leave the right to the
mercy of chance, nor wish it to prevail through the power
of the majority. There is but little virtue in the action of
masses of men. When the majority shall at length vote for
the abolition of slavery, it will be because they are indifferent
to slavery, or because there is but little slavery left to be
abolished by their vote. *They* will then be the only slaves.
Only *his* vote can hasten the abolition of slavery who asserts
his own freedom by his vote.

I hear of a convention to be held at Baltimore, or elsewhere, for the selection of a candidate for the Presidency,
made up chiefly of editors, and men who are politicians by

profession; but I think, what is it to any independent, intelligent, and respectable man what decision they may come to? Shall we not have the advantage of his wisdom and honesty, nevertheless? Can we not count upon some independent votes? Are there not many individuals in the country who do not attend conventions? But no: I find that the respectable man, so called, has immediately drifted from his position, and despairs of his country, when his country has more reason to despair of him. He forthwith adopts one of the candidates thus selected as the only *available* one, thus proving that he is himself *available* for any purposes of the demagogue. His vote is of no more worth than that of any unprincipled foreigner or hireling native, who may have been bought. O for a man who is a *man,* and, as my neighbor says, has a bone in his back which you cannot pass your hand through! Our statistics are at fault: the population has been returned too large. How many *men* are there to a square thousand miles in this country? Hardly one. Does not America offer any inducement for men to settle here? The American has dwindled into an Odd Fellow—one who may be known by the development of his organ of gregariousness, and a manifest lack of intellect and cheerful self-reliance; whose first and chief concern, on coming into the world, is to see that the almshouses are in good repair; and, before yet he has lawfully donned the virile garb, to collect a fund for the support of the widows and orphans that may be; who, in short, ventures to live only by the aid of the Mutual Insurance company, which has promised to bury him decently.

It is not a man's duty, as a matter of course, to devote himself to the eradication of any, even the most enormous wrong; he may still properly have other concerns to engage him; but it is his duty, at least, to wash his hands of it, and, if he gives it no thought longer, not to give it practically his support. If I devote myself to other pursuits and contemplations, I must first see, at least, that I do not pursue them sitting upon another man's shoulders. I must get off him first, that he may pursue his contemplations too. See what gross inconsistency is tolerated. I have heard some of my townsmen say, "I should like to have them order me out to help put down an insurrection of the slaves, or to march to Mexico;—see if I would go"; and yet these very men have each, directly by their allegiance, and so indirectly, at least, by their money, furnished a substitute. The soldier is applauded who refuses to serve in an unjust war by those who do not refuse to sustain the unjust government which makes the war; is applauded by those whose own act and authority he disregards and sets at naught; as if the state were penitent to that degree that it hired one to scourge it while it sinned, but not to that degree that it left off sinning for a moment. Thus, under the name of Order and Civil Government, we are all made at last to pay homage to and support our own meanness. After the first blush of sin comes its indifference; and from immoral it becomes, as it were, *un*moral, and not quite unnecessary to that life which we have made.

The broadest and most prevalent error requires the most disinterested virtue to sustain it. The slight reproach to which the virtue of patriotism is commonly liable, the noble are most likely to incur. Those who, while they disapprove of the character and measures of a government, yield to it their allegiance and support are undoubtedly its most conscientious supporters, and so frequently the most serious obstacles to reform. Some are petitioning the state to dissolve the Union, to disregard the requisitions of the President. Why do they not dissolve it themselves—the union between themselves and the state—and refuse to pay their quota into its treasury? Do not they stand in the same relation to the state that the state does to the Union? And have not the same reasons prevented the state from resisting the Union which have prevented them from resisting the state?

How can a man be satisfied to entertain an opinion merely, and enjoy *it?* Is there any enjoyment in it, if his opinion is that he is aggrieved? If you are cheated out of a single dollar by your neighbor, you do not rest satisfied with knowing that you are cheated, or with saying that you are cheated, or even with petitioning him to pay you your due; but you take effectual steps at once to obtain the full amount, and see that you are never cheated again. Action from principle, the perception and the performance of right, changes things and relations; it is essentially revolutionary, and does not consist wholly with anything which was. It not only divides states and churches, it divides families; ay, it divides the *individual*, separating the diabolical in him from the divine.

Unjust laws exist: shall we be content to obey them, or shall we endeavor to amend them, and obey them until we have succeeded, or shall we transgress them at once? Men generally, under such a government as this, think that they ought to wait until they have persuaded the majority to alter them. They think that, if they should resist, the remedy would be worse than the evil. But it is the fault of the government itself that the remedy is worse than the evil. *It* makes it worse. Why is it not more apt to anticipate and provide for reform? Why does it not cherish its wise minority? Why does it cry and resist before it is hurt? Why does it not encourage its citizens to be on the alert to point out its faults, and *do* better than it would have them? Why does it always crucify Christ, and excommunicate Copernicus and Luther, and pronounce Washington and Franklin rebels?

One would think, that a deliberate and practical denial of its authority was the only offense never contemplated by government; else, why has it not assigned its definite, its suitable and proportionate penalty? If a man who has no property refuses but once to earn nine shillings for the state, he is put in prison for a period unlimited by any law that I know, and determined only by the discretion of those who placed him there; but if he should steal ninety times nine shillings from the state, he is soon permitted to go at large again.

If the injustice is part of the necessary friction of the machine of government, let it go, let it go: perchance it will wear smooth—certainly the machine will wear out. If the injustice has a spring, or a pulley, or a rope, or a crank, exclusively for itself, then perhaps you may consider whether the remedy will not be worse than the evil; but if it is of such a nature that it requires you to be the agent of injustice to another, then, I say, break the law. Let your life be a counter friction to stop the machine. What I have to do is to see, at any rate, that I do not lend myself to the wrong which I condemn.

As for adopting the ways which the state has provided for remedying the evil, I know not of such ways. They take too much time, and a man's life will be gone. I have other affairs to attend to. I came into this world, not chiefly to make this a good place to live in, but to live in it, be it good or bad. A man has not everything to do, but something; and because he cannot do *everything,* it is not necessary that he should do *something* wrong. It is not my business to be petitioning the Governor or the Legislature any more than it is theirs to petition me; and if they should not hear my petition, what should I do then? But in this case the state has provided no way: its very Constitution is the evil. This may seem to be harsh and stubborn and unconciliatory; but it is to treat with the utmost kindness and consideration the only spirit that can appreciate or deserves it. So is all change for the better, like birth and death, which convulse the body.

I do not hesitate to say, that those who call themselves Abolitionists should at once effectually withdraw their support, both in person and property, from the government of Massachusetts, and not wait till they constitute a majority of one, before they suffer the right to prevail through them. I think that it is enough if they have God on their side, without waiting for that other one. Moreover, any man more right than his neighbors constitutes a majority of one already.

Josiah Warren

True Civilization and Personal Liberty [1]

Josiah Warren (1798–1874) Born in Boston, an inventor and a social philosopher, he is regarded as the first American anarchist and was descended from historically famous Puritan stock. A keen student of Owen, he with his family joined the utopian community New Harmony. He undertook an experiment known as the "time store" as it attempted to fix and regulate the amount of merchant's compensation. It gave rise to other attempts that became known as the "equity movement." He was an ingenious inventor (a lard-burning lamp, a speed press, a self-inking cylinder press, and a process for rapid and cheap production of stereotype plates). The keynote of his social philosophy was individuality. Everyone should be a law unto himself, without violating the integrity of others. He spent his last years in Boston, where he died in the home of a friend after a long illness.

[1] From *True Civilization: A Subject of Vital and Serious Interest to All People; but most Immediately to Men and Women of Labor and Sorrow*, by Josiah Warren. Clintondale (published by the author): 1869.

THE GREATEST PRACTICABLE AMOUNT OF
LIBERTY TO EACH INDIVIDUAL

Liberty! Freedom! Right! The vital principle of happiness! The one perfect law! The soul of every thing that exalts and refines us! The one sacred sound that touches a sympathetic chord in every living breast! The watchword of every revolution in the holy cause of suffering humanity! Freedom! The last lingering word whispered from the dying martyr's quivering lips! The one precious boon—the atmosphere of heaven. The "one mighty breath, which shall, like a whirlwind, scatter in its breeze the whole dark pile of human mockeries." When is LIBERTY to take up its abode on earth?

What is liberty? WHO WILL ALLOW ME TO DEFINE IT FOR HIM, AND AGREE BEFOREHAND TO SQUARE HIS LIFE BY MY DEFINITION? Who does not wish to see it first, and sit in judgment on it, and *decide for himself* as to its propriety? And who does not see that it is his *own individual* interpretation of the word that he adopts? And who will agree to square his whole life by any rule, which, although good at present, may not prove applicable to all cases? Who does not wish to preserve his *liberty* to act according to the peculiarities or INDIVIDUALITIES of future cases, and to sit in judgment on the merits of each, and to change or vary from time to time with new developments and increasing knowledge? Each individual being thus at liberty at all times, would be SOVEREIGN OF HIMSELF. NO GREATER AMOUNT OF LIBERTY CAN BE CONCEIVED—ANY LESS WOULD NOT BE LIBERTY! Liberty defined and limited by others is slavery! LIBERTY, then, is the SOVEREIGNTY OF THE INDIVIDUAL; and never shall man know liberty until each and every individual is acknowledged to be *the only legitimate sovereign of his or her person, time, and property, each living and acting at his own cost;* and not until we live in society where each can exercise this inalienable right of sovereignty at all times without clashing with, or violating that of others. This is impracticable just in proportion as we or our interests are UNITED *or combined with others*. The only ground upon which man can know liberty, is that of DISCONNECTION, DISUNION, INDIVIDUALITY.

You and I may associate together as the best of friends, as long as our interests are not too closely connected; but let our domestic arrangements be too closely *connected;* let me become responsible for your debts, or let me, by joining a society of which you are a member, become responsible for your sentiments, and the discordant effects of too close connection will immediately appear. Harmonious society can be erected on no other ground than the strictest INDIVIDUALITY of interests and responsibilities, nor can the liberty of mankind be restored upon any other principle or mode of action. How can it be otherwise? If my interest is united with yours, and we differ at any point in its management, as this difference is inevitable, one must yield, the other must decide, or, we must leave the decision to a third party. This third party is government, and thus, in UNITED INTERESTS, *government originates*. The more business there is thus committed to governmental management, the more must each of the governed surrender his liberty or his control over his own, and the greater must be the amount of power delegated to the government. When this becomes unlimited or *indefinite*, the government is absolute, and the liberty and security of the governed are annihilated; when limited or *definite,* some liberty remains to the governed. Experience has proved, *that power cannot be delegated to rulers of states and nations, in sufficient quantities for the management of business, without its becoming an indefinite quantity*, and in this *indefiniteness* have mankind been cheated out of their legitimate liberty.

Let twenty persons combine their means to build a bridge, each contributing twenty dollars—at the first meeting for business it is found that the business of such combinations can be conducted only by electing some one *individual* deciding and acting power, before any practical steps can be taken. Here each subscriber must trust his twenty dollars to the management of some one, perhaps not of his own choice, yet, as the sum is *definite* and not serious, its loss may not disturb his SECURITY, and he prefers to risk it for the prospective advantages to himself and his neighborhood. In entering his twenty dollars into this combination he submits it to the control of others, but he submits nothing more; and if he is aware beforehand, that the business of all combinations must be conducted by delegated power; and if he is not com-

pelled to submit to any conditions not contemplated beforehand; and if he can withdraw his investment at pleasure,
then there is no violation of his natural liberty or sovereignty
over his own; or, if he choose to make a permanent investment, and lay down all future control over it, for the sake
of a prospective advantage, it is a surrender of so much of
his property (not his liberty) to the control of others; but,
it being a definite quantity, and the *risks* and conditions all
being made known and voluntarily consented to beforehand,
the consequences may not be serious to him; and, although
he may discover, in the course of the business, that the *principle is wrong,* yet, he may derive ultimate advantage, under
some circumstances, from so much combination—some
may be willing to invest more and others less. If each one is
himself the supreme judge at all times of the individual case
in hand, and is free to act from his own individual estimate
of the advantages to be derived to himself or others, as in
the above instance, then the natural liberty of the individual
is not invaded; but it is when the decision or will of others is
made his rule of action, CONTRARY TO HIS VIEWS OR INCLINA-
TION, that his legitimate liberty is violated.

We eat prussic acid in a peach—*another quantity* of prussic acid is certain and sudden death. Let us learn to *dis-
criminate,* to *individualize* our ideas, even of different quantities of the same thing. The above amount of combination
may be harmless; indeed, it may give us a healthful proof
that it is wrong in principle, and admonish us not to pursue
it farther. But now let us contemplate another *degree* of
combination—combination as the basis of society, involving
all the great interests of man; his liberty, his person, his
mind, his time, his labor, his food, the soil he rests upon, his
property, his responsibilities to an indefinite extent, his
security, the education and destinies of his children, the indefinite interests of his race! In such combinations, whether
political or social, the different members can never be found
always possessing the same views and feelings on all these
subjects. Not even two persons can perform a piece of music
together in *order,* unless one of them commences or leads
individually, or, unless both agree to be governed by some
third movement, which is an individuality. Two leaders cannot lead—*the lead must be individual,* or confusion and discord will be the result. The same is true with regard to any

combined movement. In political and social combinations, men have sought to mitigate the horrid abuses of despotism by diffusing the delegated power, but they have always purchased the relief at the expense of confusion. The experience of all the world has shown, that the business of such combinations cannot be conducted by the whole of its members, but that one or a few must be set apart to lead and manage the business of the combination; to these, power must be delegated JUST IN PROPORTION TO THE AMOUNT OF BUSINESS COMMITTED TO THEIR CHARGE. These constitute the government of the combination, and to this government all must yield their INDIVIDUAL SOVEREIGNTY, or the combination cannot move one step. If their persons, their responsibilities, and all their interests are involved in the combination, as in communities of common property, all *these* must be entirely under the control of the government, whose judgment or will is the rule for all the governed, and the natural liberty or sovereignty of every member is entirely annihilated, and the government is as strong, as absolute as a government can be made, while the members are rendered as weak and as dependent on the governing few as they can be rendered, and consequently, their LIBERTY and SECURITY are reduced to the lowest practicable degree. If only half of the interests of the individual are invested in the combination, then only half the quantity of government is required, and only half of the natural liberty of the members need to be surrendered; but as this definite quantity cannot be measured and set apart from the other half, and as government once erected, either through the *indefiniteness* of the language in which the power is delegated or by other means, will steal the other half; there is no security, no liberty for mankind, but through the ABANDONMENT of COMBINATIONS as the basis of society.

If governments originate in combined interests, and if government and liberty cannot exist together, then the solution of our problem demands that there be NO COMBINED INTERESTS TO MANAGE. All interests must be individualized—all responsibilities must be *individual*, before men can enjoy complete liberty or security, and before society can be completely harmonious. We can dispense with government only in proportion as we can reduce the amount of public business to be managed. This, then, is the movement for the restoration of the liberty of mankind; it is to *disconnect,* to *individualize,* rather than to *combine* or "UNITE" our interests!

When one's person, his labor, his responsibilities, the soil he rests on, his food, his property, and all his interests are so *disconnected, disunited* from others, that he can control or dispose of these at all times, according to his own views and feelings, without controlling or disturbing others; and when his premises are sacred to himself, and his person is not approached, nor his time and attention taken up, against his inclination, then the individual may be said to be practically SOVEREIGN OF HIMSELF, and all that constitutes or pertains to his individuality. No greater scope of liberty for every individual can be conceived—any less is not the "greatest practicable amount of liberty. . . ."

CONCLUSION

I have stated the problem to be solved, I have suggested the means of its solution, and endeavored to exhibit their applications in a manner to reach the plainest understanding. I have carefully withheld comments of my own, that the mind of the reader might sit in *free* and unbiased judgment in each case, and on every point of our subject; and I now respectfully, but earnestly, invite him or her to study the adaptation of these means to their proposed ends, and to decide whether or not the problem is fully and correctly stated—whether or not the means proposed are adequate to the solution of that problem—whether or not I am correct in the following conclusions:

That *cost* is an equitable, and the only equitable principle for the government of prices in the pecuniary commerce of mankind.

That this being reduced to practice, would give to labor its legitimate reward, and its necessary and natural stimulus.

That it would convert the present clashing interests of mankind into cooperating interests, and thereby sweep away the principal cause of national prejudices and national wars —would destroy all motive in the masses to invade each other—all necessity for armies, navies, and other paraphernalia for national defense, and thereby neutralize the principal excuse for government—that by infusing into the public

mind, correct and practical principles which will give a
clear knowledge of the rights of each other, and at the same
time raise every one above the temptation to violate them,
we can put an end to the other excuse for governmental
"protection."

That by dispensing with government we shake off the
greatest invader of human rights, the nightmare of society.

That cost being made the limit of price, would give to a
washerwoman a greater income than the importer of foreign
goods—that this would entirely upset the whole of the present system of national trade—stop all wars arising out of the
scramble for the profits of trade, and demolish all tariffs,
duties, and all systems of policy that give rise to them—
would abolish all distinctions of rich and poor—would
enable every one to consume as much as he produced, and,
consequently, prevent any one from living at the cost of
another, without his or her consent.

That it would prevent the ruinous fluctuations in prices,
and in business, which are the chief elements of *insecurity,*
and which give rise to the unprincipled scramble for property
so prevalent in all civilized countries, in which, in the very
midst of the most clamorous professions of righteousness, the
rights of persons, of property, and the great interests of the
whole race are practicably forgotten or disregarded.

That upon this principle the great problem of machinery
against labor is mathematically and harmoniously solved—
and that no other principles or modes of action can thus
solve it. That upon this principle the disgusting and degrading features of our pecuniary commerce would be changed,
and men could exchange their products with each other without degrading their own characters and destroying their
self-respect in the operation.

That this principle is indispensable to the *security of person* and property—that it would put an end to the scramble
for property, which gives rise to encroachments on each
other, to restrain which, government is invented and invoked
—that these governments, instead of securing the rights of
person and property, prove in their operations the greatest
violators of all rights, and that we must work out the security
of person and property without governments.

That *cost* being made the limit of price, would necessarily
produce all the cooperation, and all the economies aimed at

by the most intelligent and devoted friends of humanity; and, by reducing the burthen of labor to a mere pastime or necessary exercise, would probably annihilate its *cost;* when, like water or amateur music, no price would be set upon it; and the highest aspirations of the best of our race would be naturally realized.

That the security of person and property demands that every one shall feel secure from any external power rising above him, and controlling his person, time, or property, or involving him in responsibilities, contrary to his own individual inclination—that he must feel that he has, and always shall have, his own destiny in his own hands—that he shall always be sovereign of himself and all his own interests—that this sovereignty of the individual is directly opposed to all external or artificial government. That this sovereignty of the individual is impracticable in national, State, Church, or reform *combinations;* and that combination is, therefore, exactly the wrong condition for the security, peace, and liberty of mankind. That the true movement for the attainment of these ends is for each individual to commence immediately to disconnect his person and all his interests from combinations of every description, and to assume the entire control of them as fast as they can be sufficiently separated from others, so that he can control his own, WITHOUT CONTROLLING THEM.

That a rational circulating medium, a definite representative of property on equitable principles, has never been known to mankind—that all the great money transactions of the world, all banks and banking operations, all stock-jobbing, all money corporations and money movements, all systems of finance, and all the money business of the world, have been based upon shells, metals, and pictures; things which are no better qualified for a circulating medium, than a floating log is fit for a boundary of a piece of land. That all the legislative action on this subject has been conducted in the most profound ignorance of what a circulating medium should be, or legislators have abused their trust, and sold the people to their enemies. That a rational and equitable circulating medium, together with *cost as the limit of price,* would strike at the root of all political, commercial, and financial corruption, and contribute largely to establish equity, security, liberty, equality, peace, and abundance, wherever it shall be introduced.

That all INTERESTS AND RESPONSIBILITIES MUST BE ENTIRELY INDIVIDUALIZED, before the legitimate liberty of mankind can be restored—before each one can be sovereign of his own without violating the sovereignty of others. That the sovereignty of every individual is not only indispensable to security, but constitutes the natural liberty of mankind, and must be restored back to each, before society can be harmonious. That the sovereignty of the individual becoming a new element in public opinion, and thereby constituting each the supreme deciding power for himself at all times, would put an end to all discordant controversies on ALL SUBJECTS—disarm all laws and governments of their desolating power; and, that with an habitual regard to this right in every one, no one's time or attention would be taken up, nor their thoughts or feelings disturbed, against his or her inclination, and that our social intercourse would thus become purified, refined, and exalted, to the very highest conceivable state of perfection.

That the natural tendency of these new elements of society is to abolish all the cause of crimes, and all the horrid inventions for punishment, and to take away the last excuse of men for their insane cruelty to each other. That the sovereignty of the individual constitutes the largest liberty to each individual—that *liberty defined and limited by others is slavery.* That every one has an inalienable right to define this and all other words for himself or herself, and, therefore, that no one has any right to define them for others; and, therefore, that all verbal institutions which demand conformity in their interpretations are as false in principle as they have proved pernicious in practice.

That the great problem of education has never been practically solved, nor can it be solved upon any of the principles upon which society is now acting; but, that the study of natural individualities, with these natural deductions from them, point out a solution at once simple, truthful, beautiful, and sublime.

Finally, that the five elements of new society herein set forth, together with other modern discoveries and inventions, are capable, if reduced to practice, of "ADJUSTING, HAR-

MONIZING, AND REGULATING THE PECUNIARY, INTELLEC-
TUAL, AND MORAL INTERCOURSE OF MANKIND," and of elevating the condition and character of our race to the fulfillment
of the highest aspirations and purest hopes of the most
devoted friends of humanity.

William Ernest Hocking **Anarchism and Consent** [1]

William Ernest Hocking (1873 ——)   Hocking was born in Cleveland, Ohio, in 1873. A graduate of Harvard University, he has
studied abroad at the Universities of Gottingen, Berlin, and
Heidelberg. He is the recipient of a great number of honorary
degrees. He is a Professor Emeritus of Philosophy and the
author of many books. Among his later works are *The Coming
World Civilization, The Meaning of Immortality in Human
Experience,* and *Strength of Men and Nations.*

The voluntary groupings of men
have life in them; some of them have capacity and intelligence enough, the pluralist tells us, to bend, or control, or
defy the policy of the government. But if this is so, why
may they not, either now or later, wholly take its place? Why
may we not look forward to a society of free, naturally inter-
lacing, self-governing private groups? This is the question
put by the philosophical anarchist.

Note that if anarchy is equivalent to chaos, the philosophical anarchist, despite his name, is no seeker of anarchy. He
calls for an end not of law but of laws and of law enforcement. Nor does he advise that government should be at once
done away, ending its force by violence. His plan (if we may
make a type of schemes so various) is that the activities of
government shall be diminished by degrees until, when only
the administering of public services is left, private associations may take them over.

In its opposition to force, anarchism is akin to the belief
that war between States can be and ought to be banished:
anarchism is pacifism in internal affairs. In its opposition to
governmental activity, it is akin to an ideal widely professed

[1] From *Man and the State,* by William Ernest Hocking. New Haven: Yale
University Press. Copyright 1926. Reprinted by permission of the publisher.

during the last century under the name of laissezfaire, and still of popular vogue in the belief that "the state governs best that governs least." Most Americans are instinctive laissezfaire-ists in the respect that they dislike being reminded of government, believing in their capacity and that of their neighbors to manage their own affairs and their mutual affairs on terms of fair play without the surveillance of public authorities; and most incline subconsciously to philosophical anarchism, in so far as they assume, with Spinoza,[2] that if man were completely socialized in his nature, as some day he may be, there would be no need for the State. Laissezfaire-ists differ from anarchists not so much in their ideal as in their view of the possibilities of human nature.[3] The former think that the self-seeking and deceitful elements of human nature will remain statistically about as they are, requiring the police functions as an irreducible minimum of State activity; the latter believe in a moral progress such that the social casing of coercion may eventually be discarded, leaving a matured, self-respecting humanity to maintain freely its order and character. They believe, further, that the gradual decrease of state pressure would hasten this event, because human nature has a bent to goodness, and gives the best account of itself when unfettered by artificial requirements.

As for the criminal, his existence is not forgotten; but it is thought that he is either such by definition only, as one who has disobeyed what *we* have commanded; or he is such by response to the unnatural environment of the State and the exaggerated inequalities which it fosters;[4] or else he is the unusual individual of determined ill will who is best dealt with by near and private hands, since the life of the will, whether for good or for evil, is always intimate, individual, and unique. The legal separation between sheep and goats

---

2 *Theologico-Political Tractate,* tr. Elwes, p. 73. [Hocking's note, as are all others in this extract.]
3 The views of Benjamin R. Tucker, presented in his journal, *Liberty* (Boston, 1881), are an ingenious blend of Proudhon and Herbert Spencer, and indicate the affiliation between them. Kropotkin in *Anarchist Communism* expressly steps off from Spencer's views to his own.
4 "Three quarters of all the acts which are brought every year before our courts have their origin, either directly or indirectly, in the present disorganized state of society with regard to the production and distribution of wealth—not in the perversity of human nature." P. Kropotkin, *Anarchist Communism,* p. 31.

is too obviously an affair of exteriors to satisfy the anarchist's thirst for inner realities.

He is not disposed to minimize the need of settling disputes, as a condition of keeping social groups alive. He is not less but rather more impressed than most men with the necessity as well as the beauty of reasonableness, self-control, and cumulative understandings among men.[5] His difference from those who hold to the state is simply that he believes that these goods should be and can be supplied by men themselves, not imposed upon them by an external power.

This faith of the anarchist in the capacity of human nature for association at once forceless and orderly is not wholly *a priori*. In the nature of the case, modern experiments in anarchism have been confined to small communities living within and under the general law of existing states. Still, communities have existed which were nearly devoid of organized public force, except such as formed itself spontaneously as occasion demanded. The early Jewish community was of this character.[6] In its case, a tenacious religious faith made possible a direction of public affairs uniquely informal and noncoercive. And while that faith cannot be reproduced, a moral equivalent is conceivable.

But the chief evidence is nearer at hand, in the same facts as lead the more cautious thinker to pluralism, namely, the abundant vital energy of voluntary groups, their natural authority, and growing capacity for self-government. Con-

---

[5] It is to be noted that an amoral and purely self-assertive anarchistic philosophy is a sporadic development, as in Aristippus or Max Stirner. It stands aside from the main current of philosophical anarchism, which relies on the inherent ethical forces of human nature to replace political control. Such is the anarchism of Zeno, the Stoic, of Vida, bishop of Alva, of Chojecki, the Hussite, of Hans Denk, the Anabaptist, of Tolstoy, of Kropotkin

"Provided that you yourselves do not abdicate your freedom; provided that you yourselves do not allow others to enslave you; and provided that to the violent and antisocial passions of this or that person *you oppose your equally vigorous social passions,* then you have nothing to fear from liberty. . . . To struggle; to look danger in the face; to live on dry bread in order to put an end to inequities that revolt us; to feel ourselves in harmony with such as are worthy of love: this for a weak philosopher perhaps means self-sacrifice. But for the man or woman filled with energy, force, vigor, and youth, it is the conscious joy of life." Kroptkin, *Anarchist Morality,* pp. 27, 33f.

[6] Lord Acton says of it, "The government of the Israelites was a Federation, held together by no political authority, but by the unity of race and faith, and founded not on physical force, but on a voluntary covenant." *History of Freedom,* p. 4.

sider, for example, the immense growth in recent years of
cooperative associations of producers, consumers, builders,
etc., including now some thirty millions of members in
Europe and America; and remember that such groups can
succeed only as they impose upon themselves the rigorous
discipline required for economic stability.[7] Consider also
how the development of codes of business practice, and the
extension of the art of voluntary agreement on business
standards, is beginning to take the place of legislation and to
relieve the burdens of the courts.[8]

Continued neighborhood and a common economy have
been from time immemorial the great teachers of natural
order to mankind. To this day, vast agricultural regions carry
on a custom-controlled life, hardly aware of the existence of
the State except as tax gatherer and conscriptionist. Agriculture is also man-culture; all normal growth is from the soil
upward. It is an empirical growth, based on experience well
mastered, and therefore sound and enduring.

Quite apart, then, from the moral force which the anarchist may feel in himself and attribute to human nature at
large, there is ground for his faith in the possibilities of an
ultimately free community. But he is moved to this alternative, whose difficulty he does not conceal from himself,
chiefly by a poignant sense of the evils to which all social
control, and especially all force-using government, is subject.

The most concrete of these evils, to the traditional anarchist, is the enforcement of economic inequity. The economy
built up from the immediate contact of individual men with
soil and region and neighbor is sound, because, as we have
said, it is empirical. The State is associated with an artificial
economy, *brought to* labor and the soil from outside, an
economy ordered about a protected mass of capital, perpetuating itself by inheritance, claiming the primacy and

---

[7] It is true, these cooperative bodies do not always refrain from force, or a
pressure that amounts to force. We recall the riots of 1923 in Fresno, where
raisin growers, needing an eighty percent of the local producers as members
of their association, adopted various devices, including ducking, tarring and
feathering, to "compel them to come in," presumably for their own benefit.
The commotive process is still, at times, savagely coercive, especially, as in
this case, to the foreigner.

[8] Herbert Hoover, Address before Cleveland Chamber of Commerce.

eternity of the general idea, a practical *a priori*. Anarchism is hostile to this inherited privilege, this self-perpetuating and cumulative mass, which it finds represented to the workers chiefly in the toll which it takes from them to support its own life, in Proudhon's view a fundamental theft.

But while the existence of capital as a social acquisition may create the motive for a capitalistic state, it is not intrinsic to the idea of the State that it should enforce capitalism or any other economic order. And hostility to capitalism is, of course, not peculiar to anarchism. The evils to which the anarchist is peculiarly sensitive lie deeper, in the very nature of a coercive society.

Social belonging is in no case an unmixed good. Every group exerts a pressure upon its members which tends to standardize them and warp them from their own true. Assuming as it must that many individuals are alike in that portion of their lives which it lives for them, the group blankets and obscures individual differences of will and power. When the state is described as "an external form given to the moral will," it might seem that government is being given a good character. But is it unquestionably good to belong to a group which assumes to do for me (even if it does it well) part of the work of my own conscience—after all, an inalienable organ. If it is indeed my own will which comes back to me through the State, why must I be compelled to accept my own as the voice of another and to live so far a vicarious life? Why must I be placed in the peril of not recognizing my own conscience in what is required of me? The inescapable pressure of the majority upon the minority, more particularly upon that omnipresent minority of *one* constituted by each one's individual judgment, becomes most intolerable when it is the moral judgment that is involved.

The effect of belonging upon character is clearly perceptible. In the wilds one feels more directly the natural man. If he is weak, the State lends him no adventitious strength: the "rights" which he has in common with every other citizen he must stand up for, if they are to count in his favor. His neighbors will not restrain themselves on behalf of a specter of unmanned legality: they restrain themselves in the presence of the man they personally respect. Thus the native forces of character must make themselves felt, and they thrive under the necessity. On the other hand, where the political environment is compact, and every moral weakling may count himself safe from violence and fraud, men of large powers may find themselves ill at ease: too much is done and willed for them—their qualities fail to tell. They may find themselves deficient in that special knack of self-alienation which enables lesser men to take firm root in the settled order. To rely on the police and the law court for protection and justice brings with it a subtle sense of shame and undue dependence.

Capacity to accept this vicarious moral living and this sharing of self-help is regarded as a part of civic virtue. Yet, other things equal, how can such renunciation of personal completeness be other than a diminishing of manhood? Unless there is an energy of personal growth great enough to carry its self-assertion into new fields, while leaving the socially shared self in the region of habit, the political man is surely in some ways less noble than the semi-anarchic pioneer.

The same "if" must be written against all social belonging. It offers at once a possibility and a danger—a possibility of growing in some directions beyond any dream of solitude, a danger of falling below the natural level by a morally parasitic and passively conforming relation to the social mentality. But in the case of the State these dangers are magnified by the element of coercion; and as the anarchist sees them, they develop into specific evils inseparable from life under government.

First of them is the *restriction of liberty;* and liberty, in the anarchist's ideal, is the chief of all political goods. If liberty is the chief political good, then no sacrifice of it for any other good can be other than a bad bargain.

Society stands to lose by every diminution of general freedom; for it runs the risk of checking its most original, and therefore most priceless, developments. Though not every divergent genius is a prophet, the prophets are bound to be among the divergent and intractable. Yet it is not in the name of the social welfare that the anarchist primarily pleads his cause. It is in the name of the individual's own destiny and right.

Life itself is individual, and the most significant things in the world—perhaps in the end the only significant things— are individual souls. Each one of these must work its own way to salvation, win its own experience, suffer from its own mistakes: "through angers, losses, ambition, ignorance, ennui," yes, and through crime and retribution, "what you are picks its way." Any rule which by running human conduct into approved grooves saves men from this salutary Odyssey thwarts the first meaning of human life.

In the second place, so far as the state requires good of men it *deprives that good of moral value.* For only that can have moral value which comes from free choice. Whatever is required by law is therefore drained of moral quality.

The actual ethical condition of the best governed states seems to confirm this criticism. Who does not recognize that in the typical political civilization of today conformity has largely replaced conscience, outer respectability takes the place of an inoperative personal conviction about conduct, and the fiber of men decays. Absence of moral originality is not the normal state of mankind: it is only in urbane communities that "what is done" becomes the complete guide to the practice of ruler and ruled alike.

Finally, there is the long history of the *abuse of power.* The unholy accompaniments of coercion, in "free" States as well as in others, the subtle poison of possessing force, the moral perdition in assuming the right to judge and punish, the blearing of the official eye to all that is individual through the pressure of business and the mechanism of the general rule, the callousness and the shifting of responsibility bred of the belief in the efficiency of the machine and the sufficiency of what has been—these are evils which are no specialties of cruel and cruder eras of mankind: they are the predictable incidents of bringing weak humanity into the false position of control over its fellows.

And the result is that enforced law shares the fate of all abnormalities—it *undermines its own position.*

For however worthy of obedience the law may be, governments, seduced by force-using, seldom are; and the disaffection from rulers extends to the law behind them. There is an element of arrogance in their wielding of principles more sacred than themselves; and if they insist on being inseparable from the law, the resentment due them will not be withheld because it strikes the law also. Law which allies itself with force begets lawlessness.

Those who justify themselves in evading the Volstead Act on the ground that it is foisted upon an unwilling majority by a group of determined bigots are not different in this respect from most other lawbreakers. They scent a personal factor in the law which is repellent to them; they extend this repulsion to the law, to its enforcers, and thus to the fabric of government. The anarchist argues that this is a psychological result which must appear in all men subject to government: sooner or later spontaneous lawfulness is destroyed.

In sum, the ultimate animus of anarchism is a deep sense of the crime which an enforced organization inflicts upon life, which is by birthright free, individual, varied.

According to the theory now before us, our wills are all included in the general will circuit we call the "State": they are included without any prior contract or consent; and yet they remain responsible for what the State does, as if they were free. This is either a contradiction or—a paradox!

The element of obvious unfreedom in the situation is aggravated by the defective quality of those deeds of the State in which we are supposed to join, deeds often unwise, occasionally unjust, at times wicked. The realistic eye which we must bring to all political theory discovers everywhere the absence of the alleged vital tie between what I will and what the State does—not unfrequently whole majorities in dissent, from the helots, slaves, churls of former days to the legally outwitted and impotent masses of today. Are the deeds of the state in any sense a part of the circuits of *their* wills? And beside these, there are the philosophical anarchists whose questions we have not yet answered, the anarchists who refuse their consent to any State, and to whom the notion of an enterprise in which all or none must join is the essence of the thing human beings ought to revolt against. The anarchist may speak for all these objectors. Where there is no consent, there can be no will.

There is no doubt about this absence of consent to many a State deed. But note that we have not been assuming consent to particular state deeds or laws, nor for that matter to the existence of any particular government. What we assert is that there is no one who does not want *the State*— if not the State here extant, then some other State including these people. Whatever the defects of any given State may be, they refer us for their remedy to State action, never to the stateless condition.

Our will toward the State is seldom one of wholesale approval, no more is our will toward our parents; and the same reflection is in order which Epictetus urged—"Did heaven owe me perfect parents?—No; it owed me parents." There is a distinction everyone learns to make in childhood between the will to play and the will to have my own way when I play. The ultimatum-temper, "I won't play unless it can be thus and so," is generally discovered to be poor building material: one should be able to maintain consent to the game together with dissent from its methods. In sterner affairs there is always a place, no doubt, for the uncompromising policy which demands "the best or nothing" or "rather no law than bad law"; but such a policy implies that one can distinguish in thought (because one refuses to distinguish in practice) between the will *that* a thing be and the will *what* it shall be. In our present case we must make still a third distinction. We must distinguish:

1) the will toward a particular law, deed, or policy;
2) the will toward the existence of the present State;
3) the will toward the existence of any State at all. And our position is that unless there is something incurably and hopelessly pernicious about particular deeds and laws, the real issue lies in the third point; and I shou d hold that in all cases this third layer of the will is necessarily affirmative, i.e., that the existence of the State *per se* is willed.

The ground for this position is simply the fact that a science of psychology is possible.

For such a science assumes that it is possible to make

some general statements about human nature, including the human will. And to make a general statement about the human will (as that human beings have innate dispositions to fear or fight or find food) is to say that there are some desires which it is not within our power *not to have*. And if there are any such desires, then, since it is necessary to have them, they are universal—or to put it otherwise, unanimous.

Now most psychologists today are inclined to attribute to the human being a large array of innate propensities. My own judgment would be that most of those which occur on such a list as that of William James appear at least temporarily in most persons, but that few of them can be said to persist through life and to be incapable of repression or transformation. That character belongs to only one instinct or disposition, namely, that one which must furnish the motive power for all such repression or transformation. The will to power, as we have defined it, would be in that position. All men have it, and always have it. And the will to power requires the State. *The will that the State exist is therefore a unanimous will;* and this proposition is independent of introspective impressions to the contrary. To include everyone within the State does no violence to the will of any individual, so long as it remains possible for him to act against the particulars to which he objects.

By the route of psychology, then, we discover that fundamental unanimity which, as many political theorists have held, must precede the right of any government, democratic or other, to impose its will upon the members of the State as "their" will. Majorities, as Rousseau clearly saw, have no natural right to dictate to minorities; whatever plan of reaching public decisions is agreed upon "presupposes unanimity once at least."[9] This unanimity is not a diplomatic achievement: it is a deliverance of human nature.

Rousseau attempted, as we have done, to unite consent with necessitation: the members of his State, if they failed to recognize their own wills in the terms of the contract or subsequent legislation were to be "compelled to be free." But consent can only be joined with necessity by way of a universal and unalterable element of the will, i.e., a char-

9 *The Social Contract*, I, ch. v.

acteristic of human nature such as we recognize in the will to power.[10] The affirmation of the state is deeper than conscious acquiescence, deeper also than fear, deep as the instinctive sense of the necessities of personal growth.

Let me remark in passing that this fundamental unanimity is not sufficient to establish the principle of majority rule.

Consent to the existence of the State carries with it only what is necessary that the State exist. To exist, it must be able to act; and to act, it must be able to reach decisions; and to reach decisions, the control by a majority is a convenient, but nowise indispensable, expedient. If one is seeking the preponderance of wisdom, rather than of force, and is not held within an artificial assumption that wisdom is equally distributed in the community, there are other and simpler ways known to politics of reaching decisions of state.

But whatever the machinery of decision, since it is to establish a deed which is the deed of all, the test of its rightness is an *eventual unanimity of approval*. No present majority, however large, can evade this ultimate test. The American Civil War, for example, will be justified, as a forcible majority decision, only if its main object, the maintenance of the Union, is eventually approved by the South as well as by the North, a condition which is approaching fulfillment.[11]

Unanimity at the beginning and at the end are the marks of a healthy and essentially free State; how the decisions that lie between are to be reached is a matter to be judged by by this standard.

The anarchist may reasonably reply to our argument that it is not enough to will that the State shall exist. All actual States are particular States, and have their life in particular deeds. If these particulars were all infected by some inherent and radical vice, the will that the State exist could not, as an

[10] Jethro Brown is right, so far as surface psychology goes, in saying that "the justification of governmental action is found not in consent but in the purpose it serves"; but to identify a necessary purpose is to discover an inevitable consent, which may belong to the deeper layers of self commonly called subconscious.

[11] Rendering patently unfair the type of criticism implied in the words of Laski: "The problem of authority may ultimately resolve itself into a question of what a section of the American people, strong enough to get its will enforced, may desire." *Authority in The Modern State,* p. 25.

abstraction or pious hope, long continue to live by itself.

There is substance in this contention. There is a tendency for common deeds to be mediocre deeds, if not vicious deeds. It is notoriously hard to maintain a high standard in any crowd; you must not be conspicuously better than your comrades; you may attack the vices of the other party, not those of your own. Further, you must accommodate yourself to the incidents of organization, whose dehumanizing tendencies we have mentioned. All organization, according to its extent, involves hierarchy, with rank and file, middledom, and overdom; and in every such ordering of men the integrity of will-impulses is falsified. It lies in the nature, not necessarily in the intention, of the middledom to be a misleading screen, a lying filter, both of facts and of desires between the rank and file and the overdom. The will that finds itself enacted in the vital circuit of any large group is a distorted version of the wills of its mass of members.

As the largest of corporate undertakings, government cannot but suffer most from these defects. By its immense momentum and the irrational elements in its connective tissue it discourages aspiration. Genius dies in its meshes; the output of government, both in tangible works and in character, bears everywhere the stamp of conventionalized mediocrity. "The history of the growth of the State, of public authority and compulsion, is the history of the decline from Florence and Nuremburg to London and New York."[12]

The conviction deepens that these vices are inherent in state action. The result is an alienation from politics on the part of growing numbers of the *"élite,"* as from an unclean thing; and a strange rapprochement between these world-fleeing idealists and the disillusioned anarchist.

If there were no other outlook we should be left with the choice of two evils, abandonment of the will to power in its fully personalized meaning, or submission to its perpetual vulgarization and corruption.

Even so, the will to power cannot be given up, and organization cannot be given up. No man, not even a religious ascetic, can be content with a parasitic relation to the history-making work of his community. The life of meditation,

12 Lowes Dickinson, *A Symposium,* p. 55.

well-justified as it is, must alternate with activities of the economic and defensive orders, if only to renew its own vigor. Any man or people that seeks a spirituality which requires a neglect of organized effort in the mastery of nature and social construction abandons, if we are right, one of the roots of an honest spirituality. There is no life immune from the incidents of establishing the frame for the will to power in the dust of fact, human fallibility, and passion.

And if it were possible to set up such a pure and sequestered life, there would be the less reason to complain of those who besmirch themselves with the abandoned activities of the state. For if the world-fleer can forget politics, he can forget who it is that pursues politics. Preemption by others of a rejected function can be no evil to the one who has rejected it.

But to despair of organization and yet to believe all things of individual human nature, as the philosophical anarchist does, is arbitrary.

The circuits of organized life impede and distort the will-impulses of the members: very well—then we have a problem in social conductivity. We demand that this distortion shall be minimized, that it shall be cured. How is this to be accomplished? That is the great field for political invention. One such invention is before the world. Democracy, as a political scheme, boasts a great advance in the conductivity of will-impulses; the will of the people pours immediately into the circuits of the State—so it is claimed. We have to examine this claim. But whether the future is with this invention or with some other, those who have no ideas to offer are hardly justified by that fact in denying that the solving ideas are possible.

For the evils which organized social life brings, organized social life may find a remedy; for the ills which attend anarchy, anarchism has no cure.

The philosophical anarchist is wholly right in his solicitude for the individual will. What he fails to see is that it is the very nature of these wills which welds their circuits together in an enforced unanimity of action for objects which they could not attain by themselves. The State lives from day to day by only so much consent as they send into it; its whole energy is drawn from the force of their demands; there is nothing in its nature which can stand in contradiction to them, nor in permanent divergence from them.

But beside the philosophical anarchist, there is the practical anarchist, a far more numerous class and found for the most part in very different quarters. Practical anarchism directly attacks the existence of the State by menacing its power to act. As a will-circuit, the existence of the State is a matter of degree: it exists as much as it can act. That power to act can be reduced to zero—for most modern States have a low resultant energy—and the result is not a State but a swarm of competing powers, no one of which is strong enough to bring the wills of the people together into a living circuit. It is by no means an axiom that a community must be capable of united action. It is not certain in advance that in a State distracted by faction a cabinet can always be found which will command a parliamentary majority. At the moment of this writing (November, 1923) it is not evident from day to day that Germany will be able to devise a public policy which will command assent either within or without her borders.

Now there are always those ready to exploit this low margin of functional energy. In our own country the balance of internal powers creates a situation in which deadlocks are always possible, while minorities and filibusterers exact their price under the threat that no action shall take place. To such wills it is "My policy or none": these are the practical anarchists. A nation of such wills would end in chaos.

But while "rule or ruin" seems to imply a willingness to accept ruin, it is like the usual temper of suicide, a perverted form of the will to live, essentially self-contradictory. It relies on the unwillingness of the great majority to let the State fail; it shares that unwillingness. Its pretence to prefer no deed, and hence in the end no state, to the deed of its momentary opponent is essentially insincere.

The amount of this perversity increases. It is necessary to recognize it for what it is, the only variety of anarchism at all likely to lead to anarchy.

Herbert Read **Anarchism and Modern Society** [1]

Herbert Edward Read (1893 ——)   Read is an important critic and
poet. The son of a farmer, he was born in Yorkshire, England,
in 1893. He studied at the University of Leeds. He has served
as a lecturer at the University of Liverpool and Professor at
the University of Edinburgh. He has written a great number of
books in art criticism and art history and many volumes of
poetry. He is a well-known advocate of mutualist anarchism.
Some of his works are *Naked Warriors, The End of a War,
Mutations of the Phoenix, The Anatomy of Art, Art and Society,* and *Poetry and Anarchism.* He also has written innumerable introductory essays for volumes by poets, art historians,
and anarchists. The most recent of his works to appear in the
United States is *To Hell with Culture.*

Capitalist is a fashionable word
used to characterize the type of economy that prevails in the
United States, Great Britain, West Germany, and France.
In these countries the union of the direct power of the State
and the productive organization of monopoly capitalism has
attained the highest standard of living that has yet been
capable of satisfying the population of these countries. Such
apparent prosperity comes accompanied by a progressive
circulative inflation, which considerably reduces the real
value of salaries, but recognizes the need for periodic revision
and has created complex machinery to adjust salaries and
prices. The result has been a general advance in the material
condition of the working classes. That the change has been
accompanied by a spiritual impoverishment is equally
evident.

That this progress in economic conditions has implied
sacrifices for a minority one cannot deny. Pensioners and all
the people who depend upon income derived from properties, investments, and credit must suffer in relation to the
rest of the community, and there is always a remnant of
unemployed, which, in a vast country like the United States,

[1] From *El anarquismo en la sociedad capitalista,* by Herbert Read *Recon-
struir,* No. 19. (July–August, 1962). Reprinted with permission of the publishers, and translated from the Spanish for this book by Ruth L. Horowitz.

can amount to two or three million people. Money for the unemployed often takes its toll on the majority, but desperate cases are many. In capitalist society, however, the public never suffers penury or never suffers it to such an extent as to constitute a threat to the economic stability of the State.

From this economic development, the politics of *resentment* that is characteristic of the eighteenth and nineteenth centuries, one discerns that it diminishes considerably from its heyday. The political parties turned to a form of socialism with no influence on the salaried of the capitalist world, whose thoughts traveled the path of domestic comfort, diversion, sport, and the excitement of the game. *Social status,* already existing in the form of sumptuous items like television sets and automobiles, is really the sought-after thing for such people, like absolute values of justice and liberty. A growing wave of materialism has spread over Europe and North America during the last twenty years and at its base all idealism has disintegrated. Crime and delinquency, currently attributed to poverty and inequality, has nevertheless proliferated and in reality displays characteristics of an acquisitive society as well as similar inevitable results from a lack of normal ethics.

From time to time the governments of these capitalist countries change name but not purposes. Foreigners look in vain for some moral or philosophical distinction in the politics of the two great parties in the United States, a country in which socialism as such has never been established as a politically active force.

I include my own country; "socialist" has never been the name of a political party, although it has been employed as a term to discredit the Labour Party. This party, which once professed socialist principles, has renounced a doctrine that might at most have alienated the prosperous worker and in reality was only anxious to maintain prosperity through means that might not endanger the economic methods that had given rise to it. Nationalization, which was once the official politics of the Labour Party, has been abandoned, except as a means of maintaining the salaries in the industries that the capitalists were willing to relinquish as dispensable. In every sphere of politics the British Labour Party pursues an action intended to maintain a high standard of living, which means, in reality, that in the whole international sphere

—disarmament, colonialism, the common market—its calculations are determined not through principles but rather through expediency.

In general, in the entire Western world, there has been a cynical abandonment of principles on the part of all political parties (even the communist parties, who are divided only over irreconcilable interpretations of the tactics of the equally closed principles of the USSR).

Politics as a practical activity has never cultivated abstracted principles of truth: it is an exercise in expedience and was defined as such by Machiavelli. Politics is the general name of various "slogans," dialectical or practical, for the acquisition and maintenance of power, and these slogans have always acted against the general welfare of the community. The only protest that can stand up against such politics of power should therefore be nonpolitics; the politics of no politics; that is, anarchism.

Anarchism is a philosophy based on this first principle, the negation of power or of force as an agent for the success of the good. Anarchism sustains the opposite principle: the principle of mutual aid. I believe that unless we support such a principle and base all our beliefs and attitudes on it, there is no future for anarchism or for humanity. Other principles take root in this fundamental one; but unless our goal is the complete elimination of force from the body politic, we are not anarchists of conviction. Whatever the consequences may be, personal and social, our obligation is primarily to maintain that the use of force is corrupting to the human mind and produces infinite damage to the community. This is the principle, enunciated by Lao-tse, Chuang-tze, Jesus Christ, Tolstoy, Kropotkin, and Gandhi, on which we can never compromise.

Against this principle, and in defense of compromise, it has been said, for example by Pascal (who was such a devotee of the principle that he was willing to let the truth rest upon a wager), that "greed and power are the causes of all of our actions: greed brings us to voluntary action, power to involuntary action." The same exegesis has stated that "justice without power is impotent, power without justice is tyranny." But such apologetics don't tell us how to reunite power and justice nor how to conciliate them nor how we can be sure that the powerful will at the same time be just. In truth, they concede that from the moment they cannot be certain that what is right is strong, people ought to behave as if what was strong was right.

An anarchist is the last one to deny the existence of evil. The use of force everywhere for thousands of years has so corrupted the minds of men that wicked thoughts have become enshrined in a custom that has taken root and behaves perversely in physical enforcement. It is on this precept of realism that we affirm our principles.

Simone Weil, in her essay on *The Iliad,* pointed out that the bitterness prevailing throughout the miraculous poem by Homer is due to the subjection of the human spirit to force; it is, in the last analysis, the subjugation of the human spirit to matter. The law of force, the power of life and death, is as cold and inflexible as the law of inert matter. And force, she says, "is as pitiless with the man that possesses it, or believes he possesses it, as it is with its victims; to the latter ultimatums are oppressive, to the former they are poisonous."

From the beginning of history man has always been subjected to force, to shame, to humiliation. That has been his tragedy. And religion has been an acceptance of this tragic focus on life, religion and perhaps also art.

Should we, as anarchists, dare to rise up against this tragic conception of life? Should we dare to affirm the dignity of life, the joy of life, the promise of life? That, I believe, is what we stand for, if we are true anarchists. We maintain that the course of history can be rechanneled if mutual aid as a principle of progress takes the place of the law of force.

Let us examine a little more carefully this concept of power or force. I have employed these terms interchangeably, but it is necessary to draw a distinction between the human practice of power and what we call "the forces of nature." Since we are human we do not inherit a paradise: on the contrary, we have been born into a world that requires incessant labor as the price of living. We hurl ourselves, you might say, against matter and the noble life is the triumph of spirit over matter. But such drudgery has dignity, and if we do not abuse Nature, Nature is benevolent and is quick to cooperate. By virtue of our labor we assure that two, or ten, or one hundred grains of wheat are planted in fertile instead of rocky soil; and Nature, if we allow ourselves to apostrophize this force, is agreeable. Mutual aid, as demonstrated so brilliantly by Kropotkin, is a force of Nature, and this force aims to be liberated through our hands.

Destructive forces and creative forces exist in Nature and in humanity; anarchism is consequently the only philosophy that upholds this distinction and insists that humanity should cooperate with Nature's creative forces and renounce the destructive forces of human vanity. The causes of our behavior ought to be conceived not as greed and power over others, but rather as conquest over the violence within ourselves and cooperation with creative forces in the natural world. The crime and delinquency that have characterized up to a point all historical societies of the past are not a mystery. They are the consequence of individual and social frustrations that inevitably surge forth from the domain of force. This empire has endured for thousands of years in the heart of man, conditioned his sentiments for egotistical aggression and the anxiety over obtaining good things. He should realize that the creative forces of nature can prevail for a long time before evil can be eliminated from man's corrupted nature. But there are foundations for hope in history: we must believe or lose hope forever.

The anarchists are always accused of a lack of realism, but aside from some Catholics, they are the only realists in the world. Because anarchists dare to affirm that truth, justice, and personal liberty are true universals, truths that can guide and form all of our thoughts and acts. From this creed one deduces that human laws and institutions have no real existence. They are conventions that should command our obedience only to the extent that they guarantee truth, justice, and personal liberty, and every time the reality of these principles may be denied, it is our duty to disobey such laws and institutions. Civil disobedience is not a question of expediency: it is the road of truth, the road of life, Nature.

Such realism comes into conflict with the utilitarianism of our political parties, and it is for that reason that the anarchists are erroneously considered unrealistic. But if we have some vision that extends beyond the present moment and that seeks an accord of society with truth, then we should repulse all political recourses and, if necessary, the State itself. The State is a fortress, an arsenal from which tyrants draw their weapons of oppression. It has no real existence:

it is a myth, a legend invented by philosophers like Plato, Machiavelli, Hegel. Unfortunately the myth of philosophy becomes converted into the fortress of politics. Ernst Cassirer asserted that it was beyond the power of philosophy to destroy the myth created by it; a myth is impenetrable to rational argument. But Cassirer also said that philosophy allows us to understand the mythic nature of political creeds. In other words, what philosophy has united can also be put asunder. The realist would say: it is better to avoid all myths. Plato's *Republic* ends like Hitler's Reich.

This is not the occasion to review the principles of anarchism. That, I presume, you all understand. The problem that I wish to treat is the application of those principles to the world in which we live: a world indifferent to truth, to justice, and to personal liberty, dedicated to a politics of utilitarianism that may be veering, with terrible certainty, toward its own destruction.

We ought to begin by realizing that anarchism can never admit to a doctrine of utilitarianism. Our principles contradict at least two thousand years of political evolution, and it is not to be supposed that we can change such a tendency in a few years through direct political means, or that we can find one or more model communities that demonstrate to the world the validity of our beliefs. The Spanish Civil War was a terrible example of this second impossibility. Anarchism in one country was rent by envy, the contemptibility or apathy of the rest of the world. The centralized power of capitalism, the centralized power of communism, the centralized power of the Church, could not tolerate within its bosom a community that promised to break up the concept of power and replace it with the opposite concept of mutual aid.

The Spanish nation was torn asunder not only by capitalism, not only by the union of fascist hordes, but rather by something common to all these forces: a conviction that power is just and that whatever defenseless country falls into a pit of confusion, there such a doctrine can be displayed.

More significant is perhaps the case of Israel. It is said that there is an artificial community, partially to accommodate the political expediency of world powers that are trying to gain possession of the oil wells in the Eastern Crescent and partially to satisfy the idealistic aspirations of the dis-

possessed Jews. In the first bloom of this idealism and under
primitive conditions, the environment offered no attraction
for the investment of capital. The principle of mutual aid
was adopted. The *kibbutzim* resulted in a blatant demonstration of the practicality of the principle. For a time it seemed,
as Martin Buber clearly pointed out, that Jerusalem was
going to be designed like one of two poles of socialism, the
other being Moscow.

The result of this great experiment may yet be uncertain
—the exactitude of external forces are inexorable; the pressure to conform to the economic standards of capitalist
society and the subjugation of ethical integrity—such is the
price demanded by capitalist society. But although one may
not consider the Jewish experiment a success, it is, as Buber
says, a "sign of no failure." "If an experiment effected under
certain conditions has been shown to be successful up to a
certain point, we are able to agree on the idea of modifying
it in other, less formidable, conditions."

Conditions in Palestine have been and continue to be
exceptional, and its destiny was bound to the rest of the
world. But what we, as anarchists, ought to observe with
satisfaction is that the communal Jewish village, as it was
established in Palestine, has demonstrated that the principle
of mutual aid is efficient when ethical idealism—"the
pioneer spirit," as it is termed—exists and supports itself
without being corrupted by political force.

Israel has existed as a social laboratory, and that existence
has been guaranteed only through the unrestrained juggling
of equilibrium of the world's political powers. Such laboratories cannot be created at will and cannot outlive the forceful dissolution of the power equilibrium. We should not
therefore consider that such an accidental event would
offer some broad hope for the realization of our principles.
The most recent example of Cuba shows that under other
conditions the powers will not tolerate an oasis in a political
desert: one or another force must occupy it and direct its
destiny just to the brink of war.

Spain, Palestine, Cuba—these are names that, despite their
tragic significance, demonstrate clearly that history is still
capable of sudden surprises—or to employ a more meaningful metaphor, that several splits or fissures have appeared in
the monolithic structure of power. This, I believe, can make

us feel secure in our faith, but it should not give us false hope.

Power continues to be the governing principle of politics throughout the whole world, and general recognition of some alternative principle is very remote. In such circumstances, what is the task of the individual anarchist?

Considered as a political movement, anarchism has remained in a disadvantageous position, provided that we don't allow its principles to ossify into something dogmatic and not even to form something of a discipline. Its goal is the most complete unfolding of individualism, combined, in Kropotkin's words, "with the most elevated development of voluntary association in all its aspects, in all of its possible gradations and for all possible purposes; an association that is always changing, that carries in itself the elements of its own perpetuity, that adopts the forms that best correspond in any given moment to the multiple efforts of all." Kropotkin was influenced by the evolutionist theories of his time and was convinced that all biological, individual, and social progress depends on resistance to conformity, fixity, and centralization. Up to what point the anarchists have a practical, immediate program is determined by these criteria. There are many little loopholes in politics that do not reveal a tendency toward centralization or individuation and our choice might have to be clear.

We can at times find ourselves in the intricate situation of resting on ostensibly reactionary politics or politics defended by political reactionaries, or of being against socialist or communist politics that tend toward the consolidation of a centralized State. Yet the "Poujadistes" can at times appear to be our allies! If we are clear in our principles and firm in our convictions, this has no importance. Other times we may rely on the capitalists, for example, in their efforts to decentralize industry. And in others, on the socialists in their efforts to improve working conditions and to reform education. We do not belong to any party because no party can represent our final goal; but some of our immediate objectives can be partially carried out, and although that is small satisfaction for our revolutionary ardor, it is better than an intransigent and impotent dogmatism.

Certain great solutions may remain that transcend politics and with which we cannot compromise. I have always maintained that to believe in mutual aid is incompatible with any form of aggression. An anarchist, by the logic of his fundamental principles, is compelled to be a pacifist. To resist war, impugn military service, oppose the use of force in international affairs, are not merely moral obligations alone, but active obligations. Such a focus is not universally accepted in the anarchist movement, and Spain, in 1936, presented us with a tragic dilemma. I still think that in the circumstances of 1936 resistance based on nonviolence would have been the best politics, but this is vain speculation. It is better to look toward India, where the faith of Gandhi is still effective and where the principles of anarchism as they were practiced by his disciples still offers the only political salvation to millions of people. India is too vast to carry out a laboratory experiment as in Israel; perhaps much too extensive for any solution that may not be tragic in its consequences. But when the country is larger and the population more extensive, the more prodigious, incompetent, and frustrating are the forces of centralization. China is more extensive than India and is already committed to a polititcs of centralization. But those politics do not give nor can give results. I have been to China and I have seen much poverty and suffering humanity, but also much courage and human solidarity. The Chinese communities, isolated for perhaps thousands of miles around from political control of the Party in Peking, restrained in its production and organized into cooperatives, might seem to be very close in practice to the cooperative communities pointed out by Kropotkin in *Fields, Factories and Workshops*. The "slogans" painted on the walls could proclaim the dogmas of an infallible party, but real life was "a society of equalitarian interchange based on regional committees, rural communities that combine agriculture with industry," which was the definition of Gustav Landauer of an anarchist community. Perhaps the words don't belong in such a context: they bear no relation to social reality, which is a brave proposal for ending what Nietzsche called "the terrible norm of necessity that up to now has gone forward with the name 'history.'" Nietzsche saw this as a task for the "new philosophers," but the philosophers could only point out the road, which is the road of truth. To the terrible norm of necessity the philosophers were only able to oppose their immutable ideals of liberation and justice.

This interpretation of the role of the anarchists in capitalist society, can seem to imply a fragmentation of the movement. But such fragmentation is already a political reality. They have converted us into an impotent political movement, those same forces that have stripped the socialist and communist movements of their idealism, by the triumph not of some variety of political principles, but rather by the ideal of middle-class comfort. The conflicting forces in the world today still defend what each one terms "a mode of life," and this way of life is measured in production statistics. A politician who might dare to solicit the public acceptance for a way of life measured by moral satisfaction would not be understood, or if it were, no attention would be paid to it. But that was the mode of life that Gandhi asked his followers to accept. The credo that despite the apparent triumph of force in the world, the opposite principle of love ought to prevail, is quite simple. Nonviolence, the only weapon in the arsenal of love, is, as Gandhi might say, the weapon of the strong. Hypocrisy would easily be weakness. Fear and love are contradictory terms. Love is fearful in delivery, free as soon as it gains response. Love struggles with the world without violence; as it scores gains, its superiority succeeds over every other sentiment. "My daily experience," declares Gandhi, "like that of those who work with me—is that all problems tend to solve themselves if we are decided on making of the law of truth and nonviolence the law of life. The law of love will triumph, in the same manner as the law of gravity will operate, accepted by us or not."

Paul Arthur Schilpp

Philosophy and the Social Crisis [1]

Paul Arthur Schilpp (1897 ——) Born in Germany in 1897, Paul Schilpp settled in the United States in 1913. He has studied at

[1] From "In Defense of Socrates' Judges," *Enquiry: A Journal of Independent Radical Thought*, Vol. 2, No. 2 (Fall, 1944). Reprinted by permission of the author.

Columbia, Northwestern, and Stanford Universities, and is an
ordained minister of the Methodist Church. He was professor
of psychology at Tacoma, Washington, and professor of philosophy at the College of the Pacific and he has lectured in
India. He has edited and sponsored many works in philosophy.
His latest are *Human Nature and Progress, The Philosophy of
Karl Jaspers,* and *Philosophy of C. D. Broad.* He edited *Philosophy of Religion* and *Dictionary of Philosophy.* Presently he is
at Northwestern University.

Philosophers, rather glibly, have
assumed it as a matter of course that in the most famous
court trial of the pre-Christian era, the trial which took place
in the City of Athens in 399 B.C., they have been (and still
are) on the side of Socrates, the convicted criminal, rather
than on the side of his triumphant judges. It does not seem to
me that this assumption is justified by the facts. Instead, the
actual attitude and conduct of philosophers in most ages
appears to me to arraign them on the side of Socrates' judges
rather than on that of Socrates himself. This, at any rate,
appears to be true of too many philosophers in the present
tragic hour in human history.

Instead of rising above the noisy clash of clans and above
the battlecries of the moment, instead of undertaking the
leadership of humanity in matters of the intellect and of
spirit, philosophers once again, as so many times before, are
busily engaged in joining the mad chorus of international
strife and in adding vehemence to its sound and fury, ready
to climb on the bandwagons of stopgap saviors. For the most
part, we are much too busy oiling the machinery of military
national defense and keeping it moving to the tune of untold
billions and in behalf of the systematic planning of human
destruction to be able either for ourselves to see things, with
Spinoza, *"sub specie aeternitatis,"* or to be fit to provide this
sadly needful humanity with the kind of critical thought and
intellectual leadership, without which not merely the present
but even the future of humanity must be largely hopeless.

At the moment I am not concerned with the detailed arguments as between Socrates and his judges. Rather, I am
concerned with the basic fact that Socrates, Athens' wisest
man, was on trial for his life on the double charge of being

a blasphemer of the gods, on the one hand, and a corrupter
of youth, on the other; and with the other equally fundamental fact that the judges of Athens who tried, convicted,
and condemned him, represented the social judgment and
conscience of the population of Athens in 399 B.C. Socrates,
practicing the real and intended role of the *philos sophiae*,
had made the fatal mistake of daring to follow the voice of
critical reflection and wisdom rather than the voice of the
demos. So far from considering it his function simply to
mirror and reflect the sentiments and fluctuating emotions of
the fickle populace—day before yesterday saying: "We were
fooled by idealistic slogans into mass murder once, but never
again," yesterday committed to all possible aid "short of
war," and today whooping it up with all the former gusto
and enthusiasm for making the world once more "safe for
democracy" by supporting the international mass murder
the second time in one generation—Socrates had the temerity
to *think* and to express his thoughts freely: a dangerous
thing to do in any age; but never so dangerous as when feelings run high and the populace is off on a rampage, whipped
up to fever heat and fury by demagogues with unholy axes
to grind. There never was a better time in our whole national
life than the present to remind ourselves of the fact that the
wisest man of Athens stood condemned by Athens' best legal
minds as a dangerous disturber of Athens' peace, as a rebel
and revolutionary, as the "fifth columnist" of his day. No
wonder they were determined to stop him! No wonder either
that they succeeded. For, the "fifth column," never more
dangerous to the State than in times of emergency and of
national crisis, must be stopped at any price. Socrates,
because he refused to prostitute his thought and speech until
it would merely have become the *ancilla populi*, had to pay
with his life for his devotion to the unpopular truth and for
his insistence upon freely speaking his mind in criticism of
the mob's emotions, thoughts, and actions.

The events of 399 B.C., however, are, unfortunately, not
unique in human—or, for that matter, even in philosophical
—history. The same sort of thing happened in Jerusalem
early in the first century (of our own time-recording) and in
Holland sixteen centuries later, simply to extract two of the
most famous repetitions of such tendencies and procedures.
No age seems to delight in the presence, within its midst, of

a gadfly, a mind that refuses to succumb to the mere mouth-
ings of the shibboleths of the period, but insists rather upon
stabbing bluntly and ruthlessly into some of the most cherished of the era's fairy tales. The year of crisis, 1944, in this
regard differs not one whit from other ages or periods. Just
because it undeniably *is* a year of crisis, it shares with other
such critical periods of human history the flare for high-
sounding slogans and for what look like very idealistic convictions and commitments. And anyone who does not immediately fall for these slogans or fails to swallow them
hook, line, and sinker, is at once being made to look very
devilish indeed. Appeaser, "fifth columnist," traitor! These
are the words heard on every side, if one even so much as
ventures to question the popular hysteria, the increasing lust
for blood, the whole mad rush over the edge of the abyss of
total war and mass murder. Not to be critical has come to be
the order of the day, and that even within philosophical
circles. Or, if one *must* be critical, then let's be critical of
nice neat little questions of epistemology, of metaphysics, of
symbolic logic, or of the methodology of science. But, in
heaven's name, let's not be critical of the mob mind and
fury, of national hysteria, of patriotic slogans or nationalistic catchwords—in short, of the State or of the direction in
which the State is moving. Whatever else we be, let's be
"good patriots!" Let no one dare to question our patriotism!
And, to be patriotic, in these days, has come to be equivalent
to accepting uncritically and without question whatever the
Great White Father in Washington has, in his divine wisdom,
chosen to do.

In other words, the inherent rightness and justice of the
decisions of the state must not be questioned. The state is
sacrosanct: above the criticism of thinkers and philosophers.
And /or *vox populi, vox dei.*

These are, of course, not new doctrines or new procedures.
They are, if not as old as the hills, at least as old as Socrates
and older. Moreover, they have, more recently, received a
quite unusual amount of—even philosophical—attention.
For example, for more than a century now, philosophers and
political scientists alike have been in the habit of chastising
Hegel for his apotheosis of the Prussian State. It has been
common practice to denounce Hegel for his easy sellout

to the Prussian powers-that-were. And, still more recently, we have heard it said on almost innumerable occasions that no self-respecting philosopher could live under a modern communistic, fascistic, or nazi regime and prostitute his mind and his profession by becoming an academic protagonist of the procedures, propaganda, commitments, and directions of the political state under which he happened to be living. Let it be said here in unequivocal fashion that the present writer has found himself in complete agreement with both of these judgments all along.

But, having made this confession, the writer never dreamed he would live to see the day when multitudes of his colleagues would turn around and adopt for themselves and for their own program of teaching the same uncritical attitude of mind which they had been in the habit of criticizing so severely in Hegel and in fascist and communist philosophers. Who could have dreamed, even three or four years ago, that the critical minds of American philosophers would shortly be converted into mere apologists either for their own (American) State or for that of the British Empire? Who, at that time, would have been believed, had he foretold that American and British philosophers would—within so short a space of time—put their own (supposedly philosophical) services just as unequivocally into the service of their own respective existing political states as Hegel had done a hundred and twenty years ago and as German, Italian, and Russian philosophers have been doing for the past decade? And who, above all, would have believed that such a complete reversal of attitude and procedure would be possible on the part of thinkers whose basic and lifelong commitment and training had more particularly qualified them for maintaining a critical attitude of mind even in the midst of national sprees of emotionalism and hysteria, and for the kind of aloofness from the mere immediacy of a situation which, first and foremost, is supposed to characterize the truly scholarly mind?

Fairness to facts demands the admission from us, therefore, that—once again, as, in the days of Hegel and of Heidegger and Gentile—philosophy is failing us at precisely the point where the only justification for philosophy, in the long run, can be found: in its ability, namely, to remain

above the noise and cry of the mob mind, critical and unperturbed, able to see, to judge, to lead—rather than to
accept, agree, and follow.

This failure of philosophy in periods of crisis is to be noted
along at least five distinct lines.

1) In the first place, it is the failure to be able to maintain
the reflective and critical attitude of mind in the presence of
great waves of popular emotionalism. In the light of what
has already been stated above, and in the light, moreover, of
what only too obviously goes on all about us, morning, noon,
and night, it is perhaps hardly necessary to establish this
point by means of elaborate demonstrations. The facts and
attitudes all about us veritably shout the truth of this assertion
into our ears.

Nor should it be necessary to argue at length that such an
attitude and procedure on the part of philosophers amounts
to an abdication of reason in favor of hyper-nationalistic
sprees of so-called patriotism. I am not asking that the philosopher should be unpatriotic or even that he should be free
from—even the emotional—attitude of deep regard and love
for his country. It is possible to be possessed of all of that
and still maintain a reflectively critical attitude of mind and
procedure. Since when does it follow that, because a parent
may find it necessary to be critical of the conduct of his child
or even to chastise that child, he therefore does not love the
child? And since when is *intelligent* patriotism the equivalent
of unquestioning acceptance of whatever the powers-that-be
in the State decide to do? I had always thought that such
an attitude was that, not of a free, but of a slave mind,
worthy, perhaps, of fascist and communist enslavement, but
not of free, democratically committed minds. Have I been
wrong in these assumptions?

2) This failure of philosophy in our present period of crisis
is, in the second place, a failure to understand the causal
relationship between means and ends. This is a very sad
confusion, indeed. For one would imagine that men who,
since the days of Hume, have spent as much time on the
problem of causality as have philosophers, would not so
easily be taken in at this point. The grandson of one of
Britain's most famous nineteenth-century philosophers,
namely Aldous Huxley, recently thought it of the utmost
importance to call the intelligent world's attention to this sad

—universal—confusion between means and ends. But, it will now have to be admitted, Huxley's cry was that of "a voice crying in the wilderness." No one has paid any serious attention to his protests or to his warnings. For, no one— under the emotional stress of the present international crisis —is willing either to admit or even to consider the so perfectly obvious fact that "whatsoever a man soweth, that shall he also reap: he who soweth to the flesh shall, from the flesh, reap corruption; and he who soweth to the spirit shall, from the spirit, reap life everlasting." If I may be permitted to translate: he who sows the instruments of destruction, shall reap what he has sown, namely destruction; whereas he who has the courage to sow the spiritual and moral qualities of justice, peace, and goodwill, shall also reap what he has sown, namely the creative fruits of such moral and spiritual endeavors and activity. There is no "hokus-pokus" in this, it is merely the inevitable operation of a universe that is orderly rather than capricious, in which causality—even though this principle remain yet unexplained in detail—is a real, experimental, and testable fact. In this kind of world it is simply the height of folly to imagine that any nation can make the "all-out" effort for the systematic development of hatred and destruction that modern "total war" requires and then expect to reap the fruits of peace, prosperity and goodwill. It would seem that one would not have to be a philosopher (or a scientist either, for that matter) to recognize this fact.

The whole doctrine of "internal relations"—that fond baby of philosophical idealism, but which has furnished plenty of fuel for philosophical discussions way beyond the boundaries of the idealistic schools—offers further evidence for the direct, immediate, and inherent relationship between means and ends. The proposition "he who takes the sword shall perish by the sword" is not true because it was uttered by the Nazarene, but rather it was uttered by the Nazarene because he found it to be true; and all human history bears witness to the fact. This is that kind of a world, a world of relationships, a world of order, a world of cause and effect. Who should know this better than philosophers? Who has meditated upon such relationships longer and more carefully than have philosophers? Is it not strange that now we are suddenly asked, by many of these same philosophers, to forget all this work and all the conclusions derived from that work? Or is it merely that—when it is academically more convenient and emotionally more satisfying—we can just blissfully overlook our conclusions derived from the careful and painstaking work of our more coldly rational and theoretical moments? I shall leave the answer to these questions to those who will find it difficult to give answers that will be at one and the same time satisfying to their emotional needs and to the requirements of truth and validity in an at least related and orderly universe.

3) The third failure of philosophy in the present crisis is a moral failure. It implies the basic surrender of faith in a moral universe, or at least in a moral human universe (for I have no intention at the moment of making the moral category a metaphysical one). The assertion (and active procedure) that evil can be overcome only by the use of more—of the same kind of—evil, though admittedly a thoroughly popular notion, obviously constitutes a fundamental betrayal of the effectiveness of moral categories. How long and how vociferously have we all denied the claim that "might makes right!" But when, in a pinch, in a crisis, it comes to action and conduct, we not only still continue to base our action on the principle, but we go out to defend our action based on such an obviously immoral principle by devious theoretical detours. Not only mankind in general, but even philosophers and moralists themselves have, apparently given up any faith they may ever have had in the effectiveness of goodness in its own right. In the light of such surrender, one cannot but wonder what teachers of courses in ethics will have to teach from now on. But, perhaps the answer to this last question is not so far to seek. For, if I remember correctly, a theological moralist (so-called) tried to find his way out of this difficulty as much as twelve years ago, when he developed a theory of morality for individual man, but claimed that on the broader social level men could not help but act immorally.[2] What such a notion will ultimately do even to so-called private morality needs not much guessing. The author of that claim has, of course, long since thrown himself into the arms of an all-powerful God, in Whom, I suppose, all these contradictions inherent in man find their blissful

---

[2] I refer, obviously, to Reinhold Niebuhr's *Moral Man and Immoral Society* (New York, 1932). [Read's note.]

(though from a merely human standpoint I suppose useless) solution. But this seems to me to be an attempt to save the moral consciousness at a point where it loses every specific human meaning. If this is all that can be said for social morality, the sooner we shall give up the whole concept of morals the better off we shall be; for we shall then at least be honest with ourselves.

Yet, in the light of such a far-reaching surrender of faith in the inherent effectiveness of goodness and truth, especially on the part of the philosophers and moralists themselves, is it really any wonder that we have had to live to see our so-called civilized modern world topple all about us in ruins? What else was to be expected in a world in which even some of the foremost advocates of morality and decency had themselves lost faith in their efficacy? It has taken men like Walter Lippmann, Aldous Huxley, and Lewis Mumford to remind us of the devastating nature of that kind of a loss of faith. And, of course, since those men do not wear the togas of the professional philosophers, we would not think of stopping to listen to their voices. All the worse for us. It isn't Nero merely who, in our day, is "fiddling while Rome is burning," it is we philosophers who are increasingly guilty of that crime. Guilty of it, because we have surrendered one of the greatest privileges and opportunities of our profession: that of being the moral leaders of the age.

4) There is still a fourth failure with which philosophy is to be charged in the present hour of crisis. This failure is due to the blemish of near-sightedness. This too is a strange charge to have to bring against philosophers. For it is the philosopher, after all, who has been claiming to "see life steadily and see it whole." It is the philosopher who is supposed to look at life and the universe *sub specie aeternitatis,* or, if not from the vantage point of eternity—a point which may, after all, be even beyond the philosopher— then at least from the long-range point of view. It is the philosopher who is expected to be able to rise above the merely "here and now," above the clatter and clanging of the momentary noises, above the sound and fury of today's immediacy and its persistently noisy but nonetheless swiftly passing claims. I say, the philosopher is "expected to." But such expectations do not seem to trouble us very seriously. When everyone else howls, we claim the right and privilege

of howling with the mob. That by so doing we have forfeited every rightful claim to leadership does not seem to trouble us very greatly.

5) And with this I have already touched upon the fifth and last failure of philosophy in the present crisis: the surrender of our intellectual leadership. In at least a practical way, this is perhaps the most serious charge of all. For, it inevitably confronts us with the question: where is humanity to look for leadership at precisely the time when it stands most seriously in need of intellectual and moral leadership, namely in a time of crisis, if, whenever a real human crisis appears, the philosophers, along with the rest of the population, start at once to run away from the facts and certainly from the light, and begin to seek refuge in Plato's ancient "Cave" or else in the equally as cavelike "blackouts" of modern civilization and culture? If philosophers can just as easily and as quickly be swept off their intellectual, moral, and spiritual feet as are the more untutored mortals, if together with the mob we readily succumb to the loud trumpetings of the moment and the noisy propaganda of the yellow press—if, at almost a moment's notice, we seem to be capable of losing all sense of balance, of perspective, of wholeness, of critical acumen, of intellectual detachment, and of moral understanding, where is humanity going to look for, much less find, the intellectual, moral, and spiritual leadership for which no time cries out so loudly as does a time of crisis? Moreover, if the world's intellectual leadership, once again, is ready to sell out to the political state (on both sides of the conflict, as we all know it did during the first world war), where is a trustworthy leadership—a leadership that would guide humanity into the new day and the new world that must be created—going to come from? Who is going to provide it? And if we cannot do so, if we must stand condemned ourselves by our own conduct in this hour of crisis, what help can we bring to those in our civilization who, because they belong to the next generation, are rightfully looking to us for leadership, for courage, for moral faith and spiritual commitment—whereas we have nothing to give them but the husks of yesterday's theories that we have let the outburst of human barbarism and savagery in Europe and Asia rob us of, because we never really did believe in their kernel and core in the first place?

I can find only one immediate answer to all these questions, and that is the frank admission that once again Socrates stands condemned: this time by the practices of his own profession. If we are really still even partially honest we ought frankly and openly to exonerate Socrates' judges from any guilt; we ought freely to come out in their defense. For, did they not save Athens' youth from "corruption" and Athens' state from radical rebellion? Did they not save the *status quo* of ancient Athens? Long live the judges of Socrates!

part two

the practice

The Historical Dimension

Gerald Brenan **Anarchism in Spain**[1]

Gerald Brenan (1894 ——) Brenan was born in England in 1894. He is a self-educated man. For his services in World War I he received the *Croix de Guerre* in 1918. Some of his works are *The Spanish Labyrinth, The Face of Spain, The Literature of the Spanish People, A Holiday By the Sea,* and *A Life of One's Own.*

We may . . . for a moment . . . consider how eminently suited anarchist organization was to Spanish conditions. The first need was to get hold of the half-starving, uneducated field laborers and factory workmen and to fill them with a consciousness of their own grievances and their own power. These men could not, as a rule, afford to pay a regular subscription, and they were suspicious of any influence from outside that might embroil them with their employers. Any regular trade-union organization with a paid secretariat, acting on orders from Barcelona or Madrid and leading its adherents like a bourgeois republican party to the polling booths, would have been doomed to failure. But the anarchist leaders were never paid

[1] From *The Spanish Labyrinth: An Account of the Social and Political Background of the Civil War,* by Gerald Brenan. Cambridge: Cambridge University Press, Copyright 1943. Reprinted by permission of the publisher.

—in 1936, when their trade union, the C.N.T., contained over a million members, it had only one paid secretary. Travelling about from place to place, on foot or mule back or on the hard seats of third-class railway carriages, or even like tramps or ambulant bullfighters under the tarpaulins of goods wagons, whilst they organized new groups or carried on propagandist campaigns, these "apostles of the idea," as they were called, lived like mendicant friars on thè hospitality of the more prosperous workmen.

Their first object was simply to enroll groups of poor workers, whatever their political or religious opinions might be, for mutual protection against employers: now and then there would be a small strike, which, if it was successful, would at once double the membership of the section and lead to other small strikes in neighboring districts. Then gradually the leaders would unfold their anarchist creed with its hatred of the Church, its wild idealism, its generous and humane outlook, and the imagination of the hearers would be kindled. Thus it happened that, at moments of enthusiasm, the number of the workers controlled by the anarchists would double and treble themselves and, when the inevitable reaction came, would shrink back to a small kernel of convinced militants. This plasticity of the anarchist movement enabled it to survive persecutions and, as soon as they were over, to reappear stronger than ever.

There is another characteristic of Spanish anarchism that goes back to the Cordova Congress. That is that all movements towards strikes or revolutionary action that develop in it come from below. What occurs is this: At some critical moment, let us say, a congress of Spanish federations is called to consider the possibility of revolutionary action. The delegates of each district will arrive at the assembly with a full knowledge of the wishes and capacities of the groups of workmen they represent. Each will get up and say what the men of his province or factory are able and prepared to do. No district will be urged to take any action for which it does not feel itself morally and materially prepared. This freedom of choice has certainly acted often to the advantage of the Government, who have been able to suppress anarchist movements at their leisure in one province after another. But, at all events until the outbreak of the Civil War, its merits have more than counterbalanced its defects. The fact that no

group has ever been overruled by another group or has had
pressure put on it to act against its private convictions, but
only in accordance with its own measure of enthusiasm and
the number of arms it has been able to collect, has meant
that the anarchists have been able to suffer defeat after defeat
and yet rise again stronger than ever. If no other European
party has shown such resistance, that is because the Spanish
anarchists have insisted upon basing their movement upon
the free and unfettered impulses of their adherents, organized in local groups, and have not allowed themselves to become enmeshed in the deadening and life-destroying net of a
party bureaucracy.

A few weeks after the conclusion of the Congress of Cordova, King Amadeo resigned from the Spanish throne and
left the country. Elections were held in March, and, owing
to the abstention of the other parties, a Republican majority
was returned. The Cortes that met on 1 June 1873 lost no
time in proclaiming a republic. It was clear from the first that
the new republic would have a federal rather than a centralized constitution and, in fact, after a few weeks hesitation,
Francisco Pi y Margall, the leader of the Federal Party, was
elected president. A period of great expansion and activity
opened for the International in Spain. But the federal movement is of such importance for the history of anarchism, and
indeed for the history of modern Spain in general, that it will
be necessary to say something about it.

The French Revolution, by the destruction of so many
local interests and privileges, completed the work of Louis
XIV and gave France a powerful and highly centralized
administration. The Liberal Revolution in Spain, as we have
already seen, imitated it. In both countries a reaction towards
a greater local and municipal liberty was inevitable. In
France this reaction was best expressed by Proudhon, who
put forward those ideas which, he believed, the French
Revolution had come into existence to fulfill, but from which
it had been diverted by the ruthless political action of the
Jacobins. In Spain, with its intense provincial feelings and
local patriotisms, one would have expected the movement
towards decentralization to be even stronger, but owing to
the prostration of the country after the Napoleonic Wars and
to the fact that Carlism drew into its own ranks many of the
forces of resistance to liberal centralism, these feelings did

not for some time make their appearance among left-wing parties. Indeed, but for the persistent preaching and writing of one man, it is possible that they would never have done so.[2]

Pi y Margall was a Catalan of lower middle-class family, who combined a small post in a Madrid bank with occasional journalism and writing books on art. But his true bent was social and political, and a reading of Proudhon (who at that time was quite unknown in Spain) showed him the way he was to go. He saw how exactly this Frenchman's ideas were suited to the aspirations of his countrymen and sat down to work out a political system that would meet their case. In 1854, a few weeks after General O'Donnell's successful *pronunciamiento* against Isabella's camarilla governments, his first book, *La Reacción y la Revolución,* came out. In spite of the haste in which it had been written and the superficial nature of many of its ideas, it constitutes a landmark in the history of Spanish political thought.

Its principal theme is the iniquity of power. Spain, it must be remembered, had been governed for two generations by force in its most brutal form—the general with his disorderly soldiers or militia, the guerrilla leader who was little better than a bandit and the firing squad. Pi y Margall finds this wicked and absurd. "Every man who has power over another is a tyrant." Discussing the meaning of "order"— that word which for more than a hundred years had been the excuse for every act of violence and injustice—he says that true order cannot be obtained by applying force.

"Order supposes arrangement, harmony, convergence of all individual and social elements: order refuses all humiliations and sacrifices. Can you call order that fictitious peace which you obtain by cutting with the sword all that you are too stupid to organize with your limited intelligence? . . . True order, let me tell you, has never existed and will never exist so long as you make such efforts to obtain it, because true order supposes cohesion, yet not a cohesion obtained

[2] The first Spanish federal seems to have been Ramón Xauradó y Fábregas, a Catalan, who began to preach republicanism in 1820. In his *Bases de una Constitución Política,* published in 1832, he advocated a federal republic. He was shot in 1837, after a rising in Barcelona. Then, according to Ramón de la Sagra (*Les Partis en Espagne*), a small anarchist and federalist group appeared at Santiago in Galicia in the early forties. Soon after, La Sagra and Antolín Faraldo were editing a federalist and socialist paper called *El Porvenir.* It was suppressed by Narváez in 1845. [Brenan's note, as are all notes in this extract.]

by the presence of exterior causes, but an intimate and spontaneous cohesion which you with all your restrictions inevitably inhibit."[3]

This indictment of the Spanish governing classes has been repeated in our own times by Ortega y Gasset. Its truth is only too obvious. The troubles of Spain come from the belief, shared by almost every element in the country, in violent remedies. Even the anarchists, who hold of course the same views on power, believe in the necessity for one supreme act of violence to end all violence. But Pi y Margall was always logical. He refused to use any means but persuasion and believed that, if he were able to form a government, he could carry out the desired state of affairs by gradual reforms.

"Since I cannot do without the system of votes, I shall universalize suffrage. Since I cannot do without supreme magistrates I shall make them as far as possible changeable. I shall divide and subdivide power, I shall make it changeable and will go on destroying it."[4] In the place of the power thus destroyed there would grow up a system of pacts between free groups and free individuals.

Pi's views, as expressed in this book, were of course pure anarchism.[5] The only thing that divided him from Bakunin was his reformism. And indeed he is regarded today by Spanish anarchists as one of their saints. But after the failure of the 1854 Revolution Pi's ideas began, like Proudhon's, to take on a more moderate and a more purely political shape. He became the leader of the new federal movement, which aimed at covering only the first lap of the long anarchist road.

This Federal movement, which first appears in the early sixties, grew up as a protest against the failure of the 1854 Revolution and the loss of everything that had been gained then. In his Program of Manzanares, General O'Donnell had demanded decentralization of local government, electoral reform, a free press, and, most significant of all, the formation of a national militia that should guard these privileges

[3] *La Reacción y La Revolución*, 1854, p. 153.
[4] *Op. cit.*, p. 196
[5] "Revolution . . . is the idea of justice. . . . It provides power quantitatively not qualitatively as our constitutionalists do. . . . It is atheist in religion and anarchist in politics: anarchist in the sense that it considers power as a very passing necessity: atheist in that it recognizes no religion, because it recognizes them all." (*op. cit.*, p. 190.) The atheism came from Proudhon and was silently dropped later.

against the encroachment of *caciques*. The success of his *pronunciamiento* had been assured by a rising of the people in Madrid and through all the towns of southern and eastern Spain, and their sentiments had been shown by lynchings of the recently established political police and by demonstrations against the Church and against conscription. In the Cortes elected that autumn there were twenty-three Republicans.

But the generals, who, like the politicians of a later date, were merely corrupt and ambitious, moved to the right as soon as they were in power, and in 1856 Narváez suppressed the national militia after some street fighting and initiated a period of severe repression. It was then that the federal idea began to grow.

The reasons for its popularity in Spain at this time are not far to seek. Federalism was first of all an expression of the Spanish devotion to the *patria chica* and a protest against the strongly centralizing policy of the "liberal" regime.[6] This desire for devolution was shared by its enemy Carlism. But it was also a protest against the autocratic and oppressive rule of these governments, which was only possible so long as they could arrange the elections as they pleased. They needed for this a highly centralized administration. Federalism, therefore, was regarded as the system best designed to preserve the rights of municipalities and to destroy the *cacique*. And there was the French influence. Ever since Louis XIV had said that there were to be no more Pyrenees, Spanish politics, both of the Right and of the Left, has followed with an exaggeration and a superficiality that are all its own the lead of France. And in France, as we have seen, the federal tendencies in the young socialist movement were vigorous. Indeed it was Pi y Margall's translation of Proudhon's *Du Principe Fédératif* in 1868, a few weeks before the Sep-

---

[6] "Federalism is a system by which diverse human groups, without losing their peculiar and particular autonomy, are associated and subordinated in conjunction with those of their kind for all common ends. . . . It is moreover the form of organization most suited to the character of our country, a nation made up of provinces which once were independent kingdoms and which even today are deeply divided by their separate laws and customs. Thus, in all the great crises through which this nation has passed since the beginning of the century, the first thing that has happened has been that the provinces have sought their safety and force within themselves, without losing from view the essential unity of the whole country." (Pi y Margall, *Las Nacionalidades*, 1882.)

tember Revolution that drove out Isabella, that gave the Spanish federals the theoretic background they needed.

From this moment enthusiasm for a federal republic grew rapidly. The *petite bourgeoisie,* who from 1840 to 1934 have been the revolutionary class *par excellence* in Spain, accepted it as their program. The advocates of a centralized republic, like those of State socialism, lost their supporters. The workers gave it their enthusiastic adherence. By the time that the constitutional monarchy, which was the solution of the liberal *bourgeoisie,* began to crack, it was obvious that a federal republic would take its place. Thus it came about that in June, 1873, Pi y Margall, a little, timid, but almost pedantically well-intentioned and honest man, found himself at the head of the Spanish State.

The federal program that was now to be applied to the most unruly and divided nation in Europe consisted in the main of a plan of extreme decentralization: the country was to be cut up into eleven autonomous cantons: these cantons were to be divided into free municipalities, and the whole bound together by voluntary pacts.[7] There was to be a Central Cortes, elected by universal suffrage, but, once the Constitution had been established, it would lose much of its authority. Conscription was to be abolished, Church and State to be separated, and free compulsory education to be provided for all. The social legislation included an eight-hour day, State inspection of factories, and regulations to control women's and children's work. There was also an agrarian program, which specified the expropriation of un-cultivated lands and the establishment on them of communities of peasants. Agrarian credit banks were to be set up and all short-term leases changed to an *enfiteusis perpetua* that should be redeemable at a fixed rate. But these social reforms never got beyond the stage of vague projects, nor

[7] The correct term was "synallagmatic, commutative and bilateral pacts." "By a federal government we understand a government founded on alliance. These alliances are contracts for whose formation it is necessary that there exist contracting parties with sufficient power or capacity to make a contract. If those who celebrate the contract are towns or states, the capacity to contract is the sovereignty: from this is deduced the fact that the federal contract can only be celebrated by sovereign peoples." (*Idea Exacta de la Federación por el Director del Estado Catalán,* 1873. Quoted by J. A. Brandt, *Toward the New Spain,* 1933.)

In Spain nothing is ever new: the various provincial juntas that sprang up during the war against Napoleon all proclaimed their absolute sovereignty.

was it decided how pressure would be brought to bear upon the autonomous cantons and municipalities, if they should refuse to carry out the reforms voted by the Cortes. For Pi y Margall's federal experiment lasted a bare two months and then collapsed in civil war and disorder.

The causes of this failure were various. In the first place the Carlist War, which had been simmering for some time on the passes of the Pyrenees, broke out with violence. This made it impossible for the Federals to disband the Army and to abolish military service. Since it was this promise which had given the Republic its popularity among the working classes, the disillusion was great.[8] Then that defect of all newly formed Spanish parties, the lack of men to fill the administrative posts, made its appearance. The federals were recruited from the lower middle classes, and the ministers, governors, and soldiers whom it threw up were either incompetent or else were unscrupulous men who had joined the party for what they could get out of it. Finally, the provinces decided not to wait for the Cortes to pass the Federal Constitution, but proceeded to set up independent cantons on their own account. With typically Iberian impatience they revolted, and the authority of the Government ceased to exist for a time in the east and south.

We must examine briefly the character of this, as it is called, Cantonalist movement. Its leaders were ambitious soldiers and local politicians: their forces were the depleted regiments under their command, and the local Republican militia known as the *Voluntarios de la Libertad*. The incentive was, to some extent, the Paris Commune, where, it will be remembered, the leading part had been played by the *Garde Nationale*. The movement broke out almost simultaneously in Málaga, Seville, Granada, Cartagena, and Valencia: Federals obtained possession of these cities and declared them to be sovereignly independent cantons: committees of public safety took over the duties of the governor. A movement of similar character broke out in Barcelona.

---

[8] The previous decade had seen a series of colonial adventures in various parts of the world that had made military service, *las quintas,* intensely unpopular. A *copla* of this time expresses this:

> Si la República viene–no habrá quintas en España–
> Por eso aquí hasta la Virgen–se vuelve Repúblicana.

As the Spanish working classes had never yet found anything that appealed to them in even a revolutionary political program, their disappointment was all the more acute.

The feeling that rises most quickly to the surface in every Spanish revolution is anticlericalism. For all the evils of the times the priests and monks are made the scapegoat. The Cantonalist movement was no exception to this. At Barcelona the churches were closed for several months. The militia turned one into a barracks, and public dances were given in another. Priests could not go about the streets in their robes. At Seville the Cantonalists declared that the cathedral would be converted into a café. Taxes were levied on the rich, and in some towns a few houses were burned. In the country districts the villagers took advantage of the general anarchy to proclaim the complete independence of their villages and to divide up the large estates or common lands. As the police wisely withdrew to their barracks, these ceremonies usually passed off quietly and without loss of life. It was only in one or two places, where resistance was offered by the landowners, that serious incidents took place. As one would expect, the movement collapsed as soon as the Government showed that it was ready to use force. In July General Pavía entered Seville with a handful of troops, and by a mixture of tact and firmness restored order in Andalusia. The Cantonalist leaders retired to Cartagena, where they defended themselves for four months. By the time the long siege was over, in January, 1874, the Cortes had been dissolved by the Captain-General of Madrid and the Republic had ceased, except in name, to exist.

But what part was played by the International in these chaotic events? As we have seen, a congress had been held at Cordova in the last days of 1872 and had been followed by a great increase in the number of members, especially in the small towns of Andalusia. The accession to power of the Federals during the summer of 1873 was naturally favorable to it. On the surface, at all events, the similarity of their programs was very striking. "We wish," says one of the resolutions adopted at the Cordova Congress, "to build on the ruins of national unity free and independent municipalities bound only by federal pacts."[9] But this identity of

[9] A. Marvaud, *La Question Sociale en Espagne*, p. 36. This had also been the language of the Internationalist groups in the Paris Commune. And on 21 October 1868 the Central Committee of the International of Geneva had issued a manifesto calling upon the Spanish people to "proclaim a Federal Republic—the only form of government that, transitorily and as a means of arriving at a social organization based on justice, offers serious guarantees of popular liberty."

aims on the purely political issue could not conceal wide differences upon the social. The intentions of the federals towards the working class did not go beyond a more or less sincere radicalism, whilst the followers of Bakunin were bound in the most specific terms to have no dealings with bourgeois political parties and to spurn all compromises in their advance towards social revolution. Yet the agreement was sufficiently great for the question of whether or not they should cooperate to invite serious consideration. Everyone knew that the Internationalists had fought alongside the *Garde Nationale* (who were not even federals) in the Paris Commune.

The decision arrived at was highly characteristic. The Internationalists refused to give any general support to the Federalist movement, but they raised no objection to their local groups or individual members cooperating with it. That is to say, they were ready to get any advantage they could out of it for themselves without compromising either their principles or their freedom of action. And when one examines the records of the Cantonalist risings one is struck by the very small part the International played in them. At Valencia they came out because the Governor had imprisoned some of their members—an early example of the famous anarchist solidarity. At Granada two of them sat on the Committee of Public Safety. (The effect of this was so to terrify the bourgeoisie that the Canton collapsed at once.) Only at one or two small towns, where they had a following of factory hands, did they do anything on their own account. It may be worthwhile to describe what happened at one of these, because it provides the first example of the Red atrocity story that was to be brought up with monotonous regularity whenever the middle classes felt their position to be threatened.

Alcoy is a small town between Valencia and Alicante, which manufactures paper. It is a historic industry—paper has been made here since the eleventh century—and in 1873 the factories employed 8000 hands. Under the influence of a school teacher called Albarracín, who had been converted

But as the conflict with Marx developed, the apoliticism of the Bakuninists became more pronounced. The final attitude of refusal to cooperate with any political party was fixed at the Congress of Saint Imier in 1872 in a resolution written by Bakunin himself and accepted by the Federal Congress at Cordova a few months later (see Guillaume, *L'Internationale*, vol. III, p. 8 for the text of this). This must be considered the fundamental doctrine of Spanish Anarchism.

to anarchism, they decided to give Spain its first example of
a general strike. The object of the strike was, in accordance
with the resolutions of the Regional Congress at Cordova, an
eight-hour day. The men came out and began to negotiate
with the owners. Whilst they were doing so the municipality
intervened, taking, as one would expect, the owners' side.
The workmen at once sent a deputation to demand the resignation of the *alcalde,* who, as they declared, had broken his
promise to remain neutral. Bands of workmen began to
march up and down the street in front of the town hall till
the police, losing their heads as in Spain they usually do,
fired a volley. A fight began that lasted twenty hours. During
the fight some dozen people were killed on each side. The
workmen were in the end victorious, and as a sign of their
victory they burned several factories and houses, shot the
offending mayor and, *more hispánico,* cut off his head and
those of the police who had been killed in the fight, and
paraded them round the town.

The events at Alcoy produced an enormous sensation. For
the first time a group that did not belong either to the Church,
the Army, or the middle classes had become revolutionary.
The whole press came out with stories of people thrown alive
from balconies, women violated, priests crucified, men
soaked in petrol and set on fire. Even the Republican papers
joined in. Such was the fear inspired by the working classes
and by their new dreaded organization the International![10]

The days of this International in Spain were now drawing
to a close. But their last months were the most glorious. In
Europe most people attributed to them the success of the
Cantonalist rising. Everywhere except in Spain reaction

[10] The fear was worked up artificially by the Carlists, who brought out two
pseudo-anarchist papers, *El Petroleo* and *Los Descamisados,* which filled their
columns with crude invocations to the people to rise and murder the bourgeois and burn their property. J. J. Morato gives some amusing extracts
from these. Under the vignette on the front páge of *Los Descamisdos* was
written· "900,000 heads! Let us tear the vault of heaven as though it were a
paper roof! Property is theft! Complete, utter social equality! Free Love!"
whilst the first number contains an article entitled "Our Program" which
begins in this style: "We, the disinherited, the pariahs, the helots, the plebs,
the dregs, the scum, the filth of society: we who have no feelings, no education, no shame declare that we have reached the depths of misery and that
the hour of our triumph is at hand. . . . War on the Rich! War on the
Powerful! War on Society! . . . Anarchy is our only formula. Everything
for everyone, from power to women. . . . But first there must be a terrible,
an extraordinary bloodbath."

It is easy to guess what use was made of these publications. Already, a year reigned and the only live revolutionary force seemed to be anarchism. In Engels' correspondence one sees how bitter was his jealousy and how great his delight when, with the disappearance of the Republic, the last glimmer of revolution in Europe was suppressed. Yet these anarchists had, in fact, accomplished very little. The federals—despised bourgeois that they were—had shown themselves a thousand times braver and more revolutionary. Perhaps the most terrible thing about the International had been its name. It had already brought them, even in those lax and disorderly years, four "persecutions," and Sagasta had gone so far as to declare their organization outlawed and they themselves under the criminal code. Even their numbers were smaller than was generally thought. It is very doubtful whether they ever mustered more than 60,000 members, of whom some 40,000 were in Andalusia.[11] When in January, 1874, General Serrano finally suppressed them, there was really no reason to suppose that they would ever be heard of again. The far more powerful federal movement disappeared for good.

The International did survive, however. For seven years it lived underground. Its assemblies ceased to be held, the links between the different sections disappeared, the Catalán trade unions were made illegal. What remained were small circles of militants in Barcelona and Madrid and groups of artisans and field laborers in Andalusia. It was Andalusia that kept the fires of anarchism alight during the next twenty years.

To get a better idea of the situation in this part of Spain,

---

before this, Cándido Nocedal, the Carlist leader in the Cortes, was saying that the country would have to choose between Don Carlos and Petrol, whilst the Liberal Minister for Home Affairs, Sagasta, firmly convinced that the International in Spain was sustained by foreign gold and by three hundred foreign emissaries, was denouncing it as a "philosophic utopia of crime."

The facts are different. When Bakunin in 1873 wished to visit Barcelona, he was unable to do so because he could not raise the few pounds necessary to pay his railway fare. The only foreign emissaries to visit Spain for the International were Fanelli and Lafargue.

[11] The Spanish delegate at the Bakuninist Congress at Geneva in September 1873 claimed for the movement 300,000 members. Francisco Mora, one of the hostile Marxist group, gave the figure as 60,000. *The Times* correspondent on 5 September gave it as 50,000. The anonymous author of an article "Del Nacimiento de las Ideas Anarcho-Colectivistas en España," published in the *Revista Social* (Madrid) on 14 February 1884, writing with an inside knowledge of the anarchist movement gave it as 30,000. But the anarchists, true Iberians that they are, have never attached much importance to numerical accuracy. "Let us have no more," wrote the editor of *Solidaridad Obrera* in 1937, "of these miserable statistics, which only freeze the brain and paralyze the blood."

one can compare it with that of Ireland in Fenian times. In both the same factors were at work. An imaginative race, a hopeless oppression and poverty, a class of landowners who when not actually absentees were regarded as foreigners, a special constabulary living in fortified barracks and armed with rifles. This constabulary, the *Guardia Civil*, was important. Narváez had created it in 1844 to take the place of the militia, who were politically unreliable: its chief function was to keep down the bandits.

The bandit had always been a feature of Andalusian life and for centuries had acted as a safety valve for popular discontent. In the eyes of the country people he was a hero, the friend of the poor and its champion against its oppressors. But the enclosure of the common lands had so increased the discontent that it became unsafe to tolerate bandits any longer. They were suppressed and risings of peasants came instead. However, on the first sign of political disturbance, the bandit reappeared again, but this time on the other side. No longer Robin Hoods (the police made that impossible), they were now the tools of the *caciques,* who needed them to protect their property and to control the elections against the rising tide of popular enthusiasm. The crop of bandits that covered Andalusia between 1868 and 1873 and made traveling without escort impossible were nearly all of this type, and since, whenever they were arrested, the *caciques* put pressure on the judges to release them, the police were powerless. Andalusia seemed to be approaching the condition that led to the appearance of the Mafia in Sicily. It was the anarchists and the Civil Guard between them that prevented this by polarizing the feelings of the oppressed and the oppressors. From now on every Civil Guard became a recruiting officer for anarchism, and, as the anarchists increased their membership, the Civil Guard also grew.[12] One has to have lived in Andalusia to understand the kind of warfare that went on between them.

This Civil Guard was one of the few really reliable and incorruptible bodies of men in Spain. Carefully picked and highly disciplined, they lived scattered in small fortified posts among the towns and villages, forbidden to intermarry

[12] See Julián de Zugasti. *El Bandolerismo,* 1878. Zugasti was Governor of Cordova from 1870 to 1874 with the special mission of suppressing brigandage. He was the originator of the famous *ley de fugas.* See also Bernaldo de Quirós, *La Mafia* and *El Espartaquismo Andaluz.*

or to associate familiarly with the local inhabitants or to
move about unarmed or alone. This rule has led to their
being known everywhere as *la Pareja,* or "the Pair." It goes
without saying that in poverty-stricken districts—that is to
say, throughout a large part of Spain—their relations with
the working classes were of open hostility and suspicion.
Living as they did among their enemies, they became un-
usually ready to shoot. Again and again mild riots and
demonstrations have become dangerous because the Civil
Guard could not keep their fingers off their triggers. And
from the moment that, in the nineties, the anarchists rather
tentatively took to violence too, the readiness of the *Guardia*
to shoot became greater than ever. After 1931 the hatred
between them and the villagers made many parts of Spain
ungovernable.

The character of the rural anarchism that grew up in the
south of Spain differed, as one would expect, from that
developed in the large cities of the north. "The idea," as it
was called, was carried from village to village by anarchist
"apostles." In the farm laborers' *gañanías* or barracks, in
isolated cottages by the light of oil *candiles,* the apostles
spoke on liberty and equality and justice to rapt listeners.
Small circles were formed in towns and villages that started
night schools where many learned to read, carried on antireligious propaganda, and often practiced vegetarianism and
teetotalism. Even tobacco and coffee were banned by some,
and one of these old apostles whom I knew maintained that,
when the age of liberty came in, men would live on unfired
foods grown by their own hand. But the chief characteristic
of Andalusian anarchism was its naive millenarianism. Every
new movement or strike was thought to herald the immediate
coming of a new age of plenty, when all—even the Civil
Guard and the landowners—would be free and happy. How
this would happen no one could say. Beyond the seizure of
the land (not even that in some places) and the burning of
the parish church, there were no positive proposals.

The underground period came to an end in 1881, when
the liberal government of Sagasta (once the Diocletian of
the Internationalists) came into office and passed a law
making trade unions and working-class organizations legal.
The socialists at once took advantage of this law to found

their party and at an anarchist congress held in Barcelona in March, the Spanish Regional Federation of the International came into existence. It was a federation of small trade unions and local sections, modeled on that set up by the Cordova Congress in 1872, with a strictly legal program of propaganda and strikes.

But meanwhile repressions and persecutions all over Europe had brought about a change in the character of anarchism. The Bakuninist International had held its last Congress in 1877. Since then a crisis in the watchmaking industry had led to the ruin of the small home industries in the Jura, and large-scale production at Geneva took its place. Thus the backbone of anarchist trade unionism in Europe was broken and in March, 1878, the *Bulletin de la Fédération Jurassienne,* which for seven years had been the chief organ of the anarchist movement, came out for the last time. *Le Révolté,* edited by Kropotkin at Geneva, took its place with a new theory—anarchist communism.

But the loss of its trade-union following owing to persecutions and other causes, and its consequent isolation from the masses, was leading to a movement that tended either to individualism or to small secret groups. In the congresses that were celebrated from time to time in different parts of Europe, it was no longer federations of workers who sent their delegates, but small groups of militants and sometimes even newspapers and isolated individuals who represented no one but themselves. Most of the groups were secret and some were terrorist.

It was the Italians who best represented this tendency. The factory worker in Italy had never taken to anarchism. Just as in Spain, it had been the *petite bourgeoisie* and the peasants of the south who had shown most susceptibility to it. Already at the Berne Congress of 1876, Malatesta was declaring that "trade unionism was a reactionary institution." But the police had become more active in Italy since then, and soon even the peasants hung back. To stir them up and to rouse their imaginations new and more striking methods were suggested. "Propaganda by deed" began to be preached as an anarchist technique. At first this did not consist in much more than organized risings or conspicuous acts of sabotage, but police repressions, accompanied sometimes

by ferocious torture in prison, led to the formation of definitely terroristic groups, which were ready to use any means
to bring down their enemies.

The assassination of the Czar in March, 1881, by Russian
social revolutionaries caused a profound sensation all over
Europe. The reactionaries everywhere took fright, and the
revolutionaries were encouraged. The anarchist congress
that met in London four months later debated under its
shadow. Many of the delegates were, in Stekloff's words,
"isolated desperadoes, lone wolves, infuriated by persecution
and out of touch with the masses." Others, the most violent
of all in their proposals, were police spies. Others again represented the new theories of "anarchist communism." But
resolutions were passed accepting "propaganda by deed" as
a useful method and recommending members to "pay more
attention to the technical and chemical sciences." The Spanish delegate, when he went back to Madrid, took several
new ideas with him.

However, the effect of this changed orientation upon their
Spanish comrades was inconsiderable. Spaniards lived then
at a great distance from the rest of Europe. Besides, anarchism had still a large proletarian following. Under such conditions terrorist action was madness and would not find any
encouragement among the workers. The new Regional Federation had in any case no need to appeal for violent methods.
Its progress during the first year or two of its existence was
rapid. A congress held at Seville in 1882 represented some
50,000 workers, of whom 30,000 came from Andalusia and
most of the rest from Catalonia.[13]

Yet the fact that there was no longer any picked body of
professed anarchists, such as had been provided by the old

[13] According to Anselmo Lorenzo, the Regional Federation was composed at
this time of 49,000 members. Of these 30,047 were from Andalusia, 13,181
from Catalonia, 2,355 from Valencia, 1,550 from Castile, 847 from Galicia, 689
from Aragon, and 710 from the Basque provinces (i.e., Bilbao). (*El Proletaria-
do Militante*, vol. II, pp. 147 and 313.)

Díaz del Moral (op. cit. pp. 122) gives a total of 57,934 members, of whom
19,181 were from eastern Andalusia, and 19,168 from western Andalusia. The
discrepancy is due to the fact that for Andalusia he is including sections that
were affiliated to the Federation but that did not send delegates to the congress
at Seville. These figures, whether correct or not in themselves, show clearly
the distribution of anarchists in different parts of the country and their huge
preponderance in the south. It was not till the end of the century that the
anarchist federations in Catalonia began to outnumber those in Andalusia. Till
then Spanish anarchism was chiefly a rural movement.

Alliance of Social Democracy, led to a serious lack of cohesion. Two tendencies stood out—the Catalán, which was reformist to the point of believing that the trade-union struggle should be kept within legal bounds and that strike funds should be accumulated, and the Andalusian, which was opposed to strike funds because it could not afford them and for that reason favored short strikes accompanied by violent action and sabotage.

The congress held at Seville in 1882 secured a formula of conciliation, but a group of Andalusians who called themselves the *Desheredados* or "Disinherited" and consisted of certain sections of workers from the vineyards of Jerez and Arcos de la Frontera dissented and left the Federation. They favored more violent action. Feeling in the country districts at that time was especially tense because the last two years had been years of severe drought and famine. The starving laborers had had to stand by and watch the crops on the large estates carried off to be sold at high prices in Seville or Cadiz. Ever since 1876 discontent had been acute and had shown itself in burnings of vineyards and in assassinations. Secret groups and societies pullulated. Then came a year of exceptionally abundant rainfall. The harvest was excellent, and a strike of reapers against piecework led to a state of excitement and expectation in the whole district. All at once the police announced that they had discovered a formidable secret society, the *Mano Negra* or "Black Hand," whose members had formed a plot to assassinate all the landowners of the district. Thousands of arrests were made, there were three hundred sentences of imprisonment and, after the usual tortures to obtain evidence, eight executions. Yet the very existence of the *Mano Negra* has been disputed. Bernaldo de Quirós, the famous sociologist sent down by the Government to investigate, doubted it. Spanish and French newspapers took it up and debated it for years. The nature of the evidence presented in court, the manifest barbarity of the procedure, and the severity of the sentences seemed to show that the whole thing was an invention of the police. New evidence has, however, come to light from which it would appear that there were secret societies that condemned to death—not landlords, but informers, and that the *Desheredados* were mixed up in this. But what is also certain is that the police enormously magnified the whole matter and took advantage of it to condemn the leading anarchists of the district without any regard to whether they were innocent or guilty.

The *Mano Negra* episode and the reaction that followed it drove underground once more the anarchist movement in Andalusia. In vain did a Congress summoned at Valencia issue anathemas against criminal activities. An outbreak of bubonic plague on the east coast led to a brief religious revival and to nightly processions of the Virgin about the streets. In Barcelona the Federation was rapidly going downhill. Its lack of fighting spirit and the bitter dissensions between the collectivists and the "anarchist communists" were disintegrating it.

This matter of collectivism and communism must be explained. The question was—in what form would the stateless society of the future be organized? In Bakunin's day the matter had been very little discussed: the word collectivism had been adopted because to French minds communism suggested the phalanstery.[14] In a collectivist society all property and instruments of labor are held in common, but each man has the right to what he can earn by his own work, or to join with other groups (collectives) who possess that right. Such a method of organization rather presupposes a primitive agrarian form of life and is at first sight not so well adapted to modern industrial conditions. Thus, though it was popular in Andalusia, it was questioned in Barcelona. Communism had the further advantage of being supported by most of the leading anarchists in Europe: Kropotkin, who had taken up what had originally been an Italian theory, had won them over to it. However, another very important idea was involved in this question—that of liberty. The new dogma struck at the conception underlying the whole Bakuninist organization—the liberty that each group had to decide what it thought best. If it were adopted it would put an end to that collaboration of convinced anarchists with large bodies of free workers which was the essence of Bakunin's system.

[14] See Kropotkin's *Memoirs of a Revolutionist*, p. 446. According to him "Spanish collectivists imply by collectivism the possesion in common of all instruments of production . . . and the liberty of each group to divide the produce as they think fit, according to communist or any other principles." (*Conquest of Bread*, p. 216.)

Here and not in some disagreement about the hypothetical form of the future society lay the real meaning of the controversy. Kropotkin stood for a purification and concentration of the anarchist ranks that would be a serious obstacle to the participation of the masses.

The result of this dispute was that, in 1888, the Regional Federation broke up. The immediate cause of its collapse was a violent discussion as to whether anarchist organizations should consist solely of convinced anarchists or should include all workers who were ready to join. This, as I have explained, was the real issue between "communists" and "collectivists," between Kropotkin and Bakunin. When, with the introduction of anarcho-syndicalism in 1909, it was finally decided in accordance with Bakunin's ideas, the question of the nature of the future form of society became less important. Whilst collectivism was retained as a working basis, the distant ideal became *comunismo libertario*.[15]

The next twenty years are the most obscure and ill-defined in the history of Spanish anarchism. For one thing there was no longer any single Anarchist federation covering Spain. In different towns there existed small groups of militants and intellectuals, generally centering round some weekly or fortnightly journal, and in Catalonia there was a trade union, the *Pacto de Solidaridad y Resistencia*, of collectivist tendencies, and a smaller *Organización Anarquista*, composed of pure anarchists who were mostly communists. Barcelona, Madrid, and a little later Corunna contained the strongest nuclei of militants, whilst in Andalusia rural anarchism pursued its usual rhythm: bursts of millenarian fervor leading up to some great strike or mass demonstration and followed by a decade of apathy.

One of these occurred in January, 1891, when, inspired by a successful strike in Barcelona, 4000 laborers armed with sticks and scythes marched into Jerez crying: "We cannot wait another day—We must be the first to begin the Revolution—Long live Anarchy!" and occupied it for several hours. On the arrival of the police they dispersed. Two shopkeepers were murdered in the course of this otherwise harmless ex-

15 The word "libertarian" was invented by Sébastien Faure in 1898, when the great anarchist periodical, *Revista Blanca*, was founded. Since at that time anarchist propaganda was forbidden, some other word had to be used to express the idea.

ploit, but the police made it the excuse for a violent repression, condemning four to death and sentencing eighteen to long terms of hard labor.[16]

The nineties were everywhere the period of anarchist terrorism. We have seen how the loss of its working-class adherents and the stupidity of police repressions led to this. But there were other causes as well. The reign of the bourgeoisie was now at its height. Their meanness, their philistinism, their insufferable self-righteousness weighed upon everything. They had created a world that was both dull and ugly and they were so firmly established in it that it seemed hopeless even to dream of revolution. The desire to shake by some violent action the complacency of this huge, inert, and stagnant mass of middle-class opinion became irresistible. Artists and writers shared this feeling. One must put such books as Flaubert's *Bouvard et Pécuchet* and Huysmans' *À Rebours,* Butler's and Wilde's epigrams, and Nietzsche's savage outbursts in the same category as the bombs of the anarchists. To shock, to infuriate, to register one's protest became the only thing that any decent or sensitive man could do.[17]

In Spain, however, the psychological atmosphere was different. The police were more brutal and governments were more tyrannous, but as they were also more inefficient and more careless, and as life still followed in the easier track of the previous century, the air could still be breathed. Bomb outrages tended less, therefore, to take the form of protests against society in general than to be strict acts of revenge for prison tortures or unjust sentences. The first bomb was

[16] Blasco Ibáñez's novel *La Bodega* is based on this rising. The saintly anarchist "apostle" who is its hero is meant as a portrait of Fermín Salvoechea, who although in prison at Cádiz at the time of the rising, was sentenced to twelve years hard labor for complicity in it. It is true that he probably organized it from the jail. The following year there was a strike in the same district at harvest time against landowners who paid "fifty centimes for sixteen hours." The landowners defeated it in the usual way, by calling in blackleg labor from the mountain villages.

[17] To register a protest! This phrase sums up almost the whole of anarchist action in Spain during the last fifty years. In their newspapers and magazines no word is so common as the word *protesta.* Spanish anarchism early adopted an attitude of moral disapproval towards the bourgeoisie and all its doings which it never relaxed. As to the assassinations, whilst there can be no doubt that Bakunin would not have approved of a *policy* of terrorism, it is also true that he did not boggle at isolated "acts of justice." In a letter to Herzen dated 23 June 1867 he writes: "Why do you call Berezovsky a fanatic? 'He is pure because he is a fanatic,' you say. What a terrible *jeu de mots!* . . . As

thrown, in 1891, at a building—the offices of the great
Catalán employers' association, the *Fomento*. A strike was
in progress and it was thought that a little "propaganda by
deed" would encourage the workers. After this Barcelona
suffered from a perfect epidemic of petards and bombs, laid
however not so much to injure as to frighten. The people responsible for this were a small group of anarchists,[18] many
of them Italians, who believed that in this way they would
raise the fighting spirit of the workmen. A book of instructions for making explosives, called the *Indicador Anarquista*,
was handed round, and a watchmaker learned to make
Orsini bombs with a time fuse. Malatesta visited Spain and
held a large meeting at Madrid. But the leading Spanish
militants held aloof.

The following year a young man called Pallás threw a
bomb at General Martínez Campos in revenge for the execution of two well-known anarchist journalists for complicity
in the Jerez rising. Martínez Campos was only slightly
wounded, but Pallás was tried by court martial and shot. His
friend Santiago Salvador avenged him with a terrible act.
He threw a bomb into the stalls of the Liceo Theatre, killing
twenty people, half of them women, and wounding many
more. The police, who at first could not find out who had
done it, arrested five leading anarchists at hazard, and,
although it was clear that they had no connection with the
terrorists, the judges found them guilty. Then Salvador was

---

if there were no right to passions in life! Berezovsky is an avenger, one of the
most legitimate *justiciers* of all the crimes, of all the tortures and of all humiliations which the Poles have suffered. Can't you understand? If such explosions of indignation did not take place in the world, one would despair of
the human race."

18 It is from now on that the small group becomes the characteristic organization. Small parties or *tertulias* of people would meet every day at some *café*
to discuss the new ideas and to make plans, and at the center of these would
be four or five initiates, usually intimate friends, who held the secrets. These
groups gave themselves names, such as *Salut, Fortuna, Avant, Benvenuto*, and
so on. Most of them confined themselves to discussion and propaganda, in
which they were highly successful. By 1892, when the bomb outrages began,
large sections of the middle classes and intellectuals in Barcelona had been
won over to sympathy with anarchist ideas. But under foreign influences other
groups became terrorists.

This group organization persisted, surviving even the importation of syndicalism, and later we see the redoubtable *Federación Anarquista Ibérica* or
F.A.I. built up of a large number of groups of like-minded persons, that
reacted on one another in a complicated manner. They had their cafés too:
the place at which most of the armed risings of the Republican period were
hatched was the *Café Tranquilidad* in the Paralelo.

caught. However, this did not prevent the five from being executed as well.[19] The inefficiency of the police on this occasion led to the creation of a new political police force, the *Brigada Social*.

The first act of this police was however a rather peculiar one. The traditional procession with the Host on Corpus Christi Day, headed by the bishop, the Captain-General and other authorities, was on its way to Santa María del Mar, when in the Calle de Cambios Nuevos a bomb was thrown from a top-story window on to it. But the bomb did not fall on the head of the procession where the leading dignitaries of the city were walking: it fell on the tail, where it killed seven working-class people and a soldier. The thrower of this bomb was never discovered, but General Weyler, of Cuban War notoriety and at that time Captain-General of Barcelona, made an immediate use of the incident. Not merely anarchists but simple anticlericals were arrested wholesale and thrown into the Montjuich dungeons, where the new police was let loose upon them. Here, without any control or any rational object, the most frightful tortures were applied. Several died under them, in addition to the official executions. Yet of those executed only one, Ascheri, had belonged to the group of bomb throwers. Of those acquitted sixty-one were sent to the penal settlements of Río de Oro, a punishment at that time almost worse than death. The Montjuich tortures shocked Europe and a young Italian anarchist called Angiolillo, then living in London, was so moved by the account he heard that he made his way to Santa Agueda, where the Prime Minister, Cánovas, was taking the waters, and shot him.

The loss of Cuba brought this wretched era to an end. Both the Government and the Army were too discredited to take the field any longer. The terrorist groups were discredited too and most of their members were either dead or in prison. A new breeze began to stir the drooping leaves of anarchism. First it began to be said that the general strike

[19] Salvador, in order to escape from the frightful tortures that were employed, pretended to repent of his act and to be converted. The Jesuits took him under their protection: one then had the extraordinary spectacle of the aristocratic ladies in Madrid and Barcelona treating him as a "poor unfortunate" and getting up petitions to the government for his reprieve. Not a word was said about saving his perfectly innocent but irreligious companions. However, the reprieve was refused, and on the scaffold Salvador threw off the mask and cried "*Viva el Anarquismo!*"

and not the bomb was the true revolutionary weapon; then it was passed round that the triumph of anarchism, like the triumph of Catholicism and the triumph of liberalism, could only come from the schools: the young must be educated in the libertarian doctrine before the conquest of power could begin. A movement for founding anarchist schools therefore grew up in various parts of the country. At Barcelona the *Escuela Moderna* was founded by Francisco Ferrer. At this children were brought up to believe in liberty, social equality, and so on, and above everything else to hate the Church, which taught false and "perverted" doctrines. There were also night schools for adults and a printing press that turned out a continuous stream of anarchist books and pamphlets. Ferrer himself, a narrow-minded pedant with few attractive qualities, professed to have given up all belief in violence and to have abjured his anarchist connections, but this need not be taken too seriously. The recent persecutions had made discretion desirable. Other schools were founded in Andalusia. Workingmen were taught to read and to abjure religion, vice, and alcoholism. A woman, Belén Sárraga, founded a society for workingwomen in the province of Málaga that had 20,000 members, mostly field laborers.

This movement corresponded to a period of intellectual expansion. Never before had Spanish anarchism contained men of education and ideas. It also began to open its ranks to the middle classes. Tarrida del Mármol, one of the leading anarchists of the period, was the director of the Polytechnic Academy at Barcelona and came from one of the best families in the city. José López Montenegro, who edited *La Huelga General,* had been a colonel in the Army. Ricardo Mella, a Galician typographer, was the only Spaniard to make any contribution to anarchist theory. Many young writers and intellectuals too were drawn into the acratic orbit. Ramiro de Maeztu and Azorín both sat for a time in their cafés and flirted with libertarian ideas. In Spain, just as in France, anarchism was the fashion. But the intense seriousness, which seemed to them narrowness and fanaticism, of the anarchists ended by driving most of these young dilettantes away, and the arrival of syndicalism closed the anarchist ranks for good and all to bourgeois sympathizers. Since 1910 the attitude of the Spanish anarchists towards the intellectuals has been consistently hostile. They have had their own writers and thinkers and have not been interested in others.

For syndicalism was now in the air: the new belief in the efficacy of the general strike was due to its influence. It led to the formation in Madrid in 1900 of a Federation of Workers of the Spanish Region, founded on the classic models of 1873 and 1881. This culminated two years later in a metallurgic strike in Barcelona in which many other workers joined. The strike failed and was followed by a temporary setback: the workmen left the anarchist unions in swarms and the Federation collapsed.[20] But it had given rise to a great deal of enthusiasm all over Spain and to an unprecedented wave of millenarian fervor in Andalusia. It was clear that it was only a matter of time before the new syndicalist methods of organization, with their superior vigor and cohesion, would cross the Pyrenees into Spain.

Richard Hostetter

Anarchism Versus the Italian State [1]

Richard Hostetter Since 1946 Hostetter has worked and researched the field of European socialism. He has contributed widely to European and American historical journals. His investigations have been conducted primarily in Italy for the last five years with the support of research grants. Hostetter took his advanced degree in Modern European History at the University of California. He has held a teaching fellowship at the University of California and served as an Associate Professor

[20] According to a Catholic economist, Sastre, who made a special study of the working-class organizations of this period, the number of workmen in Barcelona who belonged to the "societies of resistance" declined from over 45,000 in 1902 to a bare 10,000 in 1909. The total number of workmen in Barcelona at this time was 88,000. Even so not all these 45,000 were affiliated to anarchist federations: according to Buenacasa, an anarchist congress held at Madrid in 1900 represented only 50,000 members from the whole of Spain. The fact is that the oldest and most important trade unions in Barcelona, the hand-weavers, paper-makers, barrel-makers, and half the mill hands had steadily refused, since the foundation of the International, to come under anarchist influence. It was syndicalism and the foundation of the C.N.T. that brought them all in.

[1] From *The Italian Socialist Movement: Origins 1860–1882*, by Richard Hostetter. Princeton: D. Van Nostrand Company, Inc. Copyright © 1958. Reprinted by permission of the publisher.

of Modern European History at the University of Arkansas for
several years before going to Italy. His book, *The Italian Socialist Movement: Origins, 1860–1882*, represents the first of an
anticipated three-volume history of Italian socialism.

ITALIAN LIBERALISM AND THE
SOCIALIST PROBLEM

The national organization of Ital-
ian socialism at Rimini made the government's attitude toward its activity an important conditioning factor in its development. With the authoritarian-libertarian issue resolved
in favor of the anarchists, with the Mazzinian cause compromised in the eyes of radical youth by monarchical consolidation, with Garibaldi isolating himself from a movement whose program he disapproved, Cafiero, Malatesta,
Costa, and their comrades could now try to actuate their
program, no longer constrained to expend the bulk of their
energies defending themselves against these republican foes.
Opposition persisted after the summer of 1872, but the
anarchist chieftains considered it weakened sufficiently that
they no longer needed to extend themselves in decrying the
authoritarianism of Marx and the General Council, the
"political theology" of Mazzini, and Garibaldi's confusion of
socialism with the brotherhood of man. By the fall of 1872,
the ground was cleared for a new battle and a new enemy, the
bête noire indicated by their central tenet: the State. The
policy of the government in handling a movement intent on
subverting the political and social foundations of the State
constituted, so long as the movement retained its ideological
and organizational integrity, the determining external element affecting Italian anarchism's growth and development.

To keep the matter in proper perspective, it must be remembered that from the government's point of view—even
from that of the Italian middle class—the challenge of the
International, to the extent it was considered a challenge at
all, was a relatively minor one during the decade of the
1870s. Bourgeois public opinion, like that of the men in
government, saw in the Internationalist phenomenon a
symptom of discontent deriving from poverty, a discontent
susceptible, by the same token, to the curative powers of
enlightened paternalism. The threat warranted no excep-

tional measures. Not until the late 1870s did Italian industrialization and the worker unrest it brought in its wake arouse concern, not in the middle class as a whole, but among those productive groups with economic interests directly affected. By then, however, the problem no longer presented itself as a socialist or Internationalist one, for the Italian International was already being rent by the centrifugal force of defection in its own ranks. In a broad sense, the ruling classes did not take the socialist challenge seriously until, in the 1880s, they began to identify it with the workers' movement. During most of the preceding decade, the absence of an industrial proletariat in a country just emerging from an artisan production system kept Italy's political class from attributing any real political importance to the socialist International. Hence, any discussion of the government's attitude toward the movement in the early and mid-1870s must depart from the premise that, however vital to the existence of the International the government's point of view, the attitude itself reflected no sense of serious peril to bourgeois class interests.

The period extending from September, 1872, to July, 1876, featured, in succession, the planning and organizing of an armed insurrection, its attempted execution in August, 1874, and a subsequent series of Internationalist trials. As the representative, defendant, and executive arm of bourgeois class interests, the government, by all the canons of Marxist historiography, should have immediately extirpated the Italian International by the simple expedient of exceptional laws. The anarchists' program flatly challenged every ideal of middle-class society. Moreover, the constitutional Right, not the Left, was in power during this period. Government reaction to the attempted subversion should have reflected—and did, according to contemporary historians of the Marxist Left—the dynamics of class conflict, hinged on fear and unalloyed bourgeois class egotism. Yet, by July, 1876, all the Internationalists implicated in the 1874 attempt, having faced judges and juries drawn from the ranks of the possessing classes, found themselves free to reorganize their association on the same platform adopted at Rimini four years before, free to repeat their attempt to subvert the State and society by conspiracy and violence.

Several contingent reasons partially explain this outcome.

Juries were influenced to leniency by appreciation of the existing social inequities the defendants claimed had motivated their actions. The prosecution mounted woefully inept cases. There were too many instances of third-degree tactics by the police to extract confessions, of the use of *agents provocateurs,* of flimsy, irrelevant, and distorted evidence. Clever defense lawyers easily proved that their clients' actions did not fit the rigorous requirements of Italian laws defining conspiracy and attempted subversion of State security. Some of the leading defendants, in addressing the juries, proved exceedingly eloquent, masters of sentimental rhetoric, *simpatici* in their persons. Generally, they depicted themselves as the voice of popular conscience, protesting social injustice, as martyrs under the rod of reaction. By 1875–76, moreover, the government of the Right reached the pinnacle of its unpopularity, for reasons that went far beyond its social policy. Finally, the whole *Risorgimento* tradition of Mazzinian *coup de main,* of Garibaldian enterprises, of Agesilao Milano, of Felice Orsini, of Carlo Pisacane, sanctified, in the eyes of many, the actions of these latter-day paladins of the crusade against tyranny.

Still, if one goes beyond these immediate reasons for the exoneration of Internationalists who, if they did not quite qualify as culprits under the specific charges brought against them, were certainly guilty of attempted insurrection in point of fact, it becomes clear that the favorable verdicts derived from a climate of public opinion—i.e., informed, bourgeois opinion—that was contrary to any departure from strict legality in handling the anarcho-socialist phenomenon, regardless of how unequivocally the Internationalists stated their challenge to bourgeois society. Any government action against a political faction could not avoid close scrutiny by public opinion; any suspicion that such action violated the principle of liberty under law meant that no Italian government, under normal circumstances, could hope to win approval of repressive measures. So long as the Right was in power, i.e., until March, 1876, the prevailing spirit among Moderates was legalitarian and liberal, and what an Italian statesman told the French Ambassador in the summer of 1872 was generally true, even after 1876, of public opinion as well: "We have suffered so much because of arbitrary action when we lived according to the caprices of our many governments, that we want to believe in legality, now that we feel ourselves sufficiently strong to be a nation, one and free; and we are clear-sighted enough to believe in liberty only under law."

To what degree was the government of the Right, between 1872 and 1876, responsive to this spirit? The reader may judge from the ensuing record of the Italian International's experience, but certainly the meaning of that experience, in relation to the question at issue, is by no means clear except in the context of certain basic articles of faith prevalent among the men who ruled Italy. A summary of their attitude toward the social question, the International, and the general problem of how to deal with a socially subversive movement, points to the conclusion that the government reaction aroused by the insurrectional attempt of the anarchists was more maladroit than vicious, more the product of bewilderment than of class interest, certainly not aimed at the suppression of any political-economic program, not even—as Giovanni Lanza, a man of the parliamentary Right, told one of his colleagues—that inspired by the most absurd sophisms of the socialist school."

As viewed by the government, there was no real problem, in fact, as long as the propagation of these "sophisms" involved no organized attempt to overthrow the government by violence. When the anarchists actually tried "social liquidation," however, the terms of the conflict became more complex, not because suppression was technically impossible, but because men deeply attached to classical liberal principles would not adopt the only effective method of eliminating the International in Italy: exceptional laws, frankly violating constitutional liberties. The anarchists' exploitation of the government's dilemma proved only a temporary advantage, for it merely hastened the day when the government, no longer bound by liberal scruples, would treat them, not as political opponents, but as "an association of malefactors," legally in the category of common thieves and ruffians. That this development was delayed until the fall of the Right from power in 1876 attests, in itself, to the strength of the liberal idea among Moderates, such as Marco Minghetti, Giovanni Lanza, and Quintino Sella. The Italian International's war on the State from the Congress of Rimini to the summer of 1876 constituted—always within the limits

indicated at the beginning of this chapter—a challenge to
the liberal premises of Italy's ruling class. To what extent
could that class tolerate direct attack on the principles of
property, *patria,* and—in the classical sense—liberty?

Prior to the summer of 1872 the necessity of finding an
answer to such a question had probably not even occurred to
the men responsible for the government of the Italian State.
The reasons were several. In the first place, they had no
comprehension of the objective realities of the social problem, and even the term, "social question," left them perplexed. Liberalism was their religion, but it remained a moral
and juridical abstraction, only vaguely related to the framework of objective facts in which liberty might become the
possession of all. That freedom of thought, of association, of
meeting, of speech, etc., might be less than sacred to a man
with an empty stomach was a notion extraneous to their
thinking. This did not mean they were blind to the need of
ameliorating the lot of the poor. The matter was the source
of lively discussion in the pages of the *Giornale di Modena* in
the spring of 1871; Marco Minghetti, convinced that the redemption of the plebes was the supreme objective of the
century, worried about the law estate of the peasants and the
political implications of widely diffused poverty; Francesco
De Sanctis underlined the social question as the most serious
problem confronting the rulers of Italy, arguing that its solution was the only means of overcoming the public indifference and apathy implicit in parties and formulas no longer
corresponding to the realities of the situation. These exceptions, however, only underscored the fact that the great
majority of Italy's ruling class reposed their faith in paternalism and charity as the best technique of solving the social
problem. That their ideas and prejudices in regard to the
relations between capital and labor needed serious revision,
that charity, as a method of dealing with material poverty,
belonged to an outmoded era—"morally inferior to ours,"
as Mazzini would have it—these were concepts tenaciously
clung to, destined to find expression throughout the next
several decades.

Social conservatism, defense of the existing social order,
was no less a hallmark of the constitutional Left than of the
Right. The differences were only in tone, stemming mostly
from the Left's eagerness to present itself as the *vade mecum*

of the country's democratic forces. Substantially, all the parliamentary representatives of the Italian bourgeoisie agreed that property was sacred, that the middle class was the legitimate bulwark of the nation's political and social life. It was an organ of the Left, in fact, that sustained "the legitimate and merited influence of the bourgeoisie and the propertied class" in the newly created state, pointing out that in its contribution to the making of the fatherland, it did not form a class apart but actually "opened the way to complete emancipation for the worker and the rural class." If the poor man worked hard, if he showed diligence, if he saved, if he demonstrated good will and capacity, he, too, could enter the ranks of the possessing classes—and not far beneath the surface lay the implication that poverty stemmed from vice, or at least from a lack of initiative and / or ability. If the bourgeois class was open to the economically successful workers, the distinction between *borghesia* and *popolo* was merely semantic. It was argued that, if there were two opposed classes in Italian society, they consisted of those who worked and those who agitated, those who minded their own business and the professional subversives. Actually, the social problem was not one of opposed classes, but of the relations between individuals; individually, the worker was free to improve his material status, to become bourgeois.

Secondly, along with this social conservatism and the lack of understanding of the social problem that contributed to it, there was considerable bewilderment—perhaps inevitable— on the part of Italian liberal politicians as to what might be done to counteract the threatened rupture of the nexus between liberty and *patria,* their abiding article of faith in the making of Italy. Socialism had emerged as an international movement, understanding liberty as the right to ignore the principle of private property in the name of the majority's well-being. In creating Italy, the liberals thought they had demonstrated, beyond all question, the indissoluble tie between *their* liberal ideas and a free, united fatherland. Yet, the masses seemed not to have noticed; many, without any urging by the socialists, even considered the unification a hoax perpetrated on the common people for the benefit of the *signori,* that unity had actually worsened the plight of the masses—and in some regions of the peninsula there was more than a grain of truth to the assertion.

National unity did not satisfy the material aspirations of Italian workers and peasants—for that matter, they probably expected no such change in their fortunes, given their unconcern with the essentially political ideals of the *Risorgimento*. The cost of living climbed steadily in the post-unity years, and, so far as inadequate statistics indicate, the index of real wages in industry between 1870 and 1876 was generally downward. Ever since the unification, there had been strikes and peasant disturbances, all reflecting economic distress, and in the summer of 1872, between the beginning of July and the end of August, thirty-one strikes occurred in twenty-five different localities, including a nine-day general strike in Turin and a three-day general strike in Milan that took the combined efforts of the police and troops to quell.

Though the authorities concluded that the International was not the prime mover behind the strikes, there was evidence that the I.W.A. had favored them. There was concern, too, about a possible connection between the Italian strikes and contemporaneous disturbances in France. The Italian Foreign Office wanted its representative in Paris to sound out the *Quai d'Orsay* on whether the French and Italian strikes had derived from common instructions originating with the socialist International. An official of the *Pubblica Sicurezza*, in reporting on the outbreaks, concluded that they had demonstrated "anything but a subversive temper among our working classes" but cautioned that "a simple password . . . emanating from secret conventicles of obscure persons . . . can, from one moment to the next, throw thousands and thousands of deluded [people] into the piazzas."

There was no disguising the fact that insurrectionism, nonetheless, was again becoming identified with social unrest and upheaval—a disturbing reminder of an aspect of the 1848 movement that Italian liberals preferred to forget. "The fact alone," writes Chabod, "that [1848] remained in the popular tradition as synonymous with disorder and anarchy, and that a '48 became a very common expression for designating great tumult, [rioting] peoples in the piazzas and the plundering of houses, sufficiently proves how profound the impression had been." In the context of 1872, with the Italian national revolution completed, no patriotic objective remained to hallow disorder with social revolutionary overtones. Quite to the contrary, for the socialist International, the suspected inspiration of this latter-day plebeian unrest, was seen as a mortal enemy of not only private property, but of the sacred principle of *patria* as well. Where Pisacane's socialism had been patriotic and national, that of the international association cut across national boundaries, appealing to the classes against the nations.

This situation *sui generis* had no precedent in the experience of the men who had made the new Italy. But given their long-held conviction that patriotism and liberty were sufficiently impelling aspirations among all Italians to absorb any conceivable social longings of the multitudes, their reticence to draw any inference from the situation that might suggest measures inconsistent with their faith in classical liberal principles is understandable. National unity, guaranteed constitutional liberties, economic freedom, with these blessings, it was felt, no Italian could find fault with the new society. Of course, there would always be poverty, but every citizen also had the right to work out his own economic salvation in a liberal economy; his newly won political freedom guaranteed his immunity to extremist doctrines. The irreducible minimum of material suffering could be dealt with by private charity. Besides, as the constitutionalists of both Right and Left were fond of believing, Italy, with its predominantly agricultural economy, lacked the "combustible material" for a social conflagration.

More concretely, the men in government had no compelling reason to interpret economically motivated disturbances of the workers and peasants as symptoms of a social problem dangerous to the stability and security of the state. For one thing, the Italian Internationalists made no real effort to exploit the strikes of 1872 by organizing the workers for the cause of socialism. Cafiero, Malatesta, Costa, and the rest were far too involved in their feud with the London General Council to see the opportunity under their noses, a failing that Benoît Malon recalled to their chagrin several years later:

> . . . in Italy, while thousands of workers were wandering around the public squares, the chiefs were concerning themselves with discussions about the merits of *Anarchy* and about the proximity of the *Social Revolution;* instead

of acting, they philosophized, instead of throwing themselves into the fray, they conspired.

Secondly, the overall picture of the new nation's economic health was reassuring. Private wealth, after severe downward fluctuations during the decade 1860–70, appreciably increased from 1871 to 1875; in the same period, average income increased by more than 7½ percent over the average for 1866–70. Besides, in terms of dissatisfaction with the status quo, the low-income segment of Italian society was only one of several lamenting the economic and financial policies of the government. If, as a modern student of that epoch insists, the men of the Right, with social roots firmly imbedded in the agrarian proprietor class of the north-central region of Italy, were "substantially blind to the demands and appetites of the bourgeois fractions most advanced in a capitalistic sense," how much less were they prepared to interpret sporadic peasant and worker disturbances, however severe, as symptomatic of a "social problem" in the modern sense?

It is true that proletarian unrest, if channeled by the International, could conceivably develop into a real challenge to the political structure of the Italian state, whereas the opposition of bourgeois financiers and industrial pressure groups was premised on its continued existence. But even eliminating from consideration the Right's foes within the ranks of those accepting the existing political system does not bring the workers and peasants into focus as a *class* threat to the status quo. The men of the Right, with their high sense of the state, judged their opponents in essentially political terms, and the use of this criterion, in the early 1870s, led them to see a far greater threat in republicans and clericals than in the embryonic socialist movement. Significantly, the Right's discounting of the "red menace" was partly due to the clerical charge that socialism was not only the logical consequence of liberal doctrines but about to inherit the earth—unless, of course, all antisocialist forces mustered under the wing of Christ's Vicar.

Though very clear about the threat of republicanism per se, the government could not always discern exactly where republican propaganda left off and that of the socialists began. The difficulty was inescapable, since practically all

Italian socialists were ex-republicans, while many republicans were in the process of making the transition to the socialist camp. As late as the summer of 1872, many of the prominent socialists—thanks, in part, to Garibaldi's equivocal stand on the International—had still not broken with the Party of Action. Men like Celso Ceretti, Pescatori, Piccioli-Poggiali, Tito Zanardelli, and Salvatore Battaglia probably never accepted the premises that impelled Costa, Malatesta, and Cafiero to argue a dialectical incompatibility between their vision of a future society and that envisaged by a Mazzini or a Garibaldi.

In the sphere of action, as in that of propaganda, the socialist and republican currents were often intermingled, frequently causing the authorities to see the hand of the International in republican manifestations and vice versa. The purely republican disorders in Milan on July 24, 1870, and those of the following month in Genoa caused *La Perseveranza* (Milan) to remark the "strange concomitance" of a political with a social movement, of a republican effort against property. Or, again, when practically all but a handful of socialists lent their support to the Garibaldian congress project in the winter of 1871–72, it is not surprising that the authorities could not persuade themselves that the movement was essentially republican in inspiration and intent. Such confusion inhibited any clear appreciation of the socialist movement as a distinct challenge in itself; if anything, it tended to suggest that republicanism was acquiring further strength by identifying itself more closely with the economic aspirations of the humbler classes.

A more compelling reason for the Moderates of the government to see republicanism as the only conceivably serious danger on the Left was implicit in the circumstances surrounding the completion of national unity with the capture of Rome. Given the demonstrable fascination of French ideas and political developments for the Italians, the creation of the Third French Republic on September 4, 1870, suggested the possibility that the Italian republican movement would be spurred to greater and more effective efforts. The overthrow of Napoleon III was no cause for rejoicing by the Italian bourgeois press. The Florentine liberal daily, *La Nazione*, spoke for a huge segment of ruling-class opinion when, three days after the proclamation of the Third Repub-

lic, it insisted that Italy was now essentially a conservative
nation and that, to be such, meant saving Italian unity, independence, and society from those who once more wanted to
"Frenchify" Italy in the name of the republic; that now republicans must be fought in the name of national freedom,
they must be opposed as traitors to *la patria*. The monarchy
was equated with Italian patriotism; only the monarchy could
guarantee national liberty, independence, and unity. In fact,
a primary consideration motivating the government's decision to occupy Rome was precisely the fear that the republicans would take the initiative if the monarchy did not. Victor
Emmanuel and his ministers were under no illusions, furthermore, that conservative, monarchical Europe would tolerate
a revolutionary republican solution of the Italian question,
given Italy's unsavory reputation—thanks to the way in
which unity had been accomplished—as a focal point of
revolutionism in the European body politic.

Superficially viewed, the capture of Rome seemed to remove the republican peril: Mazzini's followers deserted his
cause in increasing numbers; many of the former republican
conspirators, from Francesco Crispi to Benedetto Cairoli,
accepted the Sabauda monarchy; Garibaldi, for all his republican—and even socialist—pronunciamentos, was no
longer a serious enemy. Mazzini's tirades against the Paris
Commune, his implicit alliance with the forces of conservatism against the reds, did not go unnoticed by the ruling
classes. Still, they could not fail to notice that it was precisely
this alliance that alienated many of his followers without
noticeably dampening their republican convictions and ambitions. Mazzini's personal prestige was no safe barometer
of the republican potential, in any case, since the very existence of the Third French Republic and portentous republican rumblings in Carlist Spain promised to feed the republican spirit in the peninsula far more than a tired Mazzini, now
giving his last energies to defending Italian youth against
the inroads of corrupting materialism. Republican sentiment
was plainly declining nowhere nearly as fast as the Genoese's
personal influence among his once numerous band. But it
was declining. And considering that socialism was rated far
below republicanism as a danger to the regime, the slight
degree of the Moderates' worry about the former becomes
apparent.

The most revealing test of the government's attitude toward the so-called specter of socialism was its net reaction to the Paris Commune, viewed by Italian, as well as European, bourgeois opinion as a supreme effort of the socialist International. "There is no doubt," reported the Italian Ambassador to Paris on March 22, 1871, ". . . that the Parisian movement is the exclusive work of the *International* and that its most distinctive and even determining characteristic is social and communist and nothing else." The bourgeois press of Italy fully concurred in this judgment. Nor did the government see the phenomenon of class warfare in Paris as extraneous to Italian interests. In March, 1871, it was informed by one of its consuls in France that a Garibaldian legion was being organized clandestinely in Paris, which, backed by the International, aspired to proclaim a republic in Italy and Spain and subsequently join the French Communards in a war of revenge against Germany. The Italian Foreign Minister, Visconti-Venosta, never an alarmist, was convinced that the strength of Communard resistance testified to "a real danger for Europe," especially for Italy, so close to the conflagration, with "numerous socialist elements within her borders." His conclusion, the true measure of his inquietude: that "in the presence of the common enemy, the Powers should . . . come to an understanding as to the means of reducing and disarming it."

Significantly, Visconti-Venosti's private opinion never became public policy. However initially serious their concern, whatever their fears, the misgivings of Italy's rulers entailed no extraordinary government measures against socialism. Like Cavour, they, too, put no faith in force as an antidote to a dangerous idea. The socialist school, Cavour had assured them, could not be fought effectively except by "opposing other principles to its principles. In the economic order, as in the political order, . . . ideas are combatted effectively only with ideas, principles with principles; material repression avails little. There is no doubt that, for a time, cannon and bayonets can repress theories and maintain material order, but if these theories are forced into the intellectual sphere, . . . sooner or later [they] . . . will gain the victory in the political and economic order."

Once the Commune was liquidated, the Moderates were not far behind the parliamentary Left in proclaiming Italy beyond the reach of socialist subversion and the International. The bourgeois press unanimously opined that, however much the International was to be damned, it still did not concern Italy. A Communard uprising was out of the question in Italy, declared *L'Opinione* on June 1, for the internal situation was too good to admit an effective subversion of society. *La Perseveranza* counted on the "uncorrupted" mentality of Italian workers:

> Here are lacking almost all the elements that concur to create the morbid conditions of other countries; here the threatening agglomerations of a worker population still do not exist in any city; here the corruption of customs has not yet reached that extreme limit met elsewhere; here living is cheaper and consequently needs are fewer; here the people are still not infected with that leprosy which for so long has insinuated itself among the working classes of the great European centers; here, in brief, instead of a corrupted people to be cured, we have a virginal people to be educated.

Il Diritto, organ of the Left, was certain that proletarian sufferings in France and England had no parallel in Italy; not an overabundance, but a shortage of labor was Italy's problem. Fear of social war, therefore, was unfounded.

In July, when Bismarck wanted the Italian government to join in a common action by the powers against the members of the I.W.A., the same Italian Foreign Minister who had thought well of the general idea in April was now convinced that in predominantly agrarian Italy there were only insignificant traces of the International. The only danger might arise, thought he, from a unification of the malcontents of the regime, including the Mazzinians, with the socialist nuclei, but even this was a relative peril, since the general tranquility prevailing in Italy and diffused dynastic sentiment would frustrate any Mazzinian or socialist effort.

The Minister of Interior, too, was no less convinced, on the basis of his subordinates' investigations, that the I.W.A. was having sparse success in establishing itself in Italy. As late as November 18, 1871, exactly one month after Carlo Cafiero assured Engels that "the International has possessed itself of the whole of Italy," Giovanni Lanza informed Visconti-Venosta that the socialist sect had but "a few dispersed adherents and little influence," and on May 31, 1872, he told the French Ambassador that he was perfectly informed on the activity of the socialist International in Italy, numbering no more than three to four thousand adherents. Mazzinians and socialists were at odds, and Garibaldi, aspiring to unite them, lacked the necessary organizing capacity: "He is only a name and a banner whose role has been played out in Italy." The only danger, in the Minister's view, lay in a *rapprochement* between freemasonry and the International. "The International association, especially in Italy, is . . . in a state of very rudimentary formation and is still seeking to decide on how . . . to manifest its action."

The government was more than vaguely interested, of course, in the conspiratorial activity of individual agitators. Police surveillance reports on Carlo Cafiero in 1871–72 made a fat file, representing the expenditure of considerable time, energy, and money. The British government was unsuccessfully importuned to cooperate with Rome authorities in keeping track of Italian agitators arriving in London. Paris and London sent alarming reports on the comings and goings of real or presumed agents of the I.W.A.; Italian diplomats in European capitals busied themselves making inquiries of a police nature concerning the activities of those of their compatriots abroad whom the Minister of Interior, frequently unjustifiably, claimed were anything but simple tourists.

Yet, during the pre-Rimini period, there was a definite lack of consistency in the way the government reacted to socialist activity. Cafiero was arrested when the Neapolitan section was dissolved in August, 1871, but never brought to trial. Vincenzo Pezza, arrested in late March, tried in May, and sentenced to five months in jail, was free before the end of July to conspire with Bakunin and agitate in the columns of *Il Gazzettino Rosa*. Socialist sections and newspapers proliferated during the year following the Commune; congresses were held and resolutions publicized. Arbitrary actions by the police were frequent, but more often the product of an excessive zeal on the part of prefects and local *questori* than of any pressure from Rome. The liberals running the central government had no intention of significantly abridging the right of association or political expression on the sole grounds of membership in or sympathy with the principles of the socialist International.

Basically, it was the strength of liberal ideals, however unrelated to social realities, that accounted for halfhearted repressive measures against socialists, for the token incarcerations, for the growth, not decline, of socialist newspapers, for the willingness to allow known conspirators like Cafiero, Malatesta, and Costa to unite Italian socialists at Rimini and enunciate a program calling for open war on bourgeois society. The Moderates' spirit of legality—inherent in their liberal creed—that prompted the French Ambassador to assure Paris that the Rome government would take no extraordinary measures against the Jesuits, was the same spirit animating those leaders when they undertook action—more maladroit than malign—against the anarchists only when the latter adopted violence as the primary means of propagating their doctrines.

When the Italian International took up arms, the men in government, whose liberal system had permitted socialists to organize for violent ends, tried to apply the only formula consistent with their legalitarian convictions: formal prosecution of Internationalists on charges of conspiracy and attempted subversion of state security. The net result: they found themselves held guilty by public opinion of arbitrary action, illegal suppression of ideas, and sacrificing their own liberal principles. It was an ironic turn of affairs, for the charge derived, not from any arbitrary campaign of government repression, but from the incidental features, already noted, of the trial themselves and, above all, from the unpopularity the government had brought on itself for reasons unrelated to its treatment of Internationalists. In brief, interpretation of the Italian International's experience in the four years following Rimini as the product of a bourgeois government's fear-ridden reaction to the specter of socialism simplifies the telling but ignores the facts.

THE ECLIPSE OF MARXIAN INFLUENCE

After the Rimini Congress the term "Internationalist" in Italy was synonymous with "Bakuninist"—or "antiauthoritarian collectivist," to use the anarchists' own label. Marxist penetration was practically nonexistent. In early November,

1872, Engels considered Enrico Bignami, editor of *La Plebe*, as the "only individual who has taken our part in Italy" but admitted that the Lodi publicist's support was something less than energetic: "He has printed my report on the Hague Congress and a letter that I wrote him." Bignami's tepid performance was excused on the ground that "he finds himself right in the middle of the 'autonomists' and must still take certain precautions." Two weeks later Engels was asking Sorge, the new secretary-general of the Council (now in New York), for full powers for Italy, lest the Marxist cause be completely lost. Letters to Bignami and occasional pieces of *La Plebe* were not enough.

For that matter, neither were polemical contributions, in the opinion of Bignami, who apparently wanted to give the Marxist view a fair hearing in the battle of ideas, without committing himself in the dispute. He made a distinction between personal invective and name-calling, on the one hand, and discussion of principles, on the other. Engels had sent him the antianarchist *"Les prétendues scissions"* ("The so-called schisms") early in June, but Bignami acknowledged receipt of the diatribe in a way that clearly announced he was hardly enthusiastic about its substance. Bignami made the warning explicit on November 17, when he urged Engels to "speak as you please about the International but do not engage in polemics with the friends of Rimini." This time, Engels took the hint, for late in October he sent Bignami an article entitled "On Authority," which, as a friendly analyst admits, examined anarchism, *for the first time,* on the plane of principle, going beyond "personal and contingent polemics." Marx soon followed suit with "Indifference in Political Matters," but by the time these two essays appeared in print, it was far too late for them to have any real influence on Italian socialists.

After this lone contribution to enlightening Italians on the dialectical superiority of "scientific" socialism, Engels quickly reverted to the "personal and the contingent." When Bignami was jailed for publishing a General Council circular in *La Plebe* on November 17, Engels saw the police action as proof that the Italian government considered the General Council and its supporters far more dangerous than the Bakuninists: "Nothing happier could have happened to us in Italy." In early January, 1873, he was reduced to thinking

of the success of Marxian socialism in Italy in bargain-
counter terms: a "colossal" success might be had for the sum
of $30-$50. To Sorge he wrote on January 4:

> Bignami [still in jail] bombards me with letters demanding
> help for him and three other prisoners. . . . In America
> something should be done. It is *of the highest importance*
> that Lodi be sustained from the outside: it is our most
> solid post in Italy, and, now that Turin no longer gives any
> sign of life, the only one on which we can count. In Lodi
> a much more important result can be obtained, and *with
> less money,* than with the jewelry workers' strike in Ge-
> neva. . . . With half of what would be uselessly sacri-
> ficed for Geneva, or even less, one might obtain a colossal
> success in Italy. Think of the rage of the [Bakuninists] if
> they could read in *La Plebe: Subscription for the families,
> etc.: Received from the General Council of the Int*[erna-
> tional], *New York*, so many *lire*, and if the General Coun-
> cil . . . suddenly proved its existence in this manner!
> . . . Certainly you should be able to get together 30 or
> 50 dollars; but, little or much, send *something* and *right
> away*, promising, if *possible*, still further donations. If we
> were to lose Lodi and *La Plebe*, we should no longer have
> a single foothold in Italy. . . .

When the Marxist plenipotentiary for Italy felt constrained
to seek the affirmation of Marxism and the existence of the
General Council through such petty and inconsequential
needling of the Bakuninists, it should have surprised no one
—including Engels himself, if he had faced the facts of the
situation—that Lodi and *La Plebe* were Marxism's sole
point d'appui in the peninsula.

Bignami himself was anything but a convinced Marxist.
He dickered with Marx to translate and publish *Das Kapital*
in the winter of 1872–73, he accepted money from Engels
to sustain him in his quarrels with the local authorities, he
continued to publish news and proclamations of the General Council, but when *La Plebe* resumed publication
May 15, 1873, Engels decided against contributing further
to its columns, no doubt convinced that the eclecticism displayed by Bignami in his choice of socialist writings for
La Plebe made the newspaper an unsuitable medium for the

divulgation of Marxian texts. One contemporary historian
of the Italian socialist movement interprets Bignami's entertainment of Engels' antianarchist pieces in *La Plebe* as
merely the fruit of "an intelligent curiosity for the great and
new movements of European culture," and doubts that the
Lodi publicist had assimilated the ideas expressed by his
London collaborators.

Nor were Bignami's contributors to *La Plebe* an influence
toward an understanding or acceptance of the doctrines ex-
ported from London. Benoît Malon, the French Communard
exile who exercised a notably moderating influence on Italian socialism during the next two decades, had already concluded that both Marxists and anarchists were too sectarian
in spirit, too committed to pushing their own narrow interpretations of the I.W.A.'s basic principles, to give practical
effect to the dictum that "the workers must accomplish their
own emancipation." Though Malon vigorously criticized the
anarchists and their insurrectionism, the reformist socialism
he preached—"integral socialism," as he characterized it in
later years—could never be squared with Marx's stress on
the necessity of proletarian political action.

Osvaldo Gnocchi-Viani, Bignami's other leading collabo-
rator, also had little sympathy for Bakuninism, but his unlimited faith in the efficacy of proletarian action on a purely
economic plane, in trade-unionist solidarity and resistance
as the primary means of struggle, put him as far from the
Marxist position as Malon. His consuming interest during
the period of anarchist fever in Italy was not opposing
Marxist doctrine to the influence of Bakunin, but in advancing the cause of the Universal League of Workers' Corporations, founded in Geneva in November, 1873, as a kind of
"Third International" to supplant both the anarchist and
"authoritarian" movements. Its program was almost purely
syndicalist, especially in its rejection of Marx's contention
that the first duty of the working class is the conquest of
political power. On this central point, Gnocchi-Viani was
clearly as "deviationist" as the anarchists, though for quite
different reasons. As late as November, 1875, he was to write:
"When and where I can, I definitely eliminate Politics, and
when I can not eliminate it, I not only subordinate it to the
Economic Question, but, since I contemplate it from a cer-

tain scientific point of view, it happens that I always see it
either in a sinister or at least a dubious light. . . ."

In Rome, where Gnocchi-Viani exercised his greatest
practical influence in the local I.W.A. section, his trade-
unionist preferences were reflected in the fact that until the
section was wrecked by the arrest of Gnocchi-Viani and his
fellow organizers on May 15, 1873, the group concerned itself almost exclusively with problems of economic resistance
and syndical organization. Still, the section was formally
affiliated with the anarchist Italian Federation and maintained fairly frequent contacts with the correspondence commission before the summer of 1873. On the other hand, there
is no trace of ties with Engels and/or the General Council
after Gnocchi-Viani formally notified Engels on August 18,
1872, of the section's creation. In the summer of 1873, the
leadership of the organization passed into the hands of a
group of anarchist immigrants from the Romagna and the
Marches—all disciples of "social liquidation," not trade
unionism.

In Florence, the same process of ideological clarification,
in a sense unfavorable to the General Council, occurred
within the local Internationalist nucleus. The Rimini decisions of August, 1872, proved catalytic, for it was around
them and the question of breaking with the General Council
that heated discussions revolved during the ensuing weeks.
Luigi Stefanoni resigned from the *Fascio Operaio* in late
August, not because he had softened his hostility toward the
Marxists he had condemned in the spring, but because he
had no taste for the insurrectional implications of the now
dominant brand of Italian socialism. Antonio Martinati, also
resigned and briefly entertained the notion of founding a new
section, loyal to the General Council, but it was Angelo
Dalmasso, close friend of the unsavory Terzaghi, who gave
practical effect to Martinati's project early in November.
After Dalmasso left Florence for Turin, however, the pro-
General Council section soon lost its ardor for supporting a
lost cause.

The *Fascio Operaio* itself was dissolved by the police on
December 1, 1872, but—true to time-sanctioned practice
—it was reconstituted three days later as the Florentine
Workers' Federation, an organization notably successful in

1873 in organizing and propagandizing the workers of Florence and its neighboring *paesi*. No trace of a connection with the Marxist faction is to be found, but in February, 1873, the governing council of the Federation sent a declaration of solidarity to the anarchist Jura Federation, approving its conduct vis-à-vis the New York General Council. By midsummer, the most influential figures in the Tuscan association were activists of the anarchist Italian Federation, Lorenzo Piccioli-Poggiali, Gaetano Grassi, and Francesco Natta. The only conceivable threat to their supremacy, the influence of moderates of the Stefanoni-Martinati persuasion, was about overcome. So far as the local *questore* could determine, the Florentine anarchists had nothing to fear from Martinati, for "he has lost all influence among the Internationalists, as among the republicans. . . ." The Florentine socialist movement was securely tied to the anarchist cause.

Probably the most telling evidence that the Marxists, in the post-Rimini period, had lost their foothold in Italy is the fact that they were reduced, by the end of 1873, to speculating on the possibility of making an ally of none other than Carlo Terzaghi, notwithstanding that Marx himself had made some serious charges against the Turinese in his "Alliance of Socialist Democracy," that in mid-March, 1873, the anarchists, at their Bologna Congress, expelled him as a police agent after hearing a well-documented indictment presented by Andrea Costa. Even the charitable—if not gullible—Garibaldi, long flattered by Terzaghi, had complimented Celso Ceretti on his condemnation of Terzaghi as an *agent provocateur* in police employ. In his newly founded newspaper, *La Discussione,* Terzaghi announced in September, 1873, that he had moved "bag and baggage" into the Marxist camp. Only a few weeks later, John Becker, now a Marxist luminary, urged the secretary-general of the I.W.A. to get in touch with Terzaghi without delay, "for I have reason to believe that something can be done in Italy with this fellow."

THE CONSOLIDATION OF BAKUNINISM

With respect to propaganda and organizational activity in Italy, practically all the energy expended in the name of socialism was that of the anarchists. It was their efforts, not those of the few lukewarm supporters of the General Coun-

cil, that had the government worried, Engels' wishful thinking to the contrary. In the months following the St. Imier
Congress, the key organizer and propagandist of the anarchist
International in Italy was Andrea Costa. Fanelli, Malatesta,
Cafiero, Nabruzzi, and Pezza left Switzerland for Italy after
the St. Imier meeting, but Costa remained behind, planning
the transformation of the Italian sections into a revolutionary
Apparat and elaborating, with Bakunin, a thoroughgoing
anarchist program as a guide for revolutionary action. "Since
we have full confidence in the instincts of the popular multitudes," the document stated, "our revolutionary method
consists of unleashing what are called the *brutal passions* and
the destruction of what, in the same bourgeois language, is
called *public order.*" By early October, Bakunin and Costa
had put together the first issue of *La Rivoluzione Sociale,* a
newspaper intended for clandestine distribution in Italy. The
warning that violence was to be the fruit of Italian socialist
unification again appeared: "Today, propaganda no longer
suffices, now we need to organize ourselves for the struggle."
And when the Italian sections were asked to support a republican mass meeting in favor of universal suffrage, to be held
in the Roman Colosseum in November, 1872, it was Costa
who spoke for the Italian Federation, as well as his home-
town section of Imola, when he signed a rebuff stating that
the anarchist policy was "negative," and that "the emancipation of the workers can be obtained only through the spontaneous federation of the workers' forces, freely constituted,
and not by means of a government or a constitution hier-
archically organized [*dall'alto al basso*]."

From his retreat in Locarno, Bakunin spurred his Italian
disciples to prepare for the day of social redemption, which,
to judge from his diary entries of the period, was to coincide
with the outbreak of several simultaneous uprisings in western Europe. The Swiss, Spanish, Belgian, and Italian anarchists, his most convinced followers, received lengthy collective
letters from the Russian in November. Cafiero conferred with
Bakunin for a week early in November; Fanelli called again
on November 25–27; from December 25–28, Cafiero, Fanelli, and Carmelo Palladino (the latter's first personal contact with the Russian), "approved a decision of a very secret character," which Bakunin's biographer concludes was a
project for Cafiero to buy a large Swiss residence near the

Italian border to serve as a conspiratorial headquarters for
the Italian anarchists and as a rent-free home for the chroni-
cally penurious Bakunin, who would appear as the nominal
owner of the property and provide a front of bourgeois
respectability vis-à-vis the Swiss authorities. For the first
time, two other Italian socialists' names appear in Bakunin's
diary entry of the 30th: Chiarini and Orsone, "Romagnols
of Faenza," with whom Bakunin had "fraternization."

On January 8 the anarchists lost one of their most vigorous
propagandists when Vincenzo Pezza died of consumption in
Naples. The authorities refused burial in the local Catholic
cemetery, but, under pressure from Pezza's friends, agreed
to allow interment in a peripheral area reserved for stillborn
infants, justifying the decision, it was said, on the grounds
that "he who has no religion is like one who has never lived."

As decided at Rimini, the Italian Federation's correspondence commission, early in January, 1873, convoked a second national congress in Mirandola "to affirm once more
truth, justice, and revolutionary morality, to tighten even
more the bonds of solidarity with the sister [foreign] federations, . . . to propose . . . the spontaneous union of the
workers' forces in anarchy and collectivism." Since the congress was to convene on March 15, the police had more than
enough time to make their own arrangements to forestall
any such gathering of subversives. The Mirandola section
was dissolved on March 12, as it was completing final arrangements. Celso Ceretti, member of the statistical commission, was hauled off to the police station, along with the
revealing documents he had compiled concerning the Italian
Federation. Most of the delegates to the projected congress
were diverted in time from Mirandola by the members of
the correspondence commission, so on the scheduled opening
day, 53 delegates, representing about 150 sections, met in
Bologna. On the night of the 16th, the second day of the
scheduled three-day meeting, the Bologna police broke in
and arrested Cafiero, Costa, Malatesta, and several others.
Again the conferees moved their meeting to another locale
and continued their deliberations. The Bologna, San Giovanni in Persiceto, Modena, Parma, and Imola sections
were immediately dissolved by the police, and the arrested
members imprisoned for several weeks. From the Ministry

of Interior all provincial authorities received an order to
extirpate the Italian Federation at the roots.

Government repression had little dampening effect on the
Bologna delegates. They declared:

> It is logical that the State persecutes us, . . . the con-
> sciousness of its imminent disappearance causes it to see
> an enemy in every worker. . . . we are not disturbed by
> this recrudescence of persecution, and we calmly wait for
> the work of the bourgeoisie to hasten our turn. . . . The
> arrogance of which our [arrested] comrades are victims
> shows once more how legitimate is the struggle for social
> emancipation; [the congress] sends a fraternal salute to
> the imprisoned friends but does not lament for them,
> since they are undergoing the consequences of their con-
> victions, consequences that none of the members of the
> Congress fear to affront.

The Rimini and St. Imier congresses of the preceding
summer had slammed the door in the face of Marx and his
friends, but the Bologna conferees locked it securely. The
perennial charges of authoritarianism against the General
Council were renewed, the Rimini and St. Imier resolutions
reconfirmed, and the formal excommunication pronounced
by the Hague Congress of September, 1872, declared invalid,
so far as the Italian Federation was concerned. In harmony
with their oft-repeated principle of sectional autonomy and
their insistence that general congress decisions not bind
member sections and federations, the Bologna meeting submitted its resolutions to the approval of all member sections
of the peninsula. In defining their anarchist principles, the
delegates called themselves atheist, materialist, antistatist,
federalist, collectivist, and antipolitical. No political action
has merit, "other than that which . . . directly conduces
to the actuation of [anarchist] principles." It followed that
"any cooperation or complicity with the political intrigues
of the bourgeoisie, even though called democratic and revolutionary," is to be rejected.

Bakunin's recurrent theme of enlisting the aid of the peasants was repeated in Resolution IX, which insisted that
proletarian emancipation is impossible without "the com-

plete fraternization" of city and country workers. The peasants should be propagandized by their city cousins, since "fourteen million peasants in Lombardy and the southern provinces are in agony because of fever and hunger and anxiously wait the hour of emancipation."

Finally, in a secret session, the Congress heard the charges against Terzaghi and decreed his expulsion from the Italian International and the post he had held since Rimini on the statistical commission, a vantage point unequalled for purposes of keeping the police informed on the spread of Internationalism in the peninsula. He managed to organize a small group of dissident socialists in Turin during the following months, but the Bologna Congress truncated his effective interference in the development of Italian socialism.

In addition to confirming the Italian socialists in their anarchist orientation, the Bologna Congress, by engendering government reprisals, focused popular attention on the Italian Federation as an outlet for dissatisfaction with a deteriorating economic situation. Released from jail, Bakunin's corps of agitators gave their all to maintaining that focus. Cafiero, though not contributing directly to this effort, spent most of the summer in Barletta, fighting for his share of the legacy left by his wealthy father, recently deceased. The money, of course, he intended to put at the disposal of the social revolution. When the Spanish insurrection broke out on July 9, Bakunin, anxious to show himself on the barricades, sent Malatesta to Barletta to ask Cafiero for traveling expenses, but the local police picked up the Russian's emissary the day after his arrival and started him on a six months' jail term.

Cafiero, advised of Bakunin's intentions, wrote the Russian immediately, begging him—according to Bakunin's account —not to risk his "precious person" in the Spanish enterprise. In August, when Cafiero finally arrived back in Locarno with money in hand, the Spanish affair no longer looked promising, but by this time Bakunin had another use for the Pugliese's wealth: he had contracted for the purchase of a dilapidated villa called the "Baronata," situated on a rocky hillside at the northern tip of Lake Verbano, just inside the Swiss border. Cafiero's dream of a revolutionary nerve center and hideout for Italian anarchists had at last become a reality. As agreed by Cafiero, Bakunin moved in as the nominal proprietor, to give the appearance of "a tired and disgusted revolutionary who, . . . after having lost his illusions, throws himself with passion into the material interests of property and family." The threadbare Russian agitator was to play the role with a vengeance. For his part, Cafiero made an initial payment of 14,000 francs on the property— only the first of many expenditures to establish headquarters for the social revolution.

Once out of jail, Andrea Costa resumed a feverish correspondence with sections all over the peninsula, advising, scolding, and urging the spread of anarchist principles and the organization of new sections. The revolutionary appeal to the Italian peasants and the history of police persecution of the International that appeared in the *Bollettino della Federazione Italiana* (May, 1873) may well have come from Costa's prolific pen. On July 4 he wrote the Jura anarchists:

> The Italian Federation, it is true, does not have the formidable organization of the Spanish Federation; but our principles are extremely diffused among the people and the revolutionary instincts of the Italian proletarians are better. . . . Our people are more mature than is thought, and secular servitude has not enervated revolutionary instincts among the manual workers, particularly in the small localities and . . . in the countryside.

On the organizational level, regional propaganda commissions were established throughout the country, spurring new sections into being, grouping them into local and regional federations. On June 26 the Italian correspondence commission notified the Swiss anarchists of twenty new sections and a new socialist newspaper, *Il Risveglio* of Siena. On July 26 at San Pietro in Vincoli, the Romagnol Federation was formed; on August 10, in a congress at Pietra la Croce, the Marchigian-Umbrian Federation was launched. Costa was on hand for both occasions. A few days after he advised the Florentine socialists to take a similar initiative, the local Section of Socialist Propaganda issued a circular convoking a congress to unite all Tuscan sections into a regional federation.

When the anarchist international congress convened in a

Geneva beer hall on September 1, 1873, Costa, Cesare Bert, Victor Cyrille, and Francesco Mattei represented Italy. England, France, Belgium, Holland, the Swiss Jura, and Spain had a total of nineteen delegates on hand—a formidable showing, in terms of geographical coverage, that contrasted sharply with the poorly attended and unrepresentative Marxist congress held in the same city a few days later —a "fiasco," as Marx admitted. Calling their meeting the "Sixth General Congress of the International," the anarchists revised the general statutes of the I.W.A. by giving the sections and federations full autonomy, abolished the General Council and denied general congresses the right to legislate in matters of principle.

In reporting on the development of the Italian International, Costa said it owed its existence to Mazzini's anti-Communard campaign. Despite the elimination of the Marxist opposition, enemies were still plentiful: the government, priests, "intransigents" (moderate socialists), Mazzinians ("believers in the emancipation of the workers by means of the social republic"), and Garibaldians (partisans of equivocation who "tend to substitute the prestige of one man for the strength of the Association," promoters of military dictatorship). The progress of the Italian International depended on acting revolutionarily; Italian workers wanted struggle, not theories.

With experience, Costa was to alter radically his faith in violence and insurrectionism, but for the rest of his life he was to support—often under heavy pressure—the view he expressed when the delegates asked themselves whether a distinction should be made, for purposes of admission to the International, between manual workers and "workers of the mind," i.e., bourgeois intellectuals sympathetic to the cause of the social revolution:

. . . I believe that one would restrain enormously the forces of revolution by eliminating what are called the workers of thought. When one wishes to make revolution, no force must be rejected. And I would add that if you refuse to accept all revolutionary forces, you risk seeing turn against you, at a certain moment, the forces that you have repelled. . . .

The goal of the International is the abolition of classes

and the establishment of human fraternity. Would it be
consistent with our goal to consecrate in the very bosom
of our association this distinction between classes that
we wish to abolish? How can the bourgeois be expected
to learn to sympathize with the workers and to share
their aspirations, if the workers reject them? For me,
there are only two categories of men, those who want
the revolution and those who do not; [and] there are
some bourgeois who want the revolution much more
energetically and seriously than certain workers.

Costa's premise that the bourgeois could be taught "to
sympathize with the workers and to share their aspirations"
might have been a page taken from Mazzini. But where
Mazzini had suggested that the teachers "express [their]
needs and ideas . . . without anger, without aggressiveness,
without threatening," we find Costa speaking of "the immediate struggle" and "the spontaneous uprising of the popular
multitudes, revolting to overthrow all bourgeois institutions."
The idea was echoed in Costa's report on the Geneva Congress, directed to his Italian comrades: "While our adversaries of all shades believe themselves more secure than ever
in their positions of privilege, the Italian proletariat musters
its forces, closes its ranks and awaits the first occasion to be
able to show the bourgeoisie that it knows how to do
something."
In the winter of 1873–74, Costa and his fellow Italian
anarchists were completely wedded to the notion of the
inevitability of imminent social revolution, regardless of the
illogicality of coupling Costa's essentially *anticlassista* orientation with the preaching of class warfare. The contradiction
on a theoretical plane, however, mirrored a certain incapacity
to square thought and action, to realize that effective revolutionary action depends, in a large measure, on a certain
indispensable minimum of consistency in revolutionary
theory. Costa and his friends denied the need of any theory
at all: "The Italian workers are not greatly concerned with
theories, . . . they desire struggle." And if the anarchists
excluded proletarian political action as a compromise with
the principle of authority, embodied in the state, they
spurned, with equal vigor, trade unionism as a method of
struggle. To Costa, the Italian proletariat's lack of economic

organization, far from being a disadvantage, was actually a virtue from the social revolutionary point of view. On this score, Costa revealed the full measure of the anarchist mystique, the essential romanticism of the faith in the revolutionary spontaneity of the economically oppressed. In Italy, he wrote in November, 1873:

> . . . we do not have . . . great industrial centers, where life in common is a necessity, where association is the indispensable condition of labor. In Italy, except in some localities, each one works in his own home and on his own account; . . . there exist among [the workers] no relations except physical proximity, community of interests, the desire to be emancipated, revolutionary passion. In such a state of affairs, economic organization is very difficult; but the revolutionaries lose nothing by it; on the contrary, in this economic isolation of the worker, needs make themselves felt all the more, for him the realization of our ideas is an imperious necessity, which we will be forced to obey. For the Italian proletarian, solidarity consists precisely in this sharing of woes, hopes, defeats, victories, in harmony and in the spontaneous uprising of all the living forces of social revolution, and not in a more or less mechanical assembling of all the forces of production.

On this set of assumptions was based the anarchist attempt at "social liquidation" in the summer of 1874.

Samuel Yellen

American Propagandists of the Deed [1]

Samuel Yellen (1906 ——) Yellen was born in Vilna, Russia, in 1906. He has taught Creative Writing, American Literature, and English Lyrical Poetry. He is Professor of English at Indiana University and the author of *American Labor Struggles* and *In the House and Out and Other Poems*.

[1] From *American Labor Struggles,* by Samuel Yellen. N.Y.: Harcourt, Brace & World Inc., Copyright 1936. Reprinted by permission of the publisher.

ANARCHISM AND THE CHICAGO IDEA

Just as the panic of 1873 marked the birth of a national and self-conscious labor movement, it also marked the birth of a practical and realistic socialism, to replace the remote utopian wishes of the earlier socialists, contented with lofty intellectual conversations and romantic essays. From this time the socialists, rather than hope idealistically for the morrow, began to act in the today by organizing hunger parades, unemployed demonstrations, strikes, mass meetings, and political tickets. At first they operated as the Workingmen's Party of the United States, which was formed in 1876 and which played, as we have seen, a considerable part in the railroad strikes of 1877, especially in Chicago and St. Louis. After the failure of the railroad strikes the Workingmen's Party was reorganized as the Socialist Labor Party, with political action as its principal function, although friendly relations with trade unions were to be maintained. When this change was made, the National Executive Committee of the Socialist Labor Party ordered the holding of mass meetings to present to legislative bodies resolutions for an eight-hour law, for the abolition of all conspiracy acts directed against labor, and for the purchase of railway and telegraph lines by the federal government.

But the socialist movement in America reflected the schism that had taken place in the First International, and split into two factions over questions of tactics and method. The Internationalists held for secret arming and direct preparation for the social revolution, with trade unionism and politics as auxiliary activities to be strictly watched lest they led into the treacherous waters of opportunism. The Lassalleans, on the other hand, sought the gradual achievement of a new society through education, political organization, and parliamentary procedure. For a few years the Lassalleans controlled the policies of the party, and even Chicago, the stronghold of the trade union and the revolutionary elements, dedicated itself to the ballot. A controversy soon arose, however, over the workingmen's military organizations. The largest of these, the *Lehr und Wehr Verein,* had been formed by the German Socialists in Chicago during 1875 as a protection against the physical intimidation of the older political parties at the polls; the need for its protection had further been shown during a strike of cabinetmakers in July, 1877, when the police raided peaceful meetings and attacked those present with outrageous brutality. A repudiation, therefore, of all such military organizations by the National Executive Committee of the Socialist Labor Party antagonized still more the Chicago revolutionary element. This hostility grew acute in 1880 after the discouraging slump of the socialist vote in the elections; and the revolutionaries denounced the moderates for a compromise made that year with the Greenback Party. Moreover, the single socialist alderman reelected in Chicago was barred from taking his seat, through tricky manipulation by the Democratic city council; and the revolutionaries pointed out the futility of attempting to win a new society through the ballot box. A great influx of refugees from the German antisocialist decree of 1878 augmented the revolutionary groups, and led finally to a convention of them in October, 1881, at Chicago.

Not until the arrival of Johann Most in America did the revolutionary groups precipitate into an active movement. The appearance of Most—disciple of Bakunin and Nechayeff, and founder of the anarchistic International Working People's Association, known then as the Black International—swept aside the parliamentary socialists. In theory Most was not a pure anarchist; nevertheless, in practice he advocated the anarchist tactics of terroristic action against Church and State by the individual on his own initiative, so that the entire movement might not be endangered if the actor in any single deed were captured. Arms alone, he believed, secured for the worker some sort of equality with the police and troops. He issued a pamphlet: *Science of Revolutionary Warfare. Manual for instruction in the use and preparation of nitro-glycerine and dynamite, gun cotton, fulminating mercury, bombs, fuse, poisons, etc., etc.* He urged the formation of rifle corps and the extermination of the "miserable brood," the "reptile brood," the "race of parasites." In another pamphlet, *Beast of Property,* he declared that with existing society there could be no compromise, only relentless war until the beast of property "has been pursued to its last lurking place and totally destroyed."

Spurred on by the agitational energy of Most, representatives from revolutionary antiparliamentary groups in 26 cities convened in Pittsburgh on October 14, 1883, to reorganize the International Working People's Association. Here again there were two distinct elements, united only by their opposition to political action. The delegates from New York and the eastern cities, led by Most, favored the individualistic tactics of anarchism; but those from Chicago and the western cities, under the guidance of Albert Parsons and August Spies, held for a mixture of anarchism and syndicalism that came to be known as the "Chicago idea." This modification actually approached syndicalism closer than it did anarchism, inasmuch as it recognized the trade union as the "embryonic group" of the future society and as the fighting unit against capitalism. However, the trade union was not to contend for the superficial and opportunistic benefits of high wages and short hours; it was to be satisfied with nothing less than the complete extinction of capitalism and the formation of a free society. In the struggle with capitalism it was not to resort to political action, was to distrust all central authority, and was to guard against betrayals by its leadership. All its faith was to rest in the direct action of the rank and file. Only two principles were lacking to make the "Chicago idea" conform with modern syndicalism: the general strike and sabotage, neither at that time theoretically developed.

Since the western faction was by far the larger, the convention confirmed the importance of the trade union. And direct action—force, violence—was the core of the tactics to be employed. The platform of the International, published in the *Alarm,* a Chicago paper edited by Parsons, read in part:

> The present order of society is based upon the spoliation of the non-propertied by the property owners, the capitalists buy the labor of the poor for wages, at the mere cost of living, taking all the surplus of labor. . . . Thus while the poor are increasingly deprived the opportunities of advancement, the rich grow richer through increasing robbery. . . . This system is unjust, insane, and murderous. Therefore those who suffer under it, and do not wish to be responsible for its continuance, ought to strive for its

destruction by all means and with their utmost energy.
. . . The laborers can look for aid from no outside source
in their fight against the existing system, but must achieve
deliverance through their own exertions. Hitherto, no
privileged class have relinquished tyranny, nor will the
capitalists of today forego their privilege and authority
without compulsion. . . . It is therefore self-evident that
the fight of proletarianism against the bourgeoisie must
have a violent revolutionary character; that wage conflicts
cannot lead to the goal. . . . Under all these circumstances, there is only one remedy left—force. . . . Agitation to organize, organizations for the purpose of rebellion, this is the course if the workingmen would rid themselves of their chains.

Here was a program advocating without camouflage the
annihilation of the existing economic and political order, a
program that could not be ignored.

In Chicago, thanks to the long history of police atrocities,
many workers joined the International, so that this city
alone had more than one-third of the 5,000 to 6,000 members. Moreover, the most able and intelligent leaders were
here—men like Parsons, Spies, Samuel Fielden, and Michael
Schwab. In fact, the Internationalists in Chicago published
five papers: the *Alarm* in English, with an edition of 2,000
twice a month; in German, the daily *Chicagoer Arbeiter-
Zeitung*, edited by Spies, with an edition of 3,600, the
Fackel, and the *Vorbote;* and in Bohemian, the *Budoucnost*.
This revolutionary nucleus quickly penetrated the trade-
union movement. Under its influence the local Progressive
Cigar Makers' Union in June, 1884, called upon all the
unions in the city to secede from the conservative Amalgamated Trades and Labor Assembly and to organize a new
Central Labor Union with a militant policy. Four German
unions answered the call—the metal workers, butchers, car-
penters and joiners, and cabinetmakers—and a declaration
of principles was adopted: that all land is a social heritage,
that all wealth is created by labor, that between labor and
capital there can be no harmony, and that every worker
ought to cut loose from the capitalist political parties and
devote himself to the trade union. From its inception the
Central Labor Union was in communication with the Inter-

nationalist group. The Socialist Labor Party, on the other hand, remained with the Amalgamated Trades and Labor Assembly.

For a year the growth of the new Central Labor Union was slow; nevertheless, by the end of 1885 it had 13 unions, whereas the Amalgamated Assembly had 19. Within a few months, however, by April, 1886, the Central Labor Union outstripped its rival and consisted of 22 unions, among which were the 11 largest in the city. It retained its contact with the International and united with it in processions and mass meetings. It began strong agitation for the eight-hour day, although its motives were different from those of the conservative Amalgamated Assembly and the Knights of Labor, since it regarded as paramount, not the attainment of the shorter working day, but the common labor front and the class struggle. It adopted the following resolution, introduced by Spies in October, 1885:

> Be it Resolved, That we urgently call upon the wage-earning class to arm itself in order to be able to put forth against their exploiters such an argument which alone can be effective: *Violence,* and further be it Resolved, that notwithstanding that we expect very little from the introduction of the eight-hour day, we firmly promise to assist our more backward brethren in this class struggle with all means and power at our disposal, so long as they will continue to show an open and resolute front to our common oppressors, the aristocratic vagabonds and the exploiters. Our war cry is "Death to the foes of the human race."

The initiative in the eight-hour movement in Chicago was left in the hands of an Eight-Hour Association, composed of the Amalgamated Assembly, the Socialist Labor Party, and the Knights of Labor, but the Central Labor Union cooperated energetically. On the Sunday preceding May 1 it organized a huge eight-hour demonstration, in which 25,000 took part, and at which Parsons, Spies, Fielden, and Schwab spoke. When the day of the struggle arrived, the main portion of the eight-hour movement in Chicago acted under the banner of the Central Labor Union and the International.

THE BOMB IS THROWN

The strike opened in Chicago with a display of great strength and much promise of success. Nearly 40,000 workers walked out on May 1 as prearranged, and the number jumped to 65,000 within three or four days. Nor was this the full strength of the movement in the city: more than 45,000 were granted a shorter working day without striking, the bulk of them—35,000—workers in the packinghouses. In addition, there were already several thousand men on strike at the Lake Shore, the Wabash, the Chicago, Milwaukee, and St. Paul, and other freight yards in protest against the hiring of non-union labor. With such a mass movement on foot, Chief of Police Ebersold apprehended difficulties and called upon the entire detective and police force to be on duty Saturday, May 1; and his face was augmented by Pinkerton detectives previously engaged by the railroads, and by special deputies, many of whom were selected from the Grand Army of the Potomac. In spite of these martial preparations, Saturday passed peacefully. The city, with hundreds of factories idle and thousands of strikers and their families promenading the streets, had a holiday appearance. There were processions and mass meetings, addressed in Bohemian, Polish, German, and English.

Faced with a strike of unexpected power and solidarity, the leading businessmen and manufacturers united to crush it. On April 27 the Western Boot and Shoe Manufacturers Association, with 60 firms represented in person and 160 by letter, was formed in Chicago for combined action. The chief iron and steel foundries, as also the copper and brass, declared that they would reject the eight-hour demand. A session of the principal planing mills was held on the morning of May 1 at the office of Felix Lang to determine procedure against the strikers. In the evening these were joined at the Sherman Hotel by all the lumber yards and box factories, and the lumber industry in concert decided to grant no concessions to the workmen. Nevertheless, by Monday, May 3, the spread of the strike was alarming. Lumber-laden craft blocked the river near the Lumber Exchange, and 300 more vessels with cargoes of lumber were expected to join the idle fleet. The building interests, then enjoying a boom, were suddenly paralyzed. The great metal foundries and the vast freight yards were tied up. To break the strike, aggressive action was needed. On Monday police clubs began to scatter processions and meetings.

That afternoon serious trouble arose at the McCormick Harvester Works. The soreness here was old. It had begun in the middle of February, when Cyrus McCormick locked out his 1,400 employees in reply to a demand by the men that the company quit its discrimination against certain of their fellows who had taken part in a former strike at the plant. In the following two months strikebreakers, Pinkertons, and police had attacked the locked-out men with wanton savagery. Bogart and Thompson say of this period:

> The police force of Chicago reflected the hostility of the employing class, regarding strikes *per se* as evidence that the men had placed themselves in opposition to law and order. During these months of unrest it became a pastime for a squad of mounted police, or a detachment in close formation, to disperse with the billy any gathering of workingmen. The billy was an impartial instrument: men, women, children, and shopkeeping bystanders alike composed its harvest. It was the police, aided by the Pinkertons, who added the great leaven of bitterness to the contest. To the workingmen they furnished concrete and hateful examples of the autocracy against which they protested.

But a greater police provocation was reserved for Monday afternoon, May 3. At this time 6,000 striking lumber-shovers met near Black Road, about a quarter of a mile north of the McCormick works, to appoint a committee to be sent to the lumberyard owners. While August Spies was addressing the meeting, a group of some 200 detached itself spontaneously from the crowd of strikers, marched to McCormick's, and heckled and attacked the scabs, who were just then leaving for their homes. Within 10 or 15 minutes there were more than 200 policemen on the spot. Meanwhile Spies, who was still speaking, and the strikers at the meeting, seeing patrol wagons and hearing gunfire, started toward McCormick's, but were met by the police. The clubs and

guns broke up the crowd; the police fired deliberately into
the running strikers, so that at least four were killed and
many wounded.

Spies, indignant at this fresh outrage, hurried to the
printing shop of the *Arbeiter-Zeitung* and issued a circular
in both English and German:

REVENGE!
WORKINGMEN, TO ARMS!!!
    The masters sent out their bloodhounds—the police;
they killed six of your brothers at McCormicks this afternoon. They killed the poor wretches because they, like
you, had the courage to disobey the supreme will of your
bosses. They killed them because they dared ask for the
shortening of the hours of toil. They killed them to show
you, *"Free* American Citizens" that you must be satisfied
and contented with whatever your bosses condescend to
allow you, or you will get killed!
    You have for years endured the most abject humilia-
tions; you have for years suffered unmeasurable iniquities;
you have worked yourself to death; you have endured the
pangs of want and hunger; your Children you have sacrificed to the factory lord—in short: you have been miserable and obedient slave[s] all these years: Why? To satisfy
the insatiable greed, to fill the coffers of your lazy thieving
master? When you ask them now to lessen your burdens,
he sends his bloodhounds out to shoot you, kill you!
    If you are men, if you are the sons of your grand sires,
who have shed their blood to free you, then you will rise in
your might, Hercules, and destroy the hideous monster
that seeks to destroy you. To arms we call you, to arms!
                                            YOUR BROTHERS.

A second circular called for a protest mass meeting the following evening in the old Haymarket on Randolph Street.

The morning of Tuesday, May 4, saw a police attack upon
a column of 3,000 strikers near Thirty-Fifth Street. Attacks
upon gatherings of strikers continued during the afternoon,
in particular one at Eighteenth and Morgan in the southwest
part of the city. Mayor Carter H. Harrison, however, gave
permission for the mass meeting that evening, and at 7:30

people began to assemble in Haymarket Square, the center
of the lumberyard and packinghouse district. Between eight
and nine o'clock about 3,000 persons were present, among
them Mayor Harrison, who attended as a spectator to see
that order was maintained. Only half a block distant was the
Desplaines Street police station, where a good-sized detail
of police was in readiness. The meeting was very quiet. Spies
addressed the crowd from a wagon in front of the Crane
Bros. factory. Then Parsons spoke, confining himself to the
eight-hour demand; he was followed by Fielden. Toward
10 o'clock a threatening rainstorm began to disperse the
gathering; by that time Spies and Parsons had left. Only
Fielden remained to speak to the few hundred who had not
yet gone. Mayor Harrison, having found the meeting peaceful and believing that all was over, left shortly after 10
o'clock, called in at the Desplaines Street station to report
that there had been no trouble, and went home to bed.

A few minutes after the mayor left, however, Inspector
John Bonfield, hated throughout the city for his record of
extreme brutality, led a detachment of 180 policemen to
break up what remained of the meeting. There was no excuse for this expedition, except Bonfield's desire for another
head-clubbing party, according to Governor Altgeld, who
declared " . . . that Capt. Bonfield is the man who is really
responsible for the death of the police officers." The police
halted a short distance from the speakers' wagon, and
Captain Ward commanded the gathering to disperse. Fielden
cried out that it was a peaceable meeting. As Captain Ward
turned to give an order to his men, a bomb was thrown from
a point on the sidewalk a little south of the wagon. It exploded in the midst of the policemen and wounded 66, of
whom seven later died. The police immediately opened fire
hysterically and shot round after round into the crowd, killing several and wounding 200. The neighborhood was
thrown into terror. Doctors were telephoned. Drugstores
were crowded with the wounded.

Who threw the bomb is still undetermined. There are three
possibilities. 1) Governor Altgeld, in his pardon message
of 1893, contended that the bomb was thrown by someone
as reprisal for all the atrocities committed by Bonfield and
the police:

. . . it is shown here that the bomb was, in all probability, thrown by someone seeking personal revenge; that a course had been pursued by the authorities which would naturally cause this; that for a number of years prior to the Haymarket affair there had been labor troubles, and in several cases a number of laboring people, guilty of no offense, had been shot down in cold blood by Pinkerton men, and none of the murderers were brought to justice. The evidence taken at coroners' inquests and presented here, shows that in at least two cases men were fired on and killed when they were running away, and there was consequently no occasion to shoot, yet nobody was punished; that in Chicago there had been a number of strikes in which some of the police not only took sides against the men, but without any authority of law invaded and broke up peaceable meetings, and in scores of cases brutally clubbed people who were guilty of no offense whatever.

2) The possibility of an *agent provocateur* must not be dismissed offhand. The police officials in Chicago were at this time quite equal to such a scheme. On the morning after the bombing, Inspector Bonfield declared:

We will take active measures to catch the leaders in this business. *The action of last night will show that their bombshell and dynamite talk has not been empty vaporings.* . . . The attack on us was brutal and cowardly. . . . [Roman mine.]

The emphasized sentence indicates perhaps an antecedent wish to prove that the "dynamite talk" was not "empty vaporings."

3) There is a strong possibility that Rudolph Schnaubelt, an anarchist and brother-in-law to Michael Schwab, was guilty. The circumstance that he was twice arrested and both times released, at a period when the police were arresting and holding all the anarchists and sympathizers they could lay their hands on, arouses the suspicion, almost the certainty, that the police wanted him out of the way, in order that they might be able to condemn the eight more important revolutionary leaders. In this connection Bogart and Thompson report:

In a statement now on record in the Illinois Historical Survey, made by Mr. Wallace Rice, June 25, 1919, and concurred in by Mr. Clarence S. Darrow and Mr. George A. Schilling, all of whom were in a position to know the inside history of the case, Mr. Rice says: "It was the impression of all the newspaper men informed in the premises that the fatal bomb was made by Louis Lingg and thrown by Rudolph Schnaubelt. Many of them believed further that this fact was also known to the police and that Schnaubelt was allowed to go after they had taken him into custody because he could not be connected in any way with the other men afterward condemned, with the possible exception of Lingg and of Michael Schwab, who was husband to Schnaubelt's sister. Lingg, however, was thought to be the only one of the defendants who had guilty knowledge of the bomb and its throwing. Schnaubelt, after his release by the police, went as far and as fast from the scene of the crime as he could, and when an indictment was found against him at last, was believed to be in southern California near the Mexican line, whence he could easily escape to another country. . . ."

Judge Gary, when reviewing the case seven years after the trial, admitted the strong likelihood of Schnaubelt's guilt, and the release twice by the police of the man who was the chief actual suspect. Gary added: "But whether Schnaubelt or some other person threw the bomb, is not an important question."

The newspapers, not only in Chicago, but everywhere, assumed an attitude of panic. They demanded the instantaneous execution of all subversive persons. Within a few days the police arrested the chief anarchists and revolutionaries in the city—Spies, Fielden, Schwab, Adolph Fischer, George Engel, Louis Lingg, Oscar Neebe; and many others, including the 25 printers in the *Arbeiter-Zeitung* shop, were taken into custody. The only one missing was Parsons, whom the police were unable to capture, notwithstanding a rigorous hunt. When the death of police officer Mathias J. Degan was announced, the press cried for speedy indictments by the grand jury. It kept fanning for weeks the feeling of terror aroused in the public. Its headlines screamed: Bloody Brutes, Red Ruffians, Red Ragsters, Bomb Makers, Red Flagsters,

Dynamarchists, Bloody Monsters, Bomb Slingers, Bomb Throwers. The *Chicago Tribune* wrote, May 6: "These serpents have been warmed and nourished in the sunshine of toleration until at last they have been emboldened to strike at society, law, order, and government." The *Chicago Herald,* May 6: "The rabble whom Spies and Fielden stimulated to murder are not Americans. They are offscourings of Europe who have sought these shores to abuse the hospitality and defy the authority of the country." The *Chicago Inter-Ocean,* May 6: "For months and years these pestiferous fellows have uttered their seditious and dangerous doctrines." The *Chicago Journal,* May 7: "Justice should be prompt in dealing with the arrested anarchists. The law regarding accessories to crime in this State is so plain that their trials will be short."

Stimulation of public hysteria became the main activity of the police. Inspector Bonfield and Captain Schaack, in particular, wanted to sustain the ferment of dread and hatred after the bomb-throwing, in order to keep the citizenry excited. Three years later, in an interview, Chief of Police Ebersold confessed: "It was my policy to quiet matters down as soon as possible after the 4th of May [1886]. The general unsettled state of things was an injury to Chicago. On the other hand, Capt. Schaack wanted to keep things stirring. He wanted bombs to be found here, there, all around, everywhere. . . . *After we got the anarchist societies broken up, Schaack wanted to send out men to again organize new societies right away."* The police seized the subscription lists of the *Arbeiter-Zeitung* and instituted a long series of raids. Meeting halls, printing offices, and private homes were broken into and searched; everyone suspected of the remotest connection with the radical movement was held. The police saw to it that the raids were fertile. Each day there were discovered ammunition, rifles, swords, muskets, pistols, bayonets, billies, anarchist literature, red flags, incendiary banners, cartridges, dirks, bullets, bulk lead, materials for manufacturing torpedoes, bullet molds, dynamite, bombs, shells, percussion caps, infernal engines, secret trapdoors, underground rifle ranges. Each find announced by the police was well played up by the press. A rumor was spread that Herr Most was coming from New York, evidently to take charge of further assassinations; and the police even pro-

duced a show of detectives at the railroad station. A crowd
gathered to await the dangerous arrival, but Herr Most did
not appear. The proper atmosphere for the trial was being
carefully prepared.

"LET THE VOICE OF THE PEOPLE BE HEARD!"

When the grand jury met in the middle of May, it quickly
indicted August Spies, Michael Schwab, Samuel Fielden,
Albert R. Parsons, Adolph Fischer, George Engel, Louis
Lingg, and Oscar Neebe, all prominent in the International,
for the murder of Mathias J. Degan on May 4. The trial was
set for June 21 at the criminal court of Cook County, with
Joseph E. Gary as judge. State's Attorney Julius S. Grinnell took command of the prosecution. The accused men
were represented by William P. Black, William A. Foster,
Sigmund Zeisler, and Moses Salomon. While the police were
making their alarming finds, while the newspapers poured
forth stories of anarchist plots for wholesale murder, and the
public clamored for the immediate execution of the indicted
men, the trial opened. Just as the preliminary examination
of talesmen commenced, the missing Parsons, who had baf-
fled a police search for six weeks, walked into court and surrendered himself for trial, joining his comrades on the defendants' bench.

At the outset two circumstances prevented any approxi-
mation to a fair trial. First, Judge Gary forced all eight defendants to stand trial together, increasing the danger that
all sorts of evidence would be admitted. Second, through an
extraordinary device the jury was packed: the candidates for
the jury were not chosen in the customary manner by drawing names from a box; instead, a special bailiff, nominated
by the State's Attorney, was appointed by the court to select
the candidates. A Chicago businessman, Otis S. Favor, made
affidavit that this bailiff had said to him in the presence of
witnesses: "I am managing this case, and know what I am
about. These fellows are going to be hanged as certain as
death. I am calling such men as the defendants will have to
challenge peremptorily and waste their time and challenges.
Then they will have to take such men as the prosecution
wants." By the adroit questioning of the judge, many who
openly admitted their prejudice against the defendants were

pronounced fit for jury service and had to be peremptorily
challenged by the defense. It took 21 days to select the jury:
981 talesmen were examined. Ultimately the defense exhausted all its peremptory challenges and the final 12 men
were picked, among them a relative of one of the victims of
the bomb.

The introductory speech by State's Attorney Grinnell,
after the presentation of evidence began on July 14, assured
the jury that the man who had thrown the bomb would be
produced. This, of course, the prosecution was unable to do.
It did at first, however, attempt to fabricate, by means of the
testimony of two alleged anarchists who had turned State's
evidence, a terroristic plot for the dynamiting of all police
stations when[ever] the word *"Ruhe"* appeared in the
Arbeiter-Zeitung. Under cross-examination the testimony of
these two witnesses was largely impaired. When this failed,
other strange evidence was disclosed. One witness named
Gilmer, shown by cross-examination to be a professional
liar who had in all likelihood been paid for testifying, swore
that he saw an object resembling a bomb pass between Spies,
Schwab, and Schnaubelt, and that he saw the latter throw
the bomb among the police. Also several policemen tried to
prove that Fielden had fired upon them from behind the
speakers' wagon, but their assertions were contradictory.
Regarding the witnesses and testimony produced by the
State, Governor Altgeld said in his pardon message:

> It is further shown here that much of the evidence given
> at the trial was a pure fabrication; that some of the promi-
> nent police officials, in their zeal, not only terrorized igno-
> rant men by throwing them into prison and threatening
> them with torture if they refused to swear to anything de-
> sired, but that they offered money and employment to
> those who would consent to do this. Further, that they
> deliberately planned to have fictitious conspiracies formed
> in order that they might get the glory of discovering them.
> In addition to the evidence in the record of some witnesses
> who swore that they had been paid small sums of money,
> etc., several documents are here referred to.

In spite of the generation of an emotional fog, the State, as
Altgeld remarks, never discovered who threw the bomb.

Nor was it able to show any specific conspiracy entered into by the accused men.

It soon developed that the eight men were on trial for their ideas, even though the defense was not permitted to introduce testimony concerning the theory of anarchism. On the grounds that the general principles of the anarchists urged the destruction of all capitalists, Judge Gary allowed the prosecution to establish a resultant specific conspiracy. The jury was deluged with readings from inciting articles in the *Alarm* and the *Arbeiter-Zeitung*. Furthermore, the police exhibited on a table before the jury box all fashions of dynamite and bomb, with all their infernal mechanism, although these destructive engines were found often miles from the scene of the bombing and weeks afterward and had no association with the defendants. The display produced the desired effect: it aroused terror. Time and again the defense objected to the presentation of irrelevant evidence whose purpose was the evocation of emotionalism, but it was overruled by the court. In other ways too, as Altgeld later pointed out, Judge Gary revealed his bias. While he confined the defense in its cross-examination to the specific points touched on by the State, he permitted the State to wander to matters entirely foreign to those the witnesses were examined in. Besides, he made insinuating remarks in the hearing of the jury that proved much more damaging than anything the prosecution could have produced. Foster, of the defense counsel, pleaded that there existed no proof of the influence on the bomb thrower of any spoken or written word by the defendants, nor of the instigation of the deed by the defendants. He persisted in conducting the case as one of homicide, since that was the charge; he confined himself to plain facts and law; and he wanted even to admit some criminal folly in the utterances of the defendants, but this they refused to permit.

The summing up before the jury began on August 11. It was concluded by State's Attorney Grinnell, whose final words were: "Law is upon trial. Anarchy is on trial. These men have been selected, picked out by the grand jury and indicted because they were leaders. They are no more guilty than the thousands who follow them. Gentlemen of the jury; convict these men, make examples of them, hang them and you save our institutions, our society." As was foreseen, the jury brought in on August 20 a verdict of guilty and fixed the penalty at hanging for seven of the defendants, the exception, Oscar Neebe, being given 15 years' imprisonment. A motion by the defense in September for a new trial was denied by Judge Gary, and the convicted men were called upon to speak before sentence was pronounced. They delivered eloquent speeches lasting three days, addressed beyond the court to workers everywhere. After a long summary of his beliefs, Spies said:

> Now, these are my ideas. They constitute a part of myself. I cannot divest myself of them, nor would I, if I could. And if you think that you can crush out these ideas that are gaining ground more and more every day, if you think you can crush them out by sending us to the gallows—if you would once more have people to suffer the penalty of death because they have dared to tell the truth—and I defy you to show us where we have told a lie—I say, if death is the penalty for proclaiming the truth, then I will proudly and defiantly pay the costly price! Call your hangman.

George Engel said:

> I hate and combat, not the individual capitalist, but the system that gives him those privileges. My greatest wish is that workingmen may recognize who are their friends and who are their enemies.

And with the defiance he had displayed throughout the trial, the twenty-one year old Lingg said:

> I repeat that I am the enemy of the "order" of today, and I repeat that, with all my powers, so long as breath remains in me, I shall combat it. . . . I despise you. I despise your order; your laws, your force-propped authority. Hang me for it!

On October 9 sentence, as decreed by the jury, was pronounced by Judge Gary.

Execution of the sentences was postponed while the case was carried before the Supreme Court of Illinois. After several months of consideration, the Supreme Court, although it admitted that the trial had not been free of legal error, affirmed in September, 1887, the verdict of the lower court. An attempt to appeal to the Supreme Court of the United States failed when that body decided that it had no jurisdiction. Labor organizations everywhere asked for mercy for the condemned men; the American Federation of Labor adopted such a resolution, while the Noble Order of the Knights of Labor was prevented from doing likewise only through the personal intervention of Powderly, who hated the anarchists and wanted to clear his Order of any association with them. During the last days Fielden and Schwab petitioned for executive clemency and asked for commutation of their sentence. The others demanded liberty or death. Governor Oglesby commuted the sentence of Fielden and Schwab to life imprisonment, and they joined Neebe in the State Penitentiary at Joliet. Lingg escaped the scaffold the day preceding the execution by exploding a dynamite tube in his mouth. The remaining four were hanged on November 11, 1887.

The nooses were quickly adjusted, the caps pulled down, and a hasty movement made for the traps. Then from beneath the hoods came these words:

Spies: "There will be a time when our silence will be more powerful than the voices you strangle today."

Fischer: "Hurrah for anarchy—"

Engel: "Hurrah for anarchy!"

Fischer: "This is the happiest moment of my life!"

Parsons: "Will I be allowed to speak, O men of America? Let me speak, Sheriff Matson! Let the voice of the people be heard! O—"

At the funeral 25,000 working people marched. William P. Black, who had been of the defense counsel, spoke over the graves:

. . . I loved these men. I knew them not until I came to know them in the time of their sore travail and anguish. As months went by and I found in the lives of those with whom I talked the witness of their love for the people, of their patience, gentleness, and courage, my heart was

taken captive in their cause. . . . I say that whatever of
fault may have been in them, these, the people whom they
loved and in whose cause they died, may well close the
volume, and seal up the record, and give our lips to the
praise of their heroic deeds, and their sublime self-
sacrifice.

COLLAPSE OF THE BLACK INTERNATIONAL

A portion of the public fury aroused by the Haymarket
bomb was deflected against the eight-hour strike in progress.
Confusion arose among the working people and their ranks
were split. Using the alleged discoveries of anarchist plots
as an excuse, the police attacked gatherings of strikers even
more savagely than before. Labor leaders were seized without ceremony. Within a week after May 4 the strikers began
to give in and return to their jobs. Many of them, particularly the freight handlers, found their places occupied by
scabs. Nor was this disordered surrender of the shorter day
movement confined to Chicago. *Bradstreet's* reported on
May 22, 1886, that out of the original 190,000 strikers in the
United States, no more than 80,000 remained, many of these
locked out. In Chicago only 16,000 were left of the former
65,000. While it is true that 42,000 of the 190,000 original
strikers in the country won their demands and that 150,000,
as has been stated, were granted shorter hours without striking, these concessions proved short-lived. As soon as the
strength of the movement was spent, the employers retracted
whatever they had granted. In one month the total still retaining the shorter hours either won or granted fell nearly
one-third, from approximately 200,000 to 137,000. By a
lockout in October the Chicago packers took away from their
35,000 employees the eight-hour day that had been conceded
without a strike in May. On January 8, 1887, *Bradstreet's*
was able to report for the nation: "It may be fairly assumed
. . . that so far as the payment of former wages for a shorter
day's work is concerned the grand total of those retaining the
concession will not exceed, if it equals, 15,000."

The eight-hour movement was not all that suffered under
the steady barrage kept up by the press. For many years all
radical theory and practice fell into disfavor with labor

organization. Powderly expressed his extreme antipathy to
the revolutionary elements:

A cardinal principle with the rampant Socialist and
Anarchist is to propagandize on every occasion that presents itself. If a new society of laboring men is established
these extremists become members of it, and attempt to
force their ideas to the front. In canting phrase and with
mock humility they will insinuate themselves into the
good graces of men who would scorn them were they to
disclose their real feelings, and once they gain the good
will of such, they have inserted a wedge between the
members of that society that sooner or later will drive
them apart.

THE SMOOTH-TONGUED ADVOCATE OF ANARCHY seldom
does anything himself toward furthering the ends of the
movement he is a part and parcel of. He secures the
services of dupes who do his bidding, either through
loyalty to principle or ignorance. That they will play on
the ignorance of workingmen is but too true; that they
despise every effort to lift the pall of ignorance that is
lowered over the fortunes of the toilers, is also true. If the
people become educated they will have no use for either
anarchy or monopoly. . . .

The relentless abuse by the newspapers, periodicals, and pul-
pit was more virulent than Powderly's. Cartoons by Thomas
Nast and others pictured bushy-bearded, foreign-looking,
and villainous anarchists deluding the laborer, assassinating
the respectable citizen, or hiding under a bed from the police.
The *Nation* accused the eight convicted anarchists of petty
cowardice, of being "chicken-hearted," for attempting to
appeal their case, instead of hanging bravely and cheerfully
like the more remote and romantic Russian Nihilists.

Some of the assaults upon the radical factions were less
crude, more subtle, veiled by an affected impartiality and
objectivity. Such was the pseudo-scientific study by Professor
Cesare Lombroso in the philosophical journal, the *Monist*,
in which, after an impressive but dubious parade of tables,
figures, and anthropological jargon, he concluded that anarchists and communists are of the criminal type. To arrive

at this conclusion he analyzed the physiognomies of 100 anarchists arrested at Turin, of 50 photographs of communards, and of photographs in Schaack's book about the Chicago anarchists; and he found an abundance of proof in "exaggerated plagiocephaly, facial asymmetry, other cranial anomalies (ultra-brachycephaly, etc.), very large jaw, exaggerated zygomas, enormous frontal sinus, dental anomalies, anomalies of the ears, anomalies of the nose, anomalous coloration of skin, old wounds, tattooing, neuropathological anomalies." It was left for the convicted Michael Schwab, still confined in the Joliet penitentiary, to point out to Professor Lombroso certain fundamental errors: 1) that there most likely exists no anthropological and physical criminal type that is hereditary; 2) that crime is in the main a product of the environment; 3) that in studying physiognomies, one's judgment is influenced by his emotional reactions; 4) that materials may easily and often unconsciously be selected to fit the desired conclusion; 5) that anarchism is not a distinct and definite term that permits the segregation of its supposed followers from those of communism, socialism, liberalism, etc. Nevertheless, Professor Lombroso's study soon filtered down to the more popular journals and newspapers, and furnished "scientific" support for the public attitude toward anarchists and revolutionaries.

Notwithstanding this protracted wave of hatred, an Amnesty Association was formed in 1889 to campaign for the release of Neebe, Fielden, and Schwab. But Governor Fifer, who succeeded Oglesby, refused to consider the matter, and the Amnesty Association had to wait until 1893, when John P. Altgeld became governor of Illinois. A petition bearing 60,000 signatures was presented to him. If he had pardoned the three men as an act of mercy, on the grounds that they had already served seven years in the penitentiary, the community would probably have applauded Altgeld and its conscience would have been put at ease. Instead, he insisted on a thorough investigation and discovered that an irreparable and monstrous legal wrong had been done not only the three men still in prison, but also the other five who were dead. When he wrote his pardon message, with its unanswerable proof that the eight defendants had not been given a fair trial, and that the State had failed to establish any connection whatever between them and the unknown person who threw the Haymarket bomb; when he showed that the court, the jury, and the prosecution had yielded to the hysteria deliberately generated and intensified by the press and the police of Chicago, he actually charged the community with judicial murder. His pardon of Neebe, Fielden, and Schwab, therefore, brought a storm upon his head, second only to that suffered by the anarchists themselves. "But realizing at the outset that the Governor's legal position was impregnable, the outraged guardians of society rushed to their favorite weapon and turned upon Altgeld himself such an intensive and protracted fire of personal vituperation as few other men in public life have ever faced. If his arguments could not be answered, at least his motives might be impugned, his reputation blackened, his political and business fortunes ruined; and to such ends the press, actively or passively abetted by nine-tenths of the most highly respectable persons in American life, bent its efforts with an almost fanatical fervor and persistency."

The radical factions in the labor movement were slow to recover from this period of persecution. After the Haymarket affair the Black International, as the workingmen withdrew in fear, soon dwindled to a small group of intellectuals. Although the modification known as the "Chicago idea" appeared again later, anarchism as a theory and a tactic never regained its hold on the labor movement in the United States. Workmen turned to the more conservative American Federation of Labor, which was able to point back with some satisfaction to the energetic part it had played in the eight-hour movement and to the resolution it had passed for the release of the eight condemned men. But the Noble Order of the Knights of Labor, both because of its official treachery in the strike and its official refusal to petition for the pardoning of the condemned men, was abandoned. Meanwhile, among the working class the executed anarchists were regarded as martyrs to the cause of labor, and their monument at Waldheim Cemetery became a shrine visited by thousands each year.

Barbara W. Tuchman **Anarchism in France** [1]

Barbara W. Tuchman   Barbara W. Tuchman is the author of three books of history, *The Guns of August, The Zimmerman Telegram,* and *Bible and Sword.* She is the mother of three daughters and is a graduate and trustee of Radcliffe College. This article is a shortened version of a chapter from a book on which she is now at work, dealing with the last two decades before the First World War and the quality of the world that died in 1914. The chapter in its completed form includes also the Spanish and Russian anarchists.

Aside from Kropotkin, Anarchist thought was most highly developed in France. France, in these years, had erected the tallest structure in the world, had invented the balloon, the bicycle, and radioactivity, nurtured a group of painters of genius and the most original composers of their time, gloried in the most cultivated capital, and had, naturally, the most explicit anarchists. Among a wide assortment, some serious and some frivolous, the leaders were Élisée Reclus and Jean Grave. Reclus, with a dark-bearded face of somber beauty and melancholy like that of a Byzantine Christ, was the soothsayer of the movement. He had fought on the barricades of the Commune and marched to prison down the dusty bloodstained road to Versailles. He came from a distinguished family of scholars and, besides his work as a geographer, devoted years to explaining and preaching the anarchist system through his books and through the periodicals he edited at one time or another with Kropotkin and Grave.

In contrast, Grave came from a working-class family. Once a shoemaker and then, like Proudhon, a typesetter and printer, he had in the eighties practiced making fulminate of mercury to blow up the Prefecture of Police or the Palais Bourbon, seat of the French Parliament. His book *The Dying Society and Anarchism* so persuasively argued the destruc-

[1] From "The Anarchists," by Barbara W. Tuchman. *The Atlantic Monthly,* 211:5 (May, 1963). Reprinted by permission of the author.

tion of the State and offered so many insidious suggestions that it cost him two years in prison. While there he wrote another book, *Society after the Revolution*, which he promptly printed himself and published upon his release. Being utopian, it was not considered dangerously subversive by the authorities. In a fifth-floor walk-up garret on a working-class street, the Rue Mouffetard, he now edited, largely wrote, and printed on a handpress the weekly *La Révolte*, while at the same time working on his great history, *Le Mouvement libértaire sous la troisième république*. In a room furnished with a table and two chairs, he lived and worked, dressed invariably in a French workman's long black blouse, surrounded by pamphlets and newspapers, "simple, silent, indefatigable," and so absorbed in his thought and task that "he seemed like a hermit from the Middle Ages who forgot to die 800 years ago."

The followers who were the body of the movement never formed a party but associated only in small, localized clubs and groups. A few comrades would pass out notices informing friends that, for instance, "The Anarchists of Marseilles are establishing a group to be called 'The Avengers and Famished,' which will meet every Sunday at ————. Comrades are invited to come and bring reliable friends to hear and take part in the discussions." Such groups existed not only in Paris but in most of the large cities and many small towns. Among them were "The Indomitables" of Armentières, "The Forced Labor" of Lille, the "Ever-Ready" of Blois, "Land and Independence" of Nantes, the "Dynamite" of Lyons, "The Anti-Patriots" of Charleville. With similar groups from other countries, they occasionally held congresses such as the one in Chicago during the World's Fair in 1893, but they neither organized nor federated.

Another of the leading figures was an Italian, Errico Malatesta, the firebrand of anarchism, always carrying the flame into whatever corner of the world there was an anarchist group. Ten years younger than Kropotkin, he looked like a romantic bandit who might have befriended the Count of Monte Cristo. In fact, he came from a well-off bourgeois family, and as a young medical student had been expelled from the University of Naples for participating in a student riot at the time of the Paris Commune. Thereafter, to make a living he learned the electrician's trade, joined the Italian section of the International, sided with Bakunin against Marx, led an abortive peasant revolt in Apulia, went to prison and then into exile. He tried to direct the Belgian general strike of 1891 away from its petty aim of manhood suffrage, since the vote, in the anarchist credo, was merely another booby trap of the bourgeois state. He was expelled for similar revolutionary efforts from one country after another and condemned to five years on the prison island of Lampedusa, from which he escaped in a rowboat during a storm. When confined to Italy he escaped in a packing case marked "Sewing Machines," which was loaded on a boat for Argentina, where he hoped to prospect for gold in Patagonia to provide funds for the cause, and where, in fact, he found gold, only to have his claim confiscated by the Argentine government.

Not content merely with talking about the coming disappearance of the State, Malatesta was constantly embroiled in practical attempts designed to help it disappear, which caused him to be suspected of deviating from pure anarchism and even of leaning toward Marxism. On one occasion he was shot by an Italian fellow anarchist of the extreme *anti-organizzatori* wing. Never discouraged, no matter how many of the insurrections he midwifed were stillborn, Malatesta was always just in or out of prison, fresh from some dramatic escape or desperate adventure, forever an exile without a home or hardly a room to call his own, always turning up, as Kropotkin said, "just as we saw him last, ready to renew the struggle, with the same love of man, the same absence of hatred for adversaries or jailers."

Their optimism was the outstanding characteristic of these leaders. They were certain that anarchism, because of its rightness, must triumph and the capitalist system, because of its rottenness, must fall, and they sensed a mysterious deadline in the approaching end of the century. "All are awaiting the birth of a new order of things," wrote Reclus. "The century which has witnessed so many grand discoveries in the world of science cannot pass away without giving us still greater conquests. After so much hatred we yearn to love each other and for this reason we are the enemies of private property and the despisers of law."

As formulated by men like Kropotkin, Malatesta, Jean

Grave, and Reclus, anarchism at the end of the century may
have attained, in the words of one of its recorders, "a shining moral grandeur," but only at the cost of a noticeable removal from reality. These men had all suffered prison more
than once for their beliefs. Kropotkin himself had lost his
teeth as a result of prison scurvy. They were not men of the
ivory tower, except insofar as their heads were in ivory
towers. They were able to draw blueprints of a state of universal harmony only by ignoring the evidence of human
behavior and the testimony of history. Their insistence on
revolution stemmed directly from their faith in humanity,
which, they believed, needed only a shining example and a
sharp blow to start it on its way to the golden age. They
spoke their faith aloud. The consequences were frequently
fatal.

Anarchism's new era of violence opened in France just
after the one-hundredth anniversary of the French Revolution. A two-year reign of dynamite, dagger, and gunshot
erupted, killed ordinary men as well as great ones, destroyed
property, banished safety, spread terror, and then subsided.
The signal was given in 1892 by a man whose name, Ravachol, seemed to "breathe revolt and hatred" and became the
symbol of the new era.

His act, like nearly all that followed it, was a gesture of
revenge for comrades who had suffered at the hands of the
State. On the previous May Day of 1891, at Clichy, a
working-class suburb of Paris, a workers' demonstration led
by *les anarchos* carrying red banners with revolutionary
slogans was charged by mounted police. In the melee five
police were slightly injured and three anarchist leaders,
Descamps, Dardare, and Léveillé, severely wounded.
Dragged to the police station, the anarchists were subjected,
while still bleeding and untended, to a *passage à tabac* of uncontrolled savagery, being made to pass between two lines of
policemen under kicks and blows and beatings with revolver
butts. At their trial, Bulot, the prosecuting attorney, charged
that Descamps, on the day before the riot, had called on the
workers to arm themselves and told them, "If the police
come, let no one fear to kill them like the dogs they are!
Down with Government! *Vive la révolution!*" Bulot there-

upon demanded the death penalty for all three, which, since no one had been killed, was an impossible demand that he might better not have made. It was to start a train of dynamite. For the moment, M. Benoist, the presiding judge, acquitted one defendant and sentenced the other two to five and three years' imprisonment respectively, the maximum penalty allowable in the circumstances.

Six months after the trial, on March 14, 1892, the home of M. Benoist on the Boulevard St. Germain was blown up by a bomb. Two weeks later, on March 27, another bomb blew up the home of Bulot, the prosecuting attorney, in the Rue de Clichy. Between the two explosions the police had circulated a description of the suspected criminal as a thin but muscular young man in his twenties with a bony, yellowish face, brown hair and beard, a look of ill health, and a round scar between thumb and first finger of the left hand. On the day of the second explosion a man of this appearance took dinner at the Restaurant Véry in the Boulevard Magenta, where he talked volubly to a waiter named Lhérot about the explosion, which no one in the quarter yet knew had taken place. He also expressed antimilitarist and anarchist opinions. Lhérot wondered about him but did nothing. Two days later the man returned, and this time Lhérot, noticing the scar, called the police. When they arrived to arrest him the slight young man suddenly became a giant of maniacal strength, and it required ten men and a terrific struggle to subdue him and take him prisoner.

This was Ravachol. He had adopted his mother's name in preference to Koenigstein, the name of his father, who had abandoned his wife and four children, leaving Ravachol at eight years of age as chief breadwinner of the family. At eighteen, after reading Eugene Sue's *The Wandering Jew*, he had lost faith in religion, adopted anarchist sentiments, attended their meetings, and as a result was dismissed with a younger brother from his job as a dyer's assistant. Meanwhile, his younger sister died and his older sister bore an illegitimate child. Although Ravachol found other jobs, they did not pay enough to keep the family from misery, so he took to illegal supplements but with a certain fierce pride of principle. Robbery of the rich was the right of the poor "to escape living like beasts," he said in prison. "To die of hunger is cowardly and degrading. I preferred to turn thief, counterfeiter, murderer." He had in fact been all these, and grave robber as well.

At his trial on April 26 he stated that his motive had been to avenge the anarchists of Clichy who had been beaten up by the police and "not even given water to wash their wounds," and upon whom Bulot and Benoist had imposed the maximum penalty although the jury had recommended the minimum. His manner was resolute, and his eyes had the peculiarly piercing gaze expressive of inner conviction. "My object was to terrorize so as to force society to look attentively at those who suffer," he said, putting volumes into a sentence. While the press described him as a figure of sinister violence and cunning and a "colossus of strength," witnesses testified that he had given money to the wife of one of the imprisoned Clichy anarchists and bought clothes for her children. At the end of the one-day trial he was sentenced to imprisonment at hard labor for life. But the Ravachol affair had just begun.

The waiter Lhérot, meanwhile, was winning heroic notoriety by regaling customers and journalists with his story of the scar, the recognition, and the arrest. As a result he attracted an unknown avenger of Ravachol who set off a bomb in the Restaurant Véry that killed not Lhérot but his brother-in-law, M. Véry, the proprietor. The act was hailed by *Le Père Peinard,* the most slangy and popular of the anarchist journals, with the ghoulish double pun, *"Vérification!"*

By now the police had uncovered a whole series of Ravachol's crimes, including a grave robbery for the jewelry on a corpse, the murder of a ninety-two-year-old miser and his housekeeper, the further murder of two old women who kept a hardware shop, which had netted him forty sous, and of another shopkeeper, which had netted him nothing. "See this hand?" Ravachol was quoted as saying. "It has killed as many bourgeois as it has fingers." At the same time he had been living peaceably in lodgings, teaching the little daughter of his landlord to read.

His retrial opened on June 21 in an atmosphere of terror induced by the avenger's bomb in the Restaurant Véry. Everyone expected the Palais de Justice to be blown up; it

was surrounded by troops, every entrance guarded, and
jurors, judges, and counsel heavily escorted by police. Upon
being sentenced to death, Ravachol said that what he had
done had been for the "anarchist idea" and added the terrible
words, "I know I shall be avenged."

Faced with this extraordinary person, at once a monster
of criminality and a protector and avenger of the unfortunate, the Anarchist press fell into discord. In *Le Révolté*
Kropotkin repudiated Ravachol as "not the true, the authentic" revolutionary but the "opéra-bouffe variety." These
deeds, he wrote, "are not the steady, daily work of preparation, little seen but immense, which the revolution demands.
This requires other men than Ravachols. Leave them to the
fin de siècle bourgeois whose product they are." Malatesta
likewise, in the literary anarchist journal *l'En Dehors*, rejected Ravachol's gesture.

The difficulty was that Ravachol belonged almost but not
quite to that class of ego anarchists, who had one serious
theorist in the German Max Stirner and a hundred practitioners of the *culte de moi*. They professed an extreme contempt for every bourgeois sentiment and social restraint,
recognizing only the individual's right to "live anarchisti-
cally," which included burglary or any other crime that
served the need of the moment. They were interested in
themselves, not in revolution. The unbridled operations of
these "miniature Borgias," usually ending in gun battles with
the police and flaunted under the banner of anarchism, added
much to the fear and anger of the public, which did not distinguish between the aberrant and the true variety. Ravachol
was both. There was in him a streak of genuine pity and
fellow feeling for the oppressed of his class that led one
anarchist paper to compare him to Jesus.

On July 11, calm and unrepentant, he went to the guillotine, crying at the end, *"Vive l'anarchie!"* At once the issue
was clear. Overnight he became an anarchist martyr, and
among the underworld a popular hero. *Le Révolté* reversed
itself. "He will be avenged!" it proclaimed, adding its bit to
the unfolding cycle of revenge. A verb, *ravacholiser,* meaning "to wipe out an enemy," became current, and a street
song *La Ravachole,* sung to the tune of *La Carmagnole,* carried the refrain:

It will come, it will come
Every bourgeois will have his bomb!

Ravachol's significance was not in his bombs but in his execution. Meantime, violence erupted across the Atlantic.

Anarchism, which rejected government in sexual matters as in all others, had its love affairs, and one that was to have explosive effect upon the movement in America was at this time in progress in New York. It began in 1890 at a memorial meeting for the Haymarket martyrs at which the German-born Johann Most was the speaker. An untended childhood accident had left him with a scarred and twisted face and deformed body. His scorned and lonely youth, when he wandered from place to place, sometimes starving, sometimes finding odd jobs, was natural soil for an animus against society. In Johann Most it sprouted with the energy of a weed. He learned the bookbinder's trade, wrote wrathfully for the revolutionary press, and achieved one term as deputy in the Reichstag in the seventies. But his vehemence kept him forever a wanderer, repeatedly imprisoned, repeatedly expelled, until he reached the United States in 1882 and by the force of his pen and personality took over leadership of the anarchists. In 1890 he was forty-four, a harsh, embittered man, yet so eloquent and impassioned when he spoke at the memorial meeting that his repellent appearance was forgotten. To one female member of the audience he seemed to "radiate hatred and love" (a phrase that succinctly describes anarchism).

Emma Goldman, a Russian-Jewish recent immigrant of twenty-one, with blue eyes, a rebellious soul, and a highly excitable nature, was transported. Her companion of the evening was Alexander Berkman, like herself a Russian Jew, who had lived in the United States less than three years. Persecution in Russia and poverty in America had endowed both these young people with exalted revolutionary purpose. Emma's first job in the United States was sewing in a factory ten and a half hours a day for $2.50 a week. Her room cost $3.00 a month. Berkman came from a slightly better class of family, which in Russia had been sufficiently well off to employ servants and send their son to the *gymnasium*. But

economic disaster had overtaken them; a favorite uncle of
revolutionary sentiments had been seized by the police and
never seen again, and Sasha (Alexander) had been expelled
from school for writing a nihilist and atheistic composition.
Now twenty, he had "the neck and chest of a giant," a high
studious forehead, intelligent eyes, and a severe expression.
From the "tension and fearful excitement" of Most's speech
about the martyrs, Emma sought "relief" in Sasha's arms,
and subsequently her enthusiasm led her to Most's arms as
well. The tensions of this arrangement proved no different
from those of any bourgeois triangle.

In June, 1892, in Homestead, Pennsylvania, the steel
workers' union struck in protest against a reduction of wages
by the Carnegie Steel Company. The company was determined to crush the union. Having become a philanthropist,
Andrew Carnegie discreetly retreated for the summer to a
salmon river in Scotland, leaving his manager, Henry Clay
Frick, to do battle with organized labor. No one was more
competent or more willing. A remarkably handsome man of
forty-three, with a strong black mustache merging into a
short black beard, a courteous controlled manner, and eyes
that could become "very steely" suddenly, Frick came from
a well-established Pennsylvania family. He dressed with
quiet distinction in dark blue with a hairline stripe, never
wore jewelry, and when offended by a cartoon of himself in
the Pittsburgh *Leader,* said to his secretary, "This won't do.
This won't do at all. Find out who owns this paper and buy
it." He now recruited three hundred strikebreakers from the
Pinkerton Agency and prepared to operate the mills behind
a military stockade.

On July 5, when Frick's private army advanced in ar-
mored barges across the Monongahela and prepared to land,
the strikers attacked with homemade cannon, rifles, dynamite, and burning oil. The day of furious battle ended with
ten killed, seventy wounded, and the Pinkertons thrown back
from the plant by the bleeding but triumphant workers. The
governor of Pennsylvania sent in eight thousand militia, the
country was electrified, and Frick, in the midst of smoke,
death, and uproar, issued an ultimatum declaring his refusal
to deal with the union and his intention to operate with non-
union labor and to discharge and evict from their homes any
workers who refused to return to their jobs.

"Homestead! I must go to Homestead!" shouted Berkman on the memorable evening when Emma rushed in waving the newspaper. It was, they felt, "the psychological moment for the deed. . . . The whole country was aroused against Frick and a blow aimed at him now would call the attention of the whole world to the cause." The workers were striking not only for themselves but "for all time, for a free life, for anarchism"—although they did not know it.

Berkman boarded the train for Pittsburgh bent on killing Frick but surviving long enough himself "to justify my case in court." Then, in prison he would "die by my own hand like Lingg."

On July 23 he made his way to Frick's office, where he was admitted when he presented a card on which he had written "Agent of a New York employment firm." Frick was conferring with his vice-chairman, John Leishman, when Berkman entered, pulled out a revolver, and fired. His bullet wounded Frick on the left side of his neck; he fired again, wounding him on the right side; and as he fired the third time, his arm was knocked up by Leishman, so that he missed a fatal shot again. Frick, bleeding, had risen and lunged at Berkman, who, attacked also by Leishman, fell to the floor dragging the other two men with him. Freeing one hand, he managed to extract a dagger from his pocket and stabbed Frick in the side and legs seven times before he was finally pulled off by a deputy sheriff and others who rushed into the room.

"Let me see his face!" whispered Frick, his own face ashen, his beard and clothes streaked with blood. The sheriff jerked Berkman's head back by his hair, and the eyes of Frick and his assailant met. At the police station two caps of fulminate of mercury of the same kind Lingg had used to blow himself up were found on Berkman's person (some say, in his mouth). Frick lived, the strike was broken by the militia, and Berkman went to prison for sixteen years.

All this left the country gasping, but the public shock was as nothing compared with that which rocked anarchist circles when in *Freiheit* of August 27, Johann Most, inveterate champion of violence, turned apostate to his past and denounced Berkman's attempt at tyrannicide. He said the importance of the terrorist deed had been overestimated and that it could not be effective where the revolutionary movement was inchoate and weak, and he dealt with Berkman, now a hero in anarchist eyes, in terms of contempt. When he repeated these views verbally at a meeting, a female fury rose up out of the audience. It was Emma Goldman, armed with a horsewhip, who sprang upon the platform and flayed her former lover across his face and body. The scandal was tremendous. It was clearly jealousy of Berkman as a younger rival, both in love and in the revolutionary movement, that galled Most. His splenetic attack on a fellow anarchist who had been ready to die for the deed was a stunning betrayal from which anarchism in America never fully recovered.

In France there was no pause in the assaults. On November 8, 1892, at the time of a miners' strike against the Société des Mines de Carmaux, a bomb was deposited in the Paris office of the company on the Avenue de l'Opéra. Discovered by the concierge, it was taken out to the sidewalk and carefully carried off by a policeman to the nearest precinct station in the Rue des Bons Enfants. As the policeman was bringing it in, it burst with a devastating explosion, killing five other policemen who were in the room. They were blown to fragments, blood and bits of flesh were splashed over shattered walls and windows, pieces of arms and legs lay about. Police suspicion centered on Émile Henry, younger brother of a well-known radical orator and son of Fortuné Henry, who had escaped to Spain after being condemned to death in the Commune. When Émile Henry's movements during the day were traced, it appeared impossible that he could have been in the Avenue de l'Opéra at the right moment, and for the time being no arrests were made.

The bomb in the police station put Paris in a panic; no one knew where the next bomb would hit. Anyone connected with the law or police was regarded by his neighbors—since Parisians live largely in apartments—as if he had the plague and was often given notice to leave by his landlord. The city, wrote an English visitor, was "absolutely paralyzed" with fear. The upper classes "lived again as if in the days of the Commune. They dared not go to the theatres, to restaurants, to the fashionable shops in the Rue de la Paix, or to ride in the Bois, where anarchists were suspected behind every tree."

The time was, in any case, one of public rancor and dis-

gust. Hardly had the republic warded off the Boulanger coup
d'etat when it was put to shame by the nests of corruption
revealed in the Panama scandal and the official traffic in
decorations. Day after day in Parliament during 1890–1892
the chain of Panama financing through loans, bribes, slush
funds, and sales of influence was uncovered, until, it was
said, 104 deputies were involved. Even Georges Clemenceau
was smeared by association and lost his seat in the next
election.

In proportion, as the prestige of the state sank, anarchism
flourished. Intellectuals flirted with it. The poet Laurent Tailhade hailed the future anarchist society as a "blessed time"
when aristocracy would be one of intellect and "the common
man will kiss the footprints of the poets." Scores of ephemeral journals and bulletins appeared with names like *Anti-
christ, New Dawn, Black Flag, Enemy of the People, The
People's Cry, The Torch, The Whip, New Humanity, Incorruptible, Sans-Culotte, Land and Liberty, Vengeance.* To
them the State, in its panic over the Ravachol affair, in its
rottenness revealed by the Panama affair, appeared to be
already crumbling.

In March of 1893, a man of thirty-two named August
Vaillant returned to Paris from Argentina, where he had
gone in the hope of starting a new life in the New World but
had failed to establish himself. Born illegitimate, he was ten
months old when his mother married a man not his father,
who refused to support the child. He was given to foster
parents. At twelve, the boy was on his own in Paris, living
by odd jobs, petty theft, and begging. Somehow he went to
school and found white-collar jobs. At one time he edited a
short-lived weekly called *l'Union Socialiste,* but soon, like
others among the disinherited, gravitated to anarchist circles.
As secretary of a *Fédération des groupes indépendants* he
had some contact with anarchist spokesmen like Jean Grave
and Sébastien Faure. Vaillant married, parted from his wife,
but kept with him their daughter, Sidonie, and acquired a
mistress. Not the footloose or libertarian type, he held together his tiny family until the end. After his failure in
Argentina, he tried again to make a living in Paris and, like
his contemporary, Knut Hamsun, then hungrily wandering
the streets of Christiania, experienced the humiliation of
"the frequent repulses, half-promises, the curt noes, the

cherished deluded hopes and fresh endeavors that always resulted in nothing," until the last frustration, when he no longer had any respectable clothes to wear when applying for a job. Unable to afford a new pair of shoes, Vaillant wore a pair of discarded galoshes he had picked up in the street. Finally he found work in a sugar refinery paying three francs a day, too little to support three people.

Ashamed and bitter to see his daughter and mistress go hungry, disillusioned with a world he never made, he decided to end his life. He would not go silently, but with a cry of protest, "a cry of that whole class," as he wrote the night before he acted, "which demands its rights and some day soon will join acts to words. At least I shall die with the satisfaction of knowing that I have done what I could to hasten the advent of a new era."

Not a man to kill, Vaillant planned a gesture that had some logic. He saw the disease of society exemplified by the scandal-ridden Parliament. He manufactured a bomb out of a saucepan filled with nails and with a nonlethal charge of explosive. On the afternoon of December 9, 1893, he took a seat in a public gallery of the Chambre des Deputés and threw his bomb into the midst of the debate. It detonated with the roar of a cannon, spraying the deputies with metal fragments, wounding several but killing none.

The sensation, as soon as the news was known, was enormous and was made memorable by an enterprising journalist. He asked for comment that night at a dinner given by the journal *La Plume* to a number of celebrities, including Zola, Verlaine, Mallarmé, Rodin, and Laurent Tailhade. The last-named replied grandly and in exquisite rhythm, *"Qu'importe les victimes si le geste est beau?"*—"What do the victims matter if it's a fine gesture?" Published in *Le Journal* next morning, the remark was soon to be recalled in gruesome circumstances. That same morning Vaillant gave himself up.

All France understood, and some, other than anarchists, even sympathized with his gesture. Ironically, these sympathizers came from the extreme right, whose antirepublican forces—royalists, Jesuits, floating aristocracy, and anti-Semites—despised the bourgeois State for their own reasons. Édouard Drumont, author of *La France Juive* and editor of *La Libre Parole*, who was busy raging at the Jews involved in the Panama scandal, produced a piece richly entitled, "On Mud, Blood and Gold—from Panama to Anarchism." "The men of blood," he said, "were born out of the mud of Panama."

On January 10 Vaillant came to trial before five judges in red robes and black gold-braided caps. Charged with intent to kill, he insisted that he had intended only to wound. "If I had wanted to kill I could have used a heavier charge and filled the container with bullets; instead I used only nails." Nevertheless, Vaillant received the death penalty, the first time in the nineteenth century that this had been imposed on a person who had not killed. Trial, verdict, and sentence were rushed through in a single day. Almost immediately petitions for pardon began to assail President Sadi Carnot, including one from a group of sixty deputies led by Abbé Lemire, who had been one of those wounded by the bomb. A fiery socialist, Jules Breton, predicted that if Carnot "pronounced coldly for death, not a single man in France would grieve for him if he were one day himself to be victim of a bomb." As incitement to murder, this cost Breton two years in prison and proved to be the second comment on the Vaillant affair that was to end in strange and sinister coincidence.

The government could not pardon an anarchist attack upon the state. Carnot refused to remit the sentence, and Vaillant was duly executed on February 5. 1894, crying "Death to bourgeois society! Long live anarchy!"

The train of death gathered speed. Only seven days after Vaillant went to the guillotine, he was avenged by a blow of such seemingly vicious unreason that the public felt itself in the midst of nightmare. This time the bomb was aimed not against any representative of law, property, or State but against the man in the street. It exploded in the Café Terminus of the Gare St. Lazare in the midst, as *Le Journal* wrote, "of peaceful, anonymous citizens gathered in a café to have a beer before going to bed." One was killed and twenty wounded. As later became clear, the perpetrator acted upon a mad logic of his own. Even before he came to trial, the streets of Paris rocked with more explosions. One in the Rue St. Jacques killed a passerby, one in the Faubourg St. Germain did no damage, and a third exploded in the

pocket of Jean Pauwels, a Belgian anarchist, as he was
entering the Church of the Madeleine. He was killed, and
proved to have set the other two. On April 4, 1894, a fourth
exploded in the fashionable Restaurant Foyot, where, though
it killed no one, it put out the eye of Laurent Tailhade, who
happened to be dining there and who only four months ago
had shrugged aside the victims of a "fine gesture."

Public hysteria mounted. When, at a theatrical performance, some scenery backstage fell with a clatter, half the
audience rushed for the exits screaming, *"Les anarchistes!
Une bombe!"* Newspapers took to printing a daily bulletin
under the heading *La Dynamite*. When the trial of the
bomber of the Café Terminus opened on April 27, the
terrible capacity of the anarchists' idea to be transformed
from love of mankind to hatred of men was revealed.

The accused turned out to be the same Émile Henry who
had been suspected of setting the earlier bomb in the office
of the Mines de Carmaux that had ultimately killed the five
policemen. Already charged for murder in the Café Terminus, he now claimed credit for the other deaths as well,
although no proof could be found. He stated that he had
bombed the Café Terminus to avenge Vaillant, and with full
intention to kill "as many as possible. I counted on fifteen
dead and twenty wounded." In fact, police had found in his
room enough equipment to make twelve or fifteen bombs.
In his cold passion, intellectual pride, and contempt for the
common man, Henry seemed the "St. Just of Anarchism."
At twenty-two he was, along with Berkman, the best educated
and best acquainted with anarchist theory of all the assas-
sins, and of them all, the most explicit.

In prison he wrote a long, closely reasoned account of his
experience of the cynicisim and injustice of bourgeois society, of his "too great respect for individual initiative" to
permit him to join the herdlike socialists, and of his approach
to anarchism. He showed himself thoroughly familiar with
its doctrines and with the writings of Kropotkin, Reclus,
Grave, Faure, and others, although he affirmed that anarchists were not "blind believers" who swallowed whole any or
all the ideas of the theorists.

But it was when he explained his choice of the Café
Terminus that he suddenly set himself apart. There, he said,

come "all those who are satisfied with the established order, all the accomplices and employees of Property and the State . . . all that mass of good little bourgeois who make 300 to 500 francs a month, who are more reactionary than their masters, who hate the poor and range themselves on the side of the strong. These are the clientele of the Terminus and the big cafés of its kind. Now you know why I struck where I did."

In court, when reproached by the judge for endangering innocent lives, he replied with icy hauteur, in words that should have been blazoned on some anarchist banner, "There are no innocent bourgeois."

As for the anarchist leaders, he said, who "dissociate themselves from the propaganda of the deed," like Kropotkin and Malatesta in the case of Ravachol, and "who try to make a subtle distinction between theorists and terrorists, they are cowards. . . . We who hand out death know how to take it. . . . Mine is not the last head you will cut off. You have hanged in Chicago, beheaded in Germany, garrotted at Jerez, shot in Barcelona, guillotined in Paris, but there is one thing you cannot destroy: Anarchism. . . . It is in violent revolt against the established order. It will finish by killing you."

Henry himself took death staunchly. Even the caustic Clemenceau, who witnessed the execution on May 21, 1894, was moved and disturbed. He saw Henry "with the face of a tormented Christ, terribly pale, implacable in expression, trying to impose his intellectual pride upon his child's body." The condemned man walked quickly, despite his shackles, up the steps of the scaffold, threw a glance around, and called out in a raucous strangled cry, *"Courage, camarades! Vive l'anarchie!"* Society's answer to Henry seemed to Clemenceau at that moment "an act of savagery."

Almost without pause fell the next blow, the last in the French series and the most important in its victim, although the least in its assassin. In Lyons on June 24, 1894, during a visit to the Exposition in that city, President Sadi Carnot was stabbed to death by a young Italian workman with the cry, *"Vive la révolution! Vive l' anarchie!"* The President was driving in an open carriage through crowds that lined the street and had given orders to his escort to let people approach. When a young man holding a rolled-up newspaper thrust himself forward from the front row, the guards did not stop him. They thought the newspaper contained flowers. Instead it contained a dagger, and with a terrible blow the young man plunged it six inches into the President's abdomen. Carnot died within three hours.

The assassin was a baker's apprentice, not yet twenty-one, named Santo Caserio. Born in Italy, he had become acquainted with anarchist groups in Milan, the home of political turbulence. At eighteen he was sentenced for distributing anarchist tracts to soldiers. Following the drift of other restless and troublesome characters, he went to Switzerland and then to Cette in the south of France, where he found work and a local group of anarchists, which went by the name *Les Coeurs de Chêne*—"Hearts of Oak." He was brooding over Vaillant's case and the refusal of the President to give a reprieve when he read in the newspapers of the President's forthcoming visit to Lyons. Caserio decided at once to do a "great deed." He asked for a holiday from his job and for twenty francs that were due him—and with the money bought a dagger and took the train for Lyons. There he followed the crowds until he met his opportunity.

Afterward in the hands of his captors and in court he was docile, smiling, and calm. His wan and rather common but gentle face looked to one journalist like "the white mask of a floured Pierrot illuminated by two bright little eyes, obstinately fixed. His lip was ornamented by a poor little shadow of a moustache which seemed to have sprouted almost apologetically." During his interrogation and trial he remained altogether placid and talked quite rationally about anarchist principles, by which he appeared obsessed. He described his act as a deliberate "propaganda of the deed." His only show of emotion was at mention of his mother, to whom he was greatly attached and to whom he had been writing letters regularly when away from home. When the jailer came to wake him on August 15, the day of execution, he wept for a moment and then made no further sound on the way to the guillotine. Just as his neck was placed on the block he murmured a few words that were interpreted by some as the traditional *"Vive l'anarchie!"* and by others as *"A voeni nen,"* meaning, in the Lombard dialect, "I don't want to."

When anarchism slew the very chief of state, it reached a climax in France, after which, suddenly, face to face with political realities and the facts of life in the labor movement, it retreated. At first, however, it looked as if the anarchists would be handed a magnificent opportunity for either propaganda or martyrdom. Charging to the offensive, the government on August 6 staged a mass trial of thirty of the best-known anarchists in an effort to prove conspiracy between theorists and terrorists. In the absence of evidence, however, the jury was not impressed and acquitted all except three of the burglar variety, who were given prison terms. Once again French common sense had reasserted itself, as is its peculiar way whenever things seem most deplorable and the friends of France are already preparing to celebrate her obsequies.

The jury's sensible verdict deprived anarchism of a *cause célèbre*, but a greater reason for the decline that followed was that the French working class was too realistic to be drawn into a movement suffering from self-inflicted impotence. The sterility of deeds of terror was already beginning to be recognized by leaders like Kropotkin, Malatesta, Reclus, and even Johann Most. Searching for other means of bringing down the State, they were always tripped up by the inherent paradox: Revolution demands organization, discipline, and authority; anarchism disallows them. The futility of their position was beginning to make itself felt. Yet in the end there was a kind of tragic sense in the anarchist rejection of authority. As Sébastien Faure, who had been educated by Jesuits, said in a moment of cold realism, "Every revolution ends in the reappearance of a new ruling class."

Realists of another kind during these years began to come to terms with the labor movement. It was the eight-hour day that the French working class wanted, not bombs in Parliament or murdered presidents. But it was the anarchist propaganda of the deed that woke them to recognition of what they wanted and the necessity of fighting for it. That was why Ravachol, whom they understood, became a popular hero and songs were sung about him in the streets. Ever since the massacres of the Commune, the French proletariat had been prostrate; it was the anarchist assaults that brought them to their feet. They sensed that their strength lay in collective action, and in 1895, only a year after the last of the anarchist assaults, there was formed the C.G.T., France's federation of labor.

Upon the anarchists, frustrated by their own inherent paradox, it exerted a strong pull. One by one they drifted into the trade unions, bringing with them as much of their doctrine as could be applied. This merger of anarchist theory and trade-union practice took the form known as "syndicalism," and in this altered form, though extremists of the pure kind like Jean Grave shunned it, French anarchism developed during the years 1895–1914.

Its dogma was direct action through the general strike, and its new prophet was Georges Sorel. Under his banner the general strike was to replace propaganda of the deed. The syndicalists continued to abhor the state or anyone willing, like the socialists, to cooperate with it, and they had no more use than their anarchist predecessors for halfway reformist measures. The strike was all, the general strike and nothing but the strike. They retained the sinews of the old movement; but something of its soul, its mad marvelous independence, was gone.

Public excitement over anarchist deeds, giving promise of heroic notoriety, acted as an intoxicant to unsound minds and produced the next two fatalities. The first took place on September 10, 1898, alongside the lake steamer at the Quai du Mont Blanc in Geneva. Here met, in mortal junction, as meaningless as when a stroke of lightning kills a child, two persons so unconnected, so far apart in the real world that their lives could never have touched except in a demented moment. One was the Empress Elizabeth of Austria, wife of Franz Joseph, the other Luigi Lucheni, a vagrant Italian workman.

The most beautiful and the most melancholy royal personage in Europe, married and crowned at sixteen, Elizabeth was still, at sixty-one, forever moving restlessly from one place to another in endless escape from an unquiet soul. Renowned for her loveliness, her golden-brown hair a yard long, her slender elegance and floating walk, her sparkling moods when she was the "incarnation of charm," she suffered also from "court-ball headaches" and could not appear in public without holding a fan before her face. She was "a fairies' child," wrote Carmen Sylva, the Queen of Romania, "with hidden wings, who flies away whenever she finds the world unbearable." She wrote sad romantic poetry and had seen her son's life end in the most melodramatic suicide of the century. Her insane first cousin, King Ludwig of Bavaria, had died by drowning; her husband's brother, Maximilian, by firing squad in Mexico; her sister by fire at a charity bazaar in Paris. "I feel the burden of life so heavily," she wrote her daughter, "that it is often like a physical pain and I would far rather be dead." She would rush off to England or Ireland to spend weeks in the hunting field riding recklessly over the most breakneck fences. In Vienna she took lessons in the most dangerous tricks of circus riding. What she was seeking was plain: "I long for death," she wrote her daughter four months before she reached Geneva.

On September 9 she visited the lakeside villa of the Baroness Adolfe de Rothschild, a remote enchanted world where tame miniature porcupines from Java and exotic colored birds decorated a private park planted with cedars of Lebanon. As she left her hotel next morning to take the lake steamer, the Italian, Lucheni, was waiting outside on the street.

He had come from Lausanne, where he recently had been reported to the police as a suspicious character. The orderly of a hospital where he had been taken for an injury suffered during a building job had found among his belongings a notebook containing anarchist songs and the drawing of a bludgeon labeled "anarchia" and underneath, in Italian, "for Humbert I." Accustomed to misfits, radicals, and exiles of all kinds, the Swiss police had not considered this sufficient cause for arrest or surveillance.

According to what he told the hospital orderly, Lucheni's mother, pregnant at eighteen with an illegitimate child, had made her way to Paris to give birth among the anonymous millions of a great city. Then she had returned to Italy, where she left her child in the poorhouse in Parma, and had disappeared to America. At nine years old the boy was a day laborer on an Italian railroad. Later, when drafted into a cavalry regiment of the Italian Army, he made a good record and was promoted to corporal. Upon his discharge in 1897, having neither savings nor prospects, he became manservant to his former captain, the Prince d'Aragona, but on being denied a raise, left in anger. Later he asked to come back, but the Prince, considering him too insubordinate for domestic service, refused. Resentful and jobless, Lucheni took to reading *L'Agitatore, Il Socialista, Avanti,* and other revolutionary papers and pamphlets whose theme at the moment was the rottenness of bourgeois society as demonstrated by the Dreyfus case. A single Samson, they indicated, could bring down the State at a blow. Lucheni, now in Lausanne, sent clippings from these papers with his comments to comrades in his former cavalry regiment. Apropos of a workman killed in a quarrel, he remarked to a friend at this time, "Ah, how I'd like to kill somebody. But it must be someone important so it gets into the papers."

Meanwhile, the Swiss papers reported the coming visit of the Empress Elizabeth to Geneva. Lucheni tried to buy a stiletto, but lacked the necessary twelve francs, so he fashioned a homemade dagger out of an old file, carefully sharpened and fitted to a handle made from a piece of firewood. As the Empress and her lady-in-waiting, Countess Sztaray, walked toward the Quai du Mont Blanc, Lucheni stood in their path. He rushed upon them with hand upraised, stopped and peered beneath her parasol to make sure of the Empress' identity, then stabbed her through the heart. Carried back to the hotel, she died four hours later. Lucheni, seized by two gendarmes, was caught in his great moment by an alert passerby with a camera. The picture shows him walking jauntily between his captors with a satisfied smile, almost a smirk, on his face. At the police station he eagerly described all his proceedings and preparations, and when later it was learned that the Empress had died, expressed himself as "delighted." He declared himself an anarchist and insisted on its being understood that he had acted on his own initiative and not as a member of any group or party. Asked why he had killed the Empress, he replied, "As part of the war on the rich and the great. . . . It will be Humbert's turn next."

From prison he wrote letters to the President of Switzerland and to the newspapers proclaiming his creed and the coming downfall of the State, and signing himself, "Luigi Lucheni, Anarchist, and one of the most dangerous of them." There being no death penalty in Geneva, Lucheni was sentenced to life imprisonment. Twelve years later, after a

quarrel with the warder that resulted in his being given a
term of solitary, he hanged himself by his belt.

In 1897, an anarchist blacksmith named Pietro Acciarito
had attempted to kill King Humbert of Italy, leaping upon
him in his carriage with a dagger in the identical manner not
only of Caserio upon President Carnot, but of an earlier
attempt on Humbert himself in 1878. More alert than Carnot
to these occupational hazards, the King had jumped aside,
escaped the blow, and remarking with a shrug to his escort,
"Sono gli incerti del mestiere"—"These are the risks of the
job"—he ordered his coachman to drive on.

The hatred for constituted society that seethed in the
lower classes and the helplessness of society to defend itself
against these attacks were becoming more and more apparent. As usual, the police, in wishful hunt for a "plot,"
arrested half a dozen alleged accomplices of Acciarito, none
of whom in the end could be proved to have had any connection with him. Plots by groups or parties could be dealt
with; there were always informers. But how could the sudden
spring of these solitary tigers be prevented?

The war of the rich upon the poor (or the reverse, depending on the angle of vision) went too deep. In 1899, in Italy,
it burst into the open. Taxes and an import duty on grain,
which the anarchists saw as another aspect of the war on the
poor by the State, caused bread riots in Ancona. They spread
north and south despite repressive measures and bloody
collision between troops and people. In Milan, streetcars
were overturned to make barricades, people hurled stones at
police armed with guns, women threw themselves in front
of trains to prevent the arrival of troops, a state of siege was
declared, and all Tuscany put under martial law. The cry
that at last the revolution had come brought thousands of
Italian workmen back from Spain, Switzerland, and the
south of France to take part. Control was only regained by
the dispatch of half an army corps to Milan. All socialist
and revolutionary papers were suppressed, Parliament was
prorogued, and although the government succeeded in re-
establishing order, it was only on the surface.

The inoffensive monarch who found himself presiding
over this situation had a fierce white mustache, personal

courage, a gallant soul, and no more noticeable talent for kingship than any of the House of Savoy. Humbert was passionately fond of horses and hunting, totally impervious to the arts, which he left to the patronage of his Queen, and very regular in his habits. Every afternoon he drove out in his carriage at the same hour over the same route through the Borghese Gardens. Every evening at the same hour he visited a lady to whom he had remained devotedly faithful since before his marriage thirty years earlier. On July 29, 1900, he was distributing prizes from his carriage to athletic competitors in Monza, the royal summer residence near Milan, when he was shot four times by a man who stepped up to the carriage and fired at hardly two yards' distance. The King gazed at him reproachfully for a moment, then fell over against the shoulder of his aide-de-camp, murmured *"Avanti!"* to his coachman, and expired.

The assassin, "holding his smoking weapon exultantly aloft," was immediately seized. He was identified as Gaetano Bresci, a thirty-year-old anarchist and silk weaver who had come from Paterson, New Jersey, to Italy with intent to assassinate the King. His act was the only instance of anarchist propaganda of the deed for which there is some evidence, though unproven, of previous conspiracy.

Paterson was a center of Italians and of anarchism. Certainly the anarchists of Paterson held many meetings and heatedly discussed a "deed" that would be the signal for overthrow of the oppressor. Certainly the King of Italy figured as their preferred target, but whether, as charged in reports after the event, lots were actually chosen to select the person to do the deed, or whether the discussions simply inspired Bresci to act of his own accord, is not certain. The picture of a cabal of anarchists in a cellar drawing lots to select an assassin was a favorite journalistic imagery of the time.

One imaginative reporter pictured Bresci as having been "indoctrinated" by Malatesta, "the head and moving spirit of all the conspiracies which have recently startled the world by their awful success." From the moment that Malatesta had been glimpsed quietly drinking at an Italian bar in Paterson, "anarchists everywhere recognized the group at Paterson as the most important in the world."

In fact, the police found no evidence that Bresci had ever

met Malatesta. He had, however, either obtained or been given a revolver in Paterson with which he practiced shooting in the woods while his wife and three-year-old daughter picked flowers nearby. Also, he was given by his comrades, or somehow obtained, money to buy a steerage ticket on the French Line with enough left over to make his way from Le Havre to Italy.

After the assassination, his Paterson comrades sent a congratulatory cable to him in prison. They gloried in his magnificent gesture and wore his picture on buttons in their coat lapels. They also insisted at a mass meeting in Paterson, attended by over a thousand persons, that there had been no plot.

Bresci himself suffered the same fate as other instruments of the Idea. As Italy had abolished the death penalty, he was sentenced to life imprisonment, the first seven years to be spent in solitary confinement. After the first few months he killed himself in prison.

Thomas G. Masaryk   Land and Freedom: Peasant Anarchism in Russia[1]

Thomas Garrigue Masaryk (1850–1937)   Masaryk was born in Hodonín, Moravia, to poor parents and was early in his youth apprenticed to a blacksmith. He grew up to study in Vienna and became a lecturer in philosophy at the University of Vienna. He was especially well versed in English philosophy. He was a federalist in Austro-Hungarian politics, resisting Germanization of Bohemia and also the antinationalist policy of the Austrian bureaucracy. For a time he was in exile in London, after declaring his sympathy for the Allies in 1914. As a young man he became a close student of Russian affairs. His studies resulted in the important work published in 1913, *The Spirit of Russia*. The English edition appeared shortly after the war, by which time Masaryk was president of the newborn Czechoslovakia. Some of his works in English are *Modern Man and Religion*, and *The Ideals of Humanity: How To Work*.

1 From *The Spirit of Russia*, by Thomas G. Masaryk. New York: The Macmillan Company, Copyright 1919. London: George Allen & Unwin, Ltd., 1919. Reprinted by permission of the publishers.

The great hopes which, after the Crimean catastrophe, had been founded upon the liberation of the peasantry and upon administrative reforms, were speedily dashed, and a revolutionary movement ensued, culminating in the assassination of Alexander II. The outward history of this movement is known; partial freedom stimulated aspirations for complete freedom. We have now to consider the views which found expression in and through this movement, to discuss the program disseminated by secret presses and unlawful secret societies, both in Russia and elsewhere.

1) In 1862 was established in St. Petersburg the first secret society, known as *Zemlja i Volja* (Land and Freedom). It maintained relationships with the Polish revolutionaries, and through the instrumentality of Bakunin was likewise in correspondence with Herzen, though the last-named mistrusted it.

The program of the Central Committee of the Russian People maintained the duty and the right of revolution as a means of defense against the oppression and cruelty of absolutism; it sharply counterposed the interests of the people to the interests of czarist absolutism; and appealed for the cooperation of those whom no danger could affright. The ultimate aim of the revolution was stated to be the summoning of a national assembly which was freely to decide the social organization of Russia; the activity of the society would terminate when freedom of election to the national assembly had been secured.

Another secret society, to which reference has already been made, was Velikorus' (Great Russia). Chernyshevski was said to have participated in the work of both these societies.

The secret organization of the radical revolutionary elements began at various places and assumed many different forms. A secret society came into existence in Moscow, and towards the close of 1865 was consolidated under the name of Organization. In this society, two trends were manifest, one comparatively moderate, which aimed merely at the diffusion of a socialist program, and the other more radical, desiring to bring about the revolution by direct action and if needs must by czaricide. Karakozov, who belonged to this left wing, made the first attempt upon Alexander's life on April 17, 1866. Karakozov and his associates were adherents of Chernyshevski, but the attempt was made by Karakozov upon his own initiative and in opposition to the wishes of the society.

Agitation was carried into wider circles by the proclamations issued from the newly established secret printing presses. The aim of these proclamations was not so much to formulate a program as to function as instruments of political propaganda and to promote a political awakening. Such proclamations were sometimes issued by authors and publicists of note, or were ascribed to these, rightly or wrongly. They were addressed either to the community at large or to particular strata of society, to cultured persons and to students, to soldiers, to peasants, to operatives.

As early as 1854, proclamations were issued (by Engelssohn); but not until the radical movement of the sixties was in full swing did they become an effective means for political propaganda.

Much attention was attracted by the before-mentioned proclamation *Young Russia* (May, 1862), which contained threats of a bloody and pitiless revolution; Russia was to be transformed into a republican and federative state; there were to be national and local parliaments, a judiciary appointed by popular election, just taxes, "social" factories and shops, "social" education of children, emancipation of women, abolition of marriage and the family, abolition of monasteries, provision for invalids and the elderly, increased pay for soldiers, etc. Should the czar and his party, as was to be anticipated, turn upon Young Russia, then: "Inspired with full confidence in ourselves, in our energies, in popular sympathy, in the splendid future of Russia, predestined to be the first of all countries to realize socialism, we shall sound the clarion call, "Seize your axes." Then we shall strike down the members of the czarist party, shall strike them unpityingly as they have unpityingly struck us, shall hew them down in the squares should the rout venture forth into the open, hew them down in their dwellings, in the narrow alleys of the towns, in the wide streets of the capitals, in the villages and the hamlets. When that day dawns, he that is not for us will be against us, will be our enemy, and our enemies must be destroyed root and branch. But with each new victory and in the hour of struggle, never forget to repeat, 'Long live the social and democratic Russian republic!' "

The proclamation purported to be issued by the "Revolutionary Central Committee."

The excitement aroused by this bold document was intense. The liberals, no less than the authorities, were outraged beyond measure, for the liberals were stigmatized as henchmen of the czar. Even Bakunin was ill-pleased, for he considered that those who had issued the proclamation failed to understand the situation, that they had no definite goal, and that they lacked revolutionary discipline. Herzen, who was attacked by name in the proclamation, criticized it, but did not take it too seriously, saying that it was an ebullition of youthful radicalism, that its authors had wished to instruct politicians and officials more far-seeing than themselves. The proclamation, he said, was unRussian; it was a *mixtum compositum* of undigested Schiller (Robber Moor), Gracchus Babeuf, and Feuerbach.

The proclamation is an interesting testimony to the nature of the epoch. We see that the younger radical generation of the sixties is socialistically inclined, that liberalism and its constitutionalist formulas have been found inadequate; that society is to be rebuilt from its foundations on a socialist plan.

According to the philosophy of history of the writers of the proclamation, society consisted of two classes, the members of the czarist party and the nonpossessing revolutionaries, for the existing order was based solely upon private property; the czar was merely the man standing on the highest rung of the ladder, whose lower rungs were occupied by landowners, merchants, and officials—all alike capitalists. Private property was to be abolished; above all, the land was to belong to the whole people, and therefore the *mir* with its provisional subdivision of the land was accepted; but such property as had been hitherto held privately was to be held only on terms of usufruct, and after the usufructuary's death was to accrue to the *mir*. Since every individual must belong to a village community, the social and democratic Russian republic would take the form of a federative union of the village communities.

Federation was to be free, and therefore the "brother"

Poles and Lithuanians could form independent states should they be unwilling to enter the Russian federation.

Herzen was wrong in describing the proclamation as un-Russian. Not merely may we consider Sten'ka Razin and Pugachev to have been its forerunners, but it likewise embodies the ideas of Pestel, from whom the authors learned, as well as from Chernyshevski and Bakunin.

The influence of the French socialists is likewise discernible, and perhaps also that of Marx.

The proclamation is unquestionably obscure in point of political outlook, as regards ways and means; this becomes obvious in its appeal to the people, to the "millions" of the old believers, to the army and its officers, to the Poles and the peasants, and above all to young men ("our main hope").

Analogous in its outlook was the proclamation *To the Younger Generation,* which has hitherto been ascribed to Mihailov, who was sentenced on this account and sent to Siberia. In actual fact the proclamation was written by Shelgunov.[2]

The proclamation represents the younger members "of all classes" as successors of the decabrists, animadverts against the pitiful economists "of the German text books" and against narrow-minded individualism, and repudiates the attempt to make an England out of Russia. In support of Herzen's and Chernyshevski's doctrine that Russia could skip certain stages of European development, we read: "Who can maintain that we must necessarily walk in the footsteps of Europe, in the footsteps of a Saxony, an England, or a France? The Gneists, Bastiats, Mohls, Raus, and Roschers, serve up to us masses of excrement, desiring to make the refuse of dead centuries into laws for the future. Such laws may do for them, but we shall find another law for ourselves. It is not merely that we can find something new, but it is essential that we do so. Our life is guided by principles utterly unknown to Europeans." Quite after the manner of Chaadaev and Herzen, the Russians are described as back-

---

[2] In the year 1873, Dostoyevsky referred to a proclamation, *To the Younger Generation,* which he had shown to Chernyshevski, and concerning which Chernyshevski had expressed an adverse opinion. If Dostoyevsky's statement that this proclamation was quite short is accurate, it cannot have been the one usually attributed to Mihailov. [Masaryk's note, as are all others in this extract.]

ward in their development, but are said to be competent for this very reason to undergo a different evolution, non-economic and peculiar to themselves. "Therein lies our salvation," that we are backward in our development. The Russian bourgeoisie, manufactured by Catherine II, is to be swept away, for the bourgeois are nothing but peasants, only peasants without land.

In addition to these proclamations, addresses to the czar and to the general public were circulated. Such addresses were sometimes issued by radicals, but still more by liberals and especially by some of the liberal *zemstvos*. For example, the Tver *zemstvo* issued a document of this character in 1862. Secretly printed addresses were likewise circulated for propaganda purposes. As far as political demands are concerned, these writings ask for nothing more than constitutionalist reforms.[3]

2) Bakunin is of leading importance in connection with the further development of the revolutionary movement. It is therefore necessary to consider a Bakuninist program, and we will choose for this purpose the program of the year 1868, as formulated in the *Narodnoe Delo* (The People's Cause) Bakunin's Genevese organ. Herein the liberation of the mind is proclaimed as the basis of social and political freedom; the belief in God and immortality and in "idealism of any kind" is proscribed, the spread of atheism and materialism being announced as definite party aims; religion is said to produce slaves, to paralyze the energies, and to prevent the realization of natural rights and true happiness.

The economic condition of the people is affirmed to be the "cornerstone," and this economic condition is said "to explain political existence"—thus runs a somewhat obscure formulation of economic materialism. In essence the state is based upon conquest, upon the right of inheritance, upon the *patria potestas* of the husband and father, and upon the religious consecration of all these principles. The necessary outcome of the existence of such a state is the slavery of the working majority and the dominion of the exploiting minority, of the so-called cultured class. For the abolition of

[3] There should be mentioned in this connection the plan for an address to the czar, written wholly or partly by Chernyshevski and outlined in a proclamation issued by the secret society Velikorus' (1861). In 1862, Herzen and Ogarev drafted such a document, which was condemned by Turgenev. It was never circulated.

these privileges it is necessary to do away with the inheritance of property, to secure equal rights for women, this involving the abolition of the *patria potestas* and of marriage; to maintain children until they reach full age, and to secure for them at the hands of a free society an education that shall make them equally competent for "muscular" and "nervous" work.

In ultimate analysis the basis of economic organization must rest on the two principles, that the land is the property of those who till it, the property of the village communities, and that capital and all the instruments of production belong to the workers, are the property of workers' associations. The entire political organism is to be a free federation of agricultural and manufacturing associations (artels); the state is to be destroyed. The separate peoples in Russia may, should they so desire, unite to form a free federation, becoming members "of the Russian folk," and this will affiliate with the equally free societies of Europe and the entire world.

3) Important for the further development of secret revolutionary propaganda was the Society of the People's Assize, a secret society founded by Nechaev in 1869. Nechaev, Bakunin's disciple, secured widespread notoriety through his *Catechism of Revolution*. This work was an introduction to conspiracy and to propaganda by deed, and presupposes the acceptance of Bakunin's program.[4]

In the *Catechism* the arts of the secret conspirator are urged with consummate Jesuitry, this word "Jesuitry" being understood in its most evil connotation as "political Machiavellianism." The members of the secret society have to obey their leader absolutely, and for the most part remain unknown one to another; the revolutionary conspirator must be a blind instrument, must abandon all personal interests and sentiments, must break every family tie, and must give up even his name, to devote his whole individuality to the life and death struggle; the genuine revolutionist abandons all romanticism, even hatred and personal feelings of revenge

---

4 The *Catechism* is reprinted in Dragomanov's edition of Bakunin's Correspondence, p. 371. Many regarded the *Catechism* as the work of Bakunin, who never denied the supposition. Dragomanov left this question open, and it needs reconsideration. G. Adler, in the article "Anarchism" in the *Handworterbuch der Staatwissenschaften*, 2nd edition, p. 308, adduces certain passages as doctrines and utterances of Nechaev taken from the *Catechism*, but they are in fact utterances by Bakunin and are not to be found in the *Catechism*. Cf., Dragomanov, *op. cit.*, pp. 353 and 363.

being subordinated to the revolutionary idea. The secret
conspirator may and must do anything needful for the cause;
he may lie if lying will promote the working of the revolutionary forces; he must enter into suitable relationships with
prostitutes, with the police, with "the so-called criminals,"
etc. The members of society, against which Nechaev is
campaigning, are divided by him into six categories. The
first of these consists of individuals whom the revolutionaries
have sentenced to death and who must be removed forthwith,
whereas the most evil of creatures may be left alive if his
misdeeds promote the growth of revolutionary energy. The
second class consists of persons whose lives may provision-
ally be spared. In the third category are "highly placed
beasts," wealthy individuals who are personally of no importance, but who can be exploited for the benefit of the
revolution. In the fourth class are aspiring officials and
liberals of various grades. With these the revolutionary
remains ostensibly on friendly terms that he may learn their
secrets, may compromise them, may make it impossible for
them to draw back, and may compel them to serve the
revolution. Fifthly come the doctrinaires, those who are conspirators and revolutionaries in word merely, and similar
chatterers; these must be urged to deeds and converted into
genuine revolutionaries. Women constitute the sixth category, the most important of all, and these are divided into
three subclasses: (a) those of no account must be exploited
like the men in categories three and four; (b) the enthusiasts
among them, who, however, are not yet fully won over to
the cause, must be treated like the men of the fifth category;
(c) the adepts, the genuinely revolutionary women "must be
regarded as the greatest of our treasures, without which we
could do nothing."

The real aim of the secret society is to secure perfect freedom and complete happiness for the workers. But since this
freedom and this happiness can be secured in no other way
than by an all-destroying revolution carried out by the people
as a whole, the guiding purpose of the secret society must be
to increase the existing evils in order that the people may
lose patience and may be stimulated to a mass rising.

In 1869 and 1870 Nechaev published a periodical in
Geneva. It was entitled "Narodnaja Rasprava" (The People's
Assize), and no more than two numbers appeared. Herein

was preached absolute negation and pandestruction. The formulation of plans for the future was condemned, and condemned too, therefore, was all exclusively theoretical rational activity. The only knowledge to be tolerated was that which directly promoted practice, the practice of "radical and universal pandestruction." As for reconstruction, "to upbuild is not our work, but that of those who will come after us." The immediate concrete aim was "to sweep away the czar with all his family." If, nonetheless, Alexander II was still permitted to live, this was merely because his proceedings were stimulating the revolutionary movement among the people. Nechaev was willing to leave his condemnation and punishment to the people's assize; the Russian folk was entitled to inflict a death sentence on the man who had deceived them with his lying reforms.

During 1869, Nechaev organized among the Moscow students a secret society which, under his leadership was speedily to shed blood. An alleged traitor, a student named Ivanov, was sentenced and murdered, the Bakuninist revolution having thus an ominous beginning with the assassination of one of its own adherents. Nechaev had an additional reason for this bloodletting in that he desired to intimidate his own followers, to knit them more closely together, and to promote the spread of the idea of pandestruction by the excitement which the murder would cause.

Bakunin condemned Nechaev in strong terms—though not until after Nechaev's "deed." In 1870 Bakunin spoke of Nechaev as a traitor, and in 1872 censured his Machiavellianism and Jesuitism. It is difficult to decide to what extent Nettlau is right in maintaining that Nechaev had fooled Bakunin and Ogarev. It was certainly characteristic of Bakunin that his plans for worldwide destruction laid him open to be befooled by such as Nechaev. From the very first Herzen distrusted Nechaev. In 1872 Nechaev was extradited from Switzerland as a common criminal, and in Russia was condemned to twenty years in a penitentiary, but was confined in the fortress of St. Peter and St. Paul where he died in 1882. Even had this not been his fate, he would have been unable to maintain his position in the revolutionary world. As Kropotkin shows in his *Memoirs,* Nechaev's program was promptly repudiated by Tchaikovski's adherents. Moreover, in Lavrov's program Nechaev's position is denounced.

Above all, the later members of the *Narodnaja Volja* disapproved of Nechaev's methods. Further, the anarchist followers of Nechaev and Bakunin, Tcherkesoff, for instance, the opponent of Marxism, did not accept this aspect of Nechaev's anarchism.[5] Kropotkin does not reject the idea of armed revolution, but he is opposed to all deception, whether practiced against friend or enemy.

Not until much later, when the younger generation had forgotten the facts established by Herzen against Nechaev in 1871, were certain attempts made to idealize him.

Once only was the method of Nechaev practically applied, this being in the peasant revolt of 1877 in the Chigirin district. Here a false "secret charter issued by supreme authority" was dangled before the eyes of the peasants.

4) Of a very different character was the program of those organizations which made it their business to promote the revolutionary culture of the masses as a precondition of the definitive revolution. I may refer for example to the program of the Tchaikovcy who were organized in the year 1871.[6]

For the Tchaikovcy, the social revolution was the terminal aim of all revolutionary organization, and the greatest possible number of peasants and operatives must be won over to the cause. Adherents among the operatives, returning to their native villages, would promote the spread of revolutionary ideas among the peasants. Local disturbances, such as were advocated by Bakuninist groups, were not approved, for it was held that these casual risings diverted people's attention from the terminal aim, the definitive revolution. But no objection was raised to local disturbances and local acts of resistance to government when these originated spontaneously.

The Tchaikovcy sympathized with the workers' international of Bakuninist trend, and sympathized with the Russian refugees, to whom they attributed an independent and peculiar influence upon the Russian folk.

5) The program of the Lavrovists, the adherents of Lavrov, has important bearings upon revolutionary developments during the seventies. It will be found in the periodical *Vpered* (Forward), which was published in Zurich and in

[5] *Cf.* W. Tcherkesoff, *Pages d'histoire socialiste,* I, "Doctrines et Actes de la Sociale Démocratie."

[6] N. Tchaikovski was a refugee from Russia in the year 1871, but returned to Russia in 1905. His program was revised by Kropotkin.

London in several different forms during the years 1873 to 1878.

The Lavrovist program recognizes the existence of two universal tasks, two struggles, in which every thoughtful man must participate; the struggle of the "realist" outlook against the theological and the metaphysical, the struggle of science against religion; and the struggle of labor against the idle enjoyment of the good things of life, the struggle to secure complete equality for individualities, the struggle against monopoly in all its forms. The former struggle, we are told, is nearly finished, and as far as Russia is concerned has no notable significance (!). But for the latter, the principal struggle, we must now prepare the ground and provide a realist foundation. By a realist foundation, Lavrov means positive or scientific socialism.

Lavrov opposes the conservatives and the pseudo liberals, but likewise opposes Nechaev and Bakunin, energetically rejecting falsehood as a weapon for use in the campaign to secure juster social institutions. Falsehood must be overcome, just as must all the instruments and methods of the old injustice; the new order cannot be founded upon exploitation, nor upon the dictatorial dominion of the few, nor upon the forcible appropriation of unearned wealth. Against an enemy (Lavrov emphasizes the word) it may doubtless be permissible to make use of falsehood in moments of extreme and temporary need, but the employment of such methods among equals and among persons of like views is a crime. In answer to Bakunin and Nechaev, he points out that even those who say that the end justifies the means will always add, with the exception of those means whose use will per se prevent the attainment of the end.

Lavrov declared that the social question was the first and the most important of all questions. He expressly subordinated the political problem to the social and above all to the economic problem, and he insisted that in view of the importance of the social struggle we should put all thought of nationality out of our minds. Accepting Marx's theory of the class struggle, Lavrov's primary demand was, therefore, for the organization of the "entire" working-class movement, and he was here thinking of the Russian peasants as well as of the factory operatives. An all-embracing organization was essential because isolated struggles were irrational and purposeless in view of the powerful organization of the enemy.

Lavrov was convinced that the terminal aim would not be achieved at one step; there would be intermediate stages. He therefore held very strongly that during the progress of the struggle we should never cease to pursue the possible, and to choose suitable means for the attainment of the goal.

Political programs and parties of a constitutionalist and liberal character were regarded as inadequate. Just as little as Herzen, would Lavrov accept the bourgeois republic in place of the bourgeois monarchy, for the whole principle of the bourgeoisie was faulty. It was no doubt essential to make the best possible use of liberal institutions in so far as these could be made to subserve socialist aims (Lavrov was thinking of freedom of conscience, the right of free combination, and the like); but the socialist ought not to think of making common cause with the liberal, though perhaps here and there the two might occupy common ground.

In respect of nationality, according to Lavrov's program human beings only were to be recognized, and the common aims of mankind; all the nations, therefore, were to unite for joint work, regardless of linguistic traditions. Rivalry between the Russians and the members of other nationalities was unsocialist.

In Russia, the peasants constitute a preponderant majority of the population, and consequently work for the peasant masses was the special mission of the Russian socialist. The Russian folk must not merely be the aim of the social revolution, but its instrument as well. It is the work of the Russian revolutionary, the intellectual, to expound the socialist aim to the people; he must not desire to exercise authority over the folk, for his only role is to carry into effect the universal social aspirations. It is the task of the intellectual to instill into the folk confidence in itself, conceived as an individuality, to enlighten the people concerning its own aims and activities; his work is to pave the way for the coming of Russia's better future. "Only when the course of historical events indicates that the moment of revolution is at hand and that the Russian folk is prepared for it, are we justified in appealing to the folk to realize the great transformation." Revolutions cannot be artificially evoked, for they are the issue of a long series of complicated historical processes, and are not the result of individual wills. Nevertheless, every attempt at a popular revolution, even should it prove unsuccessful, is a means of social education. "But whether a particular revolution be useful or injurious, history leads up to revolutions with inevitable fatalism." Lavrov declares in conclusion that for Russia, too, the revolutionary path is "the most probable."

For Lavrov, likewise, the *mir* seems the social and economic foundation upon which the socialistic transformation of society as a whole can be based. But it is necessary that, as a preliminary, the peasants shall receive enlightenment, for otherwise, even should the revolution prove successful, they would be exploited by the minority.

Marx and Comte versus Bakunin, such is the gist of this revolutionary program. In view of the lust of battle that animates the young Bakuninist revolutionaries, Lavrov voices the exhortation, "Look before you leap!" As against the secret-society men *(buntari)*, Lavrov emphasizes the advantages of propaganda, and the opponents of the Lavrovists therefore spoke of them contemptuously as "progressives."

6) *Nabat* (The Alarm Bell), a periodical published in Geneva, and edited by Tkachev, was the organ of Lavrov's adversaries. Tkachev was a Blanquist who took part in the opening political demonstrations of the early sixties, and was sentenced in Nechaev trial. His aim was to continue and outbid the radicalism of Bakunin and Nechaev, so that for him not Lavrov merely but even Bakunin were "bourgeois pseudo revolutionaries" in the sense of Nechaev's *Catechism*. Tkachev denominated his system, jacobinism. The immediate aim of the revolution is to seize political power, but this seizure of power is not itself the revolution, to which it is no more than a preliminary. The revolution will first be realized by the revolutionary state, which will attain to the negative and positive aims of the revolution.

The revolutionary state will strengthen itself by summoning a national assembly *(narodnaja duma)*, and will conduct revolutionary propaganda, will, that is to say, guide education in accordance with the principles of the new order. Whereas Lavrov laid the principal stress upon the education of the people for the revolution, and made the revolution dependent upon such education, Tkachev taught that the forcible overthrow of the old order would precede the revolutionary propaganda.

In matters of detail Tkachev recapitulates Bakunin's ideals. The existing *mir* with private ownership will be transformed into a completely communistic local community; all private tools and machinery for production will be expropriated; and the exchange of products will be effected directly, to the exclusion of all intermediaries. Physical, mental, and moral inequality will be abolished by degrees; all will be educated alike, in the spirit of love, equality, and fraternity; the existing family, with its subordination of woman and its indulgence of man's egoism and arbitrariness, will be abolished. The centralized state will gradually be replaced by the self-government of the communes.

Since the immediate aim of the revolutionaries is the seizure of political power, they must organize themselves in a "state conspiracy." By this Tkachev means something essentially similar to the Lavrovist "mass organization." He expressly condemns isolated revolutionary outbreaks on the part of small circles, but he demands like Bakunin a rigid hierarchical subordination to the "general leadership," for this alone "can bring definiteness of aim and can secure unity in the activity of all the members." For to Tkachev the immediate and sole program of revolutionary activity is "organization as a means for the disorganization and annihilation of the power of the existing State."

Tkachev remained editor of *Nabat* till 1877, and the paper was continued under other editors until 1881. It was disavowed by the *Narodnaja Volja* as Nechaev had been disavowed, for the bloodcurdling glorifications of terrorist deeds were too compromising.

The influence of *Nabat* in Russia does not seem to have been great, but Tkachev, writing under pseudonyms, diffused his views also in authorized radical periodicals. Though he had to choose his words carefully, in view of the censorship, he was, like other radical writers, perfectly well understood. Tkachev had an effective style as publicist and as literary and historical critic, and his writings exercised a revolutionary influence upon the young.[7]

[7] Tkachev was a consistent expounder of economic materialism. He rejected in its entirety Russian aristocratic literature with its excursions into the domain of the humiliated and the suffering. Owing to the new developments, he said, the position of writers had become economically insecure, and in their creative work this insecurity betrayed itself in the form of *Weltschmerz*. Consequently every aristocratic author exhibited two sides. For example

7) In the year 1877, a new *Zemlja i Volja* came into existence. The organs of this association advocated peaceful revolutionary propaganda. The agrarian problem was represented as the supreme social problem for Russia. The factory problem could be "left in the shade," since it did not really exist for Russia, but was the social problem of the West. In Russia, the supreme demands had always been for land and freedom. Land must be the property of those who tilled it, and must therefore be taken away from the landlords. For the Cossacks, liberty signified free self-governing communes, in which those elected to carry out the popular will were subject to recall. Quite similar were the views of the secret society *Zemlja i Volja,* as the successor of the revolutionary socialists Pugachev and Razin, men of the people. No attempt was made to formulate a more specific program; the future could take care of itself; for the time being it was necessary to realize "the revolution of the folk," that is to say to revolutionize the masses of the people, in order to render possible the socialistic organization of the Russian nation.

The organization of the society was directed towards the attainment of this aim. Its leadership was centralized, but not in accordance with the prescriptions of Bakunin and Tkachev. Where important questions had to be decided, the officers took a vote of the council, and in matters of supreme importance a ballot was taken of all the members. The council consisted of the members residing in St. Petersburg, which was the center. The league was subdivided into four groups: intellectuals (for propaganda and for the organization of university students); operatives; the village group (which contained the largest number of members); and the disorganization group. The last-named was the most important, for it had life and death powers over the members. Its duties were to help imprisoned comrades, to set them at liberty whenever possible, and to protect them against the violence of the administration; from time to time these duties brought the society into open conflict with the government, although such conflict was not a regular part of its program. As a

---

Turgenev, Goncharov, Pisemsky were great writers, but "apart from this their horizon did not extend further than the length of their noses"; with one side of his nature, Tolstoy loved the people, but with the other side he loved to chatter; Dostoyevsky was not worth mentioning; and so on.

precaution against treachery, traitors might be killed in case of need. The disorganization group kept the details of its plans and doings strictly secret, communicating them to the council in general outline merely.

In addition to the four groups there existed certain sections for special tasks, the most important of these being the "heavenly chancellery" of the central executive, whose business it was to provide passports, etc.

8) The aim of the *Zemlja i Volja* was peaceful revolution, but nevertheless the heralds of this peaceful revolution advanced to terrorist methods, the white terror evoking the red. In July, 1877, corporal punishment was administered in prison to Bogoljubov, a revolutionary, and the authorities committed a number of revengeful actions. In consequence of these, Trepov was shot by Vera Zasulich (1878), Mezencev was stabbed by Stepniak, and various other terrorist acts were committed or attempted.

In June, 1879, there was organized a declared terrorist party, *Narodnaja Volja* (People's Will) replacing the *Zemlja i Volja*. The purpose of the new party was to terrorize the government and the reactionary elements of society.

The party declared itself socialistic in the sense of the *narodniki*. Only the people's will had the right to sanction social forms; every idea that was to be realized politically and socially must "first of all traverse the consciousness and the will of the people." To this people's will, which strongly reminds us of Rousseau, the capitalist state was counterposed as oppressor. In accordance with the principles of people's weal and people's will, the *Narodnaja Volja* desired to restore power to the people by political revolution, and a legislative assembly would then undertake the reorganization of society. The leading socialistic principles, notwithstanding their infringement by the arbitrary proceedings of the monarchy, had remained alive in Russia. These principles were, the consciousness of the people that it was justly entitled to the land, communal and local self-government, the rudiments of federal organization, freedom of speech and conscience.

The political program of the *Narodnaja Volja* comprised the following items: continuous national representation; local self-government; independence of the *mir* as an economic and administrative unit; ownership of land by the folk; all factories and similar industrial enterprises to be in the hands of the operatives; absolute freedom of conscience, speech, press, assembly, combination, and electoral agitation; universal suffrage; replacement of standing armies by a militia.

More important than the program, were the organization and the work of the *Narodnaja Volja*. The leadership of the party was vested in the executive committee. The work was subdivided into the popular diffusion of the idea of a democratic revolution, and into agitation which was to give expression to the dissatisfaction of the folk and of society with the existing order. Terrorist activities were to take the form of the removal of the most noxious individualities in the government. The killing of spies was another terrorist duty.

With this end in view, small secret societies were to be organized everywhere, these being affiliated to and directed by the central executive committee. Members of the party were to endeavor to secure influential positions and ties in the administration, in the army, in society, and among the people.

Aware of the fact that a secret organization whose members comprised no more than an infinitesimal minority could not properly express and sustain the people's will, the energy of the party was concentrated upon preliminary labors, upon the preparations for a rising. "If, contrary to our expectations, this rising should prove needless, our collected forces can then be applied to the work of peace."

These general principles were incorporated in a number of specialized programs, which prescribed the work to be done among the urban operatives, in the army, in the intelligentsia, and among young people. Moreover, the party had to attempt to arouse European sympathy for its aims, and this, it was considered, could best be effected by suitable literary activities.

The *Narodnaja Volja* conducted all the terroristic attempts and enterprises, and was before all responsible for attempts made upon the life of the czar. Three such attempts had been undertaken before the society was organized, whilst the *Narodnaja Volja* was responsible for four. Despite its declared terrorist aim, "to break the charm of the administrative power" by the assassination of the most noxious members of the administration and the government, the *Narodnaja Volja* condemned the blind campaign of destruction advocated by Bakunin and Nechaev, Nechaev's methods being rejected as charlatanry. After March 13, 1881 (the assassination of Alexander II), the terrorist activity or the society came to an end. In the general belief this change of tactics was brought about by the alienation of public sympathy from the *Narodnaja Volja,* but according to Stepniak this was not the determining cause of the change. The *Narodnaja Volja,* he declares, discontinued individual outrages because it had decided to devote itself exclusively to the preliminary work of revolutionizing the masses.

It continued to exist, but seldom played any public part. (After Turgenev's death in 1883, the *Narodnaja Volja* issued a proclamation, and there were a few other manifestations of activity. During the revolutionary movement of 1905, it was reorganized as the Social Revolutionary Party.)

9) Besides the terrorist *Narodnaja Volja,* there issued in 1879 from the *Zemlja i Volja* the party of the *Chernyi Peredel* (Black Redistribution, that is to say, redistribution or reallotment of the black earth—see vol. I, p. 154). The aim of this party was to promote on agitation among the operatives and peasants. Plekhanov, who was its leader in the theoretical field, strongly condemned the methods of the *Narodnaja Volja.*

The *Chernyi Peredel* likewise declared itself representative of the *narodnichestvo,* of the revolutionary section of that movement, seeing that its members considered that the solution of the agrarian problem was the very essence of the social question, and being guided in this view by the same reasons as those which influenced the *narodavolcy.* Socialism was declared to be the last word in sociology, and collectivism was considered the goal of the "radical reformer." This radicalism must be "economic" radicalism, meaning that the radical reformer must strive to the utmost to secure the betterment of economic conditions, since these constitute the real basis of all other social and political conditions (historical materialism). In 1879, Plekhanov believed that collectivism could develop in Russia out of the *mir* and the artel, especially since captialism was preparing agriculture, too, and landownership for socialization—for in Russia as in Europe capitalism paved the way for socialism. Plekhanov and his associates in the *Chernyi Peredel* believed that capitalism in Russia would concentrate landed proprietorship, and would therefore prepare conditions for the "black redistribution" essential to the muzhik.

The *Chernyi Peredel* was likewise revolutionary, but its view of its mission differed from that of the *narodovolcy*. The members of the *Chernyi Peredel* considered that political revolutions had never secured economic freedom for the people, nor had even afforded anywhere guarantees for political freedom. Constitutions were exploited by the bourgeoisie against the monarch and against the working masses, and the same thing would happen in Russia. It was a matter of no importance whatever whether Alexander II or Alexander III did or did not serve out these "social cates" (the constitution); the bourgeoisie would eat them whilst the revolutionaries looked on. Doubtless the intelligentsia and also the folk desired political freedom; but for the *muzhik* freedom was intimately connected with economic conditions, and it was to such conditions that the *muzhik* must look in the first instance. The business of a genuinely practical revolutionary party in Russia was to awaken men intellectually and to prepare the means for the struggle. Such, at any rate, was the work of peaceful days; when the revolution came, the party would have to regulate the movement and to determine its trend. The special function of the intelligentsia was initiatory merely, the folk would do the rest for itself and would create its own leaders. But the function of the intelligentsia did not consist in the mere handing on of culture in accordance with legally authorized methods; an energetic revolutionary secret agitation must be promoted.

In 1881, the *Chernyi Peredel* was forced for a time to suspend its journalistic activities, but in 1883 the party was reorganized as the Group for the Liberation of Labor and developed henceforward along Marxist lines, in continuous and close connection with the Marxist and socialist movements in other lands and above all in Germany. In 1883, and in fuller detail in 1884, Plekhanov defined the attitude of his party towards other parties and trends, condemning from the Marxist outlook the socialism of Herzen and Chernyshevski, the anarchism of Bakunin, and the Blanquism of Tkachev. We shall have more to say about this matter when we come to discuss the history of Marxism.

George Woodcock   Anarchism in Latin America and Northern Europe [1]

George Woodcock (1912 ——)   George Woodcock was born in Winnipeg, Canada. He was educated in England, where he has worked in railway administration and as a farmer, free-lance writer, and editor. He has taught at the University of Washington and the University of British Columbia. He held a Guggenheim Fellowship in 1951–52 and since 1959 has been editor of the periodical *Canadian Literature*. He has a considerable number of books, articles, fiction, and poetry published, including biographies of Godwin, Proudhon, and Kropotkin.

Anarchism has thriven best in lands of the sun, where it is easy to dream of golden ages of ease and simplicity, yet where the clear light also heightens the shadows of existing misery. It is the men of the South who have flocked in their thousands to the black banners of anarchic revolt, the Italians and Andalusians and Ukrainians, the men of Lyons and Marseilles, of Naples and Barcelona. But though the Mediterranean countries and southern Russia have been its great strongholds, anarchism has a place that cannot be ignored in the political and intellectual life of many other countries. In a general history one cannot describe every libertarian movement as thoroughly as it might intrinsically deserve, but in this penultimate chapter I intend at least to sketch out the record of anarchism in Latin America, in Northern Europe, and particularly in Great Britain and the United States. [2]

During the nineteenth century the countries of Latin America were related to Spain and Portugal not only by cultural and linguistic ties, but also by similar social conditions. This was a relationship that favored the transmission of revolutionary ideas, and it was mostly the Spanish immi-

[1] From *Anarchism*, by George Woodcock. London: Christy & Moore, Ltd. Cleveland and New York: The World Publishing Company, 1962. Reprinted by permission of the publishers.
[2] For purposes of this volume, the sections on Great Britain and the United States have been omitted. [Editor's note.]

grants who spread anarchist ideals in Latin America, though in Argentina, as we have seen, the Italians also played an important missionary role. The earliest anarchist groups appeared in Mexico, Cuba, and Argentina at the beginning of the 1870s; these countries and Uruguay were represented at the last Congress of the Saint-Imier International in 1877, while in 1878 a Bakuninist League was founded in Mexico City.

The anarchists quickly became active in organizing craft and industrial workers throughout South and Central America, and until the early 1920s most of the trade unions in Mexico, Brazil, Peru, Chile, and Argentina were anarcho-syndicalist in general outlook; the prestige of the Spanish C.N.T. as a revolutionary organization was undoubtedly to a great extent responsible for this situation. The largest and most militant of these organizations was the *Federación Obrera Regional Argentina,* which was founded in 1901, largely under the inspiration of the Italian Pietro Gori; it grew quickly to a membership of nearly a quarter of a million, which dwarfed the rival social-democratic unions. From 1902 until 1909 the FORA waged a long campaign of general strikes against the employers and against antilabor legislation. Toward the end of this period there arose in Buenos Aires a situation in which the brutality of the authorities and the militancy of the workers incited each other to greater heights, until, on May Day, 1909, a gigantic demonstration marched through the streets of Buenos Aires and was broken up by the police, who inflicted many casualties on the trade unionists. In retaliation, a Polish anarchist killed Colonel Falcon, the Buenos Aires police chief who had been responsible for the deaths of many syndicalists. After this a rigorous antianarchist law was passed, but the FORA continued as a large and influential organization until 1929, when it finally merged with the·socialist U.G.T. into the General Confederation of Workers, and quickly shed its anarcho-syndicalist leanings.

In Mexico the anarchists played a considerable part in the revolutionary era that followed the downfall of the dictator Porfirio Díaz in 1910. One anarchist in particular, Ricardo Flores Magon, is still remembered among the fathers of the Mexican Revolution. With his brothers Jesús and Enrique he founded in 1900 an anarcho-syndicalist journal, *Regeneración,* which played a very important part during the next ten years in arousing the urban working class against the Díaz dictatorship. The Flores Magon brothers spent much of their lives in exile, carrying on propaganda from across the border in the United States, where they were several times imprisoned for their activities and where Ricardo died in jail in 1922.

Although Ricardo Flores Magon was concerned primarily with converting the urban workers to his anarcho-syndicalist ideas, he established links with the great agrarian leader Emiliano Zapata, whose activities in southern Mexico during the revolutionary era resemble remarkably those of Makhno in the Ukraine, for like Makhno he was a poor peasant who showed a remarkable power to inspire the oppressed farmers of southern Mexico and to lead them brilliantly in guerrilla warfare. The historian Henry Bamford Parkes remarked that the Zapatista army of the south was never an army in the ordinary sense, for its soldiers "spent their time plowing and reaping their newly won lands and took up arms only to repel invasion; they were an insurgent people." The philosophy of the Zapatista movement, with its egalitarianism and its desire to re-create a natural peasant order, with its insistence that the people must take the land themselves and govern themselves in village communities, with its distrust of politics and its contempt for personal gain, resembled very closely the rural anarchism that had risen under similar circumstances in Andalusia. Undoubtedly some of the libertarian ideas that inspired the trade unions in the cities and turned great Mexican painters, like Rivera and Dr. Atl, into temporary anarchists, found their way to Zapata in the South, but his movement seems to have gained its anarchic quality most of all from a dynamic combination of the leveling desires of the peasants and his own ruthless idealism. For Zapata was the one leader of the Mexican Revolution who never compromised, who never allowed himself to be corrupted by money or power, and who died as he lived, a poor and almost illiterate man fighting for justice to be done to men like himself.

In Mexico anarchy strikes one as the appropriate product of a chaotic history, a dramatic, divided land, and a localism as inveterate as that of Spain. In the Teutonic lands that face the North Sea and the Baltic, its presence is less expected, yet at least three of these countries, Germany, Holland, and Sweden, have produced libertarian movements of considerable historical interest.

German anarchism followed a course that curiously parallels the country's national development. In the 1840s, when Germany was a patchwork of kingdoms and principalities, the tendency was toward individualism, represented most extremely by Max Stirner. From the 1870s onward, it turned toward collectivism, until, in the twentieth century, the prevalent trend became a moderate anarcho-syndicalism, relatively nonviolent in practice and inspired by a respect for efficiency and intellect.

Anarchism first appeared in Germany under the influence of Hegel and Proudhon; it began in the 1840s with the very different personalities of Max Stirner and Wilhelm Weitling. Stirner, as we have seen, represented unqualified egoism; Weitling became a communist much influenced by Fourier and Saint-Simon. Like the anarchist communists he rejected both property and the wage system, and in his earlier writings, such as *Garantien der Harmonie und Freiheit* (1842), he put forward a basically phalansterian plan of a society in which liberated human desires would be harmonized for the general good. Though Weitling wished to destroy the state as it existed, there were elements of utopian regimentation in his vision of a "harmonious" communist society, but in time these were tempered by the influence of Proudhon.

After Weitling's final departure to the United States in 1849, he abandoned his communism and moved even closer to Proudhonian mutualism. In the monthly journal, *Republik der Arbeiter,* which he published in New York from 1850 to 1854, he criticized the experimental Utopian colonies that were still numerous in the United States as diversions of the workers' energy, which in his view should attack the vital problem of credit by the foundation of a Bank of Exchange. The Bank of Exchange, he tells us in truly Proudhonian tones, "is the soul of all reforms, the foundation for all cooperative efforts." It will set up stores for raw materials and finished products, and issue paper money based on labor value to facilitate their exchange. Associated with the Bank will be trade associations of journeymen for cooperative production, and the profits from exchange transactions will enable the Bank to provide for education, hospitals, and the care of the aged and the disabled. By these means, and without state intervention or the elimination of the individual producer, the Bank will destroy the monopoly of the capitalist and provide an economic structure which will render political institutions unnecessary. These later ideas of Weitling were undoubtedly much more influential in the neo-Proudhonian movement of the nineteenth-century United States than in Germany.

Several other German social theoreticians fell under the influence of Proudhonian anarchism during the 1840s. Karl Grün, possibly the most ardent convert, met Proudhon in Paris during 1844, and his *Die Soziale Bewegung in Frankreich und Belgien* was the first work to introduce Proudhon's ideas to the German public. Grün was a versatile man of letters who, like Proudhon, served a short, disillusioning period as a parliamentarian—in the Prussian National Assembly during 1849—and spent much of his life in exile, dying in Vienna in 1887. It was during his earlier period that Grün was most attracted to the mutualist philosophy; in fact, he ventured beyond it, for he criticized Proudhon for not attacking the wage system, and pointed out that the growing complexity of industry made it impossible to decide on each man's product with any accuracy or justice. Therefore consumption and production must alike depend on choice. "Let us have no right at all against the right of the individualist."

Moses Hess, another German socialist, who knew Proudhon and Bakunin in Paris during the 1840's, actually adopted the title "anarchy" for his own social philosophy, expounded in 1843 in *Die Philosophie der Tat*. Hess was a rather solitary and truculent figure who stood out among the Rhineland socialists as Marx's most important rival. He was never so close to Proudhon as Grün became, and he later quarreled bitterly with Bakunin, but he agreed with both in rejecting the State and dismissing organized religion as a form of mental bondage. Yet his doctrine was curiously muddled. In declaring that all free actions must proceed from individual impulses, unmarred by external influence, he came near to Stirner. In envisaging a social system under which men would work according to inclination and society would provide automatically for every man's reasonable needs, he anticipated Kropotkin. But he grafted on to his libertarian dream a number of features, such as universal suffrage and national workshops, that no true anarchist would entertain.

Neither Stirnerite nor Proudhonian anarchism had a lasting influence in Germany. Stirner gained no German following at all until after Nietzsche had become popular, and the interest in Proudhon's ideas disappeared in the general reaction that followed the failure of the revolutionary movements of 1848 and 1849. A whole generation now passed before the reappearance of any perceptible anarchist tendency. In the early years of the First International neither Bakunin nor Proudhon had any German supporters, and the Lassallian delegates who attended one Congress of the Saint-Imier International agreed with the anarchists only in their desire to stimulate cooperative experiments.

During the latter part of the century, however, anarchistic factions began to appear within the German Social Democratic Party. In 1878, for example, the bookbinder Johann Most, who had formerly been a fiery member of the Reichstag, was converted to anarchism while in exile in England. With Wilhelm Hasselmann, another anarchist convert, he was expelled by the Social Democrats in 1880, but his journal, *Die Freiheit,* published first in London in 1879 and then in New York, continued to wield an influence until the end of the century on the more revolutionary socialists both in Germany and in exile. A few small anarchist groups were formed under his influence in Berlin and Hamburg, but it is doubtful if their total membership in the 1880s much exceeded two hundred; the particular kind of violence preached by Most encouraged the conspiratorial group rather than the mass movement. One such group, led by a printer named Reinsdorf, plotted to throw a bomb at the Kaiser in 1883. They were unsuccessful, but all of them were executed.

Most's influence was also felt in Austria, where the powerful Radical faction of the Social Democratic Party was anarchist in all but name. Libertarian ideas also penetrated deeply into the trade unions in Austria, Bohemia, and Hungary, and for a brief period from 1880 to 1884 the Austro-Hungarian labor movement was probably more strongly impregnated with anarchist influences than any other in Europe outside Spain and Italy. More influential even than Most was the Bohemian Joseph Peukert, who published in

Vienna a paper of anarchist communist leanings called
Zukunft. When the Austrian authorities began to suppress
meetings and demonstrations in 1882, the anarchists and
radicals resisted violently, and a number of policemen were
killed. Finally, in January 1884, the authorities became so
disturbed by the spread of anarchist propaganda and the
increase of violent clashes between police and revolutionaries
that they declared a state of siege in Vienna and promulgated
special decrees against anarchists and socialists. One of the
anarchist leaders, Most's disciple Stellmacher, was executed,
and the rest, including Peukert, fled from the country. From
that time onward anarchism ceased to be a movement of any
importance in the Austrian Empire, though small propaganda groups did emerge in later years, and one libertarian
literary circle in Prague counted among its sympathizers and
occasional visitors both Franz Kafka and Jaroslav Hasek,
author of *The Good Soldier Schweik*.

In later years Germany produced at least three outstanding anarchist intellectuals, Erich Meuhsam, Rudolf Rocker,
and Gustav Landauer. Muehsam, one of the leading socially
engaged poets of the Weimar Republic, played an important
part in the Bavarian Soviet rising of 1919, and was eventually
beaten to death in a Nazi concentration camp. Rudolf
Rocker spent many years in England, about which I shall
say more in the following pages; after internment during the
First World War, he returned to Berlin, and became one of
the leaders of the anarcho-syndicalist movement during the
period up to the Nazi dictatorship. He was a prolific and able
writer, and at least one of his works, *Nationalism and Culture,* is a classic statement of the anarchist case against the
cult of the national State.

Gustav Landauer, who called himself an anarcho-socialist,
was one of those free spirits who never find a happy place
in any organized movement. As a young man during the
1890s he joined the Social Democratic Party, and became
the leader of a group of young rebels eventually expelled
because of their anarchistic leanings. For some years as a
disciple of Kropotkin, he edited *Der Sozialist* in Berlin, but
by 1900 he had shifted toward a position much closer to
Proudhon and Tolstoy, advocating passive resistance in the
place of violence and looking toward the spread of cooperative enterprises as the really constructive way to social

change. He differed from most other anarchists in appealing particularly to the intellectuals, whose role in social change he regarded as extremely important. This led to the failure of *Der Sozialist,* which never gained a mass readership, and to a growing sense of isolation on Landauer's part. Today Landauer's books—both his political commentaries and his essays in literary appreciation—seem excessively romantic. Yet he was one of those men of complete integrity and passionate love for the truth who represent anarchism at its best, perhaps all the more because they stand alone. Despite his distrust of political movements, Landauer was taken up in the wave of revolutionary excitement that swept Germany during the years immediately after the First World War, and, like Muehsam and Ernst Toller, he became one of the leaders of the Bavarian Soviet. In the repression that followed its downfall he was killed by the soldiers sent from Berlin. "They dragged him into the prison courtyard," said Ernst Toller. "An officer struck him in the face. The men shouted, 'Dirty Bolshie! Let's finish him off!' A rain of blows from rifle butts descended on him. They trampled on him till he was dead." The officer responsible for Landauer's murder was a Junker aristocrat, Major Baron von Gagern; he was never punished or even brought to trial.

Early in the present century the anarcho-syndicalist tendency quickly outgrew the small groups of anarchist communists and the circles of individualists upholding the ideas of Stirner and of John Henry Mackay.[3] Syndicalism originated in Germany with a dissident group calling themselves "Localists," who in the early 1890s opposed the centralizing tendencies of the Social Democratic trade unions and in 1897 broke away to form a federation of their own, the *Freie Vereinigung Deutscher Gewerkschaften.* In its early days most of the members of this organization still adhered politically to the Left wing of the Social Democratic Party, but in the years immediately preceding the First World War they fell under the influence of the French syndicalists and adopted an antiparliamentarian attitude. At this time the FVDG was still a small organization, with about 20,000

[3] Mackay was a wealthy Scot, born in Greenock, who became a naturalized German and, besides writing Stirner's biography, published a novel of his own, *The Anarchists: A Picture of Society at the Close of the Nineteenth Century,* which revealed him as a kind of inferior libertarian Gissing. [Woodcock's note.]

members, mostly in Berlin and Hamburg. After the war, in 1919, a congress held in Düsseldorf reorganized the federation on anarcho-syndicalist lines and renamed it the *Freie Arbeiter Union.* The reformed organization expanded rapidly in the revolutionary atmosphere of the early 1920s, and by the time of the Berlin International Syndicalist Congress of 1922 it had reached a membership of 120,000, which expanded further during the decade to a high point of 200,000. Like all other German organizations of the Left, the *Freie Arbeiter Union* was destroyed by the Nazis on their accession to power in 1933, and its militants either fled abroad or were imprisoned in the concentration camps, where many of them were killed or died of privation.

In Sweden there still exists an organization very similar to the German *Freie Arbeiter Union.* This is the *Sveriges Arbetares Central;* in the Baltic amber of Swedish neutrality it has been preserved from the disasters of oppression and war that destroyed almost every other anarcho-syndicalist organization, and today, in the 1960s, it still functions as a working federation of trade unionists.

There were anarchists in Sweden since the 1880s, when they infiltrated the newly formed Social Democratic Party, from which they were expelled in 1891 during the general purge of anarchists from parties belonging to the Second International. Thereafter, as anarcho-syndicalists, they worked within the trade unions until, after a disastrous general strike in 1909, they decided to break away and set up their own federation in imitation of the French C.G.T. In 1910 they founded the *Sveriges Arbetares Central.* It was a tiny organization at first, with a mere five hundred members, but its militant call to direct action appealed particularly to the lumbermen, miners, and construction workers, whose work was heavy and whose wages were generally low. By 1924, at the peak of its influence, the S.A.C. had 37,000 members; still, in the 1950s, it retained more than 20,000 members, published its own daily paper, *Arbetaren,* in Stockholm, and loyally kept alive the Syndicalist International Workingmen's Association.

There is a certain historical interest in considering how this rare survivor from the golden age of revolutionary syndicalism has adapted itself to the world of the 1960s, and a recent survey of world labor by American sociologists[4] includes a valuable description of the *Sveriges Arbetares Central* in the mid-twentieth century.

The structure of the federation has apparently remained that of an orthodox syndicalist organization, based on "local syndicates, each embracing all members within a geographical area without regard to trade or industry"; "the local syndicate remains the chief repository of union power," being "affiliated directly to the national center."

It seems clear, however, that union practices have been modified by changing social conditions. Theoretically, as the authors of the survey point out, collective bargaining is opposed by the Swedish syndicalists:

> As a means of exercising control over labor conditions each local syndicate has established a register committee, the function of which is to prepare wage schedules. After approval by the syndicate these schedules constitute the wages for which members may work. The failure of the register method to provide binding wages for definite periods of time enabled employers to cut rates during periods of unemployment, and some of the syndicates have been forced to enter into agreements. The syndicalists have advocated as means of enforcing their demands, the sympathetic strike, the slowdown through literal observance of working rules, shoddy work, and ca'canny. But these methods have proved incongruous in a so highly organized society as the Swedish, and, in fact, the syndicalists have practiced collective bargaining.

The survey goes on to remark that "the Swedish syndicalists have remained faithful to the political tenets of their doctrine," and that their unions "abstain strictly from political activity." Officially, "the eventual overthrow of capitalism through the revolutionary general strike" is still professed by the leaders of the S.A.C., but, the survey concludes, "as far as practical trade unionism is concerned . . . there is not a great deal of difference between the socialist and the syndicalist unions."

Theoretically, in other words, the *Sveriges Arbetares Central* has remained faithful to the kind of revolutionary syn-

[4] Walter Galenson (ed.), *Comparative Labor Movements.* New York, 1952.

dicalism preached by Pierre Monatte at the Amsterdam Congress in 1907; practically it has accepted standard modern procedures in industrial relationships; and in theory and practice alike it has gone far away from pure anarchism.

In Holland, anarchism has shared with the movements in Germany and Sweden their tendency toward syndicalism, but it has gained a character of its own from the militant pacifism of many of its leaders, and particularly of Ferdinand Domela Nieuwenhuis.

It was under the dynamic influence of Nieuwenhuis that Dutch anarchism really developed. In the first International the small Dutch Federation worked closely with the Belgians led by Caesar de Paepe; it supported Bakunin in his quarrel with Marx, opposed the centralism of the General Council, and joined the Saint-Imier International without ever becoming an organization of true anarchists. It was not, in fact, until the late 1880s that a clearly defined anarchist movement began to appear in Holland.

It arose out of the revival of the Dutch socialist movement under the inspiration of Nieuwenhuis at the end of the 1870s. Nieuwenhuis began his active life as a famous Lutheran preacher in a fashionable church of The Hague. He was still in his early thirties when he underwent a crisis of conscience rather similar to William Godwin's, and decided to leave the Church and devote his life to the cause of the workers. In 1879 he resigned his pastorate and founded a journal, *Recht voor Allen,* in which he advocated an ethical socialism based on a strong emotional revulsion against oppression and war, and a deep sense of human brotherhood; it was a distillation of Christian principles into modern social terms. Nieuwenhuis ceased to be a pastor, but he never ceased in the real sense to be a religious man. His strength of personality and his idealistic fervor soon made him the most influential personality among the scattered groups of Dutch socialists, and when they came together in 1881 to found the Socialist League, he became its undisputed leader.

The early years of the League, when it directed its efforts to antiwar propaganda and trade-union organization, were very stormy, and most of its active members were imprisoned at one time or another, including Nieuwenhuis himself, but they gained enough ground for Nieuwenhuis to be elected to parliament in 1888 as a Socialist; he remained there for three years, but, like Proudhon and Grün, he found it a saddening experience, and emerged a convinced antiparliamentarian. It was during his period in parliament that he began to turn toward anarchism, and to advocate, before French revolutionary syndicalism had been developed, the idea of industrial direct action and the general strike as means for the workers to free themselves from political and economic oppression and to combat war.

Already, at the International Socialist Congress in 1889, Nieuwenhuis had attacked the participation of socialists in parliamentary activity, and at the Zurich Congress in 1891 he raised, in violent opposition to Wilhelm Liebknecht, the idea of turning a war between nations into an international revolutionary war between classes by means of the general strike. At these congresses, and again in 1893 and 1896, he stood out in defense of the idea that the International should include socialists of every shade, from the most moderate reformists to the most extreme anarchists, and in the end he led the Dutch delegation out of the London Congress of 1896 as a final protest against the Second International's expulsion of the anarchists.

Meanwhile dissension had arisen within the Dutch Socialist League itself, between the majority, who followed Nieuwenhuis in his drift toward anarchism, and a strong minority attracted by German Social Democracy. The differences came to a head at the Groningen Congress of 1893, when the majority carried the League into the anarchist camp and the parliamentarians departed to form their own Socialist Party.

While Nieuwenhuis and his followers were winning the Socialist League to anarchism, their efforts to organize trade unions had also been largely successful, and in 1893 a syndicalist federation, the *National Arbeids Sekretariat* was created. It developed under the ideological influence of Christian Cornelissen, who eventually became one of the most important of anarcho-syndicalist theoreticians. He was particularly interested in the international organization of syndicalism, and the intellectualism of his attitude made him one of the few links between the working-class militants of the C.G.T., such as Pouget and Yvetot, with whom he was in direct contact, and the theoretical syndicalists who gathered around Sorel and Lagardelle, and to whose journal, *Le Mouvement Socialiste,* he contributed. Cornelissen's influence in the European anarchist movement was very considerable during the early years of the present century, but it dwindled away to nothing when he joined Kropotkin and Guillaume in supporting the Allies during the First World War.

For almost a decade the *National Arbeids Sekretariat,* whose membership at this time did not reach more than 20,000, remained the most active and influential organization among the Dutch trade unions. Its fall from this ascendant position came rather dramatically during the general strike of 1903, which started on the railways, spread to other industries, and then, at the moment of apparent success, collapsed suddenly when the government began to arrest the leaders and to use soldiers as blacklegs. The Social Democrats reaped the benefit of this defeat, and there was a mass exodus from the anarcho-syndicalist unions. For several years the *National Arbeids Sekretariat* maintained no more than a small bridgehead among the dock workers of Amsterdam and Rotterdam, and by 1910 its membership had shrunk to little more than 3,000.

The anarchist movement outside the trade unions also diminished in numbers and influence, but the personal prestige of Nieuwenhuis did not suffer greatly. He was the kind of idealist who does not need a movement to establish a moral influence, and he continued through the First World War and until his death in 1919 to wage his passionate antimilitarist campaigns, which were afterward continued by younger Dutch anarchist pacifists like Albert de Jong and Bart de Ligt, author of that extraordinary manual of passive resistance, *The Conquest of Violence,* which was read widely by British and American pacifists during the 1930s and led many of them to adopt an anarchistic point of view.

The Dutch anarcho-syndicalists slowly recovered some of the ground they had lost in 1903, and by 1922 the *National Arbeids Sekretariat,* though now a minority in comparison with the other trade unions, had regained its earlier membership; when it joined the International Workingmen's Association in 1922 it had almost 23,000 members. But, like the syndicalist movement in France, it soon began to suffer from the spell which Russian Communism cast over its younger militants. Eventually the organization itself was captured by the Communists, and a large minority who remained faithful to antiparliamentarian traditions broke away in 1923 to form the *Nederlandisch Syndikalistisch Vakverbond*. It never gained more than a fraction of the dominant influence which the *National Arbeids Sekretariat* had once wielded in the Dutch labor movement. After 1903, in fact, Dutch anarchism reconciled itself to having become a permanent minority movement whose widely respected leaders, like Nieuwenhuis and Cornelissen, enjoyed the prestige that in northern lands is granted to those voices crying in the wilderness which form the conveniently externalized consciences of peoples largely devoted to the acquisition and enjoyment of material prosperity.

Alexander Berkman

Kronstadt: The Final Act in Russian Anarchism [1]

Alexander Berkman (1870–1936) The youngest of four children, Berkman was born in Vilna, Russia, to a prosperous family. Attracted to radical ideas as a youth in St. Petersburg, he was expelled from school after submitting an atheistic essay to his instructors. Berkman came to the United States in 1887 and settled in New York City. He was a well-known anarchist leader in the United States and life-long friend of Emma Goldman. His dramatic attempt on the life of Henry C. Frick is considered the event that broke the back of resistance to the striking workers' demands, although it led to his imprisonment, a penalty he served for over twenty years. Among his numerous agitational writings the best-known of his books are *Prison Memoirs*, and *The Bolshevik Myth*. He died as the result of a suicide attempt induced by illness and poverty.

KRONSTADT[2]

Petrograd, February, 1921—The

cold is extreme and there is intense suffering in the city.

[1] From *The Bolshevik Myth*, by Alexander Berkman. By permission of Liveright, Publishers, New York. Copyright (c) R, 1953 by Elinor Fitzgerald.

[2] An exhaustive study of the Kronstadt tragedy, with the documents pertaining to it, will be found in the author's brochure, "The Kronstadt Rebellion," published by *Der Syndicalist*, Berlin, 1922. [Berkman's note, as are all others in this extract.]

Snowstorms have isolated us from the provinces; the supply of provisions has almost ceased. Only half a pound of bread is being issued now. Most of the houses are unheated. At dusk old women prowl about the big woodpile near the Hotel Astoria, but the sentry is vigilant. Several factories have been closed for lack of fuel, and the employees put on half rations. They called a meeting to consult about the situation, but the authorities did not permit it to take place.

The Trubotchny millworkers have gone on strike. In the distribution of winter clothing, they complain, the Communists received undue advantage over the nonpartisans. The Government refuses to consider the grievances till the men return to work.

Crowds of strikers gathered in the street near the mills, and soldiers were sent to disperse them. They were *kursanti,* Communist youths of the military academy. There was no violence.

Now the strikers have been joined by the men from the Admiralty shops and Galernaya docks. There is much resentment against the arrogant attitude of the Government. A street demonstration was attempted, but mounted troops suppressed it.

February 27—Nervous feeling in the city. The strike situation is growing more serious. The Patronny mills, the Baltiysky and Laferm factories have suspended operations. The authorities have ordered the strikers to resume work. Martial law in the city. The special Committee of Defense *(Komitet Oboroni)* is vested with exceptional powers, Zinoviev at its head.

At the Soviet session last evening a military member of the Defense Committee denounced the strikers as traitors to the Revolution. It was Lashevitch. He looked fat, greasy, and offensively sensuous. He called the dissatisfied workers "leeches attempting extortion" *(shkurniki),* and demanded drastic measures against them. The Soviet passed a resolution *locking out* the men of the Trubotchny mill. It means deprivation of rations—actual starvation.

February 28—Strikers' proclamations have appeared on the streets today. They cite cases of workers found frozen to death in their homes. The main demand is for winter cloth-

ing and more regular issue of rations. Some of the circulars
protest against the suppression of factory meetings. "The
people want to take counsel together to find means of relief,"
they state. Zinoviev asserts the whole trouble is due to
Menshevik and Social Revolutionist plotting.

For the first time a political turn is being given to the
strikes. Late in the afternoon a proclamation was posted
containing larger demands. "A complete change is necessary
in the policies of the Government," it reads. "First of all, the
workers and peasants need freedom. They don't want to live
by the decrees of the Bolsheviki; they want to control their
own destinies. We demand the liberation of all arrested
socialists and nonpartisan workingmen; abolition of martial
law; freedom of speech, press, and assembly for all who
labor; free election of shop and factory committees, of labor
union and Soviet representatives."

March 1—Many arrests are taking place. Groups of
strikers surrounded by Tchekists, on their way to prison, are
a common sight. Much indignation in the city. I hear that
several unions have been liquidated and their active members turned over to the Tcheka. But proclamations continue
to appear. The arbitrary stand of the authorities is having
the effect of rousing reactionary tendencies. The situation is
growing tense. Calls for the *Utchredilka* (Constituent Assembly) are being heard. A manifesto is circulating, signed
by the "Socialist Workers of the Nevsky District," openly
attacking the Communist regime. "We know who is afraid of
the Constituent Assembly," it declares. "It is they who will
no longer be able to rob us. Instead they will have to answer
before the representatives of the people for their deceit, their
thefts, and all their crimes."

Zinoviev is alarmed; he has wired Moscow for troops.
The local garrison is said to be in sympathy with the strikers.
Military from the provinces has been ordered to the city:
special communist regiments have already arrived. Extraordinary martial law has been declared today.

March 2—Most disquieting reports. Large strikes have
broken out in Moscow. In the Astoria I heard today that
armed conflicts have taken place near the Kremlin' and
blood has been shed. The Bolsheviki claim the coincidence

of events in the two capitals as proof of a counterrevolutionary conspiracy.

It is said that Kronstadt sailors have come to the city to look into the cause of trouble. Impossible to tell fact from fiction. The absence of a public press encourages the wildest rumors. The official papers are discredited.

March 3—Kronstadt is disturbed. It disapproves of the Government's drastic methods against the dissatisfied workers. The men of the warship *Petropavlovsk* have passed a resolution of sympathy with the strikers.

It has become known today that on February 28 a committee of sailors was sent to this city to investigate the strike situation. Its report was unfavorable to the authorities. On March 1 the crews of the First and Second Squadrons of the Baltic Fleet called a public meeting at Yakorny Square. The gathering was attended by 16,000 sailors, Red Army men, and workers. The Chairman of the Executive Committee of the Kronstadt Soviet, the communist Vassiliev, presided. The audience was addressed by Kalinin, President of the Republic, and by Kuzmin, Commissar of the Baltic Fleet. The attitude of the sailors was entirely friendly to the Soviet Government, and Kalinin was met on his arrival in Kronstadt with military honors, music, and banners.

At the meeting the Petrograd situation and the report of the sailors' investigating committee were discussed. The audience was outspoken in its indignation at the means employed by Zinoviev against the workers. President Kalinin and Commissar Kusmin berated the strikers and denounced the *Petropavlovsk* Resolution as counterrevolutionary. The sailors emphasized their loyalty to the Soviet system, but condemned the Bolshevik bureaucracy. The resolution was passed.

March 4—Great nervous tension in the city. The strikes continue; labor disorders have again taken place in Moscow. A wave of discontent is sweeping the country. Peasant uprisings are reported from Tambov, Siberia, the Ukraine, and Caucasus. The country is on the verge of desperation. It was confidently hoped that with the end of civil war the communists would mitigate the severe military regime. The Government had announced its intention of economic reconstruction, and the people were eager to cooperate. They looked forward to the lightening of the heavy burdens, the abolition of wartime restrictions, and the introduction of elemental liberties.

The fronts are liquidated, but the old policies continue, and labor militarization is paralyzing industrial revival. It is openly charged that the Communist Party is more interested in entrenching its political power than in saving the Revolution.

An official manifesto appeared today. It is signed by Lenin and Trotsky and declares Kronstadt guilty of mutiny *(myatezh)*. The demand of the sailors for free Soviets is denounced as "a counterrevolutionary conspiracy against the proletarian Republic." Members of the Communist Party are ordered into the mills and factories to "rally the workers to the support of the Government against the traitors." Kronstadt is to be suppressed.

The Moscow radio station sent out a message addressed "to all, all, all":

> Petrograd is orderly and quiet, and even the few factories where accusations against the Soviet Government were recently voiced now understand that it is the work of provocators. . . . Just at this moment, when in America a new Republican regime is assuming the reins of government and showing inclination to take up business relations with Soviet Russia, the spreading of lying rumors and the organization of disturbances in Kronstadt have the sole purpose of influencing the American President and changing his policy toward Russia. At the same time the London Conference is holding its sessions, and the spreading of similar rumors must influence also the Turkish delegation and make it more submissive to the demands of the Entente. The rebellion of the *Petropavlovsk* crew is undoubtedly part of a great conspiracy to create trouble within Soviet Russia and to injure our international position. . . . This plan is being carried out within Russia by a Czarist general and former officers, and their activities are supported by the Mensheviki and Social Revolutionists.

The whole Northern District is under martial law and all gatherings are interdicted. Elaborate precautions have been taken to protect the Government institutions. Machine guns are placed in the Astoria, the living quarters of Zinoviev and other prominent Bolsheviki. These preparations are increasing general nervousness. Official proclamations command the immediate return of the strikers to the factories, prohibit suspension of work, and warn the populace against congregating in the streets.

The Committee of Defense has initiated a "cleaning" of the city. Many workers suspected of sympathizing with Kronstadt have been placed under arrest. All Petrograd sailors and part of the garrison thought to be "untrustworthy" have been ordered to distant points, while the families of Kronstadt sailors living in Petrograd are held as hostages. The Committee of Defense notified Kronstadt that "the prisoners are kept as 'pledges' for the safety of the Commissar of the Baltic Fleet, N. N. Kusmin, the Chairman of the Kronstadt Soviet, T. Vassiliev, and other Communists. If the least harm be suffered by our comrades, the hostages will pay with their lives."

"We want no bloodshed," Kronstadt wired in reply. "Not a single Communist has been harmed by us."

The Petrograd workers are anxiously awaiting developments. They hope that the intercession of the sailors may turn the situation in their favor. The term of office of the Kronstadt Soviet is about to expire, and arrangements are being made for the coming elections.

On March 2 a conference of delegates took place, at which 300 representatives of the ships, the garrison, the labor unions and factories were present, among them also a number of Communists. The Conference approved the Resolution passed by the mass meeting the previous day. Lenin and Trotsky have declared it counterrevolutionary and proof of a White conspiracy.[3]

RESOLUTION OF THE GENERAL MEETING
OF THE CREWS OF THE FIRST AND
SECOND SQUADRONS OF THE
BALTIC FLEET

Held March 1, 1921

Having heard the report of the representatives sent by the General Meeting of Ship Crews to Petrograd to investigate the situation there, Resolved:

[3] The historic document, suppressed in Russia, is here reproduced in full.

1) In view of the fact that the present Soviets do not express the will of the workers and peasants, immediately to hold new elections by secret ballot, the pre-election campaign to have full freedom of agitation among the workers and peasants;

2) To establish freedom of speech and press for workers and peasants, for anarchists and Left socialist parties;

3) To secure freedom of assembly for labor unions and peasant organizations;

4) To call a nonpartisan conference of the workers, Red Army soldiers and sailors of Petrograd, Kronstadt, and of Petrograd Province, no later than March 19, 1921;

5) To liberate all political prisoners of socialist parties, as well as all workers, peasants, soldiers, and sailors imprisoned in connection with the labor and peasant movements;

6) To elect a commission to review the cases of those held in prison and concentration camps;

7) To abolish all *politodeli* (political bureaus) because no party should be given special privileges in the propagation of its ideas or receive the financial support of the Government for such purposes. Instead there should be established educational and cultural commissions, locally elected and financed by the Government;

8) To abolish immediately all *zagraditelniye otryadi* (Armed units organized by the Bolsheviki for the purpose of suppressing traffic and confiscating foodstuffs and other products. The irresponsibility and arbitrariness of their methods were proverbial throughout the country).

9) To equalize the rations of all who work, with the exception of those employed in trades detrimental to health;

10) To abolish the Communist fighting detachments in all branches of the Army, as well as the Communist guards kept on duty in mills and factories. Should such guards or military detachments be found necessary, they are to be appointed in the Army from the ranks, and in the factories according to the judgment of the workers;

11) To give the peasants full freedom of action in regard to their land, and also the right to keep cattle, on condition that the peasants manage with their own means; that is, without employing hired labor;

12) To request all branches of the Army, as well as our comrades, the military *kursanti*, to concur in our resolutions;

13) To demand for the latter publicity in the press;

14) To appoint a Traveling Commission of Control;

15) To permit free *kustarnoye* (individual small-scale) production by one's own efforts.

Resolution passed unanimously by Brigade Meeting, two persons refraining from voting.

PETRICHENKO, *Chairman Brigade Meeting*.

PEREPELKIN, *Secretary*.

Resolution passed by an overwhelming majority of the Kronstadt garrison.

VASSILIEV, *Chairman*.

Kalinin and Vassiliev vote against the Resolution.

March 4—Late at night. The extraordinary session of the Petro-Soviet in the Tauride Palace was packed with Communists, mostly youngsters, fanatical and intolerant. Admission by special ticket; a *propusk* (permit) also had to be secured to return home after interdicted hours. Representatives of shops and labor committees were in the galleries, the seats in the main body having been occupied by Communists. Some factory delegates were given the floor, but the moment they attempted to state their case, they were shouted down. Zinoviev repeatedly urged the meeting to give the opposition an opportunity to be heard, but his appeal lacked energy and conviction.

Not a voice was raised in favor of the Constituent Assembly. A millworker pleaded with the Government to consider the complaints of the workers who are cold and hungry. Zinoviev replied that the strikers are enemies of the Soviet regime. Kalinin declared Kronstadt the headquarters of General Kozlovsky's plot. A sailor reminded Zinoviev of the time when he and Lenin were hunted as counterrevolutionists by Kerensky and were saved by the very sailors whom they now denounce as traitors. Kronstadt demands only honest elections, he declared. He was not allowed to proceed. The stentorian voice and impassioned appeal of Yevdakimov, Zinoviev's lieutenant, wrought the Communists up to a high pitch of excitement. His resolution was passed amid a tumult of protest from the nonpartisan dele-

gates and labor men. The resolution declared Kronstadt
guilty of a counterrevolutionary attempt against the Soviet
regime and demands its immediate surrender. It is a declaration of war.

March 5—Many Bolsheviki refuse to believe that the
Soviet resolution will be carried out. It were too monstrous
a thing to attack by force of arms the "pride and glory of the
Russian Revolution," as Trotsky christened the Kronstadt
sailors. In the circle of their friends many Communists
threaten to resign from the Party should such a bloody deed
come to pass.

Trotsky was to address the Petro-Soviet last evening. His
failure to appear was interpreted as indicating that the seriousness of the situation has been exaggerated. But during the
night he arrived, and today he issued an ultimatum to
Kronstadt:

> The Workers' and Peasants' Government has decreed
> that Kronstadt and the rebellious ships must immediately
> submit to the authority of the Soviet Republic. There-
> fore, I command all who have raised their hand against
> the socialist fatherland to lay down their arms at once.
> The obdurate are to be disarmed and turned over to the
> Soviet authorities. The arrested commissars and other
> representatives of the Government are to be liberated at
> once. Only those surrendering unconditionally may count
> on the mercy of the Soviet Republic.
>
> Simultaneously I am issuing orders to prepare to quell
> the mutiny and subdue the mutineers by force of arms.
> Responsibility for the harm that may be suffered by the
> peaceful population will fall entirely upon the heads of
> the counterrevolutionary mutineers.
>
> This warning is final.
>
> > TROTSKY, ...
> > *Chairman Revolutionary Military*
> > *Soviet of the Republic.*
>
> KAMENEV,
> *Commander-in-Chief.*

The city is on the verge of panic. The factories are closed,
and there are rumors of demonstrations and riots. Threats
against Jews are becoming audible. Military forces continue

to flow into Petrograd and environs. Trotsky has sent another demand to Kronstadt to surrender, the order containing the threat: "I'll shoot you like pheasants." Even some Communists are indignant at the tone assumed by the Government. It is a fatal error, they say, to interpret the workers' plea for bread as opposition. Kronstadt's sympathy with the strikers and their demand for honest elections have been turned by Zinoviev into a counterrevolutionary plot. I have talked the situation over with several friends, among them a number of Communists. We feel there is yet time to save the situation. A commission in which the sailors and workers would have confidence, could allay the roused passions and find a satisfactory solution of the pressing problems. It is incredible that a comparatively unimportant incident, as the original strike in the Trubotchny mill, should be deliberately provoked into civil war with all the bloodshed it entails.

The Communists with whom I have discussed the suggestion all favor it, but dare not take the initiative. No one believes in the Kozlovsky story. All agree that the sailors are the staunchest supporters of the Soviets; their object is to compel the authorities to grant needed reforms. To a certain degree they have already succeeded. The *zagraditelniye otryadi*, notoriously brutal and arbitrary, have been abolished in the Petrograd province, and certain labor organizations have been given permission to send representatives to the villages for the purchase of food. During the last two days special rations and clothing have also been issued to several factories. The Government fears a general uprising. Petrograd is now in an "extraordinary state of siege"; being out of doors is permitted only till nine in the evening. But the city is quiet. I expect no serious upheaval if the authorities can be prevailed upon to take a more reasonable and just course. In the hope of opening the road to a peaceful solution, I have submitted to Zinoviev a plan of arbitration signed by persons friendly to the Bolsheviki:

To the Petrograd Soviet of Labor and Defense,

CHAIRMAN ZINOVIEV:

To remain silent now is impossible, even criminal. Recent events impel us anarchists to speak out and to declare our attitude in the present situation.

The spirit of ferment manifest among the workers and sailors is the result of causes that demand our serious attention. Cold and hunger had produced discontent, and the absence of any opportunity for discussion and criticism is forcing the workers and sailors to air their grievances in the open.

White-Guardist bands wish and may try to exploit this dissatisfaction in their own class interests. Hiding behind the workers and sailors they throw out slogans of the Constituent Assembly, of free trade, and similar demands.

We anarchists have long exposed the fiction of these slogans, and we declare to the whole world that we will fight with arms against any counterrevolutionary attempt, in cooperation with all friends of the Social Revolution and hand in hand with the Bolsheviki.

Concerning the conflict between the Soviet Government and the workers and sailors, we hold that it must be settled not by force of arms, but by means of comradely agreement. Resorting to bloodshed, on the part of the Soviet Government, will not—in the given situation—intimidate or quieten the workers. On the contrary, it will serve only to aggravate matters and will strengthen the hands of the Entente and of internal counterrevolution.

More important still, the use of force by the Workers' and Peasants' Government against workers and sailors will have a demoralizing effect upon the international revolutionary movement and will result in incalculable harm to the Social Revolution.

Comrades Bolsheviki, bethink yourselves before it is too late! Do not play with fire: you are about to take a most serious and decisive step.

We hereby submit to you the following proposition: Let a commission be selected to consist of five persons, inclusive of two anarchists. The commission is to go to Kronstadt to settle the dispute by peaceful means. In the given situation this is the most radical method. It will be of international revolutionary significance.

ALEXANDER BERKMAN
EMMA GOLDMAN
PERKUS
PETROVSKY

Petrograd, March 5, 1921.

March 6—Today Kronstadt sent out by radio a statement of its position. It reads:

> Our cause is just, we stand for the power of Soviets, not parties. We stand for freely elected representatives of the laboring masses. The substitute Soviets manipulated by the Communist Party have always been deaf to our needs and demands; the only reply we have ever received was shooting. . . . Comrades! They deliberately pervert the truth and resort to most despicable defamation. . . . In Kronstadt the whole power is exclusively in the hands of the revolutionary sailors, soldiers, and workers—not with counterrevolutionists led by some Kozlovsky, as the lying Moscow radio tries to make you believe. . . . Do not delay, Comrades! Join us, get in touch with us: demand admission to Kronstadt for your delegates. Only they will tell you the whole truth and will expose the fiendish calumny about Finnish bread and Entente offers.
>
> Long live the revolutionary proletariat and the peasantry!
>
> Long live the power of freely elected Soviets.

March 7—Distant rumbling reaches my ears as I cross the Nevsky. It sounds again, stronger and nearer, as if rolling toward me. All at once I realize that artillery is being fired. It is 6 P.M. Kronstadt has been attacked!

Days of anguish and cannonading. My heart is numb with despair; something has died within me. The people on the streets look bowed with grief, bewildered. No one trusts himself to speak. The thunder of heavy guns rends the air.

March 17—Kronstadt has fallen today.

Thousands of sailors and workers lie dead in its streets. Summary execution of prisoners and hostages continues.

March 18—The victors are celebrating the anniversary of the Commune of 1871. Trotsky and Zinoviev denounce Thiers and Gallifet for the slaughter of the Paris rebels. . . .

Hugh Thomas

Anarchist Labor Federations in the Spanish Civil War[1]

Hugh Thomas (1933———) Hugh Thomas was born in Windsor, England, in 1933. He took a degree first in history at Queen's College, Cambridge, and spent a year at the Sorbonne. He was in the Foreign Office from 1954 to 1956, and in 1957 he was lecturer in politics at the Royal Military Academy, Sandhurst. He resides in London.

The general aspirations of the Spanish anarchists in 1931 had hardly been modified since the arrival in Spain of Bakunin's first emissary in 1868. Before that time the whole body of revolutionary socialist ideas, which had already been so much discussed in northern Europe, had almost no Spanish adherents. Certain small cooperative movements did exist in Seville and in Barcelona. Several intellectuals of the clerical or artisan class had been attracted by the ideas of federalism and devolution suggested by Proudhon and Fourier. But in 1868 there arrived in Madrid Fanelli,[2] an Italian deputy, once a companion-in-arms of Garibaldi, now a passionate admirer of Bakunin, who was still the leading figure in the International. Although Fanelli spoke only Italian and French, and though only one among his audience of ten (mainly printers) understood a little French, his ideas had an extraordinary effect. By 1873, there were 50,000 followers[3] of Bakunin in Spain, at first known as "Internationals" and later by the more accurate name of "anarchists." To these a great new truth seemed to have been proclaimed. The State, being based upon ideas of obedience and authority, was morally evil. In its place, there should be self-governing bodies—municipalities, professions

---

1 From *The Spanish Civil War*, by Hugh Thomas. New York: Harper & Row, Incorporated, Copyright 1961. London: Eyre & Spottiswoode, Ltd., 1961. Reprinted by permission of the publishers.

2 His anarchism took the active form of becoming domiciled on the Italian railway, upon which, as a deputy, he had a free ticket. [Thomas' note, as are all others in this extract.]

3 *The Times*, 3.9.1873. Quoted Brenan, *Spanish Labyrinth*, 155.

or other societies—which would make voluntary pacts with
each other. Criminals would be punished by the censure of
public opinion. Bakunin was no doubt influenced, like Tolstoy, in forming such views, by a nostalgia for the Russian
village life that he had himself known in childhood. The
Spaniards, among whom his ideas so fruitfully spread, may
not fancifully be represented as subconsciously hankering
for a similar simplicity of the days before the grasping
modern State, of the mediaeval village societies and provincial autonomous units which had flourished in Spain as in the
rest of Europe.[4]

In 1871, the dispute between Marx and Bakunin in the
International caused a split in its branch in Spain. The mass
of the Spanish movement, the anarchists, continued, almost
alone in Europe, to follow Bakunin. (A minority, the socialists, formed a party of their own, following Marx.) The
first anarchist initiates—mainly printers, schoolmasters and
students—began a deliberate policy of education, directed
chiefly towards the Andalusian laborers. Revolutionary militants moved about from village to village, living like wandering friars. They organized night schools, where peasants
learned to read, to become teetotal, vegetarian, faithful to
their wives, and to discuss the moral evil of coffee and
tobacco. After trade unions were made legal in 1881, anarchism began to establish itself in Barcelona, where many
Andalusian laborers had gone to seek work.[5] The strike,
instantly and ruthlessly carried out, was the weapon that the
anarchists believed could lead to the achievement of the
anarchist society. Hence, even after the formation of the
CNT in 1911, there was no strike fund, since the anarchists
put their trust in swift and brutal action, rather than in
prolonged bargaining, requiring financial reserves. The
Andalusian workers were too poor to make regular contri-

---

[4] For the conversion of the working class of Spain to revolutionary ideas,
the Church, which was to suffer so much in consequence, had paradoxically
prepared the way. The Church's communalism, its puritan hostility to the
competitive instinct, particularly of its Spanish practitioners and apologists,
made the ideas of Fanelli seem merely an honest continuation of the old
faith. The religious character of Spain also made the converts to the new
collectivism, as it had made the liberals, more passionate, less ready to
compromise, more obstinate than any other similar group in Europe.

[5] The city had increased in population from below 100,000 to over a million
in the century.

butions. Nor, even in 1936, was there more than one paid official for the whole union.

The CNT was divided into two groups, though the divison was never properly noticed even by themselves. First, there were the workers of the cities, above all of Barcelona, who were really syndicalists, and who were groping for that "vertical" order of society first suggested in France in the late nineteenth century. The plan was for all the workers in one factory to delegate members to a "syndicate," which would negotiate with other syndicates questions of lodging, food, and entertainment. The second group were the rural anarchists, notably in Andalusia, whose theory represented an idealization of their own town, the *pueblo,* all of whose inhabitants would cooperate to form their own self-sufficient government. The significance of the ideal is suggested by the second meaning of the word *"pueblo,"* which can be translated "people," as opposed to the upper or middle classes. The inference was that these latter were essentially and inevitably foreigners in their own town.[6]

In Andalusia, anarchist strikes were frequently successful in securing higher wages or shorter hours (if not the "Golden Age" foreshadowed by their leaders), for the landowners, or their agents, feared the violence of the strikers' tactics. In Barcelona, there were long and bloody struggles between workers and factory owners, who knew that they had an unlimited labor reserve from which to draw. As a result, the anarchists turned in the 1890s increasingly towards terrorism. This was simultaneously being extensively practiced by their Russian cobelievers, with whom some of the Spanish anarchists were then connected by personal friendship.

In the early years of the present century, the anarchists hatred of, and increasing separation from, the middle class made them prize in their ranks all who made protests against middle-class society, including common felons. The organization of the FAI in 1927 meant the development of a whole army of shock troops in a more or less perpetual state of war against the rest of Spain. The FAI retained their fantastically high ideals. But they believed that it was with a pistol as well as with an encyclopedia that freedom

6 Pitt-Rivers, 18.

could be achieved. They were inclined to believe every word that they read. When they came across a passage in Bakunin suggesting that the new world would be gained when the last king was strangled in the guts of the last priest, they would be likely to wish to test immediately whether this was so. Their passionate concern was to create through "the propaganda of the deed" an atmosphere of panic among the middle class. They might do this through burning churches —as in May, 1931.[7] They might place their faith in the violent, sudden, political and perhaps general strike in one town after another. Or they might murder. They had no relations with any other movement and the notion of becoming a political party in the normal sense of the word was repugnant to them.

The movement had a clever tactical leader in the 1930s in José García Oliver. To Mr. Cyril Connolly, the English critic, he described his aim as "to eliminate the beast in man."[8] But he had himself spent years in prison for crimes of violence. During the Civil War, after he had become Minister of Justice, one of his attendants stretched out his arm to a quivering archivist and invited him to shake a hand that had killed two hundred and fifty-three men.[9] The other chief anarchist leaders were Federica Montseny, a formidable middle-class intellectual from Barcelona with remarkable powers of organization; Juan Peiró, a glassmaker; and two inseparable men of violence, Durruti and Ascaso. Durruti, a native of León, had come as a metalworker to Barcelona in his childhood. Here he had met Ascaso, a baker and café waiter. Together these two had committed many crimes of violence before fleeing from Spain, wandering through South America, and setting up an anarchist bookshop in Paris. Their most notorious crimes

[7] Church-burning is a Spanish and not a specially anarchist phenomenon. The first recorded outbreak was in 1834, about the time that the Spanish working class decided that the hierarchy at least had deserted their interests for those of the aristocracy or the new bourgeoisie.

[8] Connolly, *Condemned Playground*, 195. See his remarkable speech as Minister of Justice in January, 1937, page 368.

[9] *General Cause*, 371. This work consists of the evidence of mass lawsuit brought by the Nationalist Government at the end of the war. It is a document that for obvious reasons must be used warily. Nevertheless, much of the information in it is corroborated by other sources. This remark, attested by persons still living, does not seem *prima facie* unlikely.

had been the murder of the Archbishop of Saragossa,[10] the attempt on King Alfonso in 1921, the murder of a female lacemaker of Madrid, and the celebrated assault on the Bank of Spain at Gijón. These men, however, were not common criminals. They were dreamers with a violent mission, characters whom Dostoyevsky would have been proud to have created. Can one blame the Spanish bourgeoisie if they trembled when they knew that an army of nearly two million workers was led, though hardly controlled, by men such as these?[11]

By January the Republic could look with pride at its winter's work hitherto. But the very diminution of the crisis caused fragmentation, partly geographical, partly political. Barcelona, for instance, presented the appearance of a city at peace. Valencians would be heard grumbling that the "Catalans are not at war." Barcelona's worker-dictatorship of August had also vanished. Was Marx right after all in saying that anarchism inevitably degenerated into petty bourgeois habits? The anarchists were certainly in decline. The communists' air of possessing the future, their dynamism, their political attitude of no-nonsense, and, of course, the prestige of Russian arms made them the obvious party for ambitious people to join.[12] Their numbers had increased to probably 300,000 by the end of 1936. But had it not been for "the propaganda by sight" (Russian aircraft), as González Peña put it, they would have been far less successful. The communists of Barcelona, thanks additionally to their championship of individual ownership and opposition to revolution, were everywhere gaining ground. The PSUC

[10] A life of Durruti published during the Civil War gives this version of this crime: "Durruti and Ascaso heard that there was a condition of injustice in Saragossa. Accordingly they went up to the city from Barcelona and murdered Cardinal Soldevila, who was the leading proponent of reaction."

[11] Throughout the thirties, the CNT continued to be divided between the most extreme opponents of existing society, led by the FAI, and those syndicalists, the *Treintistas,* followers of Angel Pestaña, who favored a certain degree of cooperation with society. The controversy continued until the CNT Congress in Saragossa in 1936, when the *Treintistas* re-entered the CNT, though Pestaña remained outside.

[12] Even General Miaja told Pietro Nenni that he preferred the Second to the Third International. "I like the communists," he said, "because they are more resolute. The socialists talk first, then act. If the communists talk, they do so *after* acting. Militarily speaking, it is an advantage." (Nenni, 171.)

agitated for the dissolution of the revolutionary committees, so as to place all executive organs, both nominal and actual, under the Generalitat, which with the Esquerra, they dominated. Rivalry between the anarchists and PSUC became acute at the start of January, when the latter managed to place a veteran antianarchist, their Secretary-General Comorera, as Food Minister. Comorera immediately abolished the bread committees, led by the CNT, which had hitherto supervised the food supply of Barcelona. Henceforward, there was no State intervention in the food supply in Catalonia. Even rationing was abandoned. This brought immediate hardship, since the price of bread had gone up far more than wages. There followed a bread shortage caused by the inadequate harvesting of the previous year, but attributed by the anarchists to Comorera's inefficiency. A poster war ensued, CNT posters demanding Comorera's resignation, PSUC posters calling for "Less talk! Less Committees! More bread!" and "All power to the Generalitat." Meantime, bread queues, of 300 or 400 persons, outside closed bakeries, became a pathetic daily sight. Sometimes, when no bread could be distributed, *Asaltos* had to disperse the queues with rifle butts. Life seemed a far cry from the utopian dreams of July 19, 1936.

Down the coast at Valencia, conditions appeared more revolutionary than at Barcelona. Nearly all factories and shops were managed by their workers. But the effect of the Government's move to Valencia had been to give them control over the Levante, which, before November, had been almost independent. As for the dissident anarchists of the Levante, a force was dispatched against the "uncontrollables" of Taracón and Cuenca, who had so nearly brought the Government to a tragic end. After fighting, both towns became model socialist centers, whereas in neither had the UGT previously been strong. Here too, however, the communists and anarchists were in conflict—especially over the question of the marketing of oranges from the Valencian *huerta*. Since July, 1936, the marketing had been done by a committee of the UGT and CNT, representing all the trades who handled the crops though not the orange growers themselves. The Ministry of Agriculture paid this body fifty percent of the international price of the crop on delivery, and fifty percent after sale and deduction of expenses. The orange growers, with the support of the communist Uribe, Minister of Agriculture, argued that this committee took the profits, and that they got nothing. The committee contended that, if the orange crop were handed over to private commerce, not only would the trade unions be destroyed, but the private merchants would keep abroad the foreign currency. The violent hatred of the orange growers for the committee was shown by the revolt in January of the *pueblo* of Cullera, which suddenly declared itself independent, burned flashlights towards the Mediterranean to attract Nationalist ships, and turned guns against Valencia. The Government then had to take the same repressive measures against these peasant enemies of the anarchists as they had earlier done over different matters against the anarchists themselves.[18]

In Madrid, hostility between the communists and anarchists had different implications. On the one hand it was an aspect of the quarrel between Madrid and Valencia, and on the other the start of a dispute between the communists and Largo Caballero. After the battle of the Corunna high road, Kléber argued that the Republic should launch an attack, the International Brigades leading the offensive. But here Kléber came up against the jealousy that he had inspired in Miaja and other Spanish commanders. Largo Caballero, already jealous of the international prestige of La Pasionaria and other communists who had remained in Madrid during the siege, concluded that Kléber wished to use the International Brigades to stage a communist coup d'état. The anarchists of Madrid supported Miaja, and therefore indirectly, for the first time, Largo Caballero. Even so Kléber's ideas might have triumphed had he not incurred the suspicion of André Marty. As a result, Kléber left his command and went to live in a small hotel in Valencia. At the same time, Rosenberg for no obvious reason (he was, however, a Jew at a time when Stalin's perhaps always latent anti-Semitism came to a head) left his post as Ambassador at Valencia and went back to Moscow, where he was shortly to "disappear" in the purges now developing at cumulative speed. Other Russians in Spain were called home with similar consequences. Parties would be given in Madrid, attended by General Berzin, to bid farewell to officers summoned back in

[18] Borkenau, 198–204.

this way.[14] Eventually Berzin himself, guest of honor at these macabre gatherings, would also be recalled, with the usual results. Meantime in Spain, the communists suddenly ceased their most outspoken attacks on their enemies. Instead they struck through the NKVD, which was staffed mainly by foreign communists, since Spanish communists were considered less sound. The number of Russians in Spain never exceeded 2,000, but those who were there were placed in key positions. Barcelona radio services were under one Kolzov-Ginsberg. A certain Vladimir Birchitski was a central figure in arms production. And the general rumor of "the Russians are in control" was henceforward heard everywhere in the Republic. Undoubtedly their lack of knowledge of Spain, as well as their secretiveness, led these Russians (and other foreign communists) into grave mistakes.

The use that the communist party made of its power was to establish itself as deeply as possible in the Republican administration, to arrange that, through the agency of Orlov, the NKVD's tentacles should crowd out all private *checas,* both of the Socialist-Communist Youth and others, and to prepare the way for the same purge of communists and other Marxists in Spain as had now reached its second stage in Russia.[15] The first move in the Spanish purge was the PSUC's campaign to maneuvre the POUM out of the Catalán Generalitat. Nine eventually left on December 16. The anarchists gave this blessing since, like all the other parties, they also did not love the POUM's aggressive and self-assertive arrogance. The anarchists must, however, have been a little anxious not only at the spread of the communist party's power, but also at its threats. "So far as Catalonia is concerned," thundered *Pravda* on December 17, "the cleaning up of Trotskyists and anarchists has begun and it will be carried out with the same energy as in the USSR." However, no action was yet taken: and Antonov-Ovseenko, the Russian Consul-General (who, as an ex-Trotskyist, must have had his own fears of the future at this time), expressed publicly his admiration of the Catalán anarchists on December 22. By this time also the violence of the Popular Tribunals and *checas* had been greatly diminished, perhaps chiefly because

[14] Regler, *Owl of Minerva,* 294.
[15] Radek, Piatakov, and others were tried in Moscow between January 23 and 30, and thirteen were executed.

their work was almost completed. There were indeed few members of the old Right-wing parties of before the Civil War left in Republican Spain. But wild crimes by militiamen continued sporadically, especially in backward provinces.

The communists maintained their campaign against collectivization of land, and the anarchists continued in favor of its general application. Neither were strong enough to force their own solution. So the question of expropriated property was left suspended, most large estates being run by municipalities (or committees where these still existed separately) with the old laborers working under much the same conditions as of old. Where the anarchists had established themselves first, in Catalonia, Aragón and in certain wheat farms in La Mancha and sugarcane farms near Málaga, collectivized methods persisted. In Aragón, this included seventy-five percent of the small properties. There, all crops were placed under the control of a local committee. Wages were paid in proportion to needs. The anarchists claimed, in respect of wheat in Aragón, a thirty-percent increase in production.

The argument as to the relative advantage of the militia system or the army system continued as the chief bone of contention between communism and anarchism. Republican staff officers had suggested that the mixed brigade—a self-contained unit, with its own artillery, mortars, supply and medical services, developed during the wars in Morocco, was the best type of organization for the war. It was in fact adopted because the communist party, and the Soviet advisers, favored it. A decree ending the militias and reorganizing the army in mixed brigades was published at the end of December. The inspiration of these steps towards the formation of a regular army was the efficient Under-Secretary, General Asensio, and his advisers of the old regular Army such as Martín Blázquez. The anarchists disliked passionately these developments. The Libertarian Youth spoke of the dangers of just such an army as had rebelled in July: "a shock force knowing nothing of the cries for liberty, bread, justice of the cannon fodder." The General Council of the FAI demanded the suppression of the salute, equal pay for all in the army, newspapers at the front, and soldier councils, at all levels. *Solidaridad Obrera* grumbled about "obsession of discipline," "neo-militarism," and "psychosis of unity."

The Iron Column before Teruel rebelled against the financial implications of the decree against militias. Hitherto, the column had been paid *en bloc*. Now the men were to be paid individually. Fighting occurred before the anarchists submitted to the new regulations. The anarchists (and UGT) were naturally dubious about abandoning their militias, particularly when the dissolution of the communist Fifth Regiment was followed by the nomination of that body's commander, Lister, to lead the first mixed brigade. In fact, for some months longer, the militiamen still existed, though beginning to be classed under numbers not names. The separate political flags were still seen as often as that of the Republic. On the Aragón front, separate political columns lasted until the middle of the year. Uniforms were still non-existent, though everyone wore corduroy knee breeches and a zipper jacket. Training continued rudimentary since all the rifles were at the front; and even these continued, except for parts of the Madrid front, to be old and unreliable, while artillery was everywhere scarce. Grenades were still as liable to explode in the hands of the thrower as upon the enemy. In many places there were no maps, range finders, periscopes, field glasses, or cleaning materials. Orwell discovered, with the horror of a trained member of the Eton OTC, that no one in his POUM column had heard of a pull-through.[16] Bad marksmanship continued to be the rule. Discipline in most places continued to be based upon class loyalty, rather than orders by officers—though General Asensio Torrado, the Under-Secretary at the War Ministry and the moving spirit in the creation of the new Republican "People's" Army, insisted on correct military uniform for officers.[17]

Largo Caballero meanwhile continued to be jealous of everyone in Madrid, especially of La Pasionaria, who had had such great popular success there. His relations with Miaja and Madrid's commanders remained bad. He also began to dislike the presence of the Russian Ambassador, Rosenberg. On December 21, Stalin sent a letter to him full of brotherly and moderate advice: the parliamentary method might in Spain be more revolutionarily effective than in Russia; even so, the Russian experience might be useful in Spain—hence the dispatch of certain "military comrades"

[16] Orwell, *loc. cit.*
[17] For all the above, see Martín Blázquez, 279–90.

who had received orders to follow Spanish instructions and act only as advisers. Stalin begged Largo Caballero "as a friend" to report how successful the advisers had been, and to say whether he found Rosenberg satisfactory. The letter ended with the advice that peasants' and foreigners' property should be respected, that partisan forces should be formed behind the Nationalist lines, that the small bourgeoisie should not be attacked, and that Azaña and the Republicans should not be cold-shouldered.[18] And in fact the political moderation of the communist party in Spain now brought them a working alliance with the liberal Republicans. The Republicans' policy, insofar as one existed apart from the general aim of winning the war, was nearly that of the communist party in both military strategy and economics. It was thus in language almost identical with that of La Pasionaria that Azaña, in one of his rare public appearances, at Valencia on January 21, demanded "a war policy . . . with only one expression—discipline and obedience to the responsible Government of the Republic." [19]

Social and other reforms, Azaña and the communists could now agree, should await victory. And it was the adoption of this policy which gave the communist party much of its power. If the war was to be won, this was the way to win it. Their moderation gave them the friendship not only of the Republicans but also of many of the regular officers in the Army who thought the communists sane and well-organized. The anarchists seemed genuinely puzzled by the communists' close alignment with *bourgeois* democracy. At a National Youth Congress in Valencia in January, the Secretary-General of the Socialist-Communist Youth, Santiago Carrillo, remarked, "We are not Marxist Youth. We fight for a democratic, parliamentary republic." *Solidaridad Obrera* named this "Reformist Quackery." "If the United Socialist Youth are neither socialist, communist, nor Marxist, what are they?"

As for the socialists, the UGT (whose membership had

[18] This letter was published for the first time in the *New York Times* on June 4, 1939, by the then ferociously anticommunist Araquistain, Ambassador in Paris 1936–37. When this letter arrived in Largo Caballero's office, no one could read illegible signatures. Codovilla, the Comintern agent, was summoned. He could not read the signatures either. It took a member of Rosenberg's staff of the Russian Embassy to decypher the names of Stalin, Molotov, and Voroshilov (Gorkin, 85).
[19] Quoted by Cattell, *Communism*, 135.

risen to two million) was now well-stocked with communists, though it is impossible to know precisely how many. All winter, the communists were urging the unification of the socialist and communist parties, on the model of the existing union in Catalonia and the two youth movements. Both wings of the socialist party, Largo Caballero's as well as Prieto's, were, however, now wary of these approaches.

Even so, by the spring of 1937, Largo Caballero's Government was everywhere seeking to slow down the process of revolution. The political committees which had sprung up in all *pueblos* in July were being replaced by municipal councils. The nationalization of foreign firms ceased and of others was delayed. The Government also did all it could to end the collective management of factories. It sought to bring such concerns under State control, whether nationalized or privately managed. To ensure this, credit was made difficult for anarchist factories. Some mills therefore stopped when cotton was exhausted.

Yet when all these quarrels are understood, and this increasing stranglehold over the Republic exercized by the ruthless communists, Spanish and foreign, is taken into account, it needs also to be realized that this Government of Largo Caballero was fumbling towards a better Spain. The war might be taking up most of the Republican resources, but attention was being paid to education as never before. One hundred and forty-three million pesetas would be spent on education in the Republic in 1937 compared to only three million in 1936. That figure represents less of an increase than would appear immediately, because of the inflation of the Republican peseta. Nevertheless, the real increase must have been over fivehold.[20] The number of new schools opened in 1937 approached 1,000. There were 60,000 teachers in Republican Spain in 1937 compared with 37,000 in all Spain in 1931. In 1937, there were to be 2,000 military schools, at which over 200,000 previously illiterate militiamen learned to read. Despite the disputes over collectivization or private management, the decree of October, 1936, legalizing the expropriation of land owned by Nationalists revolutionized the life of Spain. By May, 1937, nearly four million hectares (fifteen percent of the whole area of

[20] Figures in *Education in Republican Spain* (pamphlet), published by United Editorial, 1938.

Spain) had been taken over by the Institute of Agrarian Reform. Credits of 80 million pesetas, and implements and fertilizers, had been afforded. The amount of land under cultivation increased by six percent between July 1936 and October 1937. In almost every case, the peasants of Republican Spain were by early 1937 either owners of their own land or laboring for a collectivized farm. The tenant farmers and the landless laborers dependent upon a negligent landlord had vanished. In industry, despite the uneasy compromise achieved in those concerns still nominally under private ownership,[21] production had generally increased by thirty percent and fifty percent in those industries (such as textiles) directly concerned with the war. In health, despite the demand for doctors and medical services at the front, there were over a thousand more beds for tubercular patients in the Republic than in 1936. Later in 1937, compulsory inoculation for smallpox, diphtheria, and typhoid was instituted. By the end of 1937, there were as many child-welfare centers in Republican Spain as there had been before the war in all Spain.[22] The remarkable and devoted work of the foreign medical aid organizations indeed radiated throughout the Republic, setting new standards of hygiene and efficiency. These achievements gained in the teeth of war should not lightly be ignored. In the field of ordinary (as opposed to political) justice, there was also a marked increase in the speed of the hearing of ordinary cases. The unusual figure of García Oliver, the anarchist Minister of Justice, stood behind such changes. He made, on January 3, 1937, perhaps the most remarkable speech of any law Minister at any time: "Justice," he announced, "must be burning hot, justice must be alive, justice cannot be restricted within the bounds of a profession. It is not that we definitely despise books and lawyers. But the fact is that there were [sic] too many lawyers.[23] When relations between men become what they should be, there will be no need to steal and kill. For the first time, let us admit here in Spain that the common criminal is not an enemy of society. He is more

[21] In Catalonia, a decree of January 9 made it obligatory for private owners to submit questions of wages, hours, new employees, production and distribution quotas, and monthly accounts to a committee of workers.

[22] Margaret Stewart, *Reform under Fire* (Fabian Society, 1939).

[23] The use of the past tense is ominous. According to *The General Cause,* 127 judicial functionaries had been killed in Republican Spain.

likely to be a victim of society. Who is there who says he dare not go out and steal if driven to it to feed his children and himself? Do not think that I am making a defense of robbery. But man, after all, does not proceed from God, but from the case, from the beast. Justice, I firmly believe, is so subtle a thing that to interpret one has only need of a heart." [24]

The northern Republican territories remained generally apart from the quarrels of the south. Yet they had their own difficulties. On January 4, Bilbao was raided by nine Junkers 52, escorted by Heinkels. Two of these were shot down by Russian Boeing fighters. Two Germans parachuted to the ground. One was killed by the crowd infuriated by this wanton attack. The other was saved from a similar death by a Russian pilot. In the meantime, Bilbao turned mad with anger. The rage of the people was exacerbated by hunger, since few food ships had recently managed to penetrate the Nationalist blockade. A furious mob, composed chiefly of non-Basque refugees from Asturias, Castile, and Galicia, marched to the buildings where the political prisoners of Bilbao were being kept. The prison governors telephoned the Basque Government. They said they could not much longer prevent the warders from opening the gates to the crowd. A UGT battalion was sent to hold the prison gates. But the battalion joined with the people, who were now shouting imprecations against those who had "brought the Germans to kill our children." First, the gates of the Laronga prison were thrown open, and the men of the UGT battalion began a massacre in which 94 prisoners were killed. In the second prison, at the Convent of the Angeles Custodios, 96 prisoners were killed. At the Convent of the Carmelites, which had also been converted into a prison, the prisoners, allied with six Basque guards, barricaded the staircase. Then, at a given signal, all the electric bulbs in the convent were knocked out. The crowd concluded that the convent was being bombed, and fled, having killed only four prisoners. The motorized Basque police now arrived. By tragic irony, they were commanded by Telesforo Monzón. He had recently conducted negotiations for the exchange of these same political prisoners with the Nationalists and, due to Franco's insistence on dealing with the Valencia Government, had

[24] Quoted by Berryer, *Red Justice* (London, 1937).

failed in his mission. The UGT militiamen implicated were arrested, and the crowd vanished. The Basque Government now sought to atone for this act of mob insanity. The families of the dead (most of whom were from Bilbao) were permitted to arrange funeral services and processions in the streets. Six members of the UGT battalion responsible were condemned to death and, as a public act of abasement, censorship of journalists' reports on the massacre was dropped.

On January 13, the anarchists of Bilbao sought to profit from the inevitable atmosphere of tension. Their posters demanded for them a share in the Government. They were easily controlled. A few weeks later, their newspaper, the *CNT del Norte,* was banned and their meetings were henceforward only permitted by license. The Government had purposely not sent the all-Basque police to control the mainly non-Basque crowd at the prisons, for fear of worsening relations between the Basques and the others. The ultimate consequence of the riots was that the Basque Nationalists became supreme in Vizcaya.[25]

[25] Steer, 110–22.

section two
The Sociological Dimension

Georges Sorel
Class War and the Ethics of Violence [1]

Georges Sorel (1847–1922) Sorel was a French social philosopher whose livelihood came from his practice as an engineer. His political personality has always been controversial, though he is generally accepted as the theoretician of revolutionary syndicalism. His socialism sprang more from an attack on the moral disintegration of the bourgeoisie than from the needs of the proletariat. The labor movement, however, had unique dimensions for revolution. He favored a variety of industrialism as opposed to finance capital, since it bred a discipline and potential for heroism that create the moral foundations for the proletarian revolution. For Sorel, the proletariat represented the virtues of producers and warriors. In *Reflections on Violence,* he took an antideterminist position against those who saw an "inevitable" revolution and he maintained that proletarian victory was bound up with its fighting ethics and its capacity for sustaining the "myth" of the general strike. The creative violence of the proletariat must show its superiority to the technical economic skills and force of the bourgeoisie. Some of the important works of Sorel are *Reflections on Violence, Illusions du progrès, Le Procès de Socrate, Matériaux pour une théorie du proletariat,* and *The Decomposition of Marxism.*

[1] From *Reflections on Violence* by Georges Sorel, translated by T. E. Hulme and J. Roth. New York: The Free Press of Glencoe. Copyright 1950. London: Allen & Unwin Ltd. Reprinted with permission of the publishers.

A) To most people the class war
is the *principle of socialist tactics.* That means that the
socialist party founds its electoral successes on the clashing
of interests that exist in an acute state between certain
groups, and that, if need be, it would undertake to make this
hostility still more acute; their candidates ask the poorest
and most numerous class to look upon themselves as forming
a corporation, and they offer to become the advocates of this
corporation; they promise to use their influence as representatives to improve the lot of the disinherited. Thus we are
not very far from what happened in the Greek states; parliamentary socialists are very much akin to the demagogues
who clamored constantly for the abolition of debts, and the
division of landed property, who put all public charges upon
the rich, and invented plots in order to get large fortunes
confiscated. "In the democracies in which the crowd is
above the law," says Aristotle, "the demagogues, by their
continual attacks upon the rich, always divide the city into
two camps . . . the oligarchs should abandon all swearing
of oaths like those they swear today; for there are cities in
which they have taken this oath—I will be the constant
enemy of the people, and I will do them all the evil that lies
in my power." Here, certainly, is a war between two classes
as clearly defined as it can be; but it seems to me absurd to
assert that it was in this way that Marx understood the
class war, which, according to him, was the essence of
socialism.

I believe that the authors of the French law of August 11,
1848, had their heads full of these classical reminiscenses
when they decreed punishment against all those who, by
speeches and newspaper articles, sought "to trouble the
public peace by stirring up hatred and contempt amongst
the citizens." The terrible insurrection of the month of June
was just over, and it was firmly believed that the victory of
the Parisian workmen would have brought on, if not an
attempt to put communism into practice, at least a series of
formidable requisitions on the rich in favor of the poor; it
was hoped that an end would be put to civil wars by increasing the difficulty of propagating *doctrines of hatred,* which
might raise the proletariat against the middle class.

Nowadays parliamentary socialists no longer entertain the

idea of insurrection; if they still occasionally speak of it, it is merely to give themselves airs of importance; they teach that the ballot box has replaced the gun; but the means of acquiring power may have changed without there being any change of mental attitude. Electoral literature seems inspired by the purest demagogic doctrines; socialism makes its appeal to the discontented without troubling about the place they occupy in the world of production; in a society as complex as ours, and as subject to economic upheavals, there is an enormous number of discontented people in all classes —that is why socialists are often found in places where one would least expect to meet them. Parliamentary socialism speaks as many languages as it has types of clients. It makes its appeal to workmen, to small employers of labor, to peasants; and in spite of Engels, it aims at reaching the farmers; it is at times patriotic; at other times it declares against the army. It is stopped by no contradiction, experience having shown that it is possible, in the course of an electoral campaign, to group together forces that according to Marxian conceptions, should normally be antagonistic. Besides, cannot a member of parliament be of service to electors of every economic situation?

In the end the term "proletariat" became synonymous with "oppressed"; and there are oppressed in all classes: German socialists have taken a great interest in the adventures of the Princess of Coburg. One of our most distinguished reformers, Henri Turot, for a long time one of the editors of the *Petite République* and municipal councillor of Paris, has written a book on the "proletariat of love," by which title he designates the lowest class of prostitutes. If one of these days the suffrage is granted to women, he will doubtless be called upon to draw up a statement of the claims of this special proletariat.

B) Contemporary democracy in France finds itself somewhat bewildered by the tactics of the class war. This explains why parliamentary socialism does not mingle with the main body of the parties of the extreme left.

In order to understand this situation, we must remember the important part played by revolutionary war in our history; an enormous number of our political ideas originated from war; war presupposes the union of national forces against the enemy, and our French historians have always severely criticized those insurrections which hampered the defense of the country. It seems that our democracy is harder on its rebels than monarchies are; the Vendéens are still denounced daily as infamous traitors. All the articles published by Clémenceau to combat the ideas of Hervé are inspired by the purest revolutionary tradition, and he says so himself clearly: "I stand by and shall always stand by the old-fashioned patriotism of our fathers of the Revolution." and he scoffs at people who would "suppress international wars in order to hand us *over in peace to the amenities of civil war*" (*Aurore,* May 12, 1905).

For some considerable time the Republicans denied that there was any struggle between the classes in France; they had so great a horror of revolt that they would not recognize the facts. Judging all things from the abstract point of view of the Declaration of the Rights of Man, they said that the legislation of 1789 had been created in order to abolish all distinction of class in law; for that reason they were opposed to proposals for social legislation, which, nearly always, reintroduced the idea of class and distinguished certain groups of citizens as being unfitted for the use of liberty. "The revolution was supposed to have suppressed class distinction," wrote Joseph Reinach sadly in the *Matin* of April 19, 1895, "but they spring up again at every step. . . . It is necessary to point out these aggressive returns of the past, but they must not be allowed to pass unchallenged; they must be resisted."

Electoral dealing led many republicans to recognize that the socialists obtain great successes by utilizing the passions of jealousy, of deception, or of hate, which exist in the world; thenceforward they became aware of the class war, and many have borrowed the jargon of the parliamentary socialists: in this way the party that is called Radical Socialist came into being. Clémenceau asserts even that he knows *moderates* who became socialists in twenty-four hours. "In France," he says, "the socialists that I know are excellent radicals who, thinking that social reforms do not advance quickly enough to please them, conceive that it would be good tactics to claim the greater in order to get the less. How many names and how many secret avowals I could quote to support what I say! But that would be useless, for nothing could be less mysterious" *(Aurore,* August 14, 1905).

Léon Bourgeois—who was not willing to adapt himself completely to the new methods, and who, for that reason perhaps, left the Chamber of Deputies for the Senate—said, at the congress of his party in July, 1905: "The class war is a fact, but a cruel fact. I do not believe that it is by prolonging this war that the solution of the problem will be attained; I believe that the solution rather lies in its suppression; men must be brought to look upon themselves as partners in the same work." It would therefore seem to be a question of creating social legislation, thus peace demonstrating to the poor that the Government has no greater care than that of improving their lot, and by imposing the necessary sacrifices on people who possess a fortune judged to be too great for the harmony of the classes.

Capitalist society is so rich, and the future appears to it in such optimistic colors, that it endures the most frightful burdens without complaining overmuch: in America politicians waste large taxes shamelessly; in Europe, the expenditure in military preparation increases every year, social peace might very well be bought by a few supplementary sacrifices. Experience shows that the middle classes allow themselves to be plundered quite easily, provided that a little pressure is brought to bear, and that they are intimidated by the fear of revolution; that party will possess the future which can most skillfully manipulate the specter of revolution; the radical party is beginning to understand this; but, however clever its clowns may be, it will have some difficulty in finding any who can dazzle the big Jew bankers as well as Jaurès and his friends can do.

C) The syndicalist organization gives a third value to the class war. In each branch of industry employers and workmen from antagonistic groups, which have continual discussions, which negotiate and make agreements. Socialism brings along its terminology of class war, and thus complicates conflicts that might have remained of a purely private order; corporative exclusiveness, which resembles the local or the racial spirit, is thereby consolidated, and those who represent it like to imagine that they are accomplishing a higher duty and are doing excellent work for socialism.

It is well-known that litigants who are strangers in a town are generally very badly treated by the judges of commercial courts sitting there, who try to give judgment in favor of their fellow townsmen. Railway companies pay fantastic prices for pieces of ground, the value of which is fixed by juries recruited from among the neighboring landowners. I have seen Italian sailors overwhelmed with fines, for pretended infractions of the law, by the fishing arbitrators with whom they had come to compete on the strength of ancient treaties. Many workmen are in the same way inclined to assert that in all their contests with employers, the worker has morality and justice on his side; I have heard the secretary of a syndicate (so fanatically a reformer as distinct from a revolutionary that he denied the oratorical talent of Guesde) declare that nobody had class feeling so strongly developed as he had—because he argued in the way I have just indicated —and he concluded that the revolutionaries did not possess the monopoly of the just conception of the class war.

It is quite understandable that many people have considered this corporative spirit as no better than the parish spirit, and also that they should have attempted to destroy it by employing methods very analogous to those which have so much weakened the jealousies that formerly existed in France between the various provinces. A more general culture and the intermixing with people of another region rapidly destroy provincialism: Would it not be possible to destroy the corporative feeling by frequently bringing the important men in the syndicates into connection with the employers, and by furnishing them with opportunities of taking part in discussions of a general order in mixed commissions? Experience has shown that this is feasible.

The efforts that have been made to remove the causes of hostility that exist in modern society have undoubtedly had some effect, although the peacemakers may be much deceived about the extent of their work. By showing a few of the officials of the syndicates that the middle classes are not such terrible men as they had believed, by loading them with politeness in commissions set up in ministerial offices or at the Musée Social, and by giving them the impression that there is a *natural and Republican* equity, above class prejudices and hatreds, it has been found possible to change the attitude of a few former revolutionaries. These conversions of a few of their old chiefs have caused great confusion in the mind of the working classes; the former enthusiasm of more than one socialist has given place to discouragement; many working men have wondered whether the trades-union organization was not becoming a kind of politics, a means of getting on.

But simultaneously with this evolution, which filled the heart of the peacemakers with joy, there was a recrudescence of the revolutionary spirit in a large section of the proletariat. Since the republican government and the philanthropists have taken it into their heads to exterminate socialism by developing social legislation, and by moderating the resistance of the employers in strikes, it has been observed that, more than once, the conflicts have become more acute than formerly. This is often explained away by saying that it was an accident, the result simply of the survival of old usages; people like to lull themselves with the hope that everything will go perfectly well on the day when manufacturers have a better understanding of the usages of social peace. I believe, on the contrary, that we are in the presence of a phenomenon that flows quite naturally from the conditions in which this pretended pacification is carried out.

I observe, first of all, that both the theories and action of the peacemakers are founded on the notion of duty, and that duty is something entirely indefinite—while law seeks rigid definition. This difference is due to the fact that the latter finds a real basis in the economics of production, while the former is founded on sentiments of resignation, goodness, and of sacrifices; and who can judge whether the man who submits to duty has been sufficiently resigned, sufficiently good, sufficiently self-sacrificing? The Christian is convinced that he will never succeed in doing all that the gospel enjoins on him; when he is free from economic ties (in a monastery), he invents all sorts of pious obligations, so that he may bring his life nearer to that of Christ, who loved men to such an extent that he accepted an ignominious fate that they might be redeemed.

In the economic world everybody limits his duty by his unwillingness to give up certain profits. While the employer will be always convinced that he has done the whole of his duty, the worker will be of a contrary opinion, and no argument could possibly settle the matter: The first will believe that he has been heroic, and the second will treat this pretended heroism as shameful exploitation.

Our great pontiffs of duty refuse to look upon a contract to work as being of the nature of a sale; nothing is so simple as a sale; nobody troubles himself to find out whether the grocer or his customer is right when they do not agree on the price of cheese; the customer goes where he can buy more cheaply, and the grocer is obliged to change his prices when his customers leave him. But when a strike takes place it is quite another thing. All the well-intentioned people, all the "progressives" and the friends of the Republic, begin to discuss which of the two parties is in the right: *to be in the right is to have accomplished one's whole social duty*. Le Play has given much advice on the means of organizing labor with a view to the strict fulfillment of duty; but he could not fix the extent of the mutual obligations; he left it to the tact of each, to the just estimation of the duties attaching to one's place in the social hierarchy, to the master's intelligent appreciation of the real needs of the workmen.

The employers generally agree to discuss disputes on these lines; to the claims of the workers they reply that they have already reached the limit of possible concessions—while the philanthropists wonder whether the selling price will not permit of a slight rise in wages. Such a discussion presupposes that it is possible to ascertain the exact extent of a man's social duty, and what sacrifices an employer must continue to make in order to *carry out the duties of his social position*. As there is no process of reasoning that can resolve such a problem, wiseacres suggest recourse to arbitration; Rabelais would have suggested recourse to the chance of the dice. When the strike is important, deputies loudly demand an inquiry, with the object of discovering whether the industrial leaders are properly fulfilling their *duties as good masters*.

Certain results are obtained in this way—which nevertheless seem absurd—because on the one hand the large employers of labor have been brought up with religious,

philanthropic, and civic ideas; and on the other hand because
they cannot show themselves too stubborn, when certain
demands are made by people occupying a high position in
the country. Conciliators stake their vanity on succeeding,
and they would be extremely hurt if industrial leaders prevented them from making social peace. The workmen are in
a much more favorable position, because the prestige of the
peacemakers is very much less with them than with the
capitalists; the latter give way, therefore, much more easily
than the workers, in order to allow these well-intentioned
folk the glory of ending the conflict. It is noticable that these
proceedings very rarely succeed when the matter is in the
hands of workmen who have become rich: Literary, moral,
or sociological considerations have very little effect upon
people born outside the ranks of the middle classes.

People who are called upon to intervene in disputes in this
way are misled by what they have seen of certain secretaries
of syndicates, whom they find much less irreconcilable than
they expected, and who seem to them to be ripe for a
recognition of the idea of social peace. In the course of
conciliation meetings more than one revolutionary has
shown that he aspires to become a member of the middle
class, and there are many intelligent people who imagine that
socialistic and revolutionary conceptions are only accidents
that might be avoided by establishing better relations between
the classes. They believe that the working-class world looks
at the economic question entirely from the standpoint of
duty, and they imagine that harmony would be established
if a better social education were given to the citizens.

Let us see what influences are behind the other movement
that tends to make conflicts more acute.

Workmen quickly perceive that the labor of conciliation
or of arbitration rests on no economico-judicial basis, and
their tactics have been conducted—instinctively perhaps—
in accordance with this datum. Since the feelings, and,
above all, the vanity of the peacemakers are in question, a
strong appeal must be made to their imaginations, and they
must be given the idea that they have to accomplish a titanic
task: demands are piled up, therefore, figures fixed in a rather
haphazard way, and there are no scruples about exaggerating
them; often the success of the strike depends on the clever-
ness with which a syndicalist (who thoroughly understands

the spirit of *social diplomacy*) has been able to introduce claims, in themselves very minor, but capable of giving the impression that the employers are not fulfilling their social duty. It often happens that writers who concern themselves with these questions are astonished that several days pass before the strikers have settled what exactly they have to demand, and that in the end demands are put forward that had not been mentioned in the course of the preceding negotiations. This is easily understood when we consider the bizarre conditions under which the discussion between the interested parties is carried on.

I am suprised that there are no strike professionals who would undertake to draw up a list of the workers' claims; they would obtain all the more success in conciliation councils as they would not let themselves be dazzled by fine words so easily as the workers' delegates.

When the strike is finished, the workmen do not forget that the employers at first declared that no concession was possible; they are led thus to the belief that the employers are either ignorant or liars. This result is not conducive to the development of social peace!

So long as the workers submitted without protest to the exactions of the employers, they believed that the will of their masters was completely dominated by economic necessities; they perceived, after the strike, that this necessity is not of a very rigid kind, and that if energetic pressure from below is brought to bear on the masters, the latter will find some means of liberating themselves from the pretended fetters of economic necessity; thus within practical limits capitalism appears to the workers to be unfettered, and they reason as if it were entirely so. What in their eyes restrains this liberty is not the necessities of competition but the ignorance of the employers. Thus is introduced the notion of the *inexhaustibility of production,* which is one of the postulates of the theory of class war in the socialism of Marx.

Why then speak of social duty? Duty has some meaning in a society in which all the parts are intimately connected and responsible to one another; but if capitalism is inexhaustible, joint responsibility is no longer founded on economic realities, and the workers think they would be dupes if they did not demand all they can obtain; they look upon the employer as an adversary with whom one comes to terms after a war. *Social duty no more exists than does international duty.*

These ideas are somewhat confused, I admit, in many minds; but they exist in a much more stable manner than the partisans of social peace imagine; the latter are deluded by appearances, and never penetrate to the hidden roots of the existing tendencies of socialism.

Before passing to other considerations, it must be noticed that our Latin countries present one great obstacle to the formation of social peace; the classes are more sharply separated by external characteristics than they are in Saxon countries; these separations very much embarrass syndicalist leaders when they abandon their former manners and take up a position in the official or philanthropic circles. These circles have welcomed them with great pleasure, since it has been perceived that the gradual transformation of trades union officials into members of the middle classes might produce excellent results; but their comrades distrust them. In France this distrust has become much more definite since a great number of anarchists have entered the syndicalist movement; because the anarchist has a horror of everything that recalls the proceedings of politicians—a class of people devoured by the desire to climb into superior classes, and having already the capitalist mind while yet poor.

Social politics have introduced new elements which must now be taken into account. First of all, it must be noticed that the workers *count* today in the world by the same right as the different productive groups which demand to be protected; they must be treated with solicitude just as the vine-growers or the sugar manufacturers. There is nothing settled about protectionism; the custom duties are fixed so as to satisfy the desires of very influential people who wish to increase their incomes; social politics proceed in the same manner. The protectionist Government professes to have knowledge that permits it to judge what should be granted to each group so as to defend the producers without injuring the consumers; similarly, in social politics it declares that it will take into consideration the interests of the employers and those of the workers.

Few people, outside the faculties of law, are so simple as to believe that the State can carry out such a program: in actual fact, the parliamentarians decide on a compromise that partially satisfies the interests of those who are most influential in elections without provoking too lively protests from those who are sacrificed. There is no other rule than the true or presumed interest of the electors; every day the customs commission recasts its tariffs, and it declares that it will not stop recasting them until it succeeds in securing prices that it considers remunerative to the people for whom it has undertaken the part of providence: it keeps a watchful eye on the operations of importers; every lowering of price attracts its attention and provokes inquiries with the object of discovering whether it would not be possible to raise values again artificially. Social politics are carried on in exactly the same way; on June 27, 1905, the *rapporteur* of a law on the length of the hours of work in the mines said, in the Chamber of Deputies: "Should the application of the law give rise to disappointment among the workmen, *we have undertaken* to lay a new bill before the house." This worthy man spoke exactly like the *rapporteur* of a tariff law.

There are plenty of workmen who understand perfectly well that all the trash of parliamentary literature only serves to disguise the real motives by which the Government is influenced. The protectionists succeed by subsidizing a few important party leaders or by financing newspapers that support the politics of these party leaders; the workers have no money, but they have at their disposal a much more efficacious means of action; they can inspire *fear*, and for several years past they have availed themselves of this resource.

At the time of the discussion of the law regulating labor in mines, the question of the threats addressed to the Government cropped up several times: On February 5, 1902, the president of the commission told the Chamber that those in power had "lent an attentive ear to clamorings from without; that they had been inspired by a sentiment of benevolent generosity in allowing themselves to be moved (*despite the tone* in which they were couched), by the claims of the working classes and the long cry of suffering of the workers in the mines." A little later he added: "We have accomplished a work of social justice, . . . a work of benevolence also, in going to those who toil and suffer, like friends solely desirous of working in peace and under honorable conditions, and we must not by a brutal and too egotistic refusal to unbend, allow them to give way to impulses which, *while not actual revolts,* would yet have as many victims." All these confused phrases served to hide the terrible fear which clutched this grotesque deputy. In the sitting of November 6, 1904, at the Senate, the minister declared that the Government was incapable of giving way to threats, but that it was necessary to open not only ears and mind, but also the heart "to respectful claims" (!); a good deal of water had passed under the bridges since the day when the Government had promised to pass the law under the threat of a general strike.

I could choose other examples to show that the most decisive factor in social politics is the cowardice of the Government. This was shown in the plainest possible way in the recent discussions on the suppression of registry offices, and on the law which sent to the civil courts appeals against the decisions of the arbitrators in industrial disputes. Nearly all the syndicalist leaders know how to make excellent use of this situation, and they teach the workers that it is not at all a question of demanding favors, but that they must profit by *middle-class cowardice* to impose the will of the proletariat. These tactics are supported by so many facts that they were bound to take root in the working-class world.

One of the things which appear to me to have most astonished the workers during the last few years has been the timidity of the forces of law and order in the presence of a riot; magistrates who have the right to demand the services of soldiers dare not use their power to the utmost, and officers allow themselves to be abused and struck with a patience hitherto unknown in them. It is becoming more and more evident every day that working-class violence possesses an extraordinary efficacy in strikes: prefects, fearing that they may be obliged to use force against insurrectionary violence, bring pressure to bear on employers in order to compel them to give way; the safety of factories is now looked upon as a favor that the prefect may dispense as he pleases; consequently he arranges the use of his police so as to intimidate the two parties, and skilfully brings them to an agreement.

Trades-union leaders have not been long in grasping the full bearing of this situation, and it must be admitted that they have used the weapon that has been put into their hands with great skill. They endeavor to intimidate the prefects by popular demonstrations that might lead to serious conflicts with the police, and they commend violence as the most efficacious means of obtaining concessions. At the end of a certain time the obsessed and frightened administration nearly always intervenes with the masters and forces an agreement upon them, which becomes an encouragement to the propagandists of violence.

Whether we approve or condemn what is called the *revolutionary and direct method,* it is evident that it is not on the point of disappearing; in a country as warlike as France there are profound reasons that would assure a considerable popularity for this method, even if its enormous efficacy had not been demonstrated by so many examples. This is the one great social fact of the present hour, and we must seek to understand its bearing.

I cannot refrain from noting down here a reflection made by Clémenceau with regard to our relations with Germany, which applies equally well to social conflicts when they take a violent aspect (which seems likely to become more and more general in proportion as a cowardly middle class continues to pursue the chimera of social peace): "There is no better means," he said (than the policy of perpetual concessions); "of making the opposite party ask for more and more. Every man or every power whose action consists solely in surrender can only finish by self-annihilation. Everything that lives resists; that which does not resist allows itself to be cut up piecemeal" *(Aurore,* August 15, 1905).

A social policy founded on middle-class cowardice, which consists in always surrendering before the threat of violence, cannot fail to engender the idea that the middle class is condemned to death, and that its disappearance is only a matter of time. Thus every conflict which gives rise to violence becomes a vanguard fight, and nobody can foresee what will arise from such engagements; although the great battle never comes to a head, yet each time they come to blows the strikers hope that it is the beginning of the great *Napoleonic battle* (that which will definitely crush the vanquished); in this way the practice of strikes engenders the notion of a catastrophic revolution.

A keen observer of the contemporary proletarian movement has expressed the same ideas: "They, like their ancestors (the French revolutionaries), are for struggle, for conquest; they desire to accomplish great works by force. Only, the war of conquest interests them no longer. Instead of thinking of battles, they now think of strikes; instead of setting up as their ideal a battle against the armies of Europe, they now set up the general strike in which the capitalist regime will be annihilated.

The theorists of social peace shut their eyes to these embarrassing facts; they are doubtless ashamed to admit their cowardice, just as the Government is ashamed to admit that its social politics are carried out under the threat of disturbances. It is curious that people who boast of having read Le Play have not observed that his conception of the conditions of social peace was quite different from that of his imbecile successors. He supposed the existence of a middle class of serious moral habits, imbued with the feelings of its own dignity, and having the energy necessary to govern the country without recourse to the old traditional bureaucracy. To those men, who held riches and power in their hands, he professed to teach their *social duty towards their subjects*. His system supposed an undisputed authority; it is well-known that he deplored the license of the press under Napoleon III as scandalous and dangerous; his reflections on this subject seem somewhat ludicrous to those who compare the newspaper of that time with those of today. Nobody in his time would have believed that a great country would accept peace at any price; his point of view in this matter did not differ greatly from that of Clémenceau. He would never have admitted that anyone could be cowardly and hypocritical enough to decorate with the name of social duty the cowardice of a middle class incapable of defending itself.

Middle-class cowardice very much resembles the cowardice of the English liberal party, which constantly proclaims its absolute confidence in arbitration between nations: arbitration nearly always gives disastrous results for England. But these *worthy progressives* prefer to pay, or even to compromise the future of their country, rather than face the horrors of war. The English liberal party has the word "justice" always on its lips, absolutely like our middle class; we might very well wonder whether all the high morality of our great contemporary thinkers is not founded on a degradation of the sentiment of honor.

The study we have just made has not led us to think that the theorists of "social peace" are on the way to an ethic worthy of acknowledgment. We now pass to a counterproof and enquire whether proletarian violence might not be capable of producing the effect in vain expected from tactics of moderation.

First of all, it must be noticed that modern philosophers seem to agree in demanding a kind of sublimity from the ethics of the future, which will distinguish it from the petty and insipid morality of the Catholics. The chief thing with which the theologians are reproached is that they make too great use of the conception of probabilism; nothing seems more absurd (not to say more scandalous) to contemporary philosophers than to count the opinions which have been emitted for and against a maxim, in order to find out whether we ought to shape our conduct by it or not.

Professor Durkheim said recently, at the *Société française de philosophie* (February 11, 1906), that it would be impossible to suppress the religious element in ethics, and that what characterized this element was its incommensurability with other human values. He recognized that his sociological researches led him to conclusions very near those of Kant; he asserted that utilitarian morality had misunderstood the problem of duty and obligation. I do not want to discuss these here; I simply cite them to show to what point the character of the sublime impresses itself on authors who, by the nature of their work, would seem the least inclined to accept it.

No writer has defined more forcibly than Proudhon the principles of that morality which modern times have in vain sought to realize. "To feel and to assert the dignity of man," he says, "first in everything in connection with ourselves, then in the person of our neighbor, and that without a shadow of egoism, without any consideration either of divine or communal sanction—therein lies Right. To be ready to defend that dignity in every circumstance with energy, and, if necessary, against oneself, that is Justice." Clémenceau, who doubtless can hardly be said to make a personal use of this morality, expresses the same thought when he writes: "Without the dignity of the human person, without independence, liberty, and justice, life is but a bestial state not worth the trouble of preserving" (*Aurore,* May 12, 1905).

One well-founded reproach has been brought against Proudhon, as well as against many others of the great moralists; it has been said that his maxims were admirable, but that they were doomed to remain ineffective. And, in fact, experience does prove, unfortunately, that those precepts which the historians of ideas call the most elevated precepts are, as a rule, entirely ineffective. This was evident in the case of the Stoics, it was no less remarkable in Kantism, and it does not seem as if the practical influence of Proudhon has been very noticeable. In order that a man may suppress the tendencies against which morality struggles, he must have in himself some source of conviction that must dominate his whole consciousness, and act before the calculations of reflection have time to enter his mind.

It may even be said that all the fine arguments by which authors hope to induce men to act morally are more likely to lead them down the slope of probabilism; as soon as we consider an act to be accomplished, we are led to ask ourselves if there is not some means of escaping the strict obligations of duty. A. Comte supposed that human nature would change in the future and that the cerebral organs that produce altruism (?) would destroy those which produce egoism; in saying that he very likely bore in mind the fact that moral decision is instantaneous, and, like instinct, comes from the depth of man's nature.

At times Proudhon is reduced, like Kant, to appeal to a kind of scholasticism for an explanation of the paradox of moral law. "To feel himself in others, to the point of sacrificing every other interest to this sentiment, to demand for others the same respect as for himself, and to be angry with the unworthy creature who suffers others to be lacking in respect for him, as if the care of his dignity did not concern himself alone, such a faculty at first sight seems a strange one. . . . There is a tendency in every man to develop and force the acceptance of that which is essentially himself— which is, in fact, his own dignity. It results from this, that the essential in man being identical and one for all humanity, each of us is aware of himself at the same time as individual and as species; and that an insult is felt by a third party and by the offender himself as well as by the injured person, that in consequence the protest is common. This precisely is what is meant by Justice."

Religious ethics claim to possess this source of action which is wanting in lay ethics, but here it is necessary to make a distinction if an error, into which so many authors have fallen, is to be avoided. The great mass of Christians do not carry out the real Christian ethic, that which the philosopher considers as really peculiar to their religion; worldly people who profess Catholicism are chiefly preoccupied with probabilism, mechanical rites and proceeding more or less related to magic and which are calculated to assure their present and future happiness in spite of their sins.

Theoretical Christianity has never been a religion suited to worldly people; the doctors of the spiritual life have always reasoned about those people who were able to escape from the conditions of ordinary life. "When the Council of Gangres, in 325," said Renan, "declared that the Gospel maxims about poverty, the renunciation of the family and virginity, were not intended for the ordinary Christian, the perfectionists made places apart where the evangelical life, too lofty for the common run of men, could be practiced in all its rigor." He remarks, moreover, very justly, that the "monastery took the place of martyrdom so that the precepts of Jesus might be carried out somewhere," but he does not push this comparison far enough; the lives of the great hermits were a material struggle against the infernal powers that pursue them even to the desert, and this struggle was to continue that which the martyrs had waged against their adversaries.

These facts show us the way to a right understanding of the nature of lofty moral convictions; these never depend on reasoning or on any education of the individual will, but on a state of war in which men voluntarily participate and which finds expression in well-defined myths. In Catholic countries the monks carry on the struggle against the prince of evil who triumphs in this world, and would subdue them to his will; in Protestant countries small fanatical sects take the place of the monasteries. These are the battlefields that enable Christian morality to hold its own, with that character of sublimity which today still fascinates many minds and gives it sufficient luster to beget in the community a few pale imitations.

When one considers a less accentuated state of the Christian ethic, one is struck by seeing to what extent it depends on strife. Le Play, who was an excellent Catholic, often contrasted (to the great scandal of his coreligionists) the solidity of the religious convictions he met with in countries of mixed religions, with the spirit of inactivity that prevails in the countries exclusively submitted to the influence of Rome. Among the Protestant peoples, the more vigorously the established Church is assailed by dissident sects the greater the moral fervour developed. We thus see that conviction is founded on the competition of communions, each of which regards itself as the army of truth fighting the armies of evil. In such conditions it is possible to find sublimity; but when religious warfare is much weakened, probabilism, mechanical rites having a certain resemblance to magic, take the first place.

We can point out quite similar phenomena in the history of modern liberal ideas. For a long while our fathers regarded from an almost religious point of view the Declaration of the Rights of Man, which seems to us nowadays only a colorless collection of abstract and confused formulas, without any great practical bearing. This was due to the fact that formidable struggles had been undertaken on account of the institutions that originated in this document; the clerical party asserted that it would demonstrate the fundamental error of liberalism; everywhere it organized fighting societies intended to enforce its authority on the people and on the Government; it boasted that it would be able to destroy the defenders of the Revolution before long. At the time when Proudhon wrote his book on Justice, the conflict was far from being ended; thus the whole book is written in a warlike tone astonishing to the reader of today: The author speaks as if he were a veteran in the wars of liberty; he would be revenged on the temporary conquerors who threaten the acquisitions of the Revolution; he announces the dawn of the great revolt.

Proudhon hopes that the duel will be soon, that the forces will meet with their whole strength, and that there will be a Napoleonic battle, finally destroying the opponent. He often speaks in a language that would be appropriate to an epic. He did not perceive that when later on his belligerent ideas had disappeared, his abstract reasonings would seem weak.

There is a ferment all through his soul that colors it and gives a hidden meaning to his thought, very far removed from the scholastic sense.

The savage fury with which the Church proceeded against Proudhon's book shows that the clerical camp had exactly the same conception of the nature and consequences of the conflict as he had.

As long as the "sublime" imposed itself in this way on the modern spirit, it seemed possible to create a lay and democratic ethic; but in our time such an enterprise would seem almost comic. Everything is changed now that the clericals no longer seem formidable; there are no longer any liberal convictions, since the liberals have ceased to be animated by their former warlike passions. Nowadays everything is in such confusion that the priests claim to be the best of democrats; they have adopted the *Marseillaise* as their party hymn, and if a little persuasion is exerted they will have illuminations on the anniversary of August 10, 1792. Sublimity has vanished from the ethics of both parties, giving place to a morality of extraordinary meanness.

Kautsky is evidently right when he asserts that in our time the advancement of the workers has depended on their revolutionary spirit. At the end of a study on social reform and revolution he says, "It is hopeless to try, by means of moral homilies, to inspire the English workman with a more exalted conception of life, a feeling of nobler effort. The ethics of the proletariat spring from its revolutionary aspirations, these are what give it the greatest force and elevation. It is the idea of revolution that has raised the proletariat from its degradation." It is clear that for Kautsky morality is always subordinate to the idea of sublimity.

The socialist point of view is quite different from that of former democratic literature; our fathers believed that the nearer man approached Nature the better he was, and that a man of the people was a sort of savage; that consequently the lower we descend the more virtue we find. The democrats have many times, in support of this idea, called attention to the fact that during revolutions the poorest people have often given the finest examples of heroism; they explain this by taking for granted that these obscure heroes were true children of Nature. I explain it by saying that, these men be-

ing engaged in a war that was bound to end in their triumph
or their enslavement, the sentiment of sublimity was bound
to be engendered by the conditions of the struggle. As a rule,
during a revolution the higher classes show themselves in a
particularly unfavorable light, for this reason, that, belonging to a defeated army, they experience the feelings of conquered people, suppliant, or about to capitulate.

When working-class circles are *reasonable,* as the professional sociologists wish them to be, when conflicts are confined to disputes about material interests, there is no more
opportunity for heroism than when agricultural syndicates
discuss the subject of the price of guano with manure merchants. It has never been thought that discussions about
prices could possibly exercise any ethical influence on men;
the experience of sales of livestock would lead to the supposition that in such cases those interested are led to admire
cunning rather than good faith; the *ethical values* recognized
by horse dealers have never passed for very elevated. Among
the important things accomplished by agricultural syndicates, De Rocquigny reports that in 1896, "the municipality
of Marmande having wanted to impose on beasts brought to
the fair a tax which the cattle breeders *considered iniquitous*
. . . the breeders struck, and stopped supplying the market
of Marmande, with such effect that the municipality found
itself forced to give in. This was a very peaceful procedure
which produced results profitable to the peasants; but it is
quite clear that nothing ethical was involved in such a
dispute.

When politicians intervene there is, almost necessarily, a
noticeable lowering of ethical standards, because they do
nothing for nothing and only act on condition that the favored association becomes one of their customers. We are
very far here from the path of sublimity, we are on that
which leads to the practices of the political-criminal societies.

In the opinion of many well-informed people, the transition from violence to cunning that shows itself in contemporary strikes in England cannot be too much admired. The
great object of the trades unions is to obtain a recognition
of the right to employ threats disguised in diplomatic formulas; they desire that their delegates should not be interfered
with when going the round of the workshops charged with
the mission of bringing those workmen who wish to work

to understand that it would be to their interests to follow the *directions* of the trades unions; they consent to express their desires in a form that will be perfectly clear to the listener, but that could be represented in a court of justice as a solidarist sermon. I protest I cannot see what is so admirable in these tactics, which are worthy of Escobar. In the past the Catholics have often employed similar methods of intimidation against the Liberals; I understand thus perfectly well why so many *worthy progressives* admire the trades unions, but the morality of the *worthy progressives* does not seem to me very much to be admired.

It is true that for a long time in England violence has been void of all revolutionary character. Whether corporative advantages are pursued by means of blows or by craft, there is not much difference between the two methods; yet the pacific tactics of the trades unions indicate an hypocrisy that would be better left to the *"well-intentioned progressives."* In a country where the conception of the general strike exists, the blows exchanged between workmen and representatives of the middle classes have an entirely different import, their consequences are far reaching and they may beget heroism.

I am convinced that in order to understand part, at any rate, of the dislike that Bernstein's doctrines rouse in German social democracy we must bear in mind these conclusions about the nature of the sublime in ethics. The German has been brought upon sublimity to an extraordinary extent, first by the literature connected with the wars of independence, then by the revival of the taste for the old national songs that followed these wars, then by a philosophy that pursues aims very far removed from sordid considerations. It must also be remembered that the victory of 1871 has considerably contributed toward giving Germans of every class a feeling of confidence in their strength that is not to be found to the same degree in this country at the present time; compare, for instance, the German Catholic party with the chicken-hearted creatures who form the clientele of the Church in France! Our clergy only think of humiliating themselves before their adversaries and are quite happy, provided that there are plenty of evening parties during the winter; they have no recollection of services that are rendered to them.

The German socialist party drew its strength particularly from the catastrophic idea everywhere spread by its propagandists, and which was taken very seriously as long as the Bismarckian persecutions maintained a warlike spirit in the groups. This spirit was so strong in the masses that they have not yet succeeded in understanding thoroughly that their leaders are anything but revolutionaries.

When Bernstein (who was too intelligent not to know what was the real spirit of his friends on the directing committee) announced that the grandiose hopes that had been raised must be given up, there was a moment of stupefaction; very few people understood that Bernstein's declarations were courageous and honest actions, intended to make the language of socialism accord more with the real facts. If hereafter it was necessary to be content with the policy of social reform, the parliamentary parties and the ministry would have to be negotiated with—that is, it would be necessary to behave exactly as the middle classes did. This appeared monstrous to men who had been brought up on a catastrophic theory of socialism. Many times had the tricks of the middle-class politicians been denounced, their astuteness contrasted with the candor and disinterestedness of the socialists, and the large element of artificiality and expediency in their attitude of opposition pointed out. It could never have been imagined that the disciples of Marx might follow in the footsteps of the liberals. With the new policy, heroic characters, sublimity, and convictions disappear! The Germans thought that the world was turned upside down.

It is plain that Bernstein was absolutely right in not wanting to keep up a revolutionary semblance that was in contradiction with the real state of mind of the party; he did not find in his own country the elements that existed in France and Italy; he saw no other way then of keeping socialism on a basis of reality than that of suppressing all that was deceptive in a revolutionary program that the leaders no longer believed in. Kautsky, on the contrary, wanted to preserve the veil that hid from the workmen the real activity of the socialist party; in this way he achieved much success among the politicians, but more than any one else he has helped to intensify the socialist crisis in Germany. The ideas of socialism cannot be kept intact by diluting the phrases of Marx in verbose commentaries, but by continually adapting the spout of Marx to facts that are capable of assuming a revolutionary aspect. The general strike alone can produce this result at the present day.

One serious question must now be asked: "Why is it that in certain countries acts of violence grouping themselves round the idea of the general strike produce a socialist ideology capable of inspiring sublimity, and why in others do they seem not to have that power?" Here national traditions play a great part; the examination of this problem would perhaps help to throw a strong light on the genesis of ideas; but we will not deal with it here.

Paul Goodman

On Treason Against Natural Societies [1]

Paul Goodman (1911 ——) Goodman was born in New York City in 1911. He is a graduate of the City College of New York and earned his Ph.D. at the University of Chicago. He is presently an associate of Columbia University. With his well-known brother, Percival, he is the author of *Communitas,* a classic work on the city. He has lectured widely at many universities and has taught at the University of Chicago, New York University, and Black Mountain College. He is a fellow of various associations of psychology and teaches methods of group therapy. Among his works are *Gestalt Therapy, Growing Up Absurd,* and books of poetry and fiction.

We speak of the Society, with a capital S, as "against the interests of Society," as tho it were a unitary thing, more than the loose confederation of lesser societies which also admittedly exist. The unanimity of behavior in the industrial, economic, military, educational, and mass-entertained Society certainly justifies the usage. Some philosophers call the Society "inorganic," meaning that many of the mores, e.g., traffic-congestion, are too remote from biological functions and impede them; but in the classical sense of organism, namely that the least parts mutu-

[1] From *Drawing the Line,* by Paul Goodman. N.Y.· Random House, Inc., Copyright 1946. Reprinted by permission of the publisher.

ally cause each other, the Society is more organic than societies have ever been; every action, especially the absurd
ones, can be shown to have social causes and to be a social
necessity. Disease is no less organic than health.

Yet in some of the strongest meanings of social unity, the
Society is almost chaotic; one such is the unanimity of moral
judgments in the most important personal issues. Thus ought
a girl to be a virgin at marriage? Is there a single standard
for husband and wife? Is theft within the law permissible?
Is patriotism ridiculous?—It would be possible to collect
millions of votes on either side of such questions. I have
made a practice of asking various persons what would be
their attitude to receiving an incestuous brother and sister
as overnight guests, and on *this* issue got many diverse
replies!

Of course the universal confusion and toleration in such
matters is itself a sign of social unanimity: namely, that
people have agreed to divorce (and disregard) intimate personal concerns and opinions from the public ritual that exerts
social pressure. The resulting uniformity of dress, behavior,
desire is at the same time intense and bloodless; and there is
no longer such a thing as earnest speech.

Now with regard to the legal penalty for crimes, like theft,
bigamy, incest, treason, murder, no such confusion and toleration exists. Once the case is brought to court, there is little
diversity of judgment and punishment. Yet obviously the
lack of moral pressure keeps many cases out of court, for
there is no scandal; adultery, for example, is a crime that is
never brought to court. Does not this put the criminal law in
an extraordinary position, and reduce the work of juries—
which ought to express the strength of social opinion—to the
merely logical function of judging evidence, which a judge
could do better?

But the discrepancy between the moral and legal judgment of crime reveals the following situation: On the one
hand the people, distracted by their timetable and their commodities, are increasingly less concerned with the passional
temptations that lead to crime; these are suppressed, sophisti-
catedly understood rather than felt, partially abreacted by
press and movies; they do not seem diabolic; the easy toleration of the idea goes with the total repression of the wish.

But on the other hand, the brute existence of any society whatever always in fact depends on the personal behavior of each soul. Therefore the Law is inflexible and unsophisticated. It is as tho *the Society knows the repressions that makes its existence possible, but to the members of the Society this knowledge has become unconscious. In this way is achieved the maximum of coercion by the easiest means.* The separation of personal and political and of moral and legal is a sign that to be coerced has become second nature. Thus it is that people are "protected from the cradle to the grave"!

Many (I believe most) of the so-called crimes are really free acts whose repression causes our timidity; natural society has a far shorter list of crimes. But on the contrary, *there is now an important class of acts that are really crimes and yet are judged indifferent or with approval by law and morals both. Acts that lead to unconcerned behavior are crimes. The separation of natural concern and institutional behavior is not only a sign of coercion, but it is positively destructive of natural society.* Let me give an obvious example.

Describing a bombed area and a horror-hospital in Germany, a sergeant writes: "In modern war there are crimes not criminals. In modern society there is evil but there is no devil. Murder has been mechanized and rendered impersonal. The foul deed of bloody hands belongs to a bygone era when man could commit his own sins. . . . Here, as in many other cases, the guilt belongs to the machine. Somewhere in the apparatus of bureaucracy, memoranda, and clean efficient directives, a crime has been committed." These have become familiar observations: the lofty bombardier is not a killer, just as the capitalist trapped in the market does not willingly deal slow death, etc. The system and now the machine itself! are guilty. Shall we bring into court the trimotor aeroplane?

The most blessed thing in the world is to live by faith without imputation of guilt; having the Kingdom within. Lo, these persons have no imputation of guilt, and have they the Kingdom within?—riders, as Hawthorne said, of the Celestial Railway!

The crime that these persons—we all in our degree—are

committing happens to be the most heinous in jurisprudence; it is a crime worse than murder. It is Treason. Treason against natural societies so far as they exist.

Not all commit Treason to our natural societies in the same degree; some are more the principals, some more the accomplices. But it is ridiculous to say that the crime cannot be imputed or that anyone commits it without intent and in ignorance. For everyone knows the moments in which he conforms against his nature, in which he suppresses his best spontaneous impulse, and cowardly takes leave of his heart. The steps that he takes to habituation and unconsciousness are crimes that entail every subsequent evil of enslavement and mass murder. The murder cannot be directly imputed, the sergeant is right; but the continuing treason must be imputed. (Why is he still a sergeant?)

Let us look a little at the horrible working out of this principle of imputation, which must nevertheless be declared just. We are bred into a society of mixed coercion and nature. The strongest natural influences—parental concern, childish imitation; adolescent desire to stand among his brothers and be independent; an artisan's ability to produce something and a citizen's duty—all these are unnaturally exerted to make us renounce and forget our natures. We conform to institutions that up to a certain point give great natural satisfactions, food, learning, and fellowship—then suddenly we find that terrible crimes are committed and we are somehow the agents. And some of us can even remember when it was that we compromised, were unwisely prudent, dismissed to another time a deeper satisfaction than convenient, and obeyed against our better judgment.

It is said the system is guilty, but the system is its members coerced into the system. It is also true that the system itself exercises the coercion.

Thus, a man works in a vast factory with an elaborate division of labor. He performs a repetitive operation in itself senseless. Naturally this work is irksome and he has many impulses to "go fishing," not to get up when the alarm clock rings, to find a more interesting job, to join with some other machinists in starting a small machine shop and try out certain ideas, to live in the country, etc. But against these impulses he meets in the factory itself and from his fellow workers (quite apart from home pressures) the following plausible arguments: that they must band together in that factory and as that factory, and in that industry and as that industry, to fight for "better working conditions," which mean more pay, shorter hours, accident insurance, etc.; and the more militant organizers will even demonstrate that by this means they can ultimately get control of all industry and smash the profit system. None of this quite answers the original irk of the work itself; but good! he commits himself to this program. Now, however, since no one has native wit enough to decide for a vast factory and industry, and all industry, what to demand and when to demand it, and what means are effective, our man must look to others for direction concerning his own felt dissatisfaction. He fights for more pay when perhaps he does not primarily care about improving his standard of living but wants to accomplish something of his own between the cradle and the grave; for seniority when in fact he doesn't want the job, etc., etc. The issues of the fight are now determined by vast, distant forces; the union itself is a vast structure and it is tied to the whole existing Society. Next he finds that he is committed not to strike at all, but to help manufacture machines of war. The machines are then "guilty."

True, the impulses of such a man are vague, romantic, and what is called "adolescent"; even if realizable they would not lead to full satisfaction. Nevertheless their essence is deep and natural. A program is a crime that does not meet the essence of the industrial irk, the noncreative job, but shunts across it. The worker who does a coercive job is a traitor. When he is sidetracked into a good, but irrelevant program, he is a traitor.

I have chosen a hard example that will rouse opposition. Let me choose a harder that will rouse even more.

A very young adolescent, as is usual enough, has sexual relations with his playfellows, partly satisfying their dreams of the girls, partly drawing on true homosexual desires that go back to earlier narcissism and mother-identifications of childhood. But because of what they have been taught in their parochial school and the common words of insult whose meaning they now first grasp, all these boys are ashamed of their acts; their pleasures are suppressed and in their stead appear fistfights and violence. The youth grows up, soon marries. Now there is conscription for a far-off war, whose

issues are dubious and certainly not part of his immediate
awareness and reaction. But his natural desire to oppose the
conscription is met by the strong attractiveness of getting
away from the wife he is a little tired of, back to the free
company of the boys in camp; away from the fatherly role
of too great responsibility, back to the dependence on a paternal sergeant, etc. The camp life, drawing always on a
repressed but finally thinly disguised sexuality, cements the
strongest bonds of fellowship amongst the soldiers. Yet any
overt sexual satisfaction amongst them is out of the question:
instead the pairs of buddies pick up prostitutes together,
copulate with them in the same room, and exchange boasts
of prowess. Next this violent homosexuality, so near the
surface but always repressed and thereby gathering tension,
turns into a violent sadism against the enemy: it is all knives
and guns and bayonets, and raining bombs on towns, and
driving home one's lust in the guise of anger to f——k the
Japs.

What a hard thing it is to impute the crime of treason
against natural society to these men who do not even consciously know what their impulse is. They know as boys;
shall we blame boys? And even the adults, priests, and
teachers who invidiously prevent the boys' antics, do it out
of unconscious envy and resentment. But they at least could
know better and are certainly guilty.

It is horrifying, tho not useless, thus to impute treason to
the particular persons and to trace the institutional crimes
that are but symptoms and results, back to the incidents of
coercion and acceptance. The guilty ones turn out to be little
children and dear parents, earnest radicals, men unconscious
of their intent and even ancestors who are dead. Thank God
the libertarian does not need to think of punishments, for he
knows—following Socrates of old—that the punishment
for injustice is to be what one is. The persons who separate
themselves from nature have to live every minute of their
lives without the power, joy, and freedom of nature. And we,
who apparently suffer grave sanctions from such persons,
betray on our faces that we are drawing on forces of nature.

But in fact the case is like the distinction in theology between the Old Law and the New. In the Old Law all are
guilty, in the New they may easily be saved. We see that in

fact everybody who still has life and energy is continually manifesting some natural force and is facing an unnatural coercion. And now, in some apparently trivial issue that nevertheless is a key, he draws the line! The next step for him to take is not obscure or difficult. It presents itself at once; it is even forcibly presented by the Society! Will he not soon develop in contrast to the habit of coercion, a *habit* of freedom? And positive natural acts bloom like the flowers.

Robert Presthus

The Social Dysfunctions of Organization [1]

Robert V. Presthus (1917 ——) Born Februry 25, 1917, in St. Paul, Minnesota, Presthus attended St. Olaf College and the University of Minnesota. He took his Ph.D. at the University of Chicago, and has taught at the University of Southern California (Los Angeles) and Michigan State University. Presently he is Professor of Public Administration at Cornell University. His special fields of interest are comparative administration and economic development, organizational theory and behavior, and conceptions of authority in organizations. Among his works are *The Organizational Society, Public Administration,* and *Turkish Conseil d'État.*

We have stressed the internal aspects of big organizations, particularly their impact upon the individuals who work in them. We now turn to some of their larger *social* consequences. Are their vaunted contributions to our economic power and our affluence the only grounds upon which they should be assayed? [2] Or do they have other, less positive, consequences that must be included in any assessment of their critical role in American society? Big organizations do indeed have vital social dysfunctions

---

[1] From *The Organizational Society* by Robert Presthus. Copyright (c) 1962 by Robert Presthus. Reprinted by permission of Alfred A. Knopf, Inc.

[2] These achievements, of course, rest upon factors such as natural-resource wealth, technology, capital, and a highly skilled labor force. The organization's unique contribution is to combine such factors into a productive synthesis, mainly by centralizing authority and control. [Presthus' note, as are all others in this extract.]

over and beyond their failure to provide a democratic-humanistic work environment. Significantly at this historical stage, such dysfunctions give rise to grave questions about our competitive ability in the international arena.

The dominant theme in the antiorganizational refrain has usually been that bureaucracy stifles individual demands for self-realization and autonomy. While this is all to the good, the larger implications of big organization are perhaps even more significant today, since they touch upon the very capacity of our society for survival. Certainly we have never faced a challenge comparable to that now posed by Russia and China. Our liberal, democratic values and political system are also threatened by the rise of authoritarian governments in many of the new states where for some time poverty, illiteracy, and insecurity will make democracy untenable. Meanwhile, we are confronted at this critical juncture with incontrovertible evidence of our declining superiority in atomic weapons, in the thrust to deliver them with ballistic missiles, and in comparative economic growth.

In this larger context, then, what are the dysfunctions of the organizational logic that pervades our society? This question requires some prefatory consideration of the *utility of conflict,* a concept that has come into wide disrepute during this era of conventional wisdom and good cheer. Both conflict and change have been stoutly resisted. But even the slightest historical perspective reveals that the survival chances of a society are largely a function of its ability to meet change. As Arnold Toynbee has shown, civilizations have always been confronted with successive challenges, such as the alternating cycles of drought and humidity that occur in the Eurasian and African steppes, forcing nomadic tribes to seek food by invasion of surrounding agricultural countries.[3] When unable to harness their values and institutions to the demand of social, economic, and climatic change, civilizations have rapidly declined. Challenges emerge within the existing order, while others are the result of external pressures. One might assume the former to be easier to accommodate since their elements are embedded in the existing culture, in contrast to alien influences that

[3] Arnold J. Toynbee, *A Study of History*. New York: Oxford University Press, 1934, Vol. 3, pp. 7–22, especially p. 17.

are not only novel but less amenable to control by the threatened society.

This distinction between internal and external challenge underlines the gravity of our present situation. For not only is the challenge essentially alien and novel, but as the uncertain course of our diplomacy suggests, we seem to have lost the initiative. With the grand exception of the Marshall Plan, for the past decade our diplomacy has been mainly one of parry rather than of thrust. The present conditions are unique in that, while threats to American security have traditionally occurred along a single dimension, the challenge now proceeds simultaneously along social, political, economic, technological, and military lines. Our greatest disability, moreover, seems to exist in the very areas where we have enjoyed supremacy, namely in technology and economic growth.

These unprecedented developments pose the most urgent demands for critical inquiry into time-honored patterns of organization, thought, and behavior. We can probably agree that the present challenge is not only unique, but that its successful resolution will require a major advance in creative areas. Not only in weaponry, but also in the design (or at least in the acceptance) of the new social and economic models that change is forcing upon us. Here again our very success is a potential handicap to us. This irony can be seen, for example, in the insistence of many political and business leaders that economic growth in the underdeveloped countries must follow the impressive American pattern of free enterprise. But such societies cannot afford free enterprise as we have known it, mainly because of their lack of venture capital (per capita income in these societies is less than $200 per year) and because of the complex technical and managerial skills that our system requires. If such unrealistic and nostalgic attitudes persist, what hope is there for the acceptance of new ideas here, such as the thought that our own national state may have become an anachronistic form of political organization?

In both weapons development and social organization, then, creativity is required to meet global shifts in power and to accommodate the demands of poorer countries for political and economic equality. Yet both our social values and our organizational forms inhibit the conflict and criticism which are the very beginning of creativity. Because it is so vital today, let us consider for a moment the sociology of conflict. What is its utility value; and why do organizations inhibit it?

The aversion to conflict in big organizations rests in part upon the perspective of its leaders who see the organization as a disciplined, cohesive system for achieving a common goal. They regard it as a rational instrument that binds together the interests of its members in a kind of all-for-one, one-for-all ethic. The other face of organization with its informal power centers and its function of satisfying individual needs for status and self-realization is neglected. Organizations are not defined this way by those who direct them. As Coser says: "The decision makers are engaged in maintaining and, if possible, in strengthening the organizational structures through and in which they exercise power and influence. Whatever conflicts occur within these structures will appear to them to be dysfunctional." [4] Moreover, many social scientists with a conservative bias regard conflict as anathema because they define society as an organic system in which by definition all values and groups operate smoothly as vital parts of the whole system. Conflict or disagreement about basic values or the roles assigned to each group thus tends to be regarded as destructive.

Similarly, in American political life, the liberal ideal of a cooperative society in which everyone works together for the public interest has gone virtually unchallenged. This romantic pluralism holds that there are really no basic (or at least no irreconcilable) conflicts between classes, between labor and management, between big business and small business, etc. Adjustment, not conflict, is the theme. To hold otherwise is to fall victim to an unlovely economic determinism. Thus both political and sociological analysis often has a built-in conservative bias that abhors conflict. In the everyday world, organizational leaders share this bias; and much of their time is consequently spent showing that we must all hang together or we will surely hang separately.

Organizational logic is essentially conservative, for it hon-

[4] L. A. Coser, *The Functions of Social Conflict.* Glencoe (Ill.): The Free Press, 1956, p. 27.

ors consistency, tradition, the minimizing of individual ends in favor of collective ends, and the wisdom of history rather than the wisdom of men. A resulting major quality and dysfunction of big organizations is, therefore, their inflexibility in the face of social and technological pressures for change. They resist conflict and creativity because they tend to assume that what is, is good. Perhaps the revival of conservative ideals among some American writers is a by-product of the organizational society in the sense that the organizational ethic has needed, certainly, a more compelling rationalization than mere efficiency or profit. It seems less ingenious, moreover, to praise organizations and modern technology than to attribute our national achievements to tradition, to history, and even to heredity, as conservative theory does.

In a larger social context, conflict is further inhibited by the pervasive American need to be liked, to pursue conformity for the sake of popularity. As we saw earlier, socialization inculcates conventional values to the extent that the individual feels guilty when he expresses unorthodox views. Moreover, as organizations become more systematic in their demands for predictability and conformity, the penalties for heterodoxy become more severe. When career chances are threatened by independence, independence becomes a luxury. Bureaucratization plays its part relentlessly as the trend toward spending one's work life in a single organization ties the individual more and more closely to the demands of a given organization. The piling up of fringe benefits and seniority rights encourages the tendency to rationalize one's work place as the best of all possible worlds. Professional training and commitments similarly increase one's personal mortgages and his tendency to play it safe.

In sum, big organizations typically seek control, discipline, and standardization. They apply pragmatic, often quantitative standards to measure their activities. For such reasons, basic research and the unstructured conditions that nourish it are fundamentally contrary to organizational logic. Such research is hard to control. Those engaged in it do not know what they will find, if anything, how long it will take, nor how much it will cost. As a former Secretary of Defense said: "Basic research is when you don't know what you're doing." Unfortunately, not all critical problems nor the motivations of individuals can be handled according to such logic. The very success of our mass-production system and its applied-research orientation seems to aggravate the resulting dilemma.

The consequences of conflicting values of scientists and military-organization men can usefully be presented in the context of interpersonal theory. We saw earlier that organizational conflict is often the result of distorted preceptions among its members, both of themselves and of each other. Such misperceptions, moreover, became self-enforcing, locking individuals into relationships that aggravate tension and hinder the organization's attempts to achieve its goals. In the case of the executive group reported [earlier], the self-deceptions of the men (the disparity between their self-perceptions and the way their associates saw them) made effective working relations impossible. A similar mechanism seems to be at work in the government's weapons-research program.

One way of portraying this perceptual disparity is by constructing a rough "index of alienation" based upon the common images that research scientists and military-organization men have of themselves and of each other. Such an index is necessarily crude; indeed, in a technical sense it is not precisely an index since it includes no quantitative difference among the items comprising it. The index, moreover, reflects both the selectivity of those who made the statements and the writer's selectivity in choosing the specific items which are included. However, the index is representative in the sense that the items were collected randomly from a wide variety of sources. The validity of each statement is less significant than the indication it offers of opposing definitions of reality by individuals working toward similar goals in a similar organizational context.

INDEX OF ALIENATION

Military-Organization Men	*Research Scientists*
The overriding significance and priority of the ICBM and IRBM programs dictate that special admin-	The real ruler of government-sponsored research [is] the Bureau of the Budget (university scientist).

Military-Organization Men

istration procedures and controls be established (Chief of Staff suggested draft memo).

An ounce of loyalty is worth a pound of brains (government security officer).

This [claim that military-research organizations were built up unnecessarily to provide commands for senior officers] is a frequent allegation which emanates from subordinates . . . whenever any new center is created for reasons best known to top management (Defense Department research coordinator).

John, a civilian cannot be in the chain of command (commanding general, military research center, to senior civilian scientist).

I do not necessarily mean that a PhD degree means a man is bright (government research coordinator).

Of course, the fact that a person believes in social equality doesn't *prove* that he's a communist; but it certainly makes you look twice, doesn't it? (Federal Loyalty Board member).

My observation [is] that some of the recommended organizations have been

Research Scientists

Unfortunately, secrecy and progress are mutually incompatible. This is always true of science (research physicist).

The key positions at the Center . . . were replaced by purely military people regardless of their competence (senior civilian scientist).

In the long run science is doomed if it is to be pursued in secrecy (university scientist).

The gossip of scientists who get together is the life-blood of physics (research physicist).

The exceptional officer, the one who is an original thinker, is considered a heretic (director, research organization).

The history of ideas is the history of mistakes (Alfred North Whitehead).

We're all scientists basically. We judge men not on position but on scientific

Military-Organization Men

self-serving in nature with the obvious objective of . . . [scientists] being placed in positions of considerable power and self-aggrandizement (assistant secretary, Defense Department).

It is clear that an optimum climate for research work by civilian scientists cannot be the only consideration (research coordinator, Defense Department).

That industrial laboratories exist because of the profit motive does not change the character of their basic research. . . . It guarantees the type of research which would . . . be labeled basic . . . in the academic world (research manager, industry).

The Air Force said, "It is easier just to eliminate basic research!" (manager, industrial missile research program).

Research Scientists

ability. Our goal is not to make a lot of money or to boss people around but to become competent scientists (scientist, industrial laboratory).

This company takes great pride in its engineering and technological achievements if you can believe the ads. But I also know that the executive vice-president has been heard to say on many occasions "You can hire technical brains a dime a dozen" (research engineer, industry).

The absence of tenure and freedom of inquiry does influence the work and research of laboratory people. I would have carried out certain types of important research if I were at the university (scientist, industrial laboratory).

Unless a colleague's competence or honesty becomes suspect, he is expected to make all decisions relating to his work for himself. The idea of a boss is anathema, as are the external controls imposed by industrial methods of organization—in fact they are held to be inconsistent with the basic tenets of professionalism.

Military-Organization Men

The trouble with these research people is that they go ahead and do research without any appreciation of the cost (manager, industrial laboratory).

Most of the troublesome people have left—you really can't have research people who think they're God Almighty (development engineer, industrial corporation).

Our job is to recruit individuals and to try to broaden them to the interests and the point of view of the company (research administrator, industry).

Research Scientists

Many of these people, used to command, are impervious to new ideas. . . . The same type of people, the same type of treatment as they apply to ship operation, they apply to . . . research and development. You simply can't do that (Navy research director).

The great point in the scientist's code is full and honest reporting to all his colleagues (university scientist).

My technical people would quit rather than work on anything they didn't believe in (director, research organization).

Allied with the consequences of such disparate self-images and judgments is the problem of goal displacement. We have seen that the results of organizational logic often include a reduction in the intrinsic satisfaction in work. This results from the breakdown of work and decision making into such minute compartments that any given individual finds it difficult to derive the psychic satisfaction of producing a finished product. But psychologists find that variety and complexity in most kinds of work are required for high morale and identification. Organizations tend to inhibit these satisfactions by dividing and standardizing work in order to gain control and efficiency.

The breaking down of university disciplines into departments, and then into special fields within a given department, may alienate the scholar because his work is seen as only a fragment of a larger whole. This not only prevents him from defining his field in large compass, but it interferes with his role as citizen by providing a handy rationalization that every problem has its experts who must define the issues and work out the solutions. In Veblen's phrase, he becomes a victim of "trained incapacity." By dramatizing the irrelevance of his special knowledge to vital public questions, such results tend to undercut pride in work and to divert one toward alternative rewards such as income, prestige, and leisure.

Organizations further encourage such displacement of values by the tendency to replace creative work and independence as the basis for rewards with subjective criteria of loyalty, seniority, dependence, adaptability, "personality," and community service. Traditional values tend to be displaced by a marketing ethic characterized by self-promotion, status borrowing, and mock conviviality. In creative kinds of work, where (after initial training and certification) standards of achievement are much less precise, and where, indeed, one may in effect set his own pace, the results are far-reaching. We have seen that physical scientists do not have to work for the government, and that many prefer not to. Organizational logic, which has been essentially authoritarian, has often failed to recognize this permissive aspect of highly skilled work. Like all of us, its advocates find it hard to change their ways in the face of new conditions. As the Defense Department's Special Assistant for Research and Development insisted:

> When the vital urgency of the military development and research mission is considered . . . it is clear that an optimum climate for research work by civilian scientists cannot be the only consideration. Certain disciplines are essential to insure that development schedules are met and that research remains in areas of direct relevance to the problems at hand. The investment of public funds in the production of weapons . . . represents such a large part of the national economy that certain checks and balances which may be regarded as restrictive are absolutely essential for the protection of the public interest. Some or all of these factors may occasionally lead to the frustration of an individual scientist, but this, it is feared, is inevitable under any system of management sensitive to its responsibilities to the public.

This dictum expresses well the military-organization man rationale. It points up a common premise of such thinking, namely, the assumption that organization and controls by themselves can create something. It points up also the assumption that basic research can be controlled when by its very nature it cannot. Organization's role must indeed be an auxiliary one of providing the conditions that will encourage individual creativity. Administrative and financial ground rules are surely needed, but in an arms race that uniquely demands innovation and flexibility in the face of rapid change, "an optimum climate for research by civilian scientists" is critical.

This study of weapons research dramatizes the whole problem of big organizations and their motivating assumptions. . . . It documents the tensions engendered by individual attempts to meet the conditions set down by the bureaucratic model. While the experiences of the research scientists may be exceptional, they underscore the dilemma of the creative, "task-oriented," ambivalent type in modern organization. Another significant generalization illustrated here is the tendency of organizations to resist innovation. A displacement of values, often masked by a ritualistic obeisance to the "public interest," may occur in which organizations develop an existence independent of the goals that inspire them. Latent individual and organizational interests blunt both the ability and the inclination of organizations to change. Personal and organizational goals of power and prestige challenge the larger social goals that presumably justify their existence in the first place.

In addition, there is the problem of the organization's impact on the meaning of work. We have suggested that most organization men are indifferents. Alienated to some extent by work and the work place, they have displaced their energy and their interest upon off-work activities. Even the upward-mobile, whose *élan* remains high, seems less interested in the intrinsic value of work than in its by-products of authority, status, and prestige. If meaningful work is essential to mental health, the human consequences of such orientations are disturbing.

Such larger implications of changing organizational values

are only beginning to emerge. While the upward-mobile role obviously pays off in terms of personal influence and income, its social results seem less fruitful. But the age of the "cheerful robot" is not inevitable. In weapons research and missile development, as we have seen, the testimony of distinguished scientists has revealed the strain between organizational values and the scientists' needs for autonomy. This suggests a growing awareness of the conditions that seem to be hampering our efforts to maintain parity with Russian military and space power. There is also evidence that the sprawling growth of university administrations, which aggravate existing disparities in academic status and income, is receiving more attention.

In sum, there is apparently some recognition that individual growth and creativity are often at odds with organizational logic. Even if this perspective has been forced upon us by the Russian economic and military thrust, its results may prove generally desirable. Although too much attention is undoubtedly being given to physical science, greater discrimination in our use of bureaucratic structure and norms may result. Perhaps we can retain them in mass production and applied spheres to which they are nicely suited, while sharply modifying them in art, education, and scientific research. If we can also abandon some of our pragmatic notions about "efficiency," humanistic values will benefit, and the need for a permissive work climate in creative areas may become clearer. Certainly, the first step in such a reorientation is an awareness of organizational dysfunctions.

Philip Selznick
Revolution Sacred and Profane [1]

Philip Selznick (1919———) Born January 8, 1919, in Newark, New Jersey, Selznick studied at Columbia University, where he received his Ph.D. in sociology. He has held a number of consulting positions for institutions, including the Rand Corpora-

[1] From "Revolution Sacred and Profane," by Philip Selznick. *Enquiry: A Journal of Independent Radical Thought*, Vol. 2, No. 2 (Fall, 1944). Reprinted by permission of the author.

tion and the Fund for the Republic. At present he teaches
TVA and the Grass Roots, The Organizational Weapon, and
sociology at the University of California at Berkeley. Among
his works are *Leadership in Administration.*

AUTHOR'S NOTE (November, 1963): I am grateful to the
Editor for the opportunity to say a word about "Revolution: Sacred and Profane." This was written twenty years
ago and marks a stage on the road away from socialist
politics. I apologize for the style, which can only be
called "youthful baroque." The peculiar blend of conservatism and a limited radicalism expressed in the essay
is still part of my political philosophy. But I no longer
believe that it makes sense to espouse a government take-
over of "the commanding heights" of the economy; nor
do I accept "the moral absolute of pacifism" as a guide to
responsible political decision. If the essay is read today
as more than a period piece, I hope its continuing message
will be that ideological thinking, and action based upon it,
is always a grave threat to the quest for a moral common-
wealth. Values can be sacred, but programs must be
profane.

We laboriously explore our diffi-
culties to discover: what seemed new ways are soon distilled
to the old, and we are to be rudely shouldered into channels
long since laid down. The literary dream and the individual
synthesis, freshly conceived and romantically inspired, may
illumine the edges and enrich the interstices of social life
—may even, at rare times, provide genesis and sustenance
for a new regrouping of the whole. But for the most part,
lumbering, structured society will not yield itself to the
eager Promethean hand nor readily consent to be remolded
in the name and in the image of each passing God. We
may, if we like, conjure up our goals with an artist's hand;
but that is the pattern of random proposal, of offering a
varied platter to the real arbiters of history, heedless of the
need to search out the possibilities in the given world as the
foundation stone of rational political enterprise.
    The sign and warrant of political wisdom (and in its

inversion, the brand mark of naiveté) is the recognition of the resistant, recalcitrant, limiting nature of human personality and social institutions. I am not, it is perhaps politic to add, entirely ignorant of the modern viewpoint in social psychology, with its brash plasticity complex. But it seems to make sense to insist that while much in that approach is important, affording a quickened awareness and a more accurate notion of methodology and its postulates, nevertheless serious people will not confuse the latter with the hardy truths won in the course of human experience, however poorly they may be formulated. For *action*—that kind, at least, which intervenes in events, which deals significantly with the primary stuff of social change, with classes and parties and governments—is always shaped and molded by the character of the institutions that it ventures to manipulate. The politically effective form of this impingement is the *limitation of alternatives,* or, put another way, the *presentation of historical choices.* The projected history of any given period may be infinitely various in the realm of fancy, but the real paths along which events may run are few and none too far apart. The philosopher may, if he is brilliant, have a viewpoint pretty much his own, but the philosopher-in-action must soon choose sides or retire. He cannot enter politics on his own terms; he must make his peace with that force, in effective conflict, with whose fate he has bound himself and his ideals.

The historical choice is the choice which is offered. It is the choice that may and can be made because: 1) large social forces are or can be readily mobilized in the direction desired; 2) solutions are offered to the felt problems of key groups; 3) continuity, though not identity, with the traditions, ideals, and habit patterns of the common man is maintained; and, 4) the program and its instruments are *responsible,* in the sense of a full acceptance of consequences without dissolution, at critical periods, into one or another more vigorous trend. There are, at any time, only a few different movements which can satisfy these conditions. They represent, at that time, the given historical alternatives, which devour between them those who attempt to find a median path. These alternatives tend, in practice, to polarize around absolutes, so that those who value action as intervention must lay aside, in choosing within the context of action, undue affection for the neat formulation and special interpretation. That is why the artist is not a politician; and it is what we mean when we say that a movement has become mature, has reached its level, has found its natural allies. It is a sure corollary of this conception that fundamental social change is gradual, always effectively braked by the moderating forces that great human agencies bring with them as they search out the unknown in action.

It may seem strange to read these words, so replete with conservative connotations, in the pages of a socialist magazine. But closer reflection will teach us, I believe, that this is as it should be. For socialism today is more and more becoming the receptacle, protagonist, and defender of the fundamental social ties as well as the highest ideals of our civilization. In the old days, socialists could lay their every stress on the changes, the overturns, that they wished to institute, leaving to the politically conservative factions the task of defending the principles, traditions, and institutions of social order. This division of function seemed fitting and proper. For it was natural to believe that those who defended a specific status quo, the existing political and economic order of things, should find it easy and useful to cling to the banner and extol the merits of the very principle of order and social stability itself. And so it was, for a long period. For although some branches of international socialism, nearing and reaching the heights of power, began to experience the difficulties that responsibility for the nation as a whole entails, most of the movement maintained its role of oppositional minority and social solvent.

But this timeless allocation of function, the conservative defender and radical innovator, has been robbed of its meaning by the complexity of the new relationships. No longer can we say that those who are defending particular structures shield as well the basic relations of mutual aid and fellowship which lie at the root of society. The value of the status quo as the crisis deepens and endures becomes, for those in power, defined in the realistic, self-conscious terms of naked rule and privilege. Despairing as they must of the viability of the traditional social forms and procedures for the maintenance of their power, the conservative elements become institutionally radical. They seize upon any course, any movement which will carry them on its shoulders and promise relief to fear-ridden bank accounts. In this way they effectively and finally divorce their special interests from the general interest and welfare of the community at large. For the new instrumentalities to which they turn are reckless of consequences beyond the capture of power, and are therefore subversive of the moral bonds and accustomed forms of social order.

Hence are the roles reversed. Socialists find themselves defending large areas of American culture (the principles of constitutionalism, Christian fellowship, individual liberty in conscience and politics and economics—to only begin the list) at precisely the time when most other groups, who *support* those presently in power, are in unashamed flight from those principles. The socialist program, in means as well as in ends, is keyed to those precepts and therefore becomes, on an historical plane, the culturally conservative and defensive movement.

Not without difficulties, not smoothly or free of racking, enervating problems. The law of the limitation of alternatives is unrelenting. The choice we make within the bounds it sets is hardly academic, or even transient; to act upon such a choice is to define the structure, the operative ideals, the habits, the alliances, in a word, the *character* of our movement. The classic decision that each generation of socialists has had to make is that between reformist social democracy and apocalyptic bolshevism. These are the polar trends. Both have deep roots in man's nature, both can intervene effectively in events—each to its own part, each in its own way. The characters of these two movements, as we have come to know them after long acquaintance, seem to exhaust the field of significant choice that the complex interweaving and interdependence of historical structures will allow us. There is no middle course that will not soon be drawn into the vortex of one or the other of the historical alternatives.

It is true, of course, that neither movement has been able to attain its professed goals. That is why many socialists, anxious to learn new lessons, have sought to delineate a new road that would be neither reformist nor bolshevist. Yet, while that research is commendable, insofar as it sharpens our understanding of tactics and strategy, it is unwise to hide our faces from the fact that ultimately we must take sides in the real struggle, which will deal harshly with our special programmatic qualifications. What, in action, will be the basic character of our movement? Will it be attuned to an essentially gradualist philosophy, with conservative precepts, with a due respect for those institutions already formed which protect and nourish our values and ideals? Or shall we build an altogether different movement, sustaining and ruled by radically different personalities, which will reach down into the emotional depths of society for the instruments of its nihilistic venture? Intelligence must make this choice self-consciously, for it sets the framework of all action. It is only in the light of the basic road we have chosen that a discussion of new procedures and wiser strategy can make sense.

Socialists who have come to know the spiritual roots of what they stand for will recognize immediately their affinity with the gradualist course. For while European socialism went down to defeat stumbling over its own errors and poor leadership, these movements still remained basically socialist and progressive. And since they were not the sole arbiters of history, it may be questioned whether even the wisest strategy would have led to victory. Bolshevism, on the other hand, transformed itself into an utterly alien instrument, turning toward quite different sources of strength and power, and embodying in explicit form all the merely potential culturally nihilistic elements in oppositional socialism. The social-democratic road leans on those cultural roots which we seek to defend; bolshevism is avowedly contemptuous of them. Social-democracy accepts (with due allowance for human frailty) the basic Christian-democratic values; bolshevism divorces itself from them and from any sense of proper humility which they entail.

The bolshevik revolution is in its nature *sacred,* generating an emotional emphasis that turns its adherents inward upon the apocalyptic image. This is hardly strange, for where objectives are vague and ill-defined, where the power of a given party (read: its leadership) is confused with the requirements of history, then the road to power absorbs the entire political agenda. The revolutionary upheaval and its preparation become the receptacle of all political wisdom— suffused with the discharged tensions of those who have committed themselves beyond recall to a simple, unforked road to social salvation. It is only fair to say that reformism too, like any other special method, has sought a halo of its own. But here the consequences, though sufficiently disturbing, have been relieved by the concentration upon tangible achievements in the here and now, always a reliable solvent of any vulgar mythology of redemption.

The tools of social and political action, devised with an eye toward what the world is really like, must be *profane* in character. As method, they must be secular, and therefore vulnerable to fact and logic, before the requirements of pragmatic evaluation and democratic dispute can come into effective play. The revolutionary elements in gradualist socialism must be profane and secular rather than sacred and religious, for they will be circumscribed by the established character of the movement as a whole and limited to the achievement of specific, clearly defined objectives. It should be emphasized that it is not *all action,* but the *tools* of action that must be profane. Within the general context of our movement, the revolutionary elements are tools, and in that sense subsidiary, at a second remove, from the primary, character-defining motifs. Indeed, it is just in terms of *what* is considered sacred that the most useful distinctions between movements are made. The fact that there are sacred elements in bolshevism is not, of itself, to be deprecated; it is what they hold sacred—the power mechanisms of revolutionary action, the hypostatization of what can be only a tool of significant but limited usefulness—that marks them as alien. It is well to recall that revolution is more (and less) than the sheer annihilation of traditional values. Before the subversion of accepted human relationships is the plain, practical, limited goal of transferring social and political power from the hands of those who rule the commanding heights of our economy. *The achievement of the latter by revolutionary means is dictated by the empirical context of our problem;* to employ those means with sagacity and care requires an impersonal budget of consequences, an accounting that happily is strengthened by prior knowledge of the inherent dangers of our ambivalent tools.

The gradualist emphasis is relevant primarily to *institutional* change; it deprecates the uprooting of established forms where subtle transformations are practicable, ever conscious of the limited capacity of men and structures for

the absorption of the thoroughgoing and all-pervasive. The
bolsheviks do not escape these strictures, for in expunging
the presently traditional they are far from casting men into
new molds. The most they can achieve is a return to older
forms, still founded on the enduring character of the human
materials with which they must deal. The gradualist cannot
make his peace with the bolshevik revolution, for that cuts
at the moral groundwork of his society. But he will realize
the necessity for a more limited revolt, profound in its
ultimate consequences but concentrated against only a relatively small sector of society as we know it. He will, in the
course of this action, be ready to defend those gains, received
and won, which fashion a restrained, reflective and moral
culture. To be sure the inherent tension between revolution
and reformism cannot be erased by the fiat of our own
desires; nor is it unlikely that the former will, at some stages,
spill over whatever dams we may construct. But a prior
limitation of goals, founded on a clear conception of alternative consequences, together with the steeping of our movement in a spiritual atmosphere in which only democracy
can live, can assure the preservation of its institutionally
gradualist character.

I repeat: we choose inevitably between polar trends and
this choice defines the framework and direction of our politics. Yet the very recognition of the necessity which binds
us to the existing political alternatives frees us for the more
intelligent construction of a special program that will take
into account an attempt to correct some of the cardinal
weaknesses of the trend to which we are committed. We are
still *pro*posing for history to *dis*pose, but insofar as we as
individuals and small groups can influence the course of
events, our special program, operating within the general
trend, can be effective.

The fruitful consequences of a dispraise of overoptimism
are evident in the revisions we may make in the traditional
social-democratic program. It is helpful to view the reformist's errors as largely stemming from an overly naive conception of the pliability of his environment. Failing to comprehend the weakness of men and institutions, he is blind to
the necessity of taking that weakness into account and of
shaping a program that will restrain the inevitable enfeebling

dissipation of energy and intelligence. The revisions offered in the light of this perception are basically two:

1) *The practical socialist overturn must be complete within its limited sphere.* Overoptimistic gradualism has not understood the bearing of concentrated and interdependent industrialism on socialist strategy. Gradualism collapses as an effective program when we face the coordinated, integrated structure of our mass-production economy. There the strokes must be bold and thoroughgoing, permitting a speedy reorientation of that key sector of our economy along welfare lines. The failure to recognize this urgent necessity, or to prepare for that kind of action, was a fatal weakness of the social democratic governments in Europe. Firm and decisive measures, taken against the small number of ruling families and their satellites who staff the boards of directors of the hundred-odd apex corporations, need not undermine the institutionally gradualist approach. On the contrary: this politically and economically momentous but culturally insignificant stumbling-block must be energetically set aside in order to permit reformism to operate as an advance guard and in broader fields. This is the limited, but vital, sense in which socialism must be a revolutionary movement. Not to turn the social fabric inside out, but to recognize that a slow pace in changing man's behavior and status does not require a weak and timid approach to the challenge of power in the essentially impersonal institutions of monopolistic industry and finance. The threat to the best in our civilization comes from those who rule at those heights; it is therefore conservative in its best sense to organize for decisive measures within that sphere. The socialist overturn neither ventures nor desires to root out the multitude in small industry, trade, and agriculture; our program does not envision the introduction from above of a New Order in social relationships; but we can insist that that power—and no more—which now rests in the hands of the self-perpetuating industrial empires should be swiftly transferred to the responsible representatives of democratic government.

I use "overturn" here in an obvious, rather literal sense, denoting the actual mobilization of social forces in action. This is a proximate tool, not an ultimate objective. As a tool, it must be used coldly, with detachment, free of illusions as to the concrete forms it must take or as to what can be accomplished. Such an attitude will enable us to delineate an economic program attuned to those necessities of administrative responsibility and centralized direction dictated by the integrated character of the industrial system. We shall not expect miracles of democratic procedure and structure from instrumentalities that provide their own answers and, very largely, make their own rules. Yet it is this very sobriety which will help us to discover those democratic channels, consistent with the urgencies of production, which can be built into the economic order for whose effective functioning we are responsible. These statements would be counsels of despair were it not for our assumption of the restricted relevance for society as a whole of the revolutionary elements in our program, an outlook incomprehensible to those for whom Revolution is their sacred, all-embracing method. It is partly as a hangover from the consecrated approach to the revolutionary method that many socialists still insist upon a romantic view of its nature and its possible results. At the same time, forced to discard old blinkers, the uneasiness of ambiguity has led them to leave their program in the limbo of unconcretized proposals.

2) *Socialism must adopt the moral absolute of pacifism.* If social-democracy was naive about the method required for the transfer of control over the industrial apparatus, it was equally sanguine about the ability of men to choose consistently the method that embodied their own values. The pacifist absolute is such in respect to its function, operating as a hard rule for those groups which have testified to its truth. But the judgment and conclusion that it represents are empirical insights. It is a perception that provides a political reflex of our deepest moral values and is therefore a steadying factor in political choice. Events have taught us that we are unable to permit ourselves complete freedom in the continuous recreation of political decisions. We are too deeply involved in immediate relationships, too sharply influenced by proximate consequences to be able to maintain the integrity of our ultimate aims unaided by functional absolutes. Hence the need for an act of collective faith in the enduring viability of procedures that we accept as crucial to the character of our movement. Democracy is one of these functional absolutes; pacifism must be another. The unity of democracy and pacifism as an interdependent set of means

and objectives becomes more plainly manifest as each new development in the modern world unfolds. These tenets are more than tools: where they operate they are constituent fundamentals of the movement, referrable only to the moral sources of its being. Originating in and justified by a prophetic empirical insight, they come to transcend their beginnings, to be woven into the symbolic, expressive image of our aspirations. In this way we return to an old and proven method of taking into account dependable human failings. *This* revolution, which has to do with the character of men and movements rather than with the practical mobilization of forces, is in its nature sacred, and completely consistent with the gradualist spirit it shares.

This cursory review of pressing revisions in the traditional social-democratic program, while radical, does not divorce us from the mainstream of that polar trend. We should work as political missionaries, from within, sharing inevitably what is culpable and what is undefiled in the movement as a whole. Because we have a history, we cannot offer a "spotless banner." But the clear perception of where we must take our stand, the sober appraisal of what we have to deal with and what can be done, will help to deliver us from the pseudo arena where "vacant shuttles weave the wind."

Karl Shapiro On the Revival of Anarchism [1]

Karl Jay Shapiro (1913 ——) Shapiro is a poet born in Baltimore, Maryland, in 1913. He has taught at Johns Hopkins University and is now at the University of Nebraska. His poetry is widely acclaimed, and he is the winner of many awards. He is the editor of *Prairie Schooner*. Some of his works are: *Person, Place and Thing, The Place of Love, Essay on Rime, Trial of a Poet, Beyond Criticism, Poems of a Jew*, and *In Defense of Ignorance*.

Before the 1960 elections, a gentleman from the Fund for the Republic asked me for an

[1] From "On the Revival of Anarchism," by Karl Shapiro, *Liberation*, February, 1961. Reprinted by permission of the author.

interview. He was gathering opinions about the coming Presidential contest, and he wanted the reaction of a poet or two. My first thought was to beg off. My second was to tell a white lie and give him the name of one of the two candidates, that I do not vote (except on local matters), that I am a date for the interview.

It is not easy to express one's honest views to a stranger, especially if one's political ideas happen to be of an unknown or an unpopular variety. I wanted very much not to be set down in my visitor's mind as a crackpot or a "fool poet." He had been a Washington correspondent and was a man of quick perception, charm, and great knowledge of politics (compared with mine, certainly). I mumbled and bumbled a good bit before I got out what I wanted to say. What I told him finally was that I had no choice of candidates, that I do not vote (except on local matters), that I am opposed to voting under the "two" party system, and that I even attempt to spread a no-voting propaganda among my friends and students. After which I tried to make some joke, such as "Pass the hemlock."

I had a distinct impression that my position, or lack of it, was quite familiar to my visitor. The word "anarchism" did not come up in the conversation, but we managed to discuss it without naming it. There were quotes from me out of Thoreau and mentions of the *Catholic Worker,* which I have read for many years. It was a fairly tame, academic talk, and we parted satisfied and friendly.

As a teacher and writer, I have become increasingly aware in recent years of the spread of anarchist thought among the rising generation. They do not call it by that name, or any name; they do not philosophize about the State or Nonviolence or Disaffiliation, but the interest is unmistakably there. The Beat movement symbolizes one extreme of youthful anger against the failure of modern society and government to keep peace among men. The Negro equality movement symbolizes a more dramatic failure of society and government to give the citizen his due. Throughout the world, the human right of insubordination against industrial society, colonialism, militarism, and against the entire cult of the Western Tradition (religious, sexual, esthetic) is making itself felt in a thousand ways. The governments are losing their young. The lifeblood of history is flowing away from the centers of force. Patriotism is having its long-awaited nervous breakdown.

And not only the young. The generation of the total war is also abandoning the conventional political thinking of the past, Left, Right, and liberal, and is returning to the example of individual moral force, as the world has so far known it through Thoreau, Whitman, Tolstoy, Kropotkin, and Gandhi.

At present we are going through the stage of withdrawal from the old political psychologies of organized governments. And we are witnessing the beginnings of successful passive-resistance movements in America and abroad. But no appeal has yet been made to the vast American middle class, the majority class, to detach itself from our competitive industrial insanity. It is indeed our industrial way of life that lends sanction to militarism and colonialism, Preparedness and suppression of human rights. Our enemy, strange as it may sound to American ears, is the Standard of Living. We worship at the altar of the White Rhinoceros, the American kitchen. Standard of Living is the holy of holies in whose name every other evil is committed. To lower this standard, or to equalize it among the peoples of the world, is our greatest need. And the first step is to disassociate ourselves from the industrial-scientific madness that rules our lives twenty-four hours a day.

The best government, the anarchists tell us, is the least governing. The worst government is the highly organized and centralized state, such as Franco's Spain or the USSR. The present tendency of the United States toward greater organization and centralization is a peril to every democratic freedom we know. We are drifting toward a totally organized state that is eventually cemented by a secret police, a standing army, an industrial-scientific aristocracy, and a propaganda and communications machine that lies at the very heart of government. The present competitive mania between Russia and the United States in "science" opens the way in our country for every breed of political opportunism. Whether the Eisenhower "diplomatic" Cold War changes into Kennedy's "cultural" Cold War will make little difference to the basic sense of hostility to which the central government is committed. The American people have lost the choice of a peaceful alternative. The Switchboard will tell us what to do.

My central point of reference is Gandhi, perhaps the most extraordinary man our age has produced. We are today experiencing the effects of Oriental ideas on our lives to an unprecedented degree. In Gandhi, for instance, we are presented with a new political psychology that is quite foreign to our practical Western minds, as when he says: "It is against my nature to prearrange." Or more striking, when he says of the law of nonviolent resistance, "that it is possible for a single individual to defy the whole might of an unjust empire to save his honor, his religion, his soul, and lay the foundation for that empire's fall or regeneration." Gandhi's belief in the power of right action (Truth) to prevent violence was demonstrated in his lifetime a thousand times over; this is a form of political behavior that is only now beginning to make its way in the West.

Gandhi, of course, was not a provincial Hindu but one who drew on the entire tradition of the literature of peaceful action, mystical and secular. One of his earliest works was a translation of Plato's *Apology* into Gujarati, a bitter irony when we remember Gandhi's own death. He also translated John Ruskin's *Unto This Last,* essays in what Ruskin called "First Principles of Political Economy," and of course he was deeply influenced by Thoreau and Tolstoy. The expression "the moral equivalent of war" he took from William James. But the fundamentals of nonviolence, noncooperation, and nonresistance are native to the Hindu world. *Dharma,* for instance, is the concept of moral pressure applied to an offending party through sufferings to oneself. To sit *dharma* is to sit mourning. Gandhi's application of *dharma* against British military and legal force constituted a one-man revolution against authority and resulted in the greatest awakening of a nation in modern history. His results range from the abolition of the worst superstitions of his religion, such as untouchability, to the equalization of the rights of Hindus and other dark peoples of South Africa, to national independence itself, a fantastic series of accomplishments almost incomprehensible to the Western mind. The West has so far produced no peaceful revolutionaries

of the stature of Gandhi, even if one includes Tolstoy, Godwin, or Kropotkin. The gropings of William James toward
such a solution of Gandhi's illustrate the dilemma of the
American mind with its predominant images of military
force.

James published his pamphlet "The Moral Equivalent of
War" in 1910. The article makes rather horrifying apologies
to the military and to scientific progress, yet the general
drift is impressive. "Pacifists ought to enter more deeply into
the aesthetical and ethical point of view of their opponents,"
says James. "So long as anti-militarists propose no substitute
for war's disciplinary function, no *moral equivalent* of war
. . . they fail to realize the full inwardness of the situation.
The duties, penalties, and sanctions pictured in the utopias
they paint are all too weak and tame to touch the military-
minded." James assumes that Western pacifism has no
language of communication with our society at large, which
is aggressive and ultimately militaristic. In rather quaint
psychology he seeks for some motive for human action that
is as "thrilling" (to use his word) as bloodshed. Puritani-
cally, he objects to a mere peace-economy on the grounds
that it may become no more than a "pleasure-economy."
"Martial discipline" in peace is therefore a necessity. He
would have young men "make war" upon nature—the typical Western fallacy that we know so well from our scientists
—and he would send youth to the "coal and iron mines, to
freight trains, to fishing fleets in December, to dishwashing,
clothes washing, and window washing," etc. Here we see the
cautious New Englander of the upper crust to whom dishwashing is almost as much of an epic experience as the
charge of the Light Brigade. But at bottom he is right. "The
martial type of character can be bred without war," says
James. And he ends his essay with the pathetic statement that
Fear is indeed great, but Fear is not "the only stimulus
known for awakening the higher ranges of man's spiritual
energy."

James probably supplied no more for Gandhi than the
wonderful catchphrase "the moral equivalent of war." It
was in an obscure work of Ruskin's that Gandhi found the
outline of a practical philosophy. He reduced Ruskin's message in *Unto This Last* to three principles:

1) that the good of the individual is contained in the good of all.

2) that a lawyer's work has the same value as the barber's inasmuch as all have the same right of earning their livelihood from their work.

3) that a life of labor, i.e., the life of the tiller of the soil and the handicraftsman, is the life worth living. Gandhi says: "The first of these I knew. The second I had dimly realized. The third had never occured to me. *Unto This Last* made it as clear as day to me that the second and the third were contained in the first. I arose with the dawn, ready to reduce these principles to practice."

The usual objection to Gandhi's ideas is that they are "Oriental" and do not apply to life in the West, that the conditions under which Gandhi operated in the Transvaal and in India cannot possibly apply to civilized Europe and America. The West has a good deal of fear and loathing for this little naked fakir, as Winston Churchill so elegantly called him. And the more aristocratic Hindus themselves, for instance Tagore, the Bengali poet, fought Gandhi at many crucial points. Tagore opposed the reintroduction of the spinning wheel, the key to a national economy; he opposed the burning of foreign cloth, which Gandhi advocated as a method of breaking European economic slavery. Gandhi plunged to the heart of the matter when he told Tagore, "I do not draw a . . . distinction between economics and ethics. Economics that hurt the moral well-being of an individual or a nation are immoral." Tagore eventually understood and surrendered the knighthood that the Crown had bestowed upon him.

There is a great deal of extremism in Gandhi's philosophy that the West will probably never be able to swallow. His asceticism, his puritanism, his almost violent hatred for the gains of science, extending even to the science of medicine, are things we cannot appreciate. "A multiplicity of hospitals is no test of civilization; it is rather a symptom of decay," said Gandhi, sounding much like a modern poet. Gandhi covering his belly with a band of raw earth as a cure for dysentery or constipation seems wholly irrational to us. And yet we cannot dismiss his principle of the nexus between science, government, and morality. In the West we are only beginning to examine the irresponsibility of Science, the loading of young minds with scientific and technological nonsense, the consequences of which we learn only when it is too late.

In rearing an unarmed army to disengage India from European rule, Gandhi developed a program of discipline in which the participant took these vows: Truthfulness (which is difficult to explain in Western psychology, though it closely resembles our Know Thyself); Nonviolence (which is a synonym for Soul-Force); Celibacy; Control of the Palate; Non-Thieving; Nonpossession; Fearlessness; and *Swadeshi* (encouragement of home industry). Most of these vows fall within the scope of our own traditional religions in one form or another. The one that is foreign to us and that may be of the utmost importance in the West is *Swadeshi,* the encouragement of home industries. *Swadeshi,* in fact, may be the nexus between Gandhism and the West.

The East is especially distinguished from the West in its attitude toward the natural world. The Easterner tends to regard himself as part of nature and of the cosmos. (In our view this is considered Fatalism.) The Westerner tends to regard himself as the enemy of Nature. We speak of the *conquest* of space or of new lands; we *subdue* the desert and the frontier; we *wipe out* disease. The Oriental, broadly speaking, does not feel combative with the outer world; rather he regards himself as part of a flux of life in which he is a single element. The Hebrew-Christian bible begins with the injunction that man shall have *dominion* over every living thing, an idea quite exotic to the Oriental or to the poet like Walt Whitman who says he thinks he could turn and live with animals.

Swadeshi, home industry, does not have to do with government but with self-sustaining. When Gandhi hit upon the idea of the spinning wheel, he had his major revelation. It is staggering to think that there was no one in India who knew how to spin (European civilization had destroyed the wheel) and that Gandhi had to search the country from top to bottom to find some old lady who still knew how to spin. In the same way, an Englishwoman had to search the country from end to end to discover the Indian temple dances and revive them. For it is true that mechanization destroys not only the national economy but the arts of nations.

Gandhi favored a break with machine industry, followed by a slow and considered assimilation of the machine.

Here is a great lesson for the West: to slow down machine progress, to impede science, to prevent industrialization from becoming the sole way of life. Thoreau says: "Shall we forever resign the pleasure of construction to the carpenter?" He also says: "We are in great haste to construct a magnetic telegraph from Maine to Texas; but Maine and Texas, it may be, have nothing important to communicate." As far as we can tell, Maine and Texas still have nothing important to communicate. In any event, communication in this country is private property, as in Russia it is purely state property. Communication is too valuable to industrial-scientific government to be passed around indiscriminately. It is always the policeman, the industrialist, or the diplomat who controls the wires from Maine to Texas.

True communication is a phenomenon having nothing to do with newspapers, PA systems, universal network control, and radar bouncing off the moon. The words of Gandhi were communicated largely by word of mouth throughout India and across the barriers of about twenty languages, whereas in America it is virtually impossible to find out what is going on in Cuba or in the Congo or in other places. What is called "news" in America, and probably in Europe as well, is what is left of the truth after Communications has masterminded the facts. The very term "artist" in the West has come to mean simply a man who tells the truth. Communications also has the function of controlling the moods of the people. Disaster is the bread and butter of the advertiser, newspaperman, broadcaster, and the public-relations expert. Little wonder that the Russian ruler visiting the United States had to have a standing army of bodyguards and secret service men to keep him from being assassinated. How much better off we all would be if everyone boycotted the newspaper, television, advertising, radio, and all the other self-styled media of communication.

Any gradual and immediate diminution of our involvement with the industrial system, on any level, would have a direct effect on the peace and well-being of our people. To remove ourselves from the world of competition is of paramount importance to the individual and to the nation. Competition is the terrible vice of modern society. Competition is the disease of the West and is the source of our violence. Nonviolence means noncompetition. Democracy is a nonviolent form of government that is in peril of destruction by the competition of systems of social and economic violence. *Ahimsa,* nonviolence, is a total force and a way of life. It has the power of Christian humility, upon which it is partly based. It is one of the noblest ideas advanced by modern man and it is destined to spread throughout the world. It cannot be employed by governments because governments are by definition committed to violence. Nonviolence is not a prerogative of governments but of men, even of one man. One nonviolent man, like Gandhi or Christ, can change history. Governments can only keep history on the march. *Ahimsa* can stop history.

Gandhi went so far as to encourage nonviolence to the venomous snakes of India, which take a terrible toll of life every year. One had to overcome this perfectly natural fear of the reptiles. "The rule of not killing venomous reptiles," says Gandhi, "has been practiced for the most part at Phoenix, Tolstoy Farm, and Sabarmati. At each of these places we had to settle on waste lands. We have had, however, no loss of life occasioned by snakebite." And he adds: "Even if it be a superstition to believe that complete immunity from harm for twenty-five years is not a fortuitous accident but a grace of God, I should still hug that superstition."

Without going into this deep and muddy question, we can learn something from this attitude of nonkilling. To depose the enemy was not an aim of Gandhi's; he must be deposed with dignity, without harm, even with honor. This is another concept foreign to Western thought and almost foreign to Christian practice. Nonhumiliation of the enemy means to return his humanity to him after a defeat. Vinoba Bhave, the greatest living disciple of Gandhi, who travels throughout India asking land for the peasantry from the great landlords and receiving it, says: "I desire to humiliate neither the rich nor the poor." This is the opposite of communist expropriation or of capitalist competition. Without a complete bond of love between the giver and the recipient, there can be no permanent guarantee of peace between the possessor and the dispossessed.

The specific issues for which Gandhi fought are generally accomplished in India, but the deeper meaning of his phi-

losophy and his politics may provide an alternative to the
ever-mounting states of crisis that are inherent in statesman-
ship, or what passes under that name. Modern competitive
society is incapable of keeping the peace. Modern government, committed to a society of competition, is incapable of
keeping the peace. Peace can come about only through the
nonviolent action of the people themselves. The present
tendency of governments to dissolve their empires provides
no guarantee of peace. On the contrary, the formation of
new countries modeled upon American or Russian economic
systems can do nothing but increase the danger of war. As
modern government is contingent for its power upon science
and industry, there would appear to be no hope of peace
except by the voluntary effort of people to place themselves
beyond the lure of science and industry. Standard of Living
equals Preparedness. Preparedness is always related to scientific warfare. People must, especially in the scientifically
advanced countries, act individually to weaken the power of
the industrial-scientific oligarchy over their lives. We must
"lower" the Standard of Living. We must learn how to sustain ourselves in peace and happiness beyond the influence
of the Switchboard. We must do these things without violence and with the high sense of chivalry that Gandhi incul-
cated in his followers. Instead of class war and hatred as
preached by the communists, or industrial-scientific competition preached by us, we must, to survive, behave non-
violently and in the spirit of love.

Irving L. Horowitz
A Postscript to
the Anarchists

Perhaps an ultimate test of vital ideas is their capacity to
reappear in many guises to lead us once again to reaffirm and
reexamine our fundamental commitments. The extent to
which an "ism" claims a stake in universal truth is often
measured by the heat it generates, by the sacrifices of its
adherents, by the needs, in one way or another, filled by its

presence. That presence may come in the form of a resound-
ing mass following or a single undying voice against the
wind. It may or may not find the proper soil on which it will
be nourished for any length of time. But it stubbornly
reappears to signal the continuing nature of the problem it
addresses. In this way, as such a presence, anarchism is preserved from the graveyard, for it speaks to the human condition in all of its phases. Neither lingering questions nor
dubious answers can bury its claim to being one among the
significant intellectual postures of the modern world.

As a postscript to these selections, we might survey the
anarchist past from the safety of the present. In working
on the anarchists in the preparations for this collection of
essays, I could not help but note the kinds of questions raised
about anarchism and the frequency with which the same
kinds of objections are voiced. It indicates to me the need to
confront directly critical sentiment. I should add that my
answers are highly personal, and this might be considered
incorrect by "purists" and "pragmatists" alike. Nevertheless,
the dialogue is all important and the issue a lively one.

*One of the founding fathers of modern sociology, Leonard
Hobhouse, once wrote that "there are other enemies of
liberty than the State and it is, in fact, by the State that we
have fought them." If this is correct, wouldn't the basic
premise of anarchism be decisively undermined?*

I am inclined to agree with Hobhouse on this. It is certainly the case that liberty can be thwarted by forces other
than the State; and that under very special circumstances,
the State has functioned to expand the liberties of men.
Perhaps this is far truer of English political history, with
its pluralistic emphasis and liberalist background, than of
other societies. But it must also be noted that State power as
coercive power is far more customary than State power as
public administration. From an empirical vantage point, the
anarchist argument does not rest so much on the exceptional
conditions under which the State may curb its coercive
tendencies, but on the general conditions under which the
State exercises its power over and against public desires.

Were the State a useful and good social instrument, there
would be little need to rationalize its existence. As a matter of record, even those who have held that the State is
necessary, rarely, if ever, go so far as to say that it is

also good. The perfect example of this is the great number of social-contract theories—particularly those of Hobbes, Rousseau, and Hegel—that seek to justify the existence of the State by rejecting the possibility of men's living without it in social comity. Underlying social-contract theories is a philosophical-ethical bias in favor of utilitarianism, of the selfish egoism of men; men must surrender their private sovereignty in order to preserve the commonweal. The anarchist, arguing from altruistic premises, is just as entitled to argue that the State corrupts the naturally cooperative inclinations of man, precisely because of the social contract.

The anarchist rejects all theories of social contract, all theories in which there is a notion that men contract out certain freedom in return for prearranged guarantees that the State renders. The reason for the rejection is, first, that there is no real contract made between men. This is only a convenient myth for the maintenance of the status quo or the maintenance of State authority. No one consciously enters a contract to apportion his rights. The second reason involves a justification of the need for State power because of the hedonist utilitarian acceptance of the selfishness, brutality, and warlike character of men, which really exposes its hypocritical claims about original goodness. In the purest Hobbesian or Machiavellian forms, contract theory involves the preservation of the ego, not the preservation of the society. Because of this convenient myth of social contract, the ego is persuaded that society is indeed set up to protect the person from injury. But as a matter of fact, society severed from its nature by class divisions, gives birth to the State precisely for the reverse reason. The State and not men in general is coercion, brutality, war, force. So that not only is there a mythology but a topsy-turvy mythology in which properties that are taken to be intrinsically human are in effect those of the State. The human qualities of goodness, sacrifice, control, order, protection, all of these somehow become mistakenly enshrined in the general theory of the State. Anarchism categorically rejects any theory based on the principles of contract to an impersonal bureaucratic force. On the other hand, anarchism also rejects revolutionary doctrines that project a theory of *ultimately* overthrowing the State. It insists that all theories that consider the State a necessary, even if temporary evil as justifying the existence of the State. There is a kind of shrewdness about the anarchist view. The anarchists were virtually the first to criticize the bolshevik or Leninist theory of a transitional dictatorship of the proletariat, which would then abolish itself, since this would violate the law of self-perpetuation of bureaucracy that the anarchists, even prior to the sociologists, raised to the level of a principle of modern industrial life. Roberto Michels, who along with Max Weber, was the father of the general theory of bureaucracy, was an anarchist and makes his criticisms from the point of view of the psychological insights gained from sympathies with (and ultimate rejection of) anarchist ideology. To say that the proletarian State is a temporary or necessary device in which the bourgeoisie can be permanently eliminated, is from the point of view of the anarchist inadequate reason to recreate the State in any form, since as an inherently evil thing it will reproduce in new ways all of the old exploitation. The frequently heard bolshevik claim that the anarchists are naive is readily turned upon the bolsheviks. From the anarchist point of view, the bolsheviks are naive because they mistake the purpose of revolution to begin with, which is to liberate from rule and not to replace it in new guises. For their part, the anarchists minimize the fact that, although revolutions never take place on schedule or according to blueprints, they do nevertheless open possibilities of emancipation otherwise impossible. But this dialogue between anarchism and communism can hardly be at an end—as long as the liquidation of the State is the professed aim of the communists.

It must be said on this point that the anarchist is more astute in his appreciation of the State than is commonly understood. Aside from the firm distinction between coercion as necessary to define the State and administration as necessary to define Society (which is mysteriously usurped by the State), there is another, and more forceful argument. The State, precisely because it accentuates both coercive and administrative functions, suffers a schizophrenic condition that accounts for its rare moments of genuine protectiveness as mentioned at the outset.

A forceful argument against the State is adduced by Proudhon. In his rebuff of the classical power school of political theory, against that line of thought that held that the State functions to protect human rights and property relations, Proudhon points out that perhaps the State does indeed have such a twofold purpose. However, by virtue of that, the State is lending its weight to "political incompatibilities" that accentuate rather than alleviate social conflict. The centralization of authority for the classical anarchist is also a polarization of power—separating the ordinary citizen more thoroughly than ever from the sources of power, and therefore leading to an intensification rather than a diminution of class struggles. And the State, sworn to uphold both people and property finds itself in a logical impossibility: to support people against property is to support its own overthrow directly; while to support property against people is an invitation to revolution. In any circumstance the State, far from being the cohesive cement of society, is really the irritant of society.

Isn't it true, as Plekhanov and others have insisted, that anarchism is simply a form of utopianism, a longing for a world of human perfection independent of the agencies for getting to such a perfect condition? And therefore, would it not be more rational to conceive of anarchism as a religious expression, a messianic critique, of the social world as it is?

The social philosophy of the anarchists would have to be described as a form of naturalistic millennialism or messianism. It has elements that are customarily associated with utopianism. There are, however, some important distinctions. Probably one of the best ways of finding out what anarchism is would be to distinguish its special features from utopianism as a general category, precisely because of its similarity.

Three basic distinctions have to be noted. First, there is in anarchism a rejection of those utopianisms that stress reforming, parochial or partial solutions. Utopianism applied to community-level organization is restricted to miniscule size and effect. Anarchism strives for total reorganization with little attention paid to preliminary model communities for persuasive purposes. The establishment of such communities among the anarchists has been the practice merely of small factions within the general midst and was never, as among the utopianists, the professed aim of the movement. It criticizes the utopianists for fashioning a perfect community as an end in itself, thereby narrowing the range of possibilities and deliberately involving a small number of people and always withdrawing from the field of social life as such.

A second significant feature is the critique anarchism launches against utopia as an ultimate refinement of benevolent despotism. All nonanarchist utopias attempted to demonstrate to the ruling caste the power of benevolence and enlightened self-interest. They were efforts to *persuade* and not to *overthrow* a ruling caste. They were reforming rather than revolutionizing agencies. The anarchist communities were attempts to persuade the masses to emulate them so as to isolate and render dysfunctional their bureaucratic and class tormentors. Voluntary associations were never really the central focus of anarchist activity. At most, they represented some of the occasional experiments in community living engaged in by the more pacific anarchists. The anarchists steadfastly viewed utopias to be microscopic reproductions of the frictions and fictions to be found in organized nation-States. The Owenite community does not effect a revolution in society and even tends to reproduce elite and mass divisions by relying heavily on the great man's guiding genius for instituting reform and establishing procedure. This despite the tendency of the anarchist communities to suffer from similar if not the same difficulties. With the stress of these communities on reform, they tend to blunt rather than stimulate desires for revolution and have incurred the criticism of the anarchists.

Anarchist belief, except for its Tolstoyan variety, is a form of scientism. It shares with socialism a naturalistic orientation in contrast to the metaphysical predilections of more religious types of utopian thought. Nevertheless, it should be noted that the Marxists were far more hostile to utopian reform communities than the anarchist because they took the tenets of *realpolitik* and the science of politics more seriously considering such efforts as a mere preliminary to scientific socialism and therefore historically transcended. To return to such efforts was the mark of empty nostalgia. Other marks of theoretical friction between the utopists and anarchists are summed up perhaps by taking note of the fact that the utopian communities demanded an extremely high degree of consensus, of agreement in principle, while anarchism insists on cooperation, on agreement in practice.

The utopian might say that because of its very totality, anarchism does not engage in a meaningful or possible struggle. The anarchists, for their part, declare that partial solutions, whether based on utopian communities or factory workshops, are doomed to failure precisely because of their partiality. To conclude this point, reform utopianism is an attempt at a total solution in a partial context, whereas anarchism is an attempt at a limited solution in a total context. For the utopian, the economic system determines behavior, hence this idea of solving problems in a limited sphere of operations is realizable. For the anarchist, psychological factors tend to be dominant, so that the solution is going to come to men individually, and at the same time it will occur to many at the same moment in history. Utopianism has no requirement for principles of revolutionary action. The basic requirement for utopia is that a group of like-minded spirits form a social compact. This does not carry any obligation to confront the society outside utopia. It should be stressed that the similarities between community utopianism and anarchism are very strong. Anarchism did lend itself to the attempt at structuring utopian communities. But these did not define the anarchist movement and were always of secondary importance in relation to the larger revolutionary efforts of the anarchists.

By setting the example the utopianists hoped to create the models that would gradually increase in number and influence. The assumption of gradualism is that things will get better, even if they get better slower. The utopian tradition and practice was an attempt to enshrine the theory of liberalism as a theory of emancipation. The anarchist counterclaim is willing to grant a degree of progressive improvement. His case really rests on the progressive and overall deterioration of the many as against the improved comforts of the few. These progressive advances are seen to have been paid for by the many whose fiber has been damaged in the process. Utopian theory does collapse in the face of the historical fact that little evidence exists that things get better simply because there are more efficient instrumentalities of control. In this the anarchist critique anticipates the contemporary scientific attitude on this question, namely, that the utilization of instruments may work for *or* against the benefit of man.

The existence of the harmonious "perfect" society is no guarantor of the general elevation of civilization.

Is it not so that the anarchist view of the contradictions between principles and power is simply an abstract formulation of a simplistic model of a world in which everyone is either good or evil? That is to say, don't the criticisms offered by Marx on Proudhon apply to anarchism in general; for example, the quasi-Hegelian phrasing of all problems in terms of irreconcilables—between proletariat and bourgeois, propertyless and property owner, individuality and collectivism, use value and exchange value, all of which are resolved in a grand metaphysical synthesis of pure negation, "phrases which lack common sense."

It would be difficult, and pointless, to deny that anarchism is indeed highly moralistic in both phraseology and practice. But to criticize it for being politically impracticable does not perhaps do it justice. There can be no doubt that anarchism was foredoomed to failure. And it is also undoubtedly the case that Marx was to some extent correct in viewing anarchism as a theory that glorified contradiction because contradiction is the basis of anarchist appeal, since this appeal is directed to the petty bourgeois, who is by nature "a socialist on one side and an economist on the other." But if we ignore the class invective, and even if we assume that anarchism in industrial societies stems from petty-bourgeois origins, we must still examine its claims—since these claims are matters of verification and not to be condemned by virtue of origin.

Every age confronts its own crises, and therefore it is difficult to speak of any particular time as being one of crisis. The modern world, however, has a particularly unique consciousness of crisis. Part of that consciousness originates with the critique offered by anarchist and various radical thinkers, of the paradoxical features of modern social organization. One would have to say that the basic philosophic premise, the critical schism of the modern world, as the anarchist sees it, is the contradiction between power and principles. Every specific interest dividing man is a reflection of that "contradiction"—since interests are themselves embodied in the State principle.

There are other ways of examining this. It can be framed as a struggle between reason and freedom, between the irrationality of pure reason as it manifests itself in the forms of bureaucracy on one hand and the absence of freedom, which has in effect a consequence of the rise of this new form of rationality. There are other possible perspectives. One could pose this as a problem of individualism versus collectivism. Nevertheless, the profundity of the anarchist critique is evident because there will be this paradox of power and principles under any conditions. Only at that point when power cannot enforce involuntary obedience can this particular form of crisis be resolved. It is possible to reconcile the antagonisms between individualism and collectivism without resorting to the anarchist call for total human transformation. It is even possible to settle the relationship between political action and bureaucracy without having to overhaul human nature. So there is something ultimate in the anarchist formulation. Anarchism is not so much a unified theory of social change as it is a description of the contradictory nature, the paradoxical results of this change. Little wonder, therefore, that anarchism itself would be invested with all forms of dualistic self-contradiction that would cause great skepticism in the minds of politically oriented men as to its worth.

When one argues with anarchism, one argues with an absurd point of view in a way. But its very absurdities and deficiencies seem to be not so much unique consequences of the anarchist position as they are consequences of a way of life in the twentieth century. The criticisms that can be made and will be made of anarchism are perhaps more profoundly criticisms of the society as we know it, and of the incapacity of humanity to rationalize and control its destiny as a universal community.

Anarchism is committed to the seizure of political power whether it be by means of the General Strike, mutual aid societies or the setting up of voluntary soviets. This doctrine has a theory of seizure of power. It would be naive to assume that these are simply people who are good-hearted and good-natured. They are by and large dedicated to the uses of violence on one hand and civil disobedience on the other. At the point of seizure anarchist perspective seems to fail. That is to say, in relation to socialism, which is based on a general theory of planning and political rule, anarchism stops at the point where socialists begin. There is an apocalyptic note that looks forward to the dissolution of the entire old society upon the seizure of the State apparatus. A most cogent criticism of anarchism states that, even if it were to reach a position of being able to seize power, the very fact that the anarchist is committed to a defense of principles rather than to the uses of power tends to make him someone who is intrinsically incapable of rule, of maintaining power. The dilemma for the anarchist is therefore the contrasting demands between the seizure of power and overthrowing the old on the one side, and the maintenance of power and construction of a new society on the other. Maintenance implies the existence of stability, order, and consensus. The anarchist, committed as he is to the permanence of the revolutionary state of flux and to the impermanence of all social order, is caught in a contradiction between his principles, which are those of permanent revolution, and political needs, which are those of order and stability.

Marx and the Marxists had an advantage that the anarchists tried vainly to incorporate in its later stages. The Marxists viewed technology and industry, the very productive process itself, as a determining factor in social change. It was from the productive base of society that the need emanated for certain consonant changes in the human administration of the productive process. The anarchist never confronted the problems of a vast technology and ignored them by trying to find his way back to a system of production that was satisfying to the individual producer rather than feasible for a growing mass society. The Marxist regards the present technological level, mass production, as fettered by individualistic (petty-bourgeois and capitalist) modes of control and presses for a type of social ownership that is in keeping with a mass and highly rationalized machinery of production. The anarchist is pressing for social reorganization in terms of a work integration principle of human relations. He could never comprehend "readiness" for revolution as readiness for the rationalization of technological necessities and ultimately for the smooth governance of humanity over the instruments of gaining its livelihood. This is why anarchism appears unconcerned with technology and indeed, antitechnological. The anarchist literature contains a strong element of nostalgia, a harkening back to a situation where workshops were small, where relationships were manageable, where people experienced affective responses with each other. Technology and the material benefits of science were never seriously entertained by the anarchists except in a ministerial contempt for that which destroys the natural man.

Technology has not merely expanded. Its demands transform the prevalent concepts of work. We are in a technological era that is qualitatively different, that brings forward entirely new forms of social behavior and social existence. Much as we prefer not to breed fragmented specialists, it is impossible to envision the era of hydrogen power and mass electrification in terms of simple, spontaneous association of individual craftsmen. The forms of technology moving from craft to a network of minutely separated functions have, therefore, tended to undermine the idea of the anarchist Everyman.

If we look closely at the anarchist paradox of power versus principles, we find that in the more generic sense the contradiction he finds between power and principle is really perhaps a bit more dramatic than it is descriptive. He is too willing to surrender principled strategies for principled ends as political compromise. The anarchist's formulations are therefore highly romantic and at the same time unsatisfactory explanations of the actual character of society. But politics, the goal of political behavior, asserts itself at this point. The anarchist, committed as he is to antipolitics, is therefore also cutting himself off from the possibility of developing the kinds of strategies that could lead to implementation of an anarchist social order. Their ambivalence over pacifist or violent tactics divides into absolutistic defenses of one or the other as a matter of principle rather than strategy. This problem is irreconcilable since both are elevated from strategies to the level of principles, and both involve commitments exclusive of the other. This leads to the surrender of critical judgment over choice. The advocates of violence demand a surrender of critical judgment when they call for the general strike. Perhaps Sorel was more candid than his colleagues when he referred to it as the "myth of the general strike," albeit a necessary myth. It had to be believed in suspension of judgment. It is likewise with the pacifist wing of anarchism. Pacifism was no longer a tactical device, it was the end itself. Lacking the instrumentalities of achieving the end, the instruments become the end. In the absence of strategies, the actors are compelled to live the part as if their example would achieve it, but their own conviction does not of itself achieve the sought-after end. For the "violent wing," violence becomes end and instrument and moreover, a heroic form of human fulfillment. It embodies all the "great" human qualities. The very attempt, therefore, to evade the problem of power itself becomes a form of corruption rather than a restoration of principles to human society.

Anarchism is plagued by sociological dualism. There is its militantly antireligious scientism, but this tends to have its sources and resolution not in the scientific enterprise, but in a mythic notion of the struggle between good and evil. The result is a super-mythology or a more religious religion than that of any enthusiastic sect. The same kind of thing occurs in turning over the problem of individualism versus collectivism. A return to individualistic patterns on the part of all humanity is what is sought after, but this is conceived in such rarefied individual qualities that such transformation is in fact accessible only to the most unusual of people. What was looked toward as the broadening of democracy becomes the basis of a new elitism, since it idealizes charismatic over more prosaic natures. Bereft of political solutions to political problems, idealizing individualistic rebellion, anarchism reflects the extent of our difficulties rather than effects significant alteration of them, but the will to criticize the excesses of organization is the positive note of fresh air when the breathing of these organisms becomes labored and stifling. Despite muddled inconsistency, frozen contradiction, oversimplified polarization of problems, the sense that negation ultimately makes lies in its capacity to neutralize the more prevalent excesses super-rationalized organizational life imposes.

From an historical perspective anarchism is a reactionary doctrine. Isn't it the case, as Hermann Rauschning long ago pointed out, that anarchism is the pure expression of nihilism —simply the will to universal unsettlement, an unbounded dynamism that is dangerous because it has nowhere to go?

The ideas of such modern-day anarchists as Sorel did serve as an intellectual tributary for fascist activism. However, it might just as readily be pointed out that Malatesta's view served as an intellectual source for communism; and Emma Goldman's pioneering efforts on behalf of birth control, less stringent laws governing divorce and migration, and widen-

ing the avenues of free speech, created a climate conducive
to liberalism. From an intellectual point of view the character of anarchism is certainly ambiguous. But the practices of
anarchism have been less ambiguous. Its leadership continually opposed World War I as being futile from the standpoint of laboring-class interests. It fought the rise of reaction
and fascism in Italy and Spain. It was the first to single out
and oppose "rightist" trends in the Russian Revolution. Since
the import of this question is not the effectiveness of anarchism but its principles, it seems singularly unfair to saddle
them with reaction.

Parenthetically, it might be noted that the implicit or tacit
support given by anarchism to fascism in its early stages
stemmed from the fascist proclamations of its rise as a revolutionary form of socialism based on syndicalism. Only at the
later stages, in the period of Hitlerite consolidation, did Italian fascism shift its base to corporativism. With that shift,
anarchism became decisively antifascist. And while Berkman
and Goldman denounced the subversion of the Soviets, the
smashing of the Kronstadt rebellion, they remained convinced of the necessity and possibilities of the Russian Revolution. If it is true that anarchism is an unbridled activism
with nowhere to go, it is at least not an unbridled activism
that is so convinced of where it is going that it is blinded to
the dangers of totalitarianism.

Because anarchism is antipolitical it has rarely, if ever,
been able to establish firm lines of organization. It is inhibited from being reactionary by the nature of the assumptions it makes about the wickedness of Behemoth. Nihilism
is the personal condition of uncommitted men suffering a
purposeless rage against the irrationalities of the prevailing
system of nation-States. The belief in the possibilities of life
unhampered by instruments of coercion reveals the rationalistic bias of most forms of anarchism in the exaltation of
human reasonableness and goodness, and contempt for the
irrationality of the State. In any of its variations, even those
more pregnant with irrationalism, there is of course a marginality shared with nihilism. This derives from a willful
opposition to social integration and social order. But desig-
nations such as reactionary, progressive, etc., depend entirely
upon specific activity concentrated on specific issues, or in
other words, the *role it plays* rather than *what it thinks*.

In the history of anarchism, there are two definite trends in its approach to historical change, trends that coincided with the pervasive optimism of enlightenment in the nineteenth century, and the equally widespread disillusionment with the idea of progress in the twentieth century. The assumptions of Godwin, as an illustration, state that the rationality of men will triumph over the irrationalities imposed by external State authority. The perfectibility of society was underwritten by the ability of men to make choices based on knowledge. For that reason, legislation and education were potential curatives to the worst infections of the social order.

But the world of class struggles, the world of competition between ruling and ruled classes rested not on knowledge but on interests. The change in the direction approaching nihilism reflected a general disillusionment by revolutionists in the ability of masses to make spontaneous choices based on reason. It was a shift from the patient optimism of a newborn insight to the restless pessimism of an old struggle. It was seen that class membership did not insure class action. The post-Marxian anarchists did not assume man's rationality and the State's irrationality. This mechanical picture no longer corresponded to a social world defined by the bureaucratic State.

The new anarchist emphasis stated that society is rational, and its very rationality grinds men down. Bureaucracy is the rationalization of what is humanly unreasonable. And if the purpose of the State is to redefine reason as mechanical rationality, nihilism may perform an antiseptic function. Where the bureaucratic apparatus defines reason, human freedom must become unreasoning. The classical definition of freedom as reason hence gives way to an "irrational" view of freedom as the absence of constraint or obligation. The crossover in anarchist beliefs from a political to a psychological guide reflects the fact that politics has become increasingly scientific. But it has decreasingly reflected an expression of individual needs. Mass society and mass culture become a permanent feature of the State apparatus. So that anarchy, because of its nihilistic elements, becomes a cry against manipulation. The anarchist is a man who won't be manipulated. The *de facto* separation between ordinary men and the political apparatus becomes a *de jure* defense of individual integrity. The paradox of the modern State is that, while politics more completely regulates the lives of men, participation in the decision-making process has become increasingly restrictive.

Earlier forms of anarchism fought a distinct and identifiable class protagonist. The politics of protest of any kind have been floundering in general—anarchism being but one protest doctrine to suffer confusion of target. In the search for the class enemy, since class lines have generally been if not blurred, then at least overshadowed by other social divisions, the casting about led to an attack on authority *per se*. Anarchism defends the individualist stance in more psychological terms by virtue of the difficulty of identifying the purely economic class enemy as the source of social oppression. The absence of a class enemy also means the absence of class friends. Anarchism never had consistent class lines and certainly at a time when the problem of economic classes itself had become vitiated by contemporary considerations of prestige and power is this even less the case. Anarchism becomes more free-floating and less representative of a class. For that reason it has at least the pretense of being universally applicable and appears to rise above class bias. It may well be that anarchism has descended from an ideology to a form of therapy—less nihilistic than merely isolated.

Even if we make the assumption that anarchism is politically progressive, may it not be reactionary in yet another sense? Is there not a nostalgic element attached to the anarchist conception of man—an attempt to restore Gemeinschaft *modes of living involving a preference for the community against the larger society, for the simple rural life over the complex urban life, for organic relations in preference to contractual relations, and finally for integrative patterns over differential patterns. In short, is there any feature of anarchism as a faith?*

An explicit theory of history runs through classical anarchism that preserves it from a simple yearning for the past glories of man. Any struggle against authority is taken to be evidence for the principles of mutual cooperation. Feudalism, based as it was on the iniquitous relations of lord and serf, priest and flock, could only herald the future in a distorted way. The Guilds showed the value of organic labor, but distorted this value as a result of an economy of scarcity.

The movement from a system of mutual aid based on scarcity to a system of social egoism, and then finally a return to mutual aid at a "higher level" of abundance, is of course, an ideal typification of society. It represents, as does Marxism, not so much a series of historical observations, as the use of history to develop a philosophy of history. And like all such meta-historical doctrines they tend to be overly abstract and contradictory. In anarchism this manifests itself in an undulation between naiveté and cynicism.

Man is always, if given the opportunity, a good fellow. On the other hand, when he has been given the opportunity, he has been exploitive and sometimes evil. The attributions are paradoxical. Perhaps more so in anarchism because of the assumption that, left in his natural state, man is cooperative. And yet, this natural state is as metaphysical an assumption as underlies the theories of social contract that anarchism scorned.

The foundations of human emancipation, for the anarchist, do entail a separation from concrete and immediate political goals, since concrete political aims are said never to be realized in the form in which they are anticipated and since the functioning of history is essentially a paradox and a mystery that does not yield its secrets in advance of the occurrence. Thus attempts to unite social and political emancipation tend to be doomed. Emancipation is seen in terms of the transformation of the social basis of life. The reorganization of that life eliminates all forms of human exploitation. But the consequences of this is not a unified description of sociology and psychology, or social man and private man, or public life and private problems, but only a permanent dualism, a kind of inner creative tension between these elements. Anarchism is in effect a description of historical tensions more than a theory for the overcoming of these tensions. It encourages man to act because of the psychological propensities of the actors rather than any accurate prevision of the drama. Anarchism does not demonstrate that a release from this tension will result in the practical surmounting of these problems. The anarchist is always suspicious of resolution. He is a rebel with a cause and not a program. He is always assuming the partiality of the revolutionary occurrence, whether it be Berkman commenting on the Russian Revolution, or Kropotkin on the

Paris Commune. These are necessary but only first steps.
And indeed how can they be total? The real Sisyphean element in anarchism is to pose the problem of social life as
something that cannot be resolved. To see society as a permanent contradiction and to see revolution as a particular
expression of that contradiction, is a far cry from the idea of
permanent revolution since it allows for no positive judge-
ment of every revolution *per se*. It may very well be that
anarchism can provide an intellectual guidepost by its watch-
fulness over the imperfections of every political act.

The difficulty with socialist theory is that it tends to be,
despite all of its claims, utopian. Once achieving a socialist
state system, socialists abandon the principle of contradiction for a mellow doctrine of "nonantagonistic contradiction." It thus becomes a theory of social preservation of the
status quo, much like capitalism. The anarchist, in his more
sophisticated thinking, states that there is no social system
that does not produce its genuine contradiction and therefore the possibility of further social change. Perhaps theories
based on social class are more practical in that they pose
possibilities of resolution. Yet resolution makes the problem
obsolete. To advance it beyond a certain point is reactionary.

Of course, in a sense, any critique of *Gesellschaft* relations—of the rise of the overextended bureaucracy, deper-
sonalized and detached from human problems—must run
the risk of making an appeal to a *Gemeinschaft* world that
was. And there is little doubt that anarchists look approv-
ingly and longingly on the organic solidarity feudalism was
supposed to have had. This yearning was especially height-
ened in the late nineteenth century under the persuasive
barrage of John Ruskin, William Morris, and Brooks Adams.
On the other hand, to make power manageable does in some
sense mean to decentralize it—to restore to the people most
immediately affected by power decisions the rights and responsibilities for making such decisions. In this sense, anarchism is no more and no less nostalgic than the sociological
theories of Durkheim, who saw in social solidarity the solution to the deterioration of human bonds; Mannheim, who
insisted that social planning be organic and not overridden
by rigid bureaucracy; and by Toennies himself, who felt
that although the shift from community to society was historically necessary, that we ought not to lose sight of the

advantages of community life, precisely because historical evolution dulls the senses to past patterns of human organization. In short, the anarchist response to the dysfunctional properties of large scale organization and the bureaucratic State, while surely touched by nostalgia, has as its essential core the same kinds of criticism now being offered by the leading figures in social science.[1] It was a rejection of ritualism in work, overconformity in response, lack of adaptability to change, self-protection of the organization in place of social service, etc., that was at the base of anarchist rejections of the super-State, rather than a longing for feudal honor or medieval craft.

The anarchist belief in the evil powers of State authority has received considerable support in the knowledge that State bureaucracy often turns out to be dysfunctional in operation and disgusting in its repressiveness. The anarchist insistence on the values of mutual aid has been transformed into a celebration of the worth of voluntary associations. The anarchist belief in the potential cooperation of all men as equals has received support in the new psychological understanding of the plasticity and viability of human character. The anarchist insistence on the posture of the outsider has been reinforced by the rise of strong and positive "subcultures" with norms of their own.

Anarchism may exaggerate the role of individual participation and underestimate the values of struggle for realization of partial goals. And the healthiest society in the world is one that recognizes that the tasks of society are not to insist on perfection, but to assist in the arts of perfecting. For this long-haul undertaking the ability to absorb the anarchist double insight into the need for revolutionary change and the possible cost of such change may yet turn out to be the strongest recommendation for democratic "politics."

When all is said on the subject, must it not be frankly admitted that anarchism is not so much a doctrine as a mood; and not a social and economic credo but an elaborate form of psychological therapy for the politically alienated and the

[1] *Cf.* Georges Friedman, *The Anatomy of Work.* New York: The Free Press of Glencoe, 1962; William H. Whyte, Jr., *The Organization Man.* New York: Simon and Schuster, Inc., 1956; Robert Presthus, *The Organizational Society.* New York: Alfred A. Knopf, 1962; and Herman D. Stein, "Administrative Implications of Bureaucratic Theory," *Social Work.* Vol. 6, No. 3 (July, 1961), pp. 14–21.

*intellectually disaffiliated? In short, must not anarchism be
accepted or rejected as an act of faith by virtue of its being
beyond confirmation, independent of any evidence as to its
actual worth?*

One of the frequent charges against the socialist tradition
is that it lacks a fully developed psychology of "socialist
man." This is natural since it makes much of the emergence
of a new man in support of its revolutionary claims. Apart
from the early neo-Hegelian writings of Marx on the alienation of the worker from the sources and uses of his labor,
the socialist tradition has tended to substitute organizational
directives for a theory of behavior. In this sense, the charge
that anarchism is more a mood than a doctrine reflects a reaction to this situation, an attempt to pick up where Feuerbach, Stirner, and the young Marx left off. From the anarchist viewpoint, socialist man had become bureaucratic man.
The perfect socialist is undeviating in principles, flexible in
political tactics, geared to the tasks of construction once the
political victory over capitalism has been won. The contrast
between fact and expectation was stark. The anarchist, perhaps in virtue of his "petty-bourgeois character," thought
more deeply about the type of man the future *ought* to produce on a mass scale. As the socialist became political, the
anarchist became philosophical.

The anarchist was less intent on future political victories
than he was on present psychological overhauling. This was
well expressed in the statement by Lefrançais, one of the
coworkers of Élisée Reclus in the Paris Commune. Speaking
of his associates in the International, he said that "I cannot
work with such fools as you are, but I cannot work with
anyone else. Because you fools are still the men I love best.
With you one can work, and remain one's self." The anarchists gave up their fortunes to the cause like Christian
ascetics. Men like Cafiero and Malatesta, an aristocrat and a
medical student respectively, took a strict Christian view of
money as a corrupting influence on the person. Like Luther,
the anarchists saw money as a diabolical symbol through
which corruption became inevitable.

The personal hardships of the anarchists—imprisonment,
exile, loss of family—all served to reinforce the revolutionary impulse. Personal hardship became something of a test
of personal worth. Like Christian reformers, no man was

beyond redemption. Thus, if anarchism is a mood, it is so in the same sense as other world historic forces of moral redemption that are at the same time politically unhinged.

As anarchism becomes historically "obsolete" its orientation becomes increasingly psychological. And the attraction of followers probably derives from the influence of people of extraordinary charismatic dimensions. They function to bring attention to the present existence of moral and at the same time secular men. Our special interest in them consists in evaluating their contribution to a secularized ethic. And, who, after all, is concerned with a secular ethic if not the disengaged and disaffiliated intelligentsia? The modern intellectual increasingly comes to define the concept of intelligence as such as being moral, i.e., intellect in itself has a responsibility to the world. It is thus precisely as a mood rather than as a political doctrine that anarchism derives its attraction for a sector of the intelligentsia. As an instrument of political analysis it has become sterile and scholastic. Yet the anarchists are admired if not emulated for their outstanding qualities as people. Revolutionists, whatever their suasion, have had outstanding moral characteristics in addition to a high degree of political skill. But what sets the anarchist apart is his belief in the absolute importance of the individual in history. As in Stirner's work, history is confronted and confounded by morality. For it to be otherwise is to convert history into predeterminism and morality into opportunism. The anarchist's taste for spontaneity as a revolutionary quality of higher integrity than organized political revolution reveals the extent to which the qualities of charisma, moral stature, are exalted among the anarchists. Spontaneity is romantic and apocalyptic, allowing for the fullest display of personal heroism.

This adherence to spontaneity of political action strongly flavors the nature of personal heroism, since the heroism this entails is not merely an illustration of the "laws of history" but a directly personal and lived experience. Revolution conducted by parliamentary means or party apparatus cannot command the same romanticism of heroic rebellion. This is further glamorized by extreme risks and dangers. The individual's highest faculties are sharpened in such a confrontation. In this sense anarchism adopts a therapeutic view of revolution.

The appeal of the outsider as such to the romantic imagination certainly finds the modern anarchist mood an attractive one. He does not accept social norms since they are man-made and arbitrary. Communist revolutionaries have gone to great length to adopt publicly acceptable norms in an effort to court popular acceptance. For the anarchist this is an extreme hypocrisy, and he could not compromise the romantic outsider to this extent. What in the political realm emerges as antipolitics, so in the personal realm marginality is also a virtue. The outsider's posture is of course not unique with the anarchists and certainly not confined to them. But it is a necessary feature in anarchism. It affects political activity to the extent that practical coalitions are forsaken as compromises with norms.

Criminality, aside from the popular uses of the word, is another word for someone who strives to rearrange the norm through unprescribed means. Criminality often pervaded the anarchist movement—not merely because the anarchist relied on theft, assassination, insurrection, but because of his exaltation of lawlessness. Everyone in some measure is lawless. But sham and hypocrisy insist that laws are inviolable when everyone knows that they are violable and violated with immunity. So that the claim for a higher morality on the part of the anarchist lies in his honesty. He is willing to assert lawlessness as a principle in opposition to the concept of law as such.

There are anarchist justifications for this concept of lawlessness. Civilization creates a whole superstructure of law and legal edifices that as a matter of fact, are superfluous in the functioning of the life of an ordinary human being. Natural man requires no regulation and suffers under the burden of those imposed, and this is alien to his deeper nature. In fact, for the anarchist it would be true to say, as many have who have addressed themselves to the nature of human morality, that making certain behavior illegitimate is the very cause of its performance. Forbiddenness has an attraction all its own and to treat deviation by means other than outlawing it would reduce the impulsion toward it.

The mental development of anarchism has been in an ever-increasing direction away from a mass based notion or even a class based notion to one of deracinated man. The appeal of anarchism, where any is exerted, exists for the consciously alienated worker separated as he is from the fruit of his labor, for the anomic middle-class man isolated from life's growth processes, for the intellectual conscious of outrageous infringements that organization imposes on individual rights. Naturally anarchism does not supply the sought-after guides for the many who seek identity but it serves this mood, occasionally in half-conscious form, and answers the quest of a socially conscious few. It delineates the possibilities of a new personality, one that is assertive and in a condition of harmony with other men, where the will to assertion is sublimated in the common good.

Anarchism is an optimistic mood in contrast to much that passed for the irrationalist thought of the nineteenth and twentieth centuries. Man can be reformed, man is plastic, and above all, consciousness itself becomes the very machinery at the disposal of men to overthrow the ballast of manipulative rule. The anarchist feels very positive about the future if for no other reason than that consciousness, anarchist consciousness, becomes a moral force advancing science and morality. Perhaps then the social psychology of the anarchist rests on the idea of self-consciousness acting as an improving force in the evolution of man.

What kind of man is yearned after by the sufferers of modern industrial society? He is much like an Apache, that is to say, he would probably be given to violence, active and not passive in the pursuit of his goals. He is a "natural man." He sheds certain features of historical civilization. During the summertime he goes nude. He is generous insofar as there is abundance. His "Apache" qualities are most fired by attempts to impose exploitative relations. His social world is in a state of permanent revolution, and change continually refreshes his life. His skills and ingenuity are embodied in the whole product he creates for the common good. Very important to social balance is the like mindedness of the community. He wants to restore a truly "Christian" being with little covetousness for material things. Ideas are freely exchanged without threatening the "powers that be." His contribution is heard and is part of the overall community decision-making. Competition based on invidious comparisons by class or nation is outmoded. He has a possibility of living an existence in keeping with his nature. Spurious power conflicts do not command him to take arms against strangers. His critical capacities are not blunted but welcomed. These ideal qualities enable the seeker to envision a realizable man since these are universally longed-for qualities and in part, men from time to time exhibit them. The anarchist is one who believes that, but for the accursed State, they will reassert themselves as man's truly human self. It gives the seeker and the converted believer the faith in the great horizons of human potential. And for the present he possesses the sharp and much needed weapon of criticism. And this keeps him alert as the guardian of humanity's better self. He lives without pretense and above all without superficial reverence. He is no jingoist. For those who define themselves as anarchists the self-definition performs the task of showing up our absurdities. And these criticisms are very clever. Why not use the label "Anarchy"? Why not use a designation that implies an extreme criticism of the social order and also an extreme celebration of the human being?

Let us not become so complacent about the possibilities of change that we scorn serious, even if erroneous, attempts to bring it about. Let us not become so clever that we smirk at every doctrinal inconsistency at the expense of opposing social injustices. The anarchists are a romantic, absurd breed that cannot, thank goodness, come to terms with some of the oppressive excesses of civilization.

Subject Index

tutional, 392, 398; fall of
in Italy, 394; government
of, 394
Rimini, 391, 392, 404-06,
412; Congress of, 394, 405;
decisions, 409; pre-, 404;
and St. Imier Congresses,
413
Risorgimento, 393, 397
(Il) Risveglio, 415
(La) Rivoluzione Sociale, 411
romantic pluralism, 554
romanticism, 469; nineteenth
century, 57
Rome, 99, 159, 255-56, 401,
405, 409, 540; of the Caesars, 148
Rotterdam, dock workers of,
494
ruling class, 122, 123, 128,
130-32, 136, 392, 400; and
governments, 53; interests
of, 130; of Italy, 395;
leisure of, 138; new, 189;
opinion, 400; of State, 128-
29; techniques of, 41; in
warfare, 131
Russia, 44, 53, 161-62, 236,
240, 514, 552, 574, 579;
abolition of serfdom in,
168; Bolshevist bureau-
cracy in, 189; Czarist, 24;
and dictatorship of the proletariat, 188; Imperial, 34;
nobility in, 130; parlia-
mentary method in, 517;
peasant anarchism in, 463-
81; rational State in, 266;
southern, 482
Russian anarchism, final act
of, 495-506
Russian Revolution, 593, 596

s

Saint Imier International,
411, 487, 492
Saint Loius, railroad strikes

of, 419
Saint Petersburg, 464, 477
Salut, 387f.
Sans-Culotte, 451
science, 28, 93, 122, 135,
157, 232, 239, 356, 442,
556-69, 578; academic
men of, 160; academies of,
235; against religion, 473;
and anarchism, 145-69; application of, 139; benefits
of, 590; dogmas of, 90;
economic, 157, 158f.; ex-
act, 153; first rudiments of,
146; governmental, 131-32;
and industry, 581; man of,
154, 157f.; natural, 157;
of politics, 586
*Science of Revolutionary
Warfare*, 421
scientific method, 28; of research, 153
scientists; conflicting values
of, 556; individual, 560;
research, 556-59, 561
Second Empire, 165
Second International, *see also*
International, 490, 493,
511f.
(The) Secret Agent, 194-211
secret societies, 147, 381,
464, 470-71, 475, 479
serfdom, 162; abolition of in
Russia, 168
Senate (French), 526, 534
Seville, 374; Cantonalists in,
375; congress at, 382-83;
cooperative movements in,
507
Siberia, 467
sixteenth century, Anabaptist movement of, 149
sixties, radical generation of,
466; radical movement of,
465; strikes in, 161
social contract theories, 583,
596
Social Contract, 186, 339f.

Name Index